Comprehensive Data Structures and Algorithms in C++

Learn fundamentals with 500+ code samples and problems

Suresh Kumar Srivastava

Deepali Srivastava

bpb

www.bpbonline.com

First Edition 2025

Copyright © BPB Publications, India

ISBN: 978-93-65898-576

To View Complete
BPB Publications Catalogue
Scan the QR Code:

Dedicated to

Our teachers, family and friends

About the Authors

- **Suresh Kumar Srivastava** has 20+ years of experience in software industry - Alcatel, BNY Mellon, Unisys and has worked on architecture and design of multiple products. He is the author of popular books, *C in Depth* and *Data Structures Through C in Depth*, which have helped over 250,000 students. He has completed his 'B' level at NIELIT. He has worked on the development of Compilers, Linkers, Debuggers, IDEs, System Utilities, System Management and Telecom/Mobile/ Systems tools. He runs an online learning site called CourseGalaxy, and loves doing software architecture, design, coding, and product engineering.

- **Deepali Srivastava** has a Master's degree in Mathematics and is an author and educator in computer science and programming. Her books *Ultimate Python Programming*, *C in Depth* and *Data Structures Through C in Depth* are widely used as reference materials by students, programmers and professionals looking to enhance their understanding of programming languages and data structures. In addition to her writing, Deepali Srivastava has been involved in creating online video courses on Data structures and Algorithms, Linux, and Python programming. Her books and courses have helped over 350,000 students learn computer science concepts.

Acknowledgements

We are grateful to our teachers for making an excellent foundation for us to do better in life. We also thank our family and friends for encouraging us to do better. Our special thanks to BPB Publications for considering our work and making it available to students worldwide. We thank software organizations and academic institutions for providing excellent exposure to software development, industry standards and valuable learning on theoretical concepts, technologies, and processes. We also thank students for learning and appreciating our previous works. This encourages us to come up with more and share knowledge wherever possible.

Preface

Data Structures and Algorithms is an essential subject in any university curriculum for the computer science stream. It provides an excellent tool for software engineers and plays a significant role in software design and development. It is also becoming a must-have skill for many competitions and job interviews in the software industry. Selection of appropriate data structures and algorithms makes the software better. Software developers are always advised to use them appropriately to provide better solutions. Understanding data structures and algorithms makes them better software developers and designers. The book will benefit students in their university curriculum and open opportunities to enter and excel in the software industry.

This book provides an extensive study of data structures and algorithms. The book has various topics - algorithms analysis, arrays, linked lists, stacks and queues, recursion, trees, graphs, sorting, searching, hashing, and storage management, to learn in-depth data structures and algorithms. The book provides a good understanding of concepts with implementation. Each concept is explained with well-defined steps, figures to understand it better, and immediate code samples to understand implementation for concepts. Complete programs are provided for better understanding of concepts and implementation. The book provides 500+ illustrations, examples, code samples, and problems to learn fundamentals and understand concepts and implementation well. There are exercise problems that strengthen the learning of concepts and implementation. The problems force the students to have a better thought process and solve the problems using concepts, and develop multiple solutions. It also helps them have better problem-solving skills and learn how to implement them. There is a comprehensive chapter that covers recursion in detail. This allows students to develop a recursive approach to problem-solving and enhances their overall thought process for solving problems.

The book is written in a straightforward language, carefully explaining concepts in a way that is easy to understand for both students and experienced engineers. Anyone with a basic understanding of computer science will be able to understand the Data Structures and Algorithms concepts. The implementation requires a basic knowledge of object-oriented programming in C++. The book provides good learning for students as well as experienced engineers. It is recommended that students begin with the first chapter, as some concepts will be used in subsequent chapters. The practical learning process involves first understanding the concept, then grasping its implementation, and finally applying each concept in a program. At the end of each chapter, explore the exercise problems to strengthen your understanding of concepts and implementation. The programs follow coding conventions and include comments to better understand the code and logic. All the programs of the chapter and the exercise solutions are provided. It is always suggested that the reader first try implementing the concepts and solving the exercises independently, and only then refer to the provided programs and solutions.

Here is the brief information of all the chapters of the book:

Chapter 1: Introduction – This chapter introduces data structures, algorithms, and methods to analyze the efficiency of algorithms

Chapter 2: Arrays – This chapter covers the array, its operations, and matrices.

Chapter 3: Linked Lists - This chapter discusses various linked lists and their operations in detail.

Chapter 4: Stacks and Queues – This chapter explores stacks and queues and their applications.

Chapter 5: Recursion - This chapter explains recursion in detail with many problems.

Chapter 6: Trees - This chapter covers a variety of trees and their operations.

Chapter 7: Graphs - This chapter explores graphs and various graph algorithms.

Chapter 8: Sorting - This chapter covers different sorting algorithms in detail with their efficiency.

Chapter 9: Searching and Hashing - This chapter explains searching and hashing techniques.

Chapter 10: Storage Management - This chapter introduces storage management and its different methods.

We hope the book will provide students with good learning opportunities and help them in their college curriculum and software development.

Suresh Kumar Srivastava

Deepali Srivastava

Code Bundle and Coloured Images

Please follow the link to download the
Code Bundle and the *Coloured Images* of the book:

https://rebrand.ly/c381f9

The code bundle for the book is also hosted on GitHub at

https://github.com/bpbpublications/Comprehensive-Data-Structures-and-Algorithms-in-C-Plus-Plus.
In case there's an update to the code, it will be updated on the existing GitHub repository.

We have code bundles from our rich catalogue of books and videos available at
https://github.com/bpbpublications. Check them out!

Errata

We take immense pride in our work at BPB Publications and follow best practices to ensure the accuracy of our content to provide with an indulging reading experience to our subscribers. Our readers are our mirrors, and we use their inputs to reflect and improve upon human errors, if any, that may have occurred during the publishing processes involved. To let us maintain the quality and help us reach out to any readers who might be having difficulties due to any unforeseen errors, please write to us at :

errata@bpbonline.com

Your support, suggestions and feedbacks are highly appreciated by the BPB Publications' Family.

Piracy

If you come across any illegal copies of our works in any form on the internet, we would be grateful if you would provide us with the location address or website name. Please contact us at **business@bpbonline.com** with a link to the material.

If you are interested in becoming an author

If there is a topic that you have expertise in, and you are interested in either writing or contributing to a book, please visit **www.bpbonline.com**. We have worked with thousands of developers and tech professionals, just like you, to help them share their insights with the global tech community. You can make a general application, apply for a specific hot topic that we are recruiting an author for, or submit your own idea.

Reviews

Please leave a review. Once you have read and used this book, why not leave a review on the site that you purchased it from? Potential readers can then see and use your unbiased opinion to make purchase decisions. We at BPB can understand what you think about our products, and our authors can see your feedback on their book. Thank you!

For more information about BPB, please visit **www.bpbonline.com**.

Join our book's Discord space

Join the book's Discord Workspace for Latest updates, Offers, Tech happenings around the world, New Release and Sessions with the Authors:

https://discord.bpbonline.com

Table of Contents

Introduction

Generally, any problem that has to be solved by the computer involves the use of data. If data is arranged in some systematic way, then it gets a structure and becomes meaningful. This meaningful or processed data is called information. It is essential to manage data in such a way that it can produce information. There can be many ways in which data may be organized or structured. To provide an appropriate structure to your data, you need to know about data structures. Data structures can be viewed as a systematic way to organize data, so that it can be used efficiently. The choice of proper data structures can greatly affect the efficiency of our program.

The process of program development generally requires us to represent the data efficiently and develop a step-by-step procedure that performs a given task and can be used to implement a program.

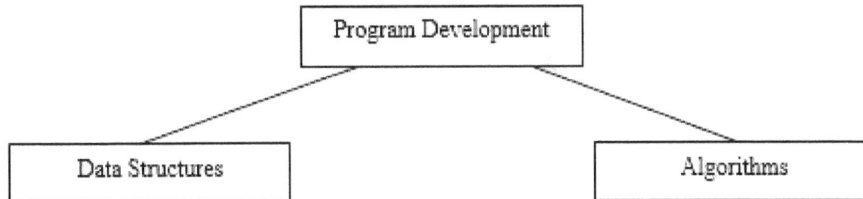

Figure 1.1 Program development

Representing the data efficiently needs the study of data structures, and the development of a step-by-step procedure requires learning about algorithms.

1.1 Data Type

A data type defines a domain of allowed values and the operations that can be performed on those values. For example, in C++, the `int` data type can take values in a range and operations that can be performed are addition, subtraction, multiplication, division, bitwise operations etc. Similarly, the data type `float` can take values in a particular range, and the operations allowed are addition, subtraction, multiplication, division, and so on (% operation and bitwise operations are not allowed). These are built-in or primitive data types and the values and operations for them are defined in the language.

If an application needs to use a data type other than the primitive data types of the language, i.e., a data type for which values and operations are not defined in the language itself, then it is the programmer's responsibility to specify the values and operations for that data type and implement it. For example, there is no built-in type for dates in C++, and if we need to process dates, we have to define and implement a data type for date.

1.2 Abstract Data Types

Abstract Data Type (ADT) is a mathematical model or concept that defines a data type logically. It specifies a set of data and a collection of operations that can be performed on that data. The definition of ADT only mentions what operations are to be performed but not how these operations will be implemented. It does not specify how data will be organized in memory and what algorithms will be used for implementing the operations. It is called "abstract" because it gives an implementation-independent view. The process of providing only the essentials and hiding the details is known as abstraction.

The user of a data type need not know how the data type is implemented; for example, we have been using `int`, `float`, `char` data types only with the knowledge of values that they can take and operations that can be performed on them without any idea of how these types are implemented. So, a user only needs to know what a data type can do but not how it will do it. We can think of ADT as a black box that hides the inner structure and design of the data type. Now, we will define three ADTs, namely List ADT, Stack ADT, and Queue ADT.

List ADT

A list contains elements of the same type arranged in sequential order and following operations can be performed on the list:

- `initialize( )`: Initialize the list to be empty.
- `get( )`: Return an element from the list at any given position.
- `insert( )`: Insert a new element at any list position.
- `remove( )`: Remove the first occurrence of any element from a non-empty list.
- `removeAt( )`: Remove the element at a specified location from a non-empty list.
- `replace( )`: Replace an element at any position with another element.
- `size( )`: Return the number of elements in the list.
- `isEmpty( )`: Return true if the list is empty; otherwise, return false.
- `isFull( )`: Return true if the list is full otherwise return false.

Stack ADT

A stack contains elements of same type arranged in sequential order and following operations can be performed on the stack:

- `initialize( )`: Initialize the stack to be empty.
- `push( )`: Insert an element at one end of the stack called top.
- `pop( )`: Remove and return the element at the top of the stack if it is not empty.
- `peek( )`: Return the element at the top of the stack without removing it if the stack is not empty.
- `size( )`: Return the number of elements in the stack.
- `isEmpty( )`: Return true if the stack is empty; otherwise, return false.
- `isFull( )`: Return true if no more elements can be pushed; otherwise, return false.

Queue ADT

A queue contains elements of the same type arranged in sequential order, and the following operations can be performed on it:

- `initialize( )`: Initialize the queue to be empty.
- `enqueue( )`: Insert an element at the end of the queue.
- `dequeue( )`: Remove and return the first element of the queue if the queue is not empty.
- `peek( )`: Return the first element of the queue without removing it if the queue is not empty.
- `size( )`: Return the number of elements in the queue.
- `isEmpty( )`: Return true if the queue is empty; otherwise, return false.
- `isFull( )`: Return true if no more elements can be inserted; otherwise, return false.

From these definitions, we can clearly see that they do not specify how these ADTs will be represented or how the operations will be carried out. There can be different ways to implement an ADT. For example, the list ADT can be implemented using arrays, single linked lists, or double linked lists. Similarly, stack

ADT and queue ADT can also be implemented using arrays or linked lists. The representation and implementation details of these ADTs are in the subsequent chapters.

The different implementations of ADT are compared for time and space efficiency, and the implementation best suited for the user's requirements is used. For example, if someone wants to use a list in a program that involves lots of insertions and deletions from the list, then it is better to use the linked list implementation of the list.

1.3 Data Structures

Data structures are data representation methods that are used to organize data. It provides a way of organizing data, so the program can use it effectively. Data structure is a programming construct used to implement an ADT. It is the physical implementation of ADT. All operations specified in ADT are implemented through functions in the physical implementation. A data structure implementing an ADT consists of a collection of variables for storing the data specified in the ADT and the algorithms for implementing the operations specified in ADT.

ADT is the logical view of data and the operations to manipulate it, while a data structure is the actual representation of data and the algorithms to manipulate it.

ADT is a specification language for data structures. ADT is a logical description, while a Data Structure is concrete. In other words, an ADT tells us **what** to do, while data structures tell us **how** to do it. The actual storage or representation of data and implementation of algorithms is done in data structures.

A program that uses a data structure is generally called a client, and the program that implements it is known as the implementation. The specification of ADT is called interface, and it is the only thing visible to the client programs that use data structure. The client programs view data structure as ADT; i.e., they have access only to the interface; the way data is represented, and operations are implemented is not visible to the client. For example, if someone wants to use a stack in the program, he can simply use the push and pop operations without any knowledge of how they are implemented. Some examples of clients of stack ADT are programs of balanced parentheses, infix to postfix, postfix evaluation.

We may change the representation or algorithm, but the client code will not be affected if the ADT interface remains the same. For example, if the implementation of the stack is changed from array to linked list, the client program should work in the same way. This helps the user of a data structure focus on his program rather than going into the details of the data structure.

Data structures can be nested; i.e., a data structure may be made up of other data structures, which may be of primitive types or user-defined types. Some of the advantages of data structures are:

- Efficiency: Proper choice of data structures makes our program efficient. For example, suppose we have some data, and we need to organize it properly and perform a search operation. If we organize our data in an array, we will have to search element by element sequentially. If the item to be searched is present at last, then we will have to visit all the elements before reaching that element. So, the use of an array is not very efficient here. There are better data structures that can make the search process efficient, like ordered arrays, binary search trees, or hash tables. Different data structures give different efficiency.

- Reusability: Data structures are reusable, i.e., once we have implemented a particular data structure, we can use it in any other place or requirement. Data structures can be formed as libraries that can be used by different clients.

- Abstraction: We have seen that a data structure is specified by an ADT, which provides a level of abstraction. The client program uses the data structure through the interface only without getting into the implementation details.

Some common operations that are performed on Data structures are-

- Insertion
- Deletion
- Traversal
- Search

There can be other operations also and the details of these operations depend on data structures. Learning about different data structures is very important because the choice of proper data structure can significantly affect the efficiency of our program.

1.3.1 Linear and Non-Linear Data Structures

A data structure is linear if all the elements are arranged in a linear order. In a linear data structure, each element has only one successor and only one predecessor. The only exceptions are the first and last elements; the first element does not have a predecessor, and the last element does not have a successor. Examples of linear data structures are arrays, strings, linked lists, stacks, and queues.

A nonlinear data structure has no linear order in the arrangement of the elements. Examples of nonlinear data structures are trees and graphs.

1.3.2 Static and Dynamic Data Structures

In a static data structure, the memory is allocated at compilation time only. Therefore, the maximum size is fixed and it cannot be changed at run time. Static data structures allow fast access to elements, but insertion and deletion are expensive. Array is an example of static data structure.

In a dynamic data structure, the memory is allocated at run time. Therefore, these data structures have flexible sizes. Dynamic data structures allow fast insertion and deletion of elements but access to elements is slow. Linked list is an example of dynamic data structure.

1.4 Algorithms

An algorithm is a procedure that contains well-defined steps for solving a particular problem. Algorithms and data structures are closely related. When we implement an algorithm, we have to choose a particular representation of data; i.e., we have to decide which data structure to use, and for using data structures, we have to develop efficient algorithms for various operations on these data structures, like searching, sorting, traversal, etc.

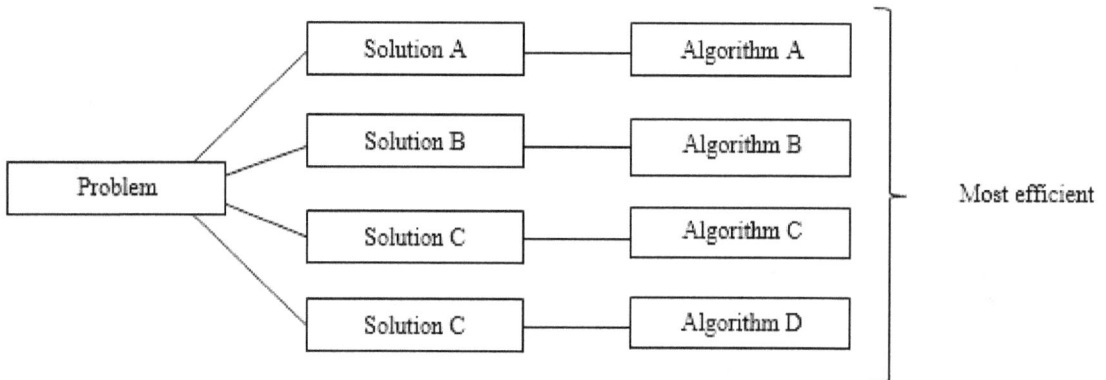

Figure 1.2 Different algorithms to solve a problem

Given a problem, there can be many ways to solve it, and these solutions are in the form of different algorithms. Hence, there can be many algorithms to solve a particular problem.

For example, there are many ways in which data can be sorted, and so we have various sorting algorithms. When we have more than one algorithm to choose from, we would like to use the most efficient algorithm or the best suited for our requirements. To decide which algorithm is best for us, we should be able to compare the algorithms and identify the most efficient one.

The efficiency of an algorithm mainly depends on these two factors:
- Running time of the algorithm
- Memory occupied by it

An efficient algorithm is one that takes less running time and occupies less memory. There can be other measures of efficiency also, like network usage or disk usage, but running time and space are the two factors which are most important. We are generally more concerned about the running time of the algorithm.

Some of the common approaches to algorithm design are explained next.

1.4.1 Greedy Algorithm

A greedy algorithm works by taking a decision that appears best at the moment, without thinking about the future. The decision, once taken, is never reconsidered. This means that a local optimum is chosen at every step in hope of getting a global optimum at the end. It is not necessary that a greedy algorithm always produce an optimal solution. Some examples where the greedy approach produces optimal solutions are Dijkstra's algorithm for single source shortest paths, Prim's and Kruskal's algorithm for minimum spanning tree, and Huffman algorithm.

1.4.2 Divide and Conquer Algorithm

A divide-and-conquer algorithm solves a problem by dividing it into smaller and similar subproblems. The solutions of these smaller problems are then combined to get the solution of the given problem. Examples of divide and conquer algorithms are merge sort, quick sort, and binary search.

1.4.3 Backtracking

In some problems we have several options, and any one of them might lead to the solution. We will take an option and try, and if we do not reach the solution, we will undo our action and select another one. The steps are retraced if we do not reach the solution; it is a trial-and-error process. An example of backtracking is the Eight Queens problem.

1.4.4 Randomized Algorithms

In a randomized algorithm, random numbers are used to make some decisions. The running time of such algorithms depends on the input as well as the random numbers that are generated. The running time may vary for the same input data. An example of randomized algorithm is a version of quick sort where a random number is chosen as the pivot.

1.5 Analysis of Algorithms

There may be many algorithms for solving any problem, and obviously, we would like to use the most efficient one. Analysis of algorithms is required to compare these algorithms and recognize the best one. As discussed previously, algorithms are generally analyzed on their time and space requirements.

1.5.1 Measuring Running Time of an Algorithm

There are two ways of measuring running time of an algorithm.

- Experimental or empirical method
- Analytical method or asymptotic analysis

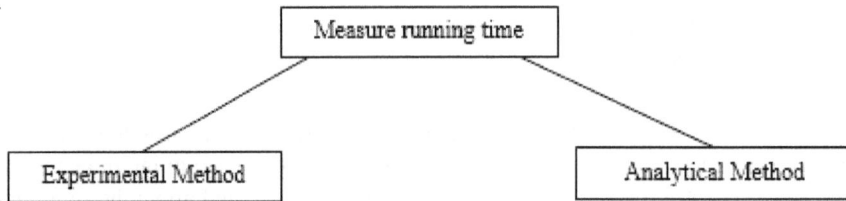

Figure 1.3 Measuring running time

1.5.1.1 Experimental Method

In the experimental method, we implement the algorithm in a programming language, run it on different inputs and record the exact running time in time units such as microseconds, seconds or minutes. This approach is not feasible, and it has certain limitations.

The first problem with this approach is that we have to implement the algorithm in a particular programming language and run it on a specific computer so that the running time becomes dependent on the software and hardware used for implementing the algorithm. This can lead to false results; for example, a bad algorithm might take less time than a good algorithm if it is run on a faster computer or is implemented in an efficient language. So, if we want to compare two algorithms and find which one is better, then we have to implement both of them using the same software and hardware environment, which might not always be possible.

Another problem is that we can run the program for only a limited number of inputs, and we might miss some inputs in which the algorithm behaves differently. The limited number of inputs on which we run the program might not indicate the proper behavior of the algorithm. The third problem is that the experimental method consumes a lot of time. Some algorithms can take hours or days to execute for a certain input, and so, in that case, this approach is not feasible.

Due to these limitations, the experimental approach is not used to measure the running time of algorithms. Instead of this, a theoretical (analytical) method is used. In this method, we analyse running time of algorithms based on their input size. This is also called asymptotic analysis. In this method, we do not calculate the exact running times, and therefore, there is no need to run the program. This approach allows us to analyse the running time of algorithms in a way that is independent of the software and hardware environments. This method also allows us to consider all possible inputs.

1.5.1.2 Asymptotic Analysis

The running time of an algorithm depends on the size of input, which is generally denoted by n. The input can have a different meaning depending on the problem that we are solving. For example, if we are searching or sorting an array, then the size of the array is the input size for the algorithm. If the input size is small, then the algorithm will take less time, and if the size of the input is big, then the running time will be more. For example, a sorting algorithm will take less time for sorting 10 numbers and more time for sorting 500 numbers. So, as the size of the input increases, the running time will also increase.

Suppose the input size of an algorithm doubles; then obviously the running time will also increase. The running time might double, or it might quadruple, or it can become 20 times or 100 times more; it depends on the algorithm. It is this behaviour of an algorithm that is studied in asymptotic analysis. So, for analysing an algorithm we will study how the running time of the algorithm increases with the increase in input size. If the running time of an algorithm increases rapidly with the input size, then that algorithm will not be considered efficient. In asymptotic analysis, we do not care about the exact running time; we are just interested in seeing what happens when the input size becomes large.

Suppose we have 2 algorithms, algorithm A and algorithm B, for solving a particular problem.

Input size n	Algorithm A	Algorithm B
2	4	4
4	8	16
7	14	49
100	200	10,000
1000	2000	1,000,000
10,000	20,000	100,000,000

Figure 1.4 Running time of the algorithms on input size

When input size is 2, both algorithms take the same running time. When input size is 4, running time for A is 8 and for B it is 16. Running times for input sizes 7, 100, 1000 and 10,000 are given in the preceding figure. We can see that running time of the algorithm B increases rapidly with input size, so for a bigger input size algorithm B will take a lot of time. For example, for input size ten thousand, A's running time is 20,000 while B's running time is 100 million. If we have to choose between Algorithm A and Algorithm B, we will definitely go with Algorithm A because the algorithm B will become inefficient for larger input.

So, to determine the efficiency of an algorithm, we have to see how it behaves when the input size is increased. How the algorithms behaves means how the running time increases with the input size. To find the rate at which running time increases, a mathematical tool called big O notation is used.

1.6 Big O Notation

Big O is the most commonly used notation to measure the performance of any algorithm by defining its order of growth. It tells us about the asymptotic behavior of a function, i.e., how fast a function $f(n)$ grows as n becomes large. The Big O examines the rate of growth of a function by comparing it with some standard functions whose rate of growth is known.

Definition

$f(n)$ is $O(g(n))$ if there exist constants c and n_0 such that,
$f(n) < cg(n)$ for all $n \geq n_0$

The definition says that the function $f(n)$ will not grow faster than function $g(n)$ for larger values of n, or we can say that $g(n)$ is an upper bound on function $f(n)$. Here $f(n)$ is the function whose rate of growth has to be examined, and $g(n)$ is the function whose rate of growth is known.

Here are some examples-

$f(n) = 5n+4$, $g(n) = n$

Let us check whether we can say that $f(n)$ is order of $g(n)$.

$5n+4 \leq cn$ for all $n \geq n_0$, this is what the definition says.

If we take c=6 and n_0=4, then the definition is satisfied, and we can say that f(n) is O(n).
$5n+4 \leq 6n$ for all $n \geq 4$

These constants are not unique, there can be many more values of c and n_0 possible which can be used to show that 5n+4 is O(n). For example, we could take c=10 and n_0=5. These values are not important because we will just say that function f(n) is O(n).

Similarly, we can show that these functions are also O(n)-
24n+5 is O(n)
3n+7 is O(n)
23n+57 is O(n)
45n is O(n)

Suppose we have-
$f(n) = 3n^2 + 4n + 7$
$g(n) = n^2$

For c=5 and n_0=6
$3n^2 + 4n + 7 \leq 5n^2$ for all $n \geq 6$
So the function $3n^2 + 4n + 7$ is $O(n^2)$.

Similarly, we can show that these functions are also $O(n^2)$-
$5n^2 + 3n$ is $O(n^2)$
$n^2 + 5$ is $O(n^2)$
$7n^2 + 3n + 65$ is $O(n^2)$

In practice, we will not find the order of a function in this way by taking some constant values and then proving this relation true. Some rules derived from this definition can be used to find the order of a fuanction. Now, let us see some functions that are commonly used in place of the function g.

We have seen that rate of growth of a function f is examined by providing an upper bound using the function g. For this function g, only some simple functional forms are used, these forms generally contain a single term in n with a coefficient of one.

$$O(1), O(\log n), O(n), O(n \log n), O(n^2), O(n^3),.....O(n^k), O(2^n), O(3^n),.....O(k^n), O(n!)$$
Slow growing ———————————————————————→ Fast growing

Figure 1.5 Growth of a function

These are some commonly used functions that provide upper bounds; i.e., we will use these functions in place of g. These functions are ordered according to their rate of growth in increasing order, so we have slow growing functions from left to faster growing functions on the right.

In the following table, we have values of some of these functions for different values of n:

n	g(n)					
	$\log_2 n$	n	$n \log_2 n$	n^2	n^3	2^n
1	0	1	0	1	1	2
2	1	2	2	4	8	4
4	2	4	8	16	64	16
8	3	8	24	64	512	256
16	4	16	64	256	4096	65536
32	5	32	160	1024	32768	4.29E+09
64	6	64	384	4096	262144	1.84E+19

Figure 1.6 Growth rate of standard functions

We can see that some functions grow faster than others. For example, the growth rate of the function n^3 is much higher than the growth rate of function n or function n log n.

So, if we have two functions, f1 and f2, where f1 is O(n), and f2 is $O(n^3)$, then we can say that the growth rate of f2 is more than that of f1 because the growth rate of function n^3 is more than that of function n. This is how we can compare two functions using big O.

1.6.1 Rules for O Notation

(1) Transitivity

If f(n) is O(g(n)) and g(n) is O(h(n)), then f(n) is O(h(n))
or we can say that O(O(h(n))) is O(h(n))

(2) If $f_1(n)$ is O(h(n)) and $f_2(n)$ is O(h(n)), then $f_1(n) + f_2(n)$ is O(h(n))

Proof :
$f_1(n)$ is O(h(n)) => there exists c_1 and n_1 such that $f_1(n) \leq c_1 h(n)$ for all $n \geq n_1$
$f_2(n)$ is O(h(n)) => there exists c_2 and n_2 such that $f_2(n) \leq c_2 h(n)$ for all $n \geq n_2$
$f_1(n) + f_2(n) \leq (c_1 + c_2) h(n)$ for all $n \geq \max(n_1, n_2)$
if $c_0 = c_1 + c_2$ and $n_0 = \max(n_1, n_2)$
$f_1(n) + f_2(n) \leq c_0 h(n)$ for all $n \geq n_0$
$f_1(n) + f_2(n)$ is O(h(n))

(3) If $f_1(n)$ is O(h(n)) and $f_2(n)$ is O(g(n)), then $f_1(n) + f_2(n)$ is max(O(h(n)),O(g(n)))

Proof :
$f_1(n)$ is O(h(n)) => there exists c_1 and n_1 such that $f_1(n) \leq c_1 h(n)$ for all $n \geq n_1$
$f_2(n)$ is O(g(n)) => there exists c_2 and n_2 such that $f_2(n) \leq c_2 g(n)$ for all $n \geq n_2$
$f_1(n) + f_2(n) \leq c_1 h(n) + c_2 g(n)$ for all $n \geq \max(n_1, n_2)$
if $c = \max(c_1, c_2)$ and $n_0 = \max(n_1, n_2)$
$f_1(n) + f_2(n) \leq c\ h(n) + c\ g(n)$ for all $n \geq n_0$
$f_1(n) + f_2(n) \leq 2c\ \max(h(n), g(n))$ for all $n \geq n_0$
$f_1(n) + f_2(n) \leq c_0 \max(h(n), g(n))$ for all $n \geq n_0$
$f_1(n) + f_2(n)$ is max(O(h(n)),O(g(n)))

(4) If $f_1(n)$ is O(h(n)) and $f_2(n)$ is O(g(n)) then $f_1(n)f_2(n)$ is O(h(n)g(n))

(5) f(n) = C => f(n) is O(1)

Proof:

$f(n) \leq C * 1$ for any n

So $f(n)$ is $O(1)$

(6) If $f(n) = C * h(n)$ where C is a constant, then $f(n)$ is $O(h(n))$

Proof:

$f(n)$ is $O(C*h(n))$

there exists constants a and b such that

$f(n) \leq a * C * h(n)$ for all $n \geq b$

Taking $c = a*C$ and $n_0 = b$

$f(n) \leq c * h(n)$ for all $n \geq n_0$

So $f(n)$ is $O(h(n))$.

(7) Any polynomial $P(n)$ of degree m is $O(n^m)$

Proof:

$P(n) = a_0 + a_1 n + a_2 n^2 + \dots\dots\dots + a_m n^m$

Let $c_0 = |a_0|, c_1 = |a_1|, c_2 = |a_2|, \dots\dots\dots c_m = |a_m|$

$P(n) \leq c_0 + c_1 n + c_2 n^2 + \dots\dots + c_m n^m = (c_0/n^m + c_1/n^{m-1} + \dots\dots + c_m) n^m$

$\leq (c_0 + c_1 + \dots\dots\dots + c_m) n^m = K n^m$

$c = K$, and $n_0 = 1$

(8) n^a is $O(n^b)$ only if a<=b, i.e., n^3 is $O(n^3)$ or $O(n^4)$ or $O(n^5)$ but n^4 is not $O(n^3)$

(9) All logarithms grow at the same rate, i.e., while computing the O notation, the base of the logarithm is not important. To justify this, we will prove that $O(\log_a n)$ is $O(\log_b n)$ and $O(\log_b n)$ is $O(\log_a n)$ for all a, b >1.

$\log_a n$ is $O(\log_b n)$

Let $xa = \log_a n$ and $yb = \log_b n$

$a^{xa} = n$ and $b^{yb} = n$

$a^{xa} = b^{yb}$

Taking $\log_a$ of both sides

$\log_a a^{xa} = \log_a b^{yb}$

$xa * \log_a a = yb * \log_a b$ (since $\log_z m^k = k * \log_z m$ for any z, m and k)

$xa = yb * \log_a b$ (since $\log_a a = 1$)

$\log_a n = \log_b n * \log_a b$ (since $xa = \log_a n$ and $yb = \log_b n$)

$\log_a n = C * \log_b n$ ($C = \log_a b$)

$\log_b n = K * \log_a n$ ($K = 1 / \log_a b$)

We have already seen that if $f(n) = C * h(n)$ where C is a constant, then $f(n)$ is $O(h(n))$.

So $\log_a n$ is $O(\log_b n)$ and $\log_b n$ is $O(\log_a n)$ for any constants a and b.

(10) log n is O(n)

log n is $O(n^a)$ for any positive constant a

Applying the definition of limits, definition of O notation is equivalent to-

$\lim_{n\to\infty} \frac{|f(n)|}{|g(n)|} = c$

L'Hospital's rule can be used for computing this form of limit, and it states that:

If $\lim_{n\to\infty} f(n) = \infty$ and $\lim_{n\to\infty} g(n) = \infty$

then $\lim_{n\to\infty} \frac{f(n)}{g(n)} = \lim_{n\to\infty} \frac{f'(n)}{g'(n)}$

where f′ and g′ represent the derivatives of f and g respectively.

If $f(n) = \log n$ and $g(n) = n$

$$\lim_{n \to \infty} \frac{\log n}{n} = \lim_{n \to \infty} \frac{1/n}{1} = 0$$

So log n is O(n).

If $f(n) = \log n$ and $g(n) = n^a$

$$\lim_{n \to \infty} \frac{\log n}{n^a} = \lim_{n \to \infty} \frac{1/n}{a n^{a-1}} = \frac{1}{a n^a} = 0 \text{ (for any positive constant a)}$$

So log n is $O(n^a)$ for any positive constant a.

(11) $\log^k n$ is O(n)

Proof:
$\log^k n$ is same as $(\log n)^k$
We have to prove that $(\log n)^k$ is O(n)
For this, we have to show that $(\log n)^k \le cn$ for $n \ge n_0$
or we have to show that $\log n \le cn^{1/k}$ for $n \ge n_0$
If we take $a = 1/k$, we have to show that $\log n \le cn^a$ for $n \ge n_0$
or we have to show that log n is $O(n^a)$
We have already proved this.

1.6.2 Finding Big O

Let us see how to find the big O for a function.

$f(n) = 3n^2 + 4n + 15$

We have to find a function g such that f(n) is O(g(n)). The rules for doing this are simple, but before using those rules we will try to understand the logic behind them.

When n=10 then f(n)=300 + 40 + 15

% due to term $3n^2$:
(300 / (300+40+15)) * 100 = 84.50%

% due to term 4n :
(40 / (300+40+15)) * 100 = 11.26%

% due to term 15 :
(15 / (300+40+15)) * 100 = 4.22%

Value of n	$3n^2$	4n	15
1	13.63%	18.18%	68.18%
10	84.50%	11.26%	4.22%
100	98.63%	1.31%	0.049%
1000	99.86%	0.13%	4.9E-04%
10000	99.98%	0.01%	4.9E-06%

Figure 1.7 Values of different terms of f(n) for different values of n

In this table, we can see the contribution of these three different terms at different values of n. We can see that as the value of n grows, the term $3n^2$ dominates the value of the function, and the term 4n and constant 15 become insignificant. This is because n^2 grows rapidly, n grows slowly and the constant 15 does not grow at all.

In Big O analysis, we are concerned with the value of the function as n becomes large. With the help of this example, we have seen that when n becomes large, the fastest-growing term in the function becomes dominant, and the lower terms and constants become insignificant, so we can just ignore them. Therefore, if we have a function that is a sum of different terms, then for finding big O for that function, we have to keep just the fastest-growing term and can discard all the lower terms and constants.

So, the **first rule** for finding Big O is to keep the fastest-growing term and discard all the lower terms and constants.

The **second rule** is that we can ignore the coefficients of the terms.
$f(n) = C*g(n) \Rightarrow f(n)$ is $O(g(n))$

For example-
$f(n) = 5n^2 \Rightarrow f(n)$ is $O(n^2)$
$f(n) = 67n \Rightarrow f(n)$ is $O(n)$

Proof:
$f(n) = C*g(n)$
$f(n)$ is $O(C*g(n))$

Some constants a and b will exist such that
$f(n) \leq a * C * g(n)$ for all $n \geq b$

Taking $c = a*C$ and $n_0 = b$
$f(n) \leq c * g(n)$ for all $n \geq n_0$

Thus $f(n)$ is $O(g(n))$

Let us see the example again:

$f(n) = 3n^2 + 4n + 15$

According to first rule, we ignore the terms 4n and 5. Thus, we are left with the term $3n^2$, and on applying the second rule, we can ignore this coefficient 3 also. Therefore, the function $f(n)$ is $O(n^2)$

The **next rule** is:
If $f(n)$ is constant, then we say that $f(n)$ is $O(1)$
$f(n) = C \Rightarrow f(n)$ is $O(1)$

These functions are $O(1)$-
$f(n) = 3$
$f(n) = 204$
$f(n) = 5556$

Proof:
$f(n) \leq C * 1$ for any n
So $f(n)$ is $O(1)$

The next rule states that while computing the O notation, the base of the logarithm is not important.
$\log_a n = \log_b n / \log_b a$

We know that logarithms with different base are related by a constant factor. Big O ignores constants, and that is why there is no need to associate any base with the logarithms while specifying the order of a function. In algorithm analysis, we will mostly encounter logarithms with base 2.

These functions are $O(\log n)$-
$f(n) = 8\log_2 n$
$f(n) = 23\log_{10} n$

Let us see some functions and big O using these rules:

$f(n) = 45$	$O(1)$
$f(n) = 6n^3 + 27\log_2 n + 2n$	$O(n^3)$
$f(n) = 8\log_2 n + 7n + 6$	$O(n)$
$f(n) = n\log_{10} n + 5n + 81n^2$	$O(n^2)$
$f(n) = \log_2 n + n\log_{10} n$	$O(n \log n)$
$f(n) = 3n + 5n^2 + 7n^3 + 2^n$	$O(2^n)$
$f(n) = 4^n + 6^n + 9n^5$	$O(6^n)$
$f(n) = 7n + 6^n + n!$	$O(n!)$

1.7 Tight and Loose Upper Bounds

This is the definition of big O:

$f(n)$ is $O(g(n))$ if there exists constants c and n_0 such that
$f(n) \leq cg(n)$ for all $n \geq n_0$

For a function $f(n)$, there can be many functions $g(n)$, such that $f(n)$ is $O(g(n))$

Let us see the function; according to definition it is correct to say:

$f(n) = 5n^2 + 4n + 8$ is $O(n^2)$ Least upper bound is the tight upper bound

Also, it is equally correct to say:

$f(n) = 5n^2 + 4n + 8$ is $O(n^3)$
is $O(n^6)$ Loose upper bounds
is $O(2^n)$
is $O(n!)$

In practice, we need to provide the least upper bound. It is also known as the tight upper bound, which is $O(n^2)$ here. All others are loose upper bounds. So, all the given statements with loose upper bounds are correct according to the definition, but they are not informative. The statement $f(n)$ is $O(g(n))$ will be informative only when the function $g(n)$ is the smallest possible function that satisfies the definition of big O. Therefore, our aim is to always provide the tight upper bound. The method we have seen earlier for finding big O will always give us the tight upper bound.

1.8 Finding Time Complexity

The running time of an algorithm is proportional to the number of primitive operations executed during run time. Some examples of these operations are:

- Comparisons
- Arithmetic operations
- Assignments
- Input and output of primary data types

To find function T, we have to express the number of primitive operations executed during run time, in terms of input size n.

Let us take an algorithm that performs some simple operations.

```
someAlgorithm(int n)
{
    Input              c1
    Assignment         c2

    for(i=0; i<n; i++)
        Comparison     c3
```

```
    Arithmetic operation       c4
}
```

Each operation in this algorithm will take a certain amount of time, depending on the computer that you are using. Suppose input takes time c1, the assignment takes time c2, the comparison takes time c3, and the arithmetic operation takes time c4. These constants can be in any unit. Now, to calculate the total running time of the algorithm, we have to add the time taken by all these operations, and for that, we have to find the number of times each operation is executed.

The input, assignment, and arithmetic operations are executed only once. The comparison operation is inside the loop, which iterates n times. The variable i goes from 0 to n-1, so there are n iterations of the loop and so the comparison is executed n times.

The total running time will be:

T = c1+c2+c3*n+c4

Now that we have found the function T that represents the running time in terms of n, the next step is to find big O for this function. We have seen that while finding big O, we can drop the constants and ignore the coefficients. So, we drop the constants c1, c2, and c4 and ignore the coefficient c3, and we can say that T is O(n).

In our big O analysis, we can ignore all the system-dependent constants, and therefore this method allows us to analyze algorithms in a way that is independent of the computer. In asymptotic analysis, we are not interested in how much time an operation takes to execute on a computer. We are interested in how many times that operation is executed. So, the exact computation of this function T is not necessary.

While writing the function T, we will be concerned only with primitive operations whose number depends on input size n because these operations can increase dramatically with an increase in input size. In asymptotic analysis, we are interested in seeing what happens when input size becomes large. So basically, we have to look for operations that are performed in those loops whose number of iterations depend on n. For example, in the preceding algorithm, we are interested only in the comparison operation, because for large values of n, this will account for most of the running time.

So, to find time complexity, we ignore all operations that are executed a constant number of times and focus only on those whose number depends on n.

1.9 Big O Analysis of Algorithms : Examples

Let us take different algorithms and calculate their time complexity.

Example 1:

```
someAlgorithm(int n)
{
        Assignment
        for(i=n-2; i>=1; i--)
                Arithmetic operation
        Output
        for(i=0; i<n; i++)
                Comparison
        for(i=0; i<6; i++)
                Assignment
}
```

In this algorithm, we will ignore the assignment and output operations as they are executed only once and do not depend on n. We can also ignore the third loop because it will always iterate 6 times only, irrespective of the size of the input. Even when n becomes 1 million, the assignment will be executed 6 times only.

The first loop will execute n-2 times because the value of i goes from n-2 to 1. Thus, the arithmetic operation will execute n-2 times. The second loop will iterate n times, so the comparison will execute n times.

So the time complexity is:

$T(n) = (n-2) + n$

$= n + n - 2$

$= 2n-2$

$T(n)$ is $O(n)$

We can ignore the constant and the coefficient. So, $T(n)$ is $O(n)$.

Example 2:

```
someAlgorithm(int n)
{
        Input
        for(i=n; i>=1; i=i-4)
                Arithmetic operation
        Output
}
```

We can ignore the input and output operations and focus on the loop. Let us find out how many times the loop will iterate.

If n = 20, then i - 20, 16, 12, 8, 4

$= \lceil 20/4 \rceil$

= 5 iterations

If n = 13, then i - 13, 9, 5, 1

$= \lceil 13/4 \rceil$

= 4 iterations

If n = 6, then i - 6, 2

$= \lceil 6/4 \rceil$

2 iterations

So the time complexity is-

$T(n) = \lceil n/4 \rceil$

$T(n)$ is $O(n)$

Example 3:

```
someAlgorithm(int n)
{
        Input
        for(i=1; i<=n; i=i+5)
                Comparison
        Output
}
```

Here in the loop, the control variable is incremented by 5 each time.

If n = 20, then i - 1, 6, 11, 16

$= \lceil 20/5 \rceil$

= 4 iterations

If n = 15, i - 1, 6, 11
= $\lceil 15/5 \rceil$
= 3 iterations

If n = 6, then i - 1, 6
= $\lceil 6/5 \rceil$
= 2 iterations

In this case, the number of loop iterations equals $\lceil n/5 \rceil$. So the time complexity is:

$T(n) = \lceil n/5 \rceil$
$T(n)$ is $O(n)$

Thus, we can say that the time complexity of loops in which the control variable is incremented or decremented by a constant number is $O(n)$.

Example 4:

```
someAlgorithm(int n)
{
        Assignment
        for(i=n; i>=1; i/=2)
                Arithmetic operation
        Output
}
```

Here, in the loop, the control variable is divided by 2 in each iteration.

If n = 51, then i - 51, 25, 12, 6, 3, 1
= $\lceil \log_2 51 \rceil$
6 iterations

If n = 20, then i - 20, 10, 5, 2, 1
= $\lceil \log_2 20 \rceil$
5 iterations

If n = 5 then i - 5, 2, 1
= $\lceil \log_2 5 \rceil$
3 iterations

The number of iterations of the loop is given by $\lceil \log_2 n \rceil$. So the time complexity is:

$T(n) = \lceil \log_2 n \rceil$
$T(n)$ is $O(\log n)$

Example 5:

```
someAlgorithm(int n)
{
        Assignment
        for(i=1; i<=n; i*=2)
                Arithmetic operation
        Output
}
```

Here, in the loop, the control variable is multiplied by 2 in each iteration.

If n = 55, then i - 1, 2, 4, 8, 16, 32
= $\lceil \log_2 55 \rceil$
6 iterations

If n = 21, then i - 1, 2, 4, 8, 16
= $\lceil \log_2 21 \rceil$
5 iterations

If n = 7, then i - 1,2,4
= $\lceil \log_2 7 \rceil$
3 iterations

The number of iterations of the loop is given by $\lceil \log_2 n \rceil$. So the time complexity is:

$T(n) = \lceil \log_2 n \rceil$
$T(n)$ is $O(\log n)$

If we divide or multiply the control variable by any other constant, then too the complexity will be O(log n).

Example 6:
```
someAlgorithm(int n)
{
        Input

        for(i=0; i<n; i++)
        {
                Assignment

                for(j=0; j<n; j++)
                        Comparison
        }
        Arithmetic operation
        Output
}
```

Here, we have nested loops. When we have nested loops, we will be interested in knowing how many times the innermost loop executes because the iterations of the innermost loop will always be more than those of outer loops. We can ignore Input, Arithmetic operation and Output operations.

The outer loop will execute n times, and for each iteration of the outer loop, the inner loop will execute n times.

Total iterations of the inner loop:
= n + n + n +........ n times = n*n = n^2

The total number of iterations is $n+n^2$ because the assignment executes n times, and the comparison executes n^2 times. So the time complexity is:

$T(n) = n + n^2$
$T(n)$ is $O(n^2)$

Example 7:
```
someAlgorithm(int n)
{
        Input
        for(i=0; i<n; i++)
        {
                for(i=n; i>=1; i/=2)
                        Arithmetic operation
                for(j=0; j<n; j++)
                        Comparison
        }
        Arithmetic operation
```

```
        Output
}
```

In this algorithm, the outer loop iterates n times, and in each iteration of the outer loop, the first inner loop iterates log n times, and the second inner loop iterates n times.

Iterations of the first inner loop:
= logn + logn + logn + ... n times = n * logn

Iterations of the second inner loop:
= n + n + n + ... n times = n * n = n^2

The inner loop arithmetic operation executes nlogn times and the comparison executes n^2 times, so the time complexity is:

$T(n) = nlogn + n^2$
$T(n)$ is $O(n^2)$

Example 8:

```
someAlgorithm(int n)
{
        input
        for(i=0; i<n; i++)
                for(j=0; j<n; j++)
                        for(k=0; k<n; k++)
                                comparison
        arithmetic operation
        for(i=0; i<n; i++)
                for(j=10; j>=1; j--)
                        assignment
}
```

In this algorithm, we have to count the number of times the comparison, and the assignment is executed because their number will depend on n.

In the first nested loop:
Iterations of outer loop = n
Iterations of the inner loop
= n + n + n + ... n times = n * n = n^2
Iterations of the innermost loop
= n + n + n + ... n^2 times = n^2 * n = n^3

In the second nested loop:
Iterations of the outer loop = n
Iterations of the inner loop
= 10 + 10 + 10 .... n times = n * 10

The comparison operation executes n^3 times and assignment operation executes 10n times, so the time complexity is:

$T(n) = n^3 + 10n$
$T(n)$ is $O(n^3)$

Example 9:

```
someAlgorithm(int n)
{
        Assignment
        for(i=0; i<n; i++)
```

```
        for(j=0; j<=i; j++)
                arithmetic operation
    output
}
```

In this algorithm, nested loops iterations of the inner loop depend on the index of the outer loop. In these cases, we cannot find the total iterations of the inner loop by just multiplying the iterations of the inner and outer loops.

For the outer loop iterations, let us see the value of i, values of j and number of iterations of inner loop.

Outer loop iterations	Value of i	Values of j	Number of iterations of inner loop
1st	0	0	1
2nd	1	0,1	2
3rd	2	0,1,2	3
....	....	....	....
(n-1)th	n-2	0,1,2,....,n-2	n-1
nth	n-1	0,1,2,....,n-2,n-1	n

Figure 1.8 Example 9 iterations values

Total iterations of inner loop $= 1 + 2 + 3 + \ldots\ldots + (n-1) + n$

$$= \frac{n(n+1)}{2} = \frac{n^2}{2} + \frac{n}{2}$$

So the time complexity is-

$$T(n) = \frac{n^2}{2} + \frac{n}{2}$$

T(n) is $O(n^2)$

Example 10:

```
someAlgorithm(int n)
{
        Assignment

        for(i=0; i<n-1; i++)
                for(j=i+1; j<n; j++)
                        arithmetic operation

        output
}
```

In this algorithm, nested loops iterations of the inner loop depend on the index of the outer loop.

For the outer loop, let us see the value of i, values of j and number of iterations of the inner loop.

Outer loop iterations	Value of i	Values of j	Number of iterations of inner loop
1st	0	1,2,3,4,....,n-2,n-1	n-1
2nd	1	2,3,4,....,n-2,n-1	n-2
3rd	2	3,4,....,n-2,n-1	n-3
....	....	....	....
(n-2)th	n-3	n-2,n-1	2
(n-1)th	n-2	n-1	1

Figure 1.9 Example 10 iterations values

Total iterations of the inner loop:

$= (n-1) + (n-2) + \ldots + 2 + 1$

$= 1 + 2 + \ldots\ldots\ldots (n-2) + (n-1)$

$= \dfrac{n(n-1)}{2} = \dfrac{n^2}{2} - \dfrac{n}{2}$

So the time complexity is:

$T(n) = \dfrac{n^2}{2} - \dfrac{n}{2}$

$T(n)$ is $O(n^2)$

This nested loop is seen in the selection sort algorithm.

Example 11:

```
someAlgorithm(int n)
{
        Assignment

        for(x=n-2; x>=0; x--)
                for(j=0; j<=x; j++)
                        arithmetic operation

        output
}
```

In this algorithm, nested loops iterations of the inner loop depend on the index of the outer loop.

For the outer loop, let us see the value of x, values of j and number of iterations of the inner loop.

Outer loop iterations	Value of x	Values of j	Number of iterations of inner loop
1st	n-2	0,1,....,n-2	n-1
2nd	n-3	0,1,....,n-3	n-2
3rd	n-4	0,1,....,n-4	n-3
....	....	....	....
(n-2)th	1	0,1	2
(n-1)th	0	0	1

Figure 1.10 Example 11 iterations values

Total iterations of the Inner loop:

$= n-1 + n-2 + \ldots\ldots + 2 + 1$

$= 1 + 2 + \ldots\ldots\ldots (n-2) + (n-1)$

$= \dfrac{n(n-1)}{2} = \dfrac{n^2}{2} - \dfrac{n}{2}$

So the time complexity is:

$T(n) = \dfrac{n^2}{2} - \dfrac{n}{2}$

$T(n)$ is $O(n^2)$

This nested loop is seen in the bubble sort algorithm.

Example 12:

```
someAlgorithm(int n)
```

```
{
        Assignment
        for(i=0; i<n; i++)
                function(i);
        output
}
```

In this algorithm, there is a function call in the loop. Let us assume the function is of O(log n).

So the time complexity is:

T(n) = n logn
T(n) is O(nlogn)

Example 13:

```
someAlgorithm(int n)
{
        for(i=0; i<n; i++)
                for(i=n-1; i>=1; i/=2)
                        Arithmetic operation
        if(condition)
        {
                for(i=0; i<n; i++)
                        for(j=0; j<n j++)
                                Comparison
        }
        else
        {
                for(i=0; i<n; i++)
                        Arithmetic Operation
        }
}
```

In this algorithm, we have a `for` loop and an `if...else` statement.

As we have seen in the earlier example, the time complexity of the `for` loop is O(nlogn). When the algorithm is executed, either `if` block or `else` block executes. While calculating time complexity, we consider the block whose order is larger. Here `if` block is $O(n^2)$ and `else` block is $O(n)$, and so we will consider the `if...else` statement as $O(n^2)$.

So the time complexity is:

T(n) = n logn + n^2
T(n) is $O(n^2)$

Example 14:

```
someAlgorithm(int n)
{
        Assignment
        for(i=0; i<5; i++)
                Arithmetic operation
        output
}
```

In this algorithm, the same number of operations are executed every time the loop is executed. Thus, the algorithm takes constant time.

The algorithm is O(1) because it will always execute a constant number of steps, whether the input size is one hundred or 1 million. The number of steps does not depend on input size n.

So the time complexity is:

T(n) is O(1)

Some examples of constant time algorithms are:

- `printFirstElement()`: prints the first element of an array of size n.
- `swapFirstLast()`: a function that swaps the first and last elements of an array of size n
- `returnStackSize()`: a function that returns the size of a stack.

These algorithms take the same time irrespective of the size of the input. Thus, they are said to take constant time and have O(1).

1.10 Worst Case, Average Case and Best Case Analysis

We have seen that the running time of an algorithm depends on the input size, but some algorithms might take a different running time for different inputs of same size. In these algorithms, the running time depends on the type of input data also.

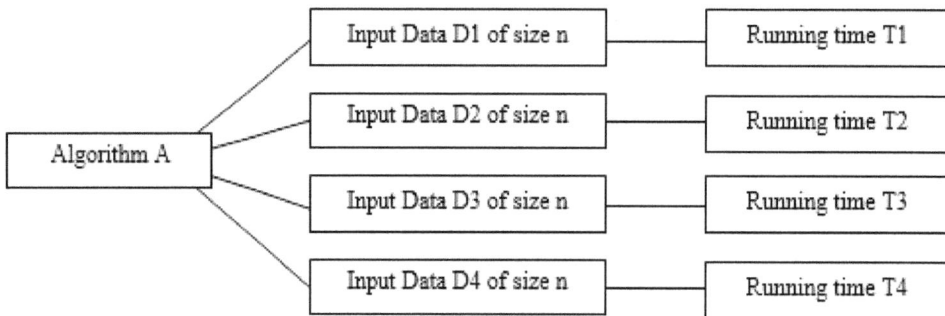

Figure 1.11 Running time of an algorithm

For example, suppose we have an algorithm with different input data sets of size n. The running time taken in all these cases is different. So, we can say that the behaviour of this algorithm depends upon the size and type of input.

Worst-case time complexity gives us a measure of the maximum running time that an algorithm will take for input size n. Similarly, best case time complexity gives us a measure of minimum running time and average case time complexity gives us a measure of average running time.

In the worst case scenario, we consider an input for which the algorithm takes the maximum time. This input causes the maximum number of operations to be executed. For example, when we search for an element in an array using linear search, the worst case scenario would be when the element to be searched is at the last place or is not present in the array. In that case, there would be n comparisons, so the worst case complexity of linear search is O(n).

In the best case, we consider an input for which the algorithm takes the minimum time. So, this input causes the minimum number of operations to be executed. In linear search, the best case would be when the element to be searched is present at the first location of the array. In this case, there would be only one comparison, and so the best case time complexity of linear search is O(1).

In the average case, we consider all possible inputs and compute an average. In this case, we have to assume certain probabilistic distribution for the input data. The most common assumption is that all possible permutations of an input are equally likely.

In practice, the worst case analysis is usually used to analyse the algorithms because in this case, we get to know the maximum time that the algorithm can take; the actual running time can never be worse than this.

The best-case analysis is not very useful as the best cases do not occur often. It is also not very informative as it gives us just the minimum time that the algorithm can take. The real running time can be much more than the minimum time. For example, an algorithm that takes some seconds in the best case might take days to execute in the worst or average case.

The average case analysis is rarely done because calculating time complexity in an average case is generally difficult.

The worst case analysis is most useful and informative and can be easily done. That is why, while analysing algorithms, we generally consider the worst case. So when we talk about the order of an algorithm, we are talking about the order in the worst case. For example we, will say that the linear search is $O(n)$, although in the best case it is $O(1)$. So, when the case is not specified, the worst case is implied.

Suppose we have an algorithm that behaves $O(n^2)$ in the worst case, $O(nlogn)$ in the average case, and $O(1)$ in the best case. We will just say that the algorithm is $O(n^2)$. To be more specific, we can explicitly state the order in these different cases.

1.11 Common Complexities

O(1) Constant
If time complexity is $O(1)$, then we say that algorithm's running time is constant. In this case, all operations are executed once or only a fixed number of times. The running time is independent of the size of input. For example, the algorithm for inserting a new element in the beginning of a linked list or getting an element from hash table will take constant time.

O(log n) logarithmic
If time complexity is $O(\log n)$, the algorithm is said to be logarithmic. This is the case in algorithms where a set of data is repeatedly divided into half, and the middle element is processed, for example, binary search.

O(n) linear
If the time complexity is $O(n)$, the algorithm is said to be linear. This is the case when each element in a data set must be processed. Here, the running time is linearly proportional to n, i.e., if the size of the input is doubled, then the running time will also be doubled. For example, the algorithm that prints all the elements of an array or the algorithm that inserts a new element at the end of a linked list will both take linear time, the worst case of linear search or the best case of bubble sort.

O(n log n) linear logarithmic
If time complexity is $O(n \log n)$, then the algorithm is said to be linear logarithmic, for example, best case of quick sort, merge sort algorithm.

O(n²) quadratic
If the time complexity is $O(n^2)$, then the algorithm is said to be quadratic. This is the case when the complete set of data has to be traversed for each element of the set, or we can say that all pairs of data items are processed. In this case, if n doubles, the run time becomes 4 times. Quadratic problems are helpful only for small sets of data because n^2 increases rapidly as n increases. This complexity generally occurs in algorithms that involve nested iterations over the input, for example, in the worst case of bubble sort and selection sort algorithms.

O(n³) cubic

If the time complexity is $O(n^3)$, then the algorithm is said to be cubic. This is the case when the algorithm processes all triplets of input data items. An example of this complexity is the matrix multiplication.

O(nᵏ) polynomial

If time complexity is $O(n^k)$ for some constant k, then the algorithm is considered polynomial.

O(aⁿ) exponential

An algorithm is called exponential if it has running time of order a^n, where a is some number more than 1. This is the case when all possible subsets of a set of data are generated. The runtime for these algorithms increases rapidly; for example, if we have an algorithm with complexity 2^n, then the running time for that algorithm will double with each additional element in the input data. An example of an exponential algorithm is the Tower of Hanoi problem. Since running times for the exponential algorithms increase rapidly, they can be used only for small input sizes and, therefore, are not of much practical use.

O(n!)

This is the case when all possible permutations of a set of data are generated.

Exercise

1. In asymptotic analysis, the exact running time is calculated.
    (a) True   (b) False

2. For analyzing an algorithm, we study how the running time of the algorithm increases with the increase in input size.
    (a) True   (b) False

3. Growth rate of n is more than growth rate of log n.
    (a) True   (b) False

4. For finding big O for a function, we have to keep the .... growing term of the function, and we can discard all the lower terms and constants.
    (a) fastest   (b) lowest

5. While computing the O notation, the base of the logarithm is not important.
    (a) True   (b) False

6. What is big O for this function?
    $f(n) = 3n^2 + 5n + 18$
    (a) $O(1)$ (b) $O(n)$ (c) $O(n^2)$

7. What is big O for this function?
    $f(n) = 100$
    (a) $O(1)$ (b) $O(n)$ (c) $O(n^2)$

8. Arrange these functions in increasing order of asymptotic complexity:
    $f1(n) = n^2 + 10n$
    $f2(n) = \log n + 89$
    $f3(n) = 2^n + n \log n$
    (a) f1,f2,f3   (b) f2,f3,f1   (c) f2,f1,f3

9. $f(n) = n^3 + 3^n$ is $O(n^3)$
    (a) True   (b) False

10. What is the run time efficiency of the following code?
    ```
    for(i=0; i<n; i++)
        a[i] = 0;
    ```
    (a) $O(n)$ (b) $O(n^2)$

11. The run time efficiency of this code is $O(n^2)$.

```
for(i=0; i<n; i++)
    for(j=0; j<5; j++)
            s = i+j;
```

(a) True   (b) False

12. Run time efficiency of this code is ....

```
for(i=0; i<n; i++)
{
    for(i=n-1; i>=1; i/=2)
            x++;
    for(j=0; j<n; j++)
            y++;
}
```

(a) $O(n \log n)$ (b) $O(n^2)$

13. For an algorithm with linear time complexity, if the input size is doubled then the running time will ....

(a) double   (b) triple   (c) quadruple

14. .... case time complexity gives us a measure of the maximum running time that an algorithm will take for input size n.

(a) Best   (b) Average   (c) Worst

15. Calculating time complexity in .... case is generally very difficult.

(a) Best   (b) Average   (c) Worst

16. If an algorithm has time complexity 2^n, then the running time for that algorithm will double with each additional element in the input data.

(a) True   (b) False

17. Which of these represents the time complexity of an algorithm that takes the same time for any input size.

(a) $O(1)$ (b) $O(\log n)$ (c) $O(n)$

18. The following two functions find the maximum element in an array. Which is the function whose behavior will depend on input data?

```
int findMax1(int a[], int n)
{
    bool isMax;
    int i,j;

    for(i=0; i<n; i++)
    {
            isMax=true;
            for(j=0; j<n; j++)
            {
                    if(a[j] > a[i])
                    {
                            isMax=false;
                            break;
                    }
            }
            if(isMax==true)
                    break;
    }
    return a[i];
}//End of findMax1()
```

```
int findMax2(int a[], int n)
{
    int i,max;
    max=a[0];
    for(i=0; i<n; i++)
    {
            if(a[i] > max)
                    max=a[i];
    }
    return max;
}//End of findMax2()
```

(a) findMax1   (b) findMax2

19. The following two functions perform the same work; which one is more efficient?

```
void sum1(int a[], int s[], int n)
{
    int i,j;
    for(i=0; i<n; i++)
    {
            s[i]=0;
            for(j=0; j<=i; j++)
                    s[i]+=a[j];
    }
}//End of sum1()
void sum2(int a[], int s[], int n)
{
    int i;
    s[0]=a[0];
    for(i=1; i<n; i++)
            s[i]=s[i-1]+a[i];
}//End of sum2()
```

(a) sum1   (b) sum2

Join our book's Discord space

Join the book's Discord Workspace for Latest updates, Offers, Tech happenings around the world, New Release and Sessions with the Authors:

https://discord.bpbonline.com

Arrays

An array is a collection of similar type of data items and each data item is called an element of the array. The data type of the elements may be any valid data type, such as char, int or float. The elements of the array share the same variable name, but each element has a different index number known as a subscript.

Consider a situation where we want to store and display the age of 100 employees. We can take an array variable `age` of type int. The size of this array variable is 100, and hence, it is capable of storing 100 integer values. The individual elements of this array are:

```
age[0], age[1], age[2], age[3], age[4],...........................age[98], age[99]
```

In C++, the subscripts start from zero, so `age[0]` is the first element, `age[1]` is the second element of the array, and so on.

Arrays can be single dimensional or multidimensional. The number of subscripts determines the dimension of array. A one-dimensional array has one subscript; two-dimensional array has two subscripts, and so on. The two-dimensional arrays are known as matrices.

2.1 One Dimensional Array

2.1.1 Declaration of 1-D Array

Like other simple variables, arrays should also be declared before they are used in the program. The syntax for the declaration of an array is:

```
datatype arrayName[size];
```

Here, `arrayName` denotes the name of the array, and it can be any valid C++ identifier; `datatype` is the data type of the elements of the array. The size of the array specifies the number of elements that can be stored in the array. It may be a positive integer constant or constant integer expression. Here are some examples of array declarations:

```
int age[100];
float salary[15];
char grade[20];
```

Here, `age` is an integer type array, which can store 100 elements of integer type. The array `salary` is a float type array of size 15, and it can hold float values. The third one is a character type array of size 20, which can hold characters. The individual elements of the above arrays are:

```
age[0],age[1],age[2],.......................................age[99]
salary[0],salary[1],salary[2],.........salary[14]
grade[0],grade[1],grade[2],....................grade[19]
```

When the array is declared, the compiler allocates space in memory sufficient to hold all the elements of the array, and so the size of array should be known at the compile time. We cannot use variables other than `const` variables to specify the array size in the declaration. For example:

```
static const int maxSize = 10;
main()
{
        int size = 15;
        float sal[maxSize]; //Valid
        int marks[size];    //Not valid
```

```
             . . . . . . . . . . . . . .
             . . . . . . . . . . . . . .
}
```

The use of the `const` variable to specify the size of the array makes it convenient to modify the program if the size of the array is to be changed later because the size has to be changed only in one place.

2.1.2 Accessing 1-D Array Elements

The elements of an array can be accessed by specifying the array name followed by the subscript in brackets. In C++, the array subscripts start from 0. Hence, if there is an array of size 5, then the valid subscripts will be from 0 to 4. The last valid subscript is one less than the size of the array. This last valid subscript is known as the upper bound of the array, and 0 is known as the lower bound of the array. Let us take an array:

```
int arr[5];      //Size of array arr is 5, can hold five integer elements
```

The elements of this array are:

```
arr[0], arr[1], arr[2], arr[3], arr[4]
```

Here, 0 is the lower bound, and 4 is the upper bound of the array.

The subscript can be any expression that yields an integer value. It can be any integer constant, integer variable, integer expression or return value (`int`) from a function call. For example, if `i` and `j` are integer variables, then these are some valid subscripted array elements-

```
arr[3], arr[i], arr[i+j], arr[2*j], arr[i++]
```

A subscripted array element is treated as any other variable in the program. We can store values in them, print their values or perform any operation that is valid for any simple variable of the same data type. For example if `arr` and `sal` are two arrays of sizes 5 and 10 respecively, then these are valid statements:

```
int arr[5];
float sal[10];
int i;
cin >> arr[1];          //input value into arr[1]
cout << sal[3];         //print value of sal[3]
arr[4] = 25;            //assign a value to arr[4]
arr[4]++;               //Increment the value of arr[4] by 1
sal[5] += 200;          //Add 200 to sal[5]
sum = arr[0]+arr[1]+arr[2]+arr[3]+arr[4]; //Add all the values of array
i=2;
cin >> sal[i];          //Input value into sal[2]
cout << sal[i];         //Print value of sal[2]
cout << sal[i++];       //Print value of sal[2] and increment the value of i
```

There is no check on bounds of the array. For example, if we have an array `arr` of size 5, the valid subscripts are only 0, 1, 2, 3, 4 and if someone tries to access elements beyond these subscripts, like `arr[5]` , `arr[10]`, the compiler will not show any error message. but this may lead to run time errors. So it is the responsibility of programmer to provide array bounds checking wherever needed.

2.1.3 Processing 1-D Arrays

For processing arrays, we generally use a `for` loop, and the loop variable is used in place of a subscript. The initial value of loop variable is taken 0 since array subscripts start from zero. The loop variable is increased by 1 each time so that we can access and process the next element in the array. The total number of passes in the loop will be equal to the number of elements in the array, and in each pass, we will process one element. Suppose `arr` is an array of type `int`:

(i) Reading values in `arr`

```
for(i=0; i<10; i++)
        cin >> arr[i];
```

(ii) Displaying values of `arr`

```
for(i=0; i<10; i++)
        cout << arr[i];
```

(iii) Adding all the elements of `arr`

```
sum=0;
for(i=0; i<10; i++)
        sum += arr[i];
//P1.cpp : Program to display the array elements.
#include <iostream>
using namespace std;

int main()
{
        int arr[5] = {10, 20, 30, 40, 50};

        cout << "The array elements are :\n";
        for(int i=0; i<5; i++)
                cout << arr[i] << " ";
        cout << "\n";

        return 0;
}//End of main()
```

2.1.4 Initialization of 1-D Array

After declaration, the elements of a local array have garbage value while the elements of global and static arrays are automatically initialized to zero. We can explicitly initialize arrays at the time of declaration. The syntax for the initialization of an array is:

```
datatype arrayName[size]={value1, value2................valueN};
```

Here, `arrayName` is the name of the array variable, `size` is the size of the array, and `value1`, `value2,................valueN` are the constant values known as initializers, which are assigned to the array elements one after another. These values are separated by commas, with a semicolon after the ending braces. For example:

```
int marks[5] = {50, 85, 70, 65, 95};
```

The values of the array elements after this initialization are:

```
marks[0]:50, marks[1]:85, marks[2]:70, marks[3]:65, marks[4]:95
```

While initializing a 1-D array, it is optional to specify the size of the array. If the size is omitted during initialization then the compiler assumes the size of array equal to the number of initializers. For example:

```
int marks[] = {99, 78, 50, 45, 67, 89};
float sal[] = {25.5, 38.5, 24.7};
```

Here, the size of the array `marks` is assumed to be 6, and that of `sal` is assumed to be 3.

If, during initialization, the number of initializers is less than the size of the array, then all the remaining elements of the array are assigned a value of zero. For example:

```
int marks[5] = {99, 78};
```

Here, the size of array is 5 while there are only 2 initializers. After this initialization, the value of the elements are:

```
marks[0]:99,  marks[1]:78,  marks[2]:0,  marks[3]:0,  marks[4]:0
```

So, if we initialize an array like this:

```
int arr[100] = {0};
```

Then all the elements of `arr` will be initialized to zero.

If the number of initializers is more than the size given in brackets, then the compiler will show an error. For example:

```
int arr[5] = {1,2,3,4,5,6,7,8};        //Error '
```

We cannot copy all the elements of an array to another array by simply assigning it to the other array. For example, if we have two arrays `a` and `b`, then:

```
int a[5] = {1,2,3,4,5};
int b[5];
b = a;  //Not valid
```

We will have to copy all the elements of the array one by one, using a `for` loop:

```
for(i=0; i<5; i++)
        b[i] = a[i];
```

In the following program, we will find out the largest and smallest number in an integer array:

```
//P2.cpp : Program to find the smallest and largest number in an array.
#include<iostream>
using namespace std;

int main()
{
        int arr[10] = {2,5,4,1,8,9,11,6,3,7};
        int small, large;

        small = large = arr[0];
        for(int i=1; i<10; i++)
        {
                if(arr[i] < small)
                        small = arr[i];
                if(arr[i] > large)
                        large = arr[i];
        }
        cout << "Smallest = " << small << ", Largest = " << large << "\n";

        return 0;
}//End of main()
```

We have taken the value of the first element as the initial value of `small` and `large`. Inside the `for` loop, we will start comparing from the second element onwards, and so this time, we have started the loop from 1 instead of 0.

The following program will reverse the elements of an array:

```
//P3.cpp : Program to reverse the elements of an array.
#include<iostream>
using namespace std;

int main()
{
        int arr[10] = {1,2,3,4,5,6,7,8,9,10};
        int i,j,temp;

        cout << "The array is :\n";
        for(i=0; i<10; i++)
                cout << arr[i] << " ";
        cout << "\n";

        for(i=0,j=9; i<j; i++,j--)
        {
```

```
            temp = arr[i];
            arr[i] = arr[j];
            arr[j] = temp;
      }
      cout << "After reversing, the array is :\n";
      for(i=0; i<10; i++)
            cout << arr[i] << " ";
      cout << "\n";

      return 0;
}//End of main()
```

In the `for` loop, we have used the comma operator and taken two variables, `i` and `j`. The variable `i` is initialized with the lower bound and `j` is initialized with upper bound. After each pass of the loop, `i` is incremented while `j` is decremented. Inside the loop, `arr[i]` is exchanged with `arr[j]`. So `arr[0]` will be exchanged with `arr[9]`, `arr[1]` with `arr[8]`, `arr[2]` with `arr[7]` and so on.

2.1.5 1-D Arrays and Functions

2.1.5.1 Passing Individual Array Elements to a Function

We know an array element is treated as any other simple variable in the program. So, like other simple variables, we can pass individual array elements as arguments to a function.

```
//P4.cpp : Program to pass array elements to a function.
#include<iostream>
using namespace std;
void checkEvenOdd(int num)
{
      if(num%2 == 0)
            cout << num << " is even\n";
      else
            cout << num << " is odd\n";
}//End of checkEvenOdd()
int main()
{
      int arr[10] = {1,2,3,4,5,6,7,8,9,10};

      for(int i=0; i<10; i++)
            checkEvenOdd(arr[i]);

      return 0;
}//End of main()
```

2.1.5.2 Passing Whole 1-D Array to a Function

We can pass the whole array as an actual argument to a function. The corresponding formal argument should be declared as an array variable of the same data type.

```
int main()
{
      int arr[10];
      ............
      ............
      func(arr); //In function call, array name is specified without brackets
}
void func(int val[10])
{
      ............
      ............
}
```

It is optional to specify the size of the array in the formal argument. For example, we may write the function definition as:

```
void func(int val[])
{
    ............
    ............
}
```

The mechanism of passing an array to a function is quite different from that of passing a simple variable. In the case of simple variables, the called function creates a copy of the variable and works on it, so that any changes made in the function do not affect the original variable. When an array is passed as an actual argument, the called function gets access to the original array and works on it, so any changes made inside the function affect the original array. Here is a program in which an array is passed to a function:

```
//P5.cpp : Program to understand the effect of passing an array to a function.
#include<iostream>
using namespace std;

void func(int val[])
{
        int sum=0;

        for(int i=0; i<6; i++)
        {
                val[i] = val[i]*val[i];
                sum += val[i];
        }
        cout << "Sum of squares = " << sum << "\n";
}//End of func()

int main()
{
        int arr[6] = {1,2,3,4,5,6};

        cout << "The array is :\n";
        for(int i=0; i<6; i++)
                cout << arr[i] << " ";
        cout << "\n";

        func(arr);

        cout << "Now the array is :\n";
        for(int i=0; i<6; i++)
                cout << arr[i] << " ";
        cout << "\n";

        return 0;
}//End of main()
```

Here, the changes made to the array inside the called function are reflected in the calling function. The name of the formal argument is different but it refers to the original array.

2.2 Two Dimensional Arrays

2.2.1 Declaration and Accessing Individual Elements of a 2-D array

The syntax of the declaration of a 2-D array is similar to that of 1-D arrays, but here we have two subscripts.

```
datatype arrayName[rowsize][columnsize];
```

Here, `rowsize` specifies the number of rows and `columnsize` represents the number of columns in the array. The total number of elements in the array are `rowsize` * `columnsize`. For example:

```
int arr[4][5];
```

Here. `arr` is a 2-D array with 4 rows and 5 columns. The individual elements of this array can be accessed by applying two subscripts, where the first subscript denotes the row number and the second subscript denotes the column number. The starting element of this array is `arr[0][0]` and the last element is `arr[3][4]`. The total number of elements in this array is 4*5 = 20.

	Col 0	Col 1	Col 2	Col 3	Col 4
Row 0	arr[0][0]	arr[0][1]	arr[0][2]	arr[0][3]	arr[0][4]
Row 1	arr[1][0]	arr[1][1]	arr[1][2]	arr[1][3]	arr[1][4]
Row 2	arr[2][0]	arr[2][1]	arr[2][2]	arr[2][3]	arr[2][4]
Row 3	arr[3][0]	arr[3][1]	arr[3][2]	arr[3][3]	arr[3][4]

2.2.2 Processing 2-D Arrays

For processing 2-D arrays, we use two nested `for` loops. The outer `for` loop corresponds to the row and the inner `for` loop corresponds to the column.

```
int arr[4][5];
```

(i) Reading values in `arr`

```
for(i=0; i<4; i++)
        for(j=0; j<5; j++)
                cin >> arr[i][j];
```

(ii) Displaying values of `arr`

```
for(i=0; i<4; i++)
        for(j=0; j<5; j++)
                cout << arr[i][j];
```

This will print all the elements in the same line. If we want to print the elements of different rows on different lines, then we can write this:

```
for(i=0; i<4; i++)
{
        for(j=0; j<5; j++)
                cout << arr[i][j];
        cout << "\n";
}
```

Here, the `cout << "\n";` statement causes the next row to begin from a new line.

```
//P6.cpp : Program to display the matrix.
#include<iostream>
#include<iomanip>
using namespace std;

static const int row=3;
static const int col=4;

int main()
{
        int mat[row][col] = { {1,2,3,4}, {5,6,7,8}, {9,10,11,12} };

        cout << "The matrix is :\n";
        for(int i=0; i<row; i++)
        {
                for(int j=0; j<col; j++)
                        cout << setw(5) << mat[i][j];
                cout << "\n";
        }
        cout << "\n";
```

```
        return 0;
}//End of main()
```

2.2.3 Initialization of 2-D Arrays

2-D arrays can be initialized in a way similar to that of 1-D arrays. For example:

```
int mat[4][3] = {11,12,13,14,15,16,17,18,19,20,21,22};
```

These values are assigned to the elements row-wise, and so the values of elements after this initialization are:

mat[0][0] : 11	mat[0][1] : 12	mat[0][2] : 13
mat[1][0] : 14	mat[1][1] : 15	mat[1][2] : 16
mat[2][0] : 17	mat[2][1] : 18	mat[2][2] : 19
mat[3][0] : 20	mat[3][1] : 21	mat[3][2] : 22

While initializing, we can group the elements row-wise using inner braces. For example:

```
int mat[4][3] = { {11,12,13}, {14,15,16}, {17,18,19}, {20,21,22} };
int mat[4][3] = {
                    {11,12,13},     //Row 0
                    {14,15,16},     //Row 1
                    {17,18,19},     //Row 2
                    {20,21,22}      //Row 3
                };
```

Here, the values in the first inner braces will be the values of Row 0, values in the second inner braces will be values of Row 1, and so on. Now consider this array initialization:

```
int mat[4][3] = {
                    {11},           //Row 0
                    {12,13},        //Row 1
                    {14,15,16},     //Row 2
                    {17}            //Row 3
                };
```

The remaining elements in each row will be assigned values 0, and so the values of elements will be:

mat[0][0] : 11	mat[0][1] : 0	mat[0][2] : 0
mat[1][0] : 12	mat[1][1] : 13	mat[1][2] : 0
mat[2][0] : 14	mat[2][1] : 15	mat[2][2] : 16
mat[3][0] : 17	mat[3][1] : 0	mat[3][2] : 0

In 2-D arrays, it is optional to specify the first dimension while initializing, but the second dimension should always be present. For example:

```
int mat[][3] = {
                    {1,10},
                    {2,20,200},
                    {3},
                    {4,40,400}
                };
```

Here, the first dimension is taken as 4 since there are 4 rows in initialization list.

A 2-D array is also known as a matrix. The next program adds two matrices; the order of both the matrices should be the same.

```
//P7.cpp : Program for addition of two matrices.
#include<iostream>
#include<iomanip>
using namespace std;

static const int row=3;
static const int col=4;
```

```
int main()
{
        int mat1[row][col] = { {1,2,8,4}, {5,6,7,8}, {3,2,1,4} };
        int mat2[row][col] = { {2,5,4,2}, {1,5,2,6}, {9,4,7,2} };
        int mat3[row][col];

        //Addition of matrices
        for(int i=0; i<row; i++)
                for(int j=0; j<col; j++)
                        mat3[i][j] = mat1[i][j]+mat2[i][j];

        cout << "Matrix 1 :\n";
        for(int i=0; i<row; i++)
        {
                for(int j=0; j<col; j++)
                        cout << setw(5) << mat1[i][j];
                cout << "\n";
        }
        cout << "\n";

        cout << "Matrix 2 :\n";
        for(int i=0; i<row; i++)
        {
                for(int j=0; j<col; j++)
                        cout << setw(5) << mat2[i][j];
                cout << "\n";
        }
        cout << "\n";

        cout << "The resultant Matrix 3 :\n";
        for(int i=0; i<row; i++)
        {
                for(int j=0; j<col; j++)
                        cout << setw(5) << mat3[i][j];
                cout << "\n";
        }
        cout << "\n";

        return 0;
}//End of main()
```

Now, we will write a program to multiply two matrices. Multiplication of matrices requires that the number of columns in the first matrix should be equal to the number of rows in the second matrix. Each row of the first matrix is multiplied with the column of the second matrix, and they are then added to get the element of resultant matrix. If we multiply two matrices of order m x n and n x p, then the multiplied matrix will be of order m x p. For example:

$$A_{2\times2} = \begin{bmatrix} 4 & 5 \\ 3 & 2 \end{bmatrix} \qquad B_{2\times3} = \begin{bmatrix} 2 & 6 & 3 \\ -3 & 2 & 4 \end{bmatrix}$$

$$C_{2\times3} = \begin{bmatrix} 4*2+5*(-3) & 4*6+5*2 & 4*3+5*4 \\ 3*2+2*(-3) & 3*6+2*2 & 3*3+2*4 \end{bmatrix} = \begin{bmatrix} -7 & 34 & 32 \\ 0 & 22 & 17 \end{bmatrix}$$

Figure 2.1 Multiplication of two matrices

```
//P8.cpp : Program for multiplication of two matrices.
#include<iostream>
#include<iomanip>
using namespace std;
```

```
static const int row1=3;
static const int col1=4;
static const int row2=col1;
static const int col2=2;

int main()
{
        int mat1[row1][col1] = { {2,1,4,3}, {5,2,7,1}, {3,1,4,2} };
        int mat2[row2][col2] = { {1,2}, {3,4}, {2,5}, {6,2} };
        int mat3[row1][col2];

        //Multiplication of matrices
        for(int i=0; i<row1; i++)
                for(int j=0; j<col2; j++)
                {
                        mat3[i][j] = 0;
                        for(int k=0; k<col1; k++)
                                mat3[i][j] += mat1[i][k]*mat2[k][j];
                }

        cout << "Matrix 1 :\n";
        for(int i=0; i<row1; i++)
        {
                for(int j=0; j<col1; j++)
                        cout << setw(5) << mat1[i][j];
                cout << "\n";
        }
        cout << "\n";

        cout << "Matrix 2 :\n";
        for(int i=0; i<row2; i++)
        {
                for(int j=0; j<col2; j++)
                        cout << setw(5) << mat2[i][j];
                cout << "\n";
        }
        cout << "\n";

        cout << "The resultant Matrix 3 :\n";
        for(int i=0; i<row1; i++)
        {
                for(int j=0; j<col2; j++)
                        cout << setw(5) << mat3[i][j];
                cout << "\n";
        }
        cout << "\n";

        return 0;
}//End of main()
```

The next program finds out the transpose of a matrix. Transpose matrix is defined as the matrix that is obtained by interchanging the rows and columns of a matrix. If a matrix is of m x n order then its transpose matrix will be of order n x m.

```
//P9.cpp : Program for transpose of matrix.
#include<iostream>
#include<iomanip>
using namespace std;

static const int row=3;
static const int col=4;

int main()
{
        int mat1[row][col] = { {3,2,1,5}, {6,5,8,2}, {9,3,4,1} };
```

```
        int mat2[col][row];

        cout << "The matrix is :\n";
        for(int i=0; i<row; i++)
        {
                for(int j=0; j<col; j++)
                        cout << setw(5) << mat1[i][j];
                cout << "\n";
        }
        cout << "\n";

        //Transpose
        for(int i=0; i<col; i++)
                for(int j=0; j<row; j++)
                        mat2[i][j] = mat1[j][i];

        cout << "Transpose of matrix is :\n";
        for(int i=0; i<col; i++)
        {
                for(int j=0; j<row; j++)
                        cout << setw(5) << mat2[i][j];
                cout << "\n";
        }
        cout << "\n";

        return 0;
}//End of main()
```

2.3 Arrays with More Than Two Dimensions

A 3-D array can thought of as an array of 2-D arrays. For example, if we have an array:

```
int arr[2][4][3];
```

We can think of this as an array consisting of two 2-D arrays, and each of those 2-D arrays has 4 rows and 3 columns.

Figure 2.2 Example of 3-D array

The individual elements are:

arr[0][0][0], arr[0][0][1], arr[0][0][2], arr[0][1][0]................arr[0][3]2]
arr[1][0][0], arr[1][0][1], arr[1][0][2], arr[1][1][0]................arr[1][3]2]

The total number of elements in the above 3-D array are:

$$= 2 * 4 * 3$$
$$= 24$$

This array can be initialized as:

```
int arr[2][4][3]={
        {
            {1,2,3},          //Matrix 0,Row 0
            {4,5},            //Matrix 0,Row 1
            {6,7,8},          //Matrix 0,Row 2
            {9}               //Matrix 0,Row 3
```

```
          },
          {
              {10,11},          //Matrix 1,Row 0
              {12,13,14},       //Matrix 1,Row 1
              {15,16},          //Matrix 1,Row 2
              {17,18,19}        //Matrix 1,Row 3
          }
     };
```

The value of elements after this initialization are:

arr[0][0][0] : 1	arr[0][0][1] : 2	arr[0][0][2] : 3
arr[0][1][0] : 4	arr[0][1][1] : 5	arr[0][1][2] : 0
arr[0][2][0] : 6	arr[0][2][1] : 7	arr[0][2][2] : 8
arr[0][3][0] : 9	arr[0][3][1] : 0	arr[0][3][2] : 0
arr[1][0][0] : 10	arr[1][0][1] : 11	arr[1][0][2] : 0
arr[1][1][0] : 12	arr[1][1][1] : 13	arr[1][1][2] : 14
arr[1][2][0] : 15	arr[1][2][1] : 16	arr[1][2][2] : 0
arr[1][3][0] : 17	arr[1][3][1] : 18	arr[1][3][2] : 19

Remember that the rule of initialization of multidimensional arrays is that the last subscript varies most frequently, and the first subscript varies least frequently.

2.3.1 Multidimensional Array and Functions

Multidimensional arrays can also be passed to functions like 1-D arrays. When passing multidimensional arrays, the first (leftmost) dimension may be omitted but all other dimensions must be specified in the function definition. For example, it would be invalid to write a function like this:

```
func(int a[],int b[][],int c[][][]) //Invalid
{
        ..............
}
```

In arrays b and c, we cannot omit all the dimensions. The correct form is:

```
func(int a[],int b[][4],int c[][3][5]) //Valid
{
        ..............
}
```

2.4 Array Operations

The array has the following operations:
- Traversal
- Search
- Insertion
- Deletion

Let us take an array of size 10, which has 5 elements:

```
int arr[10] = {10, 20, 30, 40, 50};
```

arr

10	20	30	40	50					
0	1	2	3	4	5	6	7	8	9

Figure 2.3 Array with 5 elements

2.4.1 Traversal

In an array, we can find the next element through the index number of array because every next element of an array has an index number incremented by 1 with the previous index number. Thus, we can traverse and access the array elements through array index.

Let us take the `index` value as 0. Now, the contents of `arr[index]` is 10, which is the first element of the array. We can process the next element of array by incrementing the `index` by 1.

```
index = index+1;
```

Now, `arr[index]` is 20, which is the second element of array. Therefore, we can traverse each element of array by incrementing the `index` by 1, until the `index` is not greater than the number of elements in array.

2.4.2 Search

Searching refers to finding an element in an array. For searching the element, we first traverse the array and while traversing, we compare each element of array with the given element.

We can search the element by another method named the binary search, which we will describe in the topic searching.

2.4.3 Insertion

Insertion into an array may be possible in two ways:
1. Insertion at the end
2. Insertion in between

Case 1

In the first case, we have to set the array index to the total number of elements and then insert the element. After insertion, increase the total number of elements by 1.

index = Total number of elements (5)
arr[index] = value of inserted element

Here, the element is inserted at the 6th position:

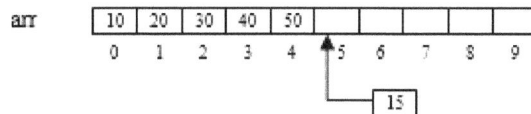

Figure 2.4 Insertion at the end

Case 2

In the second case, we have to shift right one position, all array elements from the last array element to the array element before which we want to insert the element. After insertion, increase the total number of elements by 1. Insertion at the beginning is done in the same way.

Here, the element is inserted at the 4th position:

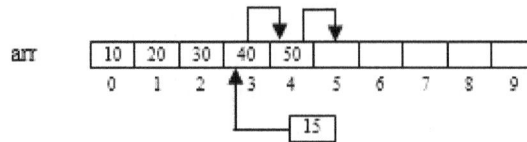

Figure 2.5 Insertion in between

2.4.4 Deletion

Deletion from an array is possible in two ways:
1. Deletion of the last element
2. Deletion in between

Case 1

First, traverse the array and compare the array element with the element that you want to delete. If the item is the last item of the array, then delete that element and decrease the total number of elements by 1.

Here, the last element is deleted:

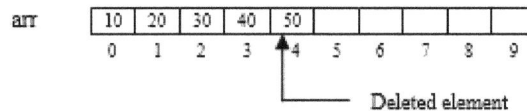

Figure 2.6 Deletion at the end

Case 2

In the second case, first traverse the array and compare the array element with the element you want to delete. If the element to be deleted is found, shift left one position from the next element to the last element of the array, and decrease the total number of elements by 1. Deletion at the beginning is done in the same way.

It is necessary to keep the status of total number of elements and the size of the array.

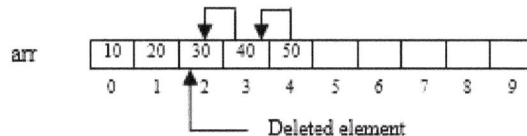

Figure 2.7 Deletion in between

The advantage of an array data structure is that we can easily compute the address of the array through index and also access the array element through index.

The disadvantage of the array is that we have to keep the total number of elements and array size. We cannot take elements more than the array size because array size is fixed. It also requires much processing in insertion and deletion because of shifting of array elements.

```
//P10.cpp : Program to rotate an array left by 1 element.
#include<iostream>
using namespace std;

static const int maxSize = 30;

int main()
{
        int arr[maxSize] = {10,20,30,40,50};
        int n=5;

        cout << "The array is :\n";
        for(int i=0; i<n; i++)
                cout << arr[i] << " ";
        cout << "\n";

        int temp = arr[0];
        for(int i=1; i<n; i++)
                arr[i-1]=arr[i];
        arr[n-1] = temp;

        cout << "After left rotation, the array is :\n";
        for(int i=0; i<n; i++)
                cout << arr[i] << " ";
        cout << "\n";

        return 0;
}//End of main()
```

2.5 Problems on Arrays

Problem 1

Write a program that scans a one-dimensional array from left to right and compares all adjacent elements. Any two adjacent elements `arr[j]` and `arr[j+1]` should be exchanged if `arr[j]` is greater than `arr[j+1]`. This procedure will always place the biggest element at the last position. Count the total number of exchanges done.

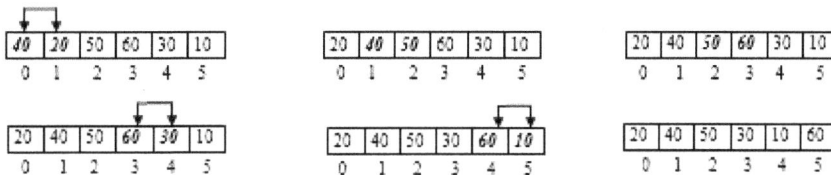

Figure 2.8 Adjacent element exchanges

```
//P11.cpp : Program to place the biggest element at the last position. Count the total
//number of exchanges done.
#include<iostream>
using namespace std;

static const int maxSize = 30;

int main()
{
        int arr[maxSize] = {40, 20, 50, 60, 30, 10, 90, 97, 70, 80};
        int n = 10, xchanges = 0;

        cout << "The array is :\n";
        for(int i=0; i<n; i++)
                cout << arr[i] << " ";
```

```cpp
        cout << "\n";

        int temp;
        for(int i=0; i<n-1; i++)
        {
                if(arr[i]>arr[i+1])
                {
                        temp = arr[i];
                        arr[i] = arr[i+1];
                        arr[i+1] = temp;
                        xchanges++;
                }
        }
        cout << "After exchanges, the array is :\n";
        for(int i=0; i<n; i++)
                cout << arr[i] << " ";
        cout << "\n";

        cout << "Total number of exchanges = " << xchanges << "\n";

        return 0;
}//End of main()
```

Problem 2

Write a program to print the Pascal triangle using a 2-D array:

1
1 1
1 2 1
1 3 3 1
1 4 6 4 1
1 5 10 10 5 1
1 6 15 20 15 6 1

We will calculate and store all the elements of Pascal triangle in a 2-D array. From the above triangle, we can observe that:

(i) All the elements of column 0 are 1.

(ii) All the elements for which row and column are the same are 1.

(iii) Any other element can be obtained by adding two elements of previous row as:

$a[i][j] = a[i-1][j-1]+a[i-1][j];$

Where, i and j represent row and column numbers.

```cpp
//P12.cpp : Program for Pascal's triangle.
#include<iostream>
#include<iomanip>
using namespace std;

static const int maxSize = 30;

int main()
{
        int arr[maxSize][maxSize];
        int n = 7; //Number of lines for triangle
        for(int i=0; i<n; i++)
        {
                for(int j=0; j<=i; j++)
                {
                        if(j==0 || i==j)
                                arr[i][j] = 1;
                        else
                                arr[i][j] = arr[i-1][j-1]+arr[i-1][j];
```

```
                }
        }
        cout << "Pascal triangle :\n";
        for(int i=0; i<n; i++)
        {
                for(int j=0; j<=i; j++)
                        cout << setw(5) << arr[i][j];
                cout << "\n";
        }
        return 0;
}//End of main()
```

Problem 3

Write a program to print the magic matrix.

(i) Magic matrix is a square matrix of order n x n, i.e., the number of rows is equal to the number of columns.
(ii) A magic matrix exists only for odd values of n.
(iii) The numbers in the matrix will be 1, 2, 3, 4......n^2, and each number can occur only once.
(iv) The sums of elements of every row, column, and diagonal are equal. This sum is always equal to $n(n^2+1)/2$.
The magic matrices for n = 3, n = 5, n = 7 are shown as follows:

2	9	4
7	5	3
6	1	8

n=3
Sum = 15

9	2	25	18	11
3	21	19	12	10
22	20	13	6	4
16	14	7	5	23
15	8	1	24	17

n=5
Sum = 65

20	11	2	49	40	31	22
12	3	43	41	32	23	21
4	44	42	33	24	15	13
45	36	34	25	16	14	5
37	35	26	17	8	6	46
29	27	18	9	7	47	38
28	19	10	1	48	39	30

n=7
Sum=175

Figure 2.9 Magic matrix

The procedure for creating a magic matrix is:

Start filling numbers from the center column of the bottom row, so initially place the number 1 in the centre column of the bottom row. Keep on placing the numbers by moving one row down and one column left (down-left) till you reach one of the following situations:

(i) If you reach the bottom left of the matrix, or a square that is already filled, then move one row up in the same column. This situation will arise when the previously placed number was divisible by n.
(ii) If you have to move left of the leftmost column, then go to the rightmost column.
(iii) If you have to move down the bottom row, then go to the topmost row.

```
//P13.cpp : Program for magic matrix.
#include<iostream>
#include<iomanip>
using namespace std;

static const int maxSize = 30;

int main()
{
        int arr[maxSize][maxSize];
        int n = 3;
```

```cpp
        int i = n-1;
        int j = (n-1)/2;
        int num;

        for(num=1; num <= n*n; num++)
        {
                arr[i][j] = num;
                i++; //move down
                j--; //move left

                if(num%n == 0)
                {
                        i-=2; //one above the previous row
                        j++;  //back to the previous column
                }
                else if(i == n)
                        i = 0; //go to topmost row
                else if(j == -1)
                        j = n-1; //go to rightmost column
        }

        cout << "Magic matrix :\n";

        for(i=0; i<n; i++)
        {
                for(j=0; j<n; j++)
                        cout << setw(5) << arr[i][j];
                cout << "\n";
        }

        return 0;
}//End of main()
```

Problem 4

Write a program to print all prime numbers less than integer n, using Sieve of Eratosthenes.

(i) Write down all integers from 2 to n sequentially.
(ii) Cross out all multiples of 2.
(iii) Find the next uncrossed number, and cross out all its multiples.
(iv) Repeat step (iii) until we find an uncrossed number whose square is greater than n.

All the uncrossed numbers are prime.

```cpp
//P14.cpp : Program to print prime numbers using Sieve of Eratosthenes.
#include<iostream>
using namespace std;

static const int maxSize = 1000;

int main()
{
        int arr[maxSize] = {0};
        int n = 50;
        int p = 2, i;

        while(p*p <= n)
        {
                for(i=2; i*p<=n; i++) //Cross out all multiples of p
                        arr[i*p] = 1;

                for(i=p+1; i<=n; i++) //Find next uncrossed
                {
                        if(arr[i] == 0)
                        {
                                p = i;
```

```
                        break;
                }
        }
    }//End of while

    //Print all uncrossed integers
    for(i=2; i<=n; i++)
    {
        if(arr[i] == 0)
            cout << i << " ";
    }
    cout << "\n";

    return 0;
}//End of main()
```

Problem 5

Write a program to print a square matrix spirally.

95	67	32	35	44	65
12	11	16	93	29	59
82	13	21	31	27	17
24	18	28	15	33	20
39	30	26	23	34	37
19	38	52	14	36	22

Figure 2.10 Square matrix

If the given matrix is printed spirally, the output would be:

95 67 32 35 44 65 59 17 20 37 22 36 14 52 38 19 39 24 82 12 11 16 93 29 27 33 34 23 26 30 18 13 21 31 15 28

The following figure shows the indices of elements and the order in which they are printed:

0,0	0,1	0,2	0,3	0,4	0,5
1,0	1,1	1,2	1,3	1,4	1,5
2,0	2,1	2,2	2,3	2,4	2,5
3,0	3,1	3,2	3,3	3,4	3,5
4,0	4,1	4,2	4,3	4,4	4,5
5,0	5,1	5,2	5,3	5,4	5,5

(0,0 to 0,5) (1,5 to 5,5) (5,4 to 5,0) (4,0 to 1,0)

1,1	1,2	1,3	1,4
2,1	2,2	2,3	2,4
3,1	3,2	3,3	3,4
4,1	4,2	4,3	4,4

(1,1 to 1,4) (2,4 to 4,4) (4,3 to 4,1) (3,1 to2,1)

2,2	2,3
3,2	3,3

(2,2 to 2,3) (3,3) (3,2)

Figure 2.11 Indices of elements and print order

```
//P15.cpp : Program to print a square matrix spirally.
#include<iostream>
```

```cpp
#include<iomanip>
using namespace std;
static const int maxSize = 10;
int main()
{
        int arr[maxSize][maxSize] =
        {
                {95,67,32,35,44,65},
                {12,11,16,93,29,59},
                {82,13,21,31,27,17},
                {24,18,28,15,33,20},
                {39,30,26,23,34,37},
                {19,38,52,14,36,22}
        };

        int n = 6;
        int i,j,start,end;

        cout << "The square matrix is :\n";
        for(i=0; i<n; i++)
        {
                for(j=0; j<n; j++)
                        cout << setw(4) << arr[i][j];
                cout << "\n";
        }

        cout << "\nPrinting the square matrix spirally :\n";

        for(start=0,end=n-1; start<=end; start++,end--)
        {
                for(i=start; i<=end; i++)
                        cout << arr[start][i] << " ";
                for(i=start+1; i<=end; i++)
                        cout << arr[i][end] << " ";
                for(i=end-1; i>=start; i--)
                        cout << arr[end][i] << " ";
                for(i=end-1; i>=start+1; i--)
                        cout << arr[i][start] << " ";
        }

        cout << "\n";

        return 0;
}//End of main()
```

Exercise

1. Write a program to exchange adjacent elements of an array.

Figure 2.12 Adjacent element exchange in array

2. Write a program to find the difference of the largest and smallest elements of an array.
3. Write a program to find the largest and second largest elements of an array.
4. Write a program to reverse only the first k elements of an array.
5. Write a program to check whether all the elements of an array are distinct.

6. Write a program to remove duplicate elements from an unsorted array.

7. Write a program to remove duplicate elements from a sorted array.

8. Write a program to find the most frequent element in a sorted array.

9. Write a program to find an element in a matrix, where the matrix is sorted row-wise and column-wise.

10. Write a program to interchange the first and last rows of a matrix.

11. Write a program to reverse the rows of a matrix.

```
1  2   3  4                13 14  15 16
5  6   7  8      ------>     9 10  11 12
9 10  11 12                 5  6   7  8
13 14 15 16                 1  2   3  4
```

Figure 2.13 Reverse the rows of a matrix

12. Write a program to interchange the first and last columns of a matrix.

13. Write a program to reverse the columns of a matrix

```
1  2   3  4                 4  3   2  1
5  6   7  8                 8  7   6  5
9 10  11 12     ------>     12 11 10  9
13 14 15 16                 16 15 14 13
```

Figure 2.14 Reverse the columns of a matrix

14. Write a program to find out whether a square matrix is symmetric or not. A square matrix is symmetric if the transpose of the matrix is equal to the matrix.

15. Write a program to find the sum of rows and columns of a 2-d array and store the sums in the same array.

```
1 2 2 1 4              1  2  2  1  4  10
5 4 3 2 5              5  4  3  2  5  19
6 3 2 1 4    ------>   6  3  2  1  4  16
3 5 4 2 3              3  5  4  2  3  17
                      15 14 11  6 16  62
```

Figure 2.15 Matrix row and column sum

16. Write a program to display a rectangular matrix spirally.

17. Write a program to display a Spiral Matrix. A spiral matrix is n x n square matrix formed by placing the numbers 1, 2, 3, 4 ……..n^2 in spiral form starting from the leftmost column and topmost row. Spiral matrices can exist for both even and odd values of n. The spiral matrices for n=3, n=4, n=7 are as follows:

1	2	3
8	9	4
7	6	5

1	2	3	4
12	13	14	5
11	16	15	6
10	9	8	7

1	2	3	4	5	6	7
24	25	26	27	28	29	8
23	40	41	42	43	30	9
22	39	48	49	44	31	10
21	38	47	46	45	32	11
20	37	36	35	34	33	12
19	18	17	16	15	14	13

n=3   n=4   n=7

Figure 2.16 Spiral matrix

18. Write a program to rotate a matrix 90 degree in a clockwise direction.

```
1 2 3              7 4 1
4 5 6      ──→      8 5 2
7 8 9              9 6 3
```

Figure 2.17 Rotatating a matrix 90 degree clockwise

19. Write a program to find the kth smallest element in an array.

20. Write a program to reverse a portion of an array.

21. Write a program to rotate left an array by k elements.

22. Write a program to display the intersection of two arrays, i.e., only the elements which are common to both the arrays.

23. Write a program to display union of two arrays, i.e., all elements of both arrays and if an element is repeated in both arrays, then display it only once.

24. Write a program to find the maximum sum of k elements subarray in an array.

25. Write a program to find if the left side sum of array elements are equal to the right side sum of array elements.

26. Write a program to find all two array elements whose sum is equal to k.

Join our book's Discord space

Join the book's Discord Workspace for Latest updates, Offers, Tech happenings around the world, New Release and Sessions with the Authors:

https://discord.bpbonline.com

Linked Lists

List is a collection of similar type of elements. There are two ways of maintaining a list in memory. The first way is to store the elements of the list in an array. However, arrays have some restrictions and disadvantages. The second way of maintaining a list in memory is through a linked list. Let us study what a linked list is, and after that, we will come to know how it overcomes the limitations of the array.

3.1 Single Linked List

A single linked list is made up of nodes where each node has two parts; the first one is the info part that contains the actual data of the list, and the second one is the link part that points to the next node of the list, or we can say, it contains the address of the next node.

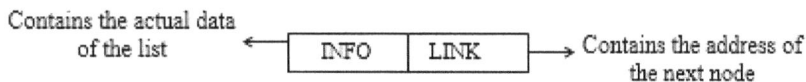

Contains the actual data
of the list | INFO | LINK | Contains the address of
the next node

Figure 3.1 Node of a single linked list

The beginning of the list is pointed by a pointer named `start`. This pointer points to the first node of the list. The link part of each node points to the next node in the list, but the link part of the last node has no next node to point to. Thus, it is made `NULL`. Hence, if we reach a node whose link part has `NULL` value, then we know that we are at the end of the list. Suppose we have a list of four integers 33, 44, 55, 66; let us see how we will represent it through a linked list"

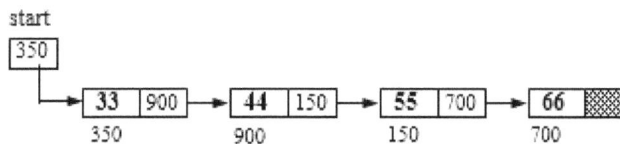

start
| 350 |

| 33 | 900 | → | 44 | 150 | → | 55 | 700 | → | 66 | ▨ |
350   900   150   700

Figure 3.2 Single linked list

From Figure 3.2, it is clear that the info part contains the integer values, and the link part contains the address of the next node. The address of the first node is contained in the pointer `start` and the link part of last node is `NULL` (represented by shaded part in the figure).

If we observe the memory addresses of the nodes, we find that the nodes are not necessarily located adjacent to each other in the memory. The following figure shows the position of nodes of the preceding list in memory:

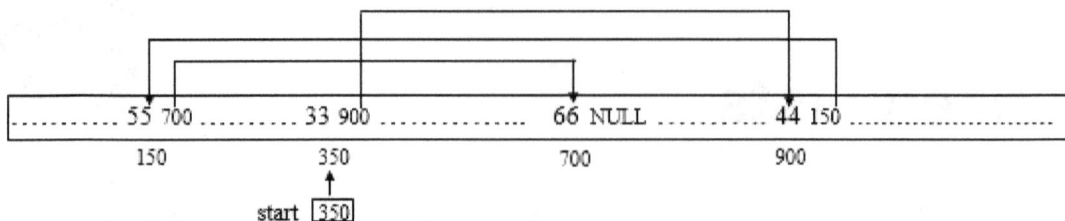

Figure 3.3 Single linked list in memory

We can see that the nodes are scattered around in memory, although they are connected to each other through the link part, which also maintains their linear order. Now, let us see the picture of memory if the same list of integers is implemented through an array:

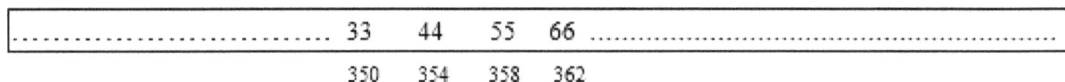

Figure 3.4 List in array

Here, the elements are stored in consecutive memory locations in the same order as they appear in the list. So, the array is a sequential representation of the list, while the linked list is a linked representation of the list. In a linked list, nodes are not stored contiguously as in an array, but they are linked through pointers (links), and we can use these links to move through the list.

Now, let us see how we can represent a node of a single linked list in C++. We will take a self-referential class for this purpose. Recall that a self-referential class is a class that contains a data member pointer to an object of the same class type. The general form of a node of linked list is:

```
class Node
{
        public:
                data member1;
                data member2;
                .......................................
                .......................................
                Node *link;  //Pointer to next node
};
```

Let us see some examples of nodes:

```
class Node
{
        public:
                int value;
                Node *link;
};
```

```
class Node
{
        public:
                char name[10];
                int code;
                float salary;
                Node *link;
};
```

```
class Node
{
        public:
                Student stu;
                Node *link;
};
```

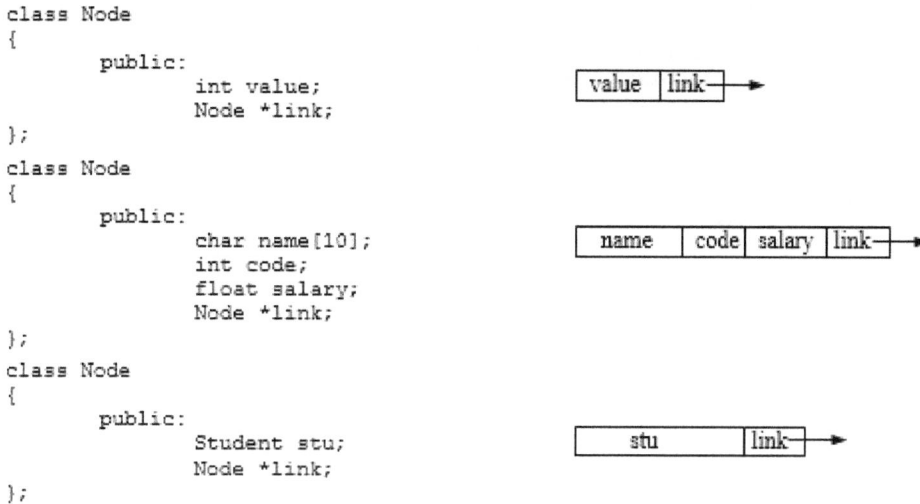

Figure 3.5 Node examples

In this chapter, we will perform all operations on linked lists that contain only an integer value in the info part of their nodes. Here is the class `Node`:

```
class Node
{
        public:
                int info;
                Node *link;
                Node(int data)
                {
                        info = data;
                        link = NULL;
                }
};//End of class Node
```

In the constructor of `Node`, data members `info` and `link` are initialized while during the creation of the node. A node will be created in this way:

```
Node *temp = new Node(10);
```

In an array, we could perform all the operations using the array name and index. In the case of the linked list, we will perform all the operations with the help of the pointer `start` of type `Node` because it is the only source through which we can access our linked list. It points to the first node of the list. The list will be considered empty if the pointer `start` contains `NULL` value. So, our first job is to declare the pointer `start` and initialize it to `NULL`. This will be in class `SingleLinkedList` which will have `start` as data member and will have member functions for operations of single linked list. Here is the class `SingleLinkedList`:

```
class SingleLinkedList
{
        private:
                Node *start;
                Node* merge1(Node *p1, Node *p2);
                Node* merge2(Node *p1, Node *p2);
                Node* divideList(Node *p);
                Node* mergeSortRec(Node *listStart);
                Node* findCycle();
```

```
public:
        SingleLinkedList();
        SingleLinkedList(const SingleLinkedList& list);
        SingleLinkedList& operator=(const SingleLinkedList& list);
        ~SingleLinkedList();

        bool isEmpty();
        void display();
        int size();
        int find(int data);
        void insertAtBeginning(int data);
        void insertAtEnd(int data);
        void insertBefore(int data, int nodeData);
        void insertAfter(int data, int nodeData);
        void insertAtPosition(int data, int position);
        void deleteAtBeginning();
        void deleteAtEnd();
        void deleteNode(int nodeData);
        void deleteAtPosition(int position);
        void reverse();

        void bubbleSortExchangeData();
        void bubbleSortExchangeLinks();
        void selectionSortExchangeData();
        void selectionSortExchangeLinks();
        void mergeLists1(const SingleLinkedList& list, SingleLinkedList&
        mergedList);
        void mergeLists2(SingleLinkedList& list, SingleLinkedList& mergedList);
        void mergeSort();
        void concatenate(SingleLinkedList& list);

        void insertCycle(int nodeData);
        bool hasCycle();
        void removeCycle();
};//End of class SingleLinkedList
```

The data member start is initialized to NULL in constructor, during the creation of the SingleLinkedList object. The start will point to the first node of list once nodes of linked lists are created. The public member functions provides the operations of the linked list and they use private member function and data member start. The SingleLinkedList object is created in this way:

```
SingleLinkedList listObj;
```

This is the constructor of class SingleLinkedList:

```
SingleLinkedList::SingleLinkedList()
{
        start = NULL;
}//End of SingleLinkedList()
```

We will discuss the following operations on a single linked list.

- Traversal of a linked list
- Searching an element
- Insertion of an element
- Deletion of an element
- Creation of a linked list
- Reversal of a linked list

The main() function is given next while the code of member functions are given with the explanation of operations.

```
//SingleLinkedList.cpp : Program of Single linked list.
#include<iostream>
```

```
using namespace std;

int main()
{
        SingleLinkedList list1;

        //Create the List
        list1.insertAtBeginning(10);
        list1.insertAtEnd(30);
        list1.insertAfter(50,30);
        list1.insertAtPosition(20,2);
        list1.insertBefore(40,50);
        cout << "List1 Items after insertion :\n";
        list1.display();

        cout << "Total items : " << list1.size() << "\n";
        cout << "find(40) = " << list1.find(40) << "\n";

        SingleLinkedList list2(list1);
        cout << "List2 Items after using copy constructor :\n";
        list2.display();

        SingleLinkedList list3;
        list3 = list1;
        cout << "List3 Items after using = operator :\n";
        list3.display();

        list1.deleteAtBeginning();
        list1.deleteAtEnd();
        list1.deleteNode(30);
        list1.deleteAtPosition(2);
        cout << "List1 Items after deletion :\n";
        list1.display();

        list2.reverse();
        cout << "List2 Items after reverse :\n";
        list2.display();

        SingleLinkedList list4;
        list4.insertAtEnd(20);
        list4.insertAtEnd(10);
        list4.insertAtEnd(50);
        list4.insertAtEnd(30);
        list4.insertAtEnd(40);
        cout << "List4 Items :\n";
        list4.display();

        SingleLinkedList list5(list4), list6(list4), list7(list4);
        list4.selectionSortExchangeData();
        cout << "List4 Items after selection sort (exchange data) :\n";
        list4.display();
        list5.selectionSortExchangeLinks();
        cout << "List5 Items after selection sort (exchange links) :\n";
        list5.display();

        list6.bubbleSortExchangeData();
        cout << "List6 Items after bubble sort (exchange data) :\n";
        list6.display();
        list7.bubbleSortExchangeLinks();
        cout << "List7 Items after bubble sort (exchange links) :\n";
        list7.display();

        SingleLinkedList list8, list9, list10, list11;
        list8.insertAtEnd(10);
        list8.insertAtEnd(20);
        list8.insertAtEnd(30);
```

```cpp
list8.insertAtEnd(40);
list8.insertAtEnd(50);
cout << "List8 Items :\n";
list8.display();

list9.insertAtEnd(15);
list9.insertAtEnd(25);
list9.insertAtEnd(35);
list9.insertAtEnd(45);
list9.insertAtEnd(55);
cout << "List9 Items :\n";
list9.display();

list8.mergeLists1(list9, list10);
cout << "List10 Items - Merged List (exchange data) :\n";
list10.display();

list8.mergeLists2(list9, list11);
cout << "List11 Items - Merged List (exchange links) :\n";
list11.display();

SingleLinkedList list12;
list12.insertAtEnd(10);
list12.insertAtEnd(5);
list12.insertAtEnd(20);
list12.insertAtEnd(15);
list12.insertAtEnd(30);
list12.insertAtEnd(25);
list12.insertAtEnd(40);
list12.insertAtEnd(35);
cout << "List12 Items :\n";
list12.display();

list12.mergeSort();
cout << "List12 Items after merge sort :\n";
list12.display();

SingleLinkedList list13, list14;
list13.insertAtEnd(10);
list13.insertAtEnd(20);
list13.insertAtEnd(30);
list13.insertAtEnd(40);
list13.insertAtEnd(50);
cout << "List13 Items :\n";
list13.display();

list14.insertAtEnd(5);
list14.insertAtEnd(15);
list14.insertAtEnd(25);
list14.insertAtEnd(35);
list14.insertAtEnd(45);
cout << "List14 Items :\n";
list14.display();

list13.concatenate(list14);
cout << "List13 Items after concatenation :\n";
list13.display();
SingleLinkedList list15;
list15.insertAtEnd(10);
list15.insertAtEnd(20);
list15.insertAtEnd(30);
list15.insertAtEnd(40);
list15.insertAtEnd(50);
list15.insertAtEnd(60);
list15.insertAtEnd(70);
```

```
        list15.insertAtEnd(80);
        cout << "find(40) = " << list15.find(40) << "\n";
        list15.insertCycle(40);
        cout << "Has cycle : " << (list15.hasCycle() ? "True" : "False") << "\n";
        list15.removeCycle();
        cout << "Has cycle : " << (list15.hasCycle() ? "True" : "False") << "\n";
        return 0;
}//End of main()
```

In the function `main()`, we are creating the `SingleLinkedList` object. So, the constructor of `SingleLinkedList` is invoked and `start` is initialized with `NULL`. The `SingleLinkedList` object is used to invoke the insertion member functions for creating the initial list of nodes. The pointer `start` will be pointing to the first node of list.

The data member `Node` pointer `start` is available to all the member functions. So, by using `start`, member functions can access the linked list.

There will be many operations which will first need to check if the list is empty or not. That can be easily done by checking the value of `start` as `start` will have value `NULL` if there is no node in the list. The following member function `isEmpty()` will return the appropriate value:

```
bool SingleLinkedList::isEmpty()
{
        return (start == NULL);
}//End of isEmpty()
```

3.1.1 Traversing a Single Linked List

Traversal means visiting each node, starting from the first node until reaching the last node. For this. we will take a `Node` pointer `ptr`, which will point to the node that is currently being visited. Initially, we have to visit the first node so `ptr` is assigned the value of `start`.

```
ptr = start;
```

Now, `ptr` points to the first node of the linked list. We can access the info part of the first node by writing `ptr->info`. Now we have to move the pointer `ptr` forward so that it points to the next node. This can be done by assigning the address of the next node to `ptr` as:

```
ptr = ptr->link;
```

Now, `ptr` has the address of the next node. Similarly, we can visit each node of the linked list through this assignment until `ptr` has a NULL value, which is the link part value of the last element. So, the linked list can be traversed as:

```
while(ptr != NULL)
{
        cout << ptr->info << "\n";
        ptr = ptr->link;
}
```

Let us take an example to understand how the assignment `ptr = ptr->link` makes the pointer `ptr` move forward. From now onwards, we will not show the addresses, we will show only the info part of the list in the figures:

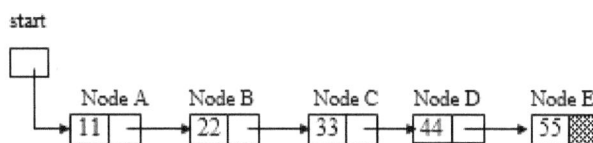

Figure 3.6 Single linked list example

In figure 3.6, node A is the first node, so `start` points to it; node E is the last node, so its link is `NULL`. Initially, `ptr` points to node A, `ptr->info` gives 11, and `ptr->link` points to node B

After the statement `ptr = ptr->link;`

`ptr` points to node B, `ptr->info` gives 22, and `ptr->link` points to node C.

After the statement `ptr = ptr->link;`

`ptr` points to node C, `ptr->info` gives 33, and `ptr->link` points to node D.

After the statement `ptr = ptr->link;`

`ptr` points to node D, `ptr->info` gives 44, and `ptr->link` points to node E.

After the statement `ptr = ptr->link;`

`ptr` points to node E, `ptr->info` gives 55, and `ptr->link` is `NULL`.

After the statement `ptr = ptr->link;`

`ptr` becomes `NULL`, i.e., we have reached the end of the list so we come out of the loop.

The following member function `display()` displays the contents of the linked list:

```cpp
void SingleLinkedList::display()
{
        Node *ptr;
        if(!isEmpty())
        {
                ptr = start;
                while(ptr != NULL)
                {
                        cout << ptr->info << "\n";
                        ptr = ptr->link;
                }
        }
        else
                cout << "List is empty\n";
}//End of display()
```

Do not think of using `start` for moving forward. If we use `start = start->link`, instead of `ptr = ptr->link`, then we will lose `start` and that is the only means of accessing our list.

The following member function `size()` returns the number of elements in the linked list.

```cpp
int SingleLinkedList::size()
{
        Node *ptr;
        int count = 0;
        ptr = start;
        while(ptr != NULL)
        {
                count++;
                ptr = ptr->link;
        }
        return count;
}//End of size()
```

3.1.2 Searching in a Single Linked List

For searching an element, we traverse the linked list and while traversing we compare the info part of each element with the given element to be searched. In the member function given below, `nodeData` is the element which we want to find:

```cpp
int SingleLinkedList::find(int nodeData)
{
        Node *ptr = start;
        int position = 0;
        while(ptr != NULL)
```

```
        {
                position++;
                if(ptr->info == nodeData)
                        return position;
                ptr = ptr->link;
        }
        return 0;
}//End of find()
```

3.1.3 Insertion in a Single Linked List

There can be four cases while inserting a node in a linked list.
- Insertion at the beginning.
- Insertion in an empty list.
- Insertion at the end.
- Insertion in between the list nodes.

To insert a node, we will initially create the `Node` object using the `new` operator. We will pass the `data` value while creating the node, so that it will be assigned to data member `info` in the constructor of `Node`.

```
Node *temp = new Node(data);
```

The `link` part of the node will be assigned `NULL` value in `Node` constructor. In our explanation, we will refer to this new node as node T.

3.1.3.1 Insertion at the Beginning of the List

We have to insert node T at the beginning of the list. Suppose the first node of list is node P. Thus, the new node T should be inserted before it.

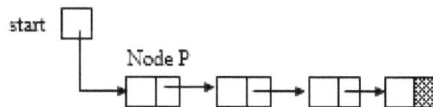

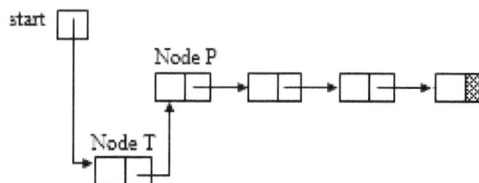

Figure 3.7 Insertion at the beginning of the list

(i) Link of node T should contain the address of node P, and we know that `start` has address of node P so we should write:

```
temp->link = start;
```

After this statement, link of node T will point to node P.

(ii) We want to make node T the first node; hence, we should update `start` so that now it points to node T.

```
start = temp;
```

The order of the above two statements is important. First, we should make the link of T equal to `start` and after that only, we should update `start`. Let us see what happens if the order of these two statements is reversed.

```
start = temp;
```

`start` points to `temp` and we lost the address of node P.

```
temp->link = start;
```

Link of `temp` will point to itself because `start` has address of `temp`. So, if we reverse the order, then the link of node T will point to itself and we will be stuck in an infinite loop when the list is processed.

The following member function `insertAtBeginning()` adds a node at the beginning of the list:

```
void SingleLinkedList::insertAtBeginning(int data)
{
        Node *temp;
        temp = new Node(data);
        if(!isEmpty())
                temp->link = start;
        start = temp;
}//End of insertAtBeginning()
```

3.1.3.2 Insertion in an Empty List

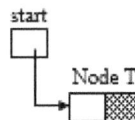

Figure 3.8 Insertion in an empty list

When the list is empty, value of `start` will be NULL. The new node that we are adding will be the only node in the list. Since it is the first node, `start` should point to this node, and it is also the last node. Thus, its link should be NULL. While creating the new node, we are already setting the link part with NULL in the Node constructor.

```
start = temp;
```

This case is taken care of in the previous case (3.1.3.1) where we are checking if list is not empty. Then only,

`temp->link` points to next node.

3.1.3.3 Insertion at the End of the List

We have to insert a new node T at the end of the list. Suppose the last node of list is node P. Then, node T should be inserted after node P:

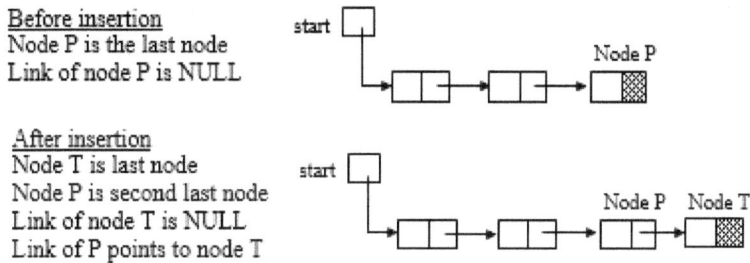

Before insertion
Node P is the last node
Link of node P is NULL

After insertion
Node T is last node
Node P is second last node
Link of node T is NULL
Link of P points to node T

Figure 3.9 Insertion at the end of the list

Suppose we have a pointer `ptr` pointing to the node P. This is the statement that should be written for this insertion:

```
ptr->link = temp;
```

`link` part of `temp` is already assigned with `NULL` while creating the node `temp`.

So, in this case we should have a pointer `ptr` pointing to the last node of the list. The only information about the linked list that we have is the pointer `start`. So, we will traverse the list till the end, to get the pointer `ptr` pointing to the last node and then do the insertion. This is how pointer `ptr` points to the last node:

```
ptr = start;
while(ptr->link != NULL)
        ptr = ptr->link;
```

In traversal of list (3.1.1) our terminating condition was `(ptr != NULL)`, because there we wanted the loop to terminate when `ptr` becomes `NULL`. Here, we want the loop to terminate when `ptr` is pointing to the last node so the terminating condition is `(ptr->link != NULL)`.

The following member function `insertAtEnd()` inserts a node at the end of the list:

```
void SingleLinkedList::insertAtEnd(int data)
{
        Node *ptr, *temp;
        temp = new Node(data);
        if(isEmpty())
                start = temp;
        else
        {
                ptr = start;
                while(ptr->link != NULL)
                        ptr = ptr->link;
                ptr->link = temp;
        }
}//End of insertAtEnd()
```

3.1.3.4 Insertion in Between the List Nodes

We have to insert a node T between nodes P and Q:

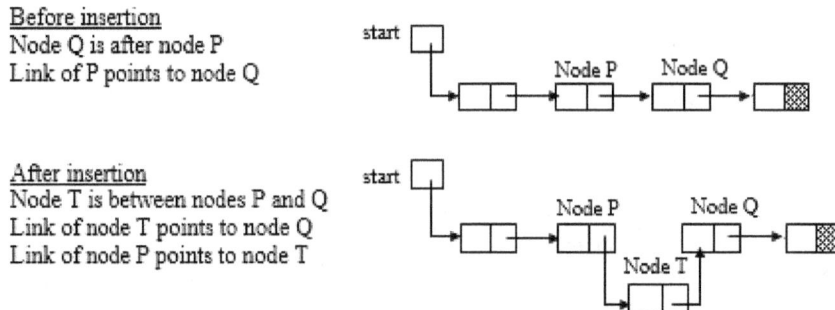

Figure 3.10 Insertion in between the list nodes

Suppose we have two pointers `ptr` and `q` pointing to nodes P and Q respectively. The two statements that should be written for insertion of node T are:

```
temp->link = q;
ptr->link = temp;
```

Before insertion, the address of node Q is in `ptr->link`, and so instead of pointer `q`, we can write `ptr->link`. Now the two statements for insertion can be written as:

```
temp->link = ptr->link;
ptr->link = temp;
```

Note: The order of these two statements is important. If you write them in the reverse order, then you will lose your links. The address of node Q is in `ptr->link`. Suppose we write the statement (`ptr->link = temp;`) first. then we will lose the address of node Q; there is no way to reach node Q and our list is broken. So first, we should assign the address of node Q to the link of node T by writing (`temp->link = ptr->link`). Now we have stored the address of node Q, and we are free to change `ptr->link`.

Now we will see three cases of insertion in between the nodes:
* Insertion after a node
* Insertion before a node
* Insertion at a given position

The two statements of insertion (`temp->link = ptr->link; ptr->link = temp;`) will be written in all three cases, but the way of finding the pointer `ptr` will be different.

3.1.3.4.1 Insertion After a Node

In this case, we are given a value from the list, and we have to insert the new node after the node that contains this value. Suppose the node P contains the given value, and node Q is its successor. We have to insert the new node T after node P, i.e., T is to be inserted between nodes P and Q. In the member function below, `data` is the new value to be inserted and `nodeData` is the value contained in node P. For writing the two statements of insertion (`temp->link = ptr->link; ptr->link = temp;`), we need pointer `ptr` to point to the node that contains `nodeData`. The procedure is the same as we have seen in searching of an element in the linked list.

```
void SingleLinkedList::insertAfter(int data, int nodeData)
{
        Node *ptr, *temp;
```

```
        ptr = start;
        if(isEmpty())
                cout << "List is empty\n";
        else
        {
                while(ptr != NULL)
                {
                        if(ptr->info == nodeData)
                        {
                                temp = new Node(data);
                                temp->link = ptr->link;
                                ptr->link = temp;
                                break;
                        }
                        ptr = ptr->link;
                }
                if(ptr == NULL)
                        cout << "Item " << nodeData << " is not in the list\n";
        }//End of else
}//End of insertAfter()
```

Let us see what happens if `nodeData` is present in the last node, and we have to insert after it. In this case, `ptr` points to the last node, and its link is `NULL`, so `temp->link` is again assigned `NULL`, and we do not have any need for a special case of insertion at the end. This member function will work correctly even if we insert it after the last node.

3.1.3.4.2 Insertion Before a Node

In this case, we are given a value from the list, and we have to insert the new node before the node that contains this value. Let us suppose that node Q contains the given value, and node P is its predecessor. We have to insert the new node T before node Q, i.e., T is to be inserted between nodes P and Q. In the member function given as follows, `data` is the new value to be inserted, and `nodeData` is the value contained in node Q. For writing the two statements of insertion (`temp->link = ptr->link; ptr->link = temp;`) we need pointer `ptr` pointing to the predecessor of the node that contains `nodeData`. Since `nodeData` is present in Q and we have to get a pointer `ptr` pointing to node P, here the condition for searching would be `if(ptr->link->info == nodeData)` and the terminating condition of the loop would be `(ptr->link != NULL)`.

```
void SingleLinkedList::insertBefore(int data, int nodeData)
{
        Node *ptr, *temp;

        ptr = start;
        if(isEmpty())
                cout << "List is empty\n";
        else if(ptr->info == nodeData) //nodeData is in first node
        {
                temp = new Node(data);
                temp->link = ptr;
                start = temp;
        }
        else
        {
                //Get the pointer to predecessor of node containing nodeData
                while(ptr->link != NULL)
                {
                        if(ptr->link->info == nodeData)
                        {
                                temp = new Node(data);
                                temp->link = ptr->link;
```

```
                                    ptr->link = temp;
                                    break;
                        }
                        ptr = ptr->link;
                }
                if(ptr->link == NULL)
                        cout << "Item " << nodeData << " is not in the List\n";
        }//End of else
}//End of insertBefore()
```

If the node is to be inserted before the first node, then that case has to be handled separately because we have to update start in this case. If the list is empty, start will be NULL and the term ptr->info (ptr initially points to start) will create problems. As such, before checking the condition if(ptr->info == nodeData) we should check for empty list.

3.1.3.4.3 Insertion at a Given Position

In this case, we have to insert the new node at a given position. The two insertion statements are same as in the previous cases (temp->link = ptr->link; ptr->link = temp;).

The way of getting pointer ptr pointing to the right node is different. If we have to insert at the first position, we will have to update start, so that case is handled separately.

```
void SingleLinkedList::insertAtPosition(int data, int position)
{
        Node *ptr, *temp;

        if(position == 1)
        {
                temp = new Node(data);
                temp->link = start;
                start = temp;
        }
        else
        {
                ptr = start;
                int index = 1;

                //Get the pointer to (position-1)th node
                while(ptr!=NULL && index < position-1)
                {
                        ptr = ptr->link;
                        index++;
                }

                if(ptr!=NULL && position>0)
                {
                        temp = new Node(data);
                        temp->link = ptr->link;
                        ptr->link = temp;
                }
                else
                        cout << "Item cannot be inserted at position : " << position <<
                        "\n";
        }//End of else
}//End of insertAtPosition()
```

3.1.4 Creation of a Single Linked List

A list can be created using insertion operations. First time, we will have to insert into an empty list, and then we will keep inserting nodes at the end of the list or insert at the beginning of the list or using any other insertion operation.

```
//Create the List
SingleLinkedList list;
list.insertAtEnd(10);
list.insertAtEnd(20);
list.insertAtEnd(30);
list.insertAtEnd(40);
list.insertAtEnd(50);
```

3.1.5 Deletion in a Single Linked List

For deletion of any node, the pointers are rearranged so that this node is logically removed from the list. To physically remove the node and return the memory occupied by it to the pool of available memory, we will use the `delete` operator. We will take a pointer variable `temp`, which will point to the node being deleted so that after the pointers have been altered, we will still have the address of that node in `temp` to free it. There can be four cases while deleting an element from a linked list.

- Deletion of first node.
- Deletion of the only node.
- Deletion in between the list.
- Deletion at the end.

In all cases, at the end we should use `delete temp;` to physically remove node T from the memory.

3.1.5.1 Deletion of First Node

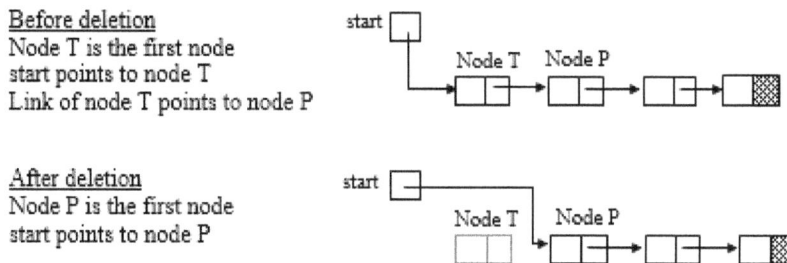

Figure 3.11 Deletion of first node

Since the node to be deleted is the first node, `temp` will be assigned the address of the first node.

```
temp = start;
```

Therefore, now `temp` points to the first node, which has to be deleted. Since `start` points to the first node of the linked list, `start->link` will point to the second node. After deletion of the first node, the second node (node P) would become the first one. Thus, `start` should be assigned the address of the node P as:

```
start = start->link;
```

After this statement, `start` points to node P, so now it is the first node of the list and then we can delete the node `temp` as:

```
delete temp;
```

The member function `deleteAtBeginning()` deletes the node at the beginning of the list.

```
void SingleLinkedList::deleteAtBeginning()
{
        Node *temp;
```

```
        if(isEmpty())
                cout << "List is empty\n";
        else
        {
                temp = start;
                start = start->link;
                delete temp;
        }
}//End of deleteAtBeginning()
```

3.1.5.2 Deletion of the Only Node

If there is only one node in the list and we have to delete it, then after deletion the list would become empty and start would have NULL value.

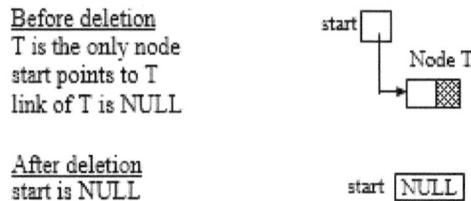

Figure 3.12 Deletion of the only node

```
temp = start;
start = NULL;
```

In the second statement, we can write start->link instead of NULL. So, this case reduces to the first one (3.1.5.1).

3.1.5.3 Deletion in Between the List Nodes

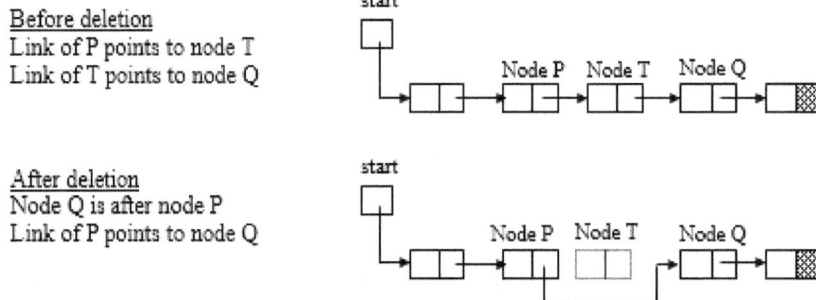

Figure 3.13 Deletion in between the list nodes

Suppose node T is to be deleted and pointer temp points to it and we have pointers ptr and q which point to nodes P and Q respectively. For deletion of node T, we will just link the predecessor of T (node P) to successor of T (node Q).

```
ptr->link = q;
```

The address of q is stored in temp->link, so instead of q, we can write temp->link or ptr->link->link in the above statement.

```
ptr->link = ptr->link->link;
```

Then we can delete the node `temp`.

Now we will see two cases of deletion in between the nodes:

- Delete a node specified with value
- Deletion of a node at a given position

The statement for deletion (`ptr->link = ptr->link->link;`) will be the same in both cases, but the way of finding the pointer `ptr` will be different.

3.1.5.3.1 Delete a Node Specified with Value

In this case, we have to find the node with specified value. The value is in node T and we need pointer `ptr` pointing to its predecessor which is node P, so our condition for searching will be `if(ptr->link->info == nodeData)`. Here, `nodeData` is the value in node to be deleted.

The member function `deleteNode()` deletes the node which has specified value.

```
void SingleLinkedList::deleteNode(int nodeData)
{
        Node *ptr, *temp;

        ptr = start;
        if(isEmpty())
                cout << "List is empty\n";
        else if(ptr->info == nodeData) //Deletion of first node
        {
                temp = ptr;
                start = ptr->link;
                delete temp;
        }
        else //Deletion in between or at the end
        {
                while(ptr->link != NULL)
                {
                        if(ptr->link->info == nodeData)
                                break;
                        ptr = ptr->link;
                }

                if(ptr->link == NULL)
                        cout << nodeData << " not found in list\n";
                else
                {
                        temp = ptr->link;
                        ptr->link = ptr->link->link;
                        delete temp;
                }
        }//End of else
}//End of deleteNode()
```

The first node deletion is handled separately because after deletion, `start` has to be updated.

3.1.5.3.2 Deletion of a Node at a Given Position

In this case, we have to delete the node at a given position. The deletion statement is same as in the previous case (`ptr->link = ptr->link->link;`).

The way of getting pointer `ptr` pointing to the right node is different. If we have to delete at the first position, then we will have to update `start`. Thus, that case is handled separately.

```
void SingleLinkedList::deleteAtPosition(int position)
```

```
{
        Node *ptr, *temp;

        ptr = start;
        if(isEmpty())
                cout << "List is empty\n";
        else if(position == 1)
        {
                temp = start;
                start = start->link;
                delete temp;
        }
        else
        {
                int index = 1;
                while(ptr->link!=NULL && index < position-1)
                {
                        ptr = ptr->link;
                        index++;
                }

                if(ptr->link!=NULL && position>0)
                {
                        temp = ptr->link;
                        ptr->link = ptr->link->link;
                        delete temp;
                }
                else
                        cout << "Node cannot be deleted at position : " << position <<
                        "\n";
        }//End of else
}//End of deleteAtPosition()
```

3.1.5.4 Deletion at the End of the List

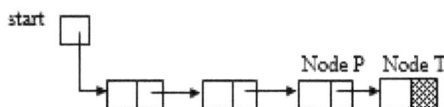

Before deletion
Node T is the last node
Link of P points to T
Link of node T is NULL

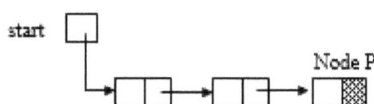

After deletion
Node P is last node
Link of node P is NULL

Figure 3.14 Deletion at the end of the list

If `ptr` is a pointer to node P, then the node T can be deleted by writing the following statement:

`ptr->link = NULL;`

Since the link of node T is NULL in the above statement, instead of NULL, we can write `temp->link` or `ptr->link->link`. Hence, we can write this statement as:

`ptr->link = ptr->link->link;`

So, we can see that this case is reduced to the previous case (3.1.5.3). Here we want the loop to terminate when `ptr` is pointing to the predecessor of the last node.

```
void SingleLinkedList::deleteAtEnd()
{
        Node *ptr, *temp;

        ptr = start;
        if(isEmpty())
                cout << "List is empty\n";
        else if(ptr->link == NULL)
        {
                temp = ptr;
                start = ptr->link;
                delete temp;
        }
        else
        {
                while(ptr->link->link != NULL)
                        ptr = ptr->link;

                temp = ptr->link;
                ptr->link = NULL;
                delete temp;
        }
}//End of deleteAtEnd()
```

The first and only node deletion is handled separately to update the `start`.

3.1.6 Destructor, Copy Constructor and Overloading of Assignment Operator (=)

Let us see the destructor, copy constructor and overloading of assignment operator (=) in a single linked list.

Here is the destructor of a single linked list:

```
SingleLinkedList::~SingleLinkedList()
{
        Node *ptr;
        while(start != NULL)
        {
                ptr = start->link;
                delete start;
                start = ptr;
        }
}//End of ~SingleLinkedList()
```

Here is the copy constructor of a single linked list:

```
SingleLinkedList::SingleLinkedList(const SingleLinkedList& list)
{
        if(list.start == NULL)
                start = NULL;
        else
        {
                Node *ptr1, *ptr2;
                ptr1 = list.start;
                ptr2 = start = new Node(ptr1->info);

                ptr1 = ptr1->link;
                while(ptr1 != NULL)
                {
                        ptr2->link = new Node(ptr1->info);
                        ptr2 = ptr2->link;
                        ptr1 = ptr1->link;
                }
```

```
        }
}//End of copy constructor
```

Here is the overloading of assignment operator (=) for a single linked list:

```
SingleLinkedList& SingleLinkedList::operator=(const SingleLinkedList& list)
{
        if(this == &list)
                return *this;

        Node *ptr;
        while(start != NULL)
        {
                ptr = start->link;
                delete start;
                start = ptr;
        }

        if(list.start == NULL)
        {
                start = NULL;
                return *this;
        }

        Node *ptr1, *ptr2;
        ptr1 = list.start;
        ptr2 = start = new Node(ptr1->info);

        ptr1 = ptr1->link;
        while(ptr1 != NULL)
        {
                ptr2->link = new Node(ptr1->info);
                ptr2 = ptr2->link;
                ptr1 = ptr1->link;
        }

        return *this;
}//End of operator=
```

3.1.7 Reversing a Single Linked List

The following changes need to be done in a single linked list for reversing it:

1. The first node should become the last node of linked list.
2. Last node should become the first node of linked list, and now start should point to it.
3. The link of 2nd node should point to 1st node; link of 3rd node should point to 2nd node and so on.

Let us take a single linked list and reverse it:

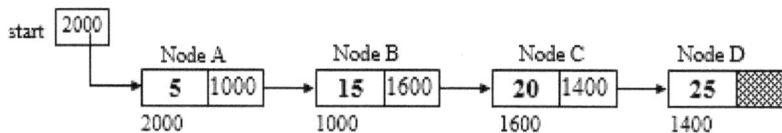

Figure 3.15 Single linked list

(i) Node A is the first node so `start` points to it.
(ii) Node D is the last node, so its link is `NULL`.
(iii) Link of A points to B, link of B points to C and link of C points to D.

After reversing, the linked list would be:

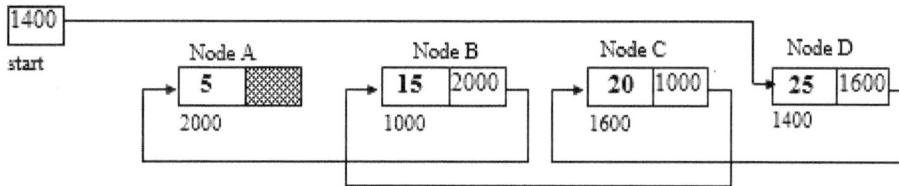

Figure 3.16 Reversed single linked list

(i) Node D is the first node so `start` points to it.
(ii) Node A is the last node, so its link is `NULL`.
(iii) Link of D points to C, link of C points to B and link of B points to A.

Now let us see how we can do the reversal of a linked list. We will take three pointers `prev`, `ptr` and `next`. Initially, the pointer `ptr` will point to `start` and `prev` will be `NULL`. In each pass, first the link of pointer `ptr` is stored in pointer `next` and after that the link of `ptr` is changed, so that it points to its previous node. The pointers `prev` and `ptr` are moved forward. Here is the member function `reverse()`, that reverses a linked list.

```
void SingleLinkedList::reverse()
{
        Node *prev, *ptr, *next;

        if(isEmpty())
                cout << "List is empty\n";
        else
        {
                ptr = start;
                prev = NULL;
                while(ptr != NULL)
                {
                        next = ptr->link;
                        ptr->link = prev;
                        prev = ptr;
                        ptr = next;
                }
                start = prev;
        }
}//End of reverse()
```

The following example shows all the steps of reversing a single linked list:

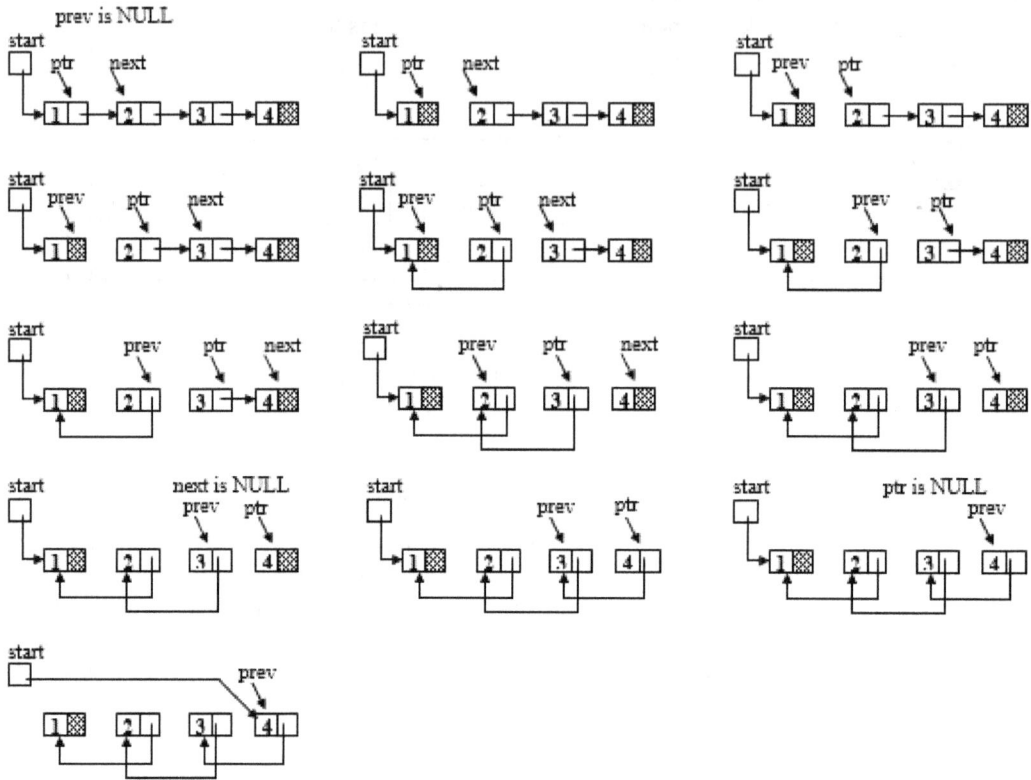

Figure 3.17 Steps of reversing a single linked list

3.2 Doubly Linked List

The linked list that we have studied contained only one link; this is why these lists are called single linked lists or one way lists. We could move only in one direction because each node has the address of the next node only. Suppose we are in the middle of a linked list, and we want the address of the previous node. Then, we have no way of doing this except repeating the traversal from the starting node. To overcome this drawback of single linked list, we have another data structure called the doubly linked list or two-way list, in which each node has two pointers. One of these pointers points to the next node and the other points to the previous node. Here is the class `Node` for doubly linked list:

```cpp
class Node
{
    public:
        int info;
        Node *prev;
        Node *next;
        Node(int data)
        {
            info = data;
            prev = NULL;
            next = NULL;
```

```
    }
};//End of class Node
```

Here, `prev` is a pointer that will contain the address of the previous node and `next` will contain the address of the next node in the list. So, we can move in both directions at any time. The `next` pointer of last node and `prev` pointer of first node are NULL.

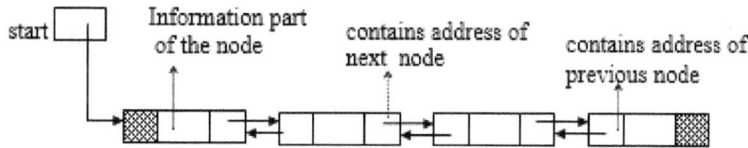

Figure 3.18 Doubly linked list

The basic logic for all operations is the same as in single linked list, but here, we have to do a little extra work because there is one more pointer that has to be updated each time. Here is the class for doubly linked list:

```
class DoublyLinkedList
{
    private:
        Node *start;
    public:
        DoublyLinkedList();
        DoublyLinkedList(DoublyLinkedList& list);
        DoublyLinkedList& operator=(DoublyLinkedList& list);
        ~DoublyLinkedList();

        bool isEmpty();
        void display();
        int size();
        int find(int data);
        void insertAtBeginning(int data);
        void insertAtEnd(int data);
        void insertBefore(int data, int nodeData);
        void insertAfter(int data, int nodeData);
        void insertAtPosition(int data, int position);
        void deleteAtBeginning();
        void deleteAtEnd();
        void deleteNode(int nodeData);
        void deleteAtPosition(int position);
        void reverse();
};//End of class DoublyLinkedList
```

The `start` will point to the first node of list once nodes of doubly linked lists are created. It will be initialized to NULL in constructor, during the creation of `DoublyLinkedList` object.

The constructor and member function `isEmpty()` will be the same as `SingleLinkedList`.

We will discuss the following operations on a doubly linked list:

- Traversal of a doubly linked list
- Searching an element
- Insertion of an element
- Deletion of an element
- Creation of a doubly linked list

- Reversal of a doubly linked list

The main() function is given here, and the code of member functions are given with the explanation of operations.

```cpp
//DoublyLinkedList.cpp : Program of Doubly linked list.
#include<iostream>
using namespace std;

int main()
{
        DoublyLinkedList list1;

        //Create the List
        list1.insertAtBeginning(10);
        list1.insertAtEnd(30);
        list1.insertAfter(50,30);
        list1.insertAtPosition(20,2);
        list1.insertBefore(40,50);
        cout << "List1 Items after insertion :\n";
        list1.display();

        cout << "Total items : " << list1.size() << "\n";
        cout << "find(40) = " << list1.find(40) << "\n";

        DoublyLinkedList list2(list1);
        cout << "List2 Items after using copy constructor :\n";
        list2.display();

        DoublyLinkedList list3;
        list3 = list1;
        cout << "List3 Items after using = operator :\n";
        list3.display();

        list1.deleteAtBeginning();
        list1.deleteAtEnd();
        list1.deleteNode(30);
        list1.deleteAtPosition(2);
        cout << "List1 Items after deletion :\n";
        list1.display();

        list2.reverse();
        cout << "List2 Items after reverse :\n";
        list2.display();

        return 0;
}//End of main()
```

3.2.1 Traversing a Doubly Linked List

Traversal of a doubly linked list is similar to traversal of a single linked list. We will use the next pointer to traverse the list. Here is the member function display():

```cpp
void DoublyLinkedList::display()
{
        Node *ptr;

        if(!isEmpty())
        {
                ptr = start;
                while(ptr != NULL)
                {
                        cout << ptr->info << "\n";
                        ptr = ptr->next;
                }
        }
```

```
        else
                cout << "List is empty\n";
}//End of display()
```

This is the member function `size()` in which we traverse the list and count the number of nodes in it:

```
int DoublyLinkedList::size()
{
        Node *ptr;
        int count = 0;

        ptr = start;
        while(ptr != NULL)
        {
                count++;
                ptr = ptr->next;
        }
        return count;
}//End of size()
```

3.2.2 Searching an Element in a Doubly Linked List

Searching an element in a doubly linked list is similar to searching for it in a single linked list. Here is the member function `find()`:

```
int DoublyLinkedList::find(int nodeData)
{
        Node *ptr = start;
        int position = 0;

        while(ptr != NULL)
        {
                position++;
                if(ptr->info == nodeData)
                        return position;
                ptr = ptr->next;
        }
        return 0;
}//End of find()
```

3.2.3 Insertion in a Doubly Linked List

We will study all four cases of insertion in a doubly linked list:
* Insertion at the beginning of the list.
* Insertion in an empty list.
* Insertion at the end of the list.
* Insertion in between the nodes

3.2.3.1 Insertion at the Beginning of the List

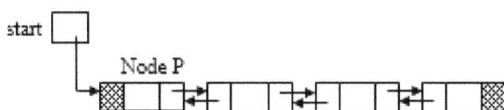

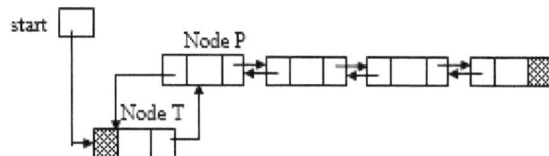

Figure 3.19 Insertion at the beginning of the list

Node T has become the first node, so its `prev` should be `NULL`, which is done in constructor while creating the new node `temp`.

The `next` part of node T should point to node P, and the address of node P is in `start`, so we should write:

```
temp->next = start;
```

Node T is inserted before node P, so the `prev` part of the node P should now point to node T:

```
start->prev = temp;
```

Now, node T has become the first node, so `start` should point to it:

```
start = temp;
void DoublyLinkedList::insertAtBeginning(int data)
{
        Node *temp;
        temp = new Node(data);
        if(!isEmpty())
        {
                temp->next = start;
                start->prev = temp;
        }
        start = temp;
}//End of insertAtBeginning()
```

3.2.3.2 Insertion in an Empty List

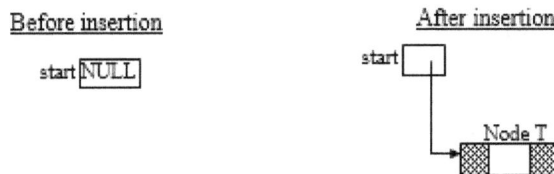

Figure 3.20 Insertion in an empty list

Node T is the first node, so its `prev` part should be `NULL`, and it is also the last node, so its `next` part should also be `NULL`. This is done in constructor while creating a new node `temp`. Node T is the first node so `start` should point to it.

```
start = temp;
```

This case is taken care of in the previous case (3.2.3.1) where we are checking if the list is not empty, then only

`temp->next` points to the next node and the next node `prev` points to `temp`.

3.2.3.3 Insertion at the End of the List

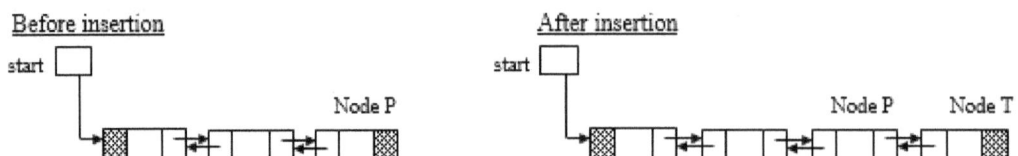

Figure 3.21 Insertion at the end of the list

Let us suppose `ptr` is a pointer pointing to the node P, which is the last node of the list.

Node T becomes the last node, so its `next` should be `NULL`, which is already assigned with `NULL`, while creating the node `temp`.

The `next` part of node P should point to node T:

```
ptr->next = temp;
```

The `prev` part of node T should point to node P:

```
temp->prev = ptr;
```

Getting the pointer `ptr` pointing to the last node P, is similar to a single linked list:

```
ptr = start;
while(ptr->next != NULL)
        ptr = ptr->next;
```

The following member function `insertAtEnd()` inserts a node at the end of the list:

```
void DoublyLinkedList::insertAtEnd(int data)
{
        Node *ptr, *temp;

        temp = new Node(data);
        if(isEmpty())
                start = temp;
        else
        {
                ptr = start;
                while(ptr->next != NULL)
                        ptr = ptr->next;

                ptr->next = temp;
                temp->prev = ptr;
        }
}//End of insertAtEnd()
```

3.2.3.4 Insertion in Between the Nodes

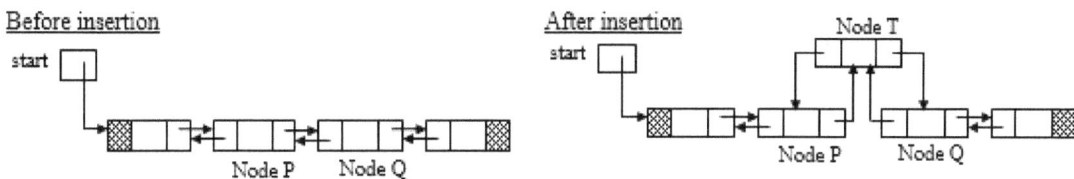

Figure 3.22 Insertion in between the nodes

Suppose pointers p and q point to nodes P and Q, respectively.

Node P is before node T, so `prev` of node T should point to node P:

```
temp->prev = p;
```

Node Q is after node T, so `next` part of node T should point to node Q:

```
temp->next = q;
```

Node T is before node Q, so `prev` part of node Q should point to node T:

```
q->prev = temp;
```

Node T is after node P, so `next` part of node P should point to node T:

`p->next = temp;`

Now we will see three cases of insertion in between the nodes:
* Insertion after a node
* Insertion before a node
* Insertion at a given position

3.2.3.4.1 Insertion After a Node

In this case, we are given a value and the new node is to be inserted after the node containing this value. Suppose node P contains this value. Thus, we have to add a new node after node P. As in single linked list, here also we can traverse the list and find a pointer `p` pointing to node P. Now, in the four insertion statements, we can replace `q` by `p->next`.

```
temp->prev = p;        ->     temp->prev = p;
temp->next = q;        ->     temp->next = p->next;
q->prev = temp;        ->     p->next->prev = temp;
p->next = temp;        ->     p->next = temp;
```

Note that `p->next` should be changed at the end because we are using it in previous statements.

In single linked list, we had seen that the case of inserting after the last node was handled automatically. But here, when we insert after the last node, the third statement (`p->next->prev = temp;`) will create problems. The pointer `p` points to the last node, so its next is NULL. Hence, the term `p->next->prev` is meaningless here. To avoid this problem, we can put a check like this:

```
if(p->next != NULL)
        p->next->prev = temp;
```

Here, is the member function `insertAfter()`. In code, we are using `ptr` instead of `p`.

```
void DoublyLinkedList::insertAfter(int data, int nodeData)
{
        Node *ptr, *temp;

        if(isEmpty())
                cout << "List is empty\n";
        else
        {
                ptr = start;
                while(ptr != NULL)
                {
                        if(ptr->info == nodeData)
                        {
                                temp = new Node(data);
                                temp->prev = ptr;
                                temp->next = ptr->next;
                                if(ptr->next != NULL) //ptr points to last node
                                        ptr->next->prev = temp;
                                ptr->next = temp;
                                break;
                        }
                        ptr = ptr->next;
                }
                if(ptr == NULL)
                        cout << "Item " << nodeData << " is not in the list\n";
        }//End of else
}//End of insertAfter()
```

3.2.3.4.2 Insertion Before a Node

In this case, we are given a value and the new node is to be inserted before the node containing this value. Suppose we have to insert the new node before node Q. We will traverse the list and find a pointer q to node Q. In a single linked list, we had to find the pointer to the predecessor, but here, there is no need to do so because we can get the address of the predecessor by q->prev. So, just replace p by q->prev in the four insertion statements.

```
temp->prev = p;          ->        temp->prev = q->prev;
temp->next = q;          ->        temp->next = q;
q->prev = temp;          ->        q->prev = temp;
p->next = temp;          ->        q->prev->next = temp;
```

q->prev should be changed at the end because it is used in other statements. Thus, the third statement should be the last one.

```
temp->prev = q->prev;
temp->next = q;
q->prev->next = temp;
q->prev = temp;
```

As in a single linked list, here also, we will have to handle the case of insertion before the first node separately. Here is the member function insertBefore(). In the code, we are using ptr instead of q:

```
void DoublyLinkedList::insertBefore(int data, int nodeData)
{
        Node *ptr, *temp;

        if(isEmpty())
                cout << "List is empty\n";
        else if(start->info == nodeData) //nodeData is in first node
        {
                temp = new Node(data);
                temp->next = start;
                start->prev = temp;
                start = temp;
        }
        else
        {
                ptr = start->next;
                while(ptr != NULL)
                {
                        if(ptr->info == nodeData)
                        {
                                temp = new Node(data);
                                temp->prev = ptr->prev;
                                temp->next = ptr;
                                ptr->prev->next = temp;
                                ptr->prev = temp;
                                break;
                        }
                        ptr = ptr->next;
                }

                if(ptr == NULL)
                        cout << "Item " << nodeData << " is not in the List\n";
        }//End of else
}//End of insertBefore()
```

3.2.3.4.3 Insertion at a Given Position

In this case, we have to insert the new node at a given position. We have to get the pointer `ptr` to (position-1)[th] node (suppose it is node P). Then insert the node. As in a single linked list, insertion at the first position is handled separately. Here is the member function `insertAtPosition()`.

```cpp
void DoublyLinkedList::insertAtPosition(int data, int position)
{
        Node *temp, *ptr;
        if(position == 1)
        {
                temp = new Node(data);
                if(!isEmpty())
                {
                        temp->next = start;
                        start->prev = temp;
                }
                start = temp;
        }
        else
        {
                ptr = start;
                int index = 1;

                //Find a pointer to (position-1)th node
                while(ptr != NULL && index < position-1)
                {
                        ptr = ptr->next;
                        index++;
                }
                if(ptr!=NULL && position>0)
                {
                        temp = new Node(data);
                        temp->prev = ptr;
                        temp->next = ptr->next;

                        if(ptr->next != NULL) //ptr points to last node
                                ptr->next->prev = temp;
                        ptr->next = temp;
                }
                else
                        cout << "Item cannot be inserted at position : " << position <<
                        "\n";
        }//End of else
}//End of insertAtPosition()
```

3.2.4 Creation of List

A doubly linked list can be created using the insertion operations. First time, we will have to insert into an empty list, and then we will keep inserting nodes at the end of the list or insert at the beginning of the list or using any other insertion operation.

```cpp
//Create the List
DoublyLinkedList list;
list.insertAtEnd(10);
list.insertAtEnd(20);
list.insertAtEnd(30);
list.insertAtEnd(40);
list.insertAtEnd(50);
```

3.2.5 Deletion from a Doubly Linked List

As in a single linked list, here also, the node is first logically removed by rearranging the pointers, and then it is physically removed using the `delete` operator. Let us study the four cases of deletion:

- Deletion of the first node.
- Deletion of the only node.
- Deletion in between the nodes.
- Deletion at the end.

In all the cases, we will take a pointer variable `temp`, which will point to the node being deleted.

3.2.5.1 Deletion of the First Node

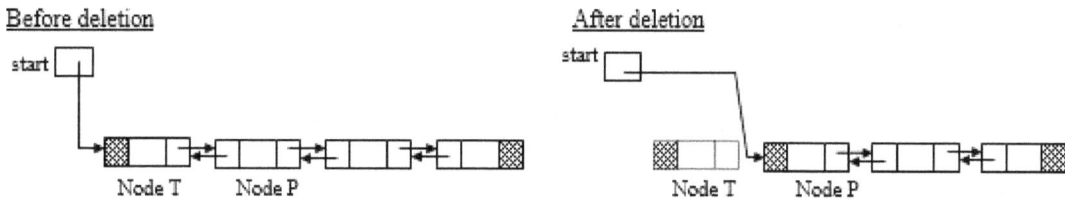

Figure 3.23 Deletion of the first node

`temp` will be assigned the address of the first node.

`temp = start;`

`start` will be updated, so that now it points to node P:

`start = start->next;`

Now, node P is the first node, so its prev part should contain `NULL`.

`start->prev = NULL;`

Here is the member function `deleteAtBeginning()`:

```
void DoublyLinkedList::deleteAtBeginning()
{
        Node *temp;

        if(isEmpty())
                cout << "List is empty\n";
        else
        {
                temp = start;
                if(start->next == NULL) //If list has only 1 node
                        start = NULL;
                else
                {
                        start = start->next;
                        start->prev = NULL;
                }
                delete temp;
        }
}//End of deleteAtBeginning()
```

3.2.5.2 Deletion of the Only Node

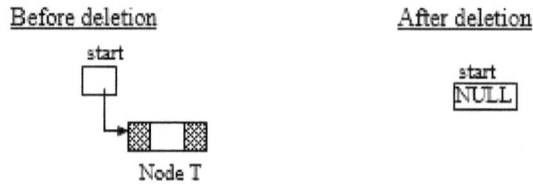

Figure 3.24 Deletion of the only node

The two statements for deletion will be:

```
temp = start;
start = NULL;
```

This case is taken care of in the previous case (3.2.5.1), where we check if the list has only one node, and then NULL is assigned to start.

3.2.5.3 Deletion in Between the Nodes

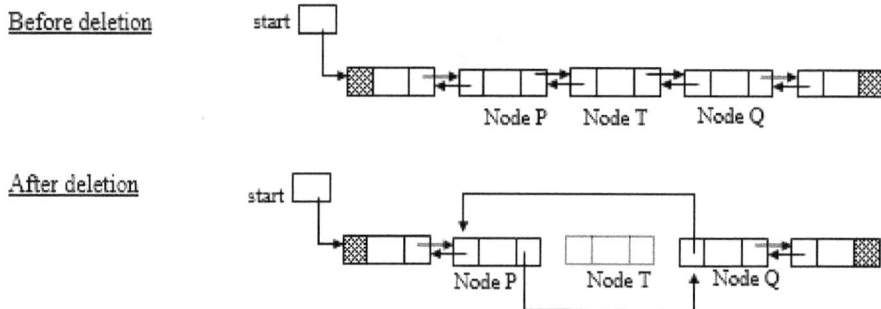

Figure 3.25 Deletion in between the nodes

Suppose we have to delete node T, and let pointers p, temp and q point to nodes P, T and Q, respectively. The two statements for deleting node T can be written as:

```
p->next = q;
q->prev = p;
```

The address of q is in temp->next so we can replace q by temp->next.

```
p->next = temp->next;
temp->next->prev = p;
```

The address of p is stored in temp->prev, so we can replace p by temp->prev.

```
temp->prev->next = temp->next;
temp->next->prev = temp->prev;
```

Thus, we need only a pointer to the node T to delete it.

Now we will see two cases of deletion in between the nodes:
- Delete a node specified with value.
- Deletion of a node at a given position.

3.2.5.3.1 Delete a Node with Specified Value

In this case, we have to find the node with a specified value. The value is in node T, and we need pointer `ptr` pointing to node T. Thus, our condition for searching will be `if(ptr->info == nodeData)`. Here, `nodeData` is the value in the node to be deleted.

The member function `deleteNode()` deletes the node with a specified value.

```
void DoublyLinkedList::deleteNode(int nodeData)
{
        Node *ptr, *temp;

        if(isEmpty())
                cout << "List is empty\n";
        else
        {
                ptr = start;
                while(ptr->next != NULL)
                {
                        if(ptr->info == nodeData)
                                break;
                        ptr = ptr->next;
                }
                if(ptr->info == nodeData)
                {
                        temp = ptr;
                        if(temp->next == NULL)
                        {
                                if(temp->prev == NULL) //First and only node
                                        start = NULL;
                                else
                                        temp->prev->next = NULL; //Last node
                        }
                        else
                        {
                                if(temp->prev == NULL) //First node
                                {
                                        temp->next->prev = NULL;
                                        start = temp->next;
                                }
                                else //Node in between
                                {
                                        temp->prev->next = temp->next;
                                        temp->next->prev = temp->prev;
                                }
                        }
                        delete temp;
                }//End of if
                else
                        cout << nodeData << " not found in list\n";
        }//End of else
}//End of deleteNode()
```

3.2.5.3.2 Deletion of a Node at a Given Position

In this case, we have to delete the node at a given position. The deletion statements are the same as explained. We have to get the pointer `ptr` pointing to the node at the specified position.

The member function `deleteAtPosition()` deletes the node at a given position:

```
void DoublyLinkedList::deleteAtPosition(int position)
{
```

```
        Node *ptr, *temp;
    if(isEmpty())
            cout << "List is empty\n";
    else
    {
            ptr = start;
            int index = 1;
            while(ptr->next != NULL)
            {
                    if(index == position)
                            break;

                    index++;
                    ptr = ptr->next;
            }

            if(position == 1)
            {
                    temp = ptr;
                    if(temp->next == NULL) //First node of only node in list
                            start = NULL;
                    else
                    {
                            temp->next->prev = NULL;
                            start = temp->next;
                    }
                    delete temp;
            }
            else if(index == position)
            {
                    temp = ptr;
                    if(temp->next == NULL)
                            temp->prev->next = NULL;
                    else
                    {
                            temp->next->prev = temp->prev;
                            temp->prev->next = temp->next;
                    }
                    delete temp;
            }
            else
                    cout << "Node cannot be deleted at position : " << position <<
                    "\n";
    }//End of else
}//End of deleteAtPosition()
```

3.2.5.4 Deletion at the End of the List

Suppose node T is to be deleted, and pointers `temp` and `ptr`, point to nodes T and P respectively. The deletion can be performed by writing the following statement:

```
ptr->next = NULL;
```

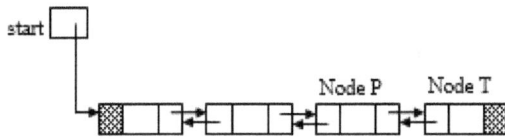

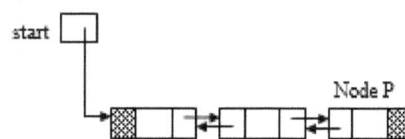

Figure 3.26 Deletion at the end of the list

The address of node P is stored in `temp->prev`, and so we can replace `ptr` with `temp->prev`.

```
temp->prev->next = NULL;
```

This is the member function `deleteAtEnd()`:

```
void DoublyLinkedList::deleteAtEnd()
{
        Node *ptr, *temp;

        if(isEmpty())
                cout << "List is empty\n";
        else
        {
                ptr = start;
                while(ptr->next != NULL)
                        ptr = ptr->next;

                temp = ptr;
                if(temp->prev != NULL)
                        temp->prev->next = NULL;
                else
                        start = NULL;
                delete temp;
        }
}//End of deleteAtEnd()
```

3.2.6 Destructor, Copy Constructor and Overloading of Assignment Operator (=)

Destructor, copy constructor and overloading of assignment operator (=) in a doubly linked list are similar to the corresponding functions in a single linked list.

Here is the destructor of a doubly linked list:

```
DoublyLinkedList::~DoublyLinkedList()
{
        Node *ptr;

        while(start != NULL)
        {
                ptr = start->next;
                delete start;
                start = ptr;
        }
}//End of ~DoublyLinkedList()
```

Here is the copy constructor of a doubly linked list:

```
DoublyLinkedList::DoublyLinkedList(DoublyLinkedList& list)
{
        if(list.start == NULL )
                start = NULL;
```

```
        else
        {
                Node *ptr1, *ptr2, *previous;
                ptr1 = list.start;
                ptr2 = start = new Node(ptr1->info);
                previous = NULL;

                ptr1 = ptr1->next;
                while(ptr1 != NULL)
                {
                        ptr2->next = new Node(ptr1->info);
                        ptr2->prev = previous;
                        previous = ptr2;
                        ptr2 = ptr2->next;
                        ptr1 = ptr1->next;
                }
                ptr2->prev = previous;
        }
}//End of copy constructor
```

Here is the overloading of assignment operator (=) in doubly linked list:

```
DoublyLinkedList& DoublyLinkedList::operator=(DoublyLinkedList& list)
{
        if(this == &list)
                return *this;

        Node *ptr;
        while(start != NULL)
        {
                ptr = start->next;
                delete start;
                start = ptr;
        }

        if(list.start == NULL)
        {
                start = NULL;
                return *this;
        }

        Node *ptr1, *ptr2, *previous;
        ptr1 = list.start;
        ptr2 = start = new Node(ptr1->info);
        previous = NULL;

        ptr1 = ptr1->next;
        while(ptr1 != NULL)
        {
                ptr2->next = new Node(ptr1->info);
                ptr2->prev = previous;
                previous = ptr2;
                ptr2 = ptr2->next;
                ptr1 = ptr1->next;
        }
        ptr2->prev = previous;

        return *this;
}//End of operator=
```

3.2.7 Reversing a Doubly Linked List

Let us take a doubly linked list and see what changes need to be made for its reversal. The following figure shows a doubly linked list and the reversed linked list:

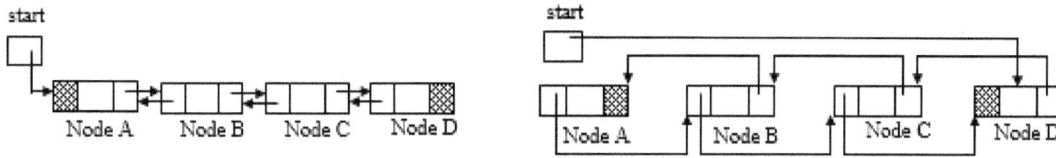

Figure 3.27 Reversing a doubly linked list

In the reversed list-

(i) `start` points to Node D.

(ii) Node D is the first node so its `prev` is `NULL`.

(iii) Node A is the last node so its `next` is `NULL`.

(iv) `next` of D points to C, `next` of C points to B and `next` of B points to A.

(v) `prev` of A points to B, `prev` of B points to C, `prev` of C points to D.

For making the function of reversal of a doubly linked list, we will need only two pointers.

```
void DoublyLinkedList::reverse()
{
        Node *ptr, *temp;

        if(isEmpty())
                cout << "List is empty\n";
        else
        {
                ptr = start;
                while(ptr->next != NULL)
                {
                        temp = ptr->next;
                        ptr->next = ptr->prev;
                        ptr->prev = temp;
                        ptr = temp;
                }
                ptr->next = ptr->prev;
                ptr->prev = NULL;
                start = ptr;
        }
}//End of reverse()
```

In a doubly linked list, we have an extra pointer, which consumes extra space, and the maintenance of this pointer makes operations lengthy and time-consuming. So doubly linked lists are beneficial only when we frequently need the predecessor of a node.

3.3 Circular Linked List

In a single linked list, for accessing any node of linked list we start traversing from first node. If we are at any node in the middle of the list, then it is not possible to access nodes that precede the given node. This problem can be solved by slightly altering the structure of a single linked list. In a single linked list, the link part of the last node is `NULL`. If we utilize this link to point to the first node, then we can have some advantages. The structure thus formed is called a circular linked list. The following figure shows a circular linked list:

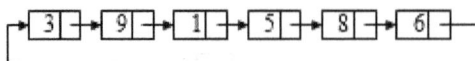

Figure 3.28 Circular linked list

Each node has a successor, and all the nodes form a ring. Now we can access any node of the linked list without going back. We can start traversal again from the first node because the list is in the form of a circle, and we can go from the last node to the first node.

We take an external pointer that points to the last node of the list. If we have a pointer `last` pointing to the last node, then `last->link` will point to the first node.

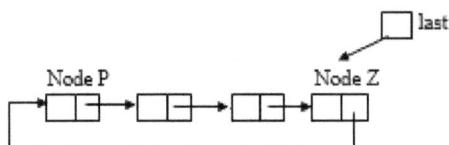

Figure 3.29 Circular list with a pointer pointing to last node

In the figure 3.29, the pointer `last` points to node Z and `last->link` points to node P. Let us see why we have taken a pointer that points to the last node instead of first node. Suppose we take a pointer `start` pointing to the first node of circular linked list. Take the case of an insertion of a node in the beginning.

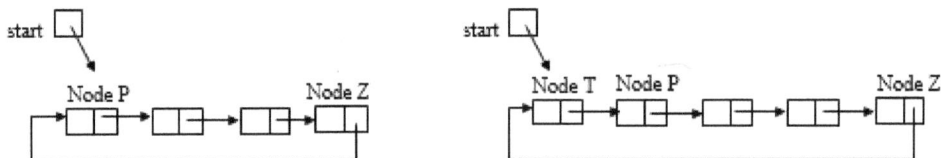

Figure 3.30 Circular list with a pointer pointing to first node

For insertion of node T in the beginning, we need the address of node Z, because we have to change the link of node Z and make it point to node T. Thus, we will have to traverse the whole list. For insertion at the end, it is obvious that the whole list has to be traversed. If instead of pointer `start`, we take a pointer to the last node. Then in both the cases, there will not be any need to traverse the whole list. So, insertion in the beginning or at the end takes constant time irrespective of the length of the list.

If the circular list is empty, the pointer last is NULL, and if the list contains only one element, then the link of `last` points to `last`.

The class `Node` is same as single linked list:

```
class Node
{
        public:
                int info;
                Node *link;
                Node(int data)
                {
                        info = data;
```

```
                                link = NULL;
                }
};//End of class Node
```

The basic logic for all operations is the same as in single linked list, but here we have to make sure that after completing any operation, the link of last node points to the first. Here is the class `CircularLinkedList` for circular linked list:

```
class CircularLinkedList
{
        private:
                Node *last;
        public:
                CircularLinkedList();
                CircularLinkedList(const CircularLinkedList& list);
                CircularLinkedList& operator=(const CircularLinkedList& list);
                ~CircularLinkedList();
                bool isEmpty();
                void display();
                void insertAtBeginning(int data);
                void insertAtEnd(int data);
                void insertBefore(int data, int nodeData);
                void insertAfter(int data, int nodeData);
                void insertAtPosition(int data, int position);
                void deleteAtBeginning();
                void deleteAtEnd();
                void deleteNode(int nodeData);
                void deleteAtPosition(int position);
                void reverse();
                void concatenate(CircularLinkedList& list);
};//End of class CircularLinkedList
```

The pointer `last` will point to the last node of list and the link of the last node will point to first node. It will be initialized to `NULL` in constructor, during the creation of `CircularLinkedList` object.

This is the constructor of class `CircularLinkedList`:

```
CircularLinkedList::CircularLinkedList()
{
        last = NULL;
}//End of CircularLinkedList()
```

The following member function `isEmpty()` returns `true` if list is empty, otherwise `false`.

```
bool CircularLinkedList::isEmpty()
{
        return (last == NULL);
}//End of isEmpty()
```

We will discuss the following operations on a circular linked list:

- Traversal of a circular linked list
- Insertion of an element
- Deletion of an element
- Creation of a circular linked list
- Reversal of a circular linked list

The `main()` function is given here, and the code of member functions are given with the explanation of operations.

```
//CircularLinkedList.cpp : Program of Circular linked list.
#include<iostream>
using namespace std;
```

```cpp
int main()
{
        CircularLinkedList list1;

        //Create the List
        list1.insertAtBeginning(10);
        list1.insertAtEnd(30);
        list1.insertAfter(50,30);
        list1.insertAtPosition(20,2);
        list1.insertBefore(40,50);
        cout << "List1 Items after insertion :\n";
        list1.display();

        CircularLinkedList list2(list1);
        cout << "List2 Items after using copy constructor :\n";
        list2.display();

        CircularLinkedList list3;
        list3 = list1;
        cout << "List3 Items after using = operator :\n";
        list3.display();

        list1.deleteAtBeginning();
        list1.deleteAtEnd();
        list1.deleteNode(30);
        list1.deleteAtPosition(2);
        cout << "List1 Items after deletion :\n";
        list1.display();

        list2.reverse();
        cout << "List2 Items after reverse :\n";
        list2.display();

        CircularLinkedList list4, list5;
        list4.insertAtEnd(10);
        list4.insertAtEnd(20);
        list4.insertAtEnd(30);
        list4.insertAtEnd(40);
        list4.insertAtEnd(50);
        cout << "List4 Items :\n";
        list4.display();

        list5.insertAtEnd(5);
        list5.insertAtEnd(15);
        list5.insertAtEnd(25);
        list5.insertAtEnd(35);
        list5.insertAtEnd(45);
        cout << "List5 Items :\n";
        list5.display();

        list4.concatenate(list5);
        cout << "List4 Items after concatenation :\n";
        list4.display();

        return 0;
}//End of main()
```

3.3.1 Traversal of a Circular Linked List

First of all, we will check if the list is empty. After that, we will take a pointer `ptr` and make it point to the first node.

```cpp
ptr = last->link;
```

The link of last node does not contain NULL, but contains the address of the first node, so here the terminating condition of our loop becomes (`ptr != last->link`).

Here is the member function `display()`:

```
void CircularLinkedList::display()
{
        Node *ptr;
        if(!isEmpty())
        {
                ptr = last->link;
                do
                {
                        cout << ptr->info << "\n";
                        ptr = ptr->link;
                }while(ptr != last->link);
        }
        else
                cout << "List is empty\n";
}//End of display()
```

We have used a `do-while` loop because if we take a `while` loop, then the terminating condition will be satisfied in the first time itself and the loop will not execute at all.

3.3.2 Insertion in a Circular Linked List

We will study all the four cases of insertion in a circular linked list:
- Insertion at the beginning of the list.
- Insertion in an empty list.
- Insertion at the end of the list.
- Insertion in between the nodes

3.3.2.1 Insertion at the Beginning of the List

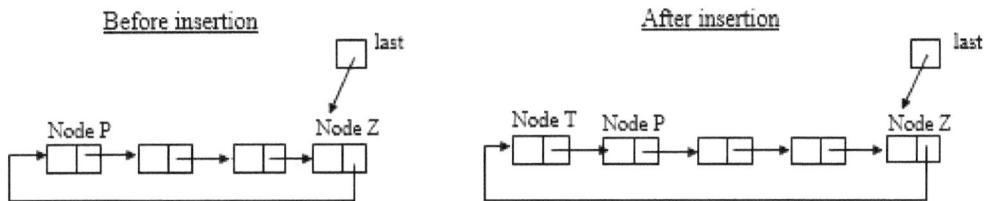

Figure 3.31 Insertion at the beginning of the list

Before insertion, P is the first node so `last->link` points to node P.

After insertion, the link of node T should point to node P and address of node P is in the `last->link`.

```
temp->link = last->link;
```

The link of the last node should point to node T:

```
last->link = temp;
void CircularLinkedList::insertAtBeginning(int data)
{
        Node *temp;
        temp = new Node(data);
        if(isEmpty())
        {
                last = temp;
                last->link = temp;
```

```
        }
        else
        {
                temp->link = last->link;
                last->link = temp;
        }
}//End of insertAtBeginning()
```

3.3.2.2 Insertion in an Empty List

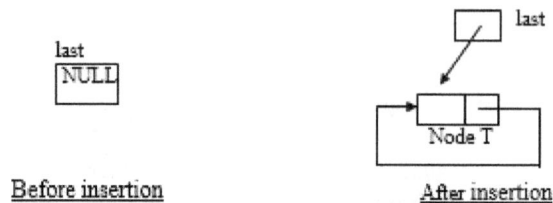

Before insertion　　　After insertion

Figure 3.32 Insertion in an empty list

After insertion, T is the last node so pointer `last` points to node T.

```
last = temp;
```

We know that `last->link` always points to the first node. Here, T is the first node so `last->link` points to node T (or `last`).

```
last->link = temp;
```

This case is taken care in the previous case (3.3.2.1) where we are checking if the list is empty, then only `last` and `last->link` both points to new inserted node `temp`.

3.3.2.3 Insertion at the End of the List

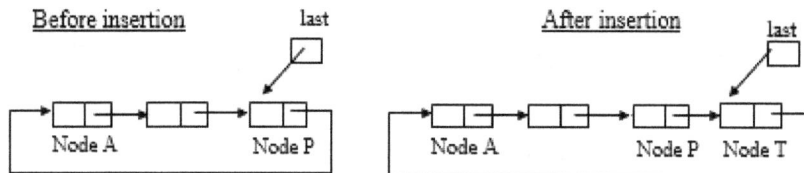

Figure 3.33 Insertion at the end of the list

Before insertion, `last` points to node P and `last->link` points to node A.

After insertion, link of T should point to node A and address of node A is in the `last->link`.

```
temp->link = last->link;
```

Link of node P should point to node T:

```
last->link = temp;
```

`last` should point to node T:

```
last = temp;
```

The order of the above three statements is important.

```
void CircularLinkedList::insertAtEnd(int data)
{
        Node *temp;
        temp = new Node(data);
        if(isEmpty())
        {
                last = temp;
                last->link = temp;
        }
        else
        {
                temp->link = last->link;
                last->link = temp;
                last = temp;
        }
}//End of insertAtEnd()
```

3.3.2.4 Insertion in Between the Nodes

The logic for insertion in between the nodes is the same as in single linked list. If the insertion is done after the last node, then the pointer `last` should be updated.

We have three cases of insertion in between the nodes:
- Insertion after a node
- Insertion before a node
- Insertion at a given position

3.3.2.4.1 Insertion After a Node

Here is the member function `insertAfter()` for insertion after a node:

```
void CircularLinkedList::insertAfter(int data, int nodeData)
{
        Node *ptr, *temp;

        if(isEmpty())
                cout << "List is empty\n";
        else
        {
                ptr = last->link;
                do
                {
                        if(ptr->info == nodeData)
                        {
                                temp = new Node(data);
                                temp->link = ptr->link;
                                ptr->link = temp;
                                if(ptr == last)
                                        last = temp;
                                break;
                        }
                        ptr = ptr->link;
                }while(ptr != last->link);

                if(ptr == last->link)
                        cout << "Item " << nodeData << " is not in the list\n";
        }//End of else
}//End of insertAfter()
```

3.3.2.4.2 Insertion Before a Node

Here is the member function `insertBefore()` for insertion before a node:

```cpp
void CircularLinkedList::insertBefore(int data, int nodeData)
{
        Node *ptr, *temp;

        ptr = last;
        if(isEmpty())
                cout << "List is empty\n";
        else if(ptr->link->info == nodeData) //nodeData is in first node
        {
                temp = new Node(data);
                temp->link = ptr->link;
                ptr->link = temp;
        }
        else
        {
                ptr = last->link;
                do
                {
                        if(ptr->link->info == nodeData)
                        {
                                temp = new Node(data);
                                temp->link = ptr->link;
                                ptr->link = temp;
                                break;
                        }
                        ptr = ptr->link;
                }while(ptr != last->link);

                if(ptr == last->link)
                        cout << "Item " << nodeData << " is not in the list\n";

        }//End of else
}//End of insertBefore()
```

3.3.2.4.3 Insertion at a Given Position

Here is the member function `insertAtPosition()` for insertion at a given position:

```cpp
void CircularLinkedList::insertAtPosition(int data, int position)
{
        Node *ptr, *temp;

        ptr = last;
        if(isEmpty())
        {
                if(position == 1)
                {
                        temp = new Node(data);
                        last = temp;
                        last->link = temp;
                }
                else
                        cout << "Item cannot be inserted at position : " << position <<
                        "\n";
        }
        else if(position == 1)
        {
                temp = new Node(data);
                temp->link = last->link;
                last->link = temp;
```

```
        }
        else
        {
                ptr = last->link;
                int index = 1;
                do
                {
                        if(index == position-1)
                        {
                                temp = new Node(data);
                                temp->link = ptr->link;
                                ptr->link = temp;
                                if(ptr == last)
                                        last = temp;
                                ptr = ptr->link;
                                break;
                        }
                        index++;
                        ptr = ptr->link;
                }while(ptr != last->link);

                if(ptr == last->link)
                        cout << "Item cannot be inserted at position : " << position <<
                        "\n";
        }//End of else
}//End of insertAtPosition()
```

3.3.3 Creation of Circular Linked List

A list can be created using insertion operations similar to those of single linked list:

```
//Create the List
CircularLinkedList list;
list.insertAtEnd(10);
list.insertAtEnd(20);
list.insertAtEnd(30);
list.insertAtEnd(40);
list.insertAtEnd(50);
```

3.3.4 Deletion in Circular Linked List

Deletion in a circular linked list is similar to deletion in a single linked list. There can be four cases while deleting an element from a circular linked list:

- Deletion of the first node.
- Deletion of the only node.
- Deletion in between the nodes.
- Deletion at the end of the list.

3.3.4.1 Deletion of the First Node

Before deletion, `last` points to node Z and `last->link` points to node T.

After deletion, the link of node Z should point to node A. Thus, `last->link` should point to node A. Address of node A is in link of node T.

```
last->link = temp->link;
```

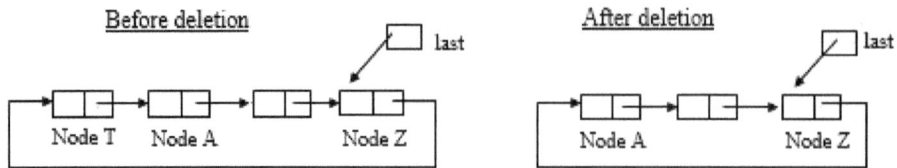

Figure 3.34 Deletion of the first node

```
void CircularLinkedList::deleteAtBeginning()
{
        Node *temp;
        if(isEmpty())
                cout << "List is empty\n";
        else if(last->link == last) //List has only one node
        {
                delete last;
                last = NULL;
        }
        else
        {
                temp = last->link;
                last->link = temp->link;
                delete temp;
        }
}//End of deleteAtBeginning()
```

3.3.4.2 Deletion of the Only Node

If there is only one element in the list, then we assign NULL value to the last pointer because after deletion there will be no node in the list.

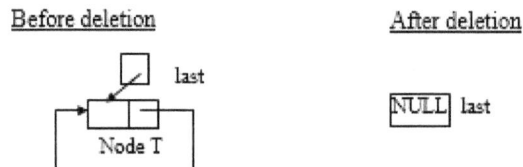

Figure 3.35 Deletion of the only node

There will be only one node in the list if the link of last node points to itself. After deletion the list will become empty, and so NULL is assigned to last.

```
last = NULL;
```

This case is taken care of in the previous case (3.3.4.1) where we are checking if the list has only one node, then first that node is deleted and then NULL is assigned to last.

3.3.4.3 Deletion in Between the Nodes

Deletion in between is the same as in the case of a single linked list. We have two cases of deletion in between the nodes:
• Delete a node specified with value
• Deletion of a node at a given position

3.3.4.3.1 Delete a Node Specified with Value

Here is the member function `deleteNode()` to delete a node specified with value:

```
void CircularLinkedList::deleteNode(int nodeData)
{
        Node *ptr, *temp;

        if(isEmpty())
                cout << "List is empty\n";
        else if(last->link->info == nodeData) //Deletion of first node
        {
                if(last->link == last) //List has only one node
                {
                        delete last;
                        last = NULL;
                }
                else
                {
                        temp = last->link;
                        last->link = temp->link;
                        delete temp;
                }
        }
        else //Deletion in between or at the end
        {
                ptr = last->link;
                while(ptr->link != last->link)
                {
                        if(ptr->link->info == nodeData)
                                break;
                        ptr = ptr->link;
                }

                if(ptr->link == last->link)
                        cout << nodeData << " not found in list\n";
                else
                {
                        temp = ptr->link;
                        if(ptr->link == last)
                                last = ptr;
                        ptr->link = ptr->link->link;
                        delete temp;
                }
        }//End of else
}//End of deleteNode()
```

3.3.4.3.2 Deletion of a Node at a Given Position

Here is the member function `deleteAtPosition()` to delete a node at a given position:

```
void CircularLinkedList::deleteAtPosition(int position)
{
        Node *ptr, *temp;

        if(isEmpty())
                cout << "List is empty\n";
        else if(position == 1) //Deletion of first node
        {
                if(last->link == last) //List has only one node
                {
                        delete last;
                        last = NULL;
                }
```

```
                else
                {
                        temp = last->link;
                        last->link = temp->link;
                        delete temp;
                }
        }
        else //Deletion in between or at the end
        {
                ptr = last->link;
                int index = 1;
                while(ptr->link != last->link)
                {
                        if(index == position-1)
                                break;
                        index++;
                        ptr = ptr->link;
                }

                if(ptr->link == last->link)
                        cout << "Node cannot be deleted at position : " << position <<
                        "\n";
                else
                {
                        temp = ptr->link;
                        if(ptr->link == last)
                                last = ptr;
                        ptr->link = ptr->link->link;
                        delete temp;
                }
        }//End of else
}//End of deleteAtPosition()
```

3.3.4.4 Deletion at the End of the List

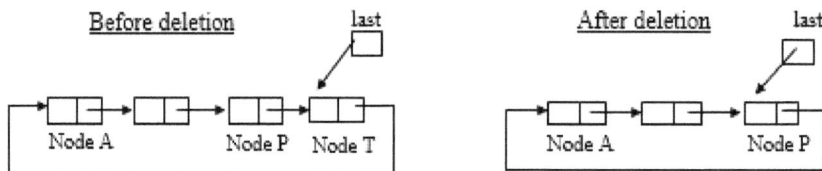

Figure 3.36 Deletion at the end of the list

Before deletion, `last` points to node T and `last->link` points to node A, `ptr` is a pointer to node P.
After deletion, the link of node P should point to node A. Address of node A is in the `last->link`.

```
ptr->link = last->link;
```

Now P is the last node, so `last` should point to node P.

```
last = ptr;
void CircularLinkedList::deleteAtEnd()
{
        Node *ptr, *temp;

        if(isEmpty())
                cout << "List is empty\n";
        else if(last->link == last) //List has only one node
        {
```

```
                delete last;
                last = NULL;
        }
        else
        {
                ptr = last->link;
                while(ptr->link != last)
                        ptr = ptr->link;

                ptr->link = last->link;
                delete last;
                last = ptr;
        }
}//End of deleteAtEnd()
```

3.3.5 Destructor, Copy Constructor and Overloading of Assignment Operator (=)

Destructor, copy constructor and overloading of assignment operator (=) in a circular linked list are similar to that in a single linked list.

Here is the destructor of a circular linked list:

```
CircularLinkedList::~CircularLinkedList()
{
        if(!isEmpty())
        {
                if(last->link == last)
                {
                        delete last;
                        last = NULL;
                }
                else
                {
                        Node *ptr;
                        do
                        {
                                ptr = last->link->link;
                                delete last->link;
                                last->link = ptr;
                        }while(ptr != last);

                        delete last;
                        last = NULL;
                }
        }//End of if
}//End of ~CircularLinkedList()
```

Here is the copy constructor of a circular linked list:

```
CircularLinkedList::CircularLinkedList(const CircularLinkedList& list)
{
        if(list.last == NULL)
                last = NULL;
        else
        {
                Node *ptr1, *ptr2;
                ptr1 = list.last->link;
                ptr2 = last = new Node(ptr1->info);
                last->link = last;

                ptr1 = ptr1->link;
                while(ptr1 != list.last->link)
```

```
                {
                        Node *temp = new Node(ptr1->info);
                        temp->link = ptr2->link;
                        ptr2->link = temp;
                        ptr2 = ptr2->link;
                        last = ptr2;
                        ptr1 = ptr1->link;
                }
        }//End of else
}//End of copy constructor
```

Here is the overloading of assignment operater (=) for a circular linked list:

```
CircularLinkedList& CircularLinkedList::operator=(const CircularLinkedList& list)
{
        if (last == list.last)
                return *this;

        if(!isEmpty())
        {
                if(last->link == last)
                {
                        delete last;
                        last = NULL;
                }
                else
                {
                        Node *ptr;
                        do
                        {
                                ptr = last->link->link;
                                delete last->link;
                                last->link = ptr;
                        }while(ptr != last);

                        delete last;
                        last = NULL;
                }
        }//End of if

        if(list.last == NULL)
                last = NULL;
        else
        {
                Node *ptr1, *ptr2;
                ptr1 = list.last->link;
                ptr2 = last = new Node(ptr1->info);
                last->link = last;

                ptr1 = ptr1->link;
                while(ptr1 != list.last->link)
                {
                        Node *temp = new Node(ptr1->info);
                        temp->link = ptr2->link;
                        ptr2->link = temp;
                        ptr2 = ptr2->link;
                        last = ptr2;
                        ptr1 = ptr1->link;
                }
        }//End of else

        return *this;
}//End of operator=
```

3.3.6 Reversing a Circular Linked List

Here is the member function `reverse()` to reverse a circular linked list:

```
void CircularLinkedList::reverse()
{
        Node *prev, *ptr, *next;

        if(isEmpty())
                cout << "List is empty\n";
        else
        {
                ptr = last->link;
                prev = last;
                while(ptr->link != last->link)
                {
                        next = ptr->link;
                        ptr->link = prev;
                        prev = ptr;
                        ptr = next;
                }
                last = ptr->link;
                last->link = ptr;
                ptr->link = prev;
        }
}//End of reverse()
```

We have studied circular lists which are singly linked. Doubly linked lists can also be made circular. In this case, the `next` pointer of last node points to the first node, and the `prev` pointer of first node points to the last node.

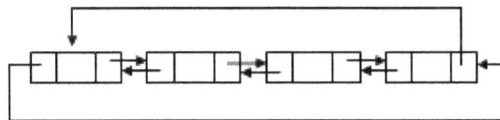

Figure 3.37 Circular doubly linked list

3.4 Linked List with Header Node

Header node is a dummy node that is present at the beginning of the list and its link part is used to store the address of the first actual node of the list. The info part of this node may be empty or can be used to contain useful information about the list such as count of elements currently present in the list. The figure 3.38 (a) shows a single linked list with 4 actual nodes and a header node, and the figure 3.38 (b) shows an empty list with a header node.

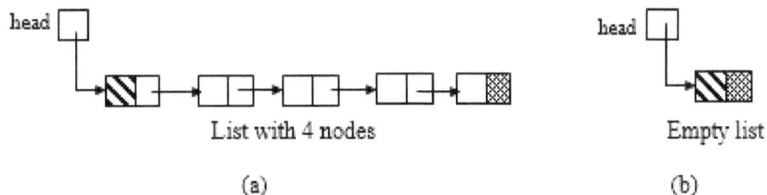

List with 4 nodes

Empty list

(a)

(b)

Figure 3.38 Single linked list with header node

The pointer `head` points to the header node and `head->link` gives the address of first true node of the list. If there is no node in the list, then `head->link` will be `NULL`.

The header node is never deleted; it exists even if the list is empty. So, it may be declared while writing the program instead of dynamically allocating memory for it.

The use of header nodes makes the program simple and faster. Since the list is never empty because the header node is always there, we can avoid some special cases of empty list and that of insertion and deletion in the beginning. For example, in the function `deleteNode()` and `insertBefore()` that we had written for single linked list, we can drop the first two cases if we take a header node in our list.

The following program performs operations on a single linked list with the header node. The logic of all operations is similar to that of single linked list without the header, but some cases have been removed.

```cpp
//SingleLinkedListH.cpp : Program of single linked list with header node.
#include<iostream>
using namespace std;
class Node
{
        public:
                int info;
                Node *link;

                Node(int data)
                {
                        info = data;
                        link = NULL;
                }
};//End of class Node
class SingleLinkedListH
{
        private:
                Node *head;
        public:
                SingleLinkedListH();
                SingleLinkedListH(const SingleLinkedListH& list);
                SingleLinkedListH& operator=(const SingleLinkedListH& list);
                ~SingleLinkedListH();
                bool isEmpty();
                void display();
                void insertAtBeginning(int data);
                void insertAtEnd(int data);
                void insertBefore(int data, int nodeData);
                void insertAfter(int data, int nodeData);
                void insertAtPosition(int data, int position);
                void deleteAtBeginning();
                void deleteAtEnd();
                void deleteNode(int nodeData);
                void deleteAtPosition(int position);
                void reverse();
};//End of class SingleLinkedListH
SingleLinkedListH::SingleLinkedListH()
{
        head = new Node(0);
}//End of SingleLinkedListH()
SingleLinkedListH::~SingleLinkedListH()
{
        Node *ptr;
        while(head != NULL)
        {
```

```
                        ptr = head->link;
                        delete head;
                        head = ptr;
        }
}//End of ~SingleLinkedListH()
SingleLinkedListH::SingleLinkedListH(const SingleLinkedListH& list)
{
        Node *ptr1, *ptr2;
        ptr1 = list.head;
        ptr2 = head = new Node(ptr1->info);

        ptr1 = ptr1->link;
        while(ptr1 != NULL)
        {
                ptr2->link = new Node(ptr1->info);
                ptr2 = ptr2->link;
                ptr1 = ptr1->link;
        }
}//End of copy constructor
SingleLinkedListH& SingleLinkedListH::operator=(const SingleLinkedListH& list)
{
        if(this == &list)
                return *this;

        Node *ptr;
        while(head != NULL)
        {
                ptr = head->link;
                delete head;
                head = ptr;
        }

        if(list.head == NULL)
        {
                head = NULL;
                return *this;
        }

        Node *ptr1, *ptr2;
        ptr1 = list.head;
        ptr2 = head = new Node(ptr1->info);

        ptr1 = ptr1->link;
        while(ptr1 != NULL)
        {
                ptr2->link = new Node(ptr1->info);
                ptr2 = ptr2->link;
                ptr1 = ptr1->link;
        }

        return *this;
}//End of operator=
bool SingleLinkedListH::isEmpty()
{
        return (head->link == NULL);
}//End of isEmpty()
void SingleLinkedListH::display()
{
        Node *ptr;
        if(!isEmpty())
        {
                ptr = head->link;
```

```cpp
                while(ptr != NULL)
                {
                        cout << ptr->info << "\n";
                        ptr = ptr->link;
                }
        }
        else
                cout << "List is empty\n";
}//End of display()
void SingleLinkedListH::insertAtBeginning(int data)
{
        Node *temp;
        temp = new Node(data);
        temp->link = head->link;
        head->link = temp;
}//End of insertAtBeginning()
void SingleLinkedListH::insertAtEnd(int data)
{
        Node *ptr, *temp;
        temp = new Node(data);
        ptr = head;
        while(ptr->link != NULL)
                ptr = ptr->link;
        ptr->link = temp;
}//End of insertAtEnd()
void SingleLinkedListH::insertBefore(int data, int nodeData)
{
        Node *ptr, *temp;

        ptr = head;
        if(isEmpty())
                cout << "List is empty\n";
        else
        {
                //Find pointer to predecessor of node containing nodeData
                while(ptr->link != NULL)
                {
                        if(ptr->link->info == nodeData)
                        {
                                temp = new Node(data);
                                temp->link = ptr->link;
                                ptr->link = temp;

                                break;
                        }
                        ptr = ptr->link;
                }
                if(ptr->link == NULL)
                        cout << "Item " << nodeData << " is not in the List\n";
        }//End of else
}//End of insertBefore()
void SingleLinkedListH::insertAfter(int data, int nodeData)
{
        Node *ptr, *temp;

        ptr = head->link;
        if(isEmpty())
                cout << "List is empty\n";
        else
        {
```

```
                        while(ptr != NULL)
                        {
                                if(ptr->info == nodeData)
                                {
                                        temp = new Node(data);
                                        temp->link = ptr->link;
                                        ptr->link = temp;
                                        break;
                                }
                                ptr = ptr->link;
                        }
                        if(ptr == NULL)
                                cout << "Item " << nodeData << " is not in the list\n";
        }//End of else
}//End of insertAfter()
void SingleLinkedListH::insertAtPosition(int data, int position)
{
        Node *ptr, *temp;
        if(position == 1)
        {
                temp = new Node(data);
                temp->link = head->link;
                head->link = temp;
        }
        else
        {
                ptr = head->link;
                int index = 1;
                //Find a pointer to (position-1)th node
                while(ptr!=NULL && index < position-1)
                {
                        ptr = ptr->link;
                        index++;
                }
                if(ptr!=NULL && position>0)
                {
                        temp = new Node(data);
                        temp->link = ptr->link;
                        ptr->link = temp;
                }
                else
                        cout << "Item cannot be inserted at position : " << position <<
                        "\n";
        }//End of else
}//End of insertAtPosition()
void SingleLinkedListH::deleteAtBeginning()
{
        Node *temp;
        if(isEmpty())
                cout << "List is empty\n";
        else
        {
                temp = head->link;
                head->link = temp->link;
                delete temp;
        }
}//End of deleteAtBeginning()
void SingleLinkedListH::deleteAtEnd()
```

```cpp
{
        Node *ptr, *temp;

        ptr = head;
        if(isEmpty())
                cout << "List is empty\n";
        else
        {
                while(ptr->link->link != NULL)
                        ptr = ptr->link;
                temp = ptr->link;
                ptr->link = NULL;
                delete temp;
        }
}//End of deleteAtEnd()
void SingleLinkedListH::deleteNode(int nodeData)
{
        Node *ptr, *temp;

        ptr = head;
        if(isEmpty())
                cout << "List is empty\n";
        else
        {
                while(ptr->link != NULL)
                {
                        if(ptr->link->info == nodeData)
                                break;
                        ptr = ptr->link;
                }
                if(ptr->link == NULL)
                        cout << nodeData << " not found in list\n";
                else
                {
                        temp = ptr->link;
                        ptr->link = ptr->link->link;
                        delete temp;
                }
        }//End of else
}//End of deleteNode()
void SingleLinkedListH::deleteAtPosition(int position)
{
        Node *ptr, *temp;

        ptr = head->link;
        if(isEmpty())
                cout << "List is empty\n";
        else if(position == 1)
        {
                temp = head->link;
                head->link = ptr->link;
                delete temp;
        }
        else
        {
                int index = 1;
                while(ptr->link!=NULL && index < position-1)
                {
                        ptr = ptr->link;
                        index++;
                }
```

```
                    if(ptr->link!=NULL && position>0)
                    {
                            temp = ptr->link;
                            ptr->link = ptr->link->link;
                            delete temp;
                    }
                    else
                            cout << "Node cannot be deleted at position : " << position <<
                            "\n";
        }//End of else
}//End of deleteAtPosition()
void SingleLinkedListH::reverse()
{
        Node *prev, *ptr, *next;

        if(isEmpty())
                cout << "List is empty\n";
        else
        {
                ptr = head->link;
                prev = NULL;
                while(ptr != NULL)
                {
                        next = ptr->link;
                        ptr->link = prev;
                        prev = ptr;
                        ptr = next;
                }
                head->link = prev;
        }
}//End of reverse()

int main()
{
        SingleLinkedListH list1;

        //Create the List
        list1.insertAtBeginning(10);
        list1.insertAtEnd(30);
        list1.insertAfter(50,30);
        list1.insertAtPosition(20,2);
        list1.insertBefore(40,50);
        cout << "List1 Items after insertion :\n";
        list1.display();

        SingleLinkedListH list2(list1);
        cout << "List2 Items after using copy constructor :\n";
        list2.display();
        SingleLinkedListH list3;
        list3 = list1;
        cout << "List3 Items after using = operator :\n";
        list3.display();

        list1.deleteAtBeginning();
        list1.deleteAtEnd();
        list1.deleteNode(30);
        list1.deleteAtPosition(2);
        cout << "List1 Items after deletion :\n";
        list1.display();

        list2.reverse();
        cout << "List2 Items after reverse :\n";
        list2.display();
```

```
        return 0;
}//End of main()
```

The header node can be attached to circular linked lists and doubly linked lists also. The following figure shows a circular single linked list with header node:

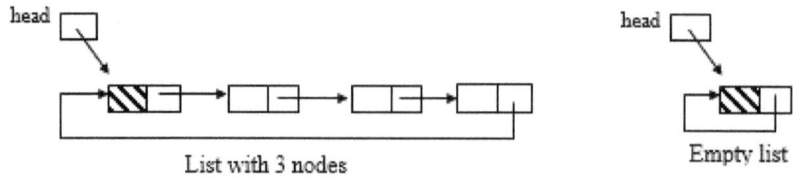

List with 3 nodes

Empty list

Figure 3.39 Circular single linked list with header

Here, the external pointer points to the header node rather than at the end.

The following figures show doubly linked list and doubly linked circular list with header nodes:

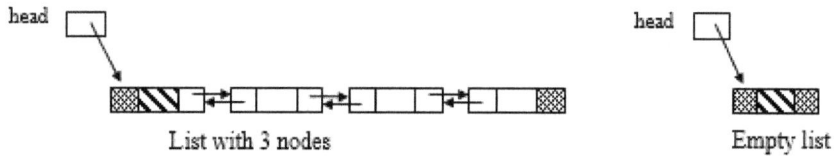

List with 3 nodes

Empty list

Figure 3.40 Doubly linked list with header

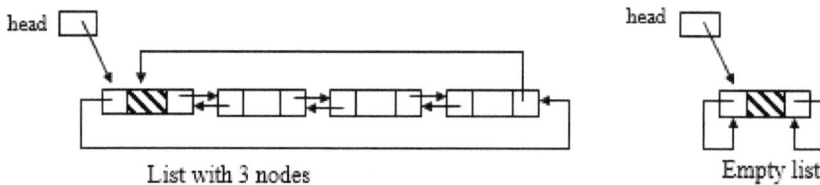

List with 3 nodes

Empty list

Figure 3.41 Doubly linked circular list with header

3.5 Sorted Linked List

In some applications, it is better if the elements in the list are kept in sorted order. For maintaining a list in sorted order, we have to insert the nodes in proper place. Let us take an ascending order linked list and insert some elements in it.

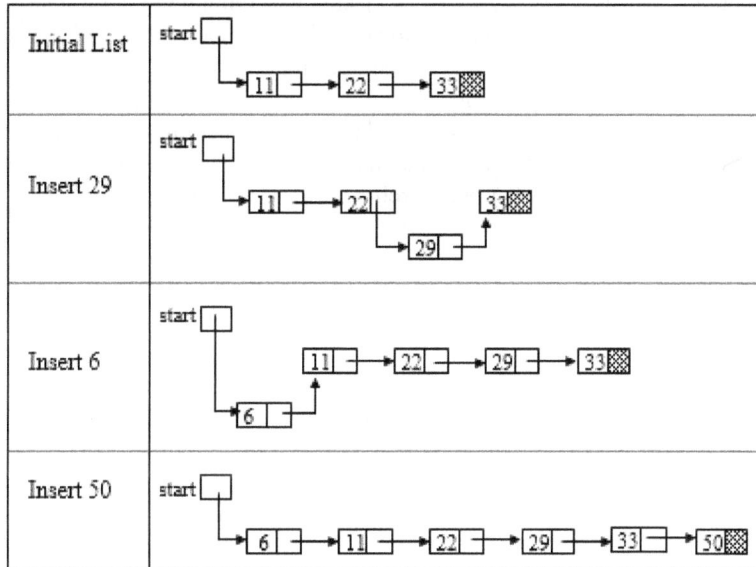

Figure 3.42 Insertion in a sorted linked list

When the element to be inserted is smaller than the first element, it will be inserted in the beginning. When the element to be inserted is greater than the last element, it will be inserted at the end. In other cases, the element will be inserted in the list at its proper place.

We will have a member function `insert()` that will insert an element in the list, such that the ascending order is maintained. We have the same 4 cases as in other lists:

- Insertion in the beginning.
- Insertion in an empty list.
- Insertion at the end.
- Insertion in between.

Since we have taken a single linked list, insertion in beginning and insertion in an empty list can be handled in the same way.

```
if(isEmpty() || data < start->info)
{
        temp->link = start;
        start = temp;
}
```

For insertion in between, we will traverse the list and find a pointer to the node after which our new node should be inserted.

```
ptr = start;
while(ptr->link!=NULL && ptr->link->info < data)
        ptr = ptr->link;
```

The new node has to be inserted after the node which is pointed by pointer `ptr`. The two lines of insertion are the same as in single linked list:

```
temp->link = ptr->link;
ptr->link = temp;
```

If the insertion is to be done at the end, then too the above statements will work.

Other member functions such as `display()`, `size()` etc., will remain the same. The member function `find()` will be altered a little because here we can stop our search as soon as we find an element with value larger than the given element to be searched. The member functions such as `insertAtBeginning()`, `insertAtEnd()`, `insertBefore()`, `insertAfter()`, `insertAtPosition()` do not make sense here because if we use these functions, then the sorted order of the list might get disturbed. The function `insert()` decides where the element has to be inserted and inserts it in the proper place. The process of deletion is the same as in single linked list but searching will be different.

```cpp
//SortedLinkedList.cpp : Program of sorted linked list.
#include<iostream>
using namespace std;

class Node
{
	public:
		int info;
		Node *link;
		Node(int data)
		{
			info = data;
			link = NULL;
		}
};//End of class Node

class SortedLinkedList
{
	private:
		Node *start;
	public:
		SortedLinkedList();
		~SortedLinkedList();

		bool isEmpty();
		void display();
		int find(int data);
		void insert(int data);
};//End of class SortedLinkedList

SortedLinkedList::SortedLinkedList()
{
	start = NULL;
}//End of SortedLinkedList()

SortedLinkedList::~SortedLinkedList()
{
	Node *ptr;

	while(start != NULL)
	{
		ptr = start->link;
		delete start;
		start = ptr;
	}
}//End of ~SortedLinkedList()

bool SortedLinkedList::isEmpty()
{
	return (start == NULL);
}//End of isEmpty()

void SortedLinkedList::display()
{
	Node *ptr;

	if(!isEmpty())
```

```
            {
                    ptr = start;
                    while(ptr != NULL)
                    {
                            cout << ptr->info << "\n";
                            ptr = ptr->link;
                    }
            }
            else
                    cout << "List is empty\n";
}//End of display()
int SortedLinkedList::find(int nodeData)
{
        Node *ptr = start;
        int position = 0;

        while(ptr!=NULL && ptr->info<=nodeData)
        {
                position++;
                if(ptr->info == nodeData)
                        return position;
                ptr = ptr->link;
        }

        return 0;
}//End of find()
void SortedLinkedList::insert(int data)
{
        Node *ptr, *temp;

        temp = new Node(data);
        //List empty or new node to be inserted before first node
        if(isEmpty() || data < start->info)
        {
                temp->link = start;
                start = temp;
        }
        else
        {
                ptr = start;
                while(ptr->link!=NULL && ptr->link->info < data)
                        ptr = ptr->link;

                temp->link = ptr->link;
                ptr->link = temp;
        }
}//End of insert()
int main()
{
        SortedLinkedList list;
        list.insert(10);
        list.insert(20);
        list.insert(30);
        list.insert(40);
        list.insert(50);
        cout << "List Items :\n";
        list.display();
        cout << "find(40) = " << list.find(40) << "\n";

        return 0;
}//End of main()
```

3.6 Sorting a Linked List

If we have a linked list in unsorted order and want to sort it, we can apply any sorting algorithm. We will use selection sort and bubble sort techniques (procedure given in Chapter 8, Sorting). In that chapter, the elements to be sorted are stored in an array, and here, the elements to be sorted are stored in a linked list. So here we can carry out the sorting in two ways-

- By exchanging the data
- By rearranging the links

Sorting by exchanging the data is similar to sorting carried out in arrays. If we have large records, then this method is inefficient since the movement of records will take more time. In a linked list, we can perform the sorting by one more method, i.e., by rearranging the links. In this case, there will be no movement of data, only the links will be changed.

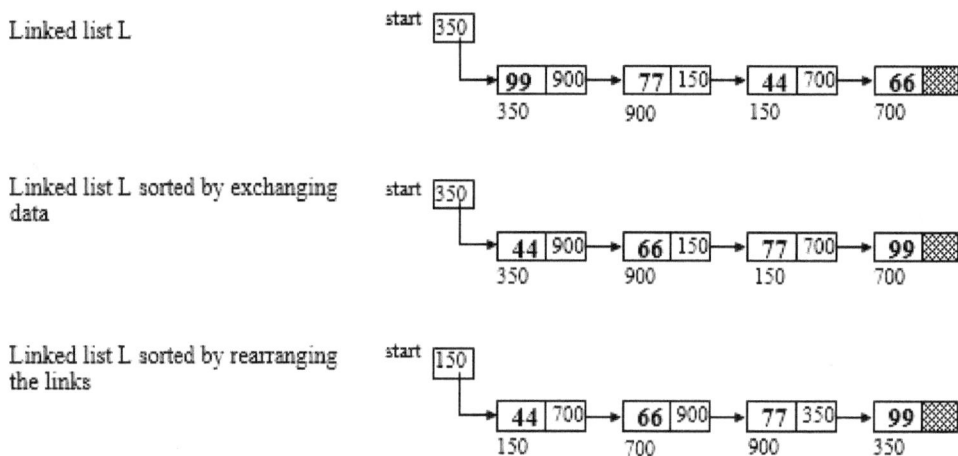

Figure 3.43 Sorting a linked list

3.6.1 Selection Sort by Exchanging Data

The procedure of sorting a linked list through selection sort is shown in the following figure 3.44.

The member function `selectionSortExchangeData()` of class `SingleLinkedList` will sort a single linked list through selection sort technique by exchanging data.

```cpp
void SingleLinkedList::selectionSortExchangeData()
{
        Node *p, *q;
        int temp;
        p = start;
        for(p=start; p->link!=NULL; p=p->link)
        {
                for(q=p->link; q!=NULL; q=q->link)
                {
                        if(p->info > q->info)
                        {
                                temp = p->info;
                                p->info = q->info;
                                q->info = temp;
                        }
                }
        }
```

```
    }
}//End of selectionSortExchangeData()
```

The terminating condition for outer loop is (p->link!=NULL), and so it will terminate when p points to the last node, i.e., it will work till p reaches second last node. The terminating condition for inner loop is (q!=NULL). Therefore, it will terminate when q becomes NULL, i.e., it will work till q reaches the last node. After each iteration of the outer loop, the smallest element from the unsorted elements will be placed at its proper place. In the following figure, the shaded portion shows the elements that have been placed at their proper place:

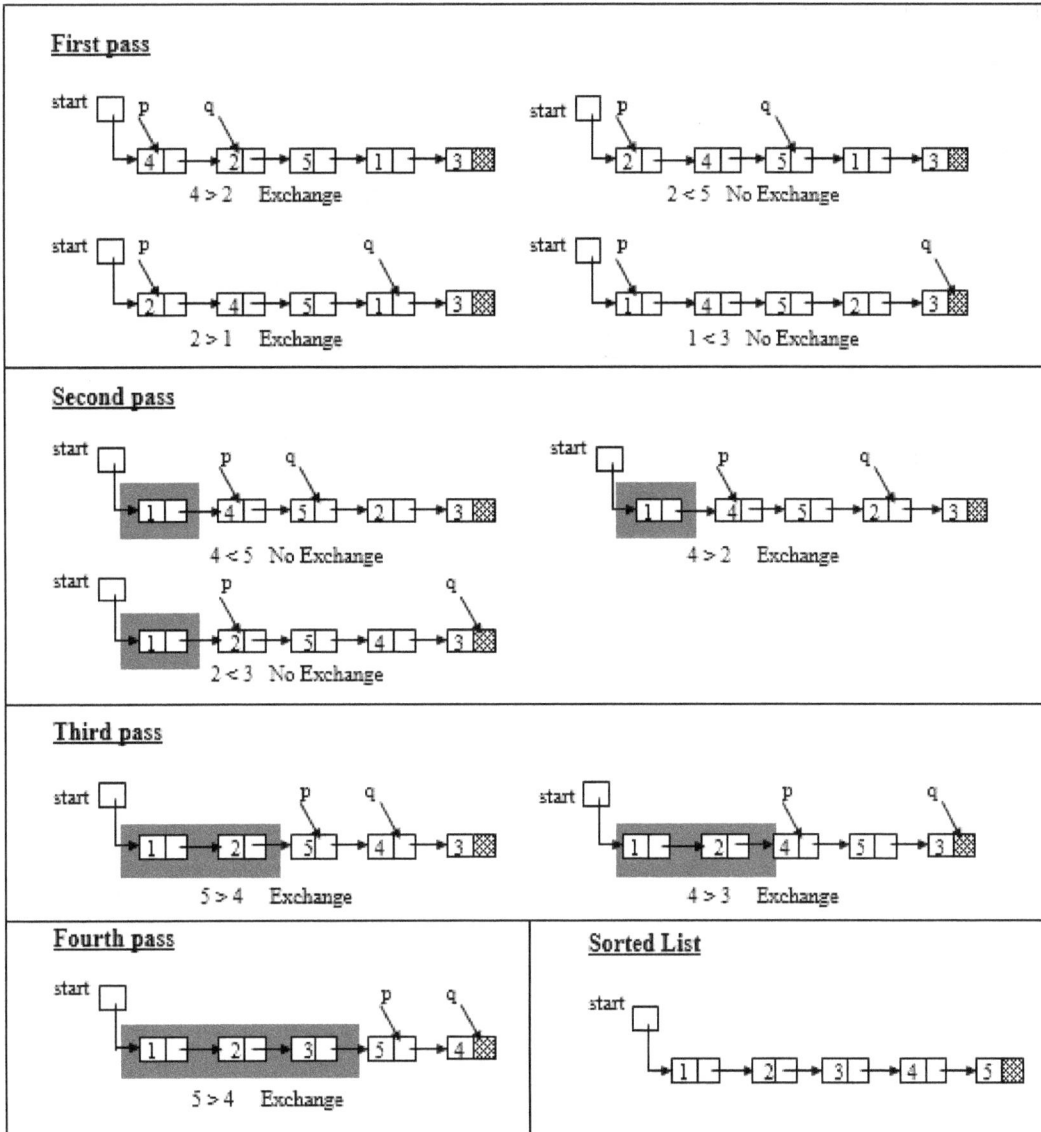

Figure 3.44 Selection sort by exchanging data

3.6.2 Bubble Sort by Exchanging Data

The procedure of sorting a linked list through bubble sort is shown in figure 3.45. After each pass, the largest element from the unsorted elements will be placed at its proper place. In the figure 3.45, the shaded portion shows the elements that have been placed at their proper place. In bubble sort, adjacent elements are compared so we will compare nodes pointed by pointers p and q where q is equal to p->link.

In each pass of the bubble sort, comparison starts from the beginning, but the end changes each time. Thus, in the inner loop, pointer p is always initialized to start. We have defined a pointer variable end, and the loop will terminate when link of p is equal to end.

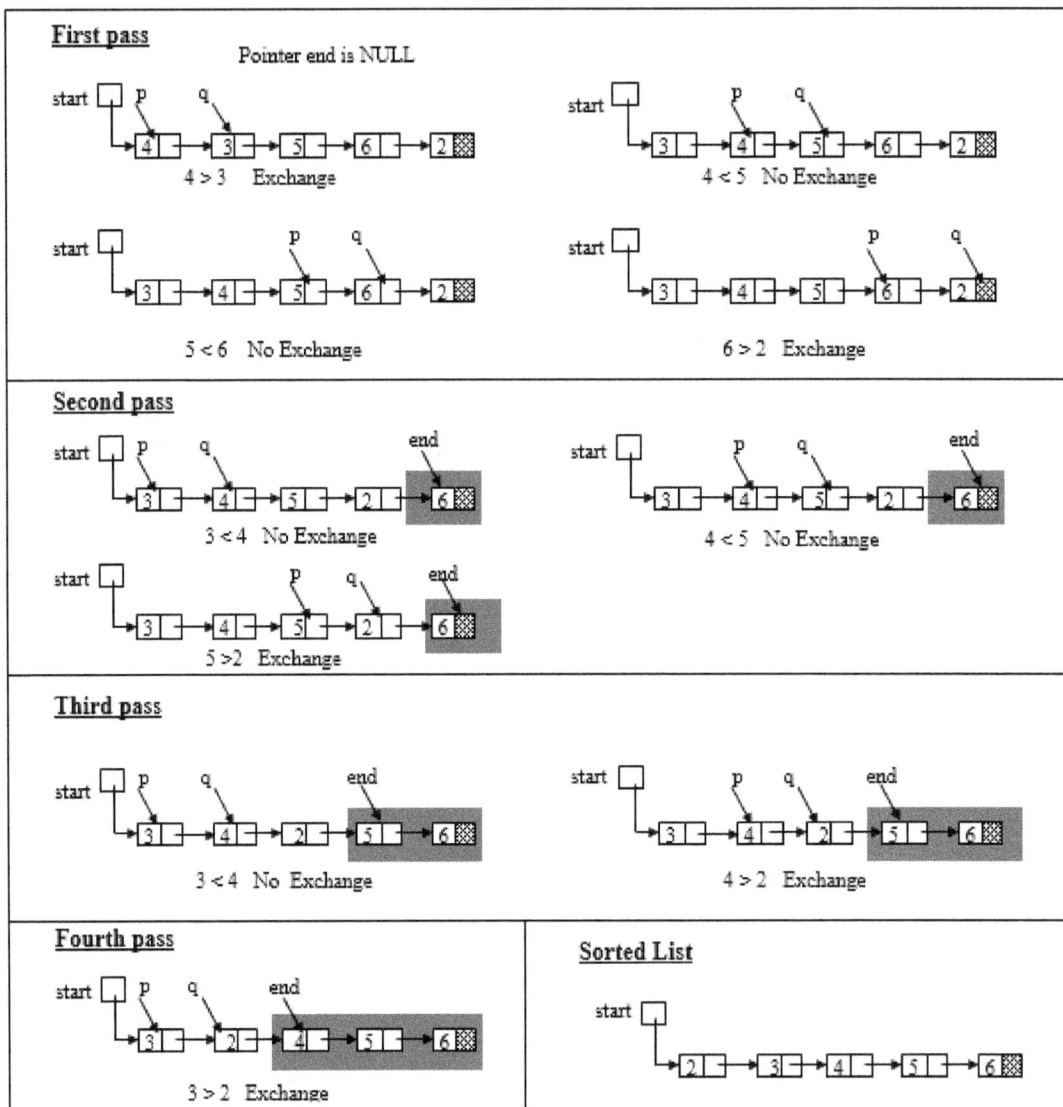

Figure 3.45 Bubble sort by exchanging data

So, the inner loop can be written as:

```
for(p=start; p->link!=end; p=p->link)
{
        q = p->link;
        if(p->info > q->info)
        {
                temp = p->info;
                p->info = q->info;
                q->info = temp;
        }
}
```

Now, we have to see how the pointer variable `end` has to be initialized and changed. This will be done in the outer loop.

```
for(end=NULL; end!=start->link; end=q)
{
        for(p=start; p->link!=end; p=p->link)
        {
                q = p->link;
                if(p->info > q->info)
                {
                        temp = p->info;
                        p->info = q->info;
                        q->info = temp;
                }
        }
}
```

The pointer variable `end` is `NULL` in the first iteration of outer loop, and so the inner loop will terminate when p points to the last node i.e., the inner loop will work only till p reaches second last node. After the first iteration, value of `end` is updated and is made equal to q. Now, `end` points to the last node. This time the inner loop will terminate when p points to the second last node i.e., the inner loop will work only till p reaches third last node.

After each iteration of the outer loop, the pointer `end` moves one node back towards the beginning. Initially the `end` is `NULL`; after the first iteration, it points to the last node; after second iteration it points to the second last node and so on. The terminating condition for outer loop is taken as (`end!=start->link`), so the outer loop will terminate when `end` points to second node, i.e., the outer loop will work only till `end` reaches the third node.

The member function `bubbleSortExchangeData()` of class `SingleLinkedList` will sort a single linked list through bubble sort technique by exchanging data.

```
void SingleLinkedList::bubbleSortExchangeData()
{
        Node *p, *q, *end;
        int temp;
        for(end=NULL; end!=start->link; end=q)
        {
                for(p=start; p->link!=end; p=p->link)
                {
                        q = p->link;
                        if(p->info > q->info)
                        {
                                temp = p->info;
                                p->info = q->info;
                                q->info = temp;
                        }
                }
```

```
        }//End of for
}//End of bubbleSortExchangeData()
```

3.6.3 Selection Sort by Rearranging Links

The pointers p and q will move in the same manner as in selection sort by exchanging data. We will compare nodes pointed by pointers p and q. If the value in node pointed by p is more than the value in node pointed by q, then we will have to change the links such that the positions of these nodes in the list are exchanged. For changing the positions, we will need the address of predecessor nodes as well. Thus, we will take two more pointers r and s, which will point to the predecessors of nodes pointed by p and q respectively. In this case, the two loops can be written as:

```
for(r=p=start; p->link!=NULL; r=p,p=p->link)
{
        for(s=q=p->link; q!=NULL; s=q,q=q->link)
        {
                if(p->info > q->info)
                {
                        ........................
                }
        }
}
```

In both the loops, pointers p and q are initialized and changed in the same way as in selection sort by exchanging data. Now let us see what is to be done if p->info is greater than q->info.

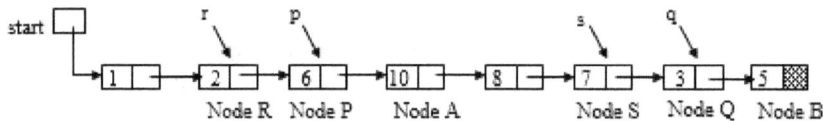

Figure 3.46 Selection sort by rearranging links - 1

The positions of nodes P and Q have to be exchanged, i.e., node P should be between nodes S and B, and node Q should be between nodes R and A.

(i) Node P should be before node B, so the link of node P should point to node B.

```
p->link = q->link;
```

(ii) Node Q should be before node A, so the link of node Q should point to node A.

```
q->link = p->link;
```

(iii) Node Q should be after node R, so the link of node R should point to node Q.

```
r->link = q;
```

(iv) Node P should be after node S, so the link of node S should point to node P.

```
s->link = p;
```

For writing the first two statements, we will need a temporary pointer, since we are exchanging p->link and q->link.

```
temp = p->link;
p->link = q->link;
q->link = temp;
```

If p points to the first node, then r also points to the first node i.e., nodes R and P both are same. In this case, there is no need of writing the third statement (r->link = q;).

We need the third statement only if the pointer p is not equal to start. So, it can be written as:

```
if(p!=start)
        r->link = q;
```

If start points to node P, then start needs to be updated and now it should point to node Q:

```
if(p==start)
        start = q;
```

After writing the above statements, the linked list will look like this:

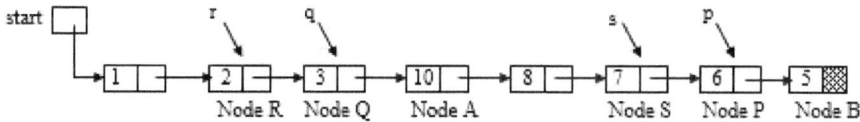

Figure 3.47 Selection sort by rearranging links - 2

The positions of nodes P and Q have changed, and this is what we want because the value in node P was more than value in node Q. Now we will bring the pointers p and q back to their positions to continue with our sorting process. For this, we will exchange the pointers p and q with the help of a temporary pointer.

```
temp = p;    p = q;    q = temp;
```

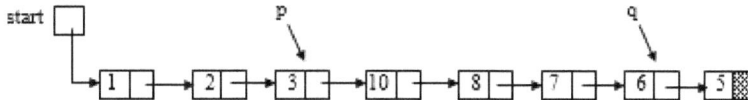

Figure 3.48 Selection sort by rearranging links - 3

The member function selectionSortExchangeLinks() of class SingleLinkedList will sort a single linked list through selection sort technique by rearranging links.

```
void SingleLinkedList::selectionSortExchangeLinks()
{
        Node *p, *q, *r, *s, *temp;

        for(r=p=start; p->link!=NULL; r=p,p=p->link)
        {
                for(s=q=p->link; q!=NULL; s=q,q=q->link)
                {
                        if(p->info > q->info)
                        {
                                temp = p->link;
                                p->link = q->link;
                                q->link = temp;

                                if(p != start)
                                        r->link = q;
                                s->link = p;

                                if(p == start)
                                        start = q;

                                temp = p;
                                p = q;
                                q = temp;
```

```
            }//End of if
        }//End of for
    }//End of for
}//End of selectionSortExchangeLinks()
```

In the previous figures, we have taken the case when p and q point to non-adjacent nodes, and we have written our code according to this case only. Now let us see whether this code will work when p and q point to adjacent nodes. The pointers p and q will point to adjacent nodes only in the first iteration of the inner loop. In that case, s and q point to same node. The following figure shows this situation:

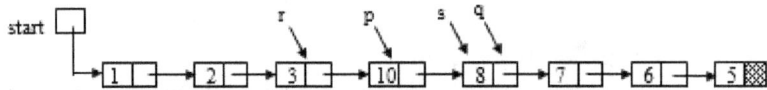

Figure 3.49 Selection sort by rearranging links - 4

You can see that the code we have written will work in this case also. Thus, there is no need to consider a separate case when nodes p and q are adjacent.

3.6.4 Bubble Sort by Rearranging Links

In bubble sort, since p and q are always adjacent, there is no need to take the predecessor of the node pointed by q. Both loops are written in the same way as in bubble sorting by exchanging data. In the inner loop, we have taken a pointer r that will point to the predecessor of the node pointed by p.

```
for(end=NULL; end!=start->link; end=q)
{
        for(r=p=start; p->link!=end; r=p,p=p->link)
        {
                q = p->link;
                if(p->info > q->info )
                {
                        ....................
                }
        }
}
```

Now let us see what is to be done if p->info is greater than q->info.

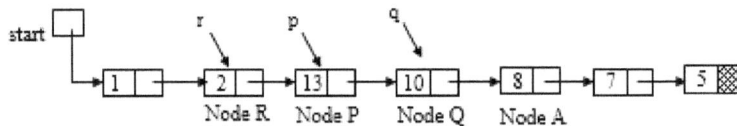

Figure 3.50 Bubble sort by rearranging links

Node P should be before node A, so the link of node P should point to node A:

```
p->link = q->link;
```

Node Q should be before node P, so the link of node Q should point to node P:

```
q->link = p;
```

Node Q should be after node R, so the link of node R should point to node Q:

```
r->link = q;
```

The member function `bubbleSortExchangeLinks()` of class `SingleLinkedList` sorts a single linked list using the bubble sort technique by rearranging links.

```
void SingleLinkedList::bubbleSortExchangeLinks()
{
        Node *p, *q, *r, *end, *temp;

        for(end=NULL; end!=start->link; end=q)
        {
                for(r=p=start; p->link!=end; r=p,p=p->link)
                {
                        q = p->link;
                        if(p->info > q->info)
                        {
                                p->link = q->link;
                                q->link = p;

                                if(p != start)
                                        r->link = q;
                                else
                                        start = q;

                                //Rearranging the position of p and q for next pass
                                temp = p;
                                p = q;
                                q = temp;
                        }//End of if
                }//End of for
        }//End of for
}//End of bubbleSortExchangeLinks()
```

3.7 Merging

If there are two sorted linked lists, then the process of combining these sorted lists into another list of sorted order is called merging. The following figure shows two sorted lists, and a third list obtained by merging them:

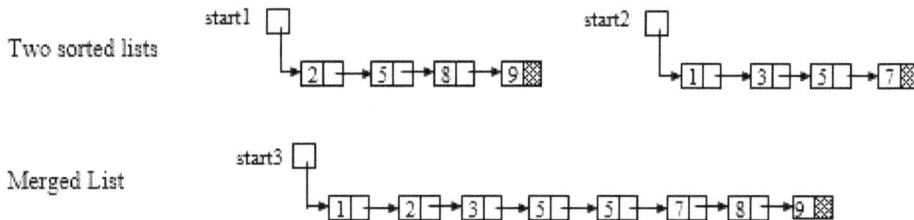

Figure 3.51 Merged linked list from two sorted linked lists

For merging, both the lists are scanned from left to right. We will take one element from each list, compare them and then take the smaller one (or equal) in the third list. This process will continue until the elements of one list are finished. Then, we will take the remaining elements of the unfinished list in the third list. The whole process for merging is shown in figure 3.52. We have taken two pointers p1 and p2, that will point to the nodes that are being compared. There can be two cases while comparing p1->info and p2->info.

1. If `(p1->info) <= (p2->info)`
The new node that is added to the resultant list has info equal to p1->info. After this, we will make p1 point to the next node of first list.

2. If `(p2->info) < (p1->info)`

The new node that is added to the resultant list has info equal to `p2->info`. After this, we will make `p2` point to the next node of second list.

The procedure of merging is shown in figure 3.52:

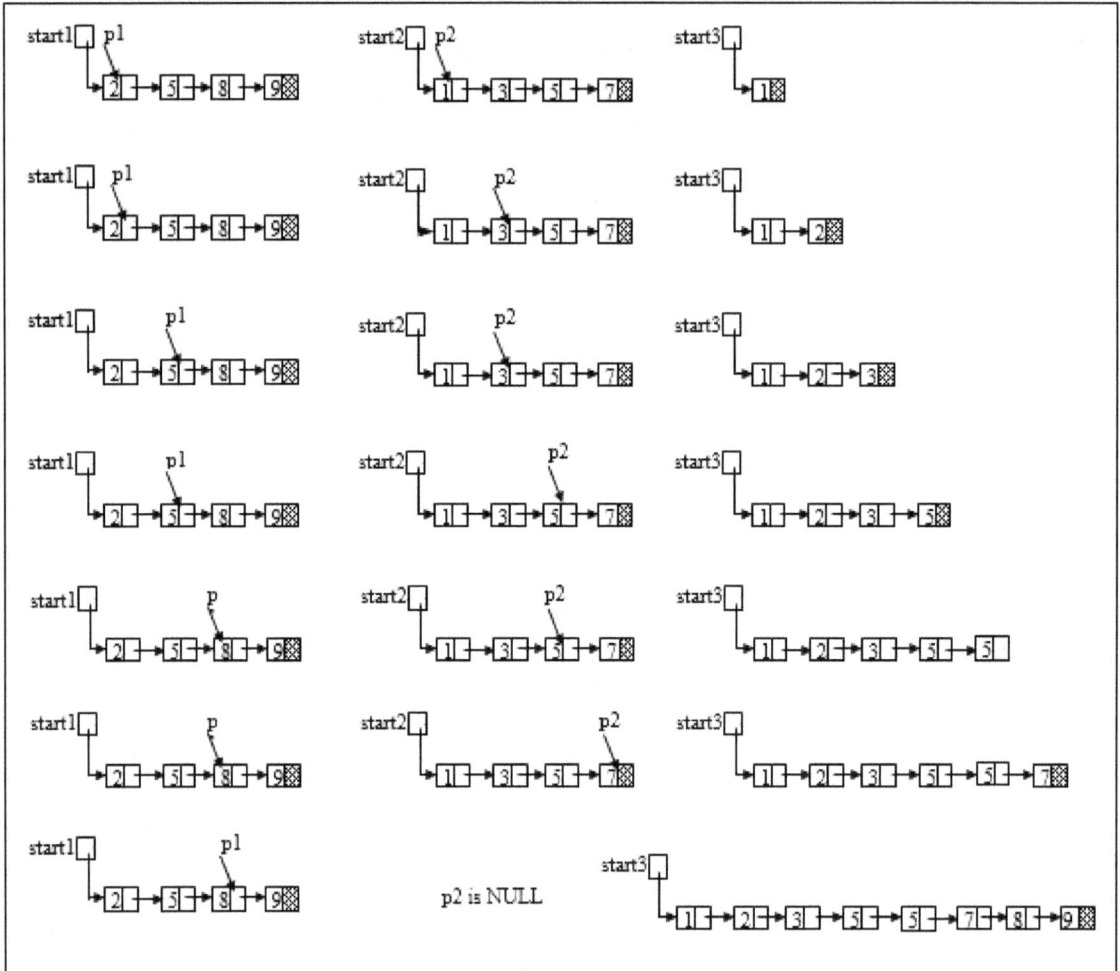

Figure 3.52 Merging of two sorted linked lists

```
while(p1!=NULL && p2!=NULL)
{
        if(p1->info <= p2->info)
        {
                pM->link = new Node(p1->info);
                p1 = p1->link;
        }
        else
        {
                pM->link = new Node(p2->info);
                p2 = p2->link;
        }
```

```
        pM = pM->link;
}
```

The above loop will terminate when any of the list will finish. Now, we have to add the remaining nodes of the unfinished list to the resultant list. If the second list has finished, then we will insert all the nodes of first list in the resultant list as:

```
while(p1 != NULL)
{
        pM->link = new Node(p1->info);
        p1 = p1->link;
        pM = pM->link;
}
```

If the first list has finished, then we will insert all the nodes of the second list in the resultant list as:

```
while(p2 != NULL)
{
        pM->link = new Node(p2->info);
        p2 = p2->link;
        pM = pM->link;
}
```

The member function `merge1()` of class `SingleLinkedList` will merge list1 and list2 in another new list.

```
//Merging 2 lists to another new list
Node* SingleLinkedList::merge1(Node *p1, Node *p2)
{
        Node *startM;
        if(p1->info <= p2->info)
        {
                startM = new Node(p1->info);
                p1 = p1->link;
        }
        else
        {
                startM = new Node(p2->info);
                p2 = p2->link;
        }

        Node *pM = startM;
        while(p1!=NULL && p2!=NULL)
        {
                if(p1->info <= p2->info)
                {
                        pM->link = new Node(p1->info);
                        p1 = p1->link;
                }
                else
                {
                        pM->link = new Node(p2->info);
                        p2 = p2->link;
                }
                pM = pM->link;
        }

        //Second list is finished. Add the elements of first list.
        while(p1 != NULL)
        {
                pM->link = new Node(p1->info);
                p1 = p1->link;
                pM = pM->link;
        }
```

```
        //First list is finished. Add the elements of second list.
        while(p2 != NULL)
        {
                pM->link = new Node(p2->info);
                p2 = p2->link;
                pM = pM->link;
        }

        return startM;
}//End of merge1()
```

The member function `merge1()` is private and will be called in the public member function `mergeLists1()` as:

```
void SingleLinkedList::mergeLists1(const SingleLinkedList& list, SingleLinkedList&
mergedList)
{
        mergedList.start = merge1(start, list.start);
}//End of mergeLists1()
```

The member function `mergeLists1()` will be used in program as:

```
list1.mergeLists1(list2, list3);
```

Here, `list1` and `list2` are sorted and will be merged in another new list `list3`:

The member function `merge2()` of class `SingleLinkedList` will merge `list1` and `list2` by rearranging links:

```
//Merging lists by exchanging links
Node* SingleLinkedList::merge2(Node *p1, Node *p2)
{
        Node *startM;
        if(p1->info <= p2->info)
        {
                startM = p1;
                p1 = p1->link;
        }
        else
        {
                startM = p2;
                p2 = p2->link;
        }

        Node *pM = startM;
        while(p1!=NULL && p2!=NULL)
        {
                if(p1->info <= p2->info)
                {
                        pM->link = p1;
                        p1 = p1->link;
                        pM = pM->link;
                }
                else
                {
                        pM->link = p2;
                        p2 = p2->link;
                        pM = pM->link;
                }
        }

        //Second list is finished. Add the remaining elements of first list
        if(p1 != NULL)
                pM->link = p1;
```

```
        //First list is finished. Add the remaining elements of second list
        if(p2 != NULL)
                pM->link = p2;

        return startM;
}//End of merge2()
```

Here, we are not creating a new node for a merged list; both the lists are merged with rearranging links. The member function `merge2()` is private and will be called in the public member function `mergeLists2()` as:

```
void SingleLinkedList::mergeLists2(SingleLinkedList& list, SingleLinkedList&
mergedList)
{
        mergedList.start = merge2(start, list.start);
        start = NULL;
        list.start = NULL;
}//End of mergeLists2()
```

The member function `mergeLists2()` will be used in program as:

```
list1.mergeLists2(list2, list3);
```

3.8 Concatenation

Suppose we have two single linked lists and we want to append one at the end of another. For this, the link of the last node of the first list should point to the first node of the second list. Let us take two single linked lists and concatenate them.

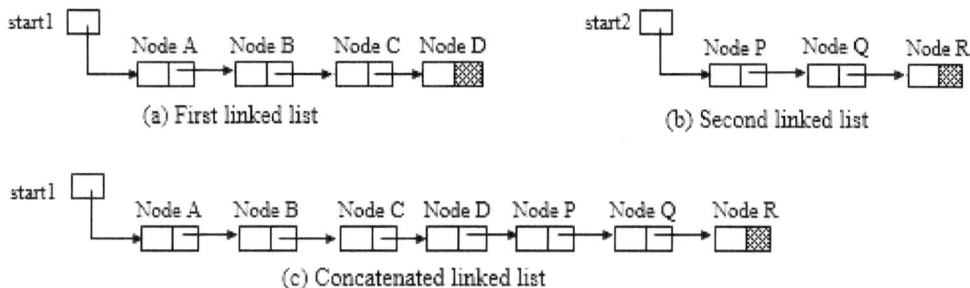

Figure 3.53 Concatenation of two linked lists

For concatenation, the link of node D should point to node P. To get the address of node D, we have to traverse the first list till the end. Suppose `ptr` points to node D, then `ptr->link` should be made equal to `start2`.

Here is the member function `concatenate()` of `SingleLinkedList`, in code `start1` is `start` and `start2` is `list.start`:

```
void SingleLinkedList::concatenate(SingleLinkedList& list)
{
        if(start == NULL)
        {
                start = list.start;
                return;
        }

        if(list.start == NULL)
                return;
```

```
            Node *ptr = start;
            while(ptr->link != NULL)
                    ptr = ptr->link;
            ptr->link = list.start;
            list.start = NULL;
}//End of concatenate()
```

This will be used in the program as:

```
list1.concatenate(list2);
```

If we have to concatenate two circular linked lists, then there is no need to traverse any of the lists. Let us take two circular linked lists:

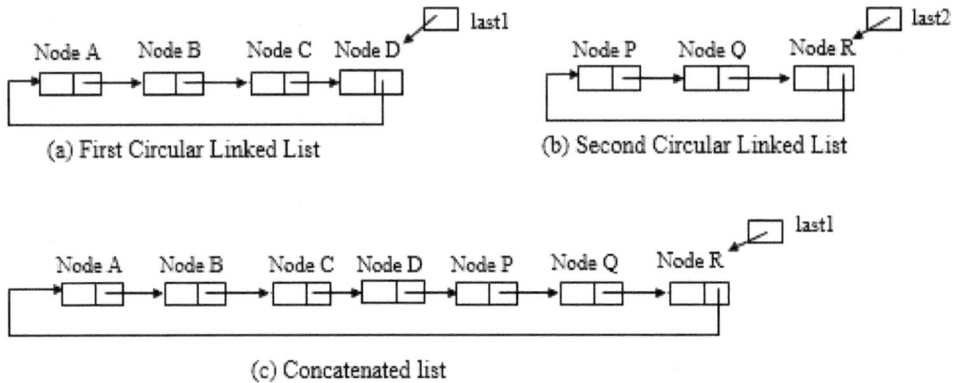

(a) First Circular Linked List
(b) Second Circular Linked List

(c) Concatenated list

Figure 3.54 Concatenation of two circular linked lists

The link of node D should point to node P:

```
last1->link = last2->link;
```

We will lose the address of node A, so before writing this statement, we should save `last1->link`.

```
ptr = last1->link;
```

The link of node R should point to node A:

```
last2->link = ptr;
```

The pointer `last1` should point to node R:

```
last1 = last2;
```

Here is the member function `concatenate()` of `CircularLinkedList`, in code `last1` is `last` and `last2` is `list.last`:

```
void CircularLinkedList::concatenate(CircularLinkedList& list)
{
        Node *ptr;

        if(last == NULL)
        {
                last = list.last;
                list.last = NULL;
        }
        else if(list.last != NULL)
        {
                ptr = last->link;
                last->link = list.last->link;
                list.last->link = ptr;
```

```
            last = list.last;
            list.last = NULL;
        }
}//End of concatenate()
```

This will be used in the program as:

```
list1.concatenate(list2);
```

3.9 Cycle Detection and Removal in Linked List

To understand cycle detection and removal, we will see the insertion, detection, and removal of the cycle.

- Insertion of a cycle
- Cycle detection
- Removal of cycle

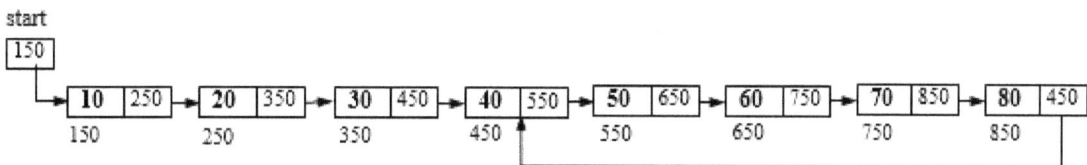

Figure 3.55 Single linked list with cycle

This list is not NULL terminated. It does not have NULL in the link part of the last node. The link part of last node has address 450 which is address of node 40. So, the list has a cycle. The nodes in the cycle are 40, 50, 60, 70, 80.

3.9.1 Insertion of a Cycle

First, we have to insert a cycle in the list for cycle detection and removal in the linked list. For insertion of the cycle, the link part of the last node should have the address of the specified node where it makes the cycle. So, we have to traverse till the specified node, which makes a cycle with the last node, keep the address of the specified node, and traverse till the last node. Then assign the address of the specified node to the link part of the last node.

Here is the member function insertCycle() of class SingleLinkedList to insert the cycle.

```
void SingleLinkedList::insertCycle(int nodeData)
{
        Node *ptr, *prev, *cyclePtr;
        cyclePtr = NULL;

        if(start==NULL || start->link==NULL)
                cout << "Cycle cannot be inserted\n";
        else
        {
                ptr = start;
                prev = start;
                while(ptr != NULL)
                {
                        if(ptr->info == nodeData)
                        {
                                cyclePtr = ptr;
                        }
                        prev = ptr;
                        ptr = ptr->link;
```

```
        }
        if(cyclePtr != NULL)
        {
                cout << "cyclePtr : " << cyclePtr << "\n";
                cout << "cyclePtr->info : " << cyclePtr->info << "\n";
                prev->link = cyclePtr;

                //Display the list (info and link)
                ptr = start;
                while(ptr != cyclePtr)
                {
                        cout << "ptr->info = " << ptr->info << "\n";
                        cout << "ptr->link = " << ptr->link << "\n";
                        ptr = ptr->link;
                }

                ptr = cyclePtr;
                do
                {
                        cout << "ptr->info = " << ptr->info << "\n";
                        cout << "ptr->link = " << ptr->link << "\n";
                        ptr = ptr->link;
                }while(ptr != cyclePtr);
        }//End of if
        else
                cout << nodeData << " is not found in the list\n";
    }//End of else
}//End of insertCycle()
```

3.9.2 Cycle Detection

There are two methods for the detection of a cycle in the list. In the first method, we can have a flag member visited in the node. Initially visited will be false, and while traversing, we will check if it is false and then make it true; otherwise, if it is true, then that is the node that makes the cycle. But here, the node requires an extra member.

The second method is the Hare and Tortoise algorithm. This is also known as Floyd's cycle detection algorithm. In this algorithm, we take two pointers: slow and fast. While traversing, the slow pointer moves one node at a time, but the fast pointer moves two nodes at a time. If the link part of the last node is NULL, then both pointers will not meet, and there is no cycle. Otherwise, both the slow and fast pointers will meet at a node in the cycle. So, if both slow and fast pointers point to the same node, then there is a cycle.

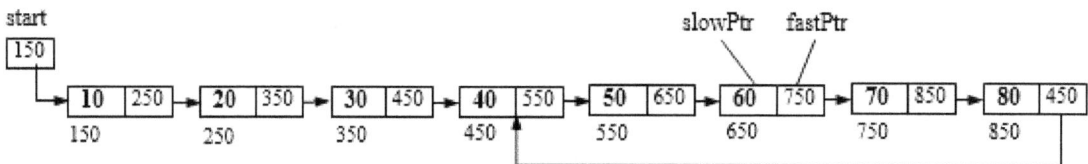

Figure 3.56 Cycle detection in a single linked list

Here is the member function findCycle() of class SingleLinkedList for cycle detection. It returns the node in the cycle where pointers slowPtr and fastPtr meet, otherwise it returns NULL if there is no cycle.

```
Node* SingleLinkedList::findCycle()
```

```
{
        Node *slowPtr, *fastPtr;
        if(start==NULL || start->link==NULL)
                return NULL;
        else
        {
                slowPtr = start;
                fastPtr = start;
                while(fastPtr!=NULL && fastPtr->link!=NULL)
                {
                        slowPtr = slowPtr->link;
                        fastPtr = fastPtr->link->link;
                        if(slowPtr == fastPtr)
                        {
                                cout << "slowPtr and fastPtr meets here\n";
                                cout << "slowPtr->info = " << slowPtr->info << "\n";
                                cout << "slowPtr->link = " << slowPtr->link << "\n";
                                cout << "fastPtr->info = " << fastPtr->info << "\n";
                                cout << "fastPtr->link = " << slowPtr->link << "\n";

                                return slowPtr;
                        }
                }//End of while

                return NULL;
        }//End of else
}//End of findCycle()
```

The member function findCycle() is used in member function hasCycle() which returns true if cycle is found, otherwise it returns false.

```
bool SingleLinkedList::hasCycle()
{
        if(findCycle() != NULL)
                return true;
        else
                return false;
}//End of hasCycle()
```

3.9.3 Removal of Cycle

Removal of the cycle requires us to know the length of the list so that we can make it a NULL terminated list by placing NULL into the link part of the last node. First, we have to use the member function findCycle() to know if there is a cycle or not. If there is a cycle, then findCycle() returns the address of the node in the cycle where both slow and fast pointers meet. We can have pointers ptr1 and ptr2 pointing to the node in the cycle returned by findCycle(). Traverse the pointer ptr1 in the cycle till the current node is pointed by ptr2 to find the length of the cycle. Now we have to find the remaining length of the list. Make pointer ptr1 point to the start of the list. Now traverse both pointers ptr1 and ptr2 till they meet. Both pointers, ptr1 and ptr2, will meet at the node where the cycle starts. The start of the list to the node before where both pointers meet, is the remaining length.

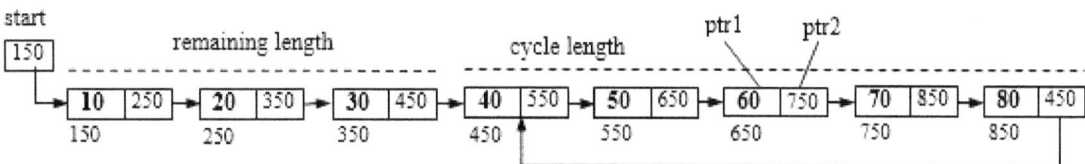

Figure 3.57 Removal of cycle in a single linked list

Adding the length of the cycle and the remaining length gives the length of the list. Now, we can traverse till the last node, and we can assign NULL in the link part of the last node of the list.

Here is the member function removeCycle() of class SingleLinkedList for the removal of a cycle.

```cpp
void SingleLinkedList::removeCycle()
{
        Node *ptr, *ptr1, *ptr2;

        ptr = findCycle();
        if(ptr == NULL)
                cout << "There is no cycle in list\n";
        else
        {
                cout << "Node where cycle was detected : " << ptr->info << "\n";
                ptr1 = ptr;
                ptr2 = ptr;

                //Find the length of cycle
                int cycleLength = 0;
                do
                {
                        cycleLength++;
                        ptr1 = ptr1->link;
                }while(ptr1 != ptr2);
                cout << "Cycle Length : " << cycleLength << "\n";

                //Find the remaining length
                int remLength = 0;
                ptr1 = start;
                while(ptr1 != ptr2)
                {
                        remLength++;
                        ptr1 = ptr1->link;
                        ptr2 = ptr2->link;
                }
                cout << "Remaining Length : " << remLength << "\n";

                int listLength = cycleLength + remLength;
                cout << "The List is : \n";
                ptr1 = start;
                for(int i=1; i<=listLength-1; i++)
                {
                        cout << ptr1->info << "\n";
                        ptr1 = ptr1->link;
                }
                cout << ptr1->info << "\n";
                ptr1->link = NULL;
        }
}//End of removeCycle()
```

3.10 Polynomial Arithmetic with Linked List

A useful application of a linked list is the representation of polynomial expressions. Let us take a polynomial expression with single variable:

$5x^4 + x^3 - 6x + 2$

In each term, we have a coefficient and an exponent. For example, in the term $5x^4$, the coefficient is 5 and the exponent is 4. The whole polynomial can be represented through a linked list where each node will represent a term of the expression.

This is the class `Node` for polynomial expression:

```
class Node
{
        public:
                int coeff;
                int expo;
                Node *link;
                Node(int coefficient, int exponent)
                {
                        coeff = coefficient;
                        expo = exponent;
                        link = NULL;
                }
};//End of class Node
```

Here, the info part of the node contains the coefficient and exponent, and the link part is the same as before and will be used to point to the next node of the list. The node representing the term $5x^4$ can be represented as:

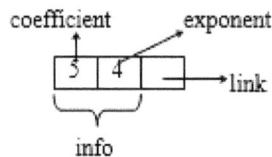

Figure 3.58 Node in polynomial expression

The polynomial $(5x^4 + x^3 - 6x + 2)$ can be represented through a linked list as:

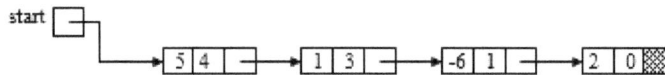

Figure 3.59 Polynomial expression in linked list

Here 2 is considered as $2x^0$ because $x^0 = 1$.

The arithmetic operations are easier if the terms are arranged in descending order of their exponents. For example, it would be better if the polynomial expression $(5x + 6x^3 + x^2 - 9 + 2x^6)$ is stored as $(2x^6 + 6x^3 + x^2 + 5x - 9)$. So, for representing the polynomial expression, we will use a sorted linked list, which would be in descending order based on the exponent. An empty list will represent zero polynomial. The following program shows the creation of polynomial linked lists and their addition and multiplication.

```
//Polynomial.cpp : Program of Polynomial expression creation, addition and multiplication
//using linked list.
#include<iostream>
using namespace std;

class Node
{
        public:
                int coeff;
                int expo;
                Node *link;
                Node(int coefficient, int exponent)
                {
```

```
                    coeff = coefficient;
                    expo = exponent;
                    link = NULL;
            }
};//End of class Node
class Polynomial
{
      private:
            Node *start;
      public:
            Polynomial();
            ~Polynomial();
            bool isEmpty();
            void display();
            int size();
            void insert(int coefficient, int exponent);
            void insertAtEnd(int coefficient, int exponent);
            void addition(Polynomial& list, Polynomial& resultList);
            void multiplication(Polynomial& list, Polynomial& resultList);
};//End of class Polynomial
Polynomial::Polynomial()
{
      start = NULL;
}//End of Polynomial()
Polynomial::~Polynomial()
{
      Node *ptr;
      while(start != NULL)
      {
            ptr = start->link;
            delete start;
            start = ptr;
      }
}//End of ~Polynomial()
bool Polynomial::isEmpty()
{
      return (start == NULL);
}//End of isEmpty()
void Polynomial::display()
{
      Node *ptr;
      if(!isEmpty())
      {
            ptr = start;
            while(ptr != NULL)
            {
                  cout << ptr->coeff;
                  if(ptr->expo == 1)
                        cout << "x";
                  else if(ptr->expo >1)
                        cout << "x^" << ptr->expo;
                  ptr = ptr->link;
                  if(ptr!=NULL)
                        cout << " + ";
            }
            cout << "\n";
      }
      else
            cout << "Zero polynomial\n";
```

```
}//End of display()
void Polynomial::insert(int coefficient, int exponent)
{
        Node *ptr, *temp;
        temp = new Node(coefficient, exponent);

        //List empty or exponent greater than first one
        if(isEmpty() || exponent > start->expo)
        {
                temp->link = start;
                start = temp;
        }
        else
        {
                ptr = start;
                while(ptr->link!=NULL && ptr->link->expo >= exponent)
                        ptr = ptr->link;

                temp->link = ptr->link;
                ptr->link = temp;
        }
}//End of insert()

//Required for addition of polynomials
void Polynomial::insertAtEnd(int coefficient, int exponent)
{
        Node *ptr, *temp;
        temp = new Node(coefficient,exponent);

        if(isEmpty())
                start = temp;
        else
        {
                ptr = start;
                while(ptr->link != NULL)
                        ptr = ptr->link;

                ptr->link = temp;
        }
}//End of insertAtEnd()

void Polynomial::addition(Polynomial& list, Polynomial& resultList)
{
        Node *p1 = start;
        Node *p2 = list.start;

        while(p1!=NULL && p2!=NULL)
        {
                if(p1->expo > p2->expo)
                {
                        resultList.insert(p1->coeff, p1->expo);
                        p1 = p1->link;
                }
                else if(p2->expo > p1->expo)
                {
                        resultList.insert(p2->coeff, p2->expo);
                        p2 = p2->link;
                }
                else if(p1->expo == p2->expo)
                {
                        resultList.insert(p1->coeff+p2->coeff, p1->expo);
                        p1 = p1->link;
                        p2 = p2->link;
                }
```

```
        }

        //If poly2 is finished and elements left in poly1
        while(p1 != NULL)
        {
                resultList.insert(p1->coeff, p1->expo);
                p1 = p1->link;
        }
        //If poly1 is finished and elements left in poly2
        while(p2 != NULL)
        {
                resultList.insert(p2->coeff, p2->expo);
                p2 = p2->link;
        }
}//End of addition()
void Polynomial::multiplication(Polynomial& list, Polynomial& resultList)
{
        Node *p1 = start;
        Node *p2 = list.start;
        Node *p2Start = p2;

        if(p1==NULL || p2==NULL)
                cout << "Multiplied polynomial is zero polynomial\n";
        else
        {
                while(p1 != NULL)
                {
                        p2 = p2Start;
                        while(p2 != NULL)
                        {
                                resultList.insert(p1->coeff*p2->coeff, p1->expo+p2->expo);
                                p2 = p2->link;
                        }
                        p1 = p1->link;
                }
        }
}//End of multiplication()
int main()
{
        Polynomial list1, list2, list3, list4;

        list1.insert(4,3);
        list1.insert(5,2);
        list1.insert(-3,1);
        cout << "Polynomial List1 :\n";
        list1.display();

        list2.insert(2,5);
        list2.insert(6,4);
        list2.insert(1,2);
        list2.insert(8,0);
        cout << "Polynomial List2 :\n";
        list2.display();

        //Polynomial addition
        list1.addition(list2, list3);
        cout << "After addition of list1 and list2 :\n";
        list3.display();

        //Polynomial multiplication
        list1.multiplication(list2, list4);
        cout << "After multiplication of list1 and list2 :\n";
```

```
        list4.display();

        return 0;
}//End of main()
```

3.10.1 Creation of Polynomial Linked List

The polynomial linked list can be created using member function `insert()`, which inserts a node in the polynomial linked list. The member function `insert()` is similar to that of sorted linked lists. The only difference is that here, our list is in descending order based on the exponent.

```
//Create a polynomial expression
Polynomial list;
list.insert(4,3);
list.insert(5,2);
list.insert(-3,1);
```

3.10.2 Addition of Two Polynomials

The procedure for addition of two polynomials represented by linked lists is somewhat similar to that of merging. Let us take two polynomial expression lists and make a third list by adding them.

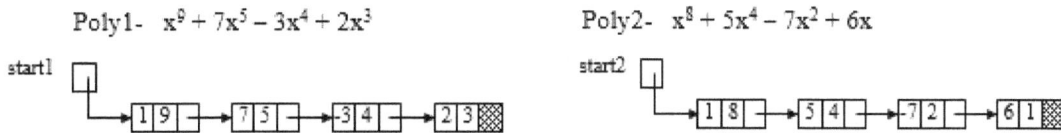

Figure 3.60 Two polynomial expressions for addition

The pointers `p1` and `p2` will point to the current nodes in the polynomials, which will be added. Both polynomials are traversed until one polynomial finishes. We can have three cases:

1. If `(p1->expo) > (p2->expo)`
The new node that is added to the resultant list has coefficient equal to `p1->coeff` and exponent equal to `p1->expo`. After this, we will make `p1` point to the next node of polynomial 1.

2. If `(p2->expo) > (p1->expo)`
The new node that is added to the resultant list has a coefficient equal to `p2->coeff` and exponent equal to
`p2->expo`. After this, we will make `p2` point to the next node of polynomial 2.

3. If `(p1->expo) == (p2->expo)`
The new node that is added to the resultant list has a coefficient equal to `(p1->coeff + p2->coeff)` and exponent equal to `p1->expo` (or `p2->expo`). After this, we will make `p1` and `p2` point to the next nodes of polynomial 1 and polynomial 2 respectively.

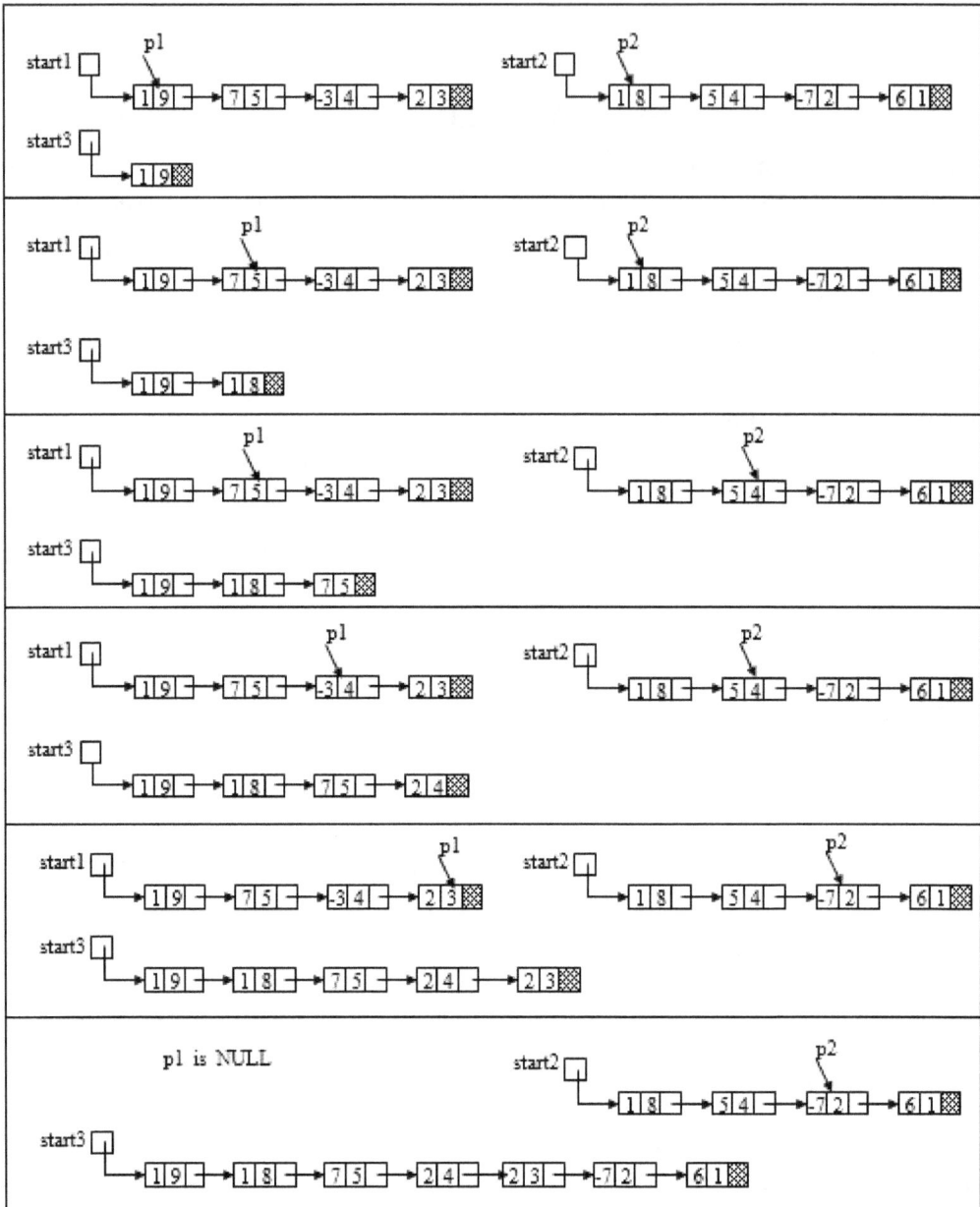

Figure 3.61 Addition of two polynomial expressions

The procedure of polynomial addition is shown in figure 3.61.

```
while(p1!=NULL && p2!=NULL)
{
        if(p1->expo > p2->expo)
        {
                resultList.insert(p1->coeff, p1->expo);
                p1 = p1->link;
```

```
        }
        else if(p2->expo > p1->expo)
        {
                resultList.insert(p2->coeff, p2->expo);
                p2 = p2->link;
        }
        else if(p1->expo == p2->expo)
        {
                resultList.insert(p1->coeff+p2->coeff, p1->expo);
                p1 = p1->link;
                p2 = p2->link;
        }
}
```

The `while` loop will terminate when any of the polynomial finish. Now, we have to add the remaining nodes of the unfinished polynomial to the resultant list. If polynomial 2 has finished, then we will put all the terms of polynomial 1 in the resultant list as:

```
while(p1 != NULL)
{
        resultList.insert(p1->coeff, p1->expo);
        p1 = p1->link;
}
```

If polynomial 1 is finished, then we will put all the terms of polynomial 2 in the resultant list as:

```
while(p2 != NULL)
{
        resultList.insert(p2->coeff, p2->expo);
        p2 = p2->link;
}
```

We can see the advantage of storing the terms in descending order of their exponents. If this were not the case, we would have to scan both lists many times.

3.10.3 Multiplication of Two Polynomials

Suppose we have to multiply the two polynomials given here:

$4x^3 + 5x^2 - 3x$

$2x^5 + 6x^4 + x^2 + 8$

For this, we have to multiply each term of the first polynomial with each term of the second polynomial. When we multiply two terms, their coefficients are multiplied, and exponents are added. The product of the above two polynomials is:

$[(4*2)x^{3+5} + (4*6)x^{3+4} + (4*1)x^{3+2} + (4*8)x^{3+0}]$ + $[(5*2)x^{2+5} + (5*6)x^{2+4} +(5*1)x^{2+2} +(5*8)x^{2+0}]$ + $[(-3*2)x^{1+5} + (-3*6)x^{1+4} + (-3*1)x^{1+2} + (-3*8)x^{1+0}]$

$8x^8 + 24x^7 + 4x^5 + 32x^3 + 10x^7 + 30x^6 + 5x^4 + 40x^2 - 6x^6 -18x^5 - 3x^3 - 24x^1$

We will have to use two nested loops: the outer loop will walk through the first polynomial, and the inner loop will walk through the second polynomial.

In the member function `multiplication()`, we have used the member function `insert()` to insert elements in the third list. If we do not do so, then the elements in the multiplied list will not be in descending order based on the exponent.

We have seen how to represent polynomial expressions with a single variable, x, through a linked list. We can extend this concept to represent expressions with multiple variables.

Another useful application of the linked list is in radix sort, which is explained in Chapter 8, Sorting.

3.11 Comparison of Array Lists and Linked lists

Now after having studied about linked lists, let us compare the two implementations of lists i.e., the array implementation and the linked implementation.

3.11.1 Advantages of Linked Lists

The advantages of linked lists are as follows:

(1) We know that the size of array is specified at the time of writing the program. This means that the memory space is allocated at compile time, and we cannot increase or decrease it during runtime according to our needs. If the amount of data is less than the size of the array, then space is wasted, while if data is more than the size of the array, then overflow occurs even if there is enough space available in memory.

Linked lists overcome this problem by using dynamically allocated memory. The size of linked list is not fixed and it can be increased or decreased during runtime. Since memory is allocated at runtime, there is no wastage of memory, and we can keep on inserting the elements till memory is available. Whenever we need a new node, we dynamically allocate it, i.e., we get it from the free storage space. When we do not need the node, we can return the memory occupied by it to the free storage space so that it can be used by other programs. We have done these two operations by using `new` and `delete` operator.

(2) Insertion and deletion inside arrays are not efficient since they require shifting of elements. For example, if we want to insert an element at the 0th position, then we have to shift all the elements of the array to the right, and if we want to delete the element present at the 0th position, then we have to shift all the elements to the left. These are the worst cases of insertion and deletion, and the efficiency is O(n). If the array consists of big records, then this shifting is even more time consuming.

In linked lists, insertion and deletion require only change in pointers. There is no physical movement of data, only the links are altered.

(3) We know that in arrays all the elements are always stored in contiguous locations. Sometimes arrays cannot be used because the amount of memory needed by them is not available in contiguous locations i.e., the total memory required by the array is available, but it is dispersed. So, in this case, we cannot create an array in spite of available memory.

In linked list, elements are not stored in contiguous locations. So, in the above case, there will be no problem in the creation of a linked list.

3.11.2 Disadvantages of Linked Lists

The disadvantages of linked lists are as follows:

(1) In arrays, we can access the nth element directly, but in linked lists, we have to pass through the first n-1 elements to reach the nth element. So, when it comes to random access, array lists are definitely better than linked lists.

(2) In linked lists, the pointer fields take extra space that could have been used for storing some more data.

(3) Writing programs for linked lists is more difficult than that for arrays.

Exercise

In all the problems assume that we have an integer in the info part of nodes.

1. Write a function to count the number of occurrences of an element in a single linked list.

2. Write a function to find the smallest and largest element of a single linked list.

3. Write a function to check if the two linked lists are identical. Two lists are identical if they have same number of elements and the corresponding elements in both lists are same.

4. Write a function to create a copy of a single linked list.

5. Given a linked list L, write a function to create a single linked list that is reverse of the list L. For example, if the list L is `1->2->3->4->5` then the new list should be `5->4->3->2->1`. The list L should remain unchanged.

6. Write a program to swap adjacent elements of a single linked list:
    (i) by exchanging info part
    (ii) by rearranging links
    For example, if a linked list is `1->2->3->4->5->6->7->8`, then after swapping adjacent elements it should become `2->1->4->3->6->5->8->7`.

7. Write a program to swap adjacent elements of a double linked list by rearranging links.

8. Write a program to swap the first and last elements of a single linked list
    (i) by exchanging info part.
    (ii) by rearranging links.

9. Write a function to move the largest element to the end of a single linked list.

10. Write a function to move the smallest element to the beginning of a single linked list.

11. Write a function for deleting all the nodes from a single linked list which have a value N.

12. Given a single linked list L1, which is sorted in ascending order, and another single linked list L2, which is not sorted, write a function to print the elements of the second list according to the first list. For example, if the first list is `1->2->5->7->8`, then the function should print the 1st, 2nd, 5th, 7th, 8th elements of second list.

13. Write a program to remove the first node of the list and insert it at the end without changing the info part of any node.

14. Write a program to remove the last node of the list and insert it in the beginning, without changing info part of any node.

15. Write a program to move a node n positions forward in a single linked list.

16. Write a function to delete a node from a single linked list. The only information we have is a pointer to the node that has to be deleted.

17. Write functions to insert a node just before and just after a node pointed to by a pointer p, without using the pointer start.

18. Write a function to remove duplicates from a sorted single linked list.

19. Write a function to remove duplicates from an unsorted single linked list.

20. Write a function to create a linked list that is the intersection of two single linked lists, i.e., it contains only the elements common to both lists.

21. Write a function to create a linked list that is a union of two single linked lists, i.e., it contains all elements of both lists and if an element is repeated in both lists, then it is included only once.

22. Given a list L1, delete all the nodes having negative numbers in the info part and insert them into list L2, and all the nodes having positive numbers into list L3. No new nodes should be created.

23. Given a linked list L1, create two linked lists, one with the odd numbers of L1 and the other with the odd numbers of L1. Do not change list L1.

24. Write a function to delete alternate nodes (even-numbered nodes) from a single linked list. For example, if the list is 1->2->3->4->5->6->7, then the resulting list should be 1->3->5->7.

25. Write a function to get the nth node from the end of a single linked list, without counting the elements or reversing the list.

26. Write a function to find the middle node of a single linked list without counting all the elements of the list.

27. Write a function to split a single linked list into two halves.

28. Write a function to split a single linked list into two lists at a node containing the given information.

29. Write a function to split a single linked list into two lists such that the alternate nodes (even numbered nodes) go to a new list.

30. Write a function to combine the alternate nodes of two null terminated single linked lists. For example, if the first list is 1->2->3->4 and the second list is 5->7->8->9, then after combining them, the first list should be 1->5->2->7->3->8->4->9 and the second list should be empty. If both lists are not of the same length, then the remaining nodes of the longer list are taken in the combined list. For example, if the first list is 1->2->3->4 and the second list is 5->7, then the combined list should be 1->5->2->7->3->4.

31. Suppose there are two null terminated single linked lists that merge at a given point and share all the nodes after that merge point (Y-shaped lists). Write a function to find the merge point (intersection point).

32. Create a double linked list in which the info part of each node contains a digit of a given number. The digits should be stored in reverse order, i.e., the least significant digit should be stored in the first node and the most significant digit in the last node. If the number is 5468132, then the linked list should be
2->3->1->8->6->4->5. Write a function to add two numbers represented by linked lists.

33. Modify the program in the previous problem so that we can store 4 digits of the given number in each node of the list. For example, if the number is 23156782913287, then the linked list would be 3287->8291->1567->23.

34. Write a function to find whether a linked list is a palindrome or not.

Join our book's Discord space

Join the book's Discord Workspace for Latest updates, Offers, Tech happenings around the world, New Release and Sessions with the Authors:

https://discord.bpbonline.com

Stacks and Queues

In linked lists and arrays, insertions and deletions can be performed at any place in the list. There can be situations when there is a need for a data structure in which operations are allowed only at the ends of the list and not in the middle. Stack and Queue are data structures that fulfill these requirements. Stack is a linear list in which insertions and deletions are allowed only at one end, while Queue is a linear list in which insertion is performed at one end and deletion is performed at the other end.

4.1 Stack

Stack is a linear list in which insertions and deletions are allowed only at one end, called the top of the stack. We can see examples of the stack in our daily life, like a stack of trays in a cafeteria, a stack of books or a stack of tennis balls. In all these cases, we can see that any object can be removed or added only at the top.

Figure 4.1 Examples of stack

The insertion and deletion operations are given special names in the case of stack. The **push** operation inserts an element in the stack, and the **pop** operation deletes an element from the stack. The figure 4.2 shows these operations with the help of an example:

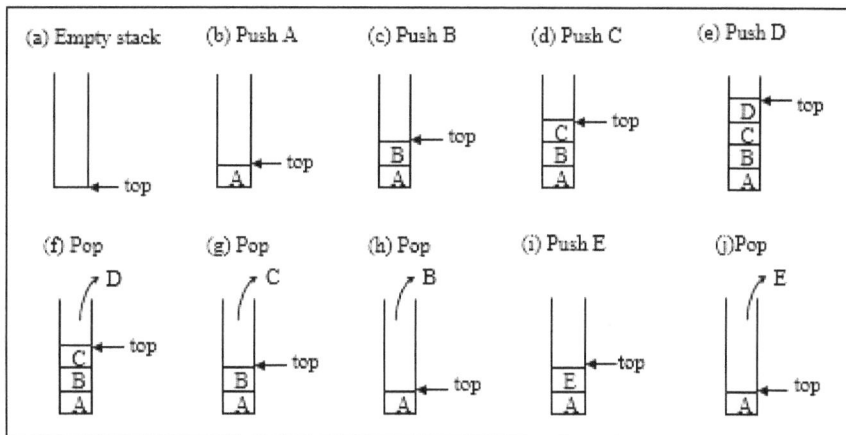

Figure 4.2 Stack operations

We can see that the element pushed last is popped first from the stack. In the example of figure 4.2, D is pushed last, but it was the first one to be popped. The behavior of stack is like last in first out, and so it is also called Last In First Out (LIFO) data structure.

Before pushing any element, we must check whether there is space in the stack or not. If there is not enough space, then the stack is said to be in an **overflow** state and the new element cannot be pushed. Similarly, before the pop operation, if the stack is empty and the pop operation is attempted, then the stack is said to be in an **underflow** state.

Since stack is a linear list, it can be implemented using arrays or linked lists. In the next two sections, we will study these two implementations of stack.

4.1.1 Array Implementation of Stack

We will take a one-dimensional array `stackArray[]` to hold the elements of the stack. In an array, elements can be added or deleted at any place, but since we are implementing a stack, we have to permit insertions and deletions at the top of the stack only. So, we take a variable `top`, which keeps the position (index) of the topmost element in the array.

Initially when the stack is empty, the value of `top` is initialized to -1. For the push operation, first the value of `top` is increased by 1, and then the new element is pushed at the position of `top`. For the pop operation, first the element at the position of `top` is popped, and then `top` is decreased by 1.

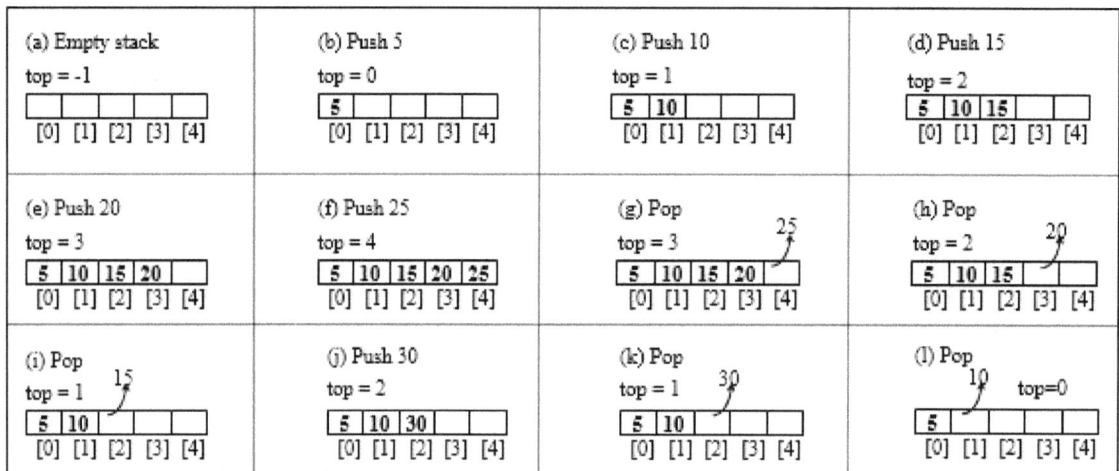

Figure 4.3 Array implementation of stack

While writing functions for push and pop operations, we have to check for overflow and underflow. If `maxSize` is the size of the array, then the stack will become full, when `top` becomes equal to `maxSize-1`. In figure 4.3, the stack is full in step (f), and the value of `top` is 4. So before pushing, we have to check for this overflow condition. The stack becomes empty when the value of `top` is -1, and so we have to check this underflow condition before popping any element from the stack.

Here is the `Stack` class:

```
class Stack
{
        private:
                int stackArray[maxSize];
```

```
                int top;
        public:
                Stack();
                bool isEmpty();
                bool isFull();
                void push(int data);
                int pop();
                int peek();
                void display();
                int size();
};//End of class Stack
```

The `Stack` class data members are:

- `stackArray`: holds the elements of the stack
- `top`: keeps the position of top most element of stack

`top` is initialized with -1 in constructor.

The `Stack` class member functions are:

- `Stack()`: constructor to initialize the `top` with -1
- `isEmpty()`: to check if the stack is empty
- `isFull()`: to check if the stack is full
- `push()`: push operation on stack
- `pop()`: pop operation on stack
- `peek()`: returns the top element of the stack without pop
- `display()`: display the elements of the stack
- `size()`: returns the size of stack

This is the program of stack using array:

```
//Stack.cpp : Program to implement stack using array.
#include <iostream>
using namespace std;

static const int maxSize = 5;

class Stack
{
        private:
                int stackArray[maxSize];
                int top;
        public:
                Stack();
                bool isEmpty();
                bool isFull();
                void push(int data);
                int pop();
                int peek();
                void display();
                int size();
};//End of class Stack

Stack::Stack()
{
        top = -1;
}//End of Stack()

bool Stack::isEmpty()
{
        return (top == -1);
}//End of isEmpty()

bool Stack::isFull()
```

```cpp
{
        return (top == maxSize-1);
}//End of isFull()
void Stack::push(int data)
{
        if(isFull())
                cout << "Stack Overflow\n";
        else
        {
                top++;
                stackArray[top] = data;
        }
}//End of push()
int Stack::pop()
{
        if(isEmpty())
                throw exception("Stack is empty");

        int retValue = stackArray[top];
        top = top-1;

        return retValue;
}//End of pop()
int Stack::peek()
{
        if(isEmpty())
                throw exception("Stack is empty");

        return stackArray[top];
}//End of peek()
int Stack::size()
{
        return (top+1);
}//End of size()
void Stack::display()
{
        if(isEmpty())
                cout << "Stack is empty\n";
        else
                for(int i=top; i>=0; i--)
                        cout << stackArray[i] << "\n";
}//End of display()
int main()
{
        Stack st;
        try
        {
                st.push(1);
                st.push(2);
                st.push(3);
                st.push(4);
                cout << "Stack Items : \n";
                st.display();

                cout << "Top Item : " << st.peek() << "\n";
                cout << "Total items : " << st.size() << "\n";
                cout << "Popped Item : " << st.pop() << "\n";
                cout << "Stack Items : \n";
                st.display();
                st.push(4);
```

```
                st.push(5);
                cout << "Stack Items : \n";
                st.display();

                cout << "Popped Item : " << st.pop() << "\n";
                cout << "Popped Item : " << st.pop() << "\n";
                cout << "Popped Item : " << st.pop() << "\n";
                cout << "Popped Item : " << st.pop() << "\n";
                cout << "Popped Item : " << st.pop() << "\n";
                cout << "Stack Items : \n";
                st.display();
        }//End of try
        catch(exception e)
        {
                cout << e.what() << "\n";
        }

        return 0;
}//End of main()
```

The function `push()` pushes an item on the stack; the function `pop()` pops an item from the stack and returns the popped item. The function `peek()` returns the top item without removing it from the stack, and so the value of `top` remains unchanged. The function `display()` displays all the elements of the stack.

4.1.2 Linked List Implementation of Stack

When the size of stack is not known in advance, it is better to implement it as a linked list. In this case, the stack will not overflow till there is space available for dynamic memory allocation. We will take a single linked list so that the class of node would be:

```
class Node
{
        public:
                int info;
                Node *link;
        Node(int data)
        {
                info = data;
                link = NULL;
        }
};//End of class Node
```

Here is the class `StackL`:

```
class StackL
{
        private:
                Node *top;
        public:
                StackL();
                bool isEmpty();
                void push(int data);
                int pop();
                int peek();
                void display();
                int size();
};//End of class StackL
```

We will take the beginning of linked list as the top of the stack. For the push operation, a node will be inserted in the beginning of the list. For the pop operation, the first node of the list will be deleted. If we take the end of the list as top of the stack, then for each push and pop operation, we will have to traverse the whole list. We will take a pointer `top` that points to the first node of the linked list. This pointer `top` is the same as the pointer `start` that we had taken in a single linked list.

For pushing an element on the stack, we follow the procedure of insertion in the beginning of the linked list. The function `push()` would be similar to the function `insertAtBeginning()` of single linked list. The stack will overflow only when there is no space left for dynamic memory allocation.

For the pop operation, we will delete the first element of the linked list. The underflow condition will arise when the linked list is empty, i.e., when `top` is equal to NULL. So, inside the function `pop()`, we will check for this underflow condition.

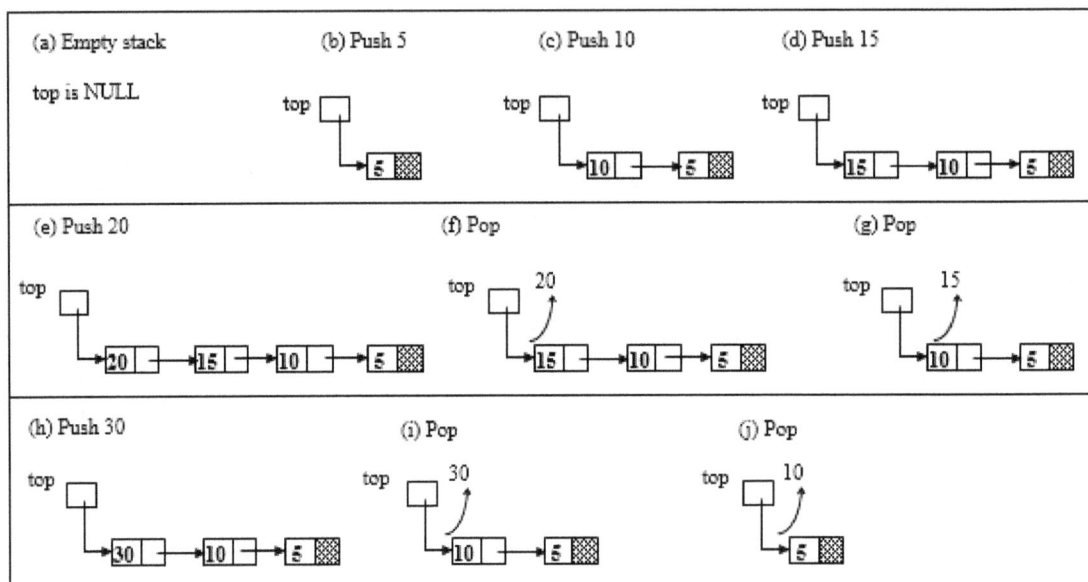

Figure 4.4 Linked list implementation of stack

```
//StackL.cpp : Program to implement stack using linked list.
#include <iostream>
using namespace std;
class Node
{
        public:
                int info;
                Node *link;
                Node(int data)
                {
                        info = data;
                        link = NULL;
                }
};//End of class Node
class StackL
{
        private:
                Node *top;
        public:
                StackL();
                bool isEmpty();
```

```
                void push(int data);
                int pop();
                int peek();
                void display();
                int size();
};//End of class StackL

StackL::StackL()
{
        top = NULL;
}//End of StackL()

bool StackL::isEmpty()
{
        return (top == NULL);
}//End of isEmpty()

void StackL::push(int data)
{
        Node *temp;
        temp = new Node(data);
        if(!isEmpty())
                temp->link = top;
        top = temp;
}//End of push()

int StackL::pop()
{
        Node *temp;
        int retValue;
        if(isEmpty())
                throw exception("Stack is empty");
        else
        {
                retValue = top->info;
                temp = top;
                top = top->link;
                delete temp;
        }
        return retValue;
}//End of pop()

int StackL::peek()
{
        if(isEmpty())
                throw exception("Stack is empty");
        return top->info;
}//End of peek()

void StackL::display()
{
        Node *ptr;
        if(!isEmpty())
        {
                ptr = top;
                while(ptr != NULL)
                {
                        cout << ptr->info << "\n";
                        ptr = ptr->link;
                }
        }
        else
                cout << "Stack is empty\n";
}//End of display()
```

```cpp
int StackL::size()
{
        Node *ptr;
        int count = 0;
        ptr = top;
        while(ptr != NULL)
        {
                count++;
                ptr = ptr->link;
        }
        return count;
}//End of size()
int main()
{
        StackL st;
        try
        {
                st.push(1);
                st.push(2);
                st.push(3);
                st.push(4);
                cout << "Stack Items : \n";
                st.display();
                cout << "Top Item : " << st.peek() << "\n";
                cout << "Total items : " << st.size() << "\n";
                cout << "Popped Item : " << st.pop() << "\n";
                cout << "Stack Items : \n";
                st.display();
                st.push(4);
                st.push(5);
                cout << "Stack Items : \n";
                st.display();
                cout << "Popped Item : " << st.pop() << "\n";
                cout << "Popped Item : " << st.pop() << "\n";
                cout << "Popped Item : " << st.pop() << "\n";
                cout << "Popped Item : " << st.pop() << "\n";
                cout << "Popped Item : " << st.pop() << "\n";
                cout << "Stack Items : \n";
                st.display();
        }//End of try
        catch(exception e)
        {
                cout << e.what() << "\n";
        }
        return 0;
}//End of main()
```

4.2 Queue

Queue is a linear list in which elements can be inserted only at one end, called the rear of the queue, and deleted only at the other end, called the front of the queue. We can see examples of the queue in daily life like a queue of people waiting at a counter or a queue of cars etc. In the queue of people and queue of cars, the person or car that enters first in the queue will be out first. The behaviour of queue is first in first out, and so it is also called First In First Out (FIFO) data structure. The following example shows that the new element is inserted at the end called rear and the deletion is done at the other end called front:

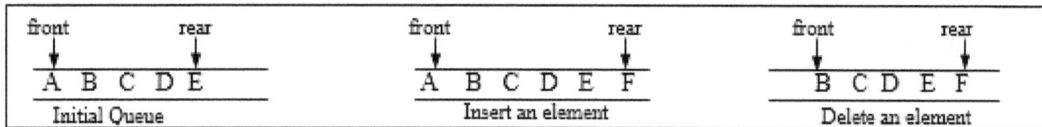

Figure 4.5 Queue operations

In a queue, the insertion operation is known as **enqueue** and deletion is known as **dequeue**. If the insert operation is attempted and there is not enough space in the queue, then this situation is called overflow and the new element cannot be inserted. If the queue is empty and the delete operation is attempted, then this situation is called underflow.

4.2.1 Array Implementation of Queue

In stack, both operations were performed at the same end, so we had to take only one variable `top`. But here, operations are performed at different ends, and so we have to take two variables to keep track of both the ends. We will take the variables named `rear` and `front`, where `rear` will hold the index of last added item in queue and `front` will hold the index of first item of queue.

(i) Initially when the queue is empty, the values of both `front` and `rear` will be -1.

(ii) For insertion, the value of `rear` is incremented by 1 and the element is inserted at the new rear position.

(iii) For deletion, the element at the front position is deleted and the value of `front` is incremented by 1.

(iv) When insertion is done in an initially empty queue, i.e., if the value of `front` and `rear` is -1, then values of `front` and `rear` are made 0.

The figure 4.6 shows insertions and deletion in a queue:

Figure 4.6 Array implementation of queue

From the figure 4.6, we can note the following things:

(i) At any time, the number of elements in the queue is equal to (`rear-front+1`), except the initial empty queue.

(ii) When `front` is equal to `rear`, there is only one element in the queue ((b), (f), (h), (j)), except the initially empty queue.

(iii) When `front` becomes equal to `(rear+1)`, the queue becomes empty ((g) and (k)). So, we can see that the queue is empty in two situations: when initially `front` is equal to -1 or when `front` becomes equal to `(rear+1)`. These are the two conditions of queue underflow.

(iv) When `rear` becomes equal to 4, it cannot be incremented further. After case (i), the value of `rear` becomes 4, and so now, it is not possible to insert any element in the queue. Hence, we can say that if the size of an array is `maxSize`, then it is not possible to insert elements after `rear` becomes equal to `maxSize-1`. This is the condition for queue overflow.

The function `enqueue()` will insert an item in the queue and the function `dequeue()` will delete an item from the queue. Inside the function `enqueue()`, we will first check the condition of overflow and then insert the element. Inside the function `dequeue()`, we will first check the condition for underflow and then delete the element. The function `peek()` returns the item at the front of the queue without removing it.

Here is the `Queue` class:

```cpp
class Queue
{
        private:
                int queueArray[maxSize];
                int front;
                int rear;
        public:
                Queue();
                bool isEmpty();
                bool isFull();
                void enqueue(int data);
                int dequeue();
                int peek();
                void display();
                int size();
};//End of class Queue
```

The `Queue` class data members are:

- `queueArray`: holds the elements of the queue
- `front`: holds the index of the first item of the queue
- `rear`: holds the index of the last added item in the queue

`front` and `rear` are initialized with -1 in the constructor.

The `Queue` class member functions are:

- `Queue()`: constructor to initialize the `front` and `rear` with -1
- `isEmpty()`: to check if the queue is empty
- `isFull()`: to check if the queue is full
- `enqueue()`: insert operation on queue
- `dequeue()`: delete operation on queue
- `peek()`: returns the front element of the queue without deleting
- `display()`: display the elements of the queue
- `size()`: returns the size of the queue

Here is the program of queue using array:

```cpp
//Queue.cpp : Program to implement queue using array.
#include <iostream>
using namespace std;
```

```
static const int maxSize = 5;
class Queue
{
        private:
                int queueArray[maxSize];
                int front;
                int rear;
        public:
                Queue();
                bool isEmpty();
                bool isFull();
                void enqueue(int data);
                int dequeue();
                int peek();
                void display();
                int size();
};//End of class Queue
Queue::Queue()
{
        front = -1;
        rear = -1;
}//End of Queue()
bool Queue::isEmpty()
{
        return (front==-1 || front==rear+1);
}//End of isEmpty()
bool Queue::isFull()
{
        return (rear == maxSize-1);
}//End of isFull()
void Queue::enqueue(int data)
{
        if(isFull())
                cout << "Queue Overflow\n";
        else
        {
                if(front == -1)
                        front = 0;

                rear = rear+1;
                queueArray[rear] = data;
        }
}//End of enqueue()
int Queue::dequeue()
{
        if(isEmpty())
                throw exception("Queue is empty");

        return queueArray[front++];
}//End of dequeue()
int Queue::peek()
{
        if(isEmpty())
                throw exception("Queue is empty");

        return queueArray[front];
}//End of peek()
void Queue::display()
{
```

```cpp
        cout << "Front = " << front << "        rear = " << rear << "\n";
        if(isEmpty())
                cout << "Queue is empty\n";
        else
                for(int i=front; i<=rear; i++)
                        cout << queueArray[i] << "\n";
}//End of display()
int Queue::size()
{
        int retValue=0;
        if(!isEmpty())
                retValue = rear-front+1;

        return retValue;
}//End of size()
int main()
{
        Queue qu;

        try
        {
                qu.enqueue(1);
                qu.enqueue(2);
                qu.enqueue(3);
                qu.enqueue(4);
                cout << "Queue Items :\n";
                qu.display();
                cout << "Front Item : " << qu.peek() << "\n";
                cout << "Total items : " << qu.size() << "\n";
                cout << "Deleted Item : " << qu.dequeue() << "\n";
                cout << "Queue Items :\n";
                qu.display();
                qu.enqueue(5);
                cout << "Queue Items :\n";
                qu.display();
                cout << "Deleted Item : " << qu.dequeue() << "\n";
                cout << "Deleted Item : " << qu.dequeue() << "\n";
                cout << "Deleted Item : " << qu.dequeue() << "\n";
                cout << "Deleted Item : " << qu.dequeue() << "\n";

                cout << "Queue Items :\n";
                qu.display();
        }//End of try
        catch(exception e)
        {
                cout << e.what() << "\n";
        }

        return 0;
}//End of main()
```

There is a drawback in this array implementation of queue. Consider the situation when the `rear` is at the last position of array and `front` is not at the 0th position:

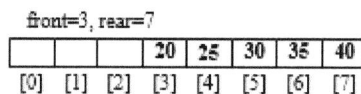

front=3, rear=7

			20	25	30	35	40
[0]	[1]	[2]	[3]	[4]	[5]	[6]	[7]

Figure 4.7 Disadvantage in array implementation of queue

There are 3 spaces for adding the elements, but we cannot insert any element in the queue because the `rear` is at the last position of array. One solution to avoid this wastage of space is that we can shift all the elements of the array to the left and adjust the values of `front` and `rear` accordingly:

front=0, rear=4

20	25	30	35	40			
[0]	[1]	[2]	[3]	[4]	[5]	[6]	[7]

Figure 4.8 Shifting of array elements of queue

This is practically not a good approach because shifting of elements will consume a lot of time. Another efficient solution to this problem is the circular queue. We will study about it later in this chapter.

4.2.2 Linked List Implementation of Queue

Queue can also be implemented through a linked list. Here is the class declaration for a node of a linked list that will be used to implement a queue:

```
class Node
{
    public:
        int info;
        Node *link;
        Node(int data)
        {
            info = data;
            link = NULL;
        }
}; //End of class Node
```

We will take the beginning of the linked list as `front`, and the end of the linked list as `rear`. So, to insert an item in our queue, we will add a node at the end of the list and to delete an item from the queue, we will delete a node from the beginning of the list. We will maintain two pointers named `front` and `rear`, where the `front` will point to the first node of the list, and, the `rear` will point to the last node of the list.

Here is the class `QueueL`:

```
class QueueL
{
    private:
                Node *front;
                Node *rear;
    public:
                QueueL();
                bool isEmpty();
                void enqueue(int data);
                int dequeue();
                int peek();
                void display();
                int size();
}; //End of class QueueL
```

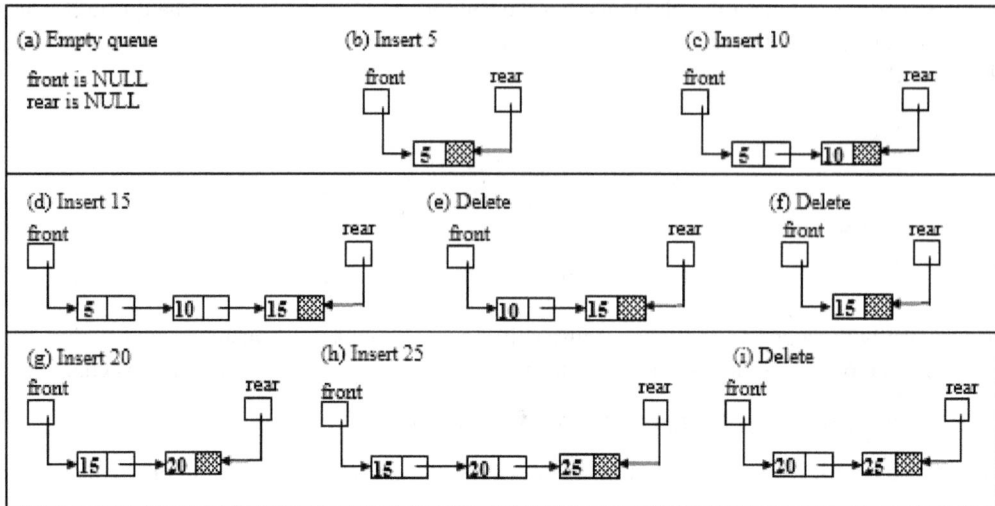

Figure 4.9 Linked list implementation of queue

```cpp
//QueueL.cpp : Program to implement queue using linked list.
#include <iostream>
using namespace std;
class Node
{
        public:
                int info;
                Node *link;
                Node(int data)
                {
                        info = data;
                        link = NULL;
                }
};//End of class Node
class QueueL
{
        private:
                Node *front;
                Node *rear;
        public:
                QueueL();
                bool isEmpty();
                void enqueue(int data);
                int dequeue();
                int peek();
                void display();
                int size();
};//End of class QueueL
QueueL::QueueL()
{
        front = NULL;
        rear = NULL;
}//End of QueueL()
bool QueueL::isEmpty()
{
```

```
                return (front == NULL);
}//End of isEmpty()
void QueueL::enqueue(int data)
{
        Node *temp;
        temp = new Node(data);
        if(isEmpty()) //If queue is empty
                front = temp;
        else
                rear->link = temp;
        rear = temp;
}//End of enqueue()
int QueueL::dequeue()
{
        Node *temp;
        int retValue;
        if(isEmpty())
                throw exception("Queue is empty");
        else
        {
                retValue = front->info;
                temp = front;
                front = front->link;
                delete temp;
        }
        return retValue;
}//End of dequeue()
int QueueL::peek()
{
        if(isEmpty())
                throw exception("Queue is empty");
        return front->info;
}//End of peek()
void QueueL::display()
{
        Node *ptr;
        if(!isEmpty())
        {
                ptr = front;
                while(ptr != NULL)
                {
                        cout << ptr->info << "\n";
                        ptr = ptr->link;
                }
        }
        else
                cout << "Queue is empty\n";
}//End of display()
int QueueL::size()
{
        Node* ptr;
        int count = 0;
        ptr = front;
        while(ptr != NULL)
        {
                count++;
                ptr = ptr->link;
        }
        return count;
```

```
}//End of size()
int main()
{
        QueueL qu;
        try
        {
                qu.enqueue(1); qu.enqueue(2);
                qu.enqueue(3); qu.enqueue(4);
                cout << "Queue Items :\n";
                qu.display();
                cout << "Front Item : " << qu.peek() << "\n";
                cout << "Total items : " << qu.size() << "\n";
                cout << "Deleted Item : " << qu.dequeue() << "\n";
                cout << "Queue Items :\n";
                qu.display();
                qu.enqueue(5);
                cout << "Queue Items :\n";
                qu.display();
                cout << "Deleted Item : " << qu.dequeue() << "\n";
                cout << "Deleted Item : " << qu.dequeue() << "\n";
                cout << "Deleted Item : " << qu.dequeue() << "\n";
                cout << "Deleted Item : " << qu.dequeue() << "\n";
                cout << "Queue Items :\n";
                qu.display();
        }//End of try
        catch(exception e)
        {
                cout << e.what() << "\n";
        }
        return 0;
}//End of main()
```

We can implement the queue with a circular linked list also; here, we take only one variable i.e., `rear`.

This is the class `QueueCL`:

```
class QueueCL
{
        private:
                Node *rear;
        public:
                QueueCL();
                bool isEmpty();
                void enqueue(int data);
                int dequeue();
                int peek();
                void display();
                int size();
};//End of class QueueCL
```

`rear` is used for inserting the item at the end of queue, and deleting the item at the front of queue.

```
//QueueCL.cpp : Program to implement queue using circular linked list.
#include <iostream>
using namespace std;

class Node
{
        public:
                int info;
                Node *link;
                Node(int data)
                {
```

```
                                info = data;
                                link = NULL;
                        }
};//End of class Node
class QueueCL
{
        private:
                Node *rear;
        public:
                QueueCL();
                bool isEmpty();
                void enqueue(int data);
                int dequeue();
                int peek();
                void display();
                int size();
};//End of class QueueCL
QueueCL::QueueCL()
{
        rear = NULL;
}//End of QueueL()
bool QueueCL::isEmpty()
{
        return (rear == NULL);
}//End of isEmpty()
void QueueCL::enqueue(int data)
{
        Node *temp;
        temp = new Node(data);
        if(isEmpty()) //If queue is empty
        {
                rear = temp;
                temp->link = rear;
        }
        else
        {
                temp->link = rear->link;
                rear->link = temp;
                rear = temp;
        }
}//End of enqueue()
int QueueCL::dequeue()
{
        Node *temp;
        int retValue;
        if(isEmpty())
                throw exception("Queue is empty");
        if(rear->link == rear) //If only one element
        {
                temp = rear;
                rear = NULL;
        }
        else
        {
                temp = rear->link;
                rear->link = rear->link->link;
        }
        retValue = temp->info;
        delete temp;
```

```
        return retValue;
}//End of dequeue()
int QueueCL::peek()
{
        if(isEmpty())
                throw exception("Queue is empty");
        return rear->link->info;
}//End of peek()
void QueueCL::display()
{
        Node *ptr;
        if(!isEmpty())
        {
                ptr = rear->link;
                do
                {
                        cout << ptr->info << "\n";
                        ptr = ptr->link;
                }while(ptr != rear->link);
        }
        else
                cout << "Queue is empty\n";
}//End of display()
int QueueCL::size()
{
        Node *ptr;
        int count = 0;
        if(!isEmpty())
        {
                ptr = rear->link;
                do
                {
                        count++;
                        ptr = ptr->link;
                }while(ptr != rear->link);
        }
        return count;
}//End of size()
int main()
{
        QueueCL qu;
        try
        {
                qu.enqueue(1); qu.enqueue(2);
                qu.enqueue(3); qu.enqueue(4);
                cout << "Queue Items :\n";
                qu.display();
                cout << "Front Item : " << qu.peek() << "\n";
                cout << "Total items : " << qu.size() << "\n";
                cout << "Deleted Item : " << qu.dequeue() << "\n";
                cout << "Queue Items :\n";
                qu.display();
                qu.enqueue(5);
                cout << "Queue Items :\n";
                qu.display();
                cout << "Deleted Item : " << qu.dequeue() << "\n";
                cout << "Deleted Item : " << qu.dequeue() << "\n";
                cout << "Deleted Item : " << qu.dequeue() << "\n";
                cout << "Deleted Item : " << qu.dequeue() << "\n";
```

```
        cout << "Queue Items :\n";
        qu.display();
}//End of try
catch(exception e)
{
        cout << e.what() << "\n";
}
return 0;
}//End of main()
```

4.3 Circular Queue

We know that when a queue is implemented as an array, insertion is not possible after the `rear` reaches the last position of array. There may be vacant positions in the array, but they cannot be utilized. To overcome this limitation, we use the concept of a circular queue.

We can think of an array to be logically circular, so that the two ends of the array wrap up to make a circle.

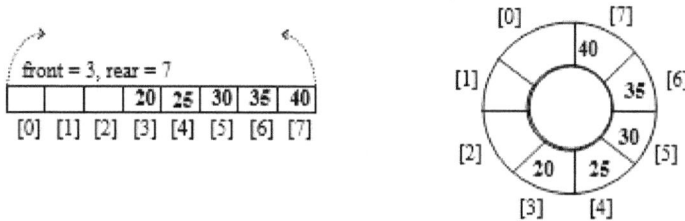

Figure 4.10 Circular queue example

Now, after the (n-1)th position, 0th position occurs. If we want to insert an element, it can be inserted at 0th position.

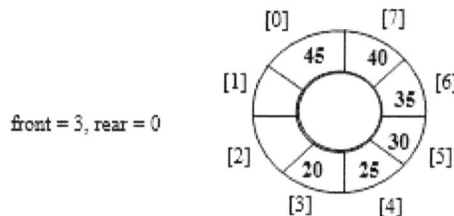

Figure 4.11 Insertion in circular queue

The insertion and deletion operations in a circular queue can be performed in a manner similar to that of queue, but we have to take care of two things. If the value of `rear` is `maxSize-1`, then instead of incrementing the `rear`, we will make it zero and then perform insertion. Similarly, when the value of `front` becomes `maxSize-1`, it will not be incremented but will be reset to zero. Let us take an example and see various operations on a circular queue.

(a) Empty queue	(b) Insert 5	(c) Insert 10
front = -1, rear = -1	front = 0, rear = 0	front = 0, rear = 1
[0] [1] [2] [3] [4]	5 [0] [1] [2] [3] [4]	5 10 [0] [1] [2] [3] [4]
(d) Delete	(e) Delete	(f) Insert 15, 20, 25
front = 1, rear = 1	front = 2, rear = 1	front = 2, rear = 4
10 [0] [1] [2] [3] [4]	[0] [1] [2] [3] [4]	15 20 25 [0] [1] [2] [3] [4]
(g) Insert 30	(h) Delete	(i) Insert 35
front = 2, rear = 0	front = 3, rear = 0	front = 3, rear = 1
30 15 20 25 [0] [1] [2] [3] [4]	30 20 25 [0] [1] [2] [3] [4]	30 35 20 25 [0] [1] [2] [3] [4]
(j) Insert 40	(k) Delete	(l) Delete
front = 3, rear = 2	front = 4, rear = 2	front = 0, rear = 2
30 35 40 20 25 [0] [1] [2] [3] [4]	30 35 40 25 [0] [1] [2] [3] [4]	30 35 40 [0] [1] [2] [3] [4]
(m) Insert 45	(n) Insert 50	(o) Delete
front = 0, rear = 3	front = 0, rear = 4	front = 1, rear = 4
30 35 40 45 [0] [1] [2] [3] [4]	30 35 40 45 50 [0] [1] [2] [3] [4]	35 40 45 50 [0] [1] [2] [3] [4]

Figure 4.12 Circular queue operations

(i) As in a simple queue, here also if the `front` is equal to `rear`, there is only one element, except initially empty queue (Cases (b) and (d)).

(ii) The circular queue will be empty in three situations; when initially `front` is equal to -1 or when `front` becomes equal to `(rear+1)`, or when `front` is equal to 0 and `rear` is equal to `maxSize-1` (Cases (a),(e) and the case when all elements deleted from the queue in case(o)).

(iii) The overflow condition in a circular queue is different from that of a simple queue. Here, overflow will occur only when all the positions of the array are occupied, i.e., when the array is full. The array will be full in two situations; when `front` is equal to 0 and `rear` is equal to `maxSize-1` (Case (n)), or when `front` is equal to `(rear+1)` (Case (j)).

From the last two points, we can see that the condition `front==(rear+1)` is true in both cases: when the queue is empty and when the queue is full. Similarly, the condition (`front==0 && rear==maxSize-1`) is true in both cases. We should make some changes in our procedure so that we can differentiate between an empty queue and a full queue.

When the only element of the queue is deleted, the `front` and `rear` are reset to -1. We can check for an empty queue just by checking the value of `front`; if the `front` is -1, then the queue is empty, otherwise not. Let us take an example and see how this is done:

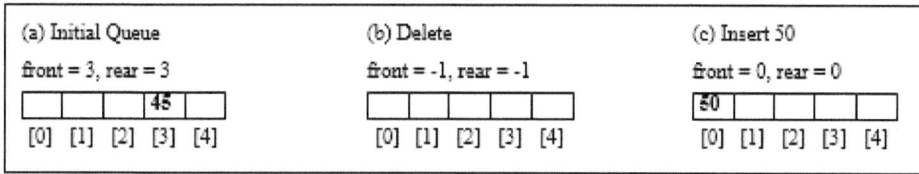

Figure 4.13 Circular queue operations example

The initial queue in figure 4.13 contains only one element. When it is deleted, the queue becomes empty, so instead of incrementing `front`, we will reset the values of `front` and `rear` to -1. We know that there is only one element in the queue when the `front` is equal to `rear`. So inside the function `dequeue()`, we can write it as:

```
if(front==rear)
{
     front = rear = -1;
}
//CQueue.cpp : Program to implement circular queue using array.
#include <iostream>
using namespace std;
static const int maxSize = 5;
class CQueue
{
     private:
             int queueArray[maxSize];
             int front;
             int rear;
     public:
             CQueue();
             bool isEmpty();
             bool isFull();
             void enqueue(int num);
             int dequeue();
             int peek();
             void display();
             int size();
};//End of class CQueue
CQueue::CQueue()
{
     front = -1;
     rear = -1;
}//End of CQueue()
bool CQueue::isEmpty()
{
     return (front == -1);
}//End of isEmpty()
bool CQueue::isFull()
{
     return ((front==0 && rear==maxSize-1) || (front==rear+1));
}//End of isFull()
void CQueue::enqueue(int num)
{
     if(isFull())
             cout << "Queue Overflow\n";
```

```cpp
        else
        {
                if(front == -1)
                        front = 0;
                if(rear == maxSize-1) //rear is at last position of queue
                        rear = 0;
                else
                        rear = rear+1;
                queueArray[rear] = num;
        }
}//End of enqueue()
int CQueue::dequeue()
{
        int retValue;
        if(isEmpty())
                throw exception("Queue is empty");
        else
        {
                retValue = queueArray[front];
                if(front == rear) //queue has only one element
                {
                        front = -1;
                        rear = -1;
                }
                else if(front == maxSize-1)
                        front = 0;
                else
                        front = front+1;
        }

        return retValue;
}//End of dequeue()
int CQueue::peek()
{
        if(isEmpty())
                throw exception("Queue is empty");
        return queueArray[front];
}//End of peek()
void CQueue::display()
{
        cout << "Front = " << front << "        rear = " << rear << "\n";
        if(isEmpty())
                cout << "Queue is empty\n";
        else
        {
                int i = front;
                if(front <= rear)
                {
                        while(i <= rear)
                                cout << queueArray[i++] << "\n";
                }
                else
                {
                        while(i <= maxSize-1)
                                cout << queueArray[i++] << "\n";
                        i=0;
                        while(i <= rear)
                                cout << queueArray[i++] << "\n";
                }
        }
```

```
}//End of display()
int CQueue::size()
{
        if(isEmpty())
                return 0;

        if(isFull())
                return maxSize-1;

        int i = front;
        int sz = 0;
        if(front <= rear)
        {
                while(i <= rear)
                {
                        sz++;
                        i++;
                }
        }
        else
        {
                while(i <= maxSize-1)
                {
                        sz++;
                        i++;
                }
                i = 0;
                while(i <= rear)
                {
                        sz++;
                        i++;
                }
        }

        return sz;
}//End of size()
int main()
{
        CQueue cq;
        try
        {
                cq.enqueue(1);
                cq.enqueue(2);
                cq.enqueue(3);
                cq.enqueue(4);
                cout << "Queue Items : \n";
                cq.display();

                cout << "Front Item : " << cq.peek() << "\n";
                cout << "Total items : " << cq.size() << "\n";
                cout << "Deleted Item : " << cq.dequeue() << "\n";
                cout << "Deleted Item : " << cq.dequeue() << "\n";
                cout << "Queue Items : \n";
                cq.display();

                cq.enqueue(5);
                cq.enqueue(6);
                cout << "Queue Items : \n";
                cq.display();

                cq.enqueue(7);
                cout << "Deleted Item : " << cq.dequeue() << "\n";
```

```
                cout << "Deleted Item : " << cq.dequeue() << "\n";
                cout << "Deleted Item : " << cq.dequeue() << "\n";
                cout << "Deleted Item : " << cq.dequeue() << "\n";
                cout << "Deleted Item : " << cq.dequeue() << "\n";
                cout << "Queue Items : \n";
                cq.display();
        }//End of try
        catch(exception e)
        {
                cout << e.what() << "\n";
        }

        return 0;
}//End of main()
```

4.4 Deque

Deque (pronounced as 'deck' or 'DQ') is a linear list in which elements can be inserted or deleted at either end of the list. The term deque is a short form of **d**ouble **e**nded **que**ue. Like a circular queue, we will implement the deque using a circular array (index 0 comes after n-1). For this, we have to take an array `queueArray[]` and two variables `front` and `rear`. The four operations that can be performed on deque are:

- Insertion at the front end.
- Insertion at the rear end.
- Deletion from the front end.
- Deletion from the rear end.

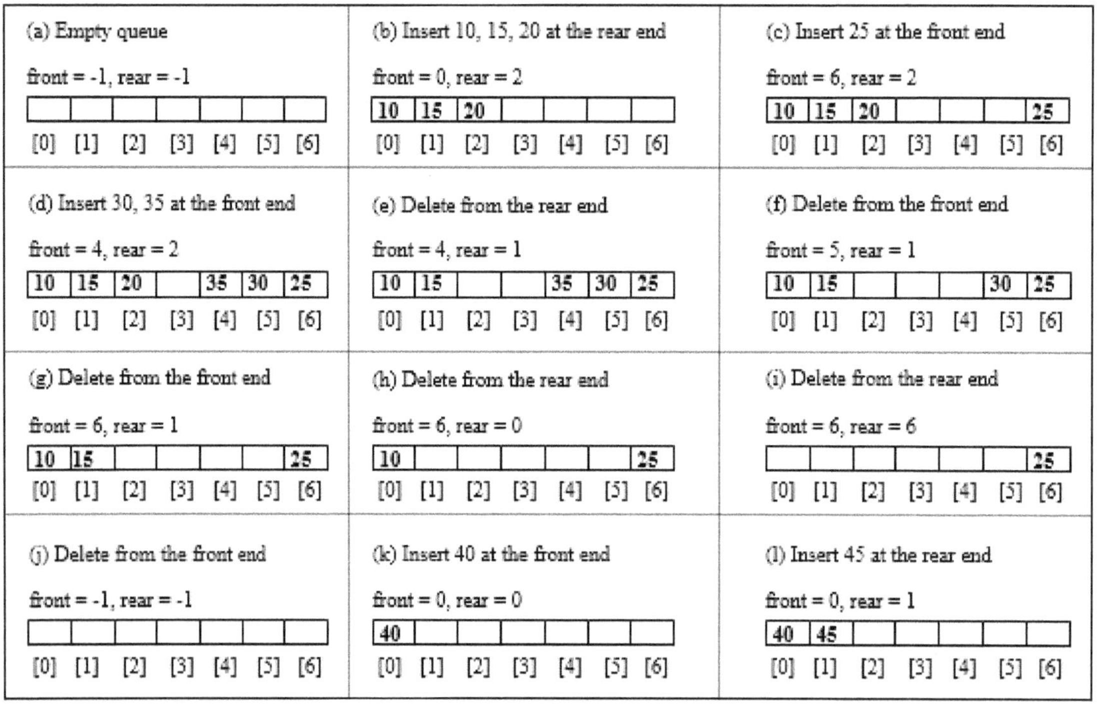

Figure 4.14 Deque operations

Insertion at the rear end and deletion from the front end are performed in similar way as in circular queue. To insert at the front end, the variable `front` is decreased by 1, and then, insertion is performed at the new position given by `front`. If the value of `front` is 0, then instead of decrementing, it is made equal to `maxSize-1`. To delete from the rear end, the variable `rear` is decreased by 1. If the value of `rear` is 0, then it is not decremented, but made equal to `maxSize-1`. The example in figure 4.14 shows various operations on a deque.

Here is the class `Deque`:

```
class Deque
{
        private:
                int queueArray[maxSize];
                int front;
                int rear;
        public:
                Deque();
                bool isEmpty();
                bool isFull();
                void insertFrontEnd(int data);
                void insertRearEnd(int data);
                int deleteFrontEnd();
                int deleteRearEnd();
                void display();
                int size();
};//End of class Deque
```

Here is the program of deque:

```
//Deque.cpp : Program to implement deque using circular array.
#include <iostream>
using namespace std;

static const int maxSize = 5;

class Deque
{
        private:
                int queueArray[maxSize];
                int front;
                int rear;
        public:
                Deque();
                bool isEmpty();
                bool isFull();
                void insertFrontEnd(int data);
                void insertRearEnd(int data);
                int deleteFrontEnd();
                int deleteRearEnd();
                void display();
                int size();
};//End of class Deque

Deque::Deque()
{
        front = -1;
        rear = -1;
}//End of Deque()

bool Deque::isEmpty()
{
        return (front == -1);
}//End of isEmpty()
```

```cpp
bool Deque::isFull()
{
        return ((front==0 && rear==maxSize-1) || (front==rear+1));
}//End of isFull()
void Deque::insertFrontEnd(int data)
{
        if(isFull())
                cout << "Queue Overflow\n";
        else
        {
                if(front == -1) //If queue is initially empty
                {
                        front = 0;
                        rear = 0;
                }
                else if(front == 0)
                        front = maxSize-1;
                else
                        front = front-1;

                queueArray[front] = data;
        }
}//End of insertFrontEnd()
void Deque::insertRearEnd(int data)
{
        if(isFull())
                cout << "Queue Overflow\n";
        else
        {
                if(front == -1) //If queue is initially empty
                {
                        front = 0;
                        rear = 0;
                }
                else if(rear == maxSize-1) //rear is at last position of queue
                        rear = 0;
                else
                        rear = rear+1;
                queueArray[rear] = data;
        }
}//End of insertRearEnd()
int Deque::deleteFrontEnd()
{
        int retValue;
        if(isEmpty())
                throw exception("Queue is empty");
        else
        {
                retValue = queueArray[front];
                if(front == rear) //queue has only one element
                {
                        front = -1;
                        rear = -1;
                }
                else if(front == maxSize-1)
                        front = 0;
                else
                        front = front+1;
        }
```

```
                return retValue;
}//End of deleteFrontEnd()
int Deque::deleteRearEnd()
{
        int retValue;
        if(isEmpty())
                throw exception("Queue is empty");
        else
        {
                retValue = queueArray[rear];
                if(front == rear) //queue has only one element
                {
                        front = -1;
                        rear = -1;
                }
                else if(rear == 0)
                        rear = maxSize-1;
                else
                        rear = rear-1;
        }

        return retValue;
}//End of deleteRearEnd()
void Deque::display()
{
        cout << "Front = " << front << "      rear = " << rear << "\n";
        if(isEmpty())
                cout << "Queue is empty\n";
        else
        {
                int i = front;
                if(front <= rear)
                {
                        while(i <= rear)
                                cout << queueArray[i++] << "\n";
                }
                else
                {
                        while(i <= maxSize-1)
                                cout << queueArray[i++] << "\n";

                        i=0;
                        while(i <= rear)
                                cout << queueArray[i++] << "\n";
                }
        }
}//End of display()
int Deque::size()
{
        if(isEmpty())
                return 0;
        if(isFull())
                return maxSize-1;

        int i = front;
        int sz = 0;

        if(front <= rear)
        {
                while(i <= rear)
                {
```

```
                    sz++;
                    i++;
            }
    }
    else
    {
            while(i <= maxSize-1)
            {
                    sz++;
                    i++;
            }
            i = 0;
            while(i <= rear)
            {
                    sz++;
                    i++;
            }
    }
    return sz;
}//End of size()
int main()
{
    Deque dq;
    try
    {
            dq.insertFrontEnd(2);
            dq.insertFrontEnd(1);
            dq.insertRearEnd(3);
            dq.insertRearEnd(4);
            cout << "Queue Items : \n";
            dq.display();

            cout << "Total items : " << dq.size() << "\n";
            cout << "Deleted Item from front : " << dq.deleteFrontEnd() << "\n";
            cout << "Deleted Item from Rear : " << dq.deleteRearEnd() << "\n";
            cout << "Queue Items : \n";
            dq.display();
            dq.insertFrontEnd(5);
            dq.insertFrontEnd(6);
            cout << "Queue Items : \n";
            dq.display();

            dq.insertRearEnd(7);
            cout << "Deleted Item : " << dq.deleteFrontEnd() << "\n";
            cout << "Deleted Item : " << dq.deleteRearEnd() << "\n";
            cout << "Deleted Item : " << dq.deleteFrontEnd() << "\n";
            cout << "Deleted Item : " << dq.deleteRearEnd() << "\n";
            cout << "Deleted Item : " << dq.deleteFrontEnd() << "\n";
            cout << "Queue Items : \n";
            dq.display();
    }//End of try
    catch(exception e)
    {
            cout << e.what() << "\n";
    }
    return 0;
}//End of main()
```

The four operations of deque are named push (insert at front end), pop (delete from front end), inject (insert at rear end), eject (delete from rear end). Deque can be of two types:

- Input restricted deque
- Output restricted deque

In Input restricted deque, elements can be inserted at only one end, but deletion can be performed from both ends. The functions valid in this case are `insertRearEnd()`, `deleteFrontEnd()`, and `deleteRearEnd()`. In Output restricted deque, elements can be inserted from both ends but deletion is allowed only at one end. The functions valid in this case are `insertFrontEnd()`, `insertRearEnd()`, and `deleteFrontEnd()`.

4.5 Priority Queue

We have seen earlier that a queue is a list of elements in which we can add the element only at one end, which is called rear of the queue, and delete the element only at the other end, which is called front of the queue. In a priority queue, every element of the queue has some priority, and it is processed based on this priority. An element with higher priority will be processed before the element which has less priority. If two elements have the same priority, then in this case, FIFO rule will follow, i.e., the element which comes first in the queue will be processed first. An example of priority queue is in CPU scheduling algorithm, in which the CPU needs to process those jobs first which have higher priority.

There are two ways of implementing a priority queue:

- Through queue: In this case, insertion is simple because the element is simply added at the rear end as usual. For performing deletion, first the element with highest priority is searched and then deleted.

- Through sorted list: In this case, insertion is costly because the element is inserted at the proper place in the list based on its priority. Here, deletion is easier since the element with the highest priority will always be in the beginning of the list.

In the first case, insertion is rapid but deletion is O(n) and in the second case, deletion is rapid, but insertion is O(n). If the priority queue is implemented using arrays, then in both the above cases, shifting of elements will be required. So, it is advantageous to use a linked list, because insertion or deletion in between the linked list is more efficient. We will implement a priority queue as a sorted linked list. Here is the class for representing a node of a linked list that implements a priority queue:

```
class Node
{
        public:
                int info;
                int priority;
                Node *link;
                Node(int data, int priority)
                {
                        info = data;
                        this->priority = priority;
                        link = NULL;
                }
};//End of class Node
```

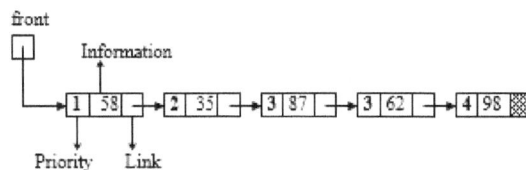

Figure 4.15 Priority queue example

Here, priority number 1 means the highest priority. If priority number of an element is 2, then it means it has priority more than the element which has priority number 3. Insertion of an element would be performed in a similar way as in a sorted linked list. Here, we insert the new element on the basis of priority of element.

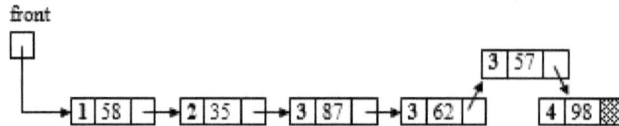

Figure 4.16 Insertion in priority queue

The delete operation will be the deletion of the first element of list, because it has more priority than other elements of queue.

Here is the class for priority queue:

```
class PQueue
{
        private:
                Node *front;
        public:
                PQueue();
                bool isEmpty();
                void enqueue(int data, int priority);
                int dequeue();
                int peek();
                void display();
                int size();
};//End of class PQueue
```

Here is the program of priority queue:

```
//PQueue.cpp : Program to implement priority queue using linked list.
#include <iostream>
using namespace std;
class Node
{
        public:
                int info;
                int priority;
                Node *link;
                Node(int data, int priority)
                {
                        info = data;
                        this->priority = priority;
                        link = NULL;
                }
};//End of class Node
class PQueue
{
        private:
                Node *front;
        public:
                PQueue();
                bool isEmpty();
                void enqueue(int data, int priority);
                int dequeue();
```

```
                int peek();
                void display();
                int size();
};//End of class PQueue

PQueue::PQueue()
{
        front = NULL;
}//End of PQueue()

bool PQueue::isEmpty()
{
    return (front == NULL);
}//End of isEmpty()

void PQueue::enqueue(int data, int priority)
{
        Node *temp, *ptr;
        temp = new Node(data, priority);
        //Queue is empty or element to be added has priority more than first element
        if(isEmpty() || priority < front->priority)
        {
                temp->link = front;
                front = temp;
        }
        else
        {
                ptr = front;
                while(ptr->link!=NULL && ptr->link->priority<=priority)
                        ptr = ptr->link;
                temp->link = ptr->link;
                ptr->link = temp;
        }
}//End of enqueue()

int PQueue::dequeue()
{
        Node *temp;
        int retValue;
        if(isEmpty())
                throw exception("Queue is empty");
        else
        {
                retValue = front->info;
                temp = front;
                front = front->link;
                delete temp;
        }

        return retValue;
}//End of dequeue()

int PQueue::peek()
{
        if(isEmpty())
                throw exception("Queue is empty");
        return front->info;
}//End of peek()

void PQueue::display()
{
        Node *ptr;
        if(!isEmpty())
        {
                cout << "Priority, Data Item\n";
```

```
                ptr = front;
                while(ptr != NULL)
                {
                        cout << ptr->priority <<", " << ptr->info << "\n";
                        ptr = ptr->link;
                }
        }
        else
                cout << "Queue is empty\n";
}//End of display()
int PQueue::size()
{
        Node* ptr;
        int count = 0;
        ptr = front;
        while(ptr != NULL)
        {
                count++;
                ptr = ptr->link;
        }

        return count;
}//End of size()
int main()
{
        PQueue pq;
        try
        {
                pq.enqueue(20,2);
                pq.enqueue(10,1);
                pq.enqueue(50,4);
                pq.enqueue(30,3);
                cout << "Queue Items : \n";
                pq.display();
                cout << "Front Item : " << pq.peek() << "\n";
                cout << "Total Items : " << pq.size() << "\n";
                cout << "Deleted Item : " << pq.dequeue() << "\n";
                cout << "Queue Items : \n";
                pq.display();
                pq.enqueue(40,5);
                cout << "Queue Items : \n";
                pq.display();
                cout << "Deleted Item : " << pq.dequeue() << "\n";
                cout << "Deleted Item : " << pq.dequeue() << "\n";
                cout << "Deleted Item : " << pq.dequeue() << "\n";
                cout << "Deleted Item : " << pq.dequeue() << "\n";
                cout << "Queue Items : \n";
                pq.display();
        }//End of try
        catch(exception e)
        {
                cout << e.what() << "\n";
        }
        return 0;
}//End of main()
```

The priority queue that we have used is a max-priority queue or descending priority queue. The other type of priority queue is a min-priority or ascending priority queue, in which, the element with lowest priority is processed first. The best implementation of priority queue is through heap tree, which we will study in the next chapter.

4.6 Applications of Stack

Some of the applications of stack that will be discussed are:
* Reversal of a string.
* Checking validity of an expression containing nested parentheses.
* Function calls.
* Conversion of infix expression to postfix form.
* Evaluation of postfix form.

4.6.1 Reversal of String

We can reverse a string by pushing each character of the string on the stack. After the whole string is pushed on the stack, we can start popping the characters from the stack and get the reversed string.

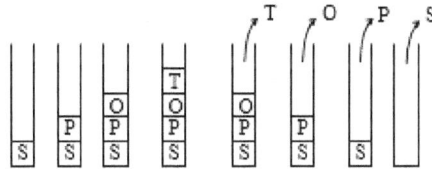

Figure 4.17 Reversal of string

We have pushed the string "SPOT" on the stack, and we get the reversed string "TOPS".

```cpp
//ReverseString.cpp : Program of reversing a string using stack.
#include<iostream>
#include<stack>
#include<string>
using namespace std;
string reverseString(string str)
{
        string temp = "";
        stack<char> st;

        for(int i=0; i<str.length(); i++)
                st.push(str[i]);

        while(!st.empty())
        {
                temp += st.top();
                st.pop();
        }

        return temp;
}//End of reverseString()
int main()
{
        string str = "algorithms";
        cout << "String is : " << str << "\n";
        cout << "Reversed string is : " << reverseString(str) << "\n";

        return 0;
}//End of main()
```

4.6.2 Checking Validity of an Expression Containing Nested Parentheses

We can use stack to check the validity of an expression that uses nested parentheses. An expression will be valid if it satisfies these two conditions:

1. The total number of left parentheses should be equal to the total number of right parentheses in the expression.
2. For every right parenthesis there should be a left parenthesis of the same type.

Some valid and invalid expressions are given below:

```
[A-B*(C+D)          Invalid
(1+5}               Invalid
[5+4*(9-2)]         Valid
[A+B -(C%D}]        Invalid
[A/(B-C)*D]         Valid
```

The procedure for checking validity of an expression containing nested parentheses is:

1. Initially take an empty stack.
2. Scan the symbols of expression from left to right.
3. If the symbol is a left parenthesis, then push it on the stack.
4. If the symbol is right parenthesis

      If the stack is empty

            Invalid : Right parentheses are more than left parentheses.

      else

            Pop an element from stack.

            If popped parenthesis does not match the parenthesis being scanned

                  Invalid : Mismatched parentheses.

5. After scanning all the symbols

If stack is empty

      Valid : Balanced Parentheses.

else

      Invalid : Left parentheses more than right parentheses.

Some examples are given below:

[A+B-{C%D}]			A-[B*(C+D)			[A/(B-C)*D]			A*(B-C)}+D	
Symbol	Stack		Symbol	Stack		Symbol	Stack		Symbol	Stack
[	[		A	Empty		[	[		A	Empty
A	[		-	Empty		A	[		*	Empty
+	[		[	[		/	[		(	(
B	[		B	[		(	[(		B	(
-	[		*	[		B	[(		-	(
{	[{		(	[(		-	[(		C	(
C	[{		C	[(		C	[(		)	Empty
%	[{		+	[(		)	[		}	Empty
D	[{		D	[(		*	[		Invalid: Scanned symbol '}' but stack is empty	
}	[		)	[		D	[			
Invalid: Scanned symbol '}' and popped symbol '(' do not match			Invalid : All symbols scanned but stack is not empty			]	Empty			
						Valid				

Figure 4.18 Parentheses validation in an expression

```cpp
//CheckParentheses.cpp : Program to check that parentheses in expression are valid or
//not.
#include<iostream>
#include<stack>
#include<string>
using namespace std;

bool matchParentheses(char leftPar, char rightPar)
{
```

```
        if(leftPar=='(' && rightPar==')')
                return true;
        if(leftPar=='{' && rightPar=='}')
                return true;
        if(leftPar=='[' && rightPar==']')
                return true;

        return false;
}//End of matchParentheses()
bool isValid(string expr)
{
        stack<char> st;

        for(int i=0; i<expr.length(); i++)
        {
                if(expr[i]=='(' || expr[i]=='{' || expr[i]=='[')
                        st.push(expr[i]);

                if(expr[i]==')' || expr[i]=='}' || expr[i]==']')
                {
                        if(st.empty())
                        {
                                cout << "Right parentheses are more than left
                                parentheses\n";
                                return false;
                        }
                        else
                        {
                                char ch = st.top();
                                st.pop();
                                if(!matchParentheses(ch, expr[i]))
                                {
                                        cout << "Parentheses are : ";
                                        cout << ch << " and " << expr[i] << "\n";
                                        return false;
                                }
                        }
                }//End of if
        }//End of for

        if(st.empty())
        {
                cout << "Balanced Parentheses\n";
                return true;
        }
        else
        {
                cout << "Left parentheses are more than right parentheses\n";
                return false;
        }
}//End of isValid()
int main()
{
        string expression = "[A/(B-C)*D]";
        cout << "Expression is : " << expression << "\n";

        try
        {
                if(isValid(expression))
                        cout << "Valid expression\n";
                else
```

```
                      cout << "Invalid expression\n";
     }
     catch(exception e)
     {
              cout << e.what() << "\n";
     }

     return 0;
}//End of main()
```

4.6.3 Function Calls

Function calls behave in LIFO manner, i.e., the function that is called first is the last one to finish execution, or, we can say that the function calls return in the reverse order of their invocation. So, the stack is the perfect data structure to implement function calls.

A stack is maintained during the execution of the program called program stack or run-time stack. Whenever a function is called, the program stores all the information associated with this call in a structure called activation record, and this activation record is pushed on the run-time stack. Activation record, also known as stack frame, consists of the following data:

(i) Parameters and local variables.

(ii) Pointer to previous activation record i.e., activation record of the caller.

(iii) Return address i.e., the instruction in the caller function, which is immediately after the function call.

(iv) Return value if function is not void.

The function whose activation record is at the top of the stack is the one that is currently being executed. Whenever a function is called, its activation record is pushed on the stack. When a function terminates, its activation record is popped from the stack and after this, the activation record of its caller comes at the top. Let us take a program example in which main() calls f1(), f1() calls f2() and f2() calls f3(). The different stages of the run-time stack in this case are shown in figure 4.19. AR in the figure denotes the activation record.

If a function calls itself, then the program creates different activation records for different calls of the same function (recursive calls). Thus, we can see that no special procedure is needed to implement recursion.

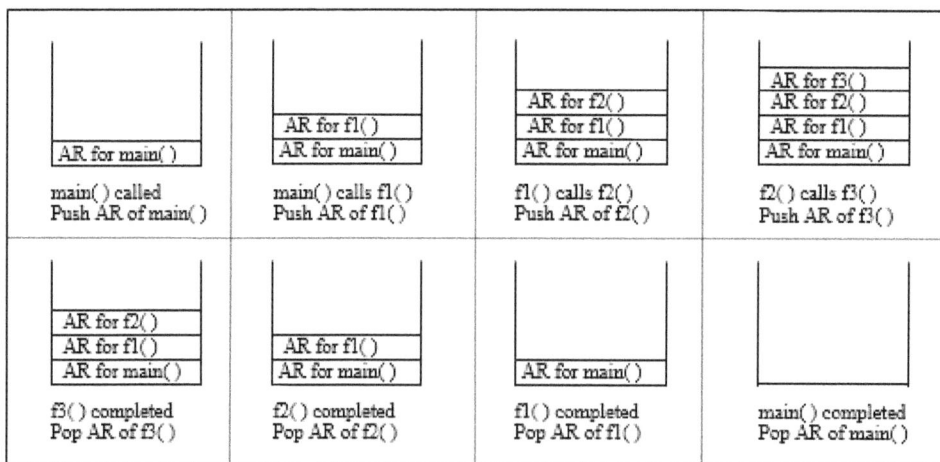

Figure 4.19 Stack for function calls

4.6.4 Polish Notation

An important application of stack is in evaluating arithmetic expressions. An arithmetic expression consists of operators and operands where operands may be either numeric constants or numeric variables. Let us take an arithmetic expression:
9+6/3

If division is performed before addition, the result would be 11, while if addition is performed before division, the result would be 5.

To avoid this ambiguity, we can use parentheses to specify which operation will be performed first.
(9+6)/3   or   9+(6/3)

Another solution is that each operation is given some priority, and the operation with the highest priority is performed first.

In our discussion, we will take five operators '+', '-', '*', '/' and '^'. The priorities of these operators would be:

Operator	Priority
^ (Exponentiation)	3
* (Multiplication) and / (Division)	2
+ (Addition) and - (Subtraction)	1

Figure 4.20 Operators with priority

So '^' has the highest priority and '+', '-' have the lowest priority. If two operators have the same priority (like '*' and '/'), then the expression is scanned from left to right and whichever operator comes first will be evaluated first. This property is called associativity and, we have assumed left to right associativity for all our operators.

Now if we apply these precedence rules to our expression 9+6/3, then we see that division should be performed before addition. Let us take an arithmetic expression and see how it can be evaluated using our precedence rules.

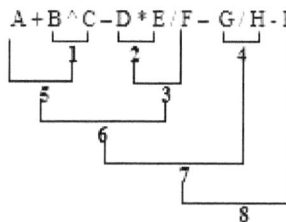

Figure 4.21 Arithmetic expression evaluation

The numbers indicate the sequence of evaluations of operators. If we want to override the precedence rules, then we can use parentheses. Anything that is between parentheses, will be evaluated first. For example, if in the above expression, we want to evaluate H-I before G/H, then we can enclose H-I within parentheses.

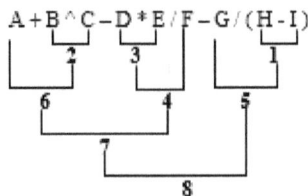

Figure 4.22 Arithmetic expression with parentheses evaluation

Here, we can see that the expression inside the parentheses is evaluated first and after that, evaluation is done on the basis of operator precedence.

This is how we can evaluate arithmetic expressions manually. We have to know the precedence rules and also take care of the parentheses. The expression has to be scanned many times, and every time, we have to reach a different place in the expression for evaluation.

Now, let us see how a computer can evaluate these expressions. If we use the same procedure, then there will be repeated scanning from left to right, which is inefficient. It would be nicer if we could transform the above expression in some form, which does not have parentheses, and all operators are arranged in proper order according to their precedence. In that case, we could evaluate the expression by just scanning the newly transformed expression once from left to right. Polish notations are used for this purpose, so let us see what these notations are.

The great Polish mathematician Jan Lukasiewicz had given a technique for the representation of arithmetic expressions in the early 1920's. According to the two notations that he gave, an operator can be placed before or after the operands. Although these notations were not very readable for humans, they proved to be very useful for compiler designers in generating machine language code for evaluating arithmetic expressions.

The conventional method of representing an arithmetic expression is known as infix, because the operator is placed in between the operands. If the operator is placed before the operands, then this notation is called prefix or Polish notation. If the operator is placed after the operands, then this notation is called postfix or reverse polish notation. So now, we have three ways to represent an arithmetic expression:

```
Infix      A+B
Prefix     +AB
Postfix    AB+
```

Let us see how to convert an infix expression into its equivalent postfix expression. The rules of parentheses and precedence would remain the same. If there are parentheses in the expression, then the portion inside the parentheses will be converted first. After this, the operations are converted according to their precedence. After we have converted a particular operation to its postfix, it will be considered as a single operand. We will use square brackets to represent these types of intermediate operands. If there are operators of equal precedence, then the operator, which is on the left, is converted first. Let us take an example:

```
A-B^C+D*E/(F+G)
A-B^C+D*E/[FG+]           Convert F+G to FG+
A-[BC^]+D*E/[FG+]         Convert B^C to BC^
A-[BC^]+[DE*]/[FG+]       Convert D*E to DE*
A-[BC^]+[DE*FG+/]         Convert [DE*]/[FG+] to DE*FG+/
[ABC^-]+[DE*FG+/]         Convert A-[BC^] to ABC^-
ABC^-DE*FG+/+             Convert [ABC^-]+[DE*FG+/] to ABC^-DE*FG+/+
```

Here are a few more examples of conversion from infix to postfix:

```
A+B/C-D*E+F          (A+B)/C*D-E^F          A^B/C*D/E^F*G
A+[BC/]-D*E+F        [AB+]/C*D-E^F          [AB^]/C*D/[EF^]*G
A+[BC/]-[DE*]+F      [AB+]/C*D-[EF^]        [AB^C/]*D/[EF^]*G
[ABC/+]-[DE*]+F      [AB+C/]*D-[EF^]        [AB^C/D*]/[EF^]*G
[ABC/+DE*-]+F        [AB+C/D*]-[EF^]        [AB^C/D*EF^/]*G
ABC/+DE*-F+          AB+C/D*EF^-            AB^C/D*EF^/G*
```

```
A-B*C+(D-E)*F/G/H    A+B/C^D-E*F/(G+H)      A+B/(C*D^E)-F*G^H
A-B*C+[DE-]*F/G/H    A+B/C^D-E*F/[GH+]      A+B/(C*[DE^])-F*G^H
A-[BC*]+[DE-F*]/G/H  A+B/[CD^]-E*F/[GH+]    A+B/[CDE^*]-F*G^H
A-[BC*]+[DE-F*G/]/H  A+[BCD^/]-[EF*]/[GH+]  A+B/[CDE^*]-F*[GH^]
A-[BC*]+[DE-F*G/H/]  A+[BCD^/]-[EF*GH+/]    A+[BCDE^*/]-[FGH^*]
[ABC*-]+[DE-F*G/H/]  [ABCD^/+]-[EF*GH+/]    [ABCDE^*/+]-[FGH^*]
ABC*-DE-F*G/H/+      ABCD^/+EF*GH+/-        ABCDE^*/+FGH^*-
```

The conversion from infix to prefix also uses the same rules, but here, the operator is placed before the operands. The following examples show the conversion of the infix form to the prefix form:

```
A+B/C-D*E+F          (A+B)/C*D-E^F          A^B/C*D/E^F*G
A+[/BC]-D*E+F        [+AB]/C*D-E^F          [^AB]/C*D/[^EF]*G
A+[/BC]-[*DE]+F      [+AB]/C*D-[^EF]        [/^ABC]*D/[^EF]*G
[+A/BC]-[*DE]+F      [/+ABC]*D-[^EF]        [*/^ABCD]/[^EF]*G
[-+A/BC*DE]+F        [*/+ABCD]-[^EF]        [/*/^ABCD^EF]*G
+-+A/BC*DEF          -*/+ABCD^EF            */*/^ABCD^EFG
```

```
A-B*C+(D-E)*F/G/H    A+B/C^D-E*F/(G+H)      A+B/(C*D^E)-F*G^H
A-B*C+[-DE]*F/G/H    A+B/C^D-E*F/[+GH]      A+B/(C*[^DE])-F*G^H
A-[*BC]+[-DE]*F/G/H  A+B/[^CD]-E*F/[+GH]    A+B/[*C^DE]-F*G^H
A-[*BC]+[*-DEF]/G/H  A+[/B^CD]-E*F/[+GH]    A+B/[*C^DE]-F*[^GH]
A-[*BC]+[/*-DEFG]/H  A+[/B^CD]-[*EF]/[+GH]  A+[/B*C^DE]-F*[^GH]
A-[*BC]+[//*-DEFGH]  A+[/B^CD]-[/*EF+GH]    A+[/B*C^DE]-[*F^GH]
[-A*BC]+[//*-DEFGH]  [+A/B^CD]-[/*EF+GH]    [+A/B*C^DE]-[*F^GH]
+-A*BC//*-DEFGH      -+A/B^CD/*EF+GH        -+A/B*C^DE*F^GH
```

We can see that the prefix and postfix forms of any expression are not mirror images of each other. In all three forms, the relative positions of the operands remain the same.

In the prefix and postfix forms, parentheses are not needed and the operators and operands are arranged in proper order according to their precedence levels. Now, let us take an infix expression and convert it to postfix and then see how this postfix expression can be evaluated. For simplicity, we will take numerical constants of single digit only.

```
3+5*(7-4)^2
3+5*[74-]^2
3+5*[74-2^]
3+[574-2^*]
3574-2^*+
```

To evaluate this postfix expression, it is scanned from left to right and as soon as we get an operator, we apply it to the last two operands.

```
3574-2^*+        Apply '-' to 7 and 4
35[3]2^*+        Apply '^' to 3 and 2
35[9]*+          Apply '*' to 5 and 9
3[45]+           Apply '+' to 3 and 45
48
```

So, we can see that in a postfix expression, the operators are evaluated in the same sequence as they appear in the expression. While evaluating a postfix expression, we are not concerned about any precedence rules or parentheses.

Now, let us see how we can write a program for the two step process of converting the infix form to postfix form and evaluating the postfix expression. The stack data structure proves helpful here and is used in both steps.

4.6.4.1 Converting Infix Expression to Postfix Expression Using Stack

We will take the operators '^', '*', '/', '+' and '-', and assume the same precedence rules as before. We know that the order of operands is the same in both infix and postfix. So the operands can be simply added to postfix. In postfix, the order of operators has to be changed, and parentheses have to be eliminated. So, a stack will be used for temporary placement of operators and left parentheses.

Let us take a string named `infix` that has an arithmetic expression in infix form and another string `postfix` that will contain the arithmetic expression in postfix form. The steps involved to convert the infix expression into postfix expression are as follows:

(1) Scan the symbols of string `infix` one by one from left to right.

    (a) If the symbol is an operand

        Add it to string `postfix`.

    (b) If the symbol is a left parenthesis '('

        Push it on the stack.

    (c) If the symbol is a right parenthesis ')'

        Pop all the operators from stack upto the first left parenthesis and add these operators to string `postfix`. Discard both left and right parentheses.

    (d) If symbol is an operator

        Pop the operators which have precedence greater than or equal to the precedence of the symbol operator, and add these popped operators to string `postfix`.

        Push the scanned symbol operator on the stack. (Assume that left parenthesis has least precedence)

(2) After all the symbols of string `infix` have been scanned, pop all the operators remaining on the stack and add them to the string `postfix`.

Let us take an infix expression and convert it into postfix:

Infix : A+B/C*(D+E)-F				
	Symbol	Action	Stack	Postfix
(1)	A	Add A to postfix	Empty	A
(2)	+	Push on the stack	+	A
(3)	B	Add B to postfix	+	AB
(4)	/	Push on the stack	+/	AB
(5)	C	Add C to postfix	+/	ABC
(6)	*	Pop / and add it to postfix and then push * on the stack	+*	ABC/
(7)	(	Push on the stack	+* (	ABC/
(8)	D	Add D to postfix	+* (	ABC/D
(9)	+	Push on the stack	+* (+	ABC/D
(10)	E	Add E to postfix	+* (+	ABC/DE
(11)	)	Pop + and add to postfix	+*	ABC/DE+
(12)	-	Pop * and +, add them to postfix and then push -	-	ABC/DE+*+
(13)	F	Add F to postfix	-	ABC/DE+*+F
(14)		Pop - and add to postfix	Empty	ABC/DE+*+F-

Figure 4.23 Converting infix expression to postfix expression

- In step (2), the operator '+' is simply pushed on the stack, since the stack is empty.

- In step (4), we will first compare the precedence of '/' with that of the top operator of the stack, which is '+'. Since the precedence of '+' is less than that of '/', we will not pop any operator and simply push '/' on the stack.

- In step (6), we will compare the precedence of '*' with that of the top operator of stack, which is '/'. Since the precedence of '*' is equal to that of '/', operator '/' is popped and added to postfix. Now the top operator of stack is '+'. Now we will compare precedence of '*' with that of '+'. Since the precedence of '+' is less than that of '*', now operator '*' is pushed on the stack.

- In step (9), '+' is simply pushed on the stack since we have assumed that the precedence of '(' is least.

- In step (11), we have to pop all the operators till the left parentheses, so '+' is popped and added to postfix.

- In step (12), the precedence of '*' is greater than that of '-', so '*' is popped and added to postfix. Now, the top operator on stack is '+' and its precedence is equal to that of '-'; so it is also popped and added to the postfix. After this, '-' is pushed on the stack.

- In step (14), all the symbols of the expression have been scanned, and so now, we have to pop all the operators from the stack and add to postfix. The only operator remaining on stack is '-', so it is popped and added to postfix.

Let us work out a few more examples to fully comprehend the process.

Infix : A^B*C/(D*E-F)		
Symbol	Stack	Postfix
A	Empty	A
^	^	A
B	^	AB
*	*	AB^
C	*	AB^C
/	/	AB^C*
(	/(	AB^C*
D	/(	AB^C*D
*	/(*	AB^C*D
E	/(*	AB^C*DE
-	/(-	AB^C*DE*
F	/(-	AB^C*DE*F
)	/	AB^C*DE*F-
	Empty	AB^C*DE*F-/

Infix : A-B/C^D*E+F/G		
Symbol	Stack	Postfix
A	Empty	A
-	-	A
B	-	AB
/	-/	AB
C	-/	ABC
^	-/^	ABC
D	-/^	ABCD
*	-*	ABCD^/
E	-*	ABCD^/E
+	+	ABCD^/E*-
F	+	ABCD^/E*-F
/	+/	ABCD^/E*-F
G	+/	ABCD^/E*-FG
	Empty	ABCD^/E*-FG/+

Figure 4.24 Infix expression to postfix expression example

Infix : 8*(5^4+2)-6^2/(9*3)		
Symbol	Stack	Postfix
8	Empty	8
*	*	8
(	*(	8
5	*(	85
^	*(^	85
4	*(^	854
+	*(+	854^
2	*(+	854^2
)	*	854^2+
-	-	854^2+*
6	-	854^2+*6
^	-^	854^2+*6
2	-^	854^2+*62
/	-/	854^2+*62^
(	-/(	854^2+*62^
9	-/(	854^2+*62^9
*	-/(*	854^2+*62^9
3	-/(*	854^2+*62^93
)	-/	854^2+*62^93*
	Empty	854^2+*62^93*/-

Infix : 7+5*3^2/(9-2^2)+6*4		
Symbol	Stack	Postfix
7	Empty	7
+	+	7
5	+	75
*	+*	75
3	+*	753
^	+*^	753
2	+*^	7532
/	+/	7532^*
(	+/(	7532^*
9	+/(	7532^*9
-	+/(-	7532^*9
2	+/(-	7532^*92
^	+/(-^	7532^*92
2	+/(-^	7532^*922
)	+/	7532^*922^-
+	+	7532^*922^-/+
6	+	7532^*922^-/+6
*	+*	7532^*922^-/+6
4	+*	7532^*922^-/+64
	Empty	7532^*922^-/+64*+

Figure 4.25 Infix expression to postfix expression more examples

4.6.4.2 Evaluation of Postfix Expression Using Stack

In a postfix expression, operators are placed after the operands. When we scan the postfix expression from left to right, first, the operands will come, and then the corresponding operator. So this time, we will need a stack to hold the operands. Whenever any operator occurs in scanning, we pop two operands from the stack and perform the operation. Here, we do not require any information of operator precedence.

Let us take a string `postfix` that has an arithmetic expression in postfix form. The steps involved to evaluate the postfix expression are:

1. Scan the symbols of string `postfix` one by one from left to right.

    (a) If symbol is an operand
          Push it on the stack
    (b) If symbol is an operator
          Pop two elements from stack and apply the operator to these two elements
          Suppose first A is popped and then B is popped
          result = B operator A
          Push result on the stack

2. After all the symbols of postfix have been scanned, pop the only element left in the stack and it is the value of postfix arithmetic expression.

Let us take a postfix expression and evaluate it:

```
Infix   : 7+5*3^2/(9-2^2)+6*4
Postfix : 7532^^*922^-/+64*+
```

Symbol	Action	Stack
7	Push 7	7
5	Push 5	7,5
3	Push 3	7,5,3
2	Push 2	7,5,3,2
^	Pop 2 and 3, Push 3^2	7,5,9
*	Pop 9 and 5, Push 5*9	7,45
9	Push 9	7,45,9
2	Push 2	7,45,9,2
2	Push 2	7,45,9,2,2
^	Pop 2 and 2, Push 2^2	7,45,9,4
-	Pop 4 and 9, Push 9-4	7,45,5
/	Pop 5 and 45, Push 45/5	7,9
+	Pop 9 and 7, Push 7+9	16
6	Push 6	16,6
4	Push 4	16,6,4
*	Pop 4 and 6, Push 6*4	16,24
+	Pop 24 and 16, Push 16+24	40

Figure 4.26 Evaluation of postfix expression

After evaluation of the postfix expression, its value is 40. Let us take the same postfix expression in infix form and evaluate it.

```
7+5*3^2/(9-2^2)+6*4
7+5*3^2/(9-4)+6*4
7+5*3^2/5+6*4
7+5*9/5+6*4
7+45/5+6*4
7+9+6*4
7+9+24
16+24
40
```

We can see the same result, but in postfix evaluation, we have no need to take care of parentheses and sequence of evaluation.

```cpp
//InfixToPostfix.cpp : Program to covert infix to postfix and evaluate the postfix
//expression. It will evaluate only single digit numbers.
#include<iostream>
#include<stack>
#include<string>
using namespace std;

string infixToPostfix(string infix);
int evaluatePostfix(string postfix);
int precedence(char symbol);
int power(int b, int a);

int power(int b, int a)
{
        int result=1;

        for(int i=1; i<=a; i++)
                result *= b;

        return result;
}//End of power()

int evaluatePostfix(string postfix)
{
        char symbol;
        int a, b, temp;
        stack<int> st;

        for(int i=0; i<postfix.length(); i++)
        {
                symbol = postfix[i];

                if(symbol-'0' >= 0 && symbol-'0' <= 9)
                {
                        st.push(symbol-'0');
                }
                else
                {
                        a = st.top();
                        st.pop();
                        b = st.top();
                        st.pop();

                        switch(symbol)
                        {
                                case '+':
                                        temp = b+a; break;
                                case '-':
                                        temp = b-a; break;
                                case '*':
                                        temp = b*a; break;
                                case '/':
                                        temp = b/a; break;
                                case '%':
                                        temp = b%a; break;
                                case '^':
                                        temp = power(b, a); break;
                        }//End of switch

                        st.push(temp);
                }//End of else
        }//End of for
```

```cpp
                return st.top();
}//End of evaluatePostfix()
int precedence(char symbol)
{
        switch(symbol)
        {
                case '(':
                        return 0;
                case '+':
                case '-':
                        return 1;
                case '*':
                case '/':
                case '%':
                        return 2;
                case '^':
                        return 3;
                default:
                        return 0;
        }
}//End of precedence()
string infixToPostfix(string infix)
{
        string postfix = "";
        char symbol;
        stack<char> st;

        for(int i=0; i<infix.length(); i++)
        {
                symbol = infix[i];

                switch(symbol)
                {
                        case '(':
                                st.push(symbol);
                                break;
                        case ')':
                                while(st.top() != '(')
                                {
                                        postfix += st.top();
                                        st.pop();
                                }
                                st.pop();
                                break;
                        case '+':
                        case '-':
                        case '*':
                        case '/':
                        case '%':
                        case '^':
                                while( !st.empty() && ( precedence(st.top()) >=
                                        precedence(symbol) ) )
                                {
                                        postfix += st.top();
                                        st.pop();
                                }
                                st.push(symbol);
                                break;
                        default:
                                postfix += symbol;
                                break;
```

```
        }//End of switch
    }//End of for

    while(!st.empty())
    {
            postfix += st.top();
            st.pop();
    }

    return postfix;
}//End of infixToPostfix()
int main()
{
    string infix = "7+5*3^2/(9-2^2)+6*4";
    string postfix;

    cout << "Infix expression is : " << infix << "\n";
    postfix = infixToPostfix(infix);
    cout << "Postfix expression is :\n";
    cout << postfix << "\n";

    cout << "Value of expression is :\n";
    cout << evaluatePostfix(postfix) << "\n";

    return 0;
}//End of main()
```

In the above discussion, we have taken all our operators as left associative for simplicity i.e., when two operators had the same precedence, then first we evaluated the operator which was on the left. However, the exponentiation operation is generally right associative. The value of expression 2^2^3 should be $2^8=256$ and not $4^3=64$. So A^B^C should be converted to ABC^^, while we are converting it to AB^C^. So let us see what change we can make in our procedure if we have any operator which is right associative. We will define two priorities in this case:

Operator	In-stack Priority	Incoming Priority
^ (Exponentiation)	3	4
* (Multiplication) and / (Division)	2	2
+ (Addition) and - (Subtraction)	1	1

Figure 4.27 Two priorities for operators

For left associative operators, both priorities will be same but for right associative operators incoming priority should be more than the in-stack priority. To incorporate this change in our program, we will make two functions instead of the function `precedence()`. Now whenever an operator comes while scanning infix, then pop the operators which have in-stack priority greater than or equal to the incoming priority of the symbol operator.

```
while(!st.empty() && (instackPrecedence(st.top()) >= incomingPrecedence(symbol)))
{
        postfix += st.top();
        st.pop();
}
```

Here `instackPrecedence()` and `incomingPrecedence()` are functions that return the in-stack and incoming priorities of operators.

Exercise

1. Implement a stack in an array A, using A[0] as the top.

2. Implement a queue in an array such that if the rear reaches the end, all the elements are shifted left.

3. Implement a stack in an array such that the stack starts from the last position of array i.e., initially the top is at the last position of the array, and it moves towards the beginning of the array as the elements are pushed.

4. Write a program to implement 2 stacks in a single array of size N. The stacks should not show overflow if there is even a single slot available in the array. Write the functions `pushA()`, `pushB()`, `popA()`, `popB()` for pushing and popping from these stacks.

5. Write a program to implement 2 queues in a single array. The queues should not show overflow if there is even a single slot available in the array.

6. Implement a queue using 2 stacks.

7. Implement a stack using 2 queues.

8. Implement a stack with one queue.

9. Reverse a stack using two stacks.

10. Reverse a stack using a queue.

11. Reverse a queue using one stack.

12. Copy the contents of a stack S1 to another stack S2 using one temporary stack.

13. Copy a queue Q1 to another queue Q2.

14. Implement a data structure that supports stack push and pop operations and returns the minimum element.

15. Write a program to convert a decimal number to binary using a stack.

16. Write a program to print all the prime factors of a number in descending order using a stack. For example, the prime divisors of 450 are 5, 5, 3, 3, 2.

17. Write a program for converting an infix expression to prefix and evaluating that prefix expression.

18. Convert the following infix expressions to equivalent postfix and prefix:
    (i) (A+B)*(C+D)   (ii) A%(C-D)+B*E   (iii) A-(B+C)*D/E   (iv) H^(J+K)*I%S

19. Convert the following infix expressions to equivalent prefix expressions and then evaluate the prefix expressions using stack:
    (i) (5+3)/4-2   (ii) 6/3+3*2^2+1   (iii) (8+2)/2 *3-2/1+3

20. Convert the following postfix expressions to prefix:
    (i) ABC*-DE-F*G/H/+   (ii) AB+C/D*EF^−   (iii) ABC^-DE*FG+/+
    Write a program for this conversion.

21. Convert the following prefix expressions to postfix:
    (i) +-+A/BC*DEF   (ii) -+A/B*C^DE*F^GH   (iii) -+A/B^CD/*EF+GH
    Write a program for this conversion.

22. Evaluate the following postfix expressions:
    (i) 593/21+*+62/-3+   (ii) 432^+18*22+/-2-   (iii) 23^1-42/6*+31+2/-

Recursion

Recursion is a process in which a problem is defined in terms of itself. The problem is solved by repeatedly breaking it into smaller problems, which are similar in nature to the original problem. The smaller problems are solved, and their solutions are applied to get the final solution to the original problem. To implement recursion technique in programming, a function should be capable of calling itself. A recursive function is a function that calls itself.

```
int main()
{
        ............
        rec();
        ............
}//End of main()
void rec()
{
        ............
        rec();              //recursive call
        ............
}//End of rec()
```

Here the function `rec()` is calling itself inside its own function body, so `rec()` is a recursive function. When `main()` calls `rec()`, the code of `rec()` will be executed and since there is a call to `rec()` inside `rec()`, again `rec()` will be executed. It seems that this process will go on infinitely but in practice, a terminating condition is written inside the recursive function which ends this recursion. This terminating condition is also known as exit condition or the base case. This is the case when function will stop calling itself and will finally start returning.

Recursion proceeds by repeatedly breaking a problem into smaller versions of the same problem, till finally we get the smallest version of the problem which is simple enough to solve. The smallest version of problem can be solved without recursion and this is actually the base case.

5.1 Writing a Recursive Function

Recursion is a way of thinking about problems, so before writing a recursive function for a problem we should be able to define the solution of the problem in terms of a similar type of a smaller problem. The two main steps in writing a recursive function are-

1. Identification of the base case and its solution, i.e. the case where solution can be achieved without recursion. There may be more than one base case.
2. Identification of the general case or the recursive case i.e. the case in which recursive call will be made.

Identifying the base case is very important because without it the function will keep on calling itself resulting in infinite recursion.

We must ensure that each recursive call takes us closer to the base case i.e. the size of problem should be diminished at each recursive call. The recursive calls should be made in such a way that finally we arrive at the base case. If we do not do so, we will have infinite recursion. So merely defining a base case will not help us avoid infinite recursion, we should implement the function such that the base case is finally reached.

5.2 Flow of Control in Recursive Functions

Before understanding the flow of control in recursive calls, first let us see how control is transferred in simple function calls.

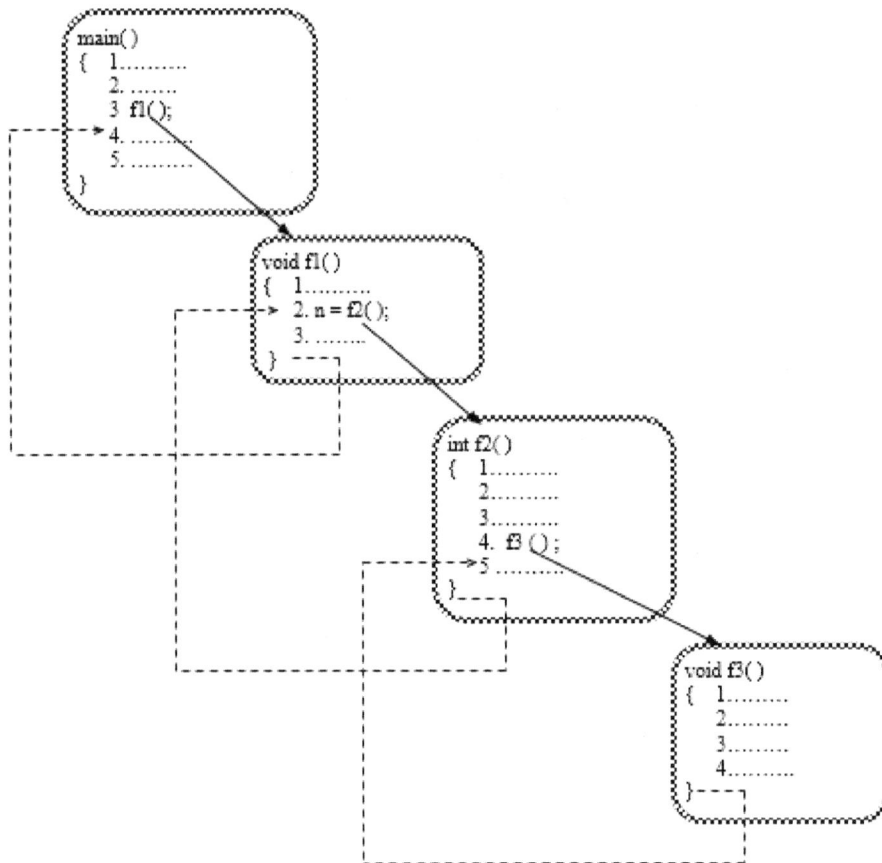

Figure 5.1 Flow of control in normal function calls

In the figure 5.1, the flow of control is-

- `main()` calls function `f1()` at line 3 so control is transferred to `f1()`.
- Inside function `f1()`, the function `f2()` is called at line 2 so control is transferred to function `f2()`.
- Inside function `f2()`, the function `f3()` is called at line 4 so control is transferred to function `f3()`.
- Inside function `f3()` no function is called so control returns back to function `f2()` at line 5.
- After finishing function `f2()`, control is returned to function `f1()` at line 2. Here control returned to line 2 because the work of assigning the return value of `f2()` to variable n still remains.
- Now after finishing the execution of function `f1()` the control is returned to `main()` at line 4.

When the execution of a function is finished we return to the caller (parent) function at the place where we had left it. Recursive calls are no different and they behave in a similar manner. In figure 5.2, the function that is being called each time is the same. We will call the different calls of `func()` as different invocations of `func()`.

- Initially `main()` calls `func()`, so in first invocation of `func()` value of formal parameter n is 5. Line 1 of this function is executed, after this the terminating condition is checked and since it is false we do not return. Now line 4 is executed and then at line 5, `func()` is called with argument 3.

- Now control transfers to the second invocation of `func()` and inside this invocation, value of n is 3. Line 1 of this second invocation of `func()` is executed, after this the terminating condition is checked and since it is false we do not return. Now line 4 is executed and then at line 5, `func()` is called with argument 1.

- Now control transfers to the third invocation of `func()` and inside this invocation, value of n is 1. Line 1 of this third invocation of `func()` is executed, after this the terminating condition is checked and since it is true, we return.

- We return to second invocation of `func()` at line 6. Note that now we are inside second invocation of `func()` so value of n is 3. After executing lines 6 and 7 we return back to the line 6 of first invocation.

- Now we are inside first invocation of `func()` so value of n is 5. After executing lines 6 and 7 of first invocation we return to `main()` at line 4.

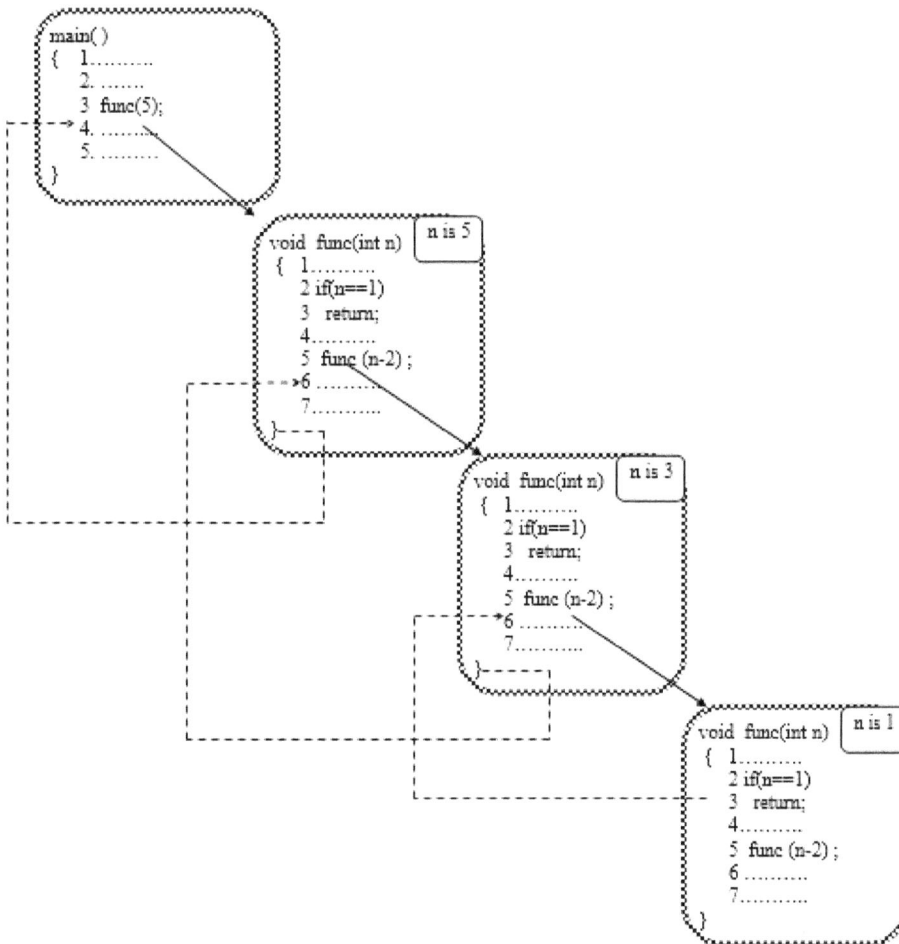

Figure 5.2 Flow of control in recursive function calls

We can see that the recursive functions are called in a manner similar to that of regular functions, but here, the same function is called each time. When execution of an invocation of recursive function is finished, we return to the previous invocation where we had left it.

We know that each function has some local variables that exist only inside that function. The local variables of the called function are active, while the local variables of the caller function are kept on hold or suspended. The same case occurs in recursion, but here, the caller function and called function are copies of the same function. When a function is called recursively, then for each invocation, a new set of formal parameters and local variables (except static) is created. Their names are the same as declared in function, but their memory locations are different and they contain different values. These values are remembered by the compiler till the end of the function call, so that these values are available while returning. In the example of figure 5.2, we can see that there are three invocations of func(), but each invocation had its own copy of formal parameter n.

The number of times that a function calls itself is known as the recursive depth of that function. In the example of figure 5.2, the depth of recursion is 3.

5.3 Winding and Unwinding Phase

All recursive functions work in two phases: winding phase and unwinding phase. Winding phase begins when the recursive function is called for the first time, and each recursive call continues the winding phase. In this phase, the function keeps on calling itself and no return statements are executed in this phase. This phase terminates when the terminating condition becomes true in a call. After this, the unwinding phase begins and all the recursive function calls start returning in reverse order till the first invocation of function returns. In the unwinding phase, the control returns through each invocation of the function.

In some algorithms, we need to perform some work while returning from recursive calls. In that case, we put that particular code in the unwinding phase i.e., just after the recursive call.

We will try to understand the concept of recursion through numerous examples. Although most of them may not be very efficient yet, they are classic examples of learning how recursion works. Initially when learning recursion, we should trace the functions and see how the control is transferred to understand the behavior of recursive functions.

5.4 Examples of Recursion

5.4.1 Factorial

We know that the factorial of a positive integer n can be found by multiplying all integers from 1 to n.
n! = 1 * 2 * 3 *..........* (n-1) * n

This is the iterative definition of factorial, and we can easily write an iterative function for it using a loop. Now, we will try to find the solution of this factorial problem recursively.

We know that: 4! = 4 * 3 * 2 * 1
We can write it as: 4! = 4 * 3!   (since 3! = 3 * 2 * 1)
Similarly, we can write: 3! = 3 * 2!
                          2! = 2 * 1!
                          1! = 1 * 0!

Therefore, in general, we can say that the factorial of a positive integer n is the product of n and the factorial of n-1.

n! = n * (n-1)!

The problem of finding out the factorial of (n-1) is similar to that of finding out the factorial of n. However, it is smaller in size. Thus, we have defined the solution of the factorial problem in terms of the problem itself. We know that the factorial of 0 is 1. This can act as the terminating condition or the base case. So, the recursive definition of factorial can be written as:

$$n! = \begin{cases} 1 & n = 0 \\ n * (n\text{-}1)! & n > 0 \end{cases}$$

Figure 5.3 Recursive definition of factorial

Now we will write a program, which finds out the factorial using a recursive function:

```cpp
//Factorial.cpp : Program to find the factorial of a number using recursion.
#include <iostream>
using namespace std;
long int factorial(int n)
{
        if(n==0)
                return 1;

        return (n * factorial(n-1));
}//End of factorial()
int main()
{
        int num = 5;

        if(num < 0)
                cout << "No factorial for negative number\n";
        else
                cout << "Factorial of " << num << " = " << factorial(num) << "\n";

        return 0;
}//End of main()
```

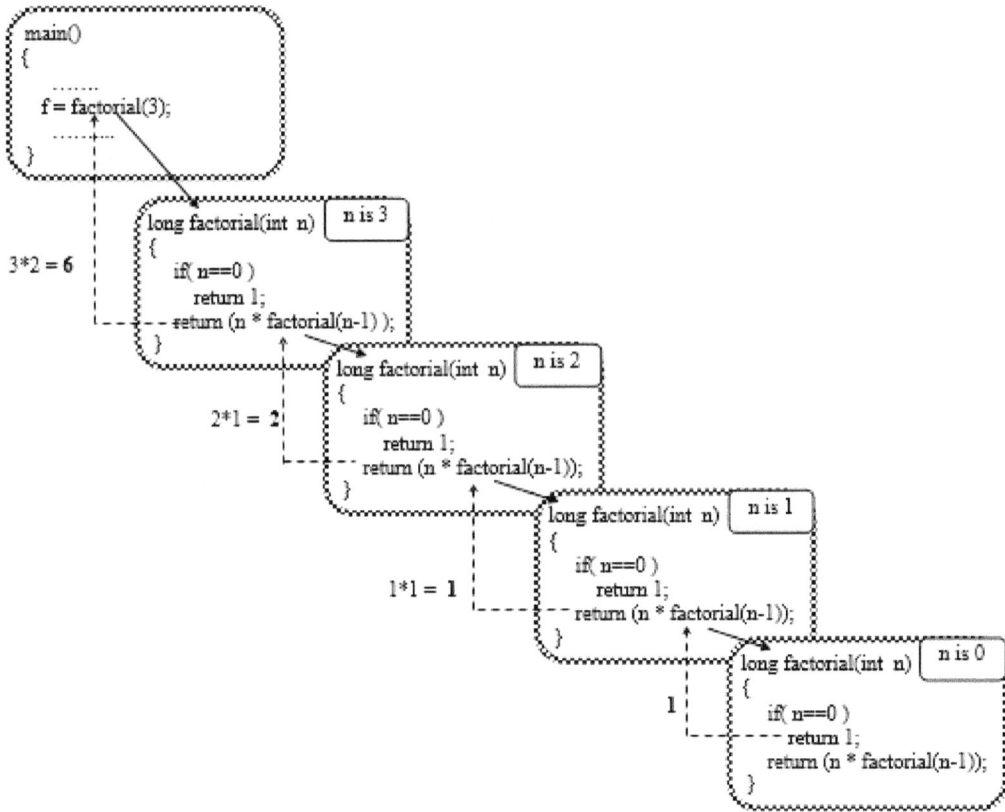

Figure 5.4 Finding factorial of a number recursively

The function `factorial()` returns 1 if the argument n is 0. Otherwise, it returns `n*factorial(n-1)`. To return `n*factorial(n-1)`, the value of `factorial(n-1)` has to be calculated for which the `factorial()` has to be called again with an argument of n-1. This process of calling `factorial()` continues till it is called with an argument of 0. Suppose we want to find out the factorial of 3.

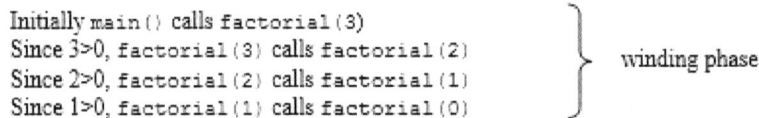

```
Initially main() calls factorial(3)
Since 3>0, factorial(3) calls factorial(2)
Since 2>0, factorial(2) calls factorial(1)
Since 1>0, factorial(1) calls factorial(0)
```
winding phase

Figure 5.5 Winding phase of fatorial function

The first time when `factorial()` is called, its argument is the actual argument given in the `main()`, which is 3. So, in the first invocation of `factorial()`, the value of n is 3. Inside this first invocation, there is a call to `factorial()` with argument n-1, and so now, `factorial()` is invoked for the second time. This time, the argument is 2. Now, the second invocation calls the third invocation of `factorial()` and this time, the argument is 1. The third invocation of `factorial()` calls the fourth invocation with an argument of 0.

When `factorial()` is called with n=0, the condition inside `if` statement becomes true, i.e., we have reached the base case. So now, the recursion stops and the statement return 1 is executed. The winding phase terminates here and the unwinding phase begins and control starts returning towards the original call.

Now every invocation of `factorial()` will return a value to the previous invocation of `factorial()`. These values are returned in the reverse order of function calls.

Value returned by `factorial(0)` to `factorial(1)` $= 1$
Value returned by `factorial(1)` to `factorial(2)` $= 1 * $ `factorial(0)` $ = 1*1 = 1$
Value returned by `factorial(2)` to `factorial(3)` $= 2 * $ `factorial(1)` $ = 2*1 = 2$ ⎫ Unwinding Phase
Value returned by `factorial(3)` to `main()` $= 3 * $ `factorial(2)` $ = 3*2 = 6$ ⎭

Figure 5.6 Unwinding phase of factorial function

The function `factorial()` is called four times. Each function call is different from another, and the argument supplied is different each time.

In the program, we have taken `long int` as the return value of `factorial()` since the value of factorial for even a small value of n exceeds the range of `int` data type.

5.4.2 Summation of Numbers from 1 to n

The next example of a recursive function that we are taking, is a function that computes the sum of integers from 1 to n. This is similar to the factorial problem; there we had to find the product of numbers from 1 to n, while here, we have to find the sum.
We can say that the sum of the numbers from 1 to n is equal to n plus the sum of numbers 1 to n-1.
summation(n) = n + summation(n-1)

$$summation(4) = 4 + summation(3)$$
$$= 4 + 3 + summation(2)$$
$$= 4 + 3 + 2 + summation(1)$$
$$= 4 + 3 + 2 + 1 + summation(0)$$

We know that the summation(0) will be equal to 0, and this can act as the base case. So, the base case occurs when the function is called with the value of n equal to 0, and in this case, the function should return 0.

```
int summation(int n)
{
        if(n == 0)
                return 0;
        return (n + summation(n-1));
}//End of summation()
```

5.4.3 Displaying Numbers from 1 to n

In the previous two examples, we found the product and sum of numbers from 1 to n. Now, we will write a recursive function to display these numbers. This function only has to display the numbers, so it will not return any value and will be of type `void`.

We have written two functions `display1()` and `display2()`, which are traced in figures 5.7 and 5.8. Let us see which one gives us the desired output.

```
void display1(int n)
{
        if(n == 0)
```

```
            return;
        cout << n << "\n";
        display1(n-1);
}//End of display1()
void display2(int n)
{
        if(n == 0)
                return;
        display2(n-1);
        cout << n << "\n";
}//End of display2()
```

The function display1() is traced in figure 5.7. Initially, the cout inside the first invocation will be executed, and in that invocation, the value of n is 3. So, 3 is displayed first. After this, the cout inside the second invocation is executed and 2 is displayed, and then cout inside the third invocation is executed and 1 is displayed. In the fourth invocation, the value of n becomes 0; we have reached the base case and the recursion is stopped. So this function displays the values from n to 1, but we wanted to display the values from 1 to n.

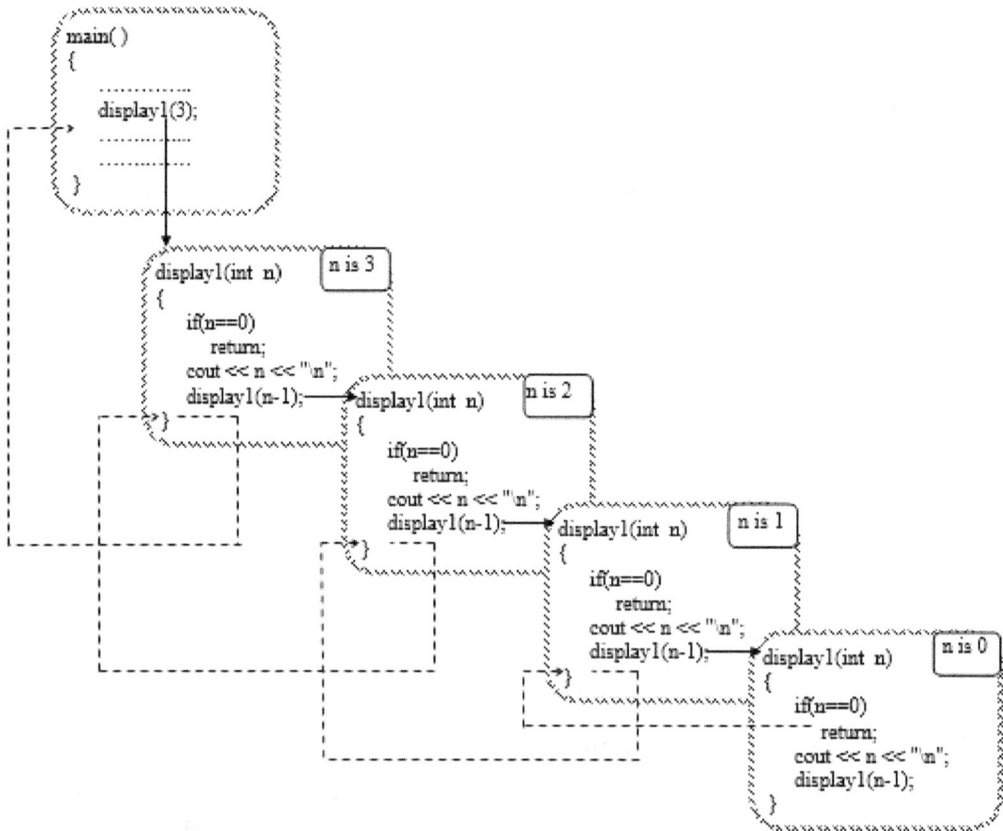

Figure 5.7 Displaying numbers from n to 1

Now, let us trace the function `display2()`.

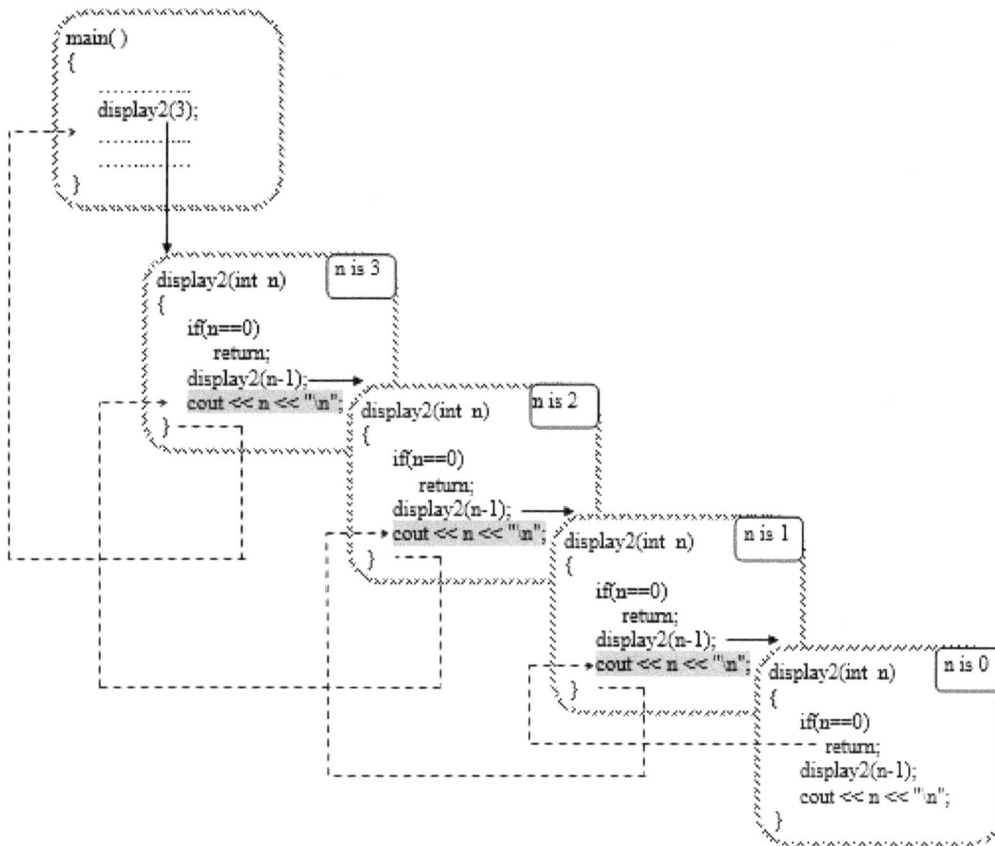

Figure 5.8 Displaying numbers from 1 to n

In `display2()`, the `cout` is after the recursive call, and so the `cout` statements are not executed in the winding phase. However, they are executed in the unwinding phase. In the unwinding phase, the calls return in reverse order, and so first of all, the `cout` of the third invocation is executed, and in this invocation. the value of n is 1. So, 1 is displayed. After this, the `cout` of the second invocation is executed, and in this invocation, the value of n is 2, so 2 is displayed. At last, the `cout` of the first invocation is executed and 3 is displayed.

5.4.4 Display and Summation of Series

Let us take a simple series of numbers from 1 to n. We want to write a recursive function that displays this series, as well as, finds the sum of this series. For example, if the number of terms is 5, then our function should give this output.

$1 + 2 + 3 + 4 + 5 = 15$

We have already seen how to display, and find the sum of numbers from 1 to n, so let us combine that logic to write a function for our series.

```
//Series.cpp : Program to display and find out the sum of series.
//Series : 1 + 2 + 3 + 4 + 5 +.......
```

```cpp
#include <iostream>
using namespace std;

int rseries(int n)
{
        if(n == 0)
                return 0;
        return n + rseries(n-1);
        cout << n << " + ";
}//End of rseries()

int main()
{
        int n = 5;
        cout << "\b\b= " << rseries(n) << "\n"; //\b to erase last + sign

        return 0;
}//End of main()
```

Let us find out whether the function `rseries()` gives us the desired output. This function will return the sum of the series but will not display any term of the series. This is because in the unwinding phase, when control returns to the previous invocation, the return statement (`return n + rseries(n-1)`) is executed. Thus, the function returns without executing the `cout` statement. To make the function work correctly, we can write it like this:

```cpp
int rseries(int n)
{
        int sum;
        if(n == 0)
                return 0;
        sum = (n + rseries(n-1));
        cout << n << " + ";

        return sum;
}//End of rseries()
```

The `cout` statement is before the `return` statement and after the recursive call, so it will always be executed in the unwinding phase.

5.4.5 Sum of Digits of an Integer and Displaying an Integer as a Sequence of Characters

The problem of finding the sum of digits of a number can be defined recursively as:

sumOfDigits(n) = least significant digit of n + sumdigits (n with least significant digit removed)

The sum of digits of a single digit number is the number itself, and it can act as the base case.

If we have to find the sum of digits of 45329, we can proceed as:

sumOfDigits(45329) = 9 + sumOfDigits(4532)
sumOfDigits(4532) = 2 + sumOfDigits(453)
sumOfDigits(453) = 3 + sumOfDigits(45)
sumOfDigits(45) = 5 + sumOfDigits(4)
sumOfDigits(4) = 4

The least significant digit of the integer n can be extracted by the expression `n%10`. The recursive call has to be made with the least significant digit removed and this is done by calling the function with `(n/10)`. The base case would be when the function is called with a one digit argument.

```cpp
//Finds the sum of digits of an integer
int sumOfDigits(long int n)
{
        if(n/10 == 0) //if n is a single digit number
```

```
                return n;
        return n%10 + sumOfDigits(n/10);
}//End of sumOfDigits()
```

We can display the digits using `n%10` and recursive call can be made with `n/10`, so that it will not have a last digit.

```
//Displays the digits of an integer
void display(long int n)
{
        if(n/10 == 0)
        {
                cout << n;
                return;
        }
        cout << n%10;
        display(n/10);
}//End of display()
```

However, this will display the digits of the number in a reverse order, as the `cout` statement is in winding phase before the recursive call. So we have to place the `cout` statement in the unwinding phase after a recursive call.

```
//Displays the digits of an integer
void display(long int n)
{
        if(n/10 == 0)
        {
                cout << n;
                return;
        }
        display(n/10);
        cout << n%10;
}//End of display()
```

We would like to combine the logic of the display of digits and the sum of digits together, as we already have the digits information from finding the sum of digits. Here is the modified `sumOfDigits()` function:

```
//Displays digits of an integer number and finds the sum of digits of that number
int sumOfDigits(long int n)
{
        int sum;
        if(n/10 == 0) //if n is a single digit number
        {
                cout << n%10;
                return n;
        }
        sum = (n%10 + sumOfDigits(n/10));
        cout << n%10;
        return sum;
}//End of sumOfDigits()
```

5.4.6 Base Conversion

Now, we will write a recursive function which will convert a decimal number to binary, octal and hexadecimal base. To do this conversion, we have to divide the decimal number repeatedly by the base, till it is reduced to 0, and print the remainders in a reverse order. If the base is hexadecimal, then we have to print the alphabets for remainder values greater than or equal to 10. We want to print the the remainders in reverse order, so that we can do this work in the unwinding phase.

```cpp
//BaseConversion.cpp : Program to convert a positive decimal number to Binary, Octal or
//Hexadecimal.
#include <iostream>
using namespace std;

void convertBase(int num, int base)
{
        int rem = num%base;
        if(num == 0)
                return;
        convertBase(num/base, base);
        if(rem < 10)
                cout << rem;
        else
                cout << char(rem-10+'A');
}//End of convertBase()

int main()
{
        int num = 20;
        cout << "Decimal number : " << num << "\n";
        cout << "Binary : ";          convertBase(num, 2);   cout << "\n";
        cout << "Octal : ";           convertBase(num, 8);   cout << "\n";
        cout << "Hexadecimal : ";     convertBase(num, 16);  cout << "\n";

        return 0;
}//End of main()
```

5.4.7 Exponentiation of a Positive Integer

The iterative definition for finding a^n is:

$a^n = a * a * a * \ldots\ldots\ldots$ n times

The recursive definition can be written as:

$$a^n = \begin{cases} 1 & n=0 \quad \text{(Base case)} \\ a * a^{n-1} & n>0 \quad \text{(Recursive case)} \end{cases}$$

Figure 5.9 Recursive definition of a^n

```cpp
//PowerOfNumber.cpp : Program to find the exponentiation of a number
//(a power n, example 2 power 3 = 8).
#include <iostream>
using namespace std;

long int power(int a, int n)
{
        if(n == 0)
                return 1;

        return (a * power(a, n-1));
}//End of power()

int main()
{
        int a=3, n=4;
        cout << a << " power " << n << " = " << power(a, n) << "\n";

        return 0;
}//End of main()
```

5.4.8 Prime Factorization

Prime factorization of a number means factoring a number into a product of prime numbers. For example, prime factors of numbers 84 and 45 are:

84 = 2 * 2 * 3 * 7
45 = 3 * 3 * 5

To find the prime factors of a number n, we check its divisibility by prime numbers 2,3,5,7,... till we get a divisor d. Now, d becomes a prime factor and the problem reduces to finding prime factors of n/d. The base case occurs when the problem reduces to finding prime factors of 1. Let us see how we can find prime factors of 84.

84 is divisible by 2, so 2 is a PF, and now the problem reduces to finding PFs of 84/2 = 42
42 is divisible by 2, so 2 is a PF, and now the problem reduces to finding PFs of 42/2=21
21 is not divisible by 2, so we check divisibility by the next prime number, which is 3
21 is divisible by 3, so 3 is PF, and now the problem reduces to finding PFs of 21/3=7.
7 is not divisible by 3, so we check divisibility by the next prime number, which is 5,
7 is not divisible by 5, so we check divisibility by the next prime number, which is 7,
7 is divisible by 7, so 7 is a PF, and now the problem reduces to finding PFs of 7/7=1

The recursive function for printing the prime factors of a number are:

```
void primeFactors(int num)
{
        int i=2;
        if(num == 1)
                return;
        while(num%i != 0)
                i++;
        cout << i << " ";
        primeFactors(num/i);
}//End of primeFactors()
```

For simplicity, we have checked the divisibility by all numbers starting from 2 (prime and non prime), but we will get only prime factors. For example, 6 is non prime factor of 84, but it has already been removed as a factor of 2 and factor of 3.

5.4.9 Greatest Common Divisor

The greatest common divisor (or highest common factor) of two integers is the greatest integer that divides both of them without any remainder. It can be found by using Euclid's remainder algorithm, which states that:

$$GCD(a, b) = \begin{cases} a & b = 0 & \text{(Base case)} \\ GCD(b, a\%b) & \text{otherwise} & \text{(Recursive case)} \end{cases}$$

Figure 5.10 Recursive definition of GCD(a,b)

GCD(35, 21)   (a = 35, b = 21)
 = GCD(21, 14) (a = 21, b = 35 % 21 = 14)
 = GCD(14, 7)   (a = 14, b = 21 % 14 = 7)
 = GCD(7, 0)   (a = 7, b = 14 % 7 = 0)
 = 7

GCD(12, 26)   (a = 12, b = 26)
 = GCD(26, 12) (a = 26, b = 12 % 26 = 12)
 = GCD(12, 2)   (a = 12, b = 26 % 12 = 2)
 = GCD(2, 0)   (a = 2, b = 12 % 2 = 0)
 = 2

The recursive function can be written as:

```
int GCD(int a, int b)
{
        if(b == 0)
                return a;
        return GCD(b, a%b);
}//End of GCD()
```

Here, nothing is to be done in the unwinding phase. The value returned by the last recursive call becomes the return value of previous recursive calls, and finally, it becomes the return value of the first recursive call.

5.4.10 Fibonacci Series

The Fibonacci series is a sequence of numbers in which the first two numbers are 1, and after that, each number is the sum of the previous two numbers.

1, 1, 2, 3, 5, 8, 13, 21, 34, 55, 89, ...

The problem of finding the nth Fibonacci number can be recursively defined as:

$$fib(n) = \begin{cases} 1 & n=0 \text{ or } n=1 \quad \text{(Base case)} \\ fib(n-1) + fib(n-2) & n>1 \qquad \text{(Recursive case)} \end{cases}$$

Figure 5.11 Recursive definition of nth fibonacci number

```
//Fibonacci.cpp : Program to generate fibonacci series.
#include <iostream>
using namespace std;

int fib(int n)
{
        if(n==0 || n==1)
                return 1;

        return (fib(n-1) + fib(n-2));
}//End of fib()
int main()
{
        int nterms=10;

        for (int i=0; i < nterms ; i++)
                cout << fib(i) << " ";
        cout << "\n";

        return 0;
}//End of main()
```

Here, the function fib() is called two times inside its own function body. The following figure shows the recursive calls of function fib() when it is called with argument 5:

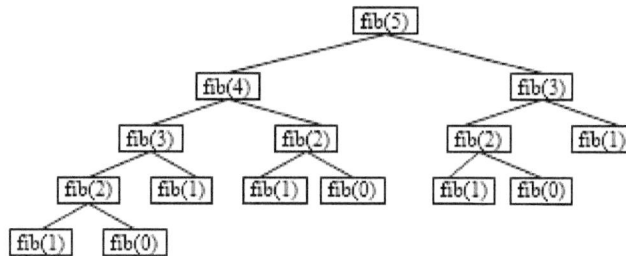

Figure 5.12 Recursive calls of function fib(5)

This implementation of Fibonacci is very inefficient because it performs same computations repeatedly. For example, in the above example, it computed the value of fib(2) 3 times.

5.4.11 Checking Divisibility by 9 and 11

We can easily check divisibility by any number using the % operator, but here we will develop functions for checking divisibility by 9 and 11, using the definitions that we have learned in mathematics, because these can help us improve our recursive thinking.

A number is divisible by 9 if and only if the sum of digits of the number is divisible by 9.

test(4968589) -> 4 + 9 + 6 + 9 + 8 + 5 + 8 + 9 = 58
test(58) -> 5 + 8 = 13
test (13) -> 1 + 3 = 4
test(4) -> not divisible by 9

test(1469358) -> 1 + 4 + 6 + 9 + 3 + 5 + 8 = 36
test(36) -> 3 + 6 = 9
test(9) -> divisible by 9

The function will be recursively called for the sum of digits of the number. The recursion will stop when the number reduces to one digit. If that digit is 9, number is divisible by 9. If that digit is less than 9, then number is not divisible by 9.

```
bool isDivisibleBy9(long int n)
{
        int sumOfDigits=0;
        if(n == 9)
                return true;
        if(n < 9)
                return false;
        while(n > 0)
        {
                sumOfDigits += n%10;
                n /= 10;
        }
        isDivisibleBy9(sumOfDigits);
}//End of isDivisibleBy9()
```

This function returns true if the number is divisible by 9. Otherwise, it returns false.

Now, let us make a function that checks divisibility by 11. A number is divisible by 11 if and only if the difference of the sums of digits at odd positions and even positions is either zero or divisible by 11.

test(91628153) -> [**28**(9+6+8+5) - 7(1+2+1+3)] = 21
test(21) -> [2 - 1] = 1

test(1) -> Not divisible by 11

62938194 -> [**32**(6+9+8+9) - **10**(2+3+1+4)] = 22
test(22) -> [2 - 2] = 0
test(0) -> divisible by 11

The function will be recursively called for the difference of sum of digits at odd and even positions. The recursion will stop when the number reduces to one digit. If that digit is 0, then the number is divisible by 11, otherwise, it is not divisible by 11.

```cpp
bool isDivisibleBy11(long int n)
{
        int s1=0, s2=0, diff;
        if(n==0)
                return true;
        if(n<10)
                return false;
        while(n>0)
        {
                s1 += n%10;
                n /= 10;
                s2 += n%10;
                n /= 10;
        }
        diff = s1>s2 ? (s1-s2) : (s2-s1);
        isDivisibleBy11(diff);
}//End of isDivisibleBy11()
```

This function returns true if number is divisible by 11, otherwise it returns false.

5.4.12 Tower of Hanoi

The problem of Tower of Hanoi is to move disks from one pillar to another using a temporary pillar. Suppose we have a source pillar A, which has a finite number of disks. These disks are placed on it in a decreasing order, that is, the largest disk is at the bottom and the smallest disk is at the top. We want to place all these disks on destination pillar C in the same order. We can use a temporary pillar B to place the disks temporarily whenever required. The conditions for this game are:

1. We can move only one disk from one pillar to another at a time.
2. A larger disk cannot be placed on a smaller disk.

Suppose the number of disks on pillar A is n. First, we will solve the problem for n=1, n=2, n=3, and then, we will develop a general procedure for the solution. Here, A is the source pillar, C is the destination pillar and B is the temporary pillar.

For n=1
Move the disk from pillar A to pillar C. (A➔C)

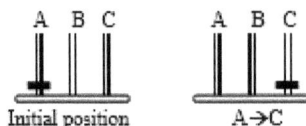

Figure 5.13 Tower of hanoi for 1 disk

For n=2

(i)   Move disk 1 from pillar A to B   (A➔B)
(ii) Move disk 2 from pillar A to C   (A➔C)
(iii) Move disk 1 from pillar B to C   (B➔C)

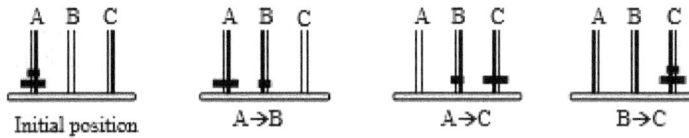

Figure 5.14 Tower of hanoi for 2 disks

For n=3

(i)   Move disk 1 from pillar A to C   (A➔C)
(ii)   Move disk 2 from pillar A to B   (A➔B)
(iii) Move disk 1 from pillar C to B   (C➔B)
(iv)   Move disk 3 from pillar A to C   (A➔C)
(v)   Move disk 1 from pillar B to A   (B➔A)
(vi)   Move disk 2 from pillar B to C   (B➔C)
(vii) Move disk 1 from pillar A to C   (A➔C)

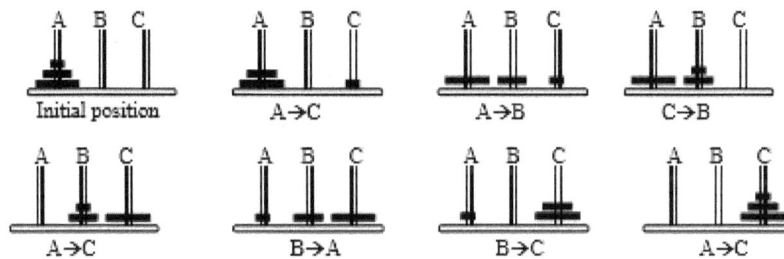

Figure 5.15 Tower of hanoi for 3 disks

These were the solutions for n=1, n=2, n=3. From these solutions, we can observe that first, we move n-1 disks from source pillar (A) to temporary pillar (B), and then move the largest(nth) disk to the destination pillar(C). So the general solution for n disks can be written as:

1. Move upper n-1 disks from A to B using C as the temporary pillar.
2. Move nth disk from A to C.
3. Move n-1 disks from B to C using A as the temporary pillar.

The base case would be when we have to move only one disk. In that case, we can simply move the disk from the source to the destination pillar and return. The recursion tree for n=5 is given as follows:

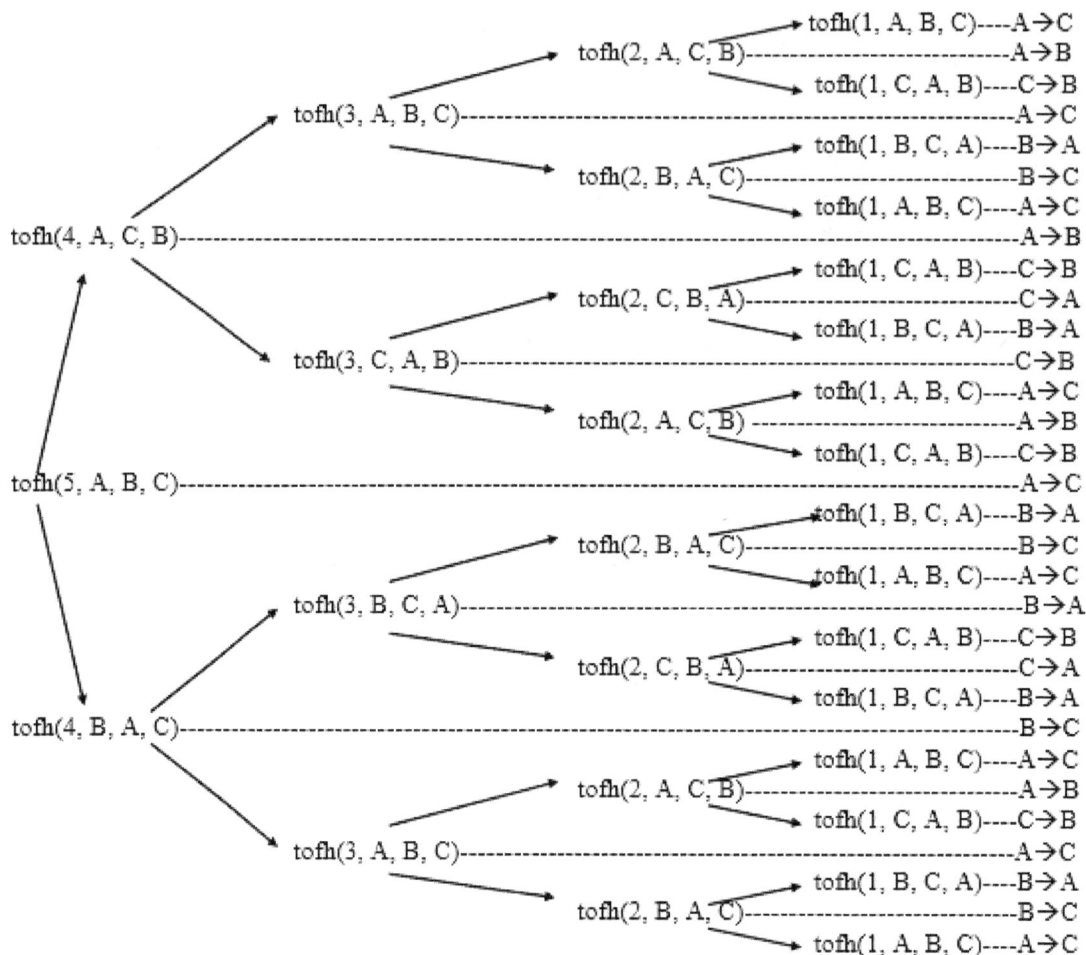

Figure 5.16 Tower of Hanoi for 5 disks

The recursive function for solving the tower of hanoi problem can be defined as:

$$tofh(\ n,\ source,\ temp,\ dest) = \begin{cases} \text{Move disk 1 from source to dest} & n=1 \\ \\ tofh(n\text{-}1,\ source,\ dest,\ temp) \\ \text{Move } n^{th} \text{ disk from source to dest} & n>1 \\ tofh(n\text{-}1,\ temp,\ source,\ dest) \end{cases}$$

Figure 5.17 Recursive definition of tower of hanoi

```cpp
//TowerOfHanoi.cpp : Program to solve Tower of Hanoi problem using recursion.
#include <iostream>
using namespace std;

void tofh(int ndisk, char source, char temp, char dest)
{
```

```
        if(ndisk == 1)
        {
                cout << "Move Disk " << ndisk << " from " << source << "-->" << dest <<
                "\n";
                return;
        }
        tofh(ndisk-1, source, dest, temp);
        cout << "Move Disk " << ndisk << " from " << source << "-->" << dest << "\n";
        tofh(ndisk-1, temp, source, dest);
}//End of tofh()
int main()
{
        char source='A', temp='B', dest='C';
        int ndisk=3;

        cout << "Sequence is :\n";
        tofh(ndisk, source, temp, dest);

        return 0;
}//End of main()
```

5.5 Recursive Data Structures

A recursive definition of a data structure defines the data structure in terms of itself. Some data structures like strings, linked lists, and trees can be defined recursively. In these types of data structures, we can take advantage of the recursive structure, and so, the operations on these data structures can be naturally implemented using recursive functions. This type of recursion is called structural recursion.

A string can be defined recursively as:
1. A string may be an empty string.
2. A string may be a character followed by a smaller string (one character less).

The string "leaf" is character 'l' followed by string "eaf". Similarly, the string "eaf" is character 'e' followed by string "af"; string "af" is character 'a' followed by string "f"; string "f" is character 'f' followed by an empty string. Thus, while defining recursive operations on strings, the case of an empty string will serve as the base case for terminating recursion.

Similarly, we can define a linked list recursively as:
(i) A linked list may be an empty linked list.
(ii) A linked list may be a node followed by a smaller linked list (one node less).

If we have a linked list containing nodes N1, N2, N3, N4, then we can say that:

linkedlist(N1-> N2-> N3-> N4) is node N1 followed by linked list(N2-> N3-> N4),
linkedlist(N2-> N3-> N4) is node N2 followed by linked list(N3-> N4),
linkedlist(N3-> N4) is node N3 followed by linked list(N4),
linkedlist(N4) is node N4 followed by an empty linked list.

While implementing operations on linked lists, we can take the case of an empty linked list as the base case for stopping recursion.

In this chapter, we will study some recursive procedures to operate on strings and linked lists. In the next chapter, we will study about another data structure called the tree, which can also be defined recursively. Some operations on trees are best defined recursively, and so, before going to that, it is better if you understand recursion in linked lists.

5.5.1 Strings and Recursion

We have seen the recursive definition of strings and the base case. Now, we will write some recursive functions for operations on strings. The first one is to find the length of a string.

The length of empty string is 0 and this will be our terminating condition. In a general case, the function is recursively called for a smaller string, which does not contain the first character of the string.

```cpp
int length(char *str)
{
        if(*str == '\0')
          ,     return 0;
        return (1 + length(str+1));
}//End of length()
```

We can print a string by printing the first character, followed by the smaller string. If the string is empty, there is nothing to be printed, and so we will do nothing and return (base case).

```cpp
void display(char *str)
{
        if(*str == '\0')
                return;
        cout << *str;
        display(str+1);
}//End of display()
```

By changing the order of printing statement and recursive call, we can get the function for displaying string in reverse order.

```cpp
void rdisplay(char *str)
{
        if(*str == '\0')
                return;
        rdisplay(str+1);
        cout << *str;
}//End of rdisplay()
```

Note that for displaying string in standard order, we have placed the printing statement before the recursive call, while during the display of numbers from 1 to n (Section 5.4.3), we had placed the printing statement after the recursive call. It is easy to understand the reason for this and if not, then trace and find out.

5.5.2 Linked Lists and Recursion

The first recursive function for linked list that we will make, is a function to find out the length of the linked list. The length of a linked list is 1 plus the length of smaller list (list without the first node), and the length of empty list is zero (base case).

```cpp
int SingleLinkedList::length(Node *ptr)
{
        if(ptr == NULL)
                return 0;
        return (1 + length(ptr->link));
}//End of length()
```

Similarly, we can make a function to find out the sum of the elements of the linked list.

```cpp
int SingleLinkedList::sum(Node *ptr)
{
        if(ptr == NULL)
                return 0;
        return (ptr->info + sum(ptr->link));
}//End of sum()
```

Next, we will make a function for printing the elements of a linked list. We can print a list by printing the first element of the list, followed by printing the smaller list; if the list is empty, there is nothing to be printed, and so, we will do nothing and return.

```
void SingleLinkedList::display(Node *ptr)
{
        if(ptr == NULL)
                return;
        cout << ptr->info << "\n";
        display(ptr->link);
}//End of display()
```

We are just walking down the list till we reach NULL, and printing the info part in the winding phase. This function will be invoked as:

```
display(start);
```

Next, we will make a function to print the list in reverse order, i.e., it will print all the elements starting from the last element.

```
void SingleLinkedList::rdisplay(Node *ptr)
{
        if(ptr == NULL)
                return;
        rdisplay(ptr->link);
        cout << ptr->info << "\n";
}//End of rdisplay()
```

The next function searches for an element in the list and if it is present, it returns true. Otherwise, it returns false.

```
bool SingleLinkedList::search(Node *ptr, int data)
{
        if(ptr == NULL)
                return false;
        if(ptr->info == data)
                return true;
        search(ptr->link, data);
}//End of search()
```

The next function inserts a node at the end of the linked list.

```
Node* SingleLinkedList::insertAtEnd(Node *ptr, int data)
{
        Node *temp;
        if(ptr == NULL)
        {
                temp = new Node(data);
                return temp;
        }
        ptr->link = insertAtEnd(ptr->link, data);
        return ptr;
}//End of insertAtEnd()
```

This function will be invoked as `start = insertAtEnd(start, data);`

The next function deletes the last node from the linked list.

```
Node* SingleLinkedList::delAtEnd(Node *ptr)
{
        if(ptr->link == NULL)
        {
                delete ptr;
                return NULL;
        }
```

```
        ptr->link = delAtEnd(ptr->link);
        return ptr;
}//End of delAtEnd()
```

This function will be invoked as `start = delAtEnd(start);`

The next function reverses the linked list.

```
Node* SingleLinkedList::reverse(Node *ptr)
{
        Node *temp;
        if(ptr->link == NULL)
                return ptr;
        temp = reverse(ptr->link);
        ptr->link->link = ptr;
        ptr->link = NULL;
        return temp;
}//End of reverse()
```

This function will be invoked as `start = reverse(start);`

5.6 Implementation of Recursion

We have seen that recursive calls execute just like normal function calls, and so, there is no special technique for implementing them. All function calls, whether recursive or non recursive, are implemented through the run time stack and in the previous chapter, we had seen how it is done. Here, we will take the example of function `factorial()` called by `main()` with argument 3, and see the changes in the run time stack as the function `factorial()` is evaluated.

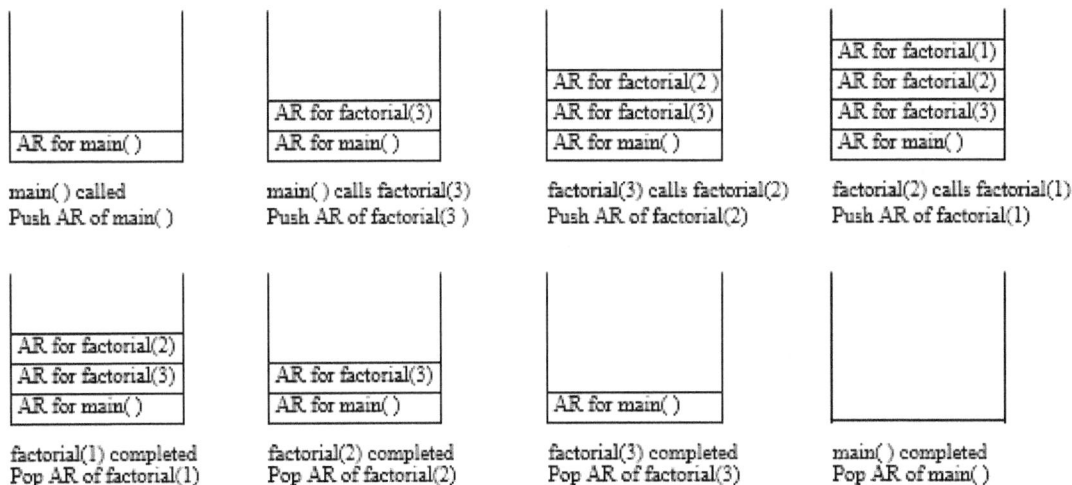

Figure 5.18 Recursive function factorial(3) evaluation in stack

In the winding phase, the stack grows as new activation records are created and pushed for each invocation of the function. In the unwinding phase, the activation records are popped from the stack in LIFO manner till the original call returns.

5.7 Recursion vs. Iteration

All repetitive problems can be implemented either recursively or iteratively. First, we will compare the workings of both the approaches.

In loops, the same block of code is executed repeatedly, and repetition occurs when the block of code is finished or a `continue` statement is encountered. In recursion, the same block of code is repeatedly executed and repetition occurs when the function calls itself.

In loops, the variables inside the loop are modified using some update statement. In recursion, the new values are passed as parameters to the next recursive call.

For the loop to terminate, there is a terminating condition, and the loop progresses in such a way that this condition is eventually hit. If this does not happen, then we get an infinite loop. For the recursion to terminate, there is a terminating condition (base case), when the function stops calling itself, and the recursion should proceed in such a way that we finally hit the base case. If this does not happen, then we will have infinite recursion, and the function will keep on calling itself till the stack is exhausted and we get stack overflow error.

Recursion involves pushing and popping activation records of all the currently active recursive calls on the stack. So, the recursive version of a problem is usually slower because of the time spent in pushing and popping these activation records. It is also expensive in terms of memory, as it uses space in the run time stack to store these activation records. If the recursion is too deep, the stack may overflow and the program will crash. On the other hand, the iterative versions do not have to pay for this function call overhead and so are faster and require less space.

Recursive solutions involve more execution overhead than their iterative counterparts, but their main advantage is that they simplify the code and make it more compact and elegant. Recursive algorithms are easier to understand because the code is shorter and clearer.

Recursion should be used when the underlying problem is recursive in nature, or when the data structure on which we are operating, is recursively defined like trees. Iteration should be used when the problem is not inherently recursive, or the stack space is limited.

For some problems which are very complex, iterative algorithms are harder to implement and it is easier to solve them recursively. In these cases, recursion offers a better way of writing our code, which is both logical and easier to understand and maintain. So sometimes, it may be worth sacrificing efficiency for code readability.

Recursion can be removed by maintaining our own stack or by using the iterative version.

5.8 Tail Recursion

Before studying about tail recursive functions, let us see what tail recursive calls are. A recursive call is tail recursive if it is the last statement to be executed inside the function.

```
void display1(int n)
{
        if(n == 0)
                return;
        cout << n << "\n";
        display1(n-1); //Tail recursive Call
}//End of display1()
void display2(int n)
{
        if(n == 0)
                return;
        display2(n-1); //Not a Tail recursive Call
```

```
        cout << n << "\n";
}//End of display2()
```

In non void functions, if the recursive call appears in the return statement and that call is not part of an expression then the call is tail recursive.

```
int GCD(int a, int b)
{
        if(b == 0)
                return a;
        return GCD(b, a%b); //Tail recursive call
}//End of GCD()
long int factorial(int n)
{
        if(n == 0)
                return 1;
        return (n * factorial(n-1)); //Not a tail recursive call
}//End of factorial()
```

Here, the call `factorial(n-1)` appears in the return statement, but it is not a tail recursive call because the call is part of an expression. Now, let us see some functions, which have more than one recursive calls.

```
void tofh(int ndisk, char source, char temp, char dest)
{
        if(ndisk == 1)
        {
                cout << "Move Disk " << ndisk << " from " << source << "-->" << dest <<
                "\n";
                return;
        }

        tofh(ndisk-1, source, dest, temp); //Not a tail recursive call
        cout << "Move Disk " << ndisk << " from " << source << "-->" << dest << "\n";
        tofh(ndisk-1, temp, source, dest); //Tail recursive call
}//End of tofh()
```

Here, the first recursive call is not a tail recursive call, while the second one is a tail recursive call. In the next function, we have two recursive calls and both are tail recursive.

```
int binarySearch(int arr[],int item, int low, int up)
{
        int mid;
        if(up < low)
                return -1;
        mid = (low+up)/2;
        if(item > arr[mid])
                return binarySearch(arr, item,mid+1, up); //Tail recursive call
        else if(item < arr[mid])
                return binarySearch(arr, item, low, mid-1); //Tail recursive call
        else
                return mid;
}//End of binarySearch()
```

Here, only one recursive call will be executed in each invocation of the function, and that recursive call will be the last one to be executed inside the function. So, both the calls in this function are tail recursive.

The two recursive calls in the fibonacci series function `fib()` are not tail recursive, because these calls are part of an expression, and after returning from the call, the return value has to be added to the return value of other recursive call.

A function is tail recursive if all the recursive calls in it are tail recursive. In the examples given earlier, the tail recursive functions are - `display1()`, `GCD()`, and `binarySearch()`. The functions `display2()`, `tofh()`, `factorial()` are not tail recursive functions.

Tail recursive functions can easily be written using loops, because as in a loop, there is nothing to be done after an iteration of the loop finishes. In tail recursive functions, there is nothing to be done after the current recursive call finishes execution. Some compilers automatically convert tail recursion to iteration for improving the performance.

In tail recursive functions, the last work that a function does is a recursive call, and so no operation is left pending after the recursive call returns. In non void tail recursive functions (like `GCD`), the value returned by the last recursive call is the value of the function. Hence in tail recursive functions, there is nothing to be done in the unwinding phase.

Since there is nothing to be done in the unwinding phase, we can jump directly from the last recursive call to the place where the recursive function was first called. So, there is no need to store the return address of the previous recursive calls and values of their local variables, parameters, return values etc. In other words, there is no need of pushing new activation record for all recursive calls.

Some modern compilers can detect tail recursion and perform tail recursion optimization. They do not push a new activation record when a recursive call occurs; rather, they overwrite the previous activation record by current activation record, while retaining the original return address. So we have only one activation record in the stack at a time, and this is for the currently executing recursive call. This improves the performance by reducing the time and memory requirement. Now, it does not matter how deep the recursion is; the space required will always be constant.

Since tail recursion can be efficiently implemented by compliers, we should try to make our recursive functions tail recursive whenever possible.

A recursive function can be written as a tail recursive function using an auxiliary parameter. The result is accumulated in this parameter and this is done in such a way that there is no pending operation left after the recursive call. For example, we can rewrite the factorial function that we have written earlier, as a tail recursive function.

```
long int trFactorial(int n, int result)
{
        if(n == 0)
                return result;
        return trFactorial(n-1, n*result);
}//End of trFactorial()
```

This function should be called as `trFactorial(n,1)`. We can make a helper function to initialize the value of result to 1. The use of this helper function hides the auxiliary parameter.

```
long int trFactorial(int n)
{
        return trFactorial(n, 1);
}//End of trFactorial()
```

Functions which are not tail recursive are called augmentive recursive functions and these types of functions have to finish the pending work after the recursive call finishes.

5.9 Indirect and Direct Recursion

If a function `f1()` calls `f2()` and the function `f2()` in turn calls `f1()`, then this is indirect recursion, because the function `f1()` is calling itself indirectly.

```
f1()
{
```

```
.........
f2();
.........
}
f2()
{

.........
f1();
.........

}
```

The chain of functions in indirect recursion may involve any number of functions. For example, f1() calls f2(), f2() calls f3(), f3() calls f4(), f4() calls f1(). If a function calls itself directly i.e., f1() is called inside its own function body, then that recursion is direct recursion. All the examples that we have seen in this chapter use direct recursion. Indirect recursion is complex and is rarely used.

Exercise

Find the output of programs from 1 to 16.

1.
```cpp
int func1(int a, int b)
{
    if(a > b)
            return 0;
    return b + func1(a, b-1);
}
int func2(int a, int b)
{
    if(a > b)
            return 0;
    return a + func2(a+1, b);
}
int main()
{
    cout << func1(3, 8) << " " << func2(3, 8) << "\n";
}
```

2.
```cpp
int func(int a, int b)
{
    if(a > b)
            return 1000;
    return a + func(a+1, b);
}
int main()
{
    cout << func(3, 8) << "\n";
}
```

3.
```cpp
int func(int a)
{
    if(a == 10)
            return a;
    return a + func(a+1);
}
int func1(int a)
{
    if(a == 0)
            return a;
    return a + func1(a+1);
```

```
    }
    int main()
    {
        cout << func(6) << "\n";
        cout << func1(6) << "\n";
    }
```

4.
```
    int func(int a, int b)
    {
        if(a == b)
                return a;
        return a + b + func(a+1, b-1);
    }
    int main()
    {
        cout << func(4, 8) << "\n";
        cout << func(3, 8) << "\n";
    }
```

5.
```
    void func1(int a, int b)
    {
        if(a > b)
                return;
        cout << b << " ";
        func1(a, b-1);
    }
    void func2(int a, int b)
    {
        if(a > b)
                return;
        func2(a, b-1);
        cout << b << " ";
    }
    int main()
    {
        func1(10, 18);
        cout << "\n";
        func2(10, 18);
        cout << "\n";
    }
```

6.
```
    void func1(int a, int b)
    {
        if(a > b)
                return;
        cout << a << " ";
        func1(a+1, b);
    }
    void func2(int a, int b)
    {
        if(a > b)
                return;
        func2(a+1, b);
        cout << a << " ";
    }
    int main( )
    {
        func1(10, 18);
        cout << "\n";
        func2(10, 18);
```

```cpp
        cout << "\n";
}
```

7.
```cpp
int func(int a, int b)
{
    if(b == 0)
            return 0;
    if(b == 1)
            return a;
    return a + func(a, b-1);
}
int main()
{
    cout << func(3, 8) << " ";
    cout << func(3, 0) << " ";
    cout << func(0, 3) << "\n";
}
```

8.
```cpp
int count(int n)
{
    if(n == 0)
            return 0;
    else
            return 1 + count(n/10);
}
int main()
{
    cout << count(17243) << "\n";
}
```

9.
```cpp
int func(int n)
{
    return (n) ? n%10 + func(n/10) : 0;
}
int main()
{
    cout << func(14837) << "\n";
}
```

10.
```cpp
int count(long int n, int d)
{
    if(n == 0)
            return 0;
    else if(n%10 == d)
            return 1 + count(n/10, d);
    else
            return count(n/10, d);
}
int main()
{
    cout << count(123212, 2) << "\n";
}
```

11.
```cpp
int func(int arr[], int size)
{
    if(size == 0)
            return 0;
    else if(arr[size-1]%2 == 0)
            return 1 + func(arr, size-1);
    else
            return func(arr, size-1);
```

```
    }
    int main( )
    {
        int arr[10] = {1,2,3,4,8,10};
        cout << func(arr, 6) << "\n";
    }
```

12.
```
int func(int arr[], int size)
{
    if(size == 0)
            return 0;
    return arr[size-1] + func(arr, size-1);
}
int main()
{
    int arr[10] = {1,2,3,4,8,10};
    cout << func(arr, 6) << "\n";
}
```

13.
```
int func(char *s, char a)
{
    if(*s == '\0')
            return 0;
    if(*s == a)
            return 1 + func(s+1, a);
    return func(s+1, a);
}
int main()
{
    char str[100] = "data structures and algorithms";
    char a = 't';

    cout << func(str, a) << "\n";
}
```

14.
```
void func1(int n)
{
    int i;
    if(n == 0)
            return;
            for(i=1; i<=n; i++)
            cout << "*";
    cout << "\n";
    func1(n-1);
}
void func2(int n)
{
    int i;
    if(n == 0)
            return;
            func2(n-1);
    for(i=1; i<=n; i++)
            cout << "*";
            cout << "\n";
}
int main( )
{
    func1(4);
    cout << "\n";
```

```
        func2(4);
    }
```

15.
```
int func(int arr[], int size)
{
    int m;
    if(size == 1)
            return arr[0];
            m = func(arr, size-1);
    if(arr[size-1] < m )
            return arr[size-1];
    else
            return m;
}
int main( )
{
    int arr[10] = {2,3,1,4,6,34};
    cout << func(arr, 6) << "\n";
}
```

16.
```
int func(int arr[], int low, int high)
{
    int mid, left, right;
    if(low == high)
            return arr[low];
            mid = (low+high)/2;
    left = func(arr, low, mid);
    right = func(arr, mid+1, high);
            if(left < right)
            return left;
    else
            return right;
}
int main( )
{
    int arr[6] = {3,4,2,11,8,10};
    cout << func(arr, 0, 5) << "\n";
}
```

17. Write a recursive function to add array of n numbers.

18. Write a recursive function to display a line of text in reverse order.

19. Write a recursive function to count all the prime numbers between numbers a and b (both inclusive).

20. A positive proper divisor of n is a positive divisor of n, which is different from n. For example 1,3,5,9,15 are positive proper divisors of 45, but 45 is not a proper divisor of 45. Write a recursive function that displays all the proper divisors of a number and returns their sum.

21. A number is perfect if the sum of all its positive proper divisors is equal to the number. For example, 28 is a perfect number since $28 = 1 + 2 + 4 + 7 + 14$. Write a recursive function that finds whether a number is perfect or not.

22. Write a recursive function to find the sum of all even numbers in an array.

23. Write a recursive function that finds the sum of all elements of an array by repeatedly partitioning it into two almost equal parts.

24. Write a recursive function to reverse the elements of an array.

25. Write a recursive function to find whether the elements of an array are in strict ascending order or not.

26. Write a recursive function that displays a positive integer in words. For example, if the integer is 2134 then it is displayed as - two one three four.

27. Write a recursive function that reverses an integer. For example if the input is 43287 then the function should return the integer 78234.

28. Write a recursive function to find the remainder when a positive integer a is divided by a positive integer b.

29. Write a recursive function to find the quotient when a positive integer a is divided by positive integer b.

30. The computation of a^n can be made efficient if we apply the following procedure instead of multiplying n times:

$a^8 = (a^2)^4$	$a^{11} = a * (a^2)^5$	$a^{19} = a * (a^2)^9$	$a^{20} = (a^2)^{10}$
$a^4 = (a^2)^2$	$a^5 = a * (a^2)^2$	$a^9 = a * (a^2)^4$	$a^{10} = (a^2)^5$
$a^2 = (a^2)^1$	$a^2 = (a^2)^1$	$a^4 = (a^2)^2$	$a^5 = a * (a^2)^2$
$a^1 = a * (a^2)^0$	$a^1 = a * (a^2)^0$	$a^2 = (a^2)^1$	$a^2 = (a^2)^1$
		$a^1 = a * (a^2)^0$	$a^1 = a * (a^2)^0$

Write a recursive function to compute a^n using this procedure.

31. Write a recursive function to multiply two numbers by the Russian peasant method. The Russian peasant method multiplies any two positive numbers using multiplication by 2, division by 2 and addition. Here, the first number is divided by 2 (integer division), and the second is multiplied by 2 repeatedly, until the first number reduces to 1. Suppose we have to multiply 19 by 25; we write the result of division and multiplication by 2 in the two columns like this:

19	25	Add
9	50	Add
4	100	
2	200	
1	400	Add
	475	

Figure 5.19 Russian peasant method to multiply two numbers

Now to get the product, we will add those values of the right hand column, for which the corresponding left column values are odd. So 25, 50, 400 will be added to get 475, which is the product of 19 and 25.

32. Write recursive functions to find values of $\lfloor \log_2 N \rfloor$ and $\lfloor \log_b N \rfloor$.

33. Write a recursive function to find the Binomial coefficient C(n,k) which is defined as:

C(n,0)=1
C(n,n)=1
C(n,k) = C(n-1,k-1) + C(n-1,k)

34. Write a recursive function to compute Ackermann's function A(m,n) which is defined as:

$$A(m,n) = \begin{cases} n+1 & \text{if } m=0 \\ A(m-1,1) & \text{if } m>0, n=0 \\ A(m-1, A(m,n-1)) & \text{otherwise} \end{cases}$$

Figure 5.20 Recursive dedinition of ackermann's function

35. Write a recursive function to count the number of vowels in a string.

36. Write a recursive function to replace each occurrence of a character by another character in a string.

37. Write a recursive function to reverse a string.

38. Write a recursive function to return the index of first occurrence of a character in a string.

39. Write a recursive function to return the index of last occurrence of a character in a string.

40. Write a recursive function to find whether a string is palindrome or not. A palindrome is a string that is read the same way forward and backward for example "radar", "hannah", "madam".

41. In the program of the previous problem, make changes so that spaces, punctuations marks, uppercase and lowercase differences are ignored. The strings "A man, a plan, a canal – Panama!", "Live Evil" should be recognized as palindromes.

42. Write a function to convert a positive integer to string.

43. Write a function to convert a string of numbers to an integer.

44. Write a function to print all possible permutations of a string. For example, if the string is "abc" then all possible permutations are abc, acb, bac, bca, cba, cab.

45. Write a function to print these pyramids of numbers:

```
1              1 2 3 4         4 3 2 1
1 2            1 2 3           3 2 1
1 2 3          1 2             2 1
1 2 3 4        1               1
```

46. A triangular number is the number of dots required to fill an equilateral triangle. The first 4 triangular numbers are 1, 3, 6, 10.

```
*        *         *            *
         * *       * *          * *
                   * * *        * * *
                                * * * *
```

Write a recursive function that returns n^{th} triangular number.

47. Write a recursive function to check if two linked lists are identical. Two lists are identical if they have the same number of elements and their corresponding elements are the same.

48. Write a recursive function to create a copy of a single linked list.

49. Write a recursive function to print alternate nodes of a single linked list.

50. Write a recursive function to delete a node from a single linked list.

51. Write a recursive function to insert a node in a sorted single linked list.

Trees

The data structures that we have studied till now, such as linked list, stack, and queue, are all linear data structures. Linked list is a good data structure from the memory point of view, but the main disadvantage with linked list is that it is a linear data structure. Every node has information of next node only. So, the searching in the linked list is sequential, which is very slow and of O(n). For searching any element in the list, we have to visit all elements of the list that come before that element. If we have a linked list of 100000 elements and the element to be searched is not present or is present at the end of the list, then we have to visit all the 100000 elements. Now, we will study a non-linear data structure, in which data is organized in a hierarchical manner. A tree structure represents a hierarchical relationship among its elements. It is very useful for information retrieval and searching in it is fast. Before going to the definition of trees, let us become familiar with the common terms used.

6.1 Terminology

We will use the tree given below in figure 6.1 to describe the terms associated with trees.

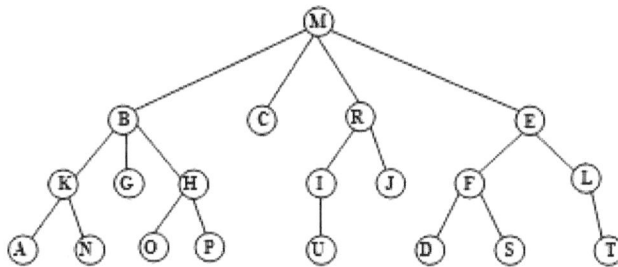

Figure 6.1 Tree

The terms are as follows:

Node: Each element of the tree is called a node. In the figure, each node is represented by a circle.

Edges: The lines connecting the nodes are called edges or branches.

Parent Node: The immediate predecessor of a node is called the parent node or the father node. For example, node M is the parent of nodes B, C, R, E and node I is the parent of node U. The grandparent is the parent of parent. For example, node E is the grandparent of node D, and node M is grandparent of node H.

Child Node: - All the immediate successors of a node are its child nodes. For example, node C is the child of node M, node D is the child of node F, and node N is the child of node K. The grandchild is the child of child node, for example, node U is grandchild of node R, node L is a grandchild of node M.

Root Node: This is a specially designated node that does not have any parent. In the example tree, node M is the root node.

Leaf node: A node that does not have any child is called a leaf node or a terminal node. All other nodes are called non-leaf nodes or non-terminal nodes. The nodes A, N, G, O, P, C, U, J, D, S, T are leaf nodes.

Level: Level of any node is defined as the distance of that node from the root. Root node is at a distance 0 from itself, so it is at level 0. The level number of any other node is 1 more than the level number of its parent node. Node M is at level 0, nodes B, C, R, E are at level 1, nodes K, G, H, I, J, F, L are at level 2, and nodes A, N, O, P, U, D, S, T are at level 3.

Height: The total number of levels in a tree is the height of the tree. So height is equal to one more than the largest level number of tree. It is also sometimes known as the depth of the tree. The largest level number in the example tree is 3, and so its height is 3+1 = 4.
(Some texts define the height of the tree equal to the largest level, and some take root at level 1. In this book, we will use the level and height as defined here.)

Siblings: Two or more nodes which have same parent are called siblings or brothers. B, C, R, E are siblings since their parent is M. All siblings are at the same level, but it is not necessary that nodes at the same level are siblings. For example, K and I are at the same level but they are not siblings, as their parents are different.

Path: The path of a node is defined as the sequence of nodes N_1, N_2, ... N_m, such that each node N_i is the parent of N_{i+1} for $1 < i < m$. In a tree, there is only one path between two nodes. The path length is defined as the number of edges on the path (m-1).

Ancestor and Descendent: Any node N_a is said to be the ancestor of node N_m, if node N_a lies in the unique path from root node to the node N_m. For example, node E is an ancestor of node S. If node N_a is ancestor of node N_m, then node N_m is said to be the descendent of node N_a.

Subtree: A tree may be divided into subtrees, which can be further divided into subtrees. The first node of the subtree is called the root of the subtree. For example, the tree in figure 6.1 may be divided into 4 subtrees: subtree BKGHANOP rooted at B, subtree C rooted at C, subtree RIJU rooted at R, and subtree EFLDST rooted at E. The subtree BKGHANOP can be further divided into three subtrees: subtree KAN rooted at K, subtree G rooted at G, and subtree HOP rooted at H. We can see that a subtree rooted at any node X consists of all the descendents of X. The root of the subtree is used to name the subtree, and so, instead of saying subtree BKGHANOP, we generally say subtree B.

Degree: The number of subtrees or children of a node is called its degree. For example, the degree of node M is 4, B is 3, F is 2, I is 1, and S is 0. The degree of a tree is the maximum degree of the nodes of the tree. The degree of the example tree is 4.

Forest: A forest is a set of n disjoint trees, where n ≥ 0. If the root of a tree is removed, we get a forest consisting of its subtrees. If in the example tree, we remove the root M, then we get a forest with four trees.

6.2 Definition of Tree

A tree can be defined recursively as follows.

A tree is a finite set of nodes such that:
(i) There is a distinguished node called root.
(ii) The remaining nodes are partitioned into n ≥ 0 disjoint sets T_1, T_2, ..., T_n, where each of these sets is a tree. The sets T_1, T_2, ..., T_n are the subtrees of the root.

6.3 Binary Tree

In a binary tree, no node can have more than two children, i.e., a node can have 0, 1 or 2 children. Each child is designated as either the left child or the right child. The terminology given for a general tree applies to binary trees also. Like tree, a binary tree can be defined recursively as follows.

A binary tree is a finite set of nodes that are:

(i) Either empty, or

(ii) Consists of a distinguished node called root, and the remaining nodes are partitioned into two disjoint sets T_1 and T_2, and both of them are binary trees. T_1 is called the left subtree and T_2 is called the right subtree.

The following five trees are examples of binary trees:

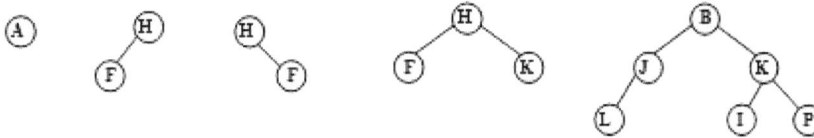

Figure 6.2 Binary tree examples

The first binary tree has only one node A, which is the root node and it has empty left and right subtrees. The second and third binary trees have 2 nodes each, but they are different because in the second binary tree, the root has a left child, while in the third tree, the root has a right child.

Two binary trees are called similar if they have a similar structure. If the structure, as well as the contents of the corresponding nodes is same, then the binary trees are said to be copies.

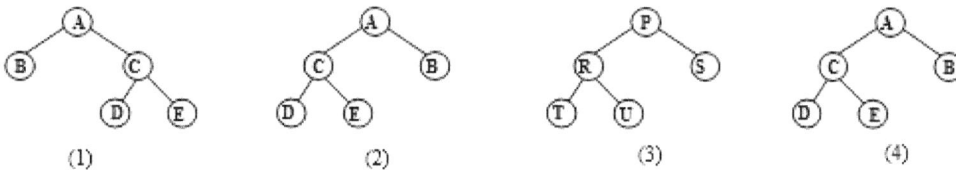

Figure 6.3 Binary trees

In figure 6.3, the trees (2), (3), and (4) are similar, as they have the same shape, while trees (2) and (4) are copies, as they have the same shape and data. Tree (1) has a different shape, and so it is not similar to the other trees.

In binary trees, we define the left and right descendent. Any node N_i is the left descendent of node N_j, if N_i belongs to the left subtree of N_j. Similarly, any node N_i is the right descendent of node N_j, if N_i belongs to the right subtree of N_j.

Now let us look at some properties of binary trees.

Property 1: The maximum number of nodes on any level i is 2^i where $i \geq 0$

Proof: This property can be proved by induction on i. The root node is the only node on level 0. So, the maximum number of nodes on level i=0 is 1, which is equal to 2^0. So, the property is true for i=0. Suppose the property is true for any level k, where k≥0, i.e., at level k, there are at most 2^k nodes. Each node in the binary tree can have at most 2 children, and so the maximum number of nodes on level k+1, will be twice the maximum number of nodes on level k, i.e., level k can have maximum $2^k \times 2 = 2^{k+1}$ nodes. So, if this property is true for any k, then it is also true for k+1. Hence proved.

Property 2: The maximum number of nodes possible in a binary tree of height h, is $2^h - 1$.

Proof: If we sum up the maximum number of nodes possible on each level, then we can get the maximum number of nodes possible in the binary tree. The first level is 0 and the last level is h-1 (from the definition of height), and at any level i the maximum number of nodes is 2^i. So, the total number of nodes possible in a binary tree of height h is given by:

$$n = \sum_{i=0}^{h-1} 2^i$$

$$= 1 + 2^1 + 2^2 + 2^3 + \dots\dots 2^{h-1} \text{ (geometric progression series)}$$

$$= \frac{2^{(h-1)+1} - 1}{2-1}$$

$$= 2^h - 1$$

Property 3: The minimum number of nodes possible in a binary tree of height h is equal to h.

Proof: A tree will have the minimum number of nodes if each level has minimum nodes. The minimum number of nodes possible on any level is 1, and there are total h levels (level 0 to level h-1). If we sum up the minimum number of nodes possible on each level, then we can get the minimum number of nodes possible in the binary tree. So, the minimum number of nodes possible in a binary tree of height h is equal to h.

The trees which have a minimum number of nodes, are called skew trees. These trees have h nodes and each tree has only one path. Some skew trees are shown as follows:

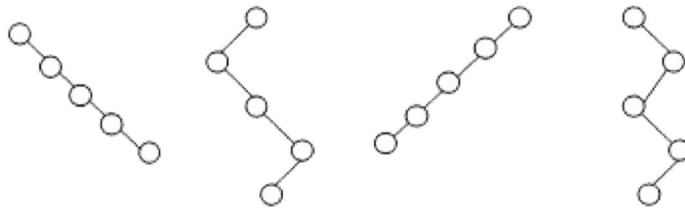

Figure 6.4 Skew trees

Property 4: If a binary tree contains n nodes, then its maximum height possible is n and the minimum height possible is $\lceil \log_2(n+1) \rceil$.

Proof: There should be at least one element on each level, so that the height cannot be more than n. A binary tree of height h can have a maximum of $2^h - 1$ nodes (from property 2). So, the number of nodes will be less than or equal to this maximum value.

$n \leq 2^h - 1$
$2^h \geq n+1$
$h \geq \log_2(n+1)$ (Taking log of both sides)
$h \geq \lceil \log_2(n+1) \rceil$ (h is an integer)

So, the minimum height possible is $\lceil \log_2(n+1) \rceil$.

Property 5: In a non-empty binary tree, if n is the total number of nodes and e is the total number of edges, then e = n-1

Proof: Every node in a binary tree has exactly one parent with the exception of root node. So, if n is the total number of nodes, then n-1 nodes have exactly one parent. There is only one edge between any child and its parent. So, the total number of edges is n-1.

Another way of proving this property is by induction on n. If there is only one node, then the number of edges is 0, i.e., the property is true for n=0, and the induction base is proved. Suppose the property is true for a tree T, whose number of nodes is k and number of edges is ed.

$k = ed+1$ ....(i)

Now, we insert one node in tree T and obtain tree T′, this will increase one edge also. Now, k′ and ed′ are the number of nodes and edges in tree T′.

$k' = k+1$

$ed' = ed+1$

So we can write:

$k = k'-1$

$ed = ed'-1$

Putting these values in equation (i) we get,

$k' = ed'+1$

So, we have proved that if the property is true for a tree T with k nodes, then it is also true for tree T′ with k+1 nodes. Hence, the property is proved.

Property 6: For any non-empty binary tree, if n_0 is the number of nodes with no child and n_2 is the number of nodes with 2 children, then $n_0 = n_2 + 1$.

Proof: Suppose n_1 is the number of nodes with 1 child. In a binary tree, any node can have 0, 1 or 2 children. So, the total number of nodes n in a binary tree is given by:

$n = n_0 + n_1 + n_2$ ....(i)

If the total number of edges is e, then from property 5, we know that:

$e = n-1$ ....(ii)

Two edges emerge from the nodes which have two children; one edge emerges from the node that has one child, and no edge emerges from the node that has no child. So, the total number of edges e can be calculated as:

$e = 0 \times n_0 + 1 \times n_1 + 2 \times n_2$

$e = n_1 + 2n_2$

Now, substitute the value of e from equation (ii):

$n - 1 = n_1 + 2n_2$

Now, substitute the value of n from equation (i):

$n_0 + n_1 + n_2 - 1 = n_1 + 2n_2$

$n_0 = n_2 + 1$

Hence, proved.

6.4 Strictly Binary Tree

A binary tree is a strictly binary tree if each node in the tree is either a leaf node or has exactly two children, i.e., there is no node with one child.

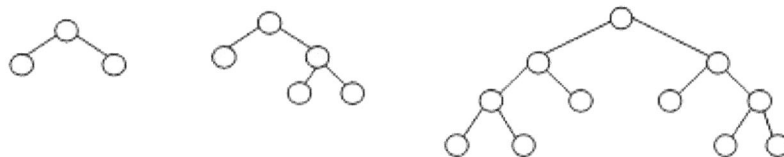

Figure 6.5 Strictly binary trees

The trees shown above are strictly binary trees, because each node has either 0 or 2 children.

Property 7: A strictly binary tree with n non-leaf nodes has n+1 leaf nodes.

Proof: We can prove this property by induction on the number of non-leaf nodes. If a binary tree consists only of the root node, then it has no non-leaf node and one leaf node, so the property is true for n=0.

We will take a strictly binary tree with k non-leaf nodes(k>0) and assume that this property is true for its left and right subtrees. Suppose the left subtree of this tree contains m non-leaf nodes. So, the right subtree will contain k-1-m non-leaf nodes. Since the property is true for both these subtrees, the left subtree will have m+1 leaf nodes, and the right subtree will have k-1-m+1 leaf nodes. So, the total leaf nodes will be m+1+k-m, i.e., k+1 nodes. Hence, the property is true for the whole tree with k non-leaf nodes.

Property 8: A strictly binary tree with n leaf nodes always has 2n-1 nodes.

Proof: From property 7, we know that if a strictly binary tree has n leaf nodes, then it has n-1 non-leaf nodes. The total number of nodes is the sum of leaf nodes and non-leaf nodes, i.e., n + n-1 = 2n-1 nodes.

6.5 Extended Binary Tree

If in a binary tree, each empty subtree (NULL link) is replaced by a special node, then the resulting tree is an extended binary tree or 2-tree.

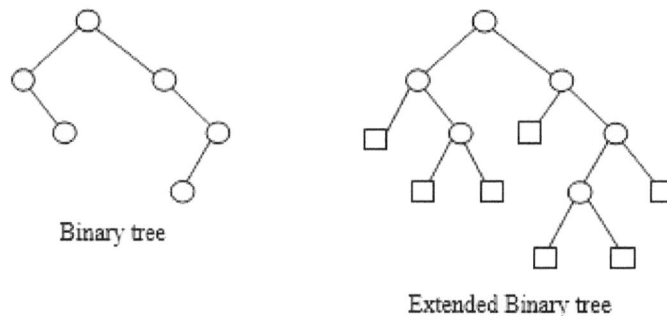

Figure 6.6 Binary tree and extended binary tree

So, we can convert a binary tree to an extended binary tree by adding special nodes to leaf nodes, and nodes that have only one child. The special nodes added to the tree are called external nodes, and the original nodes of the tree are internal nodes. Figure 6.6 shows a binary tree and the corresponding extended binary tree.

In the figure, external nodes are shown by squares and internal nodes by circles. We can see that all the external nodes are leaf nodes, while the internal nodes are non-leaf nodes.

The extended binary tree is a strictly binary tree, i.e., each node has either 0 or 2 children.

The path length for any node is the number of edges traversed from that node to the root node. This path length is equal to the level number of that node. Path length of a tree is the sum of path lengths of all the nodes of the tree.

The internal path length of a binary tree is the sum of path lengths of all internal nodes, which is equal to the sum of levels of all internal nodes. The internal path length of the tree given in figure 6.6 is:

$I = 0 + 1 + 1 + 2 + 2 + 3 = 9$

External path length of a binary tree is the sum of path lengths of all external nodes, which is equal to the sum of levels of all external nodes. The external path length of the tree given in figure 6.6 is:

$E = 2 + 2 + 3 + 3 + 3 + 4 + 4 = 21$

The internal path length and external path length will be maximum, when the tree is skewed (as in figure 6.4) and minimum when the tree is a complete binary tree (section 6.7). The following property shows the relation between internal and external path lengths.

Property 9: In an extended binary tree, if E is the external path length, I is the internal path length and n is the number of internal nodes, then E=I+2n.

Proof: This property can be proved by induction on the number of internal nodes. If the tree contains only the root, then $E = I = n = 0$, and the theorem is correct for n=0. If n=1, then there is only one internal node which is the root node. The root node will have two children, which are external nodes. So the internal path length is 0 and external path length is 2, i.e., E=2, I=0 and n=1. Hence, the property is true for n=1 also.

Suppose we have a binary tree T that has k internal nodes. Let E and I be external and internal path lengths of this tree. Let A be an internal node in this tree, such that both children of A are external nodes. Let p be the level of node A, i.e., there are p edges from the root to node A. We delete both children of node A from the tree. Node A is not an internal node now, and so the number of internal nodes is k-1. Suppose E′ and I′ are the external and internal path lengths of this resulting tree T′.

Two external nodes are deleted, which are at level (p+1), and so, the external path length decreases by 2(p+1) and node A becomes an external node, so the external path length increases by p.

$E′ = E - 2(p+1) + p$ ....(1)

Node A is not an internal node now, so the internal path length decreases by p.

$I′ = I - p$ ....(2)

Induction hypothesis : We assume that the property is true for the tree T′ that we obtain after deleting the two children of A.

$E′ = I′ + 2(k-1)$

Substituting the values of E′ and I′ from (1) and (2):

$E - 2(p+1) + p = I - p + 2(k-1)$

On simplifying this equation we get:

$E = I + 2k$

So we have proved that if the property is true for tree T′ with k-1 internal nodes, then it is also true for tree T with k internal nodes.

6.6 Full Binary Tree

A binary tree is a full binary tree if all the levels have the maximum number of nodes, i.e., if the height of the tree is h, then it will have $2^h - 1$ nodes (see property 2). The following three trees are full binary trees of heights 2, 3, and 4 and contain 3, 7, and 15 nodes respectively.

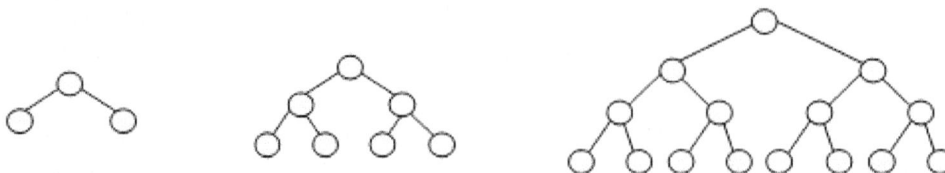

Figure 6.7 Full binary trees

The total number of nodes n in a full binary tree is $2^h - 1$, and so its height h = $\log_2(n+1)$. Suppose all nodes in a full binary tree are numbered from 1 to n, starting from the node on level 0, then nodes on level 1 and so on. Nodes on the same level are numbered from left to right. Root node is numbered 1.

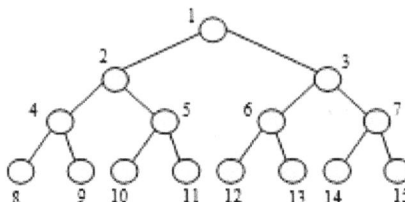

Figure 6.8 Full binary tree nodes numbered

From the figure, we can see that if the number of any node is k, then the number of its left child is 2k, the number of its right child is 2k+1, and the number of its parent is floor(k/2).

6.7 Complete Binary Tree

A complete binary tree is a binary tree where all the levels have the maximum number of nodes except possibly the last level. In the last level, the number of nodes may range from 1 to 2^{h-1}, and all these nodes are towards the left. The following three trees are complete binary trees.

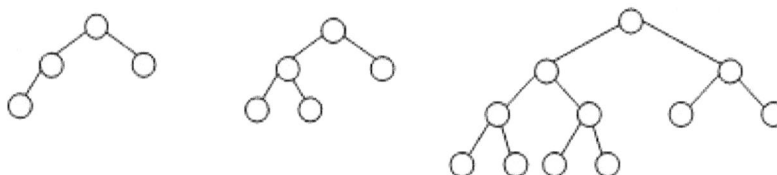

Figure 6.9 Complete binary trees

We can see that all the leaf nodes in a complete binary tree are on two adjacent levels (last level and second last level), and in the last level, all the leaf nodes appear towards the left.

The height of a complete binary tree with n nodes is $\lceil \log_2(n+1) \rceil$. If a complete binary tree contains 1000000 nodes, then its height will be only 20.

A full binary tree can be considered a special case of a complete binary tree. The numbering of nodes and formula for finding out children and parent of a node in a complete binary tree is the same as in full binary tree. In a complete binary tree, the last level may not have full nodes, and so, some nodes at the second last level may not have children. A node numbered k does not have a left child, if 2k > n, and it does not have a right child if 2k + 1 > n.

The following property for complete binary trees summarizes these points.

If a node in a complete binary tree is assigned a number k, where $1 \leq k \leq n$, then:

(i) If k = 1, then this node is the root node. If k > 1, then its parent's number is floor(k/2).

(ii) If 2k > n, then this node has no left child; otherwise, the number of left child is 2k.

(iii) If 2k+1 > n, then this node has no right child; otherwise, the number of right child is 2k+1.

Property 10: If the height of a complete binary tree is h, $h \geq 1$, then the minimum number of nodes possible is 2^{h-1} and the maximum number of nodes possible is $2^h - 1$.

Proof: The number of nodes will be maximum, when the last level also contains maximum nodes, i.e., all levels are full, and so the total nodes will be $2^h - 1$ from property 2.

The number of nodes will be minimum when the last level has only one node. In this case, the total nodes will be:

total nodes in a full binary tree of height (h – 1) + one node

$= (2^{h-1} - 1) + 1 = 2^{h-1}$

(In some texts, strictly binary trees, full binary trees, and complete binary trees are defined in a different way. In this book, we will use these terms as defined here.)

6.8 Representation of Binary Trees in Memory

Like lists, binary trees can also be implemented in two ways: one is the array representation, and the other is the linked representation.

6.8.1 Array Representation of Binary Trees

This is also called sequential representation or linear representation or contiguous representation or formula based representation of binary trees. Here, we use a one-dimensional array to maintain the nodes of the binary tree. To decide the location of nodes inside the array, we utilize the numbering scheme described in full and complete binary trees.

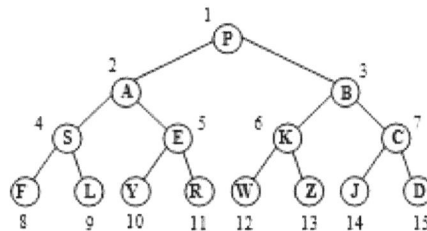

Figure 6.10 Numbering for full binary tree

We will store the nodes in the array named `tree` from index 1 onwards, and so, if a node is numbered k, then the data of this node is stored in `tree[k]`. The root node is stored in `tree[1]` and its left and right children are in `tree[2]` and `tree[3]`, respectively, and so on. So the full binary tree in figure 6.10 can be stored in array as:

tree		P	A	B	S	E	K	C	F	L	Y	R	W	Z	J	D
	0	1	2	3	4	5	6	7	8	9	10	11	12	13	14	15

Figure 6.11 Full binary tree array representation

We can easily extend this technique for other binary trees also. For this, we consider any binary tree as a complete binary tree with some missing nodes. The nodes that are missing are also numbered, and the array locations corresponding to them are left empty. For example:

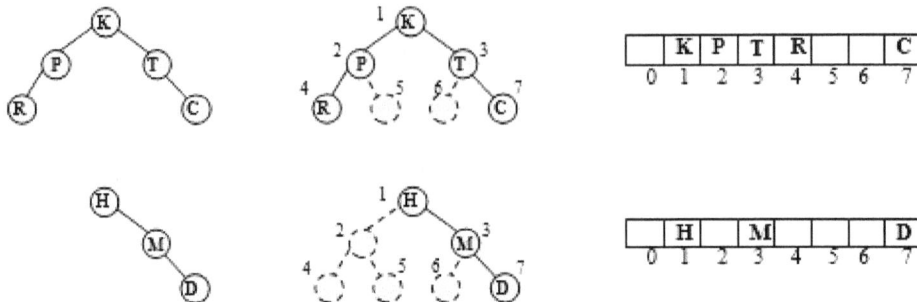

Figure 6.12 Binary trees array representation

If a node is at index k in the array, then its left child will be at index 2k, and the right child will be at index 2k+1. Its parent will be at index floor(k/2). We can see that lots of locations in the array are wasted if there are many missing nodes.

We have left location 0 empty; it may be used for some other purpose. If we want to store nodes in the array starting from index 0, then we can number the nodes from 0 to n-1. Root node is numbered 0 and stored at index 0 in the array. Now, if a node is at index k in the array, then its left child will be at index 2k+1 and the right child will be at index 2k+2. Its parent will be at index floor((k-1)/2).

The sequential representation is efficient from the execution point of view because we can calculate the index of the parent and the index of the left and right children from the index of the node. There is no need to have explicit pointers pointing to other nodes; the relationships are implicit.

We know that the maximum number of nodes possible in a binary tree of height h is $2^h - 1$. So the size of array needed is equal to $2^h - 1$. This size will be minimum if h is minimum and maximum if h is maximum. The height is minimum for complete binary trees, which is $\lceil \log_2(n+1) \rceil$. So in this case, the size of array needed is:

$2^{\lceil \log_2(n+1) \rceil} - 1$.

The height is maximum (equal to n) for skewed binary trees, and so in this case, the size of the array needed $2^n - 1$.

We have seen that a lot of space is wasted if there are many missing nodes. The maximum wastage occurs in the case of a right-skewed binary tree of height h; it would require an array of size 2^n-1, out of which, only n positions will be occupied. For example, a right skewed tree having 20 nodes (height = 20) would require an array of size 1048575, but only 20 of these locations would be used. A complete binary tree of 20 nodes (height =5) would at most require an array of size 31. So this method is not very efficient in terms of space for trees, other than complete and full binary trees.

Sequential representation is a static representation and the size of tree is restricted because of the limitation of array size. The size of array has to be known in advance and if the array size is taken too small, then overflow may occur and if array size is too large, then space may be wasted.

Insertion and deletion of nodes require a lot of movement of nodes in the array, which consumes a lot of time, so it is suitable only for data that does not change frequently.

6.8.2 Linked Representation of Binary Trees

The linked representation overcomes the problems encountered in array representation. In this representation, explicit pointers are used to link the nodes of the tree. In linked representation, we take three members in a node of the binary tree - a pointer that stores the address of the left child, info (this can be a whole record), and a pointer to store the address of the right child.

We will have a class Node for a node of the binary tree:

```
class Node
{
        public:
                char info;
                Node *lchild;
                Node *rchild;
                Node(char data)
                {
                        info = data;
                        lchild = NULL;
                        rchild = NULL;
                }
};//End of class Node
```

Here, the data members lchild and rchild are pointers of type Node, which point to the left and right children of the node. The data member info is the information field of the node. If the node has no left child, then lchild should be NULL, and if the node has no right child, then the rchild should be NULL. Leaf nodes have no children, and so, both lchild and rchild pointers will be NULL for them. Let us take a tree and see how it can be represented through linked representation.

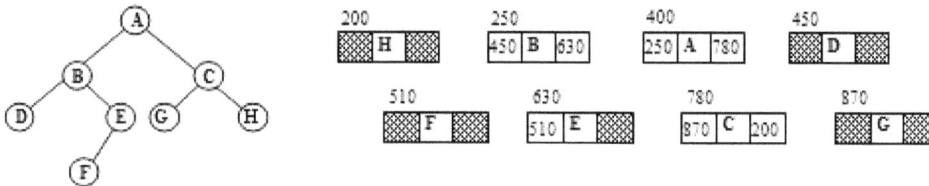

Figure 6.13 Binary tree and its nodes in memory

The nodes and their memory addresses are shown in the preceeding figure. For example, node A is located at address 400 and its left and right child pointers contain the addresses 250 and 780, which are the addresses of its left child B and right child C. For leaf nodes, the left and right pointers are NULL. We can see that the nodes of the tree are scattered here and there in memory, but still they are connected to each other through the lchild and rchild pointers, which also maintain the hierarchical order of the tree. The logical view of the linked representation of the binary tree in figure 6.13 can be shown as follows:

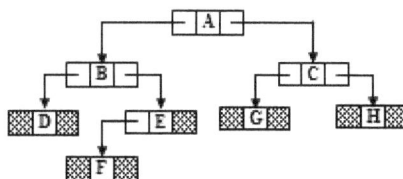

Figure 6.14 Binary tree linked representation

To access the nodes of the tree, we will maintain a data member pointer in the class of binary tree, that will point to the root node of the tree.

```
Node *root;
```

If the tree is empty, then `root` will be NULL.

If we have a pointer `ptr` pointing to a node N, then `ptr->lchild` will point to the left child of N and `ptr->rchild` will point to the right child of N. We can get a pointer to the left child of the root node by `root->lchild` and to the right child of the root node by `root->rchild`.

We can move down the tree because we have pointers to children, but we cannot find the parent of a given node. If we want this, we have to include another member in the class `Node`, which is a pointer to the parent node. However, most of the operations can be performed without the parent node information.

The linked representation uses dynamic memory allocation and so there is no restriction on the size of the tree. Insertions and deletions are also not very time-consuming compared to sequential representation. The drawback of linked representation is that it requires more memory because of the pointers. Many of the pointers would be NULL but still they are required. Later, we will see how we can use these null pointers also to store some useful information. The next property shows the number of null pointers in a binary tree.

Property 11: If there are n nodes in a binary tree, then the total number of null links will be p = n + 1.

Proof: From property 5 we know that a tree with n nodes has n-1 edges. The number of nodes is n, and so, there will be 2n links, and from these 2n links, only n-1 links will have addresses of the child nodes. So, the total null links will be 2n-(n-1) = n+1.

We can prove this property by induction also. If n=1, only the root node is there in the tree, and it has two null links. So, the property is true for n=1. If there are two nodes, then one will be the root node and the other will be the left or right child of root node. So, there will be one null link of root node and two null links of child node, i.e., total 3 null links for 2 nodes, and hence, the property is true for n=2, as well.

Suppose the property is true for a tree T with k nodes and p null links.

p = k + 1 ....(i)

We insert one more node in the tree, and this will lead to the removal of one null link, but two new null links will appear. Hence, the total null links of the tree T will increase by 1. So, the nodes and null links of new tree T′ are k′ and p′, where k′ = k + 1,   p′ = p + 1

We can write this as:

k = k′ - 1

p = p′ - 1

Putting these values in equation (i), we get:

p′ = k′ + 1

So we have proved that if the property is true for a tree T with k nodes, then it is also true for tree T′ with k+1 nodes. Hence, the property is proved.

Let us see the implementation of binary tree and its operations.

We will have the class `BinaryTree` for the binary tree:

```
class BinaryTree
{
      private:
              Node *root;
              void preorder(Node *ptr);
              void inorder(Node *ptr);
              void postorder(Node *ptr);
```

```
              int height(Node *ptr);
              void display(Node *ptr, int level);
              Node* construct(char *in, char *pre, int num);
              Node* construct1(char *in, char *post, int num);
       public:
              BinaryTree();
              ~BinaryTree(){};
              bool isEmpty();
              void createTree();
              void preorder();
              void inorder();
              void postorder();
              void levelOrder();
              int height();
              void nrecPreorder();
              void nrecInorder();
              void nrecPostorder();
              void construct(char *in, char *pre);
              void construct1(char *in, char *post);
              void display();
};//End of class BinaryTree
```

Now, we will see the explanation of all the binary tree operations and their implementations. Here is the member function `createTree()` to create the binary tree:

```
void BinaryTree::createTree()
{
       root = new Node('P');
       root->lchild = new Node('Q');
       root->rchild = new Node('R');
       root->lchild->lchild = new Node('A');
       root->lchild->rchild = new Node('B');
       root->rchild->lchild = new Node('X');
}//End of createTree()
```

The constructor of `BinaryTree` is:

```
BinaryTree::BinaryTree()
{
       root = NULL;
}//End of BinaryTree()
```

`root` is initialized with `NULL`.

6.9 Traversal in Binary Tree

Traversing a binary tree means visiting each node of the tree exactly once. Traversal of a tree gives a linear order of the nodes, i.e., all nodes can be put in one line. We have done traversal of linked list and it was very simple there because a linked list is linear, and to visit each node, we just move from start to end. In a tree, nodes are arranged in a hierarchical order and so there can be many ways in which these nodes can be visited.

If we think of a binary tree recursively, then there are three main tasks for traversing it – visiting the root node, traversing its left subtree and traversing its right subtree. These three tasks can be performed in different orders, so we have 3! = 6 ways in which a tree can be traversed. If we name these tasks as N, L, and, R, where visiting a node is N, traversing left subtree is L, and the traversing right subtree is R, then the 6 ways of traversal are NRL, NLR, LNR, LRN, RNL, and, RLN. If we follow the convention that the left subtree is traversed before the right subtree, then we are left with only three traversals, which are, NLR, LNR, and LRN. These three are standard traversals and are given special names: preorder(NLR), inorder(LNR), and postorder(LRN). The prefix *pre* in preorder means visit the root first, prefix *in* in inorder means visit the root in between the subtrees, and the prefix *post* in postorder means visit the root at the end. These traversals can be defined recursively as:

Preorder Traversal (NLR)
1. Visit the root(N).
2. Traverse the left subtree of root in preorder(L).
3. Traverse the right subtree of root in preorder(R).

Inorder Traversal (LNR)
1. Traverse the left subtree of root in inorder(L).
2. Visit the root(N).
3. Traverse the right subtree of root in inorder(R).

Postorder Traversal (LRN)
1. Traverse the left subtree of root in postorder(L).
2. Traverse the right subtree of root in postorder(R).
3. Visit the root(N).

Let us take a binary tree and apply each traversal. The numbers written outside the nodes represent the sequence in which the nodes are visited in a particular traversal.

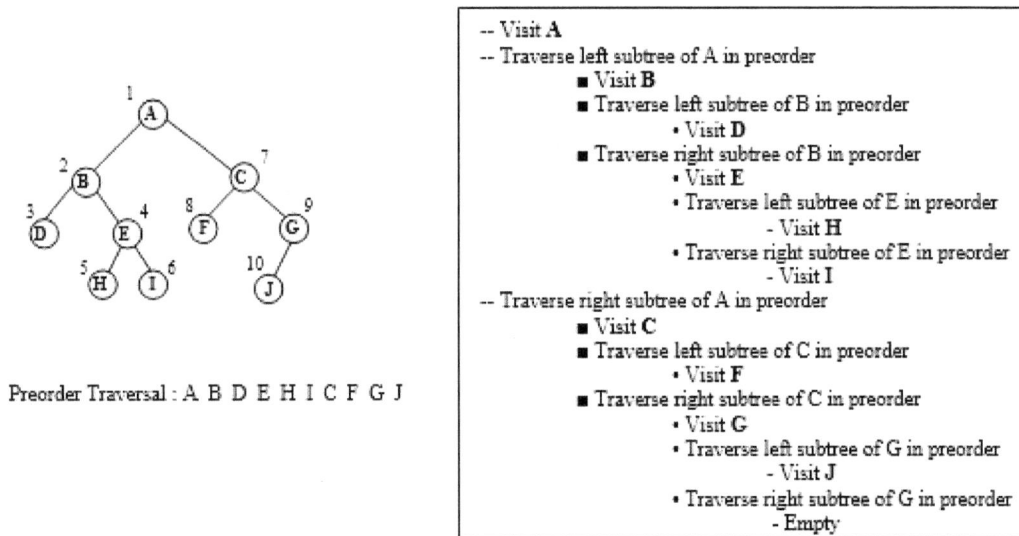

Figure 6.15 Preorder traversal

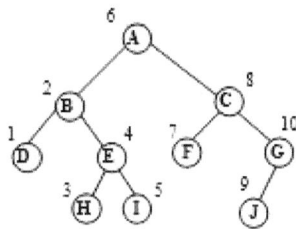

Inorder Traversal : D B H E I A F C J G

```
-- Traverse left subtree of A in inorder
        ■ Traverse left subtree of B in inorder
                    Visit D
        ■ Visit B
        ■ Traverse right subtree of B in inorder
                    • Traverse left subtree of E in inorder
                                - Visit H
                    • Visit E
                    • Traverse right subtree of E in inorder
                                - Visit I
-- Visit A
-- Traverse right subtree of A in inorder
        ■ Traverse left subtree of C in inorder
                    • Visit F
        ■ Visit C
        ■ Traverse right subtree of C in inorder
                    • Traverse left subtree of G in inorder
                                - Visit J
                    • Visit G
                    • Traverse right subtree of G in inorder
                                - Empty
```

Figure 6.16 Inorder traversal

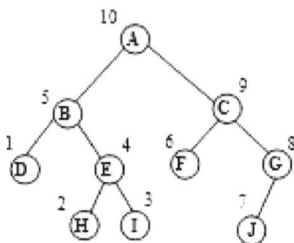

Postorder Traversal : D H I E B F J G C A

```
-- Traverse left subtree of A in postorder
        ■ Traverse left subtree of B in postorder
                    • Visit D
        ■ Traverse right subtree of B in postorder
                    • Traverse left subtree of E in postorder
                                - Visit H
                    • Traverse right subtree of E in postorder
                                - Visit I
                    • Visit E
        ■ Visit B
-- Traverse right subtree of A in postorder
        ■ Traverse left subtree of C in postorder
                    • Visit F
        ■ Traverse right subtree of C in postorder
                    • Traverse left subtree of G in postorder
                                - Visit J
                    • Traverse right subtree of G in postorder
                                - Empty
                    • Visit G
        ■ Visit C
-- Visit A
```

Figure 6.17 Postorder traversal

Let us take another example of a binary tree and apply each traversal:

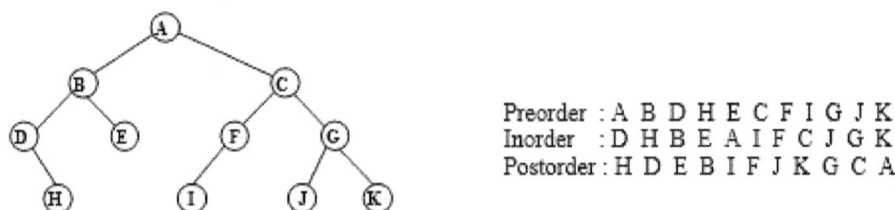

Preorder : A B D H E C F I G J K
Inorder : D H B E A I F C J G K
Postorder : H D E B I F J K G C A

Figure 6.18 Binary tree traversals

The three traversals have been defined recursively, and so they can be implemented using a stack. If we implement them recursively, then an implicit stack is used, and if we implement them non-recursively then we have to use an explicit stack. We will see both the implementations of all three traversals.

The binary tree already exists and is represented using the linked representation where the pointer `root` is a pointer to the root node of the tree. Each node of the tree has info value, and visiting a node would mean printing this value.

The recursive functions for the three traversals are given as follows. All these member functions are passed the address of the root.

```
void BinaryTree::preorder(Node *ptr)
{
        if(ptr == NULL)          //Base case
              return;
        cout << ptr->info << " ";
        preorder(ptr->lchild);
        preorder(ptr->rchild);
}//End of preorder()

void BinaryTree::inorder(Node *ptr)
{
        if(ptr == NULL)          //Base case
              return;
        inorder(ptr->lchild);
        cout << ptr->info << " ";
        inorder(ptr->rchild);
}//End of inorder()

void BinaryTree::postorder(Node *ptr)
{
        if(ptr == NULL)          //Base case
              return;
        postorder(ptr->lchild);
        postorder(ptr->rchild);
        cout << ptr->info << " ";
}//End of postorder()
```

These recursive functions will be called in these public member functions:

```
void BinaryTree::preorder()
{
        preorder(root);
        cout << "\n";
}//End of preorder()

void BinaryTree::inorder()
{
        inorder(root);
```

```
        cout << "\n";
}//End of inorder()
void BinaryTree::postorder()
{
        postorder(root);
        cout << "\n";
}//End of postorder()
```

6.9.1 Non Recursive Traversals for Binary Tree

If we want to write non-recursive functions for traversals, then we will have to use an explicit stack. The stack will store the addresses of the nodes. In the explanation when we say push or pop a node, we would actually mean push or pop the address of that node.

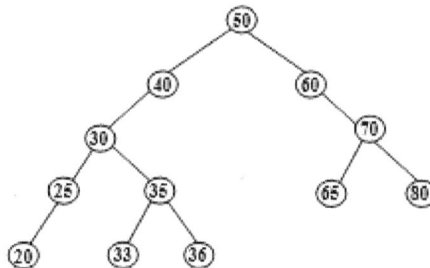

Figure 6.19 Binary tree

6.9.1.1 Preorder Traversal

The procedure for traversing a tree in preorder non recursively is:
1. Push the root node on the stack.
2. Pop a node from the stack.
3. Visit the popped node.
4. Push right child of visited node on stack.
5. Push left child of visited node on stack.
6. Repeat steps 2,3,4,5 till the stack is not empty.

If we apply this process to the tree given in figure 6.19, the steps would be:

- Push 50
- Pop 50 : Visit **50**
  Push right and left child of 50 : Push 60 , Push 40
- Pop 40 : Visit **40**
  40 has no right child so push its left child : Push 30
- Pop 30 : Visit **30**
  Push right and left child of 30 : Push 35 , Push 25
- Pop 25 : Visit **25**
  25 has no right child so push its left child : Push 20
- Pop 20 : Visit **20**
  20 has no children so nothing is pushed
- Pop 35 : Visit **35**
  Push right and left child of 35 : Push 36, Push 33
- Pop 33 : Visit **33**
  33 has no children so nothing is pushed

- Pop 36 : Visit **36**
  36 has no children so nothing is pushed
- Pop 60 : Visit **60**
  60 has no left child so push its right child : Push 70
- Pop 70 : Visit **70**
  Push right and left child of 70 : Push 80, Push 65
- Pop 65 : Visit **65**
  65 has no children so nothing is pushed
- Pop 80 : Visit **80**
  80 has no children so nothing is pushed
- Stack empty

Preorder traversal: 50 40 30 25 20 35 33 36 60 70 65 80

The member function for non-recursive preorder traversal is:

```
void BinaryTree::nrecPreorder()
{
        stack<Node *> st;
        Node *ptr = root;
        if(ptr != NULL)
        {
                st.push(ptr);
                while(!st.empty())
                {
                        ptr = st.top();
                        st.pop();
                        cout << ptr->info << " ";
                        if(ptr->rchild != NULL)
                                st.push(ptr->rchild);
                        if(ptr->lchild != NULL)
                                st.push(ptr->lchild);
                }
                cout << "\n";
        }
        else
        {
                cout << "Tree is empty\n";
        }
}//End of nrecPreorder()
```

6.9.1.2 Inorder Traversal

The procedure for traversing a tree in inorder non-recursively is:

1. Initially, `ptr` is assigned address of the root node.

2. Move along the leftmost path rooted at the node pointed by `ptr`, pushing all the nodes in the path on the stack. Stop when you reach the leftmost node, i.e., a node which has no left child; it is not pushed on the stack. Now, `ptr` points to this leftmost node.

3. If the node pointed by `ptr` has no right subtree, then visit it and pop another one from stack. Now, keep on popping and visiting the nodes till a node is popped, that has a right subtree. Now, `ptr` points to this node that has a right subtree. If the stack becomes empty, then the traversal is finished.

4. Visit the node pointed by `ptr`, and now `ptr` is assigned the address of its right child.
   Go to step 2.

Since we move along the leftmost path and push nodes, we know that whenever we pop a node, its left subtree traversal is finished. So, a node is visited just after popping it from the stack.

If we apply this process to the tree given in figure 6.19, the steps would be as follows:

(i) Move along the leftmost path rooted at 50.
- Push 50
- Push 40
- Push 30
- Push 25
- 20 is leftmost node, it has no right subtree : Visit **20** and pop
- 25 popped : it has no right subtree : Visit **25** and pop
- 30 popped : it has right subtree : Visit **30** and move to its right subtree

(ii) Move along the leftmost path rooted at 35
- Push 35
- 33 is leftmost node, it has no right subtree : Visit **33** and pop
- 35 popped : it has right subtree : Visit **35** and move to its right subtree

(iii) Move along the leftmost path rooted at 36
- 36 is leftmost node, it has no right subtree : Visit **36** and pop
- 40 popped: it has no right subtree: Visit **40** and pop
- 50 popped: it has right subtree: Visit **50** and move to its right subtree

(iv) Move along the leftmost path rooted at 60
- 60 is leftmost node, it has a right subtree : Visit **60** and move to its right subtree

(v) Move along the leftmost path rooted at 70
- Push 70
- 65 is leftmost node, it has no right subtree : Visit **65** and pop
- 70 popped : it has right subtree : Visit **70** and move to its right subtree

(vi) Move along the leftmost path rooted at 80
- 80 is leftmost node, it has no right subtree : Visit **80**, Stack empty

Inorder traversal : 20 25 30 33 35 36 40 50 60 65 70 80

The member function for non-recursive inorder traversal is:

```
void BinaryTree::nrecInorder()
{
        stack<Node *> st;
        Node *ptr = root;
        if(ptr != NULL)
        {
                while(true)
                {
                        while(ptr->lchild != NULL)
                        {
                                st.push(ptr);
                                ptr = ptr->lchild;
                        }
                        while(ptr->rchild == NULL)
                        {
                                cout << ptr->info << " ";
                                if(st.empty())
                                {
                                        cout << "\n";
                                        return;
                                }
                                ptr = st.top();
                                st.pop();
                        }
                        cout << ptr->info << " ";
                        ptr = ptr->rchild;
                }
```

```
        }
        else
        {
                cout << "Tree is empty\n";
        }
}//End of nrecInorder()
```

6.9.1.3 Postorder Traversal

In inorder traversal, we had to visit only the left subtree before visiting the node, but in postorder, we have to visit both the left and right subtrees, before visiting the node. We will make changes in the procedure of inorder, to make sure that the right subtree is also traversed before visiting the node.

In step 4 of inorder, we visited the node that has the right child, but in postorder, we will push it on the stack. So, nodes that have both left and right subtrees, are pushed on the stack twice; nodes that have only one subtree are pushed on the stack once and leaf nodes are never pushed. The procedure for traversing a tree in postorder non-recursively is:

1. Initially, `ptr` is assigned the address of the root node.

2. Move along the leftmost path rooted at node `ptr`, pushing all the nodes in the path on the stack. Stop when we reach the leftmost node, i.e., a node which has no left child; it is not pushed on the stack. Now, `ptr` points to this leftmost node.

3. If `ptr` has no right subtree or its right subtree has been traversed, then visit the node and pop another one from the stack. Now keep on popping and visiting the nodes till a node is popped, that has a right subtree, which has not been traversed. Now, `ptr` points to this node, that has an untraversed right subtree. If the stack becomes empty, then the traversal is finished.

4. Push the node pointed to by `ptr`, and now `ptr` is assigned the address of its right child.
   Go to step 2.

Since we move along the leftmost path and push nodes, we know that whenever we pop a node, its left subtree traversal is finished. In inorder, we could visit a node just after popping it from the stack, but here, we have to traverse the right subtree also. So, here the node is again pushed on stack, if it has untraversed right subtree.

If we apply this process to the tree given in figure 6.19, the steps would be as follows:

(i) Move along the leftmost path rooted at 50
 - Push 50
 - Push 40
 - Push 30
 - Push 25
 - 20 is leftmost node, it has no right subtree : Visit **20** and pop
 - 25 popped : it has no right subtree : Visit **25** and pop
 - 30 popped : it has right subtree which has not been traversed : Push 30 and move to its right subtree

(ii) Move along the leftmost path rooted at 35
 - Push 35
 - 33 is leftmost node, it has no right subtree : Visit **33** and pop
 - 35 popped : it has a right subtree which has not been traversed : Push 35 and move to its right subtree

(iii) Move along the leftmost path rooted at 36
 - 36 is leftmost node, it has no right subtree : Visit **36** and pop
 - 35 popped : it has right subtree which has been traversed : Visit **35** and pop
 - 30 popped : it has right subtree which has been traversed : Visit **30** and pop

- 40 popped : it has no right subtree : Visit **40** and pop
- 50 popped: it has right subtree which has not been traversed : Push 50 and move to its right subtree

(iv) Move along the leftmost path rooted at 60
- 60 is leftmost node, it has right subtree which has not been traversed : Push 60 and move to its right subtree

(v) Move along the leftmost path rooted at 70
- Push 70
- 65 is leftmost node, it has no right subtree : Visit **65** and pop
- 70 popped : it has right subtree which has not been traversed : Push 70 and move to its right subtree

(vi) Move along the leftmost path rooted at 80
- 80 is leftmost node, it has no right subtree : Visit **80** and pop
- 70 popped : it has right subtree which has been traversed : Visit **70** and pop
- 60 popped : it has right subtree which has been traversed : Visit **60** and pop
- 50 popped : it has right subtree which has been traversed : Visit **50**, stack empty

20 25 33 36 35 30 40 65 80 70 60 50

While writing the function for postorder, we will use a secondary pointer `visited`, to know whether the right subtree has been traversed or not.

The member function for non-recursive postorder traversal is:

```
void BinaryTree::nrecPostorder()
{
        stack<Node *> st;
        Node *ptr = root;
        Node *visited = root;
        if(ptr != NULL)
        {
                while(true)
                {
                        while(ptr->lchild != NULL)
                        {
                                st.push(ptr);
                                ptr = ptr->lchild;
                        }
                        while(ptr->rchild==NULL || ptr->rchild==visited)
                        {
                                cout << ptr->info << " ";
                                visited = ptr;
                                if(st.empty())
                                {
                                        cout << "\n";
                                        return;
                                }
                                ptr = st.top();
                                st.pop();
                        }
                        st.push(ptr);
                        ptr = ptr->rchild;
                }
        }
        else
        {
                cout << "Tree is empty\n";
        }
}//End of nrecPostorder()
```

If the right subtree of `ptr` has already been traversed, then the node visited recently would be the root of the right subtree of `ptr`. The pointer `visited` is used to store the address of the recently visited node.

6.9.2 Level Order Traversal

In level order traversal, the nodes are visited from top to bottom and from left to right. Initially, we visit the root node at level 0, then we visit all the nodes of level 1, and then all nodes of level 2, and so on, till the last level. The nodes of a particular level are visited from left to right. Let us take a tree and see its level order traversal.

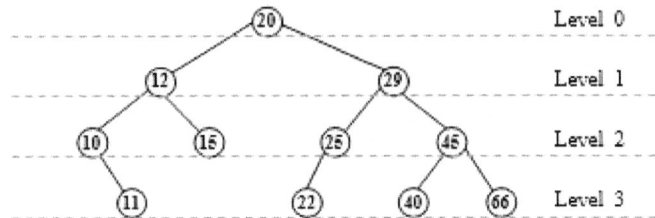

Figure 6.20 Level Order Traversal

The level order traversal of this tree is:

20 12 29 10 15 25 45 11 22 40 66

This traversal can be implemented using a queue that will store the addresses of the nodes. The procedure for level order traversal is:

1. Insert root node in the queue.
2. Delete a node from the front of queue and visit it.
3. Insert the left child of visited node in the queue at the end.
4. Insert the right child of the visited node in the queue at the end.
5. Repeat steps 2, 3, 4 till the queue is not empty.

If we apply the above procedure for the tree in figure 6.20, the steps would be as follows:

• Insert 20
• Delete 20 : Visit **20**
• Insert 12 and 29
• Delete 12 : Visit **12**
• Insert 10 and 15
• Delete 29 : Visit **29**
• Insert 25 and 45
• Delete 10 : Visit **10**
• Insert 11
• Delete 15 : Visit **15**
• Delete 25 : Visit **25**
• Insert 22
• Delete 45 : Visit **45**
• Insert 40 and 66
• Delete 11 : Visit **11**
• Delete 22 : Visit **22**
• Delete 40 : Visit **40**
• Delete 66 : Visit **66**

The member function for level order traversal is:

```
void BinaryTree::levelOrder()
{
        queue<Node *> qu;
        Node *ptr;
        qu.push(root);
        while(!qu.empty())
        {
                ptr = qu.front();
                qu.pop();
                cout << ptr->info << " ";
                if(ptr->lchild != NULL)
                        qu.push(ptr->lchild);
                if(ptr->rchild != NULL)
                        qu.push(ptr->rchild);
        }
        cout << "\n";
}//End of levelOrder()
```

6.9.3 Creation of Binary Tree from Inorder and Preorder Traversals

The inorder, preorder or postorder traversals of different binary trees may be same, and so, if we are given a single traversal, we cannot construct a unique binary tree. However, if we know the inorder and preorder traversals or inorder and postorder traversals then we can construct a unique binary tree. Note that inorder traversal is necessary for drawing the tree; we cannot draw a tree from only preorder and postorder traversals. Suppose we are given a preorder XY and postorder YX, then it is clear that X is the root, but we cannot find out whether Y is the left child or right child of X.

The procedure for constructing a binary tree from inorder and preorder traversals is:

(i) In preorder traversal, the first node is the root node, and so we get the root node by taking the first node of preorder. Now, all remaining nodes form the left and the right subtrees of the root. To divide them into left and right subtrees, we look at the inorder traversal.

(ii) In inorder traversal, root is in the middle, and nodes to the left of the root node are nodes of left subtree of node, and nodes to the right of the root node are nodes of right subtree of root node. Since we know the root node (first node of preorder), we can separate the nodes of left and right subtrees.

(iii) Now we can follow the same procedure for both left and right subtrees, till we get an empty subtree or a single node in subtree. Inorder and preorder for these subtrees can be obtained from the inorder and preorder of the whole tree.

Let us construct a binary tree from the given preorder and inorder traversals:

Preorder : A B D H E C F I G J K
Inorder : D H B E A I F C J G K

In preorder traversal, the first node is the root node. Hence, A is the root of the binary tree. From inorder, we see that nodes to the left of root node A are nodes D, H, B, E, and so, these nodes form the left subtree of A. Similarly, nodes I, F, C, J, G, and, K, form the right subtree of A, since they are to the right of A.

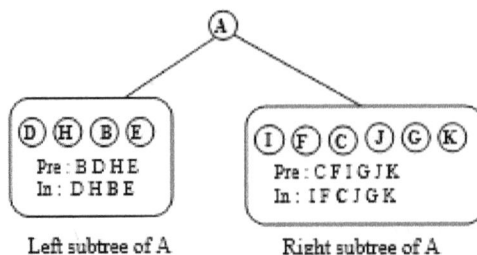

Figure 6.21 Left and right subtree of root A

Left subtree of A:
  From preorder, we get node B as root
  From inorder, we get nodes D, H in left subtree of B, and node E in right subtree of B.

Right subtree of A:
  From preorder, we get C as the root
  From inorder we get nodes I, F in left subtree of C, and nodes J, G, K in right subtree of C.

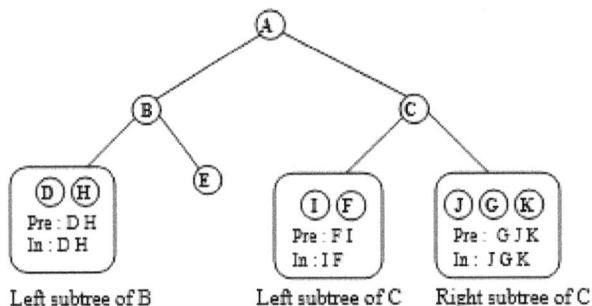

Figure 6.22 Identified left and right subtrees

Left subtree of B:
  From preorder, we get D as the root
  From inorder we get empty left subtree of D, and node H in right subtree of D.

Left subtree of C:
  From preorder, we get F as the root
  From inorder, we get node I in left subtree of F, and empty right subtree of F.

Right subtree of C :
  From preorder, we get G as the root
  From inorder, we get node J in left subtree of G, and node K in right subtree of G.

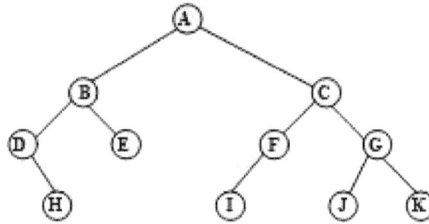

Figure 6.23 Binary tree from inoder and preorder traversal

6.9.4 Creation of Binary Tree from Inorder and Postorder Traversals

We can create a binary tree from postorder and inorder traversals using a similar procedure as described in the previous section. The only difference is that here, we get the root node by taking the last node of the postorder traversal. Let us construct a binary tree from the given postorder and inorder traversals.

Postorder : H I D J E B K F G C A
Inorder   : H D I B E J A K F C G

Node A is the last node in postorder traversal, and so it will be the root of the tree. From inorder, we see that nodes to the left of the root node A are nodes H, D, I, B, E, J. So, these nodes form the left subtree of A. Similarly, nodes K, F, C, G form the right subtree of A, since they are to the right of A.

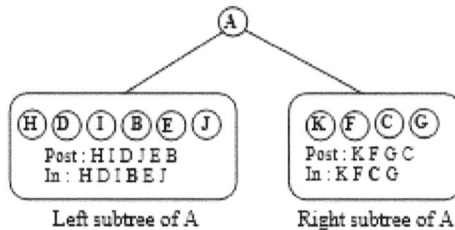

Figure 6.24 Left and right subtree of root A

Left subtree of A:
   From postorder, we get node B as root.
   From inorder, we get nodes H, D, I in the left subtree of B, and nodes E, J in the right subtree of B.

Right subtree of A :
   From postorder, we get node C as root.
   From inorder, we get nodes K, F in the left subtree of C, and node G in right subtree of C.

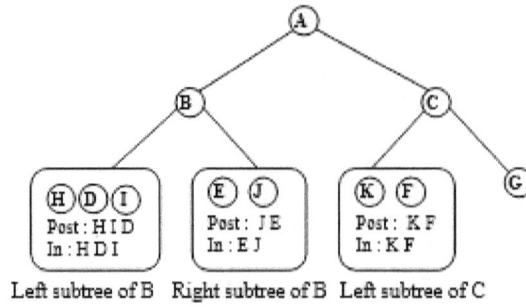

Figure 6.25 Identified left and right subtrees

Left subtree of B:
  From postorder, we get node D as root.
  From inorder, we get node H in left subtree of D, and node I in right subtree of D.

Right subtree of B:
  From postorder, we get node E as root.
  From inorder, we get empty left subtree of E, and node J in right subtree of E.

Left subtree of C:
  From postorder, we get node F as root.
  From inorder, we get node K in left subtree of F, and empty right subtree of F.

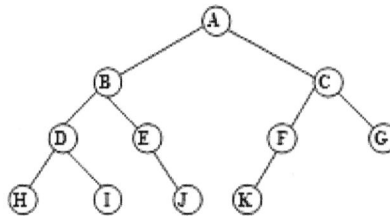

Figure 6.26 Binary tree from inorder and postorder traversal

Now we will see a quicker method of creating the tree from preorder and inorder traversal. In preorder traversal, scan the nodes one by one and keep inserting them in the tree. In inorder traversal, underline the nodes which have been inserted. To insert a node in its proper position in the tree, we will look at that node in the inorder traversal and insert it according to its position, with respect to the underlined nodes.

Preorder : A B D G H E I C F J K
Inorder : G D H B E I A C J F K

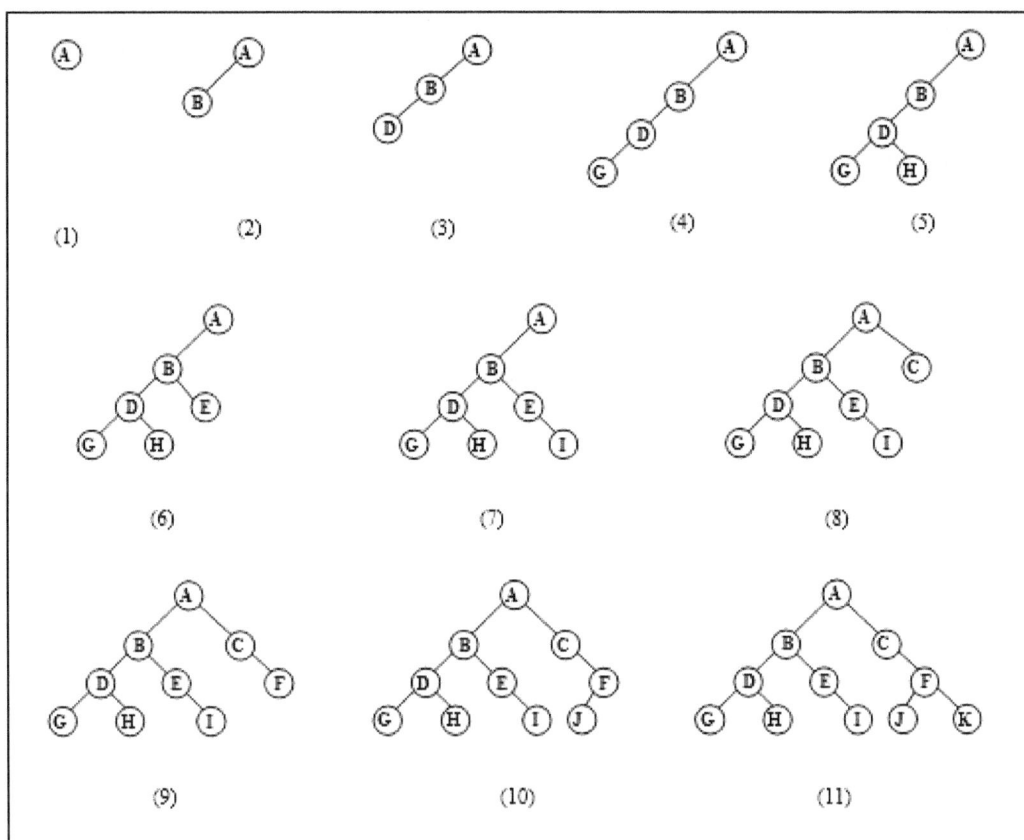

Figure 6.27 Binary tree construction from preorder and inorder traversal

1. Insert A:
G D H B E I **A** C J F K
A is the first node in preorder, hence it is root of the tree.

2. Insert B:
G D H **B** E I **A** C J F K
B is to the left of A, hence it is left child of A.

3. Insert D:
G **D** H **B** E I **A** C J F K
D is to the left of B, hence D is left child of B.

4. Insert G:
G **D** H **B** E I **A** C J F K
G is to the left of D, hence G is left child of D.

5. Insert H:
G **D** **H** **B** E I **A** C J F K
H is to the left of B and right of D, hence H is right child of D.

6. Insert E:

G D H B *E* I **A** C J F K

E is to the left of A and right of B, hence E is right child of B.

7. Insert I:

G D H B E *I* **A** C J F K

I is to the left of A and right of E, hence I is right child of E.

8. Insert C:

G D H B E I A *C* J F K

C is to the right of A, hence C is right child of A.

9. Insert F:

G D H B E I A C J *F* K

F is to the right of C, hence F is right child of C.

10. Insert J:

G D H B E I A C *J* **F** K

J is to the right of C and to left of F, hence J is left child of F.

11. Insert K:

G D H B E I A C J F *K*

K is to the right of F, hence K is right child of F.

Creation of tree from postorder and inorder by this method is the same as the creation of tree from inorder and preorder. The only difference is that in postorder, we will start scanning the nodes from the right side, i.e., the last node in the postorder will be inserted first, and the first node will be inserted at last.

The member function for constructing a tree from inorder and preorder is given next. The inorder and preorder traversals are stored in `char` arrays and passed to parameters `in` and `pre`.

```
//Creation of binary tree from inorder and preorder traversal
Node* BinaryTree::construct(char *in, char *pre, int num)
{
        Node *temp;
        char *q;
        if(num == 0)
                return NULL;
        temp = new Node(pre[0]);
        if(num == 1)    //if only one node in tree
                return temp;
        q = in;
        int i;
        for(i=0; q[0]!=pre[0]; i++)
                q++;
        //Now q points to root in inorder list and number of nodes in its left subtree
        //is i
        //For left subtree
        temp->lchild = construct(in, pre+1, i);
        //For right subtree
        int j;
        for(j=1; j<=i+1; j++)
                pre++;
        temp->rchild = construct(q+1, pre, num-i-1);

        return temp;
}//End of construct()
```

```
void BinaryTree::construct(char *in, char *pre)
{
        root = construct(in, pre, strlen(in));
}//End of construct()
```

The function for constructing a tree from inorder and postorder is:

```
//Creation of binary tree from inorder and postorder traversal
Node* BinaryTree::construct1(char *in, char *post, int num)
{
        Node *temp;
        char *q, *ptr;
        int i, j;
        if(num == 0)
                return NULL;
        ptr = post;
        for(i=1; i<num; i++)
                ptr++;
        //Now ptr points to last node of postorder which is root
        temp = new Node(ptr[0]);
        if(num == 1)    //if only one node in tree
                return temp;
        q = in;
        for(i=0; q[0]!=ptr[0]; i++)
                q++;
        //Now i denotes the number of nodes in left subtree
        //and q points to root node in inorder list
        //For left subtree
        temp->lchild = construct1(in, post, i);
        //For right subtree
        for(j=1; j<=i; j++)
                post++;
        temp->rchild = construct1(q+1, post, num-i-1);

        return temp;
}//End of construct1()
void BinaryTree::construct1(char *in, char *post)
{
        root = construct1(in, post, strlen(in));
}//End of construct1()
```

6.10 Height of Binary Tree

The recursive function to find out the height of binary tree is given as follows. It is passed the root of the binary tree and it returns the height of that tree.

```
int BinaryTree::height(Node *ptr)
{
        int hLeft, hRight;
        if(ptr == NULL)         //Base case
                return 0;
        hLeft = height(ptr->lchild);
        hRight = height(ptr->rchild);
        if(hLeft > hRight)
                return 1+hLeft;
        else
                return 1+hRight;
}//End of height()
int BinaryTree::height()
{
        return height(root);
```

```
}//End of height()
```

The height of an empty tree is 0 and this serves as the base case. In the recursive case, we can find out the height of a tree by adding 1 to the height of its left or right subtree (whichever is more). For example, suppose we have to find out the height of the given tree:

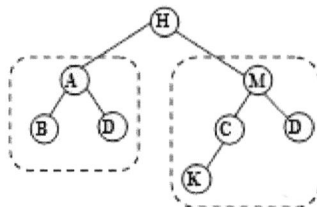

Figure 6.28 Binary tree

The heights of the left and the right subtrees rooted at H are 2 and 3 respectively. So, the height of this tree can be obtained by adding 1 to height of the right subtree, and hence, the height of this tree is 4. The height of the left and the right subtrees can be found in the same way.

The member function to display the binary tree and the `main()` function is as follows:

```
//BinaryTree.cpp : Program for Binary Tree.
#include<iostream>
#include<stack>
#include<queue>
using namespace std;
void BinaryTree::display(Node *ptr, int level)
{
        if(ptr == NULL)
                return;
        display(ptr->rchild, level+1);
        cout << "\n";
        for(int i=0; i<level; i++)
                cout << "      ";
        cout << ptr->info;
        display(ptr->lchild, level+1);
}//End of display()
void BinaryTree::display()
{
        display(root, 0);
        cout << "\n";
}//End of display()
int main()
{
        BinaryTree bnTree;
        bnTree.createTree();
        bnTree.display();
        cout << "\n";
        cout << "Preorder traversal :\n";
        bnTree.preorder();
        cout << "Inorder traversal :\n";
        bnTree.inorder();
        cout << "Postorder traversal :\n";
        bnTree.postorder();
        cout << "Level order traversal :\n";
        bnTree.levelOrder();
```

```
        cout << "Height = " << bnTree.height() << "\n";
        cout << "Non Recursive Preorder traversal :\n";
        bnTree.nrecPreorder();
        cout << "Non Recursive Inorder traversal :\n";
        bnTree.nrecInorder();
        cout << "Non Recursive Postorder traversal :\n";
        bnTree.nrecPostorder();
        char inorder[] = "GDHBEIACJFK";
        char preorder[] = "ABDGHEICFJK";
        BinaryTree bnTree1;
        cout << "Creation of binary tree from Inorder = " << inorder << ", Preorder = "
        << preorder << " :\n";
        bnTree1.construct(inorder, preorder);
        bnTree1.display();
        cout << "\n";
        char postorder[] = "GHDIEBJKFCA";
        BinaryTree bnTree2;
        cout << "Creation of binary tree from Inorder = " << inorder << ", Postorder =
        " << postorder << " :\n";
        bnTree2.construct1(inorder, postorder);
        bnTree2.display();
        cout << "\n";
        return 0;
}//End of main()
```

6.11 Expression Tree

Any algebraic expression can be represented by a tree, in which the non-leaf nodes are operators, and the leaf nodes are the operands. Almost all arithmetic operations are unary or binary, and so, the expression trees are generally binary trees. The left child represents the left operand, while the right child represents the right operand. In the case of unary minus operator, the node will have only one child. Every algebraic expression represents a unique tree. Let us take an algebraic expression and the corresponding expression tree.

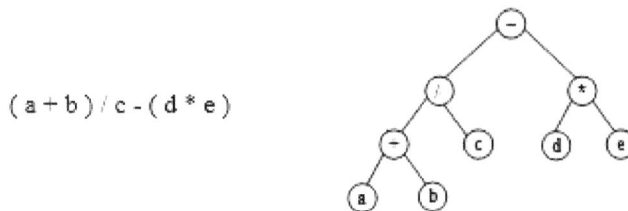

Figure 6.29 Expression tree

We can see that the leaf nodes are the variables or constants, and all the non-leaf nodes are the operators. The parentheses of the algebraic expression do not appear in the tree, but the tree retains the purpose of parentheses. For example, the + operator is applied to operands a and b, and then the / operator is applied to a+b and c.

Now, we will take an expression tree and apply each traversal.

Algebraic expression: $(a - b * c) / (d + e / f)$

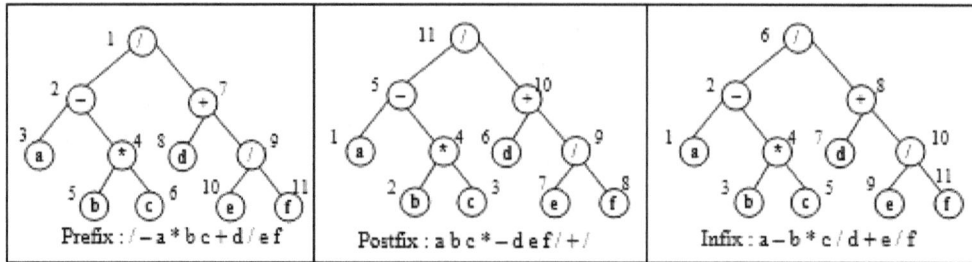

Figure 6.30 Expression tree traversals

Preorder Traversal: / – a * b c + d / e f
Inorder Traversal: a – b * c / d + e / f
Postorder Traversal: a b c * – d e f / + /

The preorder and postorder traversals give the corresponding prefix and postfix expressions of the given algebraic expression. The inorder traversal gives us an expression in which the order of operator and operands is the same as in the given algebraic expression but without the parentheses. We can get a parenthesized infix expression by following the given procedure:

- If the node is a leaf node (operand)
        Print the contents of the node
- If the node is a non leaf node (operator)
        Print ' ('
        Traverse the left subtree
        Print the contents of the node
        Traverse the right subtree
        Print ') '

Starting from the root node, the above recursive procedure will give us this expression:

((a – (b * c)) / (d + (e / f)))

This expression has many surplus pair of parentheses, but it exactly represents the algebraic expression. (a – b * c) / (d + e / f).

We can easily construct an expression tree using either the postfix expression or the prefix expression. We have already seen the procedure for converting an infix expression to postfix or prefix expression (in Chapter 4, Stacks and Queues). Now, let us see the procedure for converting a postfix expression to an expression tree. This procedure uses a stack and is somewhat similar to the procedure of evaluating a postfix expression. The postfix expression is scanned from left to right, and if the symbol scanned is an operand, then we allocate a tree node and push its pointer on the stack. If the symbol scanned is an operator, then we pop pointers to two nodes N1 and N2 from the stack and then create a new tree by making the scanned operator as the root with N1 and N2 as the children. If the pointer to N1 is popped first, then it will be the right child and N2 will be the left child. Otherwise, N2 will be the right child and N1 will be the left child. Figure 6.31 shows how we can construct the tree given in the example using the following postfix expression.

a b c * - d e f / + /

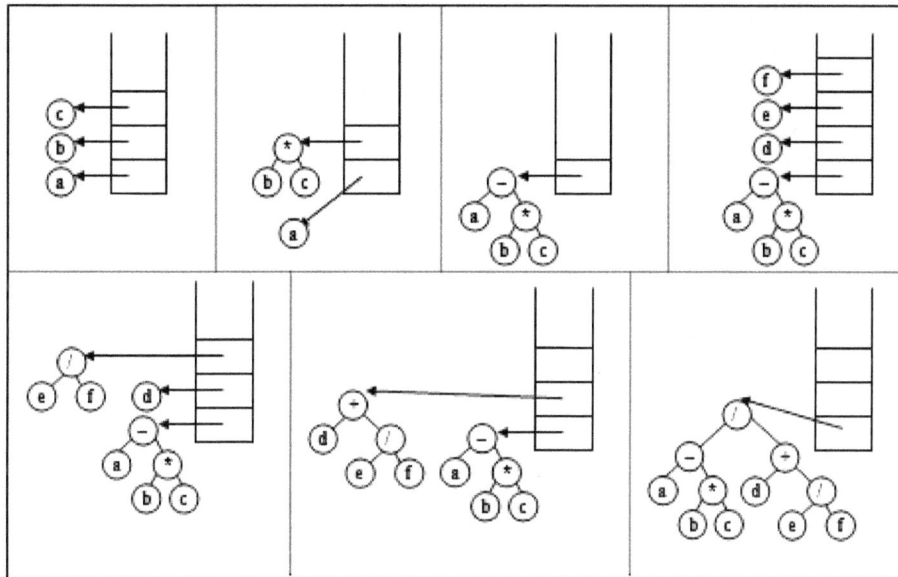

Figure 6.31 Expression tree construction from postfix expression

Here is the complete program of the expression tree:

```cpp
//ExpressionTree.cpp : Program for Expression Tree.
#include<iostream>
#include<string>
#include<stack>
using namespace std;
class Node
{
        public:
                char info;
                Node *lchild;
                Node *rchild;
                Node(char ch)
                {
                        info = ch;
                        lchild = NULL;
                        rchild = NULL;
                }
};//End of class Node
class ExpressionTree
{
        private:
                Node *root;
                bool isOperator(char ch);
                void preorder(Node *ptr);
                void postorder(Node *ptr);
                void inorder(Node *ptr);
                void display(Node *ptr, int level);
                int evaluate(Node *ptr);
                void destroy(Node *ptr);
        public:
                ExpressionTree();
```

```
                ~ExpressionTree();
                void buildTree(string postfix);
                void prefix();
                void postfix();
                void parenthesizedInfix();
                void display();
                int evaluate();
};//End of class ExpressionTree
bool ExpressionTree::isOperator(char c)
{
        if(c=='+' || c=='-' || c=='*' || c=='/')
                return true;
        return false;
}//End of isOperator();
void ExpressionTree::buildTree(string postfix)
{
        stack<Node *> treeStack;
        Node *t;
        for(int i=0; i<postfix.length(); i++)
        {
                if(isOperator(postfix[i]))
                {
                        t = new Node(postfix[i]);
                        t->rchild = treeStack.top();
                        treeStack.pop();
                        t->lchild = treeStack.top();
                        treeStack.pop();
                        treeStack.push(t);
                }
                else    //operand
                {
                        t = new Node(postfix[i]);
                        treeStack.push(t);
                }
        }
        root = treeStack.top();
        treeStack.pop();
}//End of buildTree()
void ExpressionTree::preorder(Node *ptr)
{
        if(ptr == NULL)         //Base case
                return;
        cout << ptr->info;
        preorder(ptr->lchild);
        preorder(ptr->rchild);
}//End of preorder()
void ExpressionTree::prefix()
{
        preorder(root);
        cout << "\n";
}//End of prefix()
void ExpressionTree::postorder(Node *ptr)
{
        if(ptr == NULL)         //Base case
                return;
        postorder(ptr->lchild);
        postorder(ptr->rchild);
        cout << ptr->info;
}//End of postorder()
```

```
void ExpressionTree::postfix()
{
        postorder(root);
        cout << "\n";
}//End of postfix()
void ExpressionTree::inorder(Node *ptr)
{
        if(ptr == NULL)          //Base case
                return;
        if(isOperator(ptr->info))
                cout << "(";
        inorder(ptr->lchild);
        cout << ptr->info;
        inorder(ptr->rchild);
        if(isOperator(ptr->info))
                cout << ")";
}//End of inorder()
void ExpressionTree::parenthesizedInfix()
{
        inorder(root);
        cout << "\n";
}//End of parenthesizedInfix()
int ExpressionTree::evaluate(Node *ptr)
{
        if(!isOperator(ptr->info))
                return ptr->info - 48;
        int leftValue = evaluate(ptr->lchild);
        int rightValue = evaluate(ptr->rchild);

        if(ptr->info == '+')
                return leftValue + rightValue;
        else if(ptr->info == '-')
                return leftValue - rightValue;
        else if(ptr->info == '*')
                return leftValue * rightValue;
        else if(ptr->info == '/')
                return leftValue / rightValue;
}//End of evaluate()
int ExpressionTree::evaluate()
{
        if(root == NULL)
                return 0;
        return evaluate(root);
}//End of evaluate()
int main()
{
        ExpressionTree expTree;
        string postfix = "54+12*3*-";
        expTree.buildTree(postfix);
        expTree.display();
        cout << "Prefix : ";
        expTree.prefix();
        cout << "Postfix : ";
        expTree.postfix();
        cout << "Infix : ";
        expTree.parenthesizedInfix();
        cout << "Evaluated Value : " << expTree.evaluate() << "\n";
        return 0;
}//End of main()
```

The constructor and function `display()` is the same as in the binary tree. The destructor and function `destroy()` is also the same as given in the binary search tree.

6.12 Binary Search Tree

One of the important uses of binary trees is in searching. Binary search trees are binary trees specially organized for searching. An element can be searched in average O(log N) time where N is the number of nodes. In a binary search tree, a key is associated with each node. We can define binary search trees recursively as follows.

A binary search tree is a binary tree that may be empty, and if it is not empty, then it satisfies the following properties:

1. All the keys in the left subtree of root are less than the key in the root.
2. All the keys in the right subtree of root are greater than the key in the root.
3. Left and right subtrees of root are also binary search trees.

We have assumed that all the keys of a binary search tree are distinct, although there can be a binary search tree with duplicates and in that case the operations explained here have to be changed.

For simplicity, we assume that the data part contains only an integer value, which also serves as the key. The following trees are examples of binary search trees:

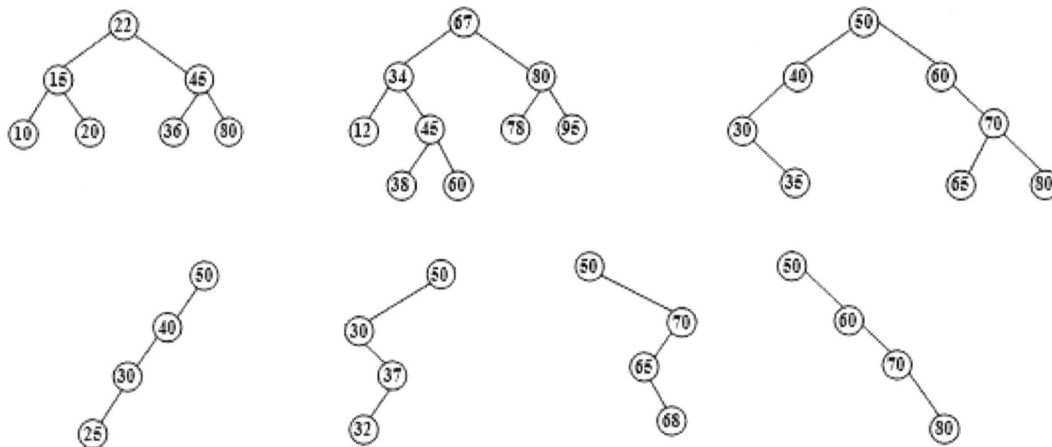

Figure 6.32 Binary search tree examples

In all these trees, we can see that for each node N in the tree, all the keys in the left subtree of node N are smaller than the key of node N, and all the keys in the right subtree of node N are greater than the key of node N.

This is the class `Node` for binary search tree:

```
class Node
{
        public:
                int info;
                Node *lchild;
                Node *rchild;
                Node(int key)
                {
```

```
                        info = key;
                        lchild = NULL;
                        rchild = NULL;
                }
};//End of class Node
```

This is the class `BinarySearchTree` for binary search tree:

```
class BinarySearchTree
{
        private:
                Node *root;
                void display(Node *ptr, int level);
                Node* insert(Node *ptr, int key);
                Node* del(Node *ptr, int key);
                Node* copy(Node *ptr);
                void destroy(Node *ptr);
                Node* search(Node *ptr, int key);
                Node* min(Node *ptr);
                Node* max(Node *ptr);
                void caseA(Node *parent, Node *ptr);
                void caseB(Node *parent, Node *ptr);
                void caseC(Node *parent, Node *ptr);
        public:
                BinarySearchTree();
                ~BinarySearchTree();
                BinarySearchTree(const BinarySearchTree &T);
                BinarySearchTree& operator=(const BinarySearchTree &T);
                bool isEmpty();
                void insert(int key);
                void insert1(int key);
                void display();
                void del(int key);
                void del1(int key);
                void del2(int key);
                bool search1(int key);
                bool search(int key);
                int min1();
                int max1();
                int min();
                int max();
};//End of class BinarySearchTree
```

The constructor is the same as in the binary tree. Here is the destructor and function `destroy()` to release the memory:

```
BinarySearchTree::~BinarySearchTree()
{
        destroy(root);
        root = NULL;
}//End of ~BinarySearchTree()
void BinarySearchTree::destroy(Node *ptr)
{
        if(ptr == NULL)
                return;
        destroy(ptr->lchild);
        destroy(ptr->rchild);
        delete ptr;
}//End of destroy()
```

The copy constructor and function `copy()` to copy the object is:

```
BinarySearchTree::BinarySearchTree(const BinarySearchTree &T)
```

```
{
        root = copy(T.root);
}//End of BinarySearchTree()
Node* BinarySearchTree::copy(Node *ptr)
{
        if(ptr == NULL)
                return NULL;
        Node *cp = new Node(ptr->info);
        cp->lchild = copy(ptr->lchild);
        cp->rchild = copy(ptr->rchild);
        return cp;
}//End of copy()
```

The overloaded assignment operator function to assign the object is:

```
BinarySearchTree& BinarySearchTree::operator=(const BinarySearchTree &T)
{
        if(this == &T)
                return *this;
        destroy(root);
        root = copy(T.root);
        return *this;
}//End of operator=()
```

The function isEmpty() returns true if there is no node in tree, otherwise returns false.

```
bool BinarySearchTree::isEmpty()
{
        return root==NULL;
}//End of isEmpty()
```

6.12.1 Traversal in Binary Search Tree

The binary search tree is a binary tree, and so the traversal methods given for binary trees apply here as well.

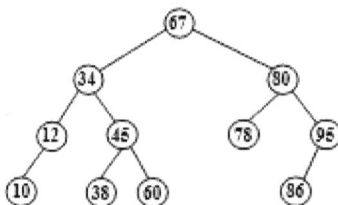

Figure 6.33 Binary search tree

The different traversals for the binary search tree in figure 6.33 are:

Preorder   : 67 34 12 10 45 38 60 80 78 95 86
Inorder   : 10 12 34 38 45 60 67 78 80 86 95
Postorder   : 10 12 38 60 45 34 78 86 95 80 67
Level order : 67 34 80 12 45 78 95 10 38 60 86

Note that the inorder traversal of a binary search tree gives us all keys of that tree in ascending order.

6.12.2 Searching in a Binary Search Tree

We start at the root node and move down the tree, and while descending when we encounter a node, we compare the desired key with the key of that node and take appropriate action:

1. If the desired key is equal to the key in the node, then the search is successful.
2. If the desired key is less than the key of the node, then we move to left child.
3. If the desired key is greater than the key of the node, then we move to right child.

In the process, if we reach a NULL left child or NULL right child, then the search is unsuccessful, i.e., the desired key is not present in the tree.

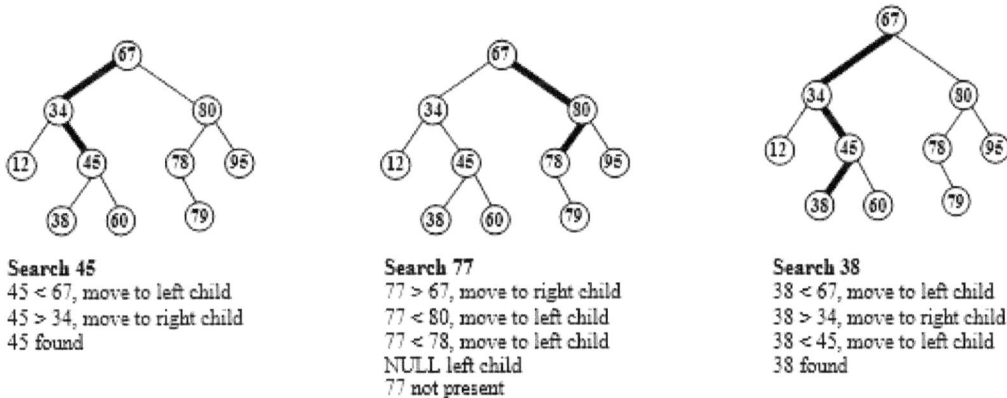

Search 45
45 < 67, move to left child
45 > 34, move to right child
45 found

Search 77
77 > 67, move to right child
77 < 80, move to left child
77 < 78, move to left child
NULL left child
77 not present

Search 38
38 < 67, move to left child
38 > 34, move to right child
38 < 45, move to left child
38 found

Figure 6.34 Searching in a binary search tree

The function for searching a key non-recursively is given as follows. This function is passed the key to be searched. It returns true if key is found; otherwise, it returns false.

```
//Non Recursive search
bool BinarySearchTree::search1(int key)
{
        Node *ptr = root;
        while(ptr != NULL)
        {
                if(key < ptr->info)
                        ptr = ptr->lchild; //Move to left child
                else if(key > ptr->info)
                        ptr = ptr->rchild; //Move to right child
                else    //key found
                        return true;
        }
        return false;
}//End of search1()
```

The search process can also be described recursively. To search a key in the tree, the key is first compared with the key in the root node. If the key is found there, then the search is successful. If the key is less than the key in the root, then the search is performed in the left subtree, because we know that all keys less than the root are stored in the left subtree. Similarly, if the key is greater than the key in the root, then the search is performed in the right subtree. In this way, the search is carried out recursively. The recursive process stops when we reach the base case of recursion. Here, we have two base cases; first, when we find the desired key (successful search), and second, when we reach a NULL subtree (unsuccessful search). The recursive function for searching a node is given as follows. This function is passed the address of the root of the tree, and the key to be searched. It returns the address of the node having the desired key, or NULL if such a node is not found.

```
//Recursive search
Node* BinarySearchTree::search(Node *ptr, int key)
```

```
{
        if(ptr == NULL)
                return NULL;     //key not found
        if(key < ptr->info)
                return search(ptr->lchild, key); //search in left subtree
        if(key > ptr->info)
                return search(ptr->rchild, key); //search in right subtree
        return ptr;      //key found
}//End of search()
bool BinarySearchTree::search(int key)
{
        return search(root, key) != NULL;
}//End of search()
```

Searching in the binary search tree is efficient because we just have to traverse a branch of the tree, and not all the nodes sequentially as in a linked list. The running time is O(h), where h is the height of the tree.

6.12.3 Finding Minimum and Maximum Key

The last node in the leftmost path starting from the root is the node with the smallest key. To find this node, we start at the root and move along the leftmost path, until we get a node with no left child. You can verify it by seeing the binary search trees in the following example. The non-recursive function to find the minimum key is shown as follows:

```
//Non Recursive to find minimum key
int BinarySearchTree::min1()
{
        if(isEmpty())
                throw exception("Tree is empty");
        Node *ptr = root;
        while(ptr->lchild != NULL)
                ptr = ptr->lchild;
        return ptr->info;
}//End of min1()
```

In the recursive function, the root of the tree is passed as parameter, and it returns the node with the minimum key:

```
//Recursive to find minimum key
Node* BinarySearchTree::min(Node *ptr)
{
        if(ptr->lchild == NULL)
                return ptr;
        return min(ptr->lchild);
}//End of min()
int BinarySearchTree::min()
{
        if(isEmpty())
                throw exception("Tree is empty");
        return min(root)->info;
}//End of min()
```

The last node in the rightmost path starting from the root is the node with the largest key. To find this node, we start at the root and move along the rightmost path until we get a node with no right child. The non-recursive function to find the maximum key is given as follows:

```
//Non Recursive to find maximum key
int BinarySearchTree::max1()
{
        if(isEmpty())
```

```
                throw exception("Tree is empty");
        Node *ptr = root;
        while(ptr->rchild != NULL)
                ptr = ptr->rchild;
        return ptr->info;
}//End of max1()
```

In the recursive function, the root of the tree is passed as the parameter and it returns the node with the maximum key:

```
//Recursive to find maximum key
Node* BinarySearchTree::max(Node *ptr)
{
        if(ptr->rchild == NULL)
                return ptr;
        return max(ptr->rchild);
}//End of max()
int BinarySearchTree::max()
{
        if(isEmpty())
                throw exception("Tree is empty");
        return max(root)->info;
}//End of max()
```

Both these operations run in O(h) time, where h is the height of the tree.

6.12.4 Insertion in a Binary Search Tree

To insert a new node, first, the key is searched. If it is not found in the tree, then it is inserted at the place where the search terminates.

We start at the root node and move down the tree and while descending, when we encounter a node, we compare the key to be inserted with the key of that node, and take appropriate action.
1. If the key to be inserted is equal to the key in the node, then there is nothing to be done, as duplicate keys are not allowed.
2. If the key to be inserted is less than the key of the node, then we move to the left child.
3. If the key to be inserted is greater than the key of the node, then we move to the right child.

We insert the new key when we reach a NULL left or right child.

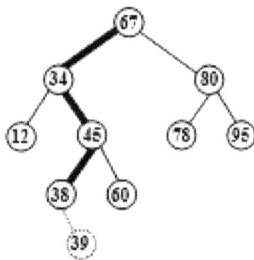

Insert 39
39 < 67, move to left child
39 > 34, move to right child
39 < 45, move to left child
39 > 38, move to right child
NULL right child
Insert as right child of 38

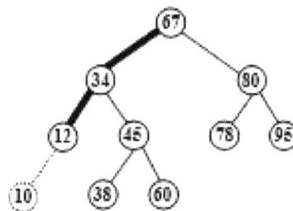

Insert 10
10 < 67, move to left child
10 < 34, move to left child
10 < 12, move to left child
NULL left child
Insert as left child of 12

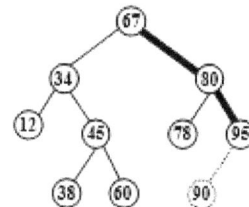

Insert 90
90 > 67, move to right child
90 > 80, move to right child
90 < 95, move to left child
NULL left child
Insert as left child of 95

Figure 6.35 Insertion in a binary search tree

To insert 39, first it is searched in the tree and the search terminates because we get NULL right subtree of 38. So, it is inserted as the right child of node 38. Let us create a binary search tree from the given keys:

50, 30, 60, 38, 35, 55, 22, 59, 94, 13, 98

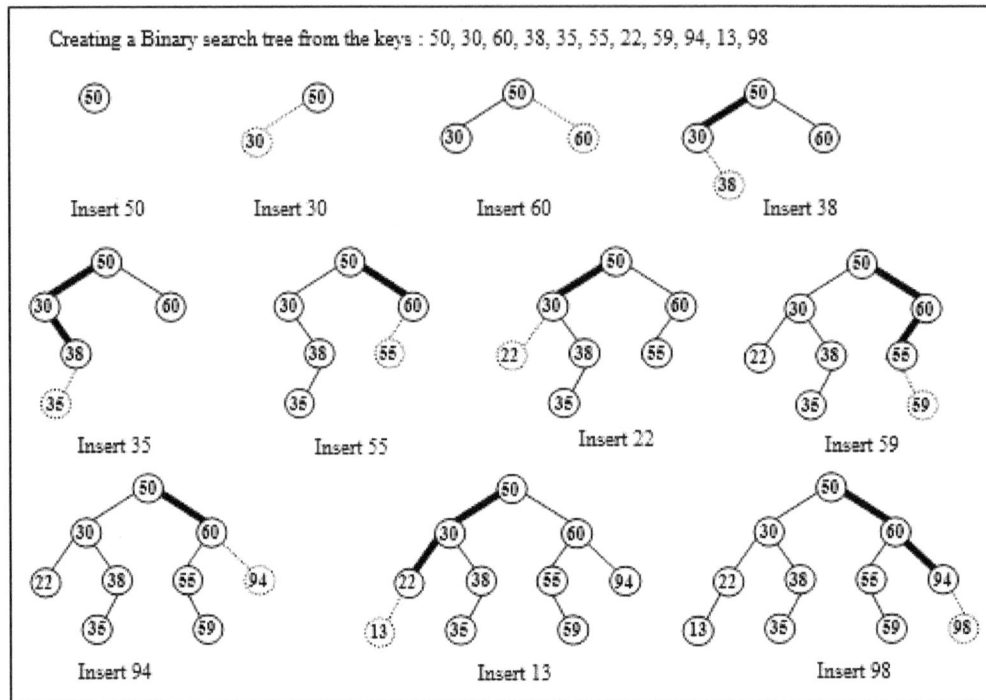

Figure 6.36 Creation of binary search tree

Note that if we alter the sequence of data, we will get different binary search trees for the same data.

The non-recursive function for the insertion of a node is given below. This function is passed the key to be inserted.

```cpp
//Non Recursive insertion
void BinarySearchTree::insert1(int key)
{
        Node *parent = NULL;
        Node *ptr = root;
        while(ptr != NULL)
        {
                parent = ptr;
                if(key < ptr->info)
                        ptr = ptr->lchild;
                else if(key > ptr->info)
                        ptr = ptr->rchild;
                else
                {
                        cout << key << " is already there\n";
                        return;
                }
        }
```

```
        Node *temp = new Node(key);
        if(parent == NULL)
                root = temp;
        else if(key < parent->info)
                parent->lchild = temp;
        else
                parent->rchild = temp;
}//End of insert1()
```

To insert in an empty tree, the root is made to point to the new node. As we move down the tree, we keep track of the parent of the node because this is required for the insertion of the new node. The pointer `ptr` walks down the path and the parent of the `ptr` is maintained through the pointer `parent`. When the search terminates unsuccessfully, `ptr` is `NULL` and `parent` points to the node whose link should be changed to insert the new node. The new node `temp` is made the left or right child of the `parent`.

The insertion of a node in a binary search tree can be described recursively as well. First, the key to be inserted is compared with the key of the root node. If the key is found there, then there is nothing to be done, and so, we return. If the key to be inserted is less than the key in the root node, then it is inserted in the left subtree. Otherwise, it is inserted in the right subtree. The same process is followed for both subtrees, till we reach a situation where we have to insert the node in an empty subtree.

The recursive function for the insertion of a node is given below. This function is passed the address of the root of the tree and the key to be inserted. It returns the address of root of the tree. The two base cases which stop the recursion are: when we find the key or when we reach a `NULL` subtree.

```
//Recursive insertion
Node* BinarySearchTree::insert(Node *ptr, int key)
{
        if(ptr == NULL) //Base Case
                ptr = new Node(key);
        else if(key < ptr->info) //Insertion in left subtree
                ptr->lchild = insert(ptr->lchild, key);
        else if(key > ptr->info) //Insertion in right subtree
                ptr->rchild = insert(ptr->rchild, key);
        else    //Base Case
                cout << key << " is already there\n";

        return ptr;
}//End of insert()
void BinarySearchTree::insert(int key)
{
        root = insert(root, key);
}//End of insert()
```

Insertion operation takes O(h) time where h is the height of the tree.

6.12.5 Deletion in a Binary Search Tree

The node to be deleted is searched in the tree. If it is found, then there can be three possibilities for that node:

A) Node has no child, i.e., it is a leaf node.
B) Node has exactly 1 child.
C) Node has exactly 2 children.

The non-recursive function for deletion of a node is given below. This function is passed the key to be deleted. Inside the function, the key is first searched, and if it is found, then the three cases are handled in three different functions `caseA()`, `caseB()`, and `caseC()`.

```
//Non Recursive deletion
void BinarySearchTree::del2(int key)
```

```
{
        Node *parent = NULL;
        Node *ptr = root;
        while(ptr != NULL)
        {
                if(ptr->info == key)
                        break;
                parent = ptr;
                if(key < ptr->info)
                        ptr = ptr->lchild;
                else
                        ptr = ptr->rchild;
        }
        if(ptr == NULL)
                cout << key << " is not in the tree\n";
        else if(ptr->lchild != NULL && ptr->rchild != NULL) //2 children
                caseC(parent, ptr);
        else if(ptr->lchild != NULL) //only left child
                caseB(parent, ptr);
        else if(ptr->rchild != NULL) //only right child
                caseB(parent, ptr);
        else    //no child
                caseA(parent, ptr);
}//End of del2()
```

Case A:

To delete a leaf node N, the link to node N is replaced by NULL. If the node is left child of its parent, then the left link of its parent is set to NULL, and if the node is the right child of its parent, then the right link of its parent is set to NULL. Then the node is deleted using the `delete` operator.

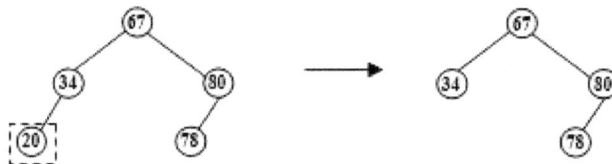

Figure 6.37 Deletion of 20

To delete 20, the left link of node 34 is set to NULL.

Figure 6.38 Deletion of 80

To delete 80, the right link of 67 is set to NULL.

If the leaf node to be deleted has no parent, i.e., it is the root node, then the pointer `root` is set to NULL.

```
void BinarySearchTree::caseA(Node *parent, Node *ptr)
{
        if(parent == NULL)      //root node to be deleted
```

```
        root = NULL;
    else if(ptr == parent->lchild)
            parent->lchild = NULL;
    else
            parent->rchild = NULL;
    delete ptr;
}//End of caseA()
```

Case B:

In this case, the node to be deleted has only one child. After deletion, this single child takes the place of the deleted node. For this, we just change the appropriate pointer of the parent node, so that after deletion, it points to the child of the deleted node. After this, the node is deleted using `delete`. Suppose N is the node to be deleted, and P is its parent and C is its child.

If N is the left child of P, then after deletion, the node C becomes the left child of P.
If N is the right child of P, then after deletion, the node C becomes the right child of P.

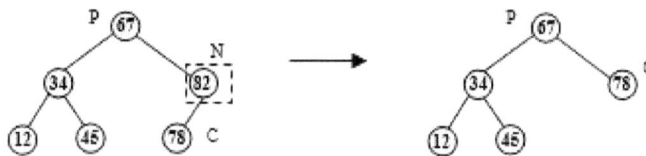

Figure 6.39 Deletion of 82

Node 82 is to be deleted from the tree. It is the right child of its parent 67, and so, the single child 78 takes the place of 82 by becoming the right child of 67.

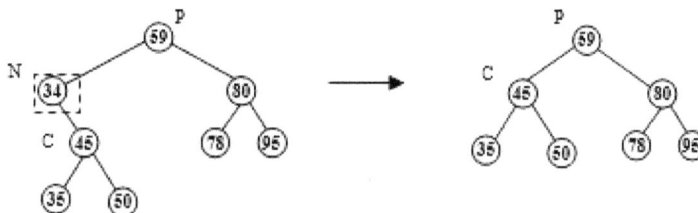

Figure 6.40 Deletion of 34

Node 34 is to be deleted from the tree. It is the left child of its parent 59, and so the single child 45 takes the place of 34 by becoming the left child of 59.

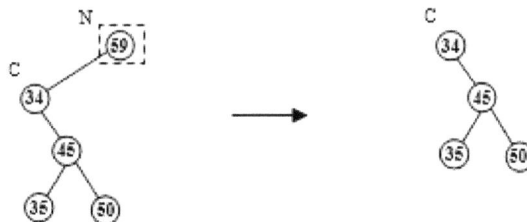

Figure 6.41 Deletion of 59

Node 59 is to be deleted from the tree. After searching, we will find that its parent is NULL because it is the root node. After deletion, the single child 34 will become the new root of the tree.

```
void BinarySearchTree::caseB(Node *parent, Node *ptr)
{
        Node *child;
        //Initialize child
        if(ptr->lchild != NULL)           //node to be deleted has left child
               child = ptr->lchild;
        else                              //node to be deleted has right child
               child = ptr->rchild;
        if(parent == NULL)                //node to be deleted is root node
               root = child;
        else if(ptr == parent->lchild)  //node is left child of its parent
               parent->lchild = child;
        else                              //node is right child of its parent
               parent->rchild = child;
        delete ptr;
}//End of caseB()
```

First we check whether the node to be deleted has a left child or right child. If it has only the left child, then we store the address of the left child, and if it has only a right child, then we store the address of the right child in pointer variable `child`.

If the node to be deleted is root node, then we assign `child` to `root`. So, the child of deleted node (root) will become the new root node. Otherwise, we check whether the node to be deleted is the left child or right child of its parent. If it is the left child, then we assign `child` to `lchild` part of its parent. Otherwise, we assign `child` to `rchild` part of its parent.

Case C:

This is the case when the node to be deleted has two children. Here, we have to find the inorder successor of the node. The data of the inorder successor is copied to the node and then the inorder successor is deleted from the tree.

Inorder successor of a node can be deleted by case A or case B because it will have either one right child or no child, it cannot have two children.

Inorder successor of a node is the node that comes just after that node in the inorder traversal of the tree. Inorder successor of a node N, having a right child is the leftmost node in the right subtree of the node N. To find the inorder successor of a node N, we move to the right child of N, and keep on moving left till we find a node with no left child. So, we can see why the inorder successor cannot have a left child.

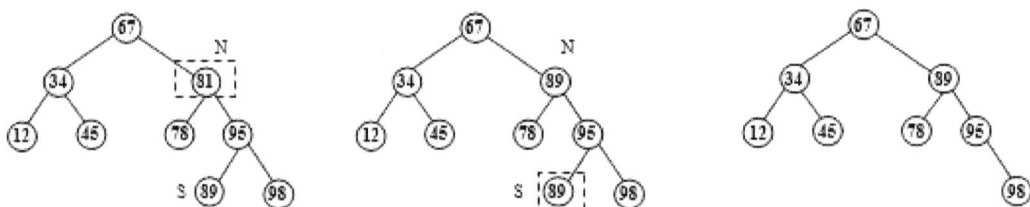

Figure 6.42 Deletion of 81

Here, node N having the key 81 is to be deleted from the tree. Its inorder successor is node S having the key 89, and so the data of node S is copied to node N. Now, node S is to be deleted from the tree. Node S can be deleted using case A because it has no child.

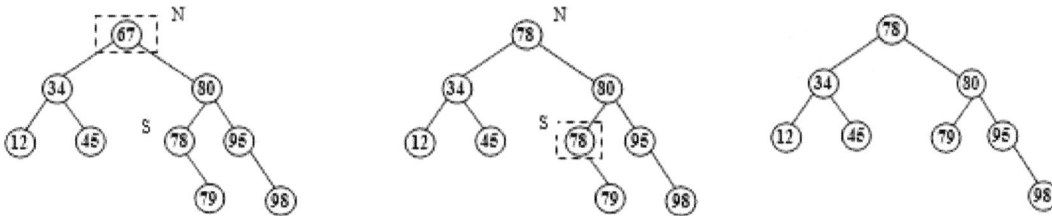

Figure 6.43 Deletion of 67

Here, node N with key 67, is to be deleted from the tree. Its inorder successor is node S having the key 78, so the data of node S is copied to node N and now node S has to be deleted from the tree. Node S can be deleted using case B because it has only one child.

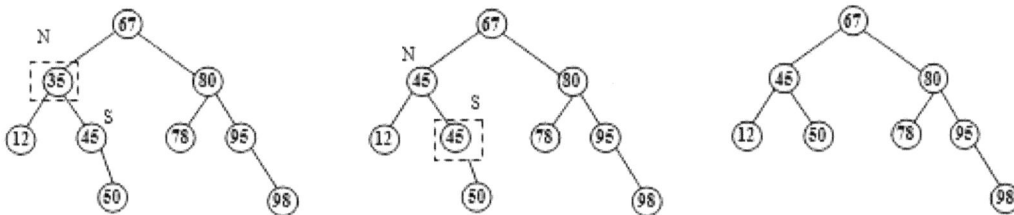

Figure 6.44 Deletion of 35

Here, node N, with key 35 is to be deleted from the tree. Its inorder successor is node S having the key 45, and so the data of node S is copied to node N, and now node S has to be deleted from the tree. Node S can be deleted using case B because it has only one child.

To delete an inorder successor, we have to call `caseA()` or `caseB()` depending on whether it has no child or one child. For deleting a node by `caseA()` or `caseB()`, we need to send the address of that node and the address of its parent. So, to delete an inorder successor, we need to find out its address and the address of its parent. In the function `caseC()`, we first find out the inorder successor and its parent, and then copy the information of successor node to the node to be deleted. After this, the successor is deleted by calling `caseA()` or `caseB()`.

```
void BinarySearchTree::caseC(Node *parent, Node *ptr)
{
        Node *s, *ps;
        //Find inorder successor and its parent
        ps = ptr;
        s = ptr->rchild;
        while(s->lchild != NULL)
        {
                ps = s;
                s = s->lchild;
        }
        ptr->info = s->info;
        if(s->lchild==NULL && s->rchild==NULL)
                caseA(ps, s);
        else
                caseB(ps, s);
}//End of caseC()
```

In the following function `del1()`, we have not created separate functions for different cases. All the cases are handled in this function only. Case A and case B are regarded as one case, because in case A, the `child` will be initialized to `NULL`.

```cpp
//Non Recursive deletion
void BinarySearchTree::del1(int key)
{
        Node *parent = NULL;
        Node *ptr = root;
        while(ptr != NULL)
        {
                if(ptr->info == key)
                        break;
                parent = ptr;
                if(key < ptr->info)
                        ptr = ptr->lchild;
                else
                        ptr = ptr->rchild;
        }
        if(ptr == NULL)
        {
                cout << key << " is not in the tree\n";
                return;
        }
        //Case C : 2 children
        //Find inorder successor and parent
        Node *s, *ps;
        if(ptr->lchild!=NULL && ptr->rchild!=NULL)
        {
                ps = ptr;
                s = ptr->rchild;
                while(s->lchild != NULL)
                {
                        ps = s;
                        s = s->lchild;
                }
                ptr->info = s->info;
                ptr = s;
                parent = ps;
        }
        //Case B and Case A : 1 or no child
        Node *child;
        if(ptr->lchild != NULL)          //Node to be deleted has left child
                child = ptr->lchild;
        else     //Node to be deleted has right child or no child
                child = ptr->rchild;
        if(parent == NULL)               //Node to be deleted is root node
                root = child;
        else if(ptr == parent->lchild) //Node is left child of its parent
                parent->lchild = child;
        else     //Node is right child of its parent
                parent->rchild = child;
        delete ptr;
}//End of del1()
```

The recursive function for deletion from binary search tree is as follows:

```cpp
//Recursive deletion
Node* BinarySearchTree::del(Node *ptr, int key)
{
        Node *child, *s, *temp;
        if(ptr == NULL)
```

```
        {
                cout << key << " not found\n";
                return ptr;
        }
        if(key < ptr->info)              //Delete from left subtree
                ptr->lchild = del(ptr->lchild, key);
        else if(key > ptr->info)         //Delete from right subtree
                ptr->rchild = del(ptr->rchild, key);
        else
        {
                //Key to be deleted is found
                if(ptr->lchild!=NULL && ptr->rchild!=NULL) //2 children
                {
                        s = ptr->rchild;
                        while(s->lchild != NULL)
                                s = s->lchild;
                        ptr->info = s->info;
                        ptr->rchild = del(ptr->rchild, s->info);
                }
                else    //1 child or no child
                {
                        if(ptr->lchild != NULL)        //Only left child
                                child = ptr->lchild;
                        else    //Only right child or no child
                                child = ptr->rchild;
                        temp = ptr;
                        ptr = child;
                        delete temp;
                }
        }//End of else

        return ptr;
}//End of del()
void BinarySearchTree::del(int key)
{
        root = del(root, key);
}//End of del()
```

We can use the inorder predecessor instead of inorder successor in case C, and in that case, we get a different binary search tree. Inorder predecessor of a node N is the rightmost node in the left subtree of node N. Like other operations, deletion also takes O(h) running time where h is the height of the tree.

The main() function for binary search tree is as follows:

```
//BinarySearchTree.cpp : Program for Binary Search Tree.
#include<iostream>
using namespace std;

int main()
{
        BinarySearchTree bst;
        try
        {
                cout << "Insertion to create the BST :\n";
                bst.insert1(80);
                bst.insert1(70);
                bst.insert1(65);
                bst.insert1(75);
                bst.insert1(90);
                bst.insert1(85);
                bst.insert1(95);
                bst.display();
```

```
                cout << "\n";
                cout << "After deleting 95 :\n";
                bst.del(95);
                bst.display();
                cout << "\n";
                cout << "Copy constructor :\n";
                BinarySearchTree bst1(bst);
                bst1.display();
                cout << "\n";
                cout << "Overloading assignment operator :\n";
                BinarySearchTree bst2;
                bst2 = bst;
                bst2.display();
                cout << "\n";
                //Search (Iterative)
                cout << "search1(75) : " << (bst.search1(75) ? "True" : "False");
                cout << "\n";
                //Search (Recursive)
                cout << "search(75) : " << (bst.search(75) ? "True" : "False");
                cout << "\n";
                cout << "Min key (Iterative) = " << bst.min1() << "\n";
                cout << "Min key (Recursive) = " << bst.min() << "\n";
                cout << "Max key (Iterative) = " << bst.max1() << "\n";
                cout << "Max key (Recursive) = " << bst.max() << "\n";
        }//End of try
        catch(exception e)
        {
                cout << e.what() << "\n";
        }
        return 0;
}//End of main()
```

The functions for traversals, display and height are the same as given in the binary tree.

6.13 Threaded Binary Tree

We had written the traversals of binary tree in two ways: recursive and non-recursive. Both types of algorithms required the use of stacks. The recursive version used a run-time stack, and the non-recursive version used a user defined stack. Traversal is a common operation, and if the tree has to be traversed frequently, then using a stack is inefficient since extra time and space are needed to maintain the stack. The traversals can be implemented more efficiently if we can avoid the use of stack. We can do this by maintaining threads in the binary tree.

A binary tree with n nodes has 2n pointers, out of which, n+1 are always NULL (Property 11). So, we can see that about half the space allocated for pointers is wasted. We can utilize this wasted space to contain some useful information. A left NULL pointer can be used to store the address of inorder predecessor of the node and a right NULL pointer can be used to store the address of the inorder successor of the node. These pointers are called threads, and a binary tree which implements these pointers is called a threaded binary tree.

If only the left NULL pointers are used as threads, then the binary tree is called a left in-threaded binary tree; if only right NULL pointers are used as threads, then the binary tree is called a right in-threaded binary tree; and if both left and right NULL pointers are used as threads, then the binary tree is called fully in-threaded tree or inthreaded tree. The following figure shows these threadings in a binary tree:

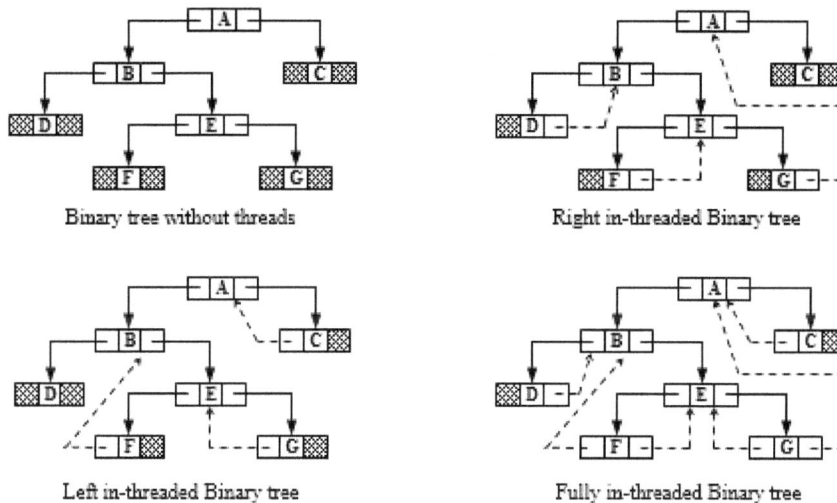

Figure 6.45 Threaded binary tree

The inorder traversal of the tree in figure 6.45 is [D B F E G A C].

D's right link is NULL and its successor is B, so the right pointer of D is made a thread.
F's right link is NULL and its successor is E, so the right pointer of F is made a thread.
G's right link is NULL and its successor is A, so the right pointer of G is made a thread.
F's left link is NULL and its predecessor is B, so the left pointer of F is made a thread.
G's left link is NULL and its predecessor is E, so the left pointer of G is made a thread.
C's left link is NULL and its predecessor is A, so the left pointer of C is made a thread.

D's left link is NULL but it has no predecessor, and C's right link is NULL but it has no successor, and so, both these pointer fields are NULL in the fully threaded tree.

Similar threading can be done corresponding to the other two traversals also, i.e., postorder and preorder. In our discussion, we will take inorder threading only.

While implementing a threaded binary tree, we should be able to distinguish real children pointers from threads. For this, we can attach two boolean variables to each node, and these variables will be used to determine whether the left and right pointers of that node are thread or child pointers.

The class Node in a fully in-threaded binary tree will be as follows:

```
class Node
{
        public:
                int info;
                Node *lchild;
                Node *rchild;
                bool lthread;
                bool rthread;
                Node(int key)
                {
                        info = key;
                        lchild = NULL;
                        rchild = NULL;
                        lthread = true;
                        rthread = true;
                }
```

```
};//End of class Node
```

Here, we have taken two boolean members: `lthread` and `rthread`, to differentiate between a thread and child pointer. If `lthread` is true, then the left pointer is a thread to inorder predecessor. Otherwise, it contains the address of the left child. Similarly, if `rthread` is true, then the right pointer is a thread to the inorder successor; otherwise, it contains the address of the right child.

The first node in inorder traversal has no predecessor, and the last node has no successor. So, the left pointer of the first node and the right pointer of the last node in inorder traversal contain NULL. For consistency, the `lthread` field of first node and `rthread` field of last node are set to true.

The class `ThreadedBinaryTree` of a fully in-threaded binary tree is as follows:

```
class ThreadedBinaryTree
{
        private:
                Node *root;
                Node* inorderPredecessor(Node *ptr);
                Node* inorderSuccessor(Node *ptr);
        public:
                ThreadedBinaryTree();
                ~ThreadedBinaryTree(){};
                bool isEmpty();
                void insert(int key);
                void del(int key);
                void inorder();
                void preorder();
};//End of class ThreadedBinaryTree
```

6.13.1 Finding Inorder Successor of a Node in an in-threaded Tree

If the right pointer of the node is a thread, then there is no need to do anything because the right thread points to the inorder successor. If the node's right pointer is not a thread, i.e., the node has a right child, then to find the inorder successor, we move to this right child and keep on moving left, till we find a node with no left child.

```
Node* ThreadedBinaryTree::inorderSuccessor(Node *ptr)
{
        if(ptr->rthread == true)
        {
                return ptr->rchild;
        }
        else
        {
                ptr = ptr->rchild;
                while(ptr->lthread == false)
                        ptr = ptr->lchild;
                return ptr;
        }
}//End of inorderSuccessor()
```

6.13.2 Finding Inorder Predecessor of a Node in an in-threaded Tree

If the left pointer is a thread, then this thread will point to the inorder predecessor. If the left pointer is not a thread, i.e., the node has a left child, then to find the inorder predecessor, we move to this left child and keep on moving right till we find a node with no right child.

```
Node* ThreadedBinaryTree::inorderPredecessor(Node *ptr)
{
        if(ptr->lthread == true)
        {
```

```
                return ptr->lchild;
        }
        else
        {
                ptr = ptr->lchild;
                while(ptr->rthread == false)
                        ptr = ptr->rchild;
                return ptr;
        }
}//End of inorderPredecessor()
```

6.13.3 Inorder Traversal of in-threaded Binary Tree

The first node to be visited in the inorder traversal is the last node in the leftmost branch starting from the root. So, we start from the root and move left till we get a node with no left child, and this node is visited. Now, we find the inorder successor of each node and visit it. The right pointer of last node is NULL, and we have marked it as thread. So, we stop our process when we get a node whose right thread is NULL.

```
void ThreadedBinaryTree::inorder()
{
        if(root == NULL)
        {
                cout << "Tree is empty\n";
                return;
        }
        //Find the leftmost node of the tree
        Node *ptr = root;
        while(ptr->lthread == false)
                ptr = ptr->lchild;
        while(ptr != NULL)
        {
                cout << ptr->info << " ";
                if(ptr->rthread == true)
                        ptr = ptr->rchild;
                else
                {
                        ptr = ptr->rchild;
                        while(ptr->lthread == false)
                                ptr = ptr->lchild;
                }
        }
}//End of inorder()
```

6.13.4 Preorder Traversal of in-threaded Binary Tree

In preorder traversal, first the root is visited. Thus, we start from the root node. If the node has a left child, then that left child will be visited. Otherwise, if the node has a right child, then that right child will be visited. If the node has neither left child nor right child (it is a leaf node), then with the help of right threads, we will reach that inorder successor of the node, which has a right subtree. Now this subtree will be traversed in preorder in the same way.

```
void ThreadedBinaryTree::preorder()
{
        if(root == NULL)
        {
                cout << "Tree is empty\n";
                return;
        }
        Node *ptr = root;
        while(ptr != NULL)
```

```
        {
                cout << ptr->info << " ";
                if(ptr->lthread == false)
                        ptr = ptr->lchild;
                else if(ptr->rthread == false)
                        ptr = ptr->rchild;
                else
                {
                        while(ptr!=NULL && ptr->rthread==true)
                                ptr = ptr->rchild;
                        if(ptr != NULL)
                                ptr = ptr->rchild;
                }
        }
}
}//End of preorder()
```

6.13.5 Insertion and Deletion in a Threaded Binary Tree

Insertion and deletion in a threaded binary tree will be the same as insertion and deletion in a binary tree, but we will have to adjust the threads after these operations. We will take the example of a threaded binary search tree and see how the nodes can be inserted and deleted from it.

6.13.5.1 Insertion

As in a binary search tree, here too, we will first search for the key value in the tree; if it is already present, then we return. Otherwise, the new key is inserted at the point where search terminates. In BST, search terminates either when we find the key, or when we reach a NULL left or right pointer. Here, all left and right NULL pointers are replaced by threads, except the left pointer of the first node, and the right pointer of the last node. So, here the search will be unsuccessful when we reach a NULL pointer or a thread.

The new node `temp` will be inserted as a leaf node, and so its left and right pointers will both be threads.

```
Node *temp = new Node(key);
```

The constructor of the `Node` will set the value of `info`, `lchild`, `rchild`, `lthread`, and `rthread` of `temp`.

```
Node(int key)
{
        info = key;
        lchild = NULL;
        rchild = NULL;
        lthread = true;
        rthread = true;
}
```

Case 1: Insertion in empty tree.

Both left and right pointers of `temp` will be set to NULL, and the new node becomes the root.

```
root = temp;
```

The `lchild` and `rchild` of `temp` is already set to NULL in the `Node` constructor.

```
lchild = NULL;
rchild = NULL;
```

Case 2: When the new node is inserted as the left child.

After inserting the node at its proper place, we have to make its left and right threads point to the inorder predecessor and successor respectively. The node which was the inorder predecessor of the parent, is now the inorder predecessor of this node `temp`. The parent of `temp` is its inorder successor. So, the left and right threads of the new node will be:

```
temp->lchild = parent->lchild;
temp->rchild = parent;
```

Before insertion, the left pointer of the parent was a thread, but after insertion, it will be a link pointing to the new node.

```
parent->lthread = false;
parent->lchild = temp;
```

The following example shows a node being inserted as the left child of its parent.

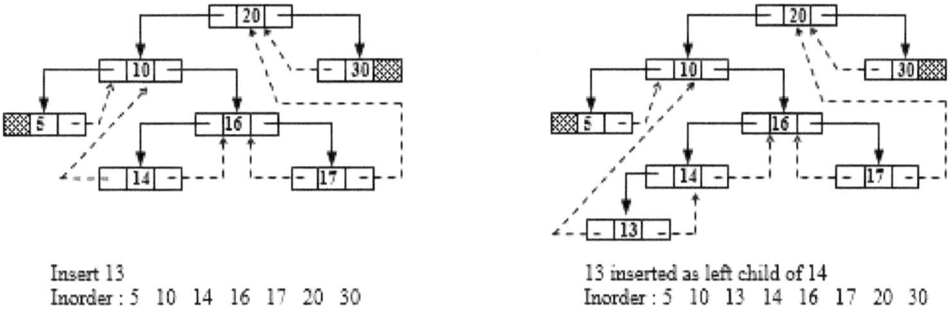

Insert 13
Inorder : 5 10 14 16 17 20 30

13 inserted as left child of 14
Inorder : 5 10 13 14 16 17 20 30

Figure 6.46 Insertion of 13

The predecessor of 14 becomes the predecessor of 13, and so the left thread of 13 points to 10.
The successor of 13 is 14, and so, the right thread of 13 points to 14.
The left pointer of 14 is not a thread now; it points to the left child, which is 13.

Case 3: When the new node is inserted as the right child.

The parent of `temp` is its inorder predecessor. The node which was the inorder successor of the parent, is now the inorder successor of this node `temp`. So, the left and right threads of the new node will be:

```
temp->lchild = parent;
temp->rchild = parent->rchild;
```

Before insertion, the right pointer of the parent was a thread, but after insertion, it will be a link pointing to the new node.

```
parent->rthread = false;
parent->rchild = temp;
```

The following example shows a node being inserted as the right child of its parent.

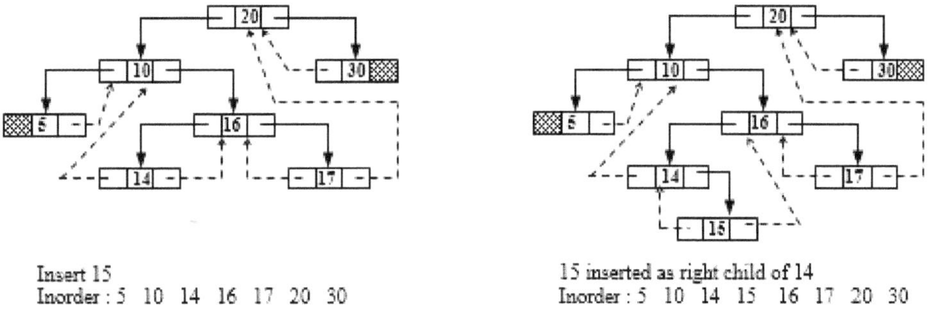

Insert 15
Inorder : 5 10 14 16 17 20 30

15 inserted as right child of 14
Inorder : 5 10 14 15 16 17 20 30

Figure 6.47 Insertion of 15

The successor of 14 becomes the successor of 15, and so, the right thread of 15 points to 16.

The predecessor of 15 is 14, and so, the left thread of 15 points to 14.

The right pointer of 14 is not a thread now, and it points to the right child, which is 15.

```cpp
void ThreadedBinaryTree::insert(int key)
{
        Node *parent = NULL;
        Node *ptr = root;
        while(ptr != NULL)
        {
                parent = ptr;
                if(key < ptr->info)
                {
                        if(ptr->lthread == false)
                                ptr = ptr->lchild;
                        else
                                break;
                }
                else if(key > ptr->info)
                {
                        if(ptr->rthread == false)
                                ptr = ptr->rchild;
                        else
                                break;
                }
                else
                {
                        cout << key << " is already there\n";
                        return;
                }
        }//End of while

        Node *temp = new Node(key);
        if(parent == NULL)
                root = temp;
        else if(key < parent->info)    //Inserted as left child
        {
                temp->lchild = parent->lchild;
                temp->rchild = parent;
                parent->lthread = false;
                parent->lchild = temp;
        }
        else    //Inserted as right child
        {
                temp->lchild = parent;
                temp->rchild = parent->rchild;
                parent->rthread = false;
                parent->rchild = temp;
        }
}//End of insert()
```

6.13.5.2 Deletion

First, the key to be deleted is searched, and then there are different cases for deleting the node in which the key is found.

```cpp
void ThreadedBinaryTree::del(int key)
{
        Node *parent = NULL;
        Node *ptr = root;
        while(ptr != NULL)
        {
```

```
                if(ptr->info == key)
                        break;
                parent = ptr;
                if(key < ptr->info)
                {
                        if(ptr->lthread == false)
                                ptr = ptr->lchild;
                        else
                                break;
                }
                else
                {
                        if(ptr->rthread == false)
                                ptr = ptr->rchild;
                        else
                                break;
                }
        }//End of while

        if(ptr!=NULL && ptr->info!=key)
        {
                cout << key << " not found\n";
                return;
        }

        //Case C : 2 children
        if(ptr->lthread==false && ptr->rthread==false)
        {
                //Find inorder successor and its parent
                Node *ps = ptr;
                Node *s = ptr->rchild;

                while(s->lthread == false)
                {
                        ps = s;
                        s = s->lchild;
                }
                ptr->info = s->info;
                ptr = s;
                parent = ps;
        }

        //Case A : no child
        if(ptr->lthread==true && ptr->rthread==true)
        {
                if(parent == NULL)      //key to be deleted is in root node
                        root = NULL;
                else if(ptr == parent->lchild)
                {
                        parent->lthread = true;
                        parent->lchild = ptr->lchild;
                }
                else
                {
                        parent->rthread = true;
                        parent->rchild = ptr->rchild;
                }
                delete ptr;
                return;
        }

        //Case B : 1 child
        Node *child;
```

```
            //Initialize child
            if(ptr->lthread == false)          //Node to be deleted has left child
                    child = ptr->lchild;
            else    //Node to be deleted has right child
                    child = ptr->rchild;
            if(parent == NULL)                 //Node to be deleted is root node
                    root = child;
            else if(ptr == parent->lchild) //Node is left child of its parent
                    parent->lchild = child;
            else    //Node is right child of its parent
                    parent->rchild = child;
            Node *pred = inorderPredecessor(ptr);
            Node *succ = inorderSuccessor(ptr);
            if(ptr->lthread == false) //If ptr has left child, right is a thread
                    pred->rchild = succ;
            else    //ptr has right child, left is a thread
                    succ->lchild = pred;
            delete ptr;
}//End of del()
```

Case A: Leaf node to be deleted.

In BST, for deleting a leaf node, the left or right pointer of parent was set to NULL. Here, instead of setting the pointer to NULL, it is made a thread.

If the leaf node to be deleted is the left child of its parent, then after deletion, the left pointer of the parent should become a thread pointing to its predecessor. The node which was the inorder predecessor of the leaf node before deletion, will become the inorder predecessor of the parent node after deletion.

```
parent->lthread = true;        parent->lchild = ptr->lchild;
```

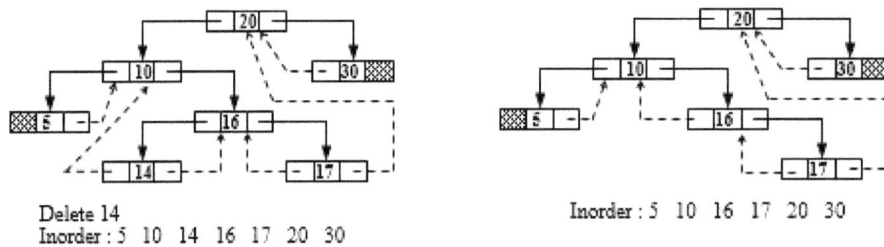

Delete 14
Inorder : 5 10 14 16 17 20 30

Inorder : 5 10 16 17 20 30

Figure 6.48 Deletion of 14

If the leaf node to be deleted is the right child of its parent, then after deletion, the right pointer of the parent should become a thread pointing to its successor. The node which was the inorder successor of the leaf node before deletion, will become the inorder successor of the parent node after deletion.

```
parent->rthread = true;        parent->rchild = ptr->rchild;
```

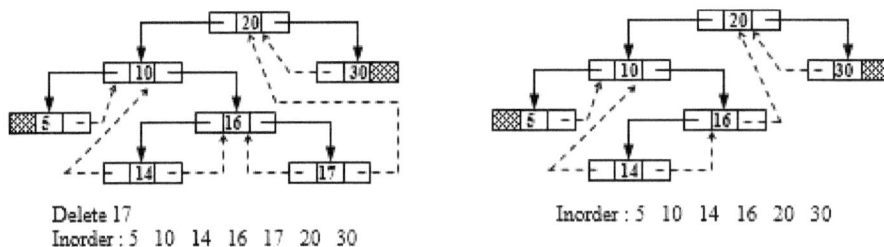

Delete 17
Inorder : 5 10 14 16 17 20 30

Inorder : 5 10 14 16 20 30

Figure 6.49 Deletion of 17

```
//Case A : no child
if(ptr->lthread==true && ptr->rthread==true)
{
        if(parent == NULL)       //key to be deleted is in root node
                root = NULL;
        else if(ptr == parent->lchild)
        {
                parent->lthread = true;
                parent->lchild = ptr->lchild;
        }
        else
        {
                parent->rthread = true;
                parent->rchild = ptr->rchild;
        }
        delete ptr;
        return;
}
```

Case B : Node to be deleted has only one child.

After deleting the node as in a BST, the inorder predecessor and inorder successor of the node are found out.

```
Node *pred = inorderPredecessor(ptr);
Node *succ = inorderSuccessor(ptr);
```

If the node to be deleted has a left subtree, then after deletion, the right thread of its predecessor should point to its successor.

```
pred->rchild = succ;
```

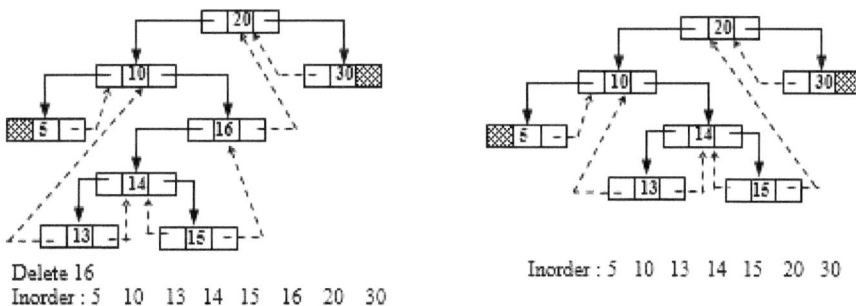

Delete 16
Inorder : 5 10 13 14 15 16 20 30

Inorder : 5 10 13 14 15 20 30

Figure 6.50 Deletion of 16

Before deletion, 15 is the predecessor and 20 is the successor of 16. After deletion of 16, the node 20 becomes the successor of 15, and so, the right thread of 15 will point to 20.

If the node to be deleted has a right subtree, then after deletion, the left thread of its successor should point to its predecessor.

```
succ->lchild = pred;
```

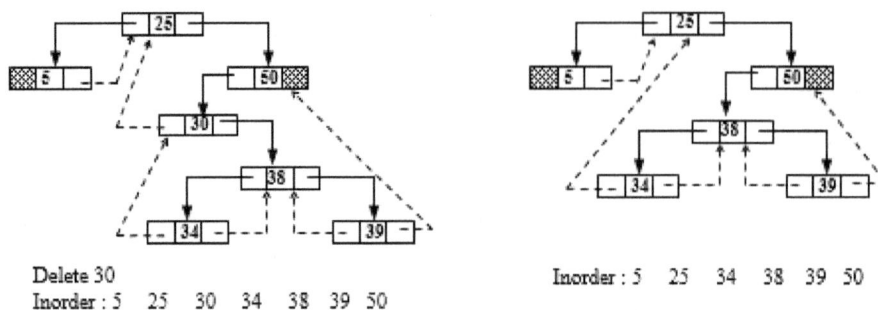

Delete 30
Inorder : 5   25   30   34   38   39   50

Inorder : 5   25   34   38   39   50

Figure 6.51 Deletion of 30

Before deletion, 25 is the predecessor and 34 is the successor of 30. After deletion of 30, the node 25 becomes the predecessor of 34, and so, the left thread of 34 will point to 25.

```
//Case B : 1 child
Node *child;
//Initialize child
if(ptr->lthread == false)          //Node to be deleted has left child
      child = ptr->lchild;
else    //Node to be deleted has right child
      child = ptr->rchild;
if(parent == NULL)                 //Node to be deleted is root node
      root = child;
else if(ptr == parent->lchild) //Node is left child of its parent
      parent->lchild = child;
else    //Node is right child of its parent
      parent->rchild = child;
Node *pred = inorderPredecessor(ptr);
Node *succ = inorderSuccessor(ptr);
if(ptr->lthread == false) //If ptr has left child, right is a thread
      pred->rchild = succ;
else    //ptr has right child, left is a thread
      succ->lchild = pred;
delete ptr;
```

Case C: Node to be deleted has two children.

Suppose node N is to be deleted. First, we will find the inorder successor of node N, and then copy the information of this inorder successor into node N. After this, the inorder successor node is deleted using either case A or case B.

```
//Case C : 2 children
if(ptr->lthread==false && ptr->rthread==false)
{
      //Find inorder successor and its parent
      Node *ps = ptr;
      Node *s = ptr->rchild;
      while(s->lthread == false)
      {
            ps = s;
            s = s->lchild;
      }
      ptr->info = s->info;
      ptr = s;
      parent = ps;
}
```

The `main()` function for threaded binary tree is as follows:

```
//ThreadedBinaryTree.cpp : Program for Threaded Binary Tree.
#include<iostream>
using namespace std;

int main()
{
        ThreadedBinaryTree threadedTree;
        threadedTree.insert(67);
        threadedTree.insert(34);
        threadedTree.insert(81);
        threadedTree.insert(12);
        threadedTree.insert(45);
        threadedTree.insert(78);
        threadedTree.insert(95);
        threadedTree.insert(20);
        threadedTree.insert(40);
        threadedTree.insert(89);
        threadedTree.insert(98);

        cout << "Inorder traversal :\n";
        threadedTree.inorder();
        cout << "\n";
        cout << "Preorder traversal :\n";
        threadedTree.preorder();
        cout << "\n";

        threadedTree.del(81);           //Case C
        cout << "Inorder traversal after deleting 81 :\n";
        threadedTree.inorder();
        cout << "\n";
        threadedTree.del(45);           //Case B (left child)
        cout << "Inorder traversal after deleting 45 :\n";
        threadedTree.inorder();
        cout << "\n";
        threadedTree.del(20);           //Case B (right child)
        cout << "Inorder traversal after deleting 20 :\n";
        threadedTree.inorder();
        cout << "\n";
        threadedTree.del(40);           //Case A (leaf node)
        cout << "Inorder traversal after deleting 40 :\n";
        threadedTree.inorder();
        cout << "\n";
        threadedTree.del(67);           //Case C (root node)
        cout << "Inorder traversal after deleting 67 :\n";
        threadedTree.inorder();
        cout << "\n";
        return 0;
}//End of main()
```

6.13.6 Threaded Tree with Header Node

In the inorder traversal, the first node has no predecessor and the last node has no successor. So in an in-threaded binary tree, the left pointer of the first node and the right pointer of the last node are NULL. To make the threading consistent, we can take a dummy node called the header node, which can act as the predecessor of the first node and the successor of the last node. Now, the left pointer of the first node and the right pointer of the last node will be threads pointing to this header node.

The binary tree can be represented as the left subtree of this header node. The left pointer of this header node will point to the root node of our tree, and the right pointer will point to itself. If we take a header node in the in-threaded tree of figure 6.45, the tree will look like this:

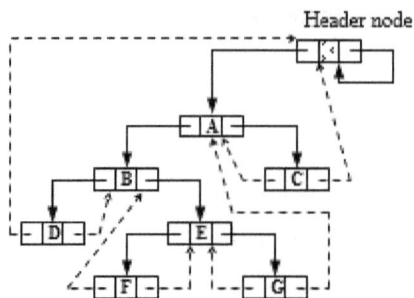

Figure 6.52 Threaded tree with header node

In an empty tree, the left pointer of the header node will be a thread pointing to itself:

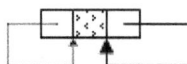

Figure 6.53 Empty threaded tree with header node

6.14 AVL Tree

A set of data can produce different binary search trees if the sequence of insertion of elements is different. Suppose we have data that consists of numbers from 1 to 9. If we insert the data in sequence $\{1, 2, 3, 4, 5, 6, 7, 8, 9\}$, then we get a binary search tree shown in figure 6.54 (a), while if we insert the data in sequence $\{4, 2, 6, 1, 3, 5, 8, 7, 9\}$, we get a binary search tree shown in figure 6.54 (b). Let us compare the search efficiency of these two trees. For this, we will find out the average number of comparisons that have to be done to reach a node.

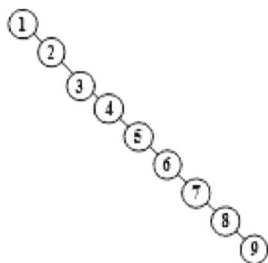

(a) Average number of comparisons to reach a node
= (1+2+3+4+5+6+7+8+9) / 9 = 45/9 = 5

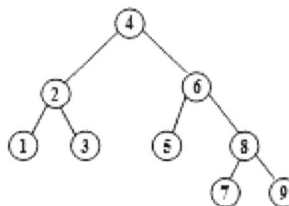

(b) Average number of comparisons to reach a node
= (1+2+2+3+3+3+3+4+4) = 25/9 = 2.77

Figure 6.54 Comparisons in binary search trees

In tree (a), we need one comparison to reach node 1, two comparisons to reach node 2, and nine comparisons to reach node 9. Therefore, the average number of comparisons to reach a node is 5. In tree (b), we need one comparison to reach node 4, two comparisons each to reach node 2 or 6, three comparisons each to reach node 1, 3, 5 or 8, and four comparisons each to reach node 7 or 9. In this tree, the average number of comparisons is 2.77.

We can see that the tree (b) is better than tree (a) from the searching point of view. In fact, tree (a) is a form of linear list and searching is O(n). Both the trees have the same data, but their structures are different because of a different sequence of insertion of elements. It is not possible to control the order of insertion, and so, the concept of height balanced binary search trees came in. The technique for balancing a binary search tree was introduced by Russian mathematicians G. M. Adelson-Velskii and E. M. Landis in 1962. The height balanced binary search tree is called AVL tree in their honour.

The main aim of the AVL tree is to perform efficient search, insertion, and deletion operations. Searching is efficient when the heights of left and right subtrees of the nodes are almost the same. This is possible in a full or complete binary search tree, which is an ideal situation and is not always achievable. This ideal situation is very nearly approximated by AVL trees.

An AVL tree is a binary search tree, where the difference in the height of the left and right subtrees of any node can be at most 1. Let us take a binary search tree and find out whether it is AVL tree or not.

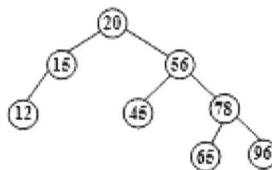

Figure 6.55 Binary search tree

For the leaf nodes 12, 45, 65 and 96, the left and right subtrees are empty, and so, the difference of heights of their subtrees is 0.

For node 20, height of left subtree is 2 and height of right subtree is 3, so difference is 1.
For node 15, height of left subtree is 1 and height of right subtree is 0, so difference is 1.
For node 56, height of left subtree is 1 and height of right subtree is 2, so difference is 1.
For node 78, height of left subtree is 1 and height of right subtree is 1, so difference is 0.

In this binary search tree, the difference in the height of left and right subtrees of any node is at most 1, and so it is an AVL tree. Now, let us take another binary search tree.

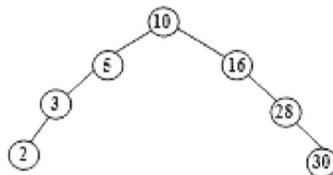

Figure 6.56 Binary search tree

For leaf nodes 2 and 30, left and right subtrees are empty so difference is 0.
For node 10, height of left subtree is 3 and height of right subtree is 3, so difference is 0.
For node 5, height of left subtree is 2 and height of right subtree is 0, so difference is 2.
For node 3, height of left subtree is 1 and height of right subtree is 0, so difference is 1.
For node 16, height of left subtree is 0 and height of right subtree is 2, so difference is 2.
For node 28, height of left subtree is 0 and height of right subtree is 1, so difference is 1.

This tree is not an AVL tree since there are two nodes for which the difference in heights of left and right subtrees exceeds 1.

Each node of an AVL tree has a balance factor, which is defined as the difference between the heights of the left subtree and the right subtree of a node.

Balance factor of a node = Height of its left subtree - Height of its right subtree

From the definition of AVL tree, it is evident that the only possible values for the balance factor of any node are -1, 0, 1.

A node is called right heavy or right high, if the height of its right subtree is one more than the height of its left subtree. A node is called left heavy or left high, if the height of its left subtree is one more than the height of its right subtree. A node is called balanced if the heights of its right and left subtrees are the same. The balance factor is 1 for left high, -1 for right high, and 0 for balanced node.

So, while writing the program for the AVL tree, we will take an extra member in the binary search tree node, which will store the balance factor of the node.

This is the class `Node` of AVL tree:

```
class Node
{
        public:
                int info;
                int balance;
                Node *lchild;
                Node *rchild;
                Node(int key)
                {
                        info = key;
                        balance = 0;
                        lchild = NULL;
                        rchild = NULL;
                }
};//End of class Node
```

As in a binary search tree, we will take an integer value in the info part of the node, which will serve as the key.

The three trees in figure 6.57 are examples of AVL trees. The balance factor of each node is shown outside the node. In all these trees, the balance factor of each node is -1, 0 or 1.

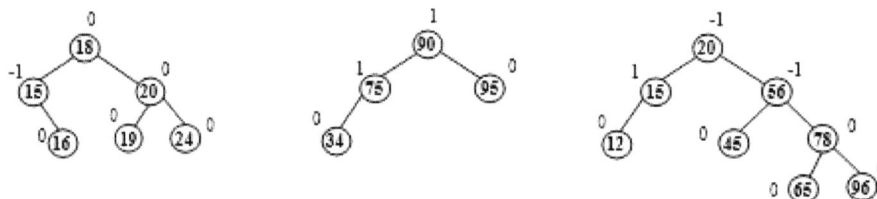

Figure 6.57 AVL trees with balance factor

Let us see some binary search trees that are not AVL trees:

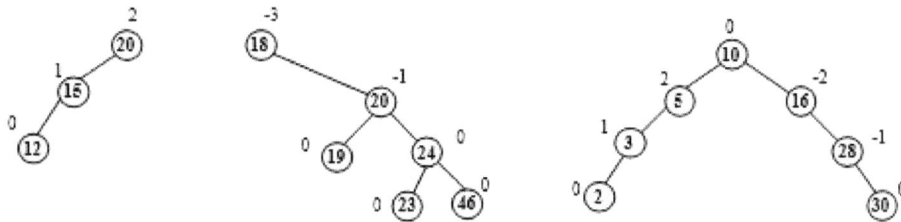

Figure 6.58 Binary search trees (Non-AVL trees) with balance factor

Now we will see the implementation of AVL tree and its operations.

This is the class `AVLTree` for AVL tree:

```
class AVLTree
{
        private:
                Node *root;
                bool taller;
                bool shorter;
                void display(Node *ptr, int level);
                void inorder(Node *ptr);
                Node* insert(Node *ptr, int key);
                void destroy(Node *ptr);
                Node* insertionLeftSubtreeCheck(Node *p);
                Node* insertionRightSubtreeCheck(Node *p);
                Node* insertionLeftBalance(Node *p);
                Node* insertionRightBalance(Node *p);
                Node* rotateRight(Node *p);
                Node* rotateLeft(Node *p);
                Node* del(Node *ptr, int key);
                Node* deletionLeftSubtreeCheck(Node *p);
                Node* deletionRightSubtreeCheck(Node *p);
                Node* deletionRightBalance(Node *p);
                Node* deletionLeftBalance(Node *p);
        public:
                AVLTree();
                ~AVLTree();
                bool isEmpty();
                void display();
                void inorder();
                void insert(int key);
                void del(int key);
};//End of class AVLTree
```

6.14.1 Searching and Traversal in AVL tree

Searching and traversal in AVL tree is done the same way as in Binary search tree.

6.14.2 Tree Rotations

After insertion or deletion operations, the balance factor of the nodes is affected and the tree might become unbalanced. The balance of the tree is restored by performing rotations, and so, before studying the insertion and deletion operations in an AVL tree, we need to know about tree rotations. Rotations are simple manipulation of pointers, which convert the tree in such a way that the new converted tree retains the binary search tree property with the inorder traversal, same as that of the original tree. Now, let us see how right rotation and left rotation are performed in binary search trees.

6.14.2.1 Right Rotation

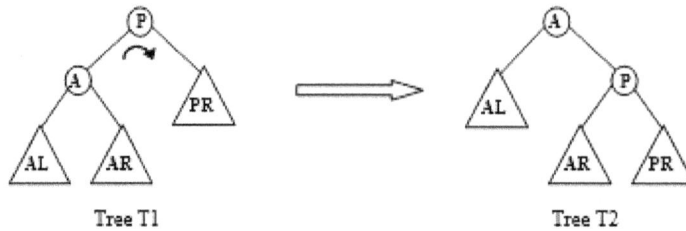

Tree T1   Tree T2

Figure 6.59 Right rotation

In the tree T1, A is the left child of node P and subtrees AL, AR are subtrees of node A. The subtree PR is the right subtree of node P. Since T1 is a binary search tree, we can write:

keys(AL) < key(A) < keys(AR) < key(P) < keys (PR) ....(1)

The inorder traversal of tree T1 will be:

inorder(AL), A, inorder(AR), P, inorder (PR)

Now, we perform a right rotation about the node P and the tree T1 will be transformed to tree T2 as shown in figure 6.59. The changes that take place are:
(i) The right subtree of A becomes the left subtree of P.
(ii) P becomes the right child of A.
(iii) A becomes the new root of the tree.

If tree T2 has to satisfy the property of a binary search tree, then the relationship among the keys should be:

keys(AL) < key(A) < keys(AR) < key(P) < keys (PR)

We have seen that this relation is true (from (1)), and so, tree T2 is also a binary search tree. The inorder traversal of tree T2 will be:

inorder(AL), A, inorder(AR), P, inorder (PR)

This is the same as the inorder traversal of tree T1.

Here, T1 could be a binary search tree or a subtree of any node of a binary search tree. Let us illustrate this rotation with an example.

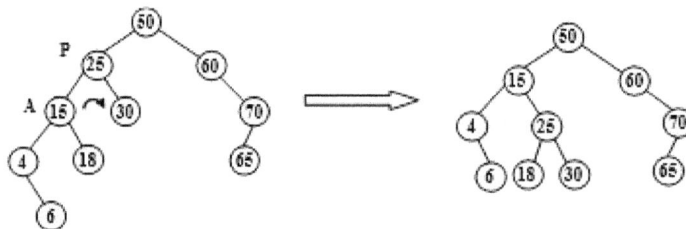

Figure 6.60 Right rotation about node 25

Here, we are performing the right rotation about node 25. If we compare this figure with the figure 6.59, then node 25 is the node P and node 15 is the node A. The subtree AL consists of nodes 4 and 6, while subtree AR consists of only node 18. The subtree PR consists of only node 30. The changes that take place due to right rotation are:

(i) The right subtree of node 15 becomes left subtree of node 25.

(ii) Node 25 becomes the right child of node 15.

(iii) The subtree which was rooted at node 25, is now rooted at node 15. So previously, the root of left subtree of node 50 was node 25, while after rotation the root of left subtree of node 50 is node 15.

Let us see two more examples of right rotation.

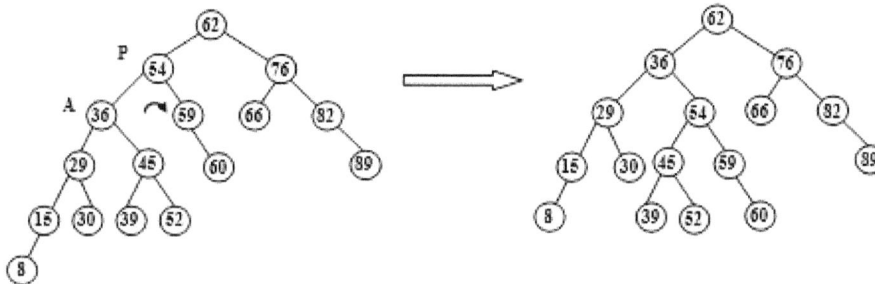

Figure 6.61 Right rotation about node 54

Here, the right rotation is performed about node 54. The subtree PR consists of nodes 59 and 60, subtree AL consists of nodes 29, 15, 30, 8, and subtree AR consists of nodes 45, 39, 52.

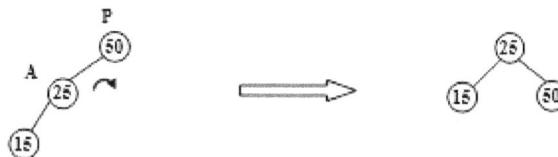

Figure 6.62 Right rotation about node 50

Here, the right rotation is performed about node 50. The subtrees PR and AR are empty, while the subtree AL consists of node 15.

The function for right rotation is simple; it takes a pointer to node P, performs rotation, and returns the pointer to node A, which is the new root of the subtree initially rooted at P.

```
Node* AVLTree::rotateRight(Node *p)
{
        Node *a;
        a = p->lchild;        //A is left child of P
        p->lchild = a->rchild; //Right child of A becomes left child of P
        a->rchild = p;        //P becomes right child of A
        return a;             //A is the new root of the subtree initially rooted at P
}//End of rotateRight()
```

6.14.2.2 Left Rotation

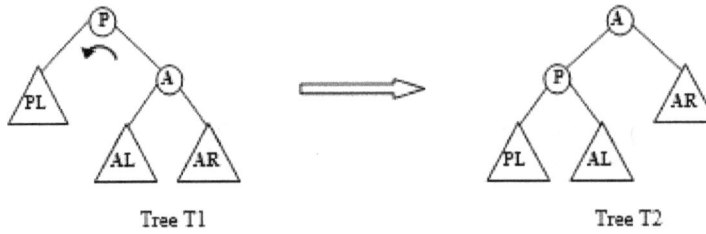

Figure 6.63 Left rotation

In the tree T1, A is the right child of node P and subtrees AL, AR are subtrees of node A. The subtree PL is the left subtree of node P. Since T1 is a binary search tree, we can write:

keys(PL) < key(P) < keys(AL) < key(A) < keys(AR) ....(2)

The inorder traversal of this tree would be:

inorder(PL), P, inorder(AL), A, inorder(AR)

Now, we perform a left rotation about the node P, and the tree T1 will be transformed to tree T2. The changes that take place are:
(i) The left subtree of A becomes the right subtree of P.
(ii) P becomes the left child of A.
(iii) A becomes the new root of the tree.

If tree T2 has to satisfy the property of a binary search tree, then the relationship among the keys should be:

keys(PL) < key(P) < keys(AL) < key(A) < keys(AR)

We have seen that this relation is true (from (2)), and so, tree T2 is also a binary search tree. The inorder traversal of binary search tree T2 will be:

inorder(PL), P, inorder(AL), A, inorder(AR)

This is the same as the inorder traversal of the tree T1. Here is an example of left rotation:

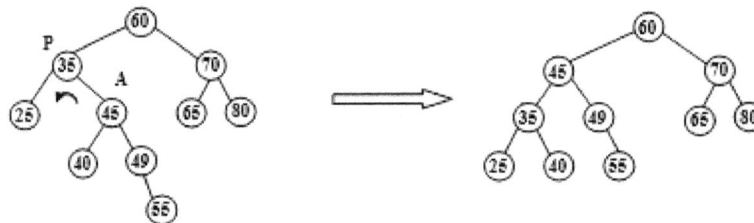

Figure 6.64 Left rotation about node 35

Here, we are performing the left rotation about node 35. If we compare it with the figure 6.63, then node 35 is node P, and node 45 is node A. The subtree AL consists of only node 40 and subtree AR consists of nodes 49 and 55. The subtree PL consists of only node 25. The changes that take place due to rotation are:

(i) The left subtree of node 45 becomes the right subtree of node 35.
(ii) Node 35 becomes the left child of node 45.
(iii) The subtree which was rooted at node 35 is now rooted at node 45.

Let us now see two more examples of left rotation:

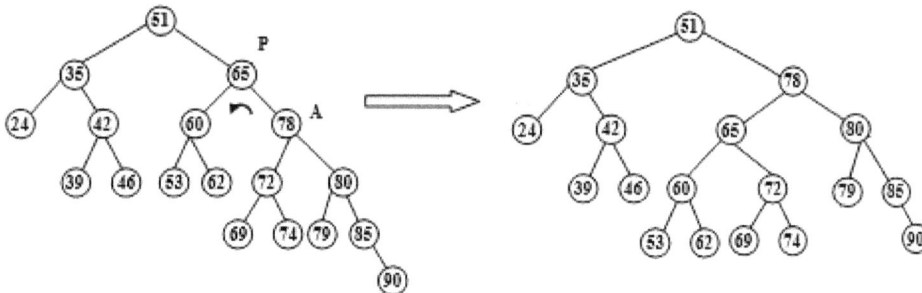

Figure 6.65 Left rotation about node 65

Here, we are performing the left rotation about node 65. The subtree PL consists of nodes 60, 53, and 62; subtree AL consists of nodes 72, 69, and 74; and subtree AR consists of nodes 80, 79, 85, and 90.

Figure 6.66 Left rotation about node 15

Here we are performing the left rotation about node 15. The subtrees PL and AL are empty while subtree AR consists of node 50. The function for left rotation is:

```
Node* AVLTree::rotateLeft(Node *p)
{
        Node *a;
        a = p->rchild;           //A is right child of P
        p->rchild = a->lchild; //Left child of A becomes right child of P
        a->lchild = p;          //P becomes left child of A
        return a;               //A is the new root of the subtree initially rooted at P
}//End of rotateLeft()
```

Now we will see how to perform insertion and deletion operations in an AVL tree.

6.14.3 Insertion in an AVL Tree

The basic insertion algorithm is similar to that of the binary search tree. We will search for the position where the new node is to be inserted and then insert the node at its proper place. After insertion, the balance factors of some nodes might change, and so, we have to record these changes. We know that the permissible balance factors in an AVL tree are 1, 0, -1, and so, if the balance factor of any node becomes 2 or -2, then we have to do additional work to restore the property of the AVL tree. Let us take an AVL tree (T) and see the effect of inserting some nodes in it.

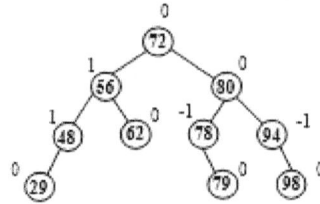

Figure 6.67 AVL tree (T)

We will insert the nodes 77, 58, 35, 99 in the tree T one by one and observe the change in balance factors.

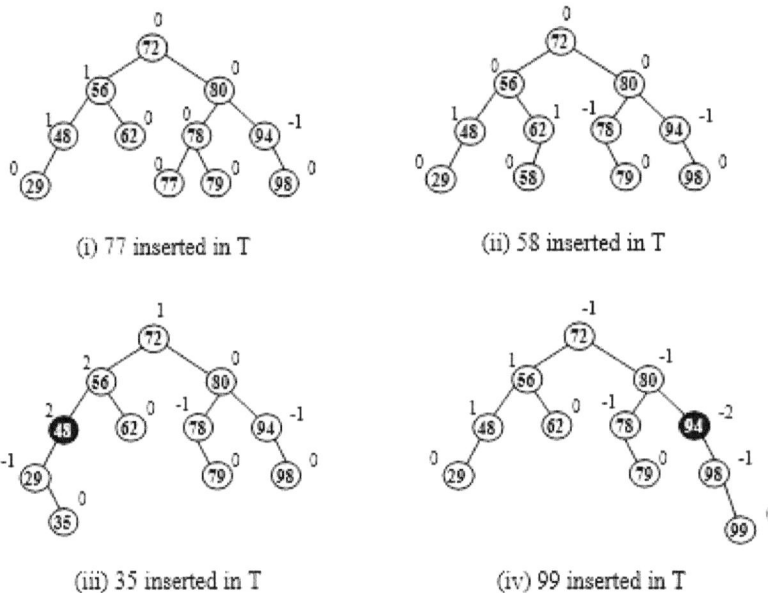

(i) 77 inserted in T

(ii) 58 inserted in T

(iii) 35 inserted in T

(iv) 99 inserted in T

Figure 6.68 Insertion in AVL tree

The nodes are inserted in the appropriate place following the same procedure as in a binary search tree. In all the four cases of figure 6.68, we can see that the balance factors of only ancestor nodes are affected, i.e., only those nodes are affected which are in the path from the inserted node to the root node. If the value of the balance factor of each node on this path is -1, 0, or 1 after insertion, then the tree is balanced and has not lost its AVL tree property after the insertion of the new node. Therefore, there is no need to do any extra work. If the balance factor of any node in this path becomes 2 or -2, the tree becomes unbalanced. The first node on this path that becomes unbalanced (balance factor 2 or -2) is marked as the pivot node. So a pivot node is the nearest unbalanced ancestor of the inserted node.

In the first two cases (insertion of 77 and 58), the tree remains AVL after the insertion of new node, while in the last two cases (insertion of 35 and 99), the balance factors of some nodes become 2 or -2, thus violating the AVL property. In the third case, 48 is marked as the pivot node, since it is the nearest unbalanced ancestor of the inserted node. Similarly, in the fourth case, 94 is marked as the pivot node.

After the insertion of the new node in the tree, we examine the nodes in the path, starting from the newly inserted node to the root. For each node in this path, the following three cases can occur:

(A) Before insertion, the node was balanced(0), and now it becomes left heavy(1) or right heavy(-1). The height of the subtree rooted at this node changes, and hence, the balance factor of the parent of this node will change. So, we need to check the balance factor of the parent node. Thus, in this case, we update the balance factor of the node and then check the balance factor of the next node in the path.

(B) Before insertion, the node was left heavy(1) or right heavy(-1), and the insertion is done in the shorter subtree. So, the node becomes balanced(0). We will update the balance factor of the node. The height of the subtree rooted at this node does not change, and hence, the balance factors of the ancestors of this node will remain unchanged. Therefore, we can stop the procedure of checking balance factors, i.e., there is no need to go upto the root and examine balance factors of all the nodes.

(C) Before insertion, the node was left heavy(1) or right heavy(-1), and the insertion is done in the heavy subtree. So, the node becomes unbalanced(2 or -2). Since the balance factor of 2 or -2 is not permitted in an AVL tree, we will not directly update the balance factor unlike the other two cases. This node is marked as the pivot node and balancing is required. The balancing is done by performing rotations at this pivot node and updating the balance factors accordingly. The balancing is done in such a way that the height of the subtree rooted at the pivot node is the same before and after insertion. Therefore, the balance factors of ancestors will not change and we can stop the procedure of checking balance factors.

Now let us apply these cases in the four insertions that we have done:

(i) **Insertion of 77 in tree T:** Nodes to be checked are 78, 80 and 72. Firstly, node 78 is examined. Before insertion, it was right heavy and now it has become balanced. This is Case B; we will change the balance factor to 0, and stop checking of balance factors. The balance factors of all the ancestors of this node will remain the same as they were before insertion. This is because the height of the subtree rooted at 78 did not change after insertion.

(ii) **Insertion of 58 in tree T:** Nodes to be checked are 62, 56 and 72. Firstly, node 62 is examined. Before insertion, it was balanced, and now, it has become left heavy. This is Case A. So, we will change the balance factor to 1 and now check node 56. Node 56 was left heavy before insertion and now it became balanced (Case B), and so, we will change the balance factor of node 56 to 0, and now we can stop procedure of checking balance factors.

(iii) **Insertion of 35 in tree T:** Nodes to be checked are 29, 48, 56 and 72. Firstly, node 29 is examined. Before insertion, it was balanced and now it has become right heavy. This is Case A. So, we will change the balance factor to -1 and check the next node, which is 48. This node was left heavy before insertion, and insertion is done in its left subtree. So now, it has become unbalanced (pivot node). This is case C, and so now, balancing will have to be done and after balancing, we can stop checking of balance factors.

(iv) **Insertion of 99 in T:** Nodes to be checked are 98, 94, 80 and 72. Firstly, node 98 is examined. Before insertion, it was balanced, and now it has become right heavy. This is Case A. So, we will change the balance factor to -1 and check the next node, which is 94. This node was right heavy before insertion, and insertion is done in its right subtree. So now, it has become unbalanced (pivot node). This is case C. Now, balancing will have to be done and after balancing, we can stop checking of balance factors.

This was an outline of the insertion process. Now, we will look at how we can write the function for insertion. In the binary search tree, we had written both recursive and non-recursive functions for insertion. Here, we will write the recursive version, because we can easily check the balance factors of ancestors in the unwinding phase. We will take the recursive insert function of BST as the base, and make some additions in it, so that the tree remains balanced after insertion. Here is the function for insertion in an AVL tree:

```
Node* AVLTree::insert(Node *ptr, int key)
{
        if(ptr == NULL)                 //Base case
        {
```

```
                ptr = new Node(key);
                taller = true;
        }
        else if(key < ptr->info)        //Insertion in left subtree
        {
                ptr->lchild = insert(ptr->lchild, key);
                if(taller == true)
                        ptr = insertionLeftSubtreeCheck(ptr);
        }
        else if(key > ptr->info)        //Insertion in right subtree
        {
                ptr->rchild = insert(ptr->rchild, key);
                if(taller == true)
                        ptr = insertionRightSubtreeCheck(ptr);
        }
        else    //Base case
        {
                cout << key << " is already there\n";
                taller = false;
        }

        return ptr;
}//End of insert()
void AVLTree::insert(int key)
{
        root = insert(root, key);
}//End of insert()
```

There are two recursive calls in the recursive `insert()` function. After the recursion stops, we will pass through each node in the path starting from inserted node to the root node, i.e., in the unwinding phase, we will pass through each ancestor of the inserted node.

The functions `insertionLeftSubtreeCheck()` and `insertionRightSubtreeCheck()` are written after the recursive calls, and so they will be called in the unwinding phase. The function `insertionLeftSubtreeCheck()` will be called to check and update the balance factors, when insertion is done in the left subtree of the current node. If insertion is done in the right subtree of the current node, then the function `insertionRightSubtreeCheck()` will be called for this purpose. These functions are not always called; they are called only when the flag `taller` is true. Now, let us see what this `taller` is and why are these functions called conditionally.

In the three cases that we have studied earlier, we know that we can stop checking if case B or case C occurs at any ancestor node. So, `taller` is a flag which is initially set to true when the node is inserted, and when any of the last two cases (B or C) are encountered, we will make it false (inside `insertionLeftSubtreeCheck()` or `insertionRightSubtreeCheck()`). The process of checking balance factors stops when `taller` becomes false.

Now, we will try to understand the working of this function with the help of an example. Let us take the example of insertion of node 58 in tree T (figure 6.68(ii)). The recursive calls are shown in the figure 6.69.

There are 4 invocations of `insert()` and the recursion stops when `insert()` is called with `ptr` as NULL. In this case, a new node is created and is assigned to `ptr`. All the fields of this node are set to proper values in the `Node` constructor. The value of flag `taller` is set to true. The value of `ptr` is returned and the unwinding phase begins.

The control returns to the previous invocation (3rd call) of `insert()`, and since `taller` is true, the function `insertionLeftSubtreeCheck()` is called (insertion in left subtree of 62). Inside this function, the appropriate action will be taken according to the case that occurs. We have seen earlier that case A occurs at this point, so inside `insertionLeftSubtreeCheck()`, the balance factor of node 62 will be reset. We know that when case A occurs, we do not stop the procedure of checking balance factors. Thus, the value of flag `taller` will remain true.

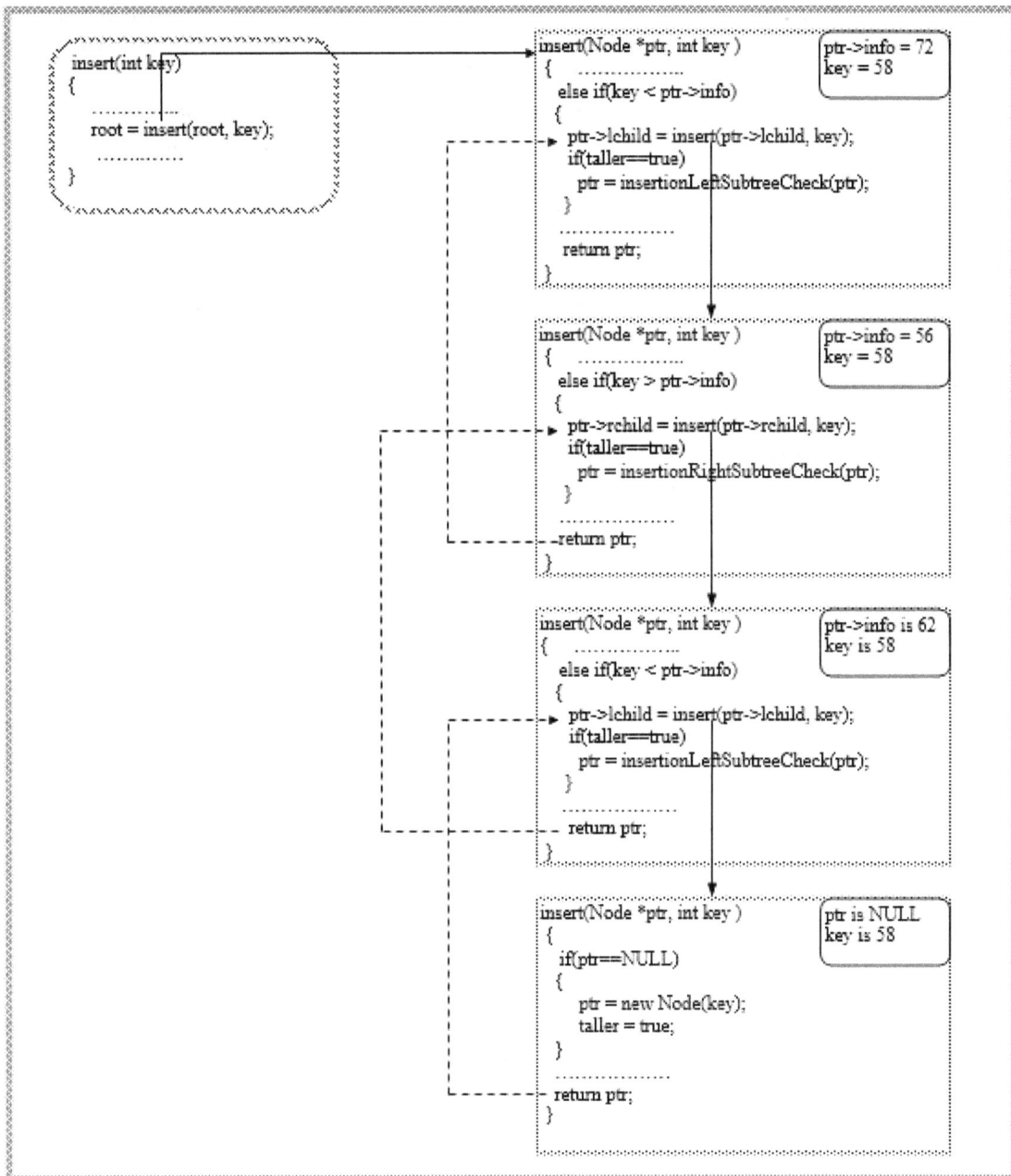

Figure 6.69 Recursive calls for inserting 58

Now, control returns to the previous invocation (2nd call) of `insert()` and since the value of `taller` is true, the function `insertionRightSubtreeCheck()` is called (insertion in right subtree of 56). This time case B occurs, and so, inside `insertionRightSubtreeCheck()`, we will reset the balance factor of node 56. Now, we have to stop the process of checking balance factors. For this, we will make the value of `taller` false inside the function `insertionRightSubtreeCheck()`. This will ensure that the functions `insertionLeftSubtreeCheck()` and `insertionRightSubtreeCheck()` will not be called in the remaining invocations of `insert()`.

Now control returns to the first invocation of `insert()`, and since now the value of `taller` is false, the function `insertionLeftSubtreeCheck()` will not be called. After this, the control returns to the public member function `insert()`, where the recursive `insert()` function is called.

If the key to be inserted is already present, then it is not inserted in the tree and so there is no need of checking the balance factors in the unwinding phase. Hence, the value of `taller` is made false in the case of duplicate key.

Now let us study in detail the different cases to be handled inside the functions `insertionLeftSubtreeCheck()` and `insertionRightSubtreeCheck()`.

6.14.3.1 Insertion in Left Subtree

When insertion is done in the left subtree of the current node, we use `insertionLeftSubtreeCheck()` to check and update the balance factors in unwinding phase. So, before writing this function, let us study the various cases involved in it. As stated earlier, initially, the value of flag `taller` will be true.

P is the current node whose balance factor is being checked. PL and PR denote the left and right subtrees of P. Insertion is done in left subtree of P. We will consider a subtree rooted at the node P.

Case L_A:

Before insertion: bf(P) = 0

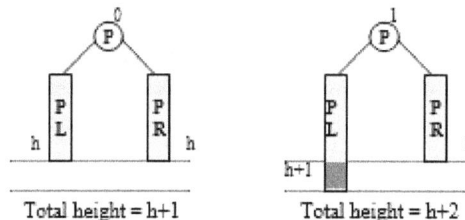

Figure 6.70 Case L_A

After insertion: bf(P) = 1
The height of the subtree rooted at node P has increased. This means that the balance factor of parent of node P will definitely change, and so we need to continue the process of checking the balance factors. Hence, the value of `taller` remains true.

Case L_B:

Before insertion: bf(P) = -1

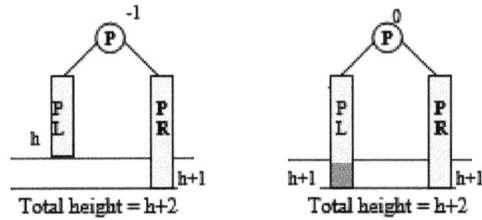

Figure 6.71 Case L_B

After insertion bf(P) = 0

Height of the subtree rooted at node P has not increased. This means that the balance factors of parent and ancestors of node P will not change. So, we can stop the process of checking balance factors. Therefore, the value of `taller` is made false.

Case L_C:

Before insertion bf(P) = 1

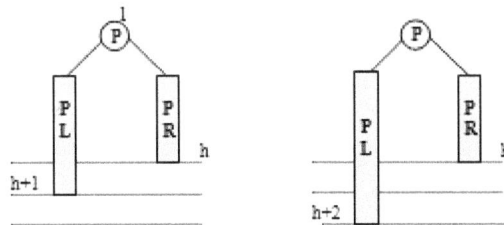

Figure 6.72 Case L_C

After insertion, the balance factor of P will become 2, and this is not a permissible value for balance factor in an AVL tree. So, we will not update it. The node P becomes unbalanced and it is the first node to become unbalanced. So, it is the pivot node. Now, left balancing is required to restore the AVL property of the tree.

Let us now see how we can balance the tree in this case by performing rotations. We will further explore the left subtree of the pivot node. Let A be the root of subtree PL, and AL, AR be the left and right subtrees of A. Therefore, the subtree rooted at the pivot node before insertion is:

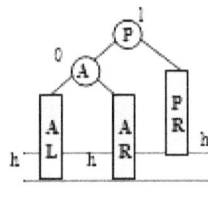

Figure 6.73 Root A for subtree PL

The balance factor of A before insertion will definitely be zero (1 or -1 is not possible). We will discuss the reason for it afterwards. Now, we can have two cases, depending on whether the insertion is done in AL or AR.

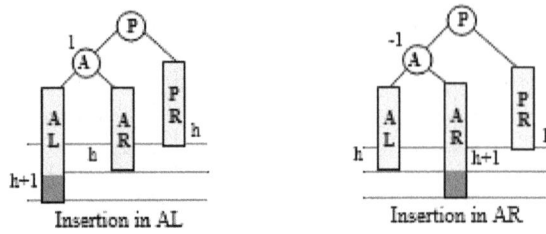

Figure 6.74 Two cases of insertion

Currently, we are checking the balance factor of node P. This means that we have travelled till node A and updated all balance factors. So, at this point, the balance factor of A will be 1, if the insertion is done in AL or -1, if the insertion is done in AR. The balance factor of the pivot node is the same as was before insertion (it is still 1); we have not updated it to 2. Now, we have two subcases depending on the balance factor of node A.

Case L_C1:

Insertion done in the left subtree of the left child of node P (in AL)
Before insertion: bf(P) = 1, bf(A) = 0
After insertion, updated balance factor of A = 1
A single right rotation about P is performed.

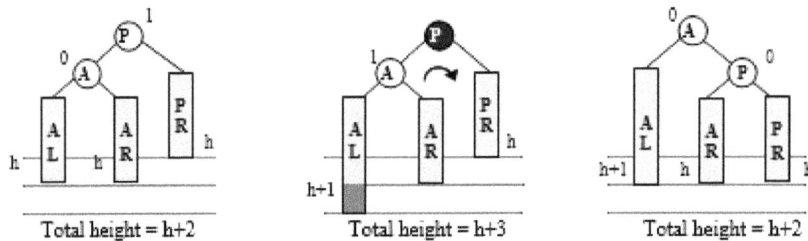

Figure 6.75 Case L_C1

After balancing: bf(P) = 0, bf(A) = 0

The first figure shows the initial tree before insertion. The second figure shows the tree after insertion at the point when we have updated balance factors till A, and found that P has become unbalanced. The third figure shows the tree after rotation. After rotating, the balance factors of both pivot node P and node A become zero, and now, node A is the new root of this subtree.

Here are two examples of case L_C1 (right rotation).

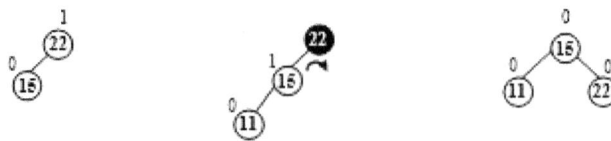

Figure 6.76 Insertion of 11

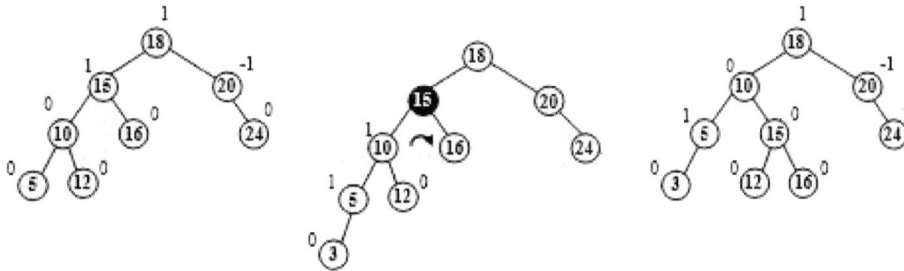

Figure 6.77 Insertion of 3

Case L_C2:

Insertion done in right subtree of left child of node P (in AR)
Before insertion: bf(P) = 1, bf(A) = 0
After insertion updated balance factor of A = -1
LeftRight rotation performed

In this case, we need to explore the right subtree of A. Let B be the root of subtree AR, and let BL, BR be the left and right subtrees of B, respectively. Before insertion, the balance factor of B will definitely be zero.

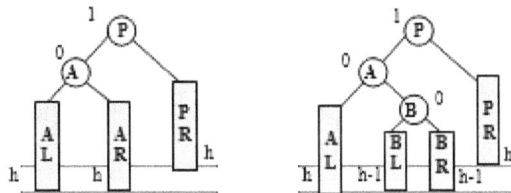

Figure 6.78 Case L_C2

Here, we can have two cases depending on whether insertion is done in BL or BR. It is possible that the subtree AR is empty before insertion, and so in this case, the newly inserted node is none other than B. This is our third case. So we have 3 subcases:
L_C2a: New node is inserted in BR   (bf(B) = -1)
L_C2b: New node is inserted in BL   (bf(B) = 1)
L_C2c: B is the newly inserted node (bf(B) = 0)

These 3 subcases are considered just to calculate the resulting balance factor of the nodes; otherwise, the rotation performed is similar in all three cases.

A single rotation about the pivot node will not balance the tree, and so we have to perform double rotation here. First, we will perform a left rotation about node A, and then we will perform a right rotation about the pivot node P.

Case L_C2a:

New node is inserted in BR,
After insertion, updated balance factor of B = -1

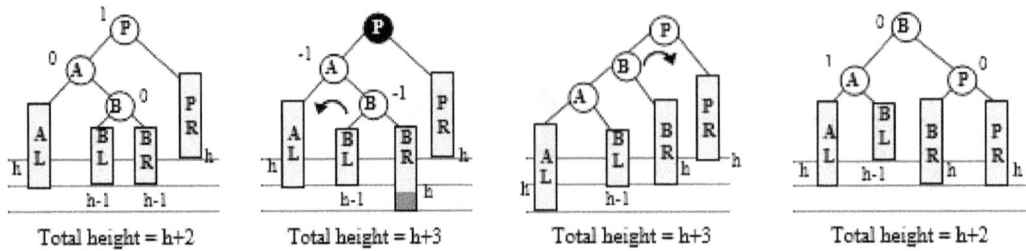

Figure 6.79 Case L_C2a

After balancing: bf(P) = 0, bf(A) = 1, bf(B) = 0

The first figure shows the initial tree before insertion, with AR further explored. The second figure shows the tree after insertion at the point when we have updated balance factors till A and found that P has become unbalanced. The third figure shows the tree after a left rotation about A, and the last figure shows the tree after a right rotation about P.

Case L_C2b:

New node is inserted in BL
After insertion, updated balance factor of B = 1

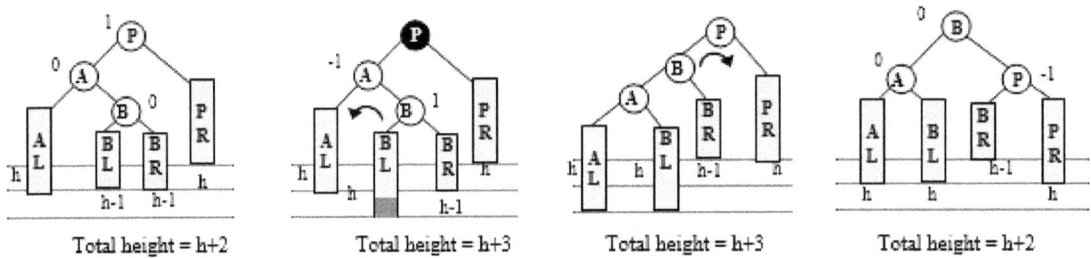

Figure 6.80 Case L_C2b

After balancing: bf(P) = -1, bf(A) = 0, bf(B) = 0

Case L_C2c:

B is the newly inserted node, so balance factor of B = 0

In figure 6.78, if the newly inserted node is B, it means that AR was empty before insertion, or we can say that the value of h is zero. Since AL and PR also have height h, they will also be empty before insertion.

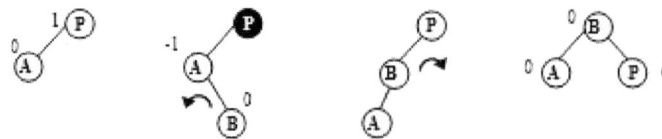

Figure 6.81 Case L_C2c

After balancing: bf(P) = 0, bf(A) = 0, bf(B) = 0

Here are two examples of case L_C2 (LeftRight rotation).

Figure 6.82 Insertion of 17

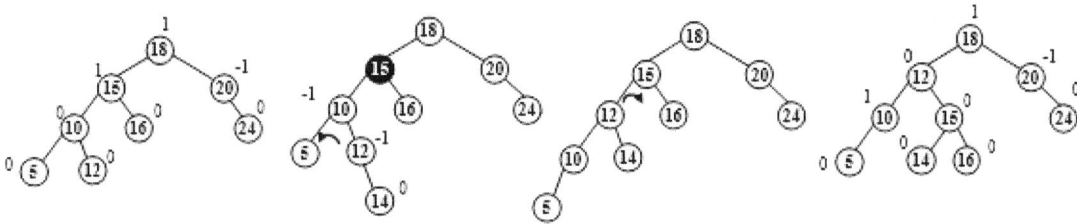

Figure 6.83 Insertion of 14

In case L_A, the value of `taller` remained true because the height of the subtree rooted at P had increased, and in case L_B, the value of `taller` is made false, because the height of the subtree rooted at P did not change. In case L_C, the subtree rooted at P gets a new root but the height of this subtree remains the same (in all subcases of L_C, height before insertion and after balancing is h+2) and so `taller` is made false. The function `insertionLeftSubtreeCheck()` is:

```
Node* AVLTree::insertionLeftSubtreeCheck(Node *p)
{
        switch(p->balance)
        {
            case 0:         //Case L_A : was balanced
                    p->balance = 1; //now left heavy
                    break;
            case -1:        //Case L_B : was right heavy
                    p->balance = 0; //now balanced
                    taller = false;
                    break;
            case 1:         //Case L_C : was left heavy
                    p = insertionLeftBalance(p); //left balancing
                    taller = false;
                    break;
        }
        return p;
}//End of insertionLeftSubtreeCheck()
```

The function `insertionLeftBalance()` is:

```
Node* AVLTree::insertionLeftBalance(Node *p)
{
        Node *a, *b;
        a = p->lchild;
        if(a->balance == 1)    //Case L_C1 : Insertion in AL
        {
                p->balance = 0;
                a->balance = 0;
                p = rotateRight(p);
        }
        else    //Case L_C2 : Insertion in AR
        {
                b = a->rchild;
                switch(b->balance)
                {
                        case -1:       //Case L_C2a : Insertion in BR
                                p->balance = 0;
                                a->balance = 1;
                                break;
                        case 1:        //Case L_C2b : Insertion in BL
                                p->balance = -1;
                                a->balance = 0;
                                break;
                        case 0:        //Case L_C2c : B is the newly inserted node
                                p->balance = 0;
                                a->balance = 0;
                                break;
                }
                b->balance = 0;
                p->lchild = rotateLeft(a);
                p = rotateRight(p);
        }
        return p;
}//End of insertionLeftBalance()
```

In the function `insertionLeftBalance()`, we have updated the balance factors before performing rotations. This is because rotations are done through functions `rotateRight()` and `rotateLeft()` and after calling these functions, p no longer points to node P, but it points to the new root of the subtree.

The following information summarizes all of the cases explained, and it includes the situation when the insertion is done in the right subtree.

A new node is inserted and taller = true
P is the node whose balance factor is being checked.

    If Insertion in left subtree of the node P (Insertion in PL)
    Case L_A : If node P was balanced before insertion
                Node P becomes left heavy
    Case L_B : If node P was right heavy before insertion
                Node P becomes balanced, taller = false
    Case L_C : If node P was left heavy before insertion
                Node P becomes unbalanced, Left Balancing required, taller = false
                P is the pivot node and its left child is A
                Case L_C1 : If insertion in left subtree of A (in AL)
                        Right Rotation (right about P)
                Case L_C2 : If insertion in right subtree of A (in AR)
                        LeftRight Rotation (left about A then right about P)
                        B is the right child of A
                        Case L_C2a : If insertion in right subtree of B (in BR)
                                  $bf(P) = 0$, $bf(A) = 1$
                        Case L_C2b : If insertion in left subtree of B (in BL)
                                  $bf(P) = -1$, $bf(A) = 0$
                        Case L_C2c : If B is the newly inserted node.
                                  $bf(P) = 0$, $bf(A) = 0$

    If Insertion in right subtree of the node P (Insertion in PR)
    Case R_A : If node P was balanced before insertion
                Node P becomes right heavy
    Case R_B : If node P was left heavy before insertion
                 Node P becomes balanced, taller = false
    Case R_C : If node P was right heavy before insertion
                 Node P becomes unbalanced, Right Balancing required, taller = false
                P is the pivot node and its right child is A
                Case R_C1 : If Insertion in right subtree of A (in AR)
                        Left Rotation (left about P)
                Case R_C2 : Insertion in left subtree of A (in AL)
                        RightLeft Rotation (right about A then left about P)
                        B is the left child of A
                        Case R_C2a : If insertion in right subtree of B (in BR)
                                    $bf(P) = 1$, $bf(A) = 0$
                        Case R_C2b : If insertion in left subtree of B (in BL)
                                  $bf(P) = 0$, $bf(A) = -1$
                        Case R_C2c : If B is the newly inserted node.
                                $bf(P) = 0$, $bf(A) = 0$

Figure 6.84 Insertion in an AVL tree

6.14.3.2 Insertion in Right Subtree

In this case, insertion is done in the right subtree of P.

Case R_A:

Before insertion: $bf(P) = 0$

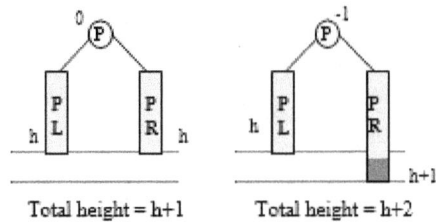

Figure 6.85 Case R_A

After insertion: bf(P) = -1
Height of the subtree rooted at pivot node changes, and so, `taller` remains true.

Case R_B:

Before insertion: bf(P) = 1

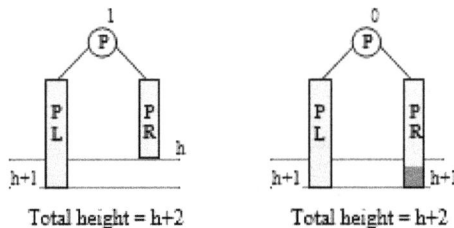

Figure 6.86 Case R_B

After insertion: bf(P) = 0
Height of the subtree rooted at the pivot node does not change, and so, the `taller` is made false.

Case R_C:

Before insertion: bf(P) = -1

After insertion, node P will become unbalanced(-2). So P becomes the pivot node and balancing is required. We will explore the subtree PR and let A be the root, and AL, AR the left and right subtrees of A. Like in case L_C, here also we have two cases depending on whether the insertion is done in AL or AR.

Case R_C1:

Insertion done in the right subtree of the right child of node P (in AR).
After insertion updated balance factor of A = -1
Left rotation about node P is performed.

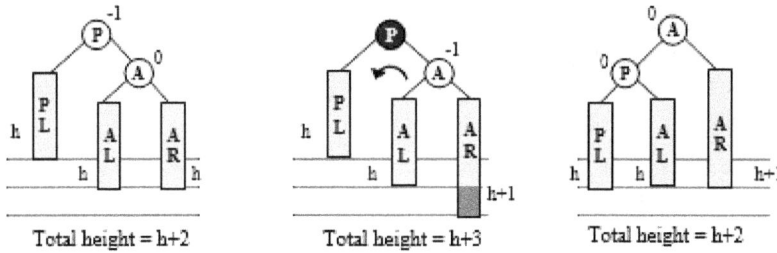

Figure 6.87 Case R_C1

After balancing: bf(P) = 0, bf(A) = 0

Here are two examples of case R_C1(left rotation).

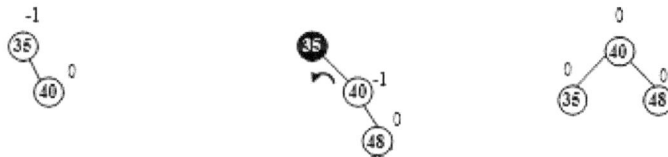

Figure 6.88 Insertion of 48

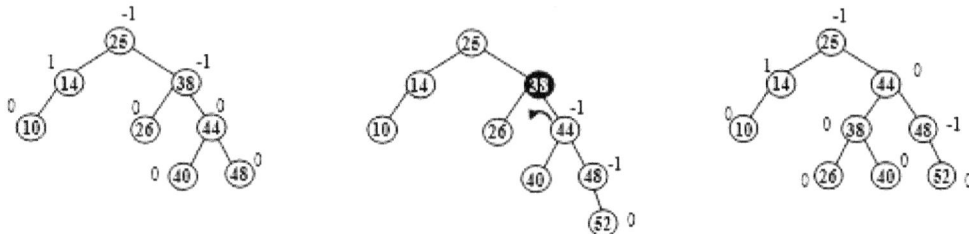

Figure 6.89 Insertion of 52

Case R_C2:

Insertion done in the left subtree of the right child of node P (in AL).
After insertion updated balance factor of A = 1
RightLeft rotation performed.

We will further explore the left subtree of A. Let B be the root of subtree AL, and, let BL, BR be the left and right subtrees of B, respectively. Before insertion, the balance factor of B will definitely be zero.

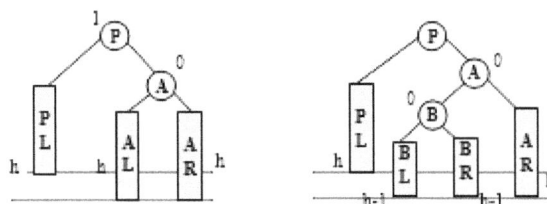

Figure 6.90 Case R_C2

There can be 3 subcases:

R_C2a: New node is inserted in BR   (bf(B) = -1)
R_C2b: New node is inserted in BL   (bf(B) = 1)
R_C2c: B is the newly inserted node (bf(B) = 0)

Like case L_C2, here also double rotation is performed. First, we will perform a right rotation about node A, and then we will perform a left rotation about the pivot node P. We can see that this is the mirror image of a case of left to right rotation.

Case R_C2a:

New node is inserted in BR.
After insertion updated balance factor of B = -1

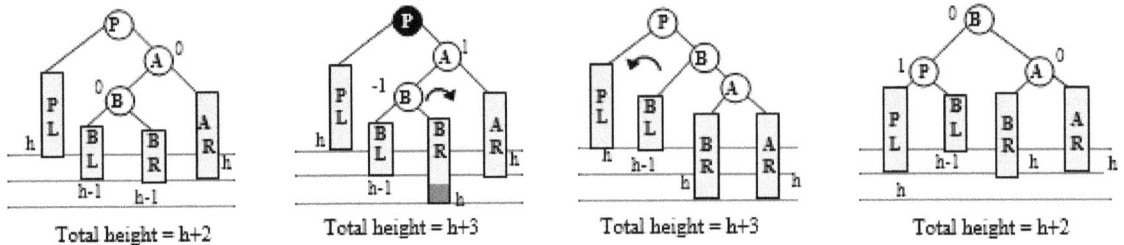

Figure 6.91 Case R_C2a

After balancing: bf(P) = 1, bf(A) = 0, bf(B) = 0

Case R_C2b:

New node is inserted in BL
After insertion updated balance factor of B = 1

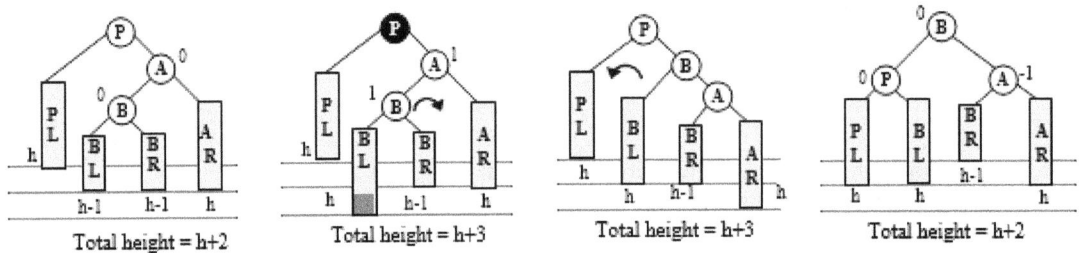

Figure 6.92 Case R_C2b

After balancing: bf(P) = 0, bf(A) = -1, bf(B) = 0

Case R_C2c:

B is the newly inserted node, so balance factor of B = 0

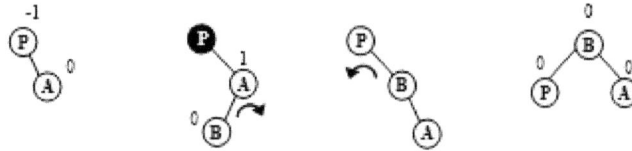

Figure 6.93 Case R_C2c

After balancing: bf(P) = 0, bf(A) = 0, bf(B) = 0

Here are two examples of case R_C2 (RightLeft rotation).

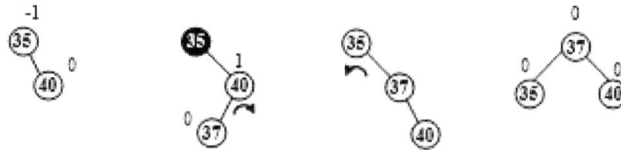

Figure 6.94 Insertion of 37

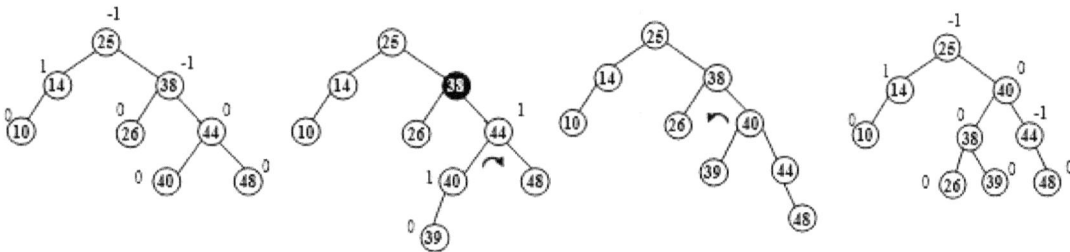

Figure 6.95 Insertion of 39

The function `insertionRightSubtreeCheck()` is:

```
Node* AVLTree::insertionRightSubtreeCheck(Node *p)
{
      switch(p->balance)
      {
            case 0:          //Case R_A : was balanced
                  p->balance = -1; //now right heavy
                  break;
            case 1:          //Case R_B : was left heavy
                  p->balance = 0; //now balanced
                  taller = false;
                  break;
            case -1:         //Case R_C : was right heavy
                  p = insertionRightBalance(p); //right balancing
                  taller = false;
                  break;
      }
      return p;
}//End of insertionRightSubtreeCheck()
```

The function `insertionRightBalance()` is:

```
Node* AVLTree::insertionRightBalance(Node *p)
{
        Node *a, *b;
        a = p->rchild;
        if(a->balance == -1)    //Case R_C1 : Insertion in AR
        {
                p->balance = 0;
                a->balance = 0;
                p = rotateLeft(p);
        }
        else    //Case R_C2 : Insertion in AL
        {
                b = a->lchild;
                switch(b->balance)
                {
                        case -1:        //Case R_C2a : Insertion in BR
                                p->balance = 1;
                                a->balance = 0;
                                break;
                        case 1:         //Case R_C2b : Insertion in BL
                                p->balance = 0;
                                a->balance = -1;
                                break;
                        case 0:         //Case R_C2c : B is the newly inserted node
                                p->balance = 0;
                                a->balance = 0;
                                break;
                }
                b->balance = 0;
                p->rchild = rotateRight(a);
                p = rotateLeft(p);
        }
        return p;
}//End of insertionRightBalance()
```

In all the 4 cases of rotation (Right, RightLeft, Left, LeftRight), the height of the subtree rooted at the pivot remains the same as was before insertion. So, the balance factors of ancestors of pivot remain unchanged. Hence, there is no need of checking balance factors of the ancestors. Only one single or double rotation is sufficient to balance the whole tree.

In the above discussion, we have assumed that the balance factors of A and B before insertion will definitely be zero. Let us see why this is so.

Whenever we find an unbalanced node (pivot node), it is definite that all the nodes in the path from newly inserted node to this pivot node had a balance factor of 0 prior to insertion. This is because if any node in this path had a balance factor of 1 or -1 before insertion, then after insertion, either this node will become balanced (bf = 0, case B), or it will become unbalanced (bf = 2 or -2, case C). We know that in both these cases, we stop checking balance factors. This is the reason for assuming the balance factors of A and B to be zero before insertion.

Let us take some numbers and construct an AVL tree from them.

50, 40, 35, 58, 48, 42, 60, 30, 33, 25

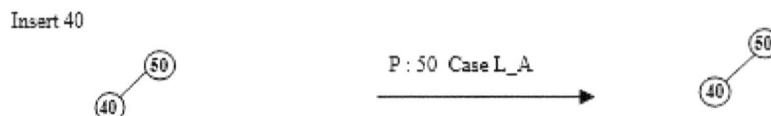

Figure 6.96 Insert 40

Insert 35

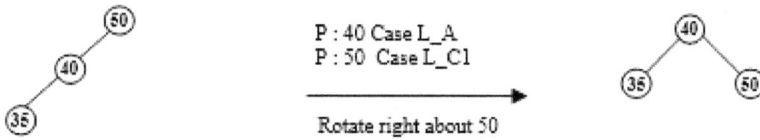

P : 40 Case L_A
P : 50 Case L_C1

Rotate right about 50

Figure 6.97 Insert 35

Insert 58

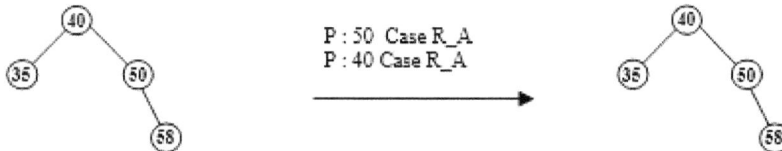

P : 50 Case R_A
P : 40 Case R_A

Figure 6.98 Insert 58

Insert 48

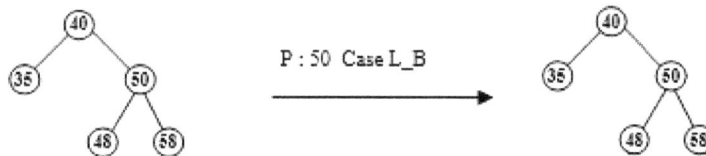

P : 50 Case L_B

Figure 6.99 Insert 48

Insert 42

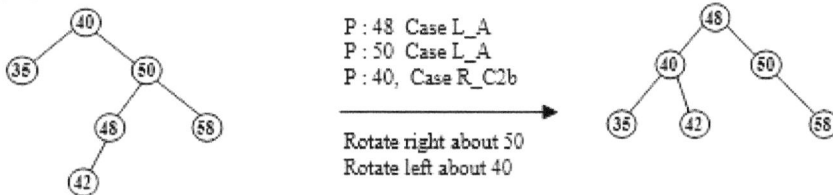

P : 48 Case L_A
P : 50 Case L_A
P : 40, Case R_C2b

Rotate right about 50
Rotate left about 40

Figure 6.100 Insert 42

Insert 60

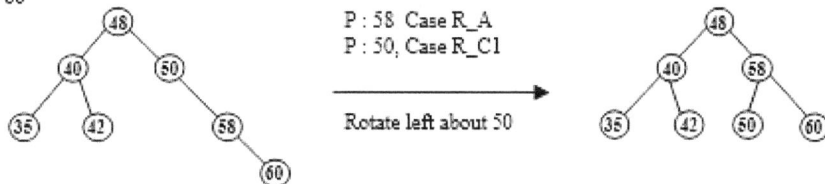

P : 58 Case R_A
P : 50, Case R_C1

Rotate left about 50

Figure 6.101 Insert 60

Insert 30

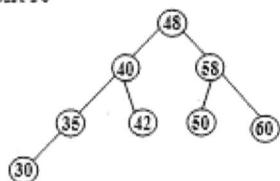

P : 35, Case L_A
P : 40, Case L_A
P : 48, Case L_A

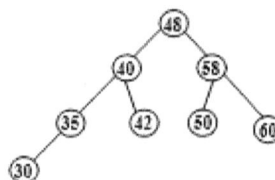

Figure 6.102 Insert 30

Insert 33

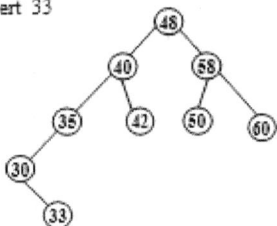

P : 30, Case R_A
P : 35, Case L_C2c

Rotate left about 30
Rotate right about 35

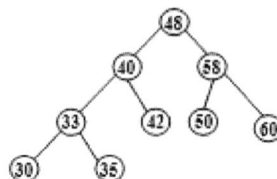

Figure 6.103 Insert 33

Insert 25

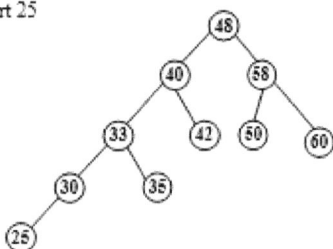

P : 30, Case L_A
P : 33, Case L_A
P : 40, Case L_C1

Rotate right about 40

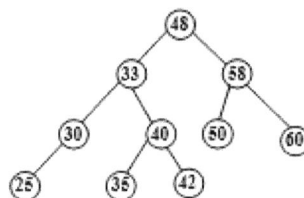

Figure 6.104 Insert 25

While inserting in an AVL tree, there is no need to remember all the cases. We just need to update the balance factors of the ancestor nodes, and if any node becomes unbalanced, we can perform the appropriate rotations.

6.14.4 Deletion in AVL Tree

Deletion is performed using the same logic as in Binary search tree. After deletion, the tree may become unbalanced in some cases, and so we have to identify these cases and arrange for restoring the balance of the tree. We can take the deletion algorithm of BST as the base and modify it, so that the AVL property is retained after deletion.

The node is deleted from the tree using recursive algorithm and in the unwinding phase, we check the balance factors of the nodes in the path from deleted node to the root node. There can be three cases for each node in this path:

(A) Before deletion, the node was balanced, and after deletion, it becomes left heavy or right heavy. We will update the balance factor of the node. In this case, the balance factors of the ancestors of this node will remain unchanged. Therefore, we can stop the procedure of checking balance factors.

(B) Before deletion, the node was left heavy or right heavy, and the deletion is performed in the heavy subtree. So after deletion, the node becomes balanced. We will update the balance factor of the node and then check the balance factor of the next node in the path.

(C) Before deletion, the node was left heavy or right heavy, and the deletion is performed in the shorter subtree. So after deletion, the node becomes unbalanced. In this case, balancing is required, which is performed using the same rotations that were done in insertion. There are 3 subcases in the case C. In one subcase, we will stop the procedure of checking balance factors, while in the other two subcases, we will continue our checking.

The function for deletion of a node from AVL tree is as follows:

```
Node* AVLTree::del(Node *ptr, int key)
{
      Node *succ, *temp;

      if(ptr == NULL)                //Base case
      {
            cout << key << " not found\n";
            shorter = false;
            return ptr;
      }

      if(key < ptr->info)            //Delete from left subtree
      {
            ptr->lchild = del(ptr->lchild, key);
            if(shorter == true)
                  ptr = deletionLeftSubtreeCheck(ptr);
      }
      else if(key > ptr->info)       //Delete from right subtree
      {
            ptr->rchild = del(ptr->rchild, key);
            if(shorter == true)
                  ptr = deletionRightSubtreeCheck(ptr);
      }
      else    //key to be deleted is found, Base case
      {

            if(ptr->lchild!=NULL && ptr->rchild!=NULL) //2 children
            {
                  succ = ptr->rchild;
                  while(succ->lchild != NULL)
                        succ = succ->lchild;

                  ptr->info = succ->info;
                  ptr->rchild = del(ptr->rchild, succ->info);
                  if(shorter == true)
                        ptr = deletionRightSubtreeCheck(ptr);
            }
            else    //1 child or no child
            {
                  temp = ptr;
                  if(ptr->lchild != NULL) //Only left child
                        ptr = ptr->lchild;
                  else    //Only right child or no child
                        ptr = ptr->rchild;

                  delete temp;
                  shorter = true;
            }
      }

      return ptr;
```

```
}//End of del()
void AVLTree::del(int key)
{
        root = del(root, key);
}//End of del()
```

The recursive del() function is similar to the function for deletion in a BST, except for a few changes required to retain the balance of the tree after deletion. The flag shorter serves the same purpose as taller did in insert(). It is initially set to true when the node is deleted, and it is made false inside deletionLeftSubtreeCheck() or deletionRightSubtreeCheck(). The process of checking balance factors stops when shorter becomes false. When the item to be deleted is not found in the tree, then also shorter is made false because in this case, we do not want any checking of balance factors in the unwinding phase.

6.14.4.1 Deletion from Left Subtree

P is the current node whose balance factor is being checked, and PL, PR are its left and right subtrees, respectively. The deletion is done from the left subtree of P.

Case L_A:

Before deletion: bf(P) = 0

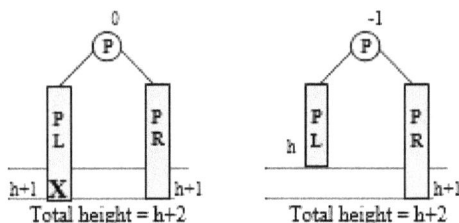

Figure 6.105 Case L_A

After deletion: bf(P) = -1
The height of the subtree rooted at P does not change after deletion, and so, shorter is made false.

Case L_B:

Before deletion: bf(P) = 1

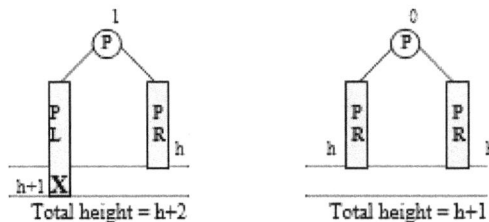

Figure 6.106 Case L_B

After deletion: bf(P) = 0
The height of the subtree rooted at P is decreased, and so, shorter remains true.

Case L_C:

Before deletion: bf(P) = -1

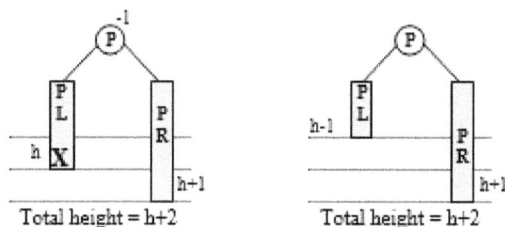

Figure 6.107 Case L_C

After deletion, node P will become unbalanced, so we will not update its balance factor directly. P becomes the pivot node, and balancing is required. We will explore the right subtree of P. Let A be the root of PR, and let AL, AR be the left and right subtrees of A.

Note that while insertion, we had explored the subtree in which insertion was done, while here, we are exploring the subtree other than the one from which the node is deleted. So, if deletion is performed from the left subtree of the pivot node, then right balancing is required.

The balance factors of only those nodes will be affected by deletion, which lie in the path from the deleted node to the root node. Presently, we are at the point when we have deleted the node and updated all the balance factors in PL, and now, we have found that P has become unbalanced. The balance factors of nodes in PR will remain unaffected after deletion, since it is not in the path from the deleted node to the root. Node A is the root of PR and so, its balance factor will be the same before and after deletion. Now, we can have three cases depending on the three different values of the balance factor of A.

Note that in insertion we had only two cases because there the balance factor of A before insertion was definitely 0. This was so because there A was in the path that was affected by insertion. In deletion, node A could have any of the three values (-1, 0, 1) before deletion since it is not in the path that is affected by deletion.

Case L_C1:

Before deletion bf(P) = -1, bf(A) = 0
Left rotation about P is performed.

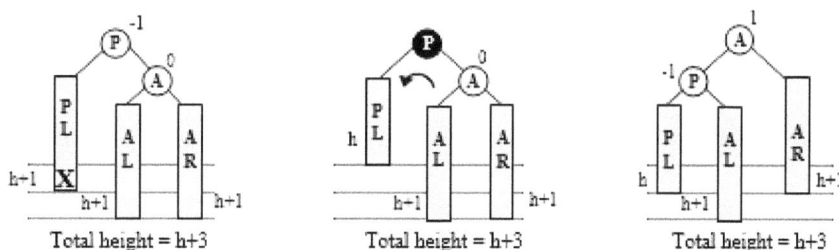

Figure 6.108 Case L_C1

After balancing: bf(P) = -1, bf(A) = 1

The first figure shows the initial tree, second figure shows the tree after deletion at the point when we have updated all the balance factors in PL and found that P has become unbalanced. The third figure shows the tree after rotation. The height of the subtree rooted at P does not change, and so, `shorter` is made false.

Case L_C2:

Before deletion bf(P) = -1, bf(A) = -1
Left rotation about P performed.

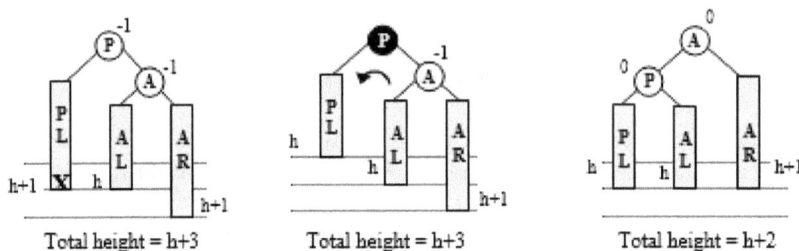

Figure 6.109 Case L_C2

After balancing: bf(P) = 0, bf(A) = 0
In this case, the height of the subtree has decreased, and so `shorter` remains true.

Case L_C3:

Before deletion: bf(P) = -1, bf(A) = 1
RightLeft rotation performed.

In this case, a single rotation will not suffice, and so, double rotation is performed. Now, we will explore the left subtree of A and let B be the root node of AL.

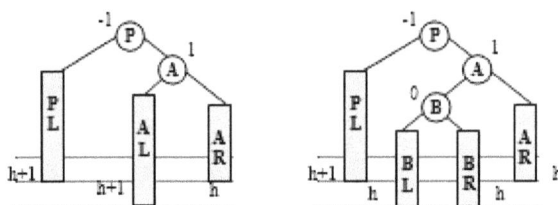

Figure 6.110 Case L_C3

We can have three subcases depending on the three different balance factors of B. The rotation performed is the same in all three cases (RightLeft rotation) but the resulting balance factors of P and A are different.

Case L_C3a:

Before deletion: bf(P) = -1, bf(A) = 1, bf(B) = 0

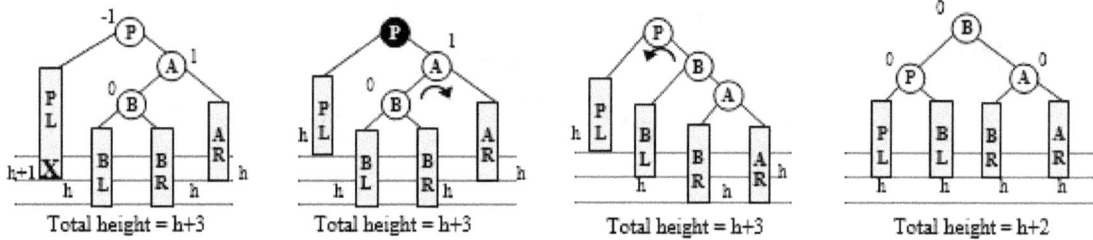

Figure 6.111 Case L_C3a

After balancing: bf(P) = 0, bf(A) = 0, bf(B) = 0

Case L_C3b:

Before deletion: bf(P) = -1, bf(A) = 1, bf(B) = 1

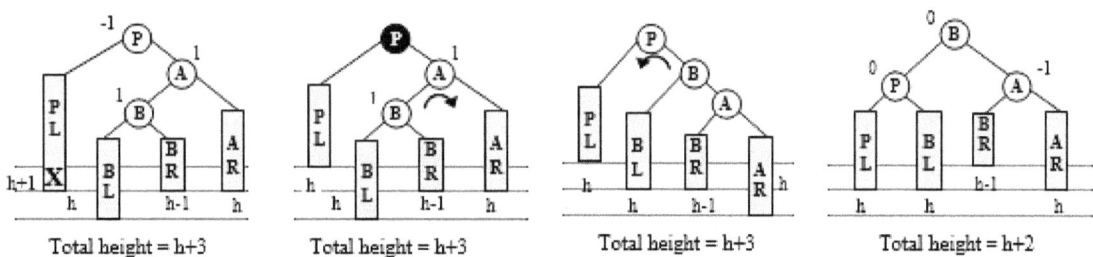

Figure 6.112 Case L_C3b

After balancing: bf(P) = 0, bf(A) = -1, bf(B) = 0

Case L_C3c:

Before deletion: bf(P) = -1, bf(A) = 1, bf(B) = -1

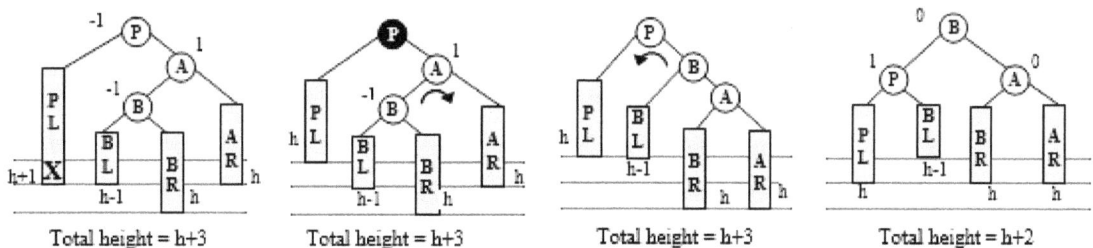

Figure 6.113 Case L_C3c

After balancing: bf(P) = 1, bf(A) = 0, bf(B) = 0

The height of the subtree decreases, and so the value of `shorter` remains true in case L_C3.

The functions `deletionLeftSubtreeCheck()` and `deletionRightBalance()` are given as follows:

```cpp
Node* AVLTree::deletionLeftSubtreeCheck(Node *p)
{
        switch(p->balance)
        {
                case 0:         //Case L_A : was balanced
                        p->balance = -1;            //now right heavy
                        shorter = false;
                        break;
                case 1:         //Case L_B : was left heavy
                        p->balance = 0;             //now balanced
                        break;
                case -1:        //Case L_C : was right heavy
                        p = deletionRightBalance(p);  //right balancing
                        break;
        }
        return p;
}//End of deletionLeftSubtreeCheck()

Node* AVLTree::deletionRightBalance(Node *p)
{
        Node *a, *b;
        a = p->rchild;
        if(a->balance == 0)         //Case L_C1
        {
                a->balance = 1;
                shorter = false;
                p = rotateLeft(p);
        }
        else if(a->balance == -1)     //Case L_C2
        {
                p->balance = 0;
                a->balance = 0;
                p = rotateLeft(p);
        }
        else                        //Case L_C3
        {
                b = a->lchild;
                switch(b->balance)
                {
                        case 0:         //Case L_C3a
                                p->balance = 0;
                                a->balance = 0;
                                break;
                        case 1:         //Case L_C3b
                                p->balance = 0;
                                a->balance = -1;
                                break;
                        case -1:        //Case L_C3c
                                p->balance = 1;
                                a->balance = 0;
                                break;
                }
                b->balance = 0;
                p->rchild = rotateRight(a);
                p = rotateLeft(p);
        }
        return p;
}//End of deletionRightBalance()
```

6.14.4.2 Deletion from Right Subtree

Case R_A:

Before deletion: bf(P) = 0

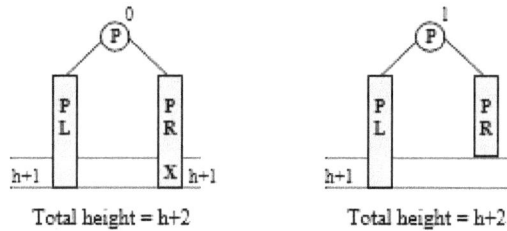

Figure 6.114 Case R_A

After deletion: bf(P) = 1
shorter = false

Case R_B:

Before deletion: bf(P) = -1

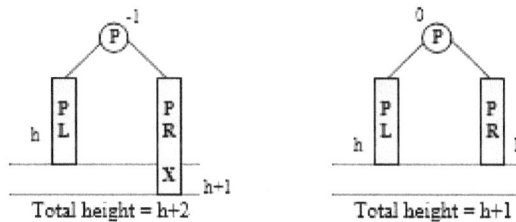

Figure 6.115 Case R_B

After deletion: bf(P) = 0
`shorter` remains true,

Case R_C:

Before deletion: bf(P) = 1
Node P becomes unbalanced, balancing required.

Case R_C1:

Before deletion: bf(P) = 1, bf(A) = 0
Right rotation about P performed.

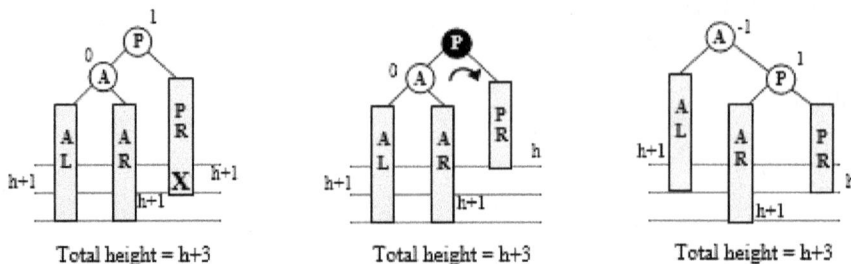

Figure 6.116 Case R_C1

After balancing: bf(P) = 1, bf(A) = -1
shorter = false

Case R_C2:

Before deletion: bf(P) = 1, bf(A) = 1
Right rotation performed.

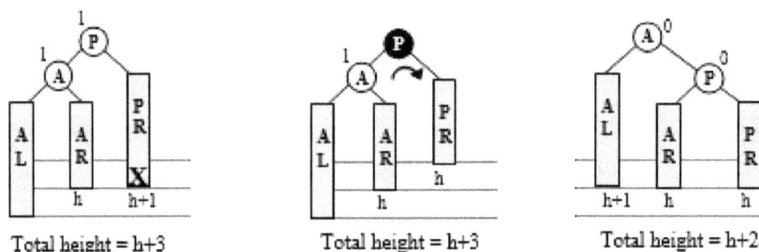

Figure 6.117 Case R_C2

After balancing: bf(P) = 0, bf(A) = 0
shorter remains true.

Case R_C3:

Before deletion: bf(P) = 1, bf(A) = -1
LeftRight rotation performed.

Case R_C3a:

Before deletion: bf(P) = 1, bf(A) = -1, bf(B) = 0

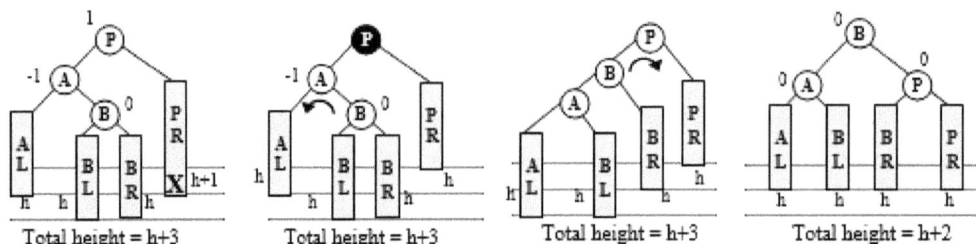

Figure 6.118 Case R_C3a

After balancing: bf(P) = 0, bf(A) = 0, bf(B) = 0

Case R_C3b:

Before deletion: bf(P) = 1, bf(A) = -1, bf(B) = 1

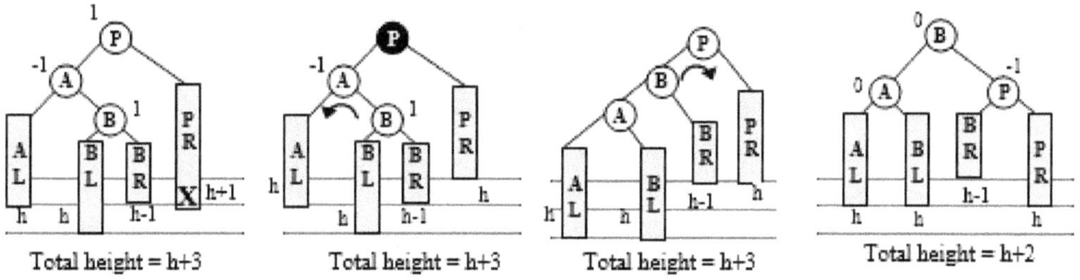

Figure 6.119 Case R_C3b

After balancing: bf(P) = -1, bf(A) = 0, bf(B) = 0

Case R_C3c :

Before deletion: bf(P) = 1, bf(A) = -1, bf(B) = -1

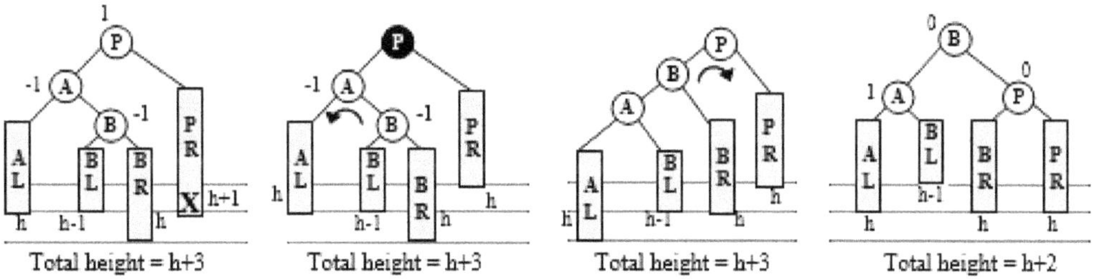

Figure 6.120 Case R_C3c

After balancing: bf(P) = 0, bf(A) =1, bf(B) = 0

The height of the subtree decreases, and so the value of `shorter` remains true in case R_C3.

The functions `deletionRightSubtreeCheck()` and `deletionLeftBalance()` are:

```
Node* AVLTree::deletionRightSubtreeCheck(Node *p)
{
        switch(p->balance)
        {
                case 0:         //Case R_A : was balanced
                        p->balance = 1;                 //now left heavy
                        shorter = false;
                        break;
                case -1:        //Case R_B : was right heavy
                        p->balance = 0;                 //now balanced
                        break;
                case 1:         //Case R_C : was left heavy
                        p = deletionLeftBalance(p);   //left balancing
                        break;
        }
```

```
        return p;
}//End of deletionRightSubtreeCheck()
Node* AVLTree::deletionLeftBalance(Node *p)
{
        Node *a, *b;
        a = p->lchild;
        if(a->balance == 0)              //Case R_C1
        {
                a->balance = -1;
                shorter = false;
                p = rotateRight(p);
        }
        else if(a->balance == 1)         //Case R_C2
        {
                p->balance = 0;
                a->balance = 0;
                p = rotateRight(p);
        }
        else                             //Case R_C3
        {
                b = a->rchild;
                switch(b->balance)
                {
                        case 0:          //Case R_C3a
                                p->balance = 0;
                                a->balance = 0;
                                break;
                        case 1:          //Case R_C3b
                                p->balance = -1;
                                a->balance = 0;
                                break;
                        case -1:         //Case R_C3c
                                p->balance = 0;
                                a->balance = 1;
                                break;
                }
                b->balance = 0;
                p->lchild = rotateLeft(a);
                p = rotateRight(p);
        }
        return p;
}//End of deletionLeftBalance()
```

All the cases and subcases of deletion are shown in figure 6.121.

Note that in the case of insertion, after making one rotation (single or double), the variable `taller` was made false and there was no need to proceed further. From the discussion of deletion, we can see that `shorter` is not always made false after rotations. For example, rotations are performed in cases L_C2, L_C3, R_C2, R_C3, but `shorter` is not made false. This means that even after performing rotation, we may have to proceed and check the balance factors of other nodes. So, in deletion, one rotation may not suffice to balance the tree, unlike the case of insertion. In the worst case, each node in the path from the deleted node to the root node may need balancing.

A new node is deleted and shortrer = true
P is the node whose balance factor is being checked.

If deletion from left subtree of the node P (deletion from PL)

Case L_A : If node P was balanced before deletion
Node P becomes right heavy, shorter = false
Case L_B : If node P was left heavy before deletion
Node P becomes balanced
Case L_C : If node P was right heavy before deletion
Node P becomes unbalanced, Right Balancing required
A is right child of P
Case L_C1 : If bf(A) = 0
Left Rotation, shorter = false
bf(P) = -1, bf(A) = 1
Case L_C2 : If bf(A) = -1
Left Rotation
bf(P) = 0, bf(A) = 0
Case L_C3 : If bf(A) = 1
RightLeft Rotation (right about A, left about P)
B is the left child of A
BL and BR are left and right subtrees of B
Case L_C3a : if bf(B) == 0
bf(P) = 0, bf(A) = 0
Case L_C3b : If bf(B) == 1
bf(P) = 0, bf(A) = -1
Case L_C3c : If bf(B) == -1
bf(P) = 1, bf(A) = 0

If deletion from right subtree of the node P (deletion from PR)

Case R_A : If node P was balanced before deletion
Node P becomes left heavy, shorter = false
Case R_B : If node P was right heavy before deletion
Node P becomes balanced
Case R_C : If node P was left heavy before deletion
Node P becomes unbalanced, left Balancing required
A is left child of P
Case R_C1 : If bf(A) = 0
Right Rotation, shorter = false
bf(P) = 1, bf(A) = -1
Case R_C2 : If bf(A) = 1
Right Rotation
bf(P) = 0, bf(A) = 0
Case R_C3 : If bf(A) = -1
LeftRight Rotation (left about A, right about P)
B is the right child of A
Case R_C3a : If bf(B) == 0
bf(P) = 0, bf(A) = 0
Case R_C3b : If bf(B) == 1
bf(P) = -1, bf(A) = 0
Case R_C3c : If bf(B) == -1
bf(P) = 0, bf(A) = 1

Figure 6.121 Deletion in an AVL tree

Now we will take an AVL tree and delete some nodes from it one by one:

Delete 60

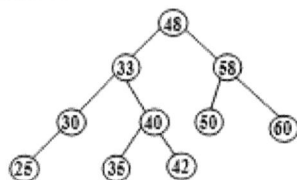
P : 58, Case R_A
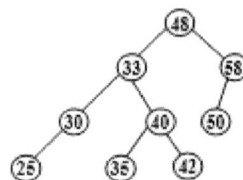

Figure 6.122 Delete 60

Delete 48

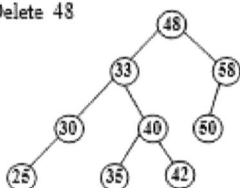
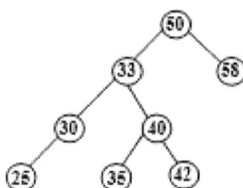

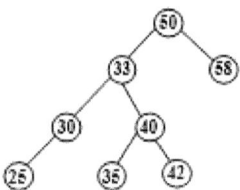
P : 58, Case L_B
P : 50, Case R_C1

Rotate right about 50
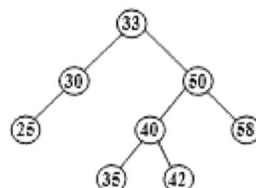

Figure 6.123 Delete 48

48 is not a leaf node, so its inorder successor 50 is copied at its place, and the node 50 is deleted from the tree.

Delete 25

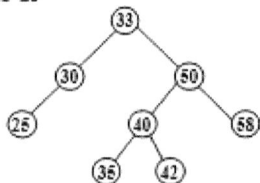
P : 30, Case L_B
P : 33, Case L_C3a

Rotate right about 50
Rotate left about 33
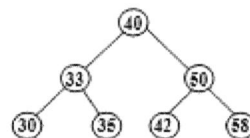

Figure 6.124 Delete 25

Delete 30

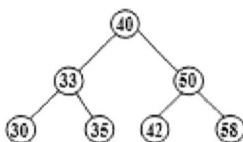
P : 33, Case L_A
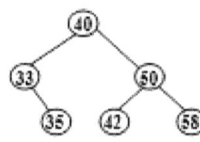

Figure 6.125 Delete 30

Delete 35

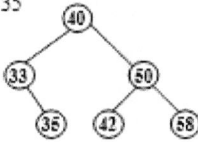

P : 33, Case R_B,
P : 40, Case L_A

——————————————→

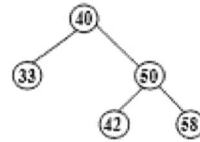

Figure 6.126 Delete 35

Delete 33

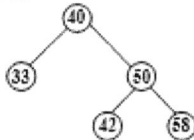

P : 40, Case L_C1

——————————————→

Rotate left about 40

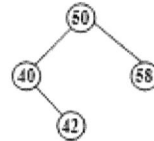

Figure 6.127 Delete 33

Delete 58

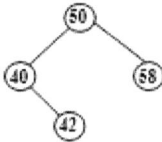

P : 50, Case R_C3a

——————————————→

Rotate left about 40
Rotate right about 50

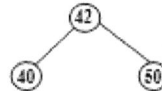

Figure 6.128 Delete 58

The `main()` function for the AVL tree is as follows:

```
//AVLTree.cpp : Program for AVL Tree.
#include<iostream>
using namespace std;

int main()
{
        AVLTree avlTree;
        avlTree.insert(50);
        cout << "Tree after inserting 50\n";
        avlTree.display();
        cout << "\n";
        avlTree.insert(40);
        cout << "Tree after inserting 40\n";
        avlTree.display();
        cout << "\n";
        avlTree.insert(35);
        cout << "Tree after insertiing 35\n";
        avlTree.display();
        cout << "\n";
        avlTree.insert(58);
        cout << "Tree after inserting 58\n";
        avlTree.display();
        cout << "\n";
        avlTree.insert(48);
        cout << "Tree after inserting 48\n";
        avlTree.display();
        cout << "\n";
```

```
        avlTree.insert(42);
        cout << "Tree after inserting 42\n";
        avlTree.display();
        cout << "\n";
        avlTree.insert(60);
        cout << "Tree after inserting 60\n";
        avlTree.display();
        cout << "\n";
        avlTree.insert(30);
        cout << "Tree after inserting 30\n";
        avlTree.display();
        cout << "\n";
        avlTree.insert(33);
        cout << "Tree after inserting 33\n";
        avlTree.display();
        cout << "\n";
        avlTree.insert(25);
        cout << "Tree after inserting 25\n";
        avlTree.display();
        cout << "\n";

        avlTree.del(60);
        cout << "Tree after deleting 60\n";
        avlTree.display();
        cout << "\n";
        avlTree.del(48);
        cout << "Tree after deleting 48\n";
        avlTree.display();
        cout << "\n";
        avlTree.del(25);
        cout << "Tree after deleting 25\n";
        avlTree.display();
        cout << "\n";
        avlTree.del(30);
        cout << "Tree after deleting 30\n";
        avlTree.display();
        cout << "\n";
        avlTree.del(35);
        cout << "Tree after deleting 35\n";
        avlTree.display();
        cout << "\n";
        avlTree.del(33);
        cout << "Tree after deleting 33\n";
        avlTree.display();
        cout << "\n";
        avlTree.del(58);
        cout << "Tree after deleting 58\n";
        avlTree.display();
        cout << "\n";
        return 0;
}//End of main()
```

The constructor, destructor, `destroy()`, `display()` and traversals functions are the same as given in binary search tree.

6.15 Red Black Trees

A red black tree is a balanced binary search tree, in which every node is colored either red or black. Properties of this tree can be explained best in terms of an extended binary tree. Recall that an extended binary tree is a tree in which all NULL links are replaced by special nodes that are called external nodes.

The properties of a red black tree are:

(P1) Root is always black.

(P2) All external nodes are black.

(P3) A red node cannot have red children; it can have only black children. There is no restriction on the color of the children of a black node, i.e., a black node can have red or black children.

(P4) For each node N, all paths from node N to external nodes contain the same number of black nodes. This number is called the black height of that node.

Black height of a node N is defined as the number of black nodes from N to an external node (without counting node N). The black height of the root node is called the black height of the tree. The black height of all external nodes is 0.

Following are two examples of red black trees; the black height of each node is shown outside the node.

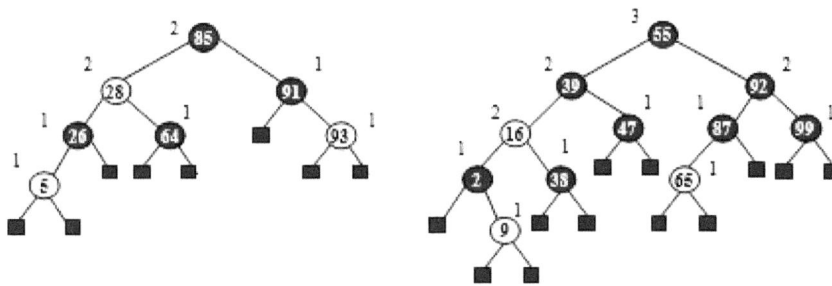

Figure 6.129 Red black trees

The root node is black in both trees, and so property P1 is satisfied for both of them. None of the red nodes has a red child, so property P3 is also satisfied for them. Property P4 is also satisfied for both the trees. The black height of the first tree is 2 and the black height of the second tree is 3. Now, let us see some trees that do not satisfy these properties.

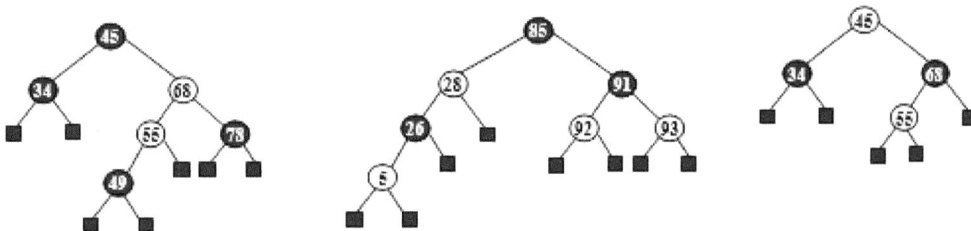

Figure 6.130 Trees violating red black tree properties

In the first tree, property P3 is violated since node 68 is red and it has a red child. We will refer to this problem as the double red problem. In the second tree, property P4 is violated for nodes 28 and 85. We will refer to this problem as the black height problem. In the third tree, property P1 is violated since the root is red.

According to property P4, all paths from a node N to any external node have the same number of black nodes. This is true for the root node as well, i.e., any path from the root node to any external node will have the same number of black nodes. Now suppose the black height of the root node is k.

If a path from the root to the external node has all the black nodes, then it will be the smallest possible path. If in a path, the black and red nodes occur alternately, then it will be the longest possible path. Since the black height of root node is k, each path will have k black nodes. Therefore, the total nodes in the shortest possible path will be k and the total nodes in the longest possible path will be 2k. Thus, we see that no path in a red black tree can be more than twice the another path of the tree. Hence, a red black tree always remains balanced. The height of a red black tree with n internal nodes is at most $2\log_2(n+1)$.

In the class Node of a red black tree, we will take an extra member color that can take two values, red or black. We will also need to maintain a parent pointer that will point to the parent of the node.

```
class Node
{
        public:
                enum {black, red} color;
                int info;
                Node *lchild;
                Node *rchild;
                Node *parent;
                Node(int key)
                {
                        info = key;
                        lchild = NULL;
                        rchild = NULL;
                        parent = NULL;
                }
};//End of class Node
```

Before proceeding further, let us define some terms we will use in the insertion and deletion operations:

Grandparent: Grandparent of a node is the parent of the parent node.

Sibling: Sibling of a node is the other child of parent node.

Uncle: Uncle is the sibling of parent node.

Nephews: Nephews of a node are the children of its sibling node.

Near Nephew: If node is a left child, then the left child of sibling node is near nephew and if node is a right child, then the right child of the sibling node is near nephew.

Far Nephew: The nephew which is not the near nephew is the far nephew. In the figure 6.131, the nephew that appears closer to the node is the near nephew and the other one is far nephew.

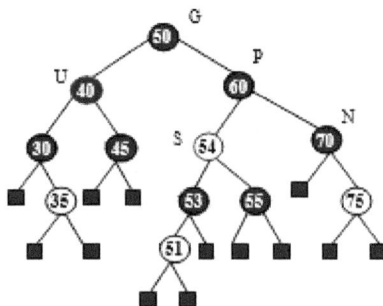

Figure 6.131 Relatives of node 70

In the tree given in figure 6.131, we have marked the relatives of node 70. Its parent is node 60, grandparent is node 50, uncle is node 40, sibling is node 54, near nephew is node 55 and far nephew is node 53.

6.15.1 Searching

Since the red black tree is a binary search tree, the procedure for searching is the same as in a binary search tree. The searching operation does not modify the tree, so there is no need for any extra work.

6.15.2 Insertion

Initially, the key is inserted in the tree following the same procedure as in a binary search tree. Each node in a red black tree should have a color, and so now, we have to decide upon the color of this newly inserted node. If we color this new node black, then it is certain that property P4 will be violated, i.e., we will have a black height problem (you can verify this yourself). If we color the new node red, then property P1 or P3 may be violated. The property P1 will be violated if this new node is the root node, and property P3 will be violated (double red problem) if the new node's parent is red. Thus, when we give the red color to the new node, we will have some cases where no property will be violated after insertion, while if we color it black, it is guaranteed that property P4 will be violated. Therefore, the better option is to color the newly inserted node red.

We have decided to color the new node red, and so we will never have any violation of property P4. If the node is inserted in an empty tree, i.e., the new node is the root node, then property P1 will be violated, and to fix this problem, we will have to color the new node black. If the new node's parent is black, then no property will be violated. If the new node's parent is red, then we will have a double red problem, and now we will study this case in detail.

We have two situations, depending on whether the parent is the left child or right child. In both situations, we have symmetric cases. The outline of all the subcases in this case is given as follows:

Parent is Red
      -Parent is left child,
            Case L_1: Uncle is red
                        Recolor
            Case L_2: Uncle is Black
                Case L_2a: Node is right child
                        Rotate left about parent and transform to case L_2b
                Case L_2b: Node is left child
                        Recolor and Rotate right about the grandparent.
      -Parent is right Child
            Case R_1: Uncle is red
                      Recolor
            Case R_2: Uncle is black
                Case R_2a: Node is left child
                        Rotate right about parent and transform to case R_2b
                Case R_2b: Node is right child
                        Recolor and Rotate left about the grandparent.

Now, let us take all the cases one by one. In the figures, we have marked the current node as N, its parent as P, its grandparent as G, and its uncle as U. Initially, the current node is the newly inserted node, but we will see that in some cases, the double red problem is moved upwards. So the current node also moves up.

The left and right rotations performed are similar to those in AVL trees.

Case L_1: Parent is left child and Uncle is red.

In this case, we just recolor the parent and uncle to black and recolor the grandparent to red. The following figures show this recoloring. The same recoloring is done if the node is right child.

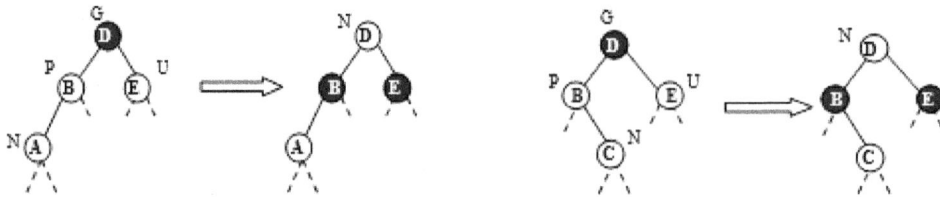

Figure 6.132 Case L_1

Looking at the recolored figures, it seems that we do not have any double red problems now. However, remember that this is only a part of the tree, and node D might have a parent and grandparent. If the parent of node D is black, then we are done, but if the parent of node D is red, then again, we have a double red problem at node D. We have just moved the double red problem one level up.

Now, the grandparent node is the node that needs to be checked for the double red problem. So after recoloring, we make the grandparent as the new current node; we have marked it N in the recolored figure. Any of the 6 cases (L_1, L_2a, L_2b, R_1, R_2a, R_2b) may be applicable to this new current node.

It might happen that we repeatedly encounter this case (or case R_1), and we move the double red problem upwards by recoloring and ultimately, we end up coloring the root red. In that case, we can just color the root black and our double red problem would be removed (insertion of 40 and insertion of 51 given in the examples of insertion).

Case L_2: Uncle is black and rotation needs to be done.

Case L_2a: Parent is left child, Uncle is black and Node is right child.

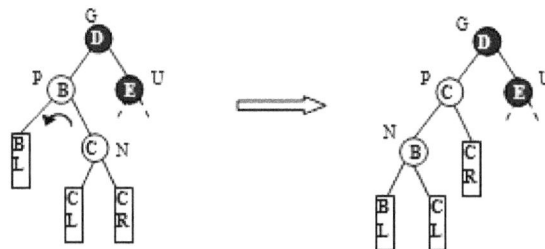

Figure 6.133 Case L_2a

This case is transformed to case L_2b by performing a rotation. We perform a left rotation about the parent node B, and after rotation, node C becomes the parent node, and node B becomes the current node. Now, the parent is the left child, the node is the left child, and the uncle is black, and this is case L_2b.

Case L_2b: Parent is left child, Uncle is black and Node is left child.

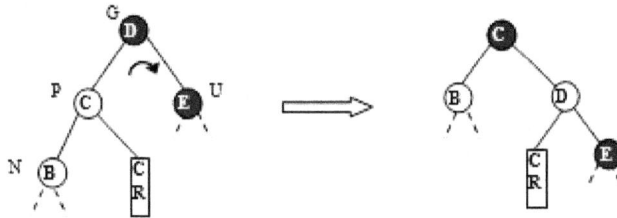

Figure 6.134 Case L_2b

In this case, the parent is recolored black, grandparent is recolored red, and a right rotation is performed about the grandparent node, and this removes the double red problem.

The other three cases occur when the parent is the right child; they are symmetric to the previous three cases, and only the figures for these cases are given.

Case R_1: Parent is right child and uncle is red.

Figure 6.135 Case R_1

Case R_2: Uncle is black.

Case R_2a: Parent is right child, uncle is black and node is left child.

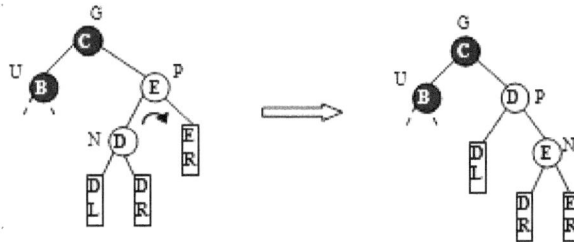

Figure 6.136 Case R_2a

Case R_2b: Parent is right child, uncle is black and node is right child.

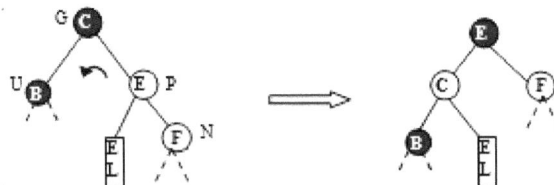

Figure 6.137 Case R_2b

Now, we will see examples of inserting some nodes in an initially empty red black tree. The explanation of each insertion is given at the end. While inserting, we will first check the color of the parent. If it is black, there is nothing to be done. If the parent is red, we have a double red problem, and we will check the color of the uncle. If the uncle is red, we will recolor and move up, and if the uncle is black, we will perform appropriate rotations and recoloring.

Insert 50

Figure 6.138 Insert 50

Insert 60

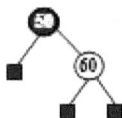

Figure 6.139 Insert 60

Insert 70

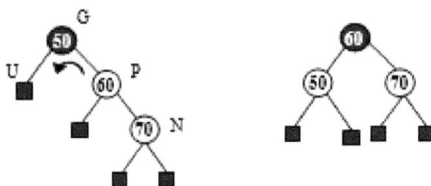

Figure 6.140 Insert 70

Insert 40

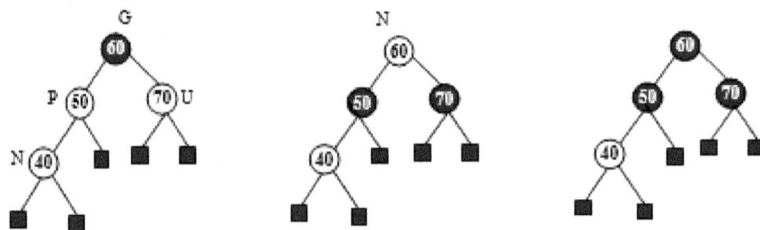

Figure 6.141 Insert 40

Insert 55, 75

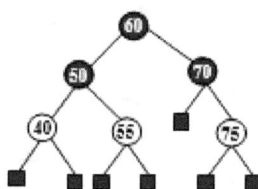

Figure 6.142 Insert 55, 75

Insert 53

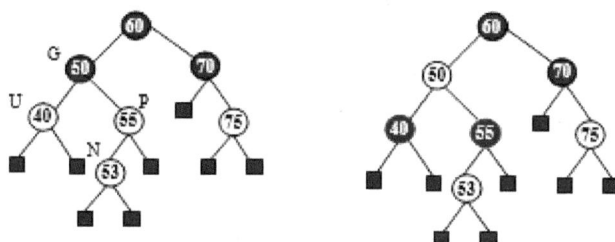

Figure 6.143 Insert 53

Insert 54

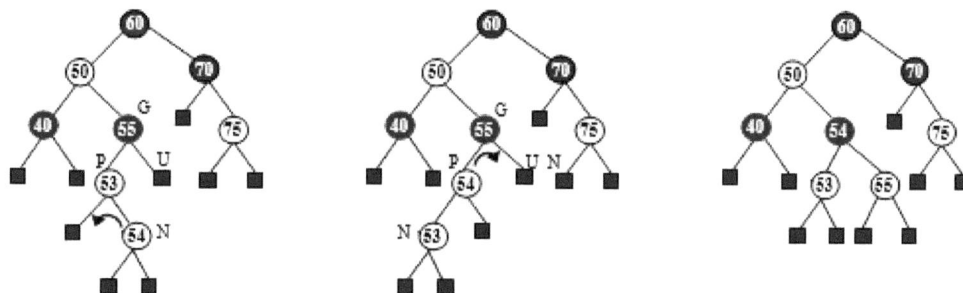

Figure 6.144 Insert 54

Insert 30, 45

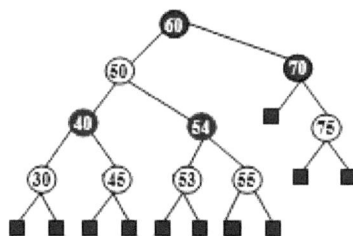

Figure 6.145 Insert 30, 45

Insert 35

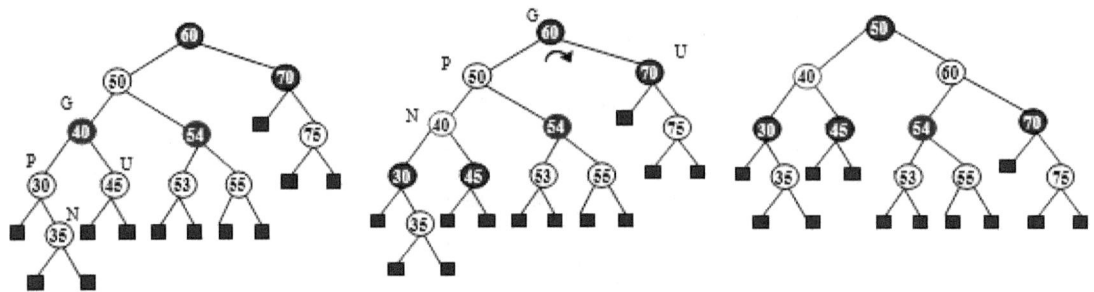

Figure 6.146 Insert 35

Insert 51

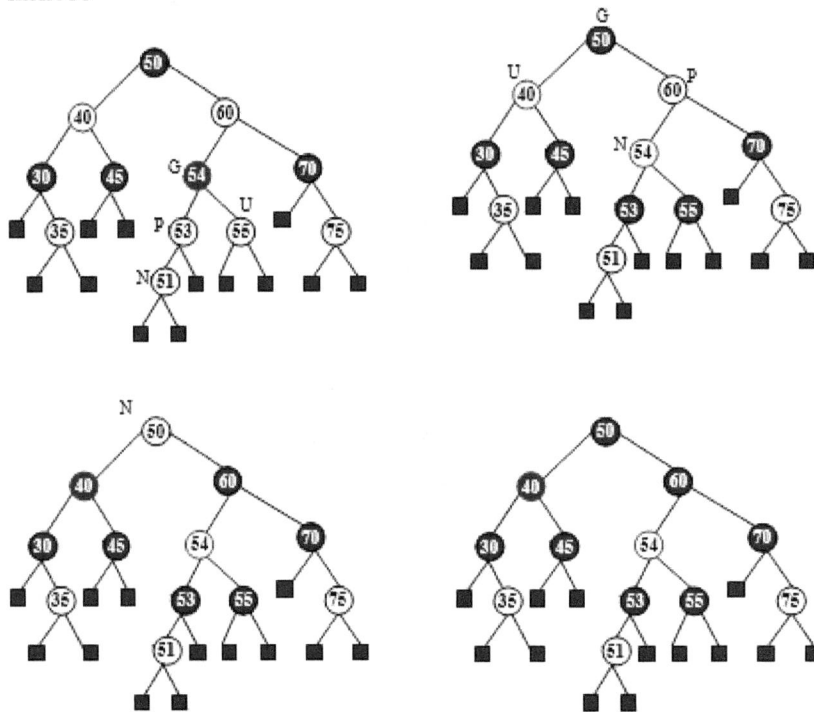

Figure 6.147 Insert 51

Insertion of 50: Newly inserted node is the root node, so color it black.
Insertion of 60: Parent is black so no violation of property.
Insertion of 70: Parent is red, double red problem.
      Uncle is black, parent is right child, node is right child (case R_2b).
      Recolor and Rotate left about grandparent(50).
Insertion of 40: Parent is red, double red problem. Uncle is red, recolor. Now node 60 is the current node.
      We have colored the root red so color it black and we are done.
Insertion of 55: Parent is black so no violation of property.
Insertion of 75: Parent is black so no violation of property.

Insertion of 53: Parent is red, double red problem. Uncle is red, recolor. Now node 50 is the current node.
 Parent of 50 is black so we are done.
Insertion of 54: Parent is red, double red problem.
 Uncle is black, parent is left child, node is right child (case L_2a).
 Rotate left about parent node and transform to case L_2b.
 Recolor and rotate right about grandparent.
Insertion of 30: Parent is black so no violation of property.
Insertion of 45: Parent is black so no violation of property.
Insertion of 35: Parent is red, double red problem. Uncle is red, recolor. Now node 40 is the current node.
 Parent(50) is red, double red problem.
 Uncle is black, parent is left child, node is left child(case L_2b).
 Recolor and rotate right about grandparent.
Insertion of 51: Parent is red, double red problem. Uncle is red, recolor. Now node 54 is the current node.
 Parent is red, double red problem. Uncle is red, recolor. Now node 50 is the current node.
 We have colored the root red so color it black and we are done.

6.15.3 Deletion

Initially, the deletion of node is performed following the same procedure as in a binary search tree. We know that in a BST, if the node to be deleted has two children, then its information is replaced by the information of inorder successor and then the successor is deleted. The successor node will have either no child or only right child. Thus, the case when the node to be deleted has two children, is reduced to the case when the node to be deleted has only one right child or no child.

Therefore, in our discussion, we will take the case of only those nodes that have only one right child or no child. This means that the node to be deleted is always a parent of an external node, i.e., the node to be deleted has either one external node as a left child, or two external nodes as children.

Suppose A is the node that has to be deleted. Then, we can think of six cases, some of which are not possible.

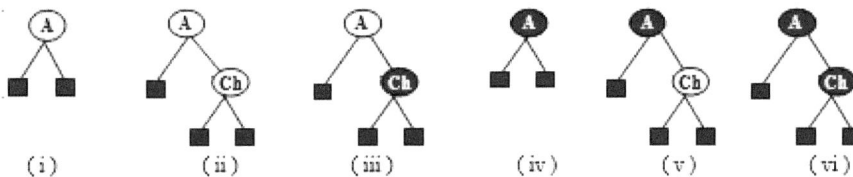

Figure 6.148 Deletion cases

(i) A is red and has no children
No property violated and the tree remains red black after deleting node A.

(ii) A is red, and its only child is red
Impossible case, because it means that there was a double red problem in the tree.

(iii) A is red, and its only child is black
Impossible case, because this means node A was violating property P4.

(iv) A is black and has no children
In this case, after deletion the black height property would be violated and we need to restore this property. There are many subcases to be considered which we will study in detail.

(v) A is black, and its only child is red

In this case, the node A is deleted and its red child takes its place. This might create a double red problem if A had a red parent. The black height problem will definitely be introduced. Both these problems can be removed just by coloring this child black.

(vi) A is black, and its only child is black.

Impossible case, because this means node A was violating property P4.

So, the three possible cases are (i), (iv) and (v). The actions to be taken in these three possible cases are:

- In Case (i), Node is red with no children.
  Delete the node
- In Case (iv), Node is black with no children.
  Delete the node and restore the black height property.
- In Case (v), Node is black and has a red child.
  Delete the node and color the child black

Now we will study case (iv) in detail. When the node to be deleted is a black node without any children. We will take N as the current node, i.e., it is the root of the subtree, which is one black node short. Initially, N will be the external node that replaced the node to be deleted, and as we proceed, we might move the current node upwards, i.e., we might move the black height problem upwards. There can be different cases depending on the color of the sibling, nephews, and the parent.

Case 1: N's sibling is Red.

Case 2: N's sibling is black, both nephews are black.
        Case 2a: Parent is Red
        Case 2b: Parent is Black

Case 3: N's sibling is black, at least one nephew is red.
        Case 3a: Far nephew is black, other nephew will be red.
        Case 3b: Far nephew is red, other nephew may be either red or black.

If the node is a left child, then we will name the cases as L_1, L_2a, L_2b, L_3a, L_3b, and if node is a right child, then we will have symmetric cases R_1, R_2a, R_2b, R_3a, R_3b.

Case L_1: N's sibling is Red

In this case, the parent and both nephews will definitely be black (by property P3).

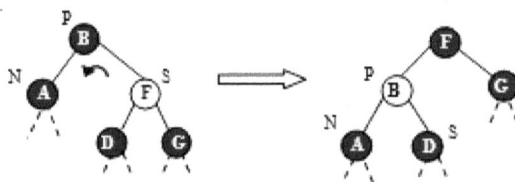

Figure 6.149 Case L_1

A left rotation is performed, and the new sibling is D, which is black, and so, this case is now converted to case 2 or case 3.

Case L_2: N's sibling and both nephews are black.

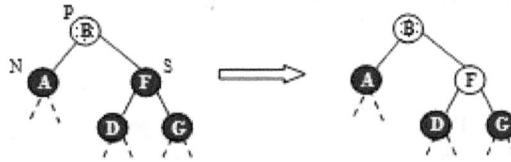

Figure 6.150 Case L_2

Node B is shaded, which means that the parent can be of either color. In this case, we color the sibling red. After that, we take different steps depending on the color of the parent.

Case L_2a: Parent is red

If the parent is red, then after coloring the sibling red, we have a double red problem. To remove this double red problem, we color the parent black.

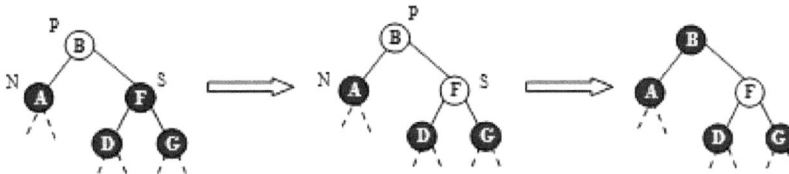

Figure 6.151 Case L_2a

In the initial figure, the subtree rooted at node A was one black node short. In the final figure, we have introduced a black node in its path, and so, now it is not a black node short. Since we colored node F red, the black height of the other subtree did not change.

Thus, by removing the double red problem, we have removed the problem of shorter black height also and there is no need to proceed further. Note that when we enter case 2 from case 1, then we will enter case 2a only and not case 2b.

Case L_2b: Parent is black.

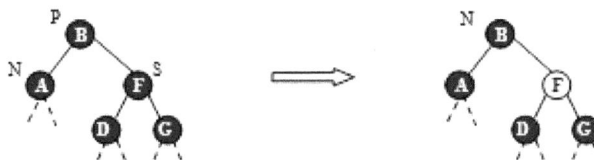

Figure 6.152 Case L_2b

In this case, the sibling is colored red and now the subtree rooted at A and the subtree rooted at F both are one black node short. So, we can say that the subtree rooted at B is one black node short. Now, we make node B the current node, and any of the cases may apply to this node. Thus, in this case, we have moved the problem of the shorter black height upwards.

Case L_3: Sibling is black, and at least one nephew is red.

Case L_3a: Sibling is black, Far nephew is black, and other nephew will be red.

This case is converted to case L_3b by performing a right rotation.

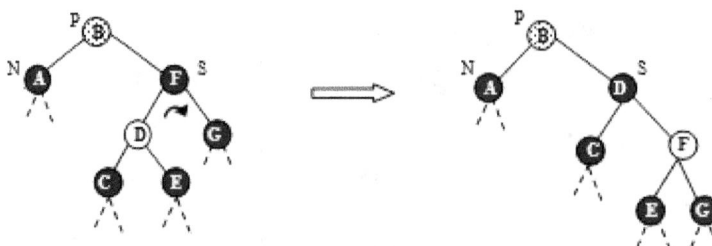

Figure 6.153 Case L_3a

The near nephew D is recolored black, sibling F is recolored red, and a right rotation is performed about the sibling node. After the rotation, node A's far nephew is node F, which is red, and so this case is converted to case L_3b.

Case L_3b: Sibling is black, Far nephew is red, and other nephew may be either red or black.

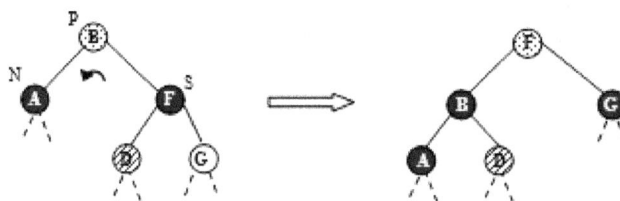

Figure 6.154 Case L_3b

The parent node B and far nephew G are recolored black, and the node F is given the color of node B. Then, a left rotation is performed about the parent node and the black height problem is solved.

The figures of other symmetric cases are given next.

Case R_1: N's sibling is Red.

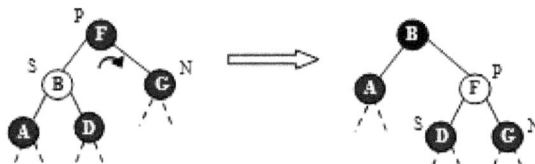

Figure 6.155 Case R_1

Case R_2a: N's sibling and both nephews are black, parent is red.

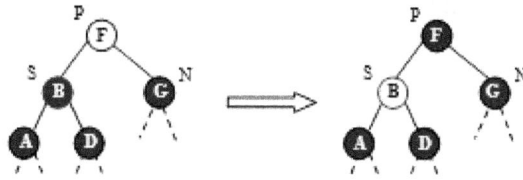

Figure 6.156 Case R_2a

Case R_2b: N's sibling and both nephews are black, parent is black.

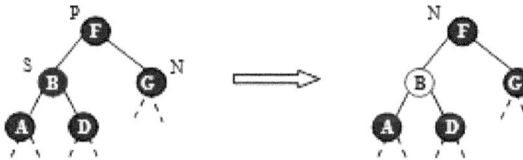

Figure 6.157 Case R_2b

Case R_3a: Sibling is black, Far nephew is black, and other nephew will be red.

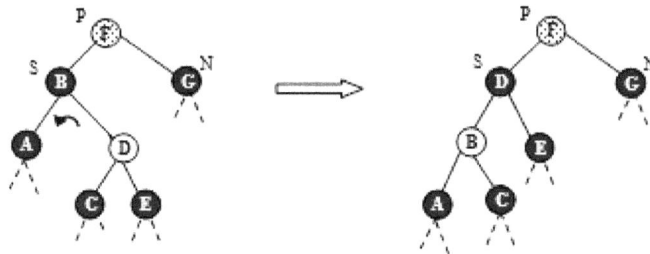

Figure 6.158 Case R_3a

Case R_3b: Sibling is black, Far nephew is red, and other nephew may be either red or black.

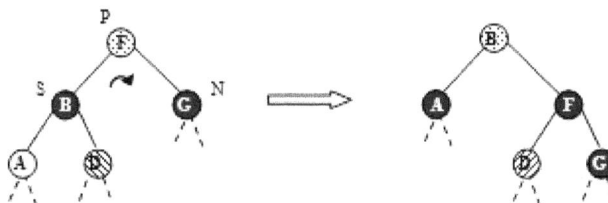

Figure 6.159 Case R_3b

Now, we will see some examples of deletion.

(i) Delete 55

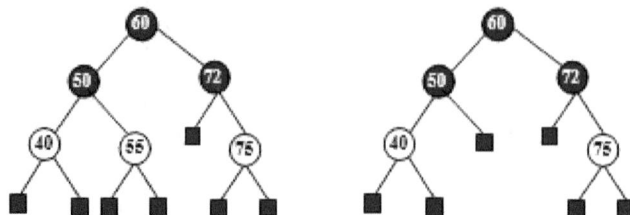

Figure 6.160 Delete 55

Here, the node to be deleted is a red node and so there is no violation of any property after deletion.

(ii) Delete 72

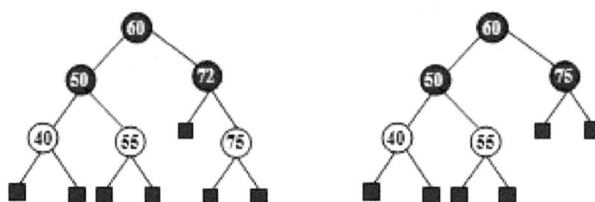

Figure 6.161 Delete 72

Here, the node to be deleted is a black node with a red child, and so, after deletion, the child is painted black.

(iii) Delete 70

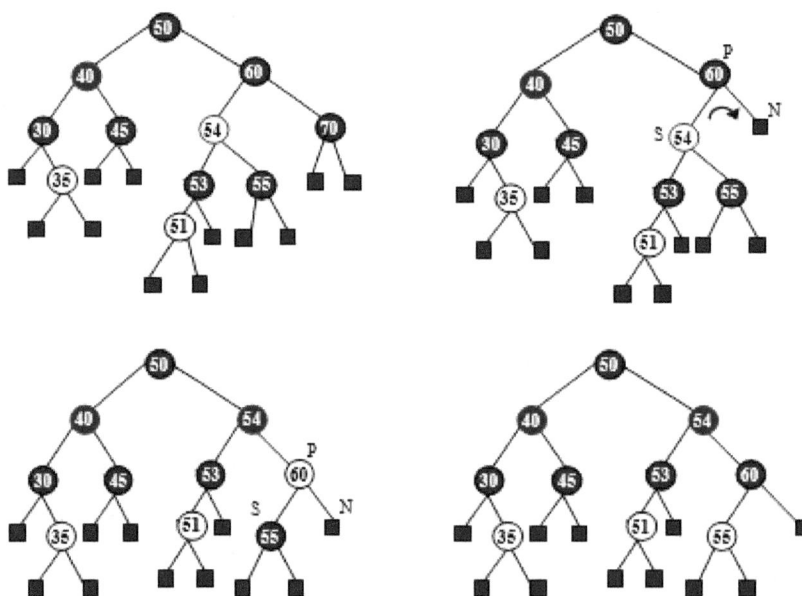

Figure 6.162 Delete 70

Node's sibling is red, and so, case R_1 applies. Perform a right rotation, and now, sibling is 55, which is black. Both nephews are also black, parent is red and this is case R_2a. Color the sibling red and parent black and we are done.

(iv) Delete 45

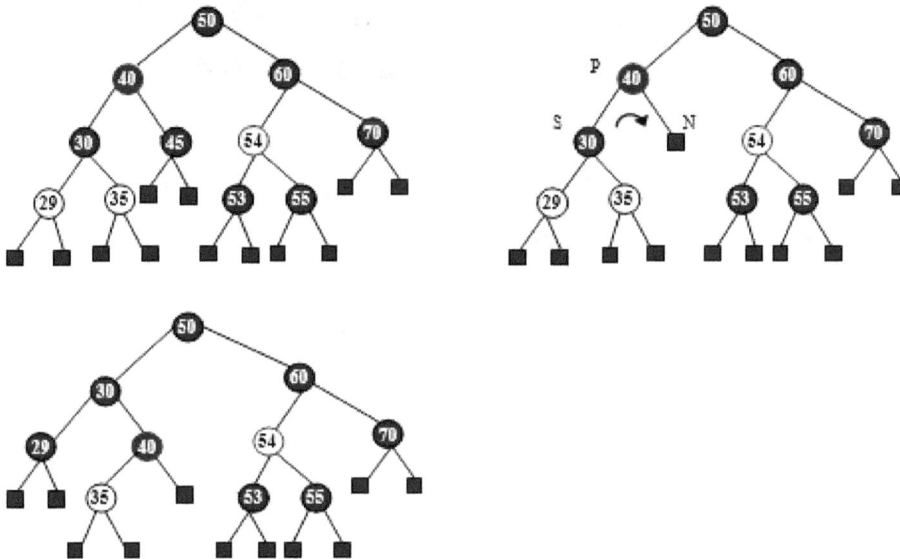

Figure 6.163 Delete 45

Here, N has a black sibling. Far nephew is red, so case R_3b applies and a right rotation and recoloring is done.

(v) Delete 53

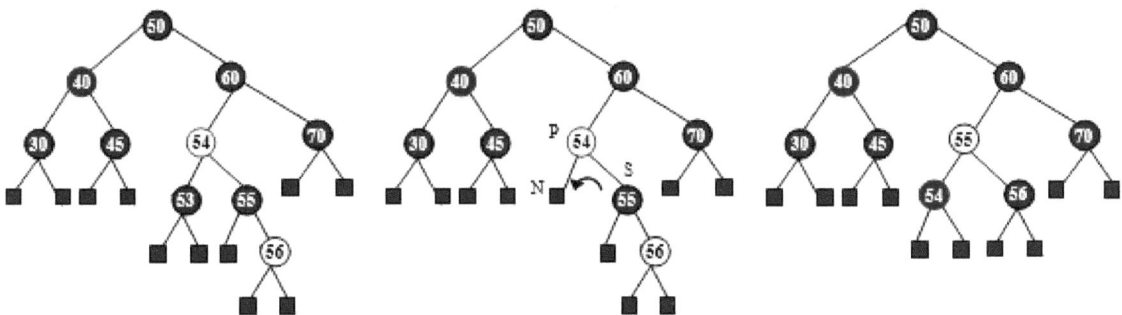

Figure 6.164 Delete 53

Here, N has a black sibling and the far nephew is red, so case L_3b applies and a left rotation and recoloring is done.

(vi) Delete 30

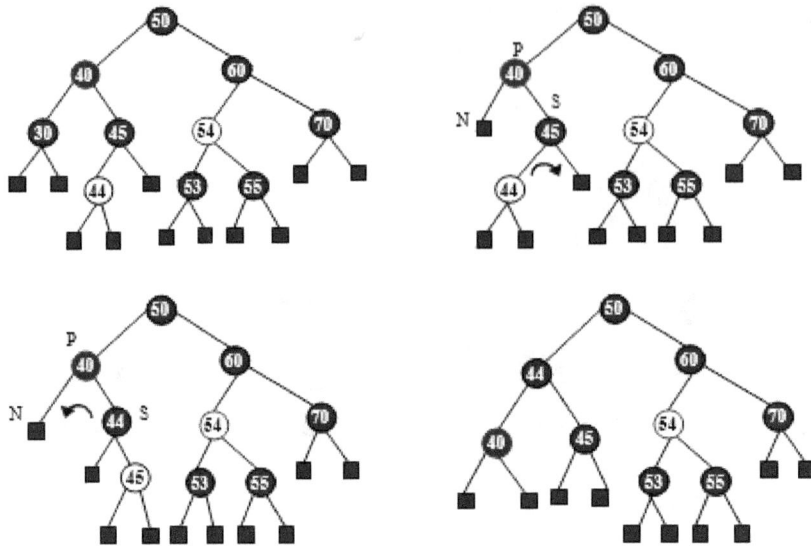

Figure 6.165 Delete 30

Here, node N has a black sibling, the far nephew is black and the near nephew is red, and so, case L_3a applies which is converted to case L_3b.

(vii) Delete 75

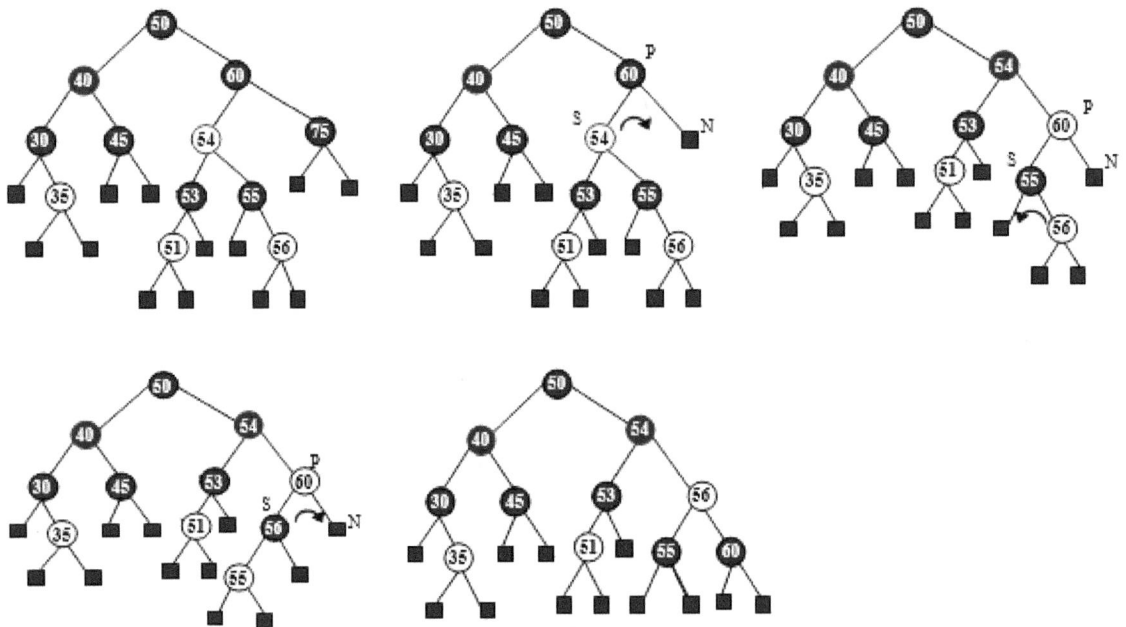

Figure 6.166 Delete 75

Here, node N's sibling is red, and so, the first case R_1 applies, which is converted to case R_3 after a rotation. After this, case R_3a applies, which is converted to case R_3b.

(viii) Delete 25

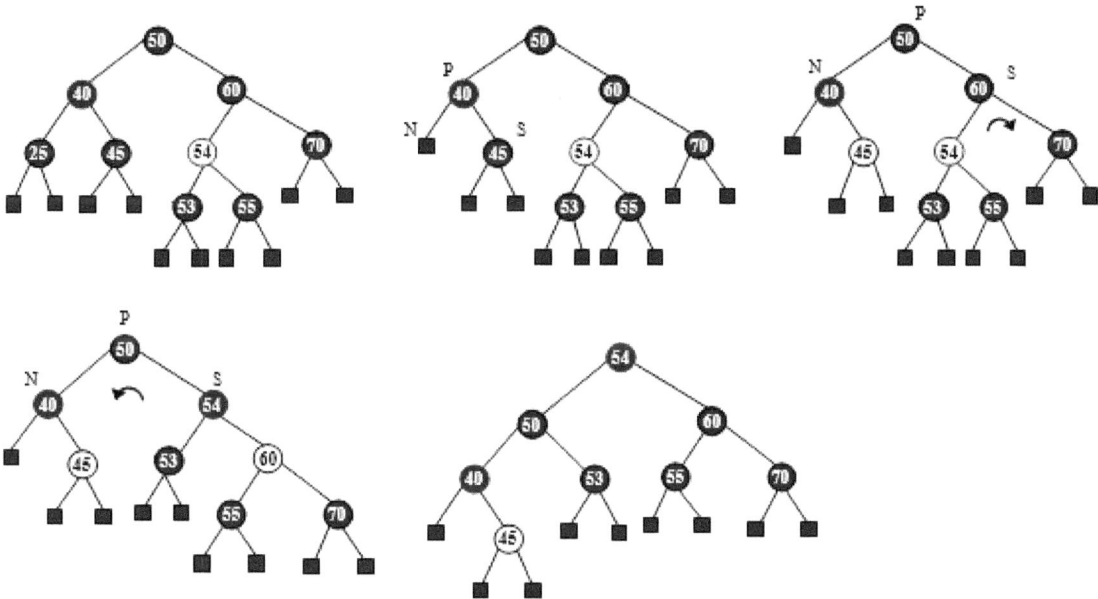

Figure 6.167 Delete 25

Here, node N's sibling, both nephews and parent are black, so case L_2b applies. Sibling node 45 is colored red, and then case L_3a applies, which is converted to case L_3b.

In the implementation, the external nodes are represented by a single sentinel node to save space, and this sentinel node also serves as the parent of the root node. The sentinel node is like any other node of the tree, and it is colored black, while the values of other fields are insignificant.

```cpp
//RedBlackTree.cpp : Program for Red Black Tree.
#include<iostream>
using namespace std;
class Node
{
        public:
                enum {black, red} color;
                int info;
                Node *lchild;
                Node *rchild;
                Node *parent;
                Node(int key)
                {
                        info = key;
                        lchild = NULL;
                        rchild = NULL;
                        parent = NULL;
                }
};//End of class Node
class RedBlackTree
```

```cpp
{
    private:
            Node *root;
            Node *sentinel; //will be parent of root and replace NULL
            bool find(int key, Node **location);
            void insertionBalance(Node *n);
            void deletionBalance(Node *n);
            void rotateRight(Node *p);
            void rotateLeft(Node *p);
            Node* getSuccessor(Node *location);
            void inorder(Node *ptr);
            void display(Node *ptr, int level);
    public:
            RedBlackTree();
            ~RedBlackTree(){};
            void insert(int key);
            void del(int key);
            void inorder();
            void display();
};//End of class RedBlackTree
RedBlackTree::RedBlackTree()
{
    sentinel = new Node(-1);
    sentinel->color = Node::black;
    root = sentinel;
}//End of RedBlackTree()
bool RedBlackTree::find(int key, Node **location)
{
    Node *ptr;
    if(root == sentinel) //Tree is empty
    {
            *location = sentinel;
            return false;
    }
    if(key == root->info) //key is at root
    {
            *location = root;
            return true;
    }

    //Initialize ptr
    if(key < root->info)
            ptr = root->lchild;
    else
            ptr = root->rchild;

    while(ptr != sentinel)
    {
            if(key == ptr->info)
            {
                    *location = ptr;
                    return true;
            }
            if(key < ptr->info)
                    ptr = ptr->lchild;
            else
                    ptr = ptr->rchild;
    }//End of while

    *location = sentinel; //key not found
    return false;
```

```
}//End of find()
void RedBlackTree::insert(int key)
{
        Node *parent = sentinel;
        Node *ptr = root;
        while(ptr != sentinel)
        {
                parent = ptr;
                if(key < ptr->info)
                        ptr = ptr->lchild;
                else if(key > ptr->info)
                        ptr = ptr->rchild;
                else
                {
                        cout << key << " is already there\n";
                        return;
                }
        }

        Node *temp = new Node(key);
        temp->lchild = sentinel;
        temp->rchild = sentinel;
        temp->color = Node::red;
        temp->parent = parent;

        if(parent == sentinel)
                root = temp;
        else if(temp->info < parent->info)
                parent->lchild = temp;
        else
                parent->rchild = temp;

        insertionBalance(temp);
}//End of insert()
void RedBlackTree::insertionBalance(Node *n)
{
        Node *uncle, *parent, *grandParent;

        while(n->parent->color == Node::red)
        {
                parent = n->parent;
                grandParent = parent->parent;

                if(parent == grandParent->lchild)
                {
                        uncle = grandParent->rchild;
                        if(uncle->color == Node::red) //Case L_1
                        {
                                parent->color = Node::black;
                                uncle->color = Node::black;
                                grandParent->color = Node::red;
                                n = grandParent;
                        }
                        else    //uncle is black
                        {
                                if(n == parent->rchild) //Case L 2a
                                {
                                        rotateLeft(parent);
                                        n = parent;
                                        parent = n->parent;
                                }
                                parent->color = Node::black; //Case L_2b
```

```
                                    grandParent->color = Node::red;
                                    rotateRight(grandParent);
                            }
                    }//End of if
                    else
                    {
                            if(parent == grandParent->rchild)
                            {
                                    uncle = grandParent->lchild;
                                    if(uncle->color == Node::red) //Case R_1
                                    {
                                            parent->color = Node::black;
                                            uncle->color = Node::black;
                                            grandParent->color = Node::red;
                                            n = grandParent;
                                    }
                                    else    //uncle is black
                                    {
                                            if(n == parent->lchild) //Case R_2a
                                            {
                                                    rotateRight(parent);
                                                    n = parent;
                                                    parent = n->parent;
                                            }
                                            parent->color = Node::black; //Case R_2b
                                            grandParent->color = Node::red;
                                            rotateLeft(grandParent);
                                    }
                            }//End of if
                    }//End of else
            }//End of while
            root->color = Node::black;
}//End of insertionBalance()
Node* RedBlackTree::getSuccessor(Node *location)
{
        Node *ptr = location->rchild;
        while(ptr->lchild != sentinel)
                ptr = ptr->lchild;
        return ptr;
}//End of getSuccessor()
void RedBlackTree::del(int key)
{
        Node *ptr;
        if(!find(key, &ptr))
        {
                cout << "Key not present\n";
                return;
        }
        if(ptr->lchild!=sentinel && ptr->rchild!=sentinel)
        {
                Node *succ = getSuccessor(ptr);
                ptr->info = succ->info;
                ptr = succ;
        }

        Node *child;
        if(ptr->lchild != sentinel)
                child = ptr->lchild;
        else
                child = ptr->rchild;
```

```
                child->parent = ptr->parent;
                if(ptr->parent == sentinel)
                        root = child;
                else if(ptr == ptr->parent->lchild)
                        ptr->parent->lchild = child;
                else
                        ptr->parent->rchild = child;
                if(child == root)
                        child->color = Node::black;
                else if(ptr->color == Node::black) //black node
                {
                        if(child != sentinel) //one child which is red
                                child->color = Node::black;
                        else    //no child
                                deletionBalance(child);
                }
                delete ptr;
}//End of del()
void RedBlackTree::deletionBalance(Node *n)
{
        Node *sib;
        while(n != root)
        {
                if(n == n->parent->lchild)
                {
                        sib = n->parent->rchild;
                        if(sib->color == Node::red) //Case L_1
                        {
                                sib->color = Node::black;
                                n->parent->color = Node::red;
                                rotateLeft(n->parent);
                                sib = n->parent->rchild; //new sibling
                        }
                        if(sib->lchild->color==Node::black && sib->rchild->color==Node::black)
                        {
                                sib->color = Node::red;
                                if(n->parent->color == Node::red) //Case L 2a
                                {
                                        n->parent->color = Node::black;
                                        return;
                                }
                                else
                                        n = n->parent; //Case L_2b
                        }
                        else
                        {
                                if(sib->rchild->color == Node::black) //Case L_3a
                                {
                                        sib->lchild->color = Node::black;
                                        sib->color = Node::red;
                                        rotateRight(sib);
                                        sib = n->parent->rchild;
                                }
                                sib->color = n->parent->color; //Case L_3b
                                n->parent->color = Node::black;
                                sib->rchild->color = Node::black;
                                rotateLeft(n->parent);
                                return;
                        }
                }
```

```cpp
            }//End of if
            else
            {
                    sib = n->parent->lchild;
                    if(sib->color == Node::red) //Case R_1
                    {
                            sib->color = Node::black;
                            n->parent->color = Node::red;
                            rotateRight(n->parent);
                            sib = n->parent->lchild;
                    }
                    if(sib->rchild->color==Node::black && sib->lchild-
                    >color==Node::black)
                    {
                            sib->color = Node::red;
                            if(n->parent->color == Node::red) //Case R_2a
                            {
                                    n->parent->color = Node::black;
                                    return;
                            }
                            else
                                    n = n->parent; //Case R_2b
                    }
                    else
                    {
                            if(sib->lchild->color == Node::black) //Case R 3a
                            {
                                    sib->rchild->color = Node::black;
                                    sib->color = Node::red;
                                    rotateLeft(sib);
                                    sib = n->parent->lchild;
                            }

                            sib->color = n->parent->color; //Case R_3b
                            n->parent->color = Node::black;
                            sib->lchild->color = Node::black;
                            rotateRight(n->parent);
                            return;
                    }
            }//End of else
        }//End of while
}//End of deletionBalance()
void RedBlackTree::rotateRight(Node *p)
{
        Node *a;
        a = p->lchild; //A is left child of P
        p->lchild = a->rchild; //Right child of A becomes left child of P
        if(a->rchild != sentinel)
                a->rchild->parent = p;
        a->parent = p->parent;
        if(p->parent == sentinel)
                root = a;
        else if(p == p->parent->rchild)
                p->parent->rchild = a;
        else
                p->parent->lchild = a;
        a->rchild = p;          //P becomes right child of A
        p->parent = a;
}//End of rotateRight()
```

```
void RedBlackTree::rotateLeft(Node *p)
{
        Node *a;
        a = p->rchild; //A is right child of P
        p->rchild = a->lchild; //Left child of A becomes right child of P
        if(a->lchild != sentinel)
                a->lchild->parent = p;
        a->parent = p->parent;
        if(p->parent == sentinel)
                root = a;
        else if(p == p->parent->lchild)
                p->parent->lchild = a;
        else
                p->parent->rchild = a;
        a->lchild = p; //P becomes left child of A
        p->parent = a;
}//End of rotateLeft()

void RedBlackTree::inorder(Node *ptr)
{
        if(ptr != sentinel)
        {
                inorder(ptr->lchild);
                cout << ptr->info;
                inorder(ptr->rchild);
        }
}//End of inorder()

void RedBlackTree::inorder()
{
        inorder(root);
}//End of inorder()

void RedBlackTree::display(Node *ptr, int level)
{
        if(ptr != sentinel)
        {
                display(ptr->rchild, level+1);
                cout << "\n";
                for(int i=0; i<level; i++)
                        cout << "    ";
                cout << ptr->info;
                if(ptr->color == Node::red)
                        cout << "^";
                else
                        cout << "*";
                display(ptr->lchild, level+1);
        }
}//End of display()

void RedBlackTree::display()
{
        display(root, 1);
}//End of display()

int main()
{
        RedBlackTree rbTree;
        cout << "Tree after inserting 50\n";
        rbTree.insert(50);
        rbTree.display();
        cout << "\n";
        cout << "Tree after inserting 60\n";
        rbTree.insert(60);
```

```
        rbTree.display();
        cout << "\n";
        cout << "Tree after inserting 70\n";
        rbTree.insert(70);
        rbTree.display();
        cout << "\n";
        rbTree.insert(40);
        cout << "Tree after inserting 40\n";
        rbTree.display();
        cout << "\n";
        cout << "Tree after inserting 55\n";
        rbTree.insert(55);
        rbTree.display();
        cout << "\n";
        cout << "Tree after inserting 75\n";
        rbTree.insert(75);
        rbTree.display();
        cout << "\n";
        cout << "Tree after inserting 53\n";
        rbTree.insert(53);
        rbTree.display();
        cout << "\n";
        cout << "Tree after inserting 54\n";
        rbTree.insert(54);
        rbTree.display();
        cout << "\n";
        cout << "Tree after inserting 30\n";
        rbTree.insert(30);
        rbTree.display();
        cout << "\n";
        cout << "Tree after inserting 45\n";
        rbTree.insert(45);
        rbTree.display();
        cout << "\n";
        cout << "Tree after inserting 35\n";
        rbTree.insert(35);
        rbTree.display();
        cout << "\n";
        cout << "Tree after inserting 51\n";
        rbTree.insert(51);
        rbTree.display();
        cout << "\n";

        cout << "Tree after deleting 55\n";
        rbTree.del(55);
        rbTree.display();
        cout << "\n";
        cout << "Tree after deleting 50\n";
        rbTree.del(50);
        rbTree.display();
        cout << "\n";
        cout << "Tree after deleting 75\n";
        rbTree.del(75);
        rbTree.display();
        cout << "\n";
        cout << "Tree after deleting 45\n";
        rbTree.del(45);
        rbTree.display();
        cout << "\n";
        return 0;
}//End of main()
```

6.16 Heap

Heap is a binary tree which satisfies the following two properties:

(i) Structure property: All the levels have the maximum number of nodes except possibly the last level. In the last level, all the nodes occur to the left.

(ii) Heap order property: The key value in any node N is greater than or equal to the key values in both its children.

From the structure property, we can see that a heap is a complete binary tree, and so its height is $\lceil \log_2(n+1) \rceil$. From the heap order property, we can say that the key value in any node N is greater than or equal to the key value in each successor of node N. This means that the root node will have the highest key value.

The heap we have defined above is called max heap or descending heap. Similarly, we can define a min heap or ascending heap. If in the second property, we change "greater" to "smaller" then we get a min heap. In a min heap, the root will have the smallest key value. The trees in figure 6.168 are max heaps, and the trees in figure 6.169 are min heaps.

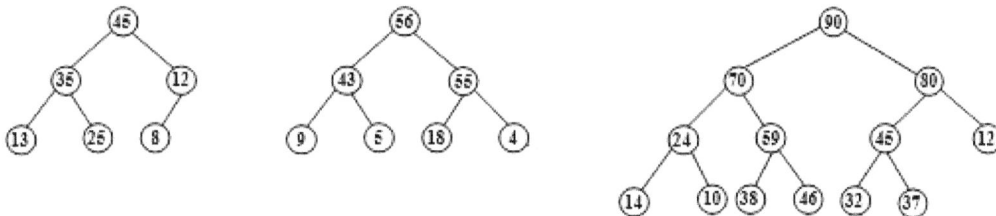

Figure 6.168 Max heaps

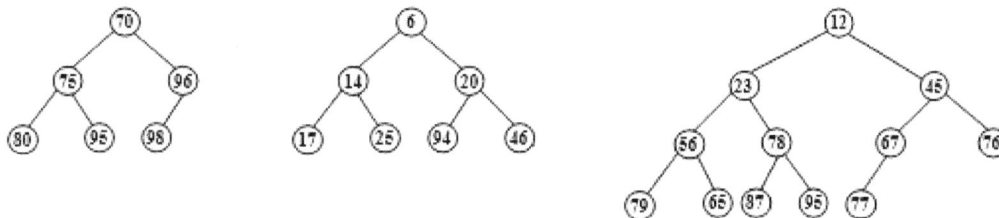

Figure 6.169 Min heaps

The nodes in a heap are partially ordered, i.e., there is no ordering of left and right child; any of the two children can be greater than the other. So a heap is not a search tree.

Heap can be used in problems where the largest (or smallest) value has to be determined quickly. The largest or smallest value can also be determined by sorting the data in descending or ascending order, and picking up the first element. But in that case, we have to do more work than required, because we just need to find the largest (or smallest) element. For that, we have to keep all the elements in order. From now onwards, in our discussions, we will use max heap only.

Heap is a complete binary tree, and sequential representation is efficient for these types of trees. Thus, heaps are implemented using arrays. Another advantage in sequential representation is that we can easily move up and down the tree, while in linked representation, we would have to maintain an extra pointer in each node to move up the tree.

If the root is stored at index 1 of the array, then the left and the right child of any node N located at index i, will be located at indices 2i and 2i+1, and the parent of node N will be at index floor(i/2).

While implementing the heap in an array, we will maintain a variable to represent the size of the heap, i.e., the number of nodes currently in the heap. If n is the heap size, then nodes of heap are stored in `arr[1], arr[2].......arr[n]`. The elements of array after `arr[n]` may contain valid entries, but they are not part of the heap.

If the value of 2i or 2i+1 is greater than the heap size, then the corresponding child does not exist. The following figure shows the array representation of a heap of size 12.

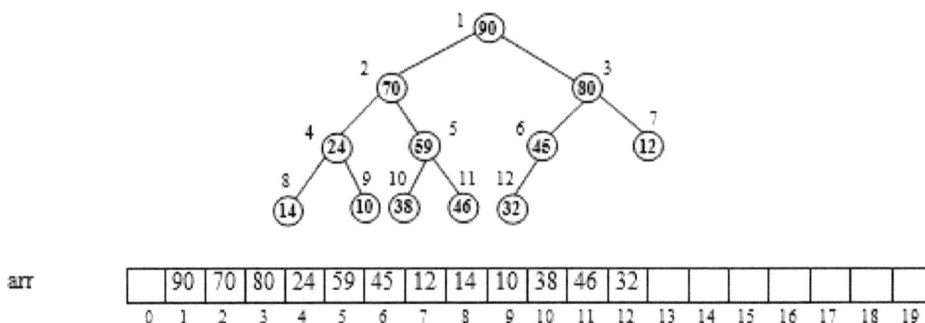

Figure 6.170 Array representation of a heap

Node 45 does not have a right child because 2*6+1=13 is greater than the heap size, which is 12. In location 0 of the array, we can store a sentinel value.

Now, we will see how to insert and delete elements from a heap. This is the class `HeapTree` for a heap tree:

```
class HeapTree
{
        private:
                int heapArr[maxSize];
                int n; //Number of elements in heap
                void restoreUp(int i);
                void restoreDown(int i);
        public:
                HeapTree();
                ~HeapTree(){}
                bool isEmpty();
                void insert(int key);
                int deleteHeap();
                void display();
};//End of class HeapTree
```

The data member array `heapArr` represents the heap, and the data member n denotes the number of elements in it.

This is the constructor of `HeapTree`:

```
HeapTree::HeapTree()
{
        n = 0;
        heapArr[0] = 9999;
}//End of HeapTree()
```

The data member n is initialized to 0. The 0th index of the array `heapArr` is stored with the maximum value, which serves as the sentinel value. All the values in the heap should be less than this value.

6.16.1 Insertion in Heap

We should insert the new key in such a way that both properties hold true after insertion also. If n is the size of heap before insertion, then it is increased to n+1, and the new key is inserted in `heapArr[n+1]`. This location is the next leaf node in the heap, and thus, the heap remains a complete binary tree after insertion as well. Suppose we have to insert key 70 in the heap tree given below:

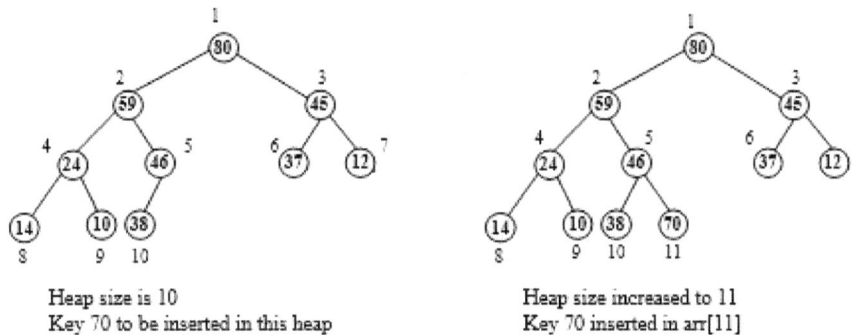

Heap size is 10
Key 70 to be inserted in this heap

Heap size increased to 11
Key 70 inserted in arr[11]

Figure 6.171 Insert 70

Insertion in this way ensures that the resulting tree fulfills the structure property, i.e., the tree remains a complete binary tree, but the second property may be violated. For example, in this case, we can see that 70 is greater than its parent 46, which is a violation of the heap order property. To restore the heap order property, we perform a procedure called `restoreUp`, in which we will move the newly inserted key up the heap and place it in its appropriate place.

Suppose k is the key that violates the heap order property and needs to be moved up. Compare k with the key in the parent node; if the parent key is smaller than k, then the parent key is moved down. Now, we try to insert k in the parent's place, and for this, k is compared with the key of the new parent. This procedure stops when we get a parent key, which is greater than k, or when we reach the root node. This way, we place the key k at its proper place in the heap.

We had inserted the key 70 in the last leaf node of the heap, and it violated the heap order property. Now, let us see how we can place the key 70 in the appropriate place using the procedure `restoreUp`.

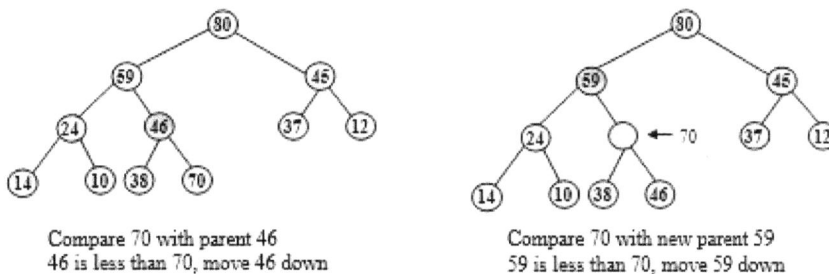

Compare 70 with parent 46
46 is less than 70, move 46 down

Compare 70 with new parent 59
59 is less than 70, move 59 down

Compare 70 with new parent 80
80 is greater than 70, proper place for 70 found

70 placed in appropriate place

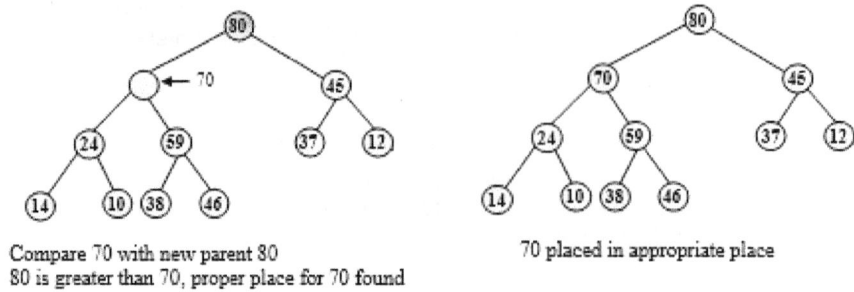

Figure 6.172 Placing 70 at appropriate place

Let us see two more examples of insertion in heap:

(i) Insert 90

Insert 90 in this heap tree

37 is less than 90, move 37 down

45 is less than 90, move 45 down

80 is less than 90, move 80 down

Reached the root node

90 placed in root node

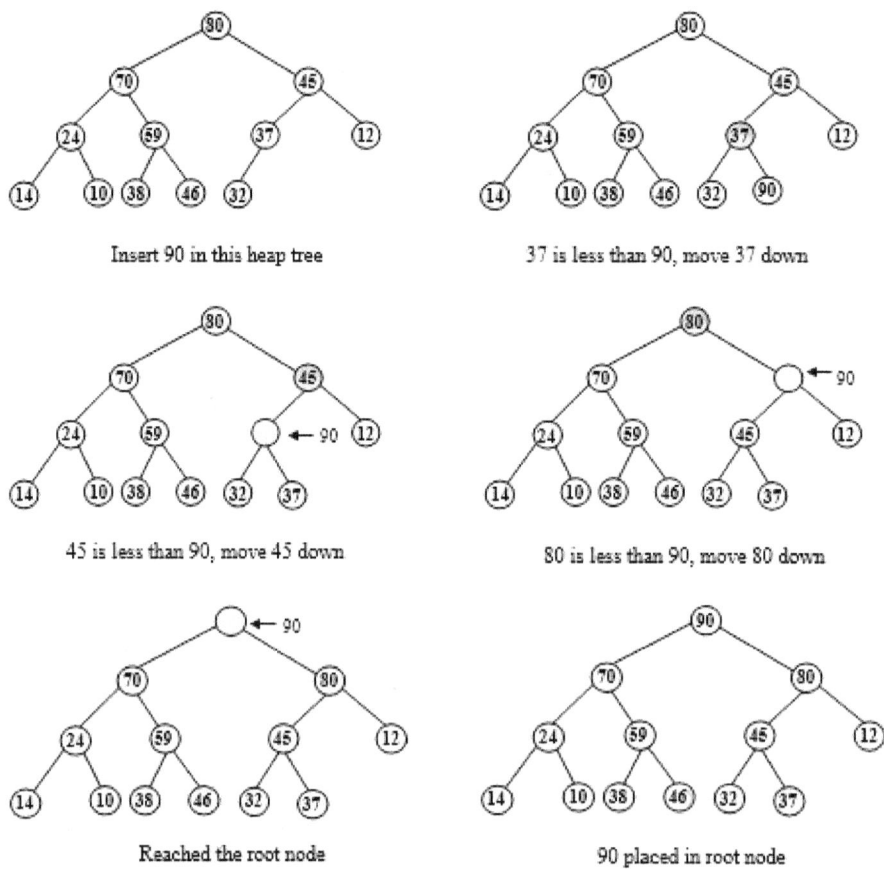

Figure 6.173 Insert 90

(ii) Insert 32

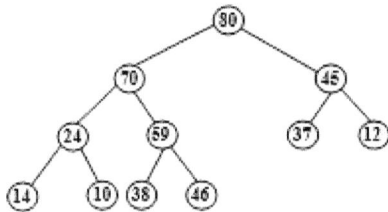

Insert 32 in this heap tree   37 is greater than 32, hence 32 is at proper place

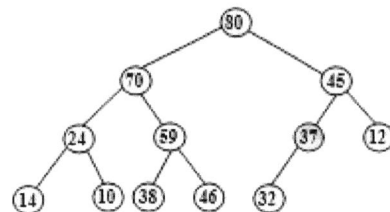

Figure 6.174 Insert 32

We can write the insert() function as:

```
void HeapTree::insert(int key)
{
        n++; //Increase the heap size by 1
        heapArr[n] = key;
        restoreUp(n);
}//End of insert()
```

Here, the heap size is first increased, then the key is inserted in the last position, and the function restoreUp() is called. The function restoreUp() can be written as:

```
void HeapTree::restoreUp(int i)
{
        int k = heapArr[i];
        int iParent = i/2;

        while(heapArr[iParent] < k)
        {
                heapArr[i] = heapArr[iParent];
                i = iParent;
                iParent = i/2;
        }
        heapArr[i] = k;
}//End of restoreUp()
```

We come out of the while loop when the exact place for the key is found. Suppose the key is the largest and has to be placed in the root node. Value of i and iParent will be 1 and 0 respectively. In this case also, the while loop terminates because we have stored a very large sentinel value in the location 0 of the array heapArr. If we do not store this value in heapArr[0], then we have to add one more condition in the while loop.

```
while(iParent>=1 && heapArr[iParent]<k)
        .........................
```

So, the use of sentinel avoids checking of one condition per loop iteration. Now, we will take some keys and insert them in an initially empty heap tree.

Keys to be inserted in Heap : 25 35 18 9 46 70 48

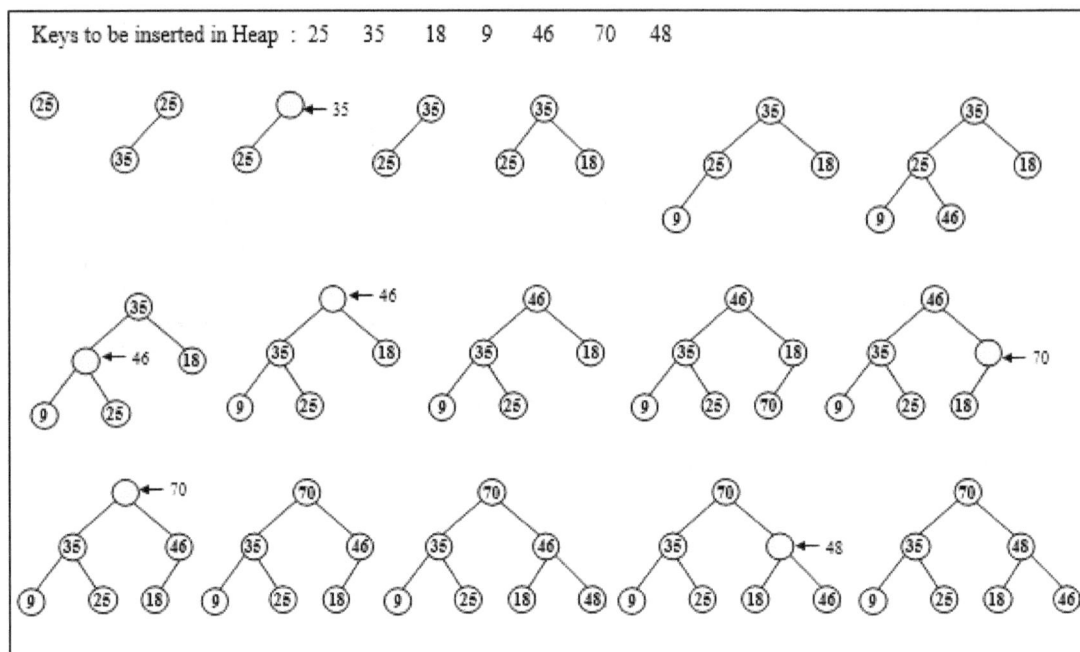

Figure 6.175 Inserting keys in heap tree

For insertion, we move on a single path from the leaf node towards the root, and hence, complexity is O(h). The height of heap is $\lceil \log_2(n+1) \rceil$, and so, complexity is O(log n). The best case of insertion is when the key can be inserted at the last position, i.e., there is no need to move it up. The worst case is when the key to be inserted is maximum; it has to be inserted in the root.

6.16.2 Deletion

Any node can be deleted from the heap but deletion of the root node is meaningful because it contains the maximum value.

Suppose we have to delete the root node from a heap of size n. The key in the root can be assigned to some variable so that it can be processed. Then we copy the key in the last leaf node, i.e., the key in location `heapArr[n]` to the root node. After this, the size of the heap is decreased to n-1. Hence, the last leaf node is deleted from the heap. Let us see how we delete root from the heap in the given figure:

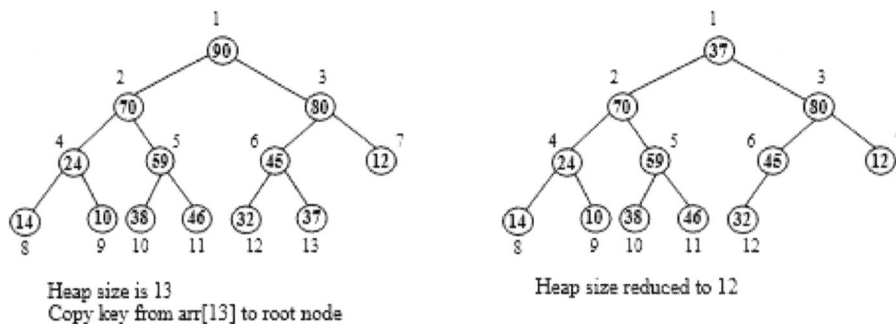

Heap size is 13
Copy key from arr[13] to root node

Heap size reduced to 12

Figure 6.176 Deleting root key from a heap

The resulting structure after deleting the root in this way is a complete binary tree, and so the first property still holds true. However, the heap order property may be violated if the key in the root node is smaller than any of its child. In the above example, key 37 is not at the proper place because it is smaller than both of its children. The procedure `restoreDown` will move the key down and place it at its proper place.

Suppose the key k violates the heap order property. Compare k with both the left and the right child. If both children are smaller than k, then we are done. If one child is greater than k, then move this greater child up. If both left and right child are greater than k, then move the larger of the two children up. After moving the child up, we try to insert the key k in this child's place, and for this, we compare it with its new children. The procedure stops when both children of k are smaller than k, or when we reach a leaf node.

Now, let us see how we can place key 37 in the appropriate place using the procedure `restoreDown`:

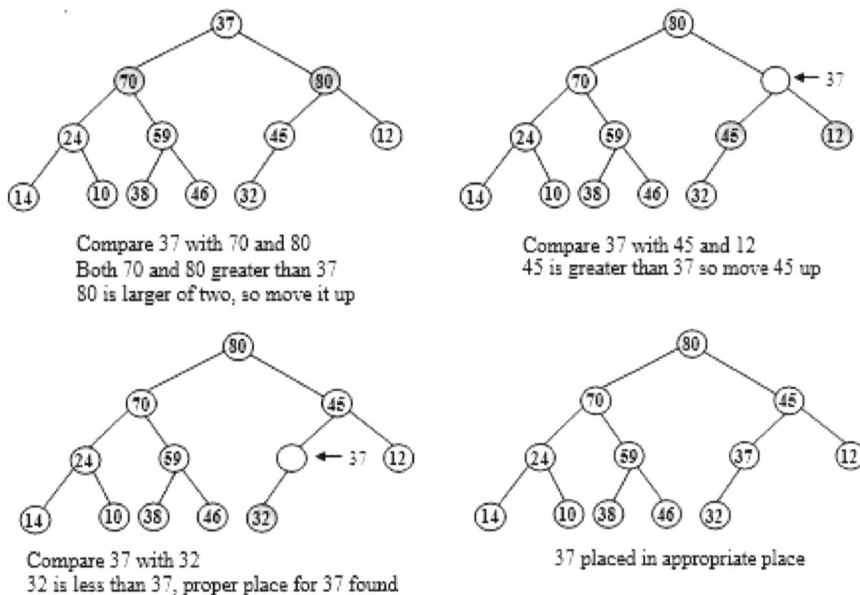

Compare 37 with 70 and 80
Both 70 and 80 greater than 37
80 is larger of two, so move it up

Compare 37 with 45 and 12
45 is greater than 37 so move 45 up

Compare 37 with 32
32 is less than 37, proper place for 37 found

37 placed in appropriate place

Figure 6.177 Placing key 37 at appropriate place

Let us see one more example of deletion of the root from the heap:

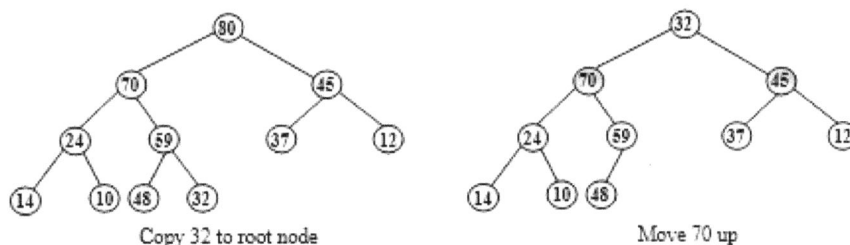

Copy 32 to root node

Move 70 up

Move 59 up

Move 48 up

Reached leaf node

Place 32 in leaf node

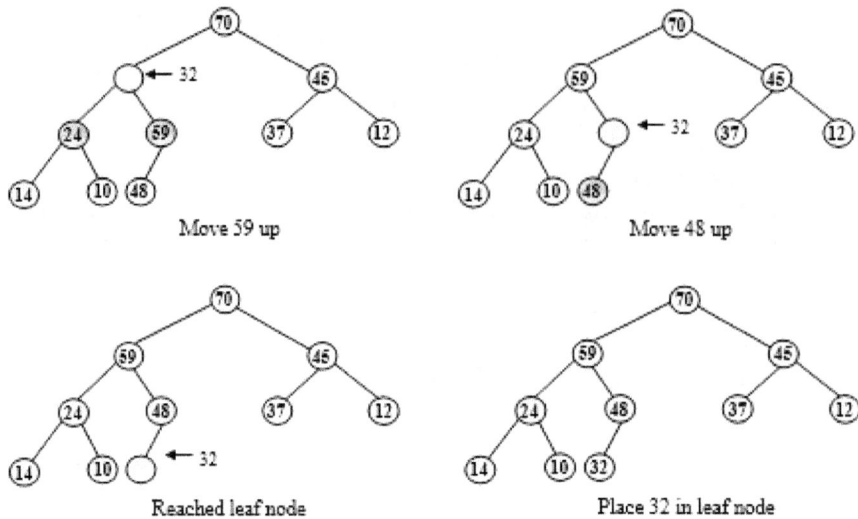

Figure 6.178 Example of deletion of root from the heap

The functions `deleteHeap()` and `restoreDown()` are:

```cpp
int HeapTree::deleteHeap()
{
        if(isEmpty())
                throw exception("Tree is empty\n");
        int maxValue = heapArr[1];    //Save the element present at the root
        heapArr[1] = heapArr[n];      //Place the last element in the root
        n--;                          //Decrease the heap size by 1
        restoreDown(1);
        return maxValue;
}//End of deleteHeap()

void HeapTree::restoreDown(int i)
{
        int k = heapArr[i];
        int lchild = 2*i;
        int rchild = lchild+1;

        while(rchild <= n)
        {
                if(heapArr[lchild]<=k && heapArr[rchild]<=k)
                {
                        heapArr[i] = k;
                        return;
                }
                else if(heapArr[lchild] > heapArr[rchild])
                {
                        heapArr[i] = heapArr[lchild];
                        i = lchild;
                }
                else
                {
                        heapArr[i] = heapArr[rchild];
                        i = rchild;
                }
                lchild = 2*i;
                rchild = lchild+1;
```

```
        }//End of while
        //If number of nodes is even
        if(lchild==n && k<heapArr[lchild])
        {
                heapArr[i] = heapArr[lchild];
                i = lchild;
        }
        heapArr[i] = k;
}//End of restoreDown()
```

When the number of nodes in the heap is odd, all nodes have either 2 children or are leaf nodes, and when the number of nodes is even, then there is one node that has only a left child. For example, if the number of nodes is 10, then the node at index 5 has only a left child, which is at index 10. In the function restoreDown(), we check for this condition separately.

For deletion, we move on a single path from root node towards the leaf. Hence, complexity is O(h). The height of heap is $\lceil \log_2(n+1) \rceil$, and so complexity is O(log n).

The functions isEmpty() and display() are:

```
bool HeapTree::isEmpty()
{
        return n==0;
}//End of isEmpty()
void HeapTree::display()
{
        for(int i=1; i<=n; i++)
                cout << heapArr[i] << " ";
        cout << "\n";
        cout << "Number of elements = " << n << "\n";
}//End of display()
```

This is the main() function:

```
//HeapTree.cpp : Program for Heap Tree.
#include<iostream>
using namespace std;

static const int maxSize = 30;

int main()
{
        HeapTree heapTree;
        try
        {
                heapTree.insert(25);
                heapTree.display();
                heapTree.insert(35);
                heapTree.display();
                heapTree.insert(18);
                heapTree.display();
                heapTree.insert(9);
                heapTree.display();
                heapTree.insert(46);
                heapTree.display();
                heapTree.insert(70);
                heapTree.display();
                heapTree.insert(48);
                heapTree.display();
                heapTree.insert(23);
                heapTree.display();
                heapTree.insert(78);
                heapTree.display();
```

```
                    heapTree.insert(12);
                    heapTree.display();
                    heapTree.insert(95);
                    cout << "After Insertion :\n";
                    heapTree.display();

                    cout << "After Deletion :\n";
                    cout << "Maximum Element : " << heapTree.deleteHeap() << "\n";
                    heapTree.display();
                    cout << "Maximum Element : " << heapTree.deleteHeap() << "\n";
                    heapTree.display();
            }
        catch(exception e)
        {
                    cout << e.what() << "\n";
        }
        return 0;
}//End of main()
```

6.16.3 Building a Heap

If we have to form a heap from some n elements, we can start with an empty heap and insert the elements sequentially n times. The `insert()` function will be called n times to build a heap in this way.

Now, let us see how we can form a heap from an array. Suppose we have an array `arr` of size n in which data is in random order, and we have to convert it to a heap of size n.

We start with a heap of size 1, i.e., initially only `arr[1]` is in the heap and after that, we insert all the remaining elements of the array (`arr[2]......arr[n]`) in the heap one by one. We insert `arr[2]` in heap of size 1, then `arr[3]` in heap of size 2, and so on, till `arr[n]` is inserted in heap of size n-1, and finally we get a heap of size n.

Since the elements are already in an array, there is no need to call `insert()`. We just increase the size of the heap and call `restoreUp()` for the next element of the array.

```
void buildHeapTopDown(int arr[], int n)
{
        for(int i=2; i<=n; i++)
                    restoreUp(i, arr);
}//End of buildHeapTopDown()
```

This method of building a heap by inserting elements one by one is a top-down approach.

The worst case is when data is in ascending order, i.e., each new key has to rise up to the root, and so, the worst case time for this approach is proportional to O(n log n). We can build a heap in O(n) time by using a bottom-up approach.

In this method, the array is considered to be representing a complete binary tree. Suppose we have an array of 11 elements stored in `arr[1].........arr[11]`, and we want to convert this array into a heap.

arr

25	35	18	9	46	70	48	23	78	12	95
1	2	3	4	5	6	7	8	9	10	11

Figure 6.179 Array of elements for building a heap

We can think of this array representing a complete binary tree, as shown in figure 6.180:

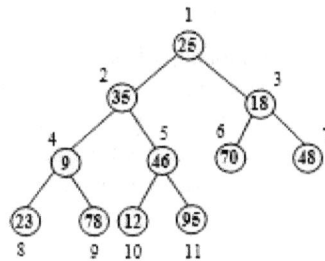

Figure 6.180 Array representing a complete binary tree

This structure satisfies the first property. To convert it to a heap, we have to make sure that the second property is also satisfied. For this, we start from the first non-leaf node and call `restoreDown()` for each node of the heap, till the root node.

The first non-leaf node is always present at index floor(n/2) of the array (if root stored at index 1 and heap size is n). So the function `restoreDown()` is called for all the nodes, with indices floor(n/2), floor(n/2)-1, floor(n/2)-2 ...... 2, 1. In our example, the heap size is 11, hence the first non-leaf node is 46 present at index 5. So, in this case, `restoreDown()` is called for `arr[5]`, `arr[4]`, `arr[3]`, `arr[2]`, `arr[1]`.

First, `restoreDown()` is called for 46. The right child of 46 is 95, which is greater than 46. So, 95 is moved up and 46 is moved down. Similarly, `retsoreDown()` is called for 9, 18, 35, and 25, and all of them are placed at the proper places. Finally, we get a heap of size 11.

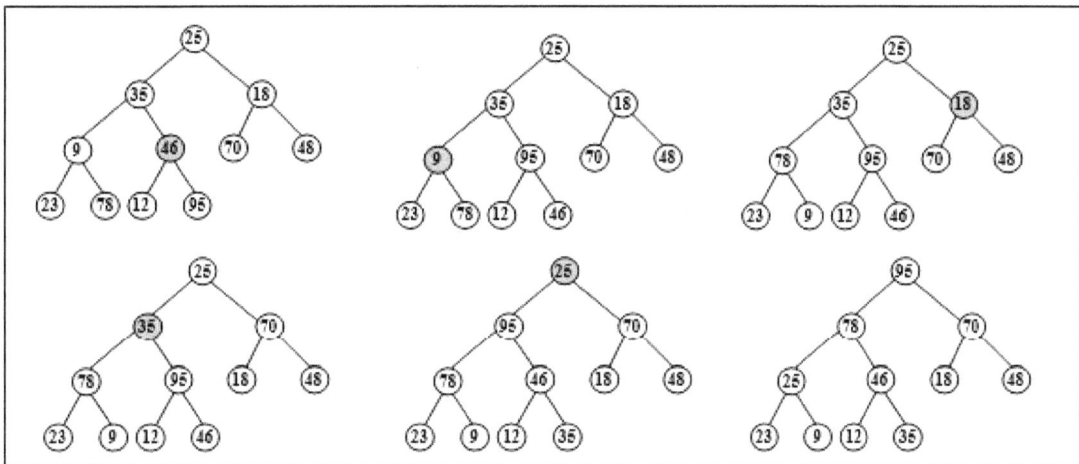

Figure 6.181 Building heap using bottom up approach

The function `buildHeapBottomUp()` using the bottom-up approach is:

```
void buildHeapBottomUp(int arr[], int n)
{
        for(int i=n/2; i>=1; i--)
                restoreDown(i, arr, n);
```

```
}//End of buildHeapBottomUp()
```

This was the procedure of building a heap through bottom-up approach; now let us understand how we are able to get a heap by applying this procedure.

The heap is constructed by making smaller subheaps from bottom-up. Each leaf node is a heap of size 1, and so we start working from the first non-leaf node. Since we are working from bottom to up, whenever we analyze a node, its left and right subtrees will be heaps. Starting from the first non leaf node, each node N is considered as the root of a subtree, whose left and right subtrees are heaps, and `restoreDown()` is called for that node, so that the whole subtree rooted at node N also becomes a heap.

There are three main applications of heap:

1. Selection algorithm
2. Implementation of priority queue
3. Heap sort

This is the complete program to build the heap:

```cpp
//BuildHeap.cpp : Program to build the heap.
#include<iostream>
using namespace std;
void restoreDown(int i, int arr[], int n)
{
        int k = arr[i];
        int lchild = 2*i;
        int rchild = lchild+1;
        while(rchild <= n)
        {
                if(k>=arr[lchild] && k>=arr[rchild])
                {
                        arr[i] = k;
                        return;
                }
                else if(arr[lchild] > arr[rchild])
                {
                        arr[i] = arr[lchild];
                        i = lchild;
                }
                else
                {
                        arr[i] = arr[rchild];
                        i = rchild;
                }
                lchild = i*2;
                rchild = lchild+1;
        }//End of while
        //If number of nodes is even
        if(lchild==n && k<arr[lchild])
        {
                arr[i] = arr[lchild];
                i = lchild;
        }
        arr[i] = k;
}//End of restoreDown()
void buildHeapBottomUp(int arr[], int n)
{
        for(int i=n/2; i>=1; i--)
                restoreDown(i, arr, n);
}//End of buildHeapBottomUp()
```

```
void restoreUp(int i, int arr[])
{
        int k = arr[i];
        int iParent = i/2;
        while(arr[iParent] < k)
        {
                arr[i] = arr[iParent];
                i = iParent;
                iParent = i/2;
        }
        arr[i] = k;
}//End of restoreUp()
void buildHeapTopDown(int arr[], int n)
{
        for(int i=2; i<=n; i++)
                restoreUp(i, arr);
}//End of buildHeapTopDown()
int main()
{
        int arr1[] = {9999, 25, 35, 18, 9, 46, 70, 48, 23, 78, 12, 95};
        int n1 = 11;
        cout << "Building Heap Botton Up :\n";
        buildHeapBottomUp(arr1, n1);
        for(int i=1; i<=n1; i++)
                cout << arr1[i] << " ";
        cout << "\n";
        int arr2[] = {9999, 25, 35, 18, 9, 46, 70, 48, 23, 78, 12, 95};
        int n2 = 11;
        cout << "Building Heap Top Down :\n";
        buildHeapTopDown(arr2, n2);
        for(int i=1; i<=n2; i++)
                cout << arr2[i] << " ";
        cout << "\n";
        return 0;
}//End of main()
```

6.16.4 Selection Algorithm

There are two ways to find the kth largest element in a list. The first method is to sort the whole list in descending order, and the element at k^{th} location will be the kth largest element. The second approach uses a heap and is more efficient. First, a heap is built from the elements, and then k elements are deleted from the heap. The last element deleted is the kth largest element.

6.16.5 Implementation of Priority Queue

We have already studied about the priority queue. If we implement it through a queue, then deletion is O(n), while insertion is O(1). If we implement it through a sorted list, then insertion is O(n), while deletion is O(1). If a heap is used to implement a priority queue, then both these operations can be performed in O(log n) time. A max or min heap can be used to implement a max or min priority queue. If we make a max heap from the priorities of nodes, then the node with the highest priority will always be at the root node. The find operation in the priority queue finds the node with the highest priority, and the delete operation deletes the node with the highest priority.

The third application heap sort will be discussed in Chapter 8, Sorting.

6.17 Weighted Path Length

Suppose every external node in an extended binary tree is assigned some non-negative weight. Then the external weighted path length of the tree can be calculated as:

$$P = W_1 P_1 + W_2 P_2 + \ldots\ldots\ldots\ldots + W_n P_n$$

Where, W_i denotes the weight and P_i denotes the path length of an external node.

If we create different trees that have same weights on external nodes, then it is not necessary that they have the same external weighted path length.

Let us take the weights 4, 7, 8, 12 and create three different trees:

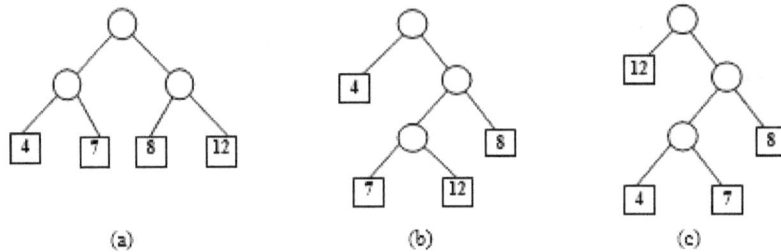

Figure 6.182 Extended binary trees with weights

The weighted path lengths of these trees is:

Weighted Path Length of (a): $P_1 = 4*2 + 7*2 + 8*2 + 12*2 = 8 + 14 + 16 + 24 = 62$
Weighted Path Length of (b): $P_2 = 4*1 + 7*3 + 12*3 + 8*2 = 4 + 21 + 36 + 16 = 77$
Weighted Path Length of (c): $P_3 = 12*1 + 4*3 + 7*3 + 8*2 = 12 + 12 + 21 + 16 = 61$

The three different trees have different external weighted path lengths. Now, our aim is to obtain an extended binary tree, which has the minimum weighted external path length for n external nodes with weights $w_1, w_2, w_3, \ldots\ldots w_n$. This tree can be created by Huffman algorithm and is thus named the Huffman tree, in honor of its inventor, David Huffman.

6.18 Huffman Tree

The Huffman tree is built from bottom-up, rather than top-down, i.e., the creation of trees starts from leaf nodes and proceeds upwards.

Suppose we have n elements with weights $w_1, w_2 \ldots\ldots w_n$, and we want to construct a Huffman tree for this set of weights.

For each element, we create a tree with a single root node. So initially, we have a forest of n trees, and each data item with its weight is placed in its own tree.

In each step of the algorithm, we pick up two trees T_i and T_j with the smallest weights (w_i and w_j), and combine them into a new tree T_k. The two trees T_i and T_j become subtrees of this new tree T_k, and the weight of this new tree is the sum of the weights of the trees T_i and T_j, i.e., $w_i + w_j$. After each step, the number of trees in our forest will decrease by 1. The process is continued till we get a single tree, and this is the final Huffman tree. The leaf nodes of this tree contain the elements and their weights. Let us take 7 elements with weights and create an extended binary tree using the Huffman algorithm.

	A	B	C	D	E	F	G
Weight	16	11	7	20	23	5	15

(i) Initially we have a forest of 7 single node trees.

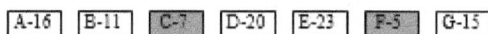

A-16 B-11 C-7 D-20 E-23 F-5 G-15

Figure 6.183 Forest of 7 single node trees

The two trees with the smallest weights are trees weighted 7 and 5 (shaded in the figure).

(ii) The trees weighted 7 and 5 are combined to form a new tree weighted 12.

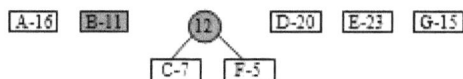

Figure 6.184 7 Trees weighted 7 and 5 are combined

We have arbitrarily made the tree weighted 7, as the left child. Any tree can be made left or right child. Now, the two trees with the smallest weights are trees weighted 11 and 12.

(iii) The trees weighted 11 and 12 are combined to form a new tree weighted 23.

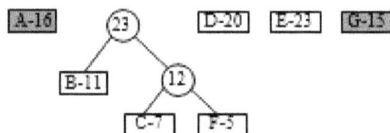

Figure 6.185 Trees weighted 11 and 12 are combined

Now the two trees with the smallest weights are trees weighted 16 and 15.

(iv) The trees weighted 16 and 15 are combined to form a new tree weighted 31.

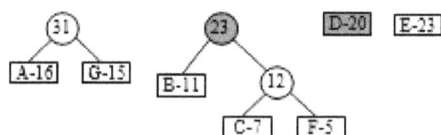

Figure 6.186 Trees weighted 16 and 15 are combined

Now, the two smallest weights are 20 and 23, but there are two trees with weight 23. We can break this tie arbitrarily and choose any one of them for combining.

(v) The trees weighted 20 and 23 are combined to form a new tree weighted 43.

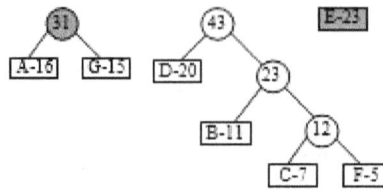

Figure 6.187 Trees weighted 20 and 23 are combined

Now, the two trees with the smallest weights are trees weighted 31 and 23.

(vi) The trees weighted 31 and 23 are combined to form a new tree weighted 54.

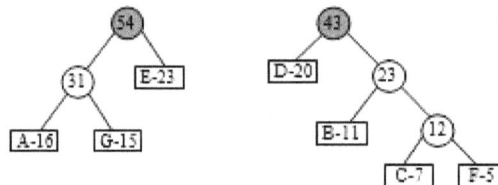

Figure 6.188 Trees weighted 31 and 23 are combined

Now the two trees with the smallest weights are the trees weighted 54 and 43.

(vii) The trees weighted 54 and 43 are combined to form a new tree weighted 97.

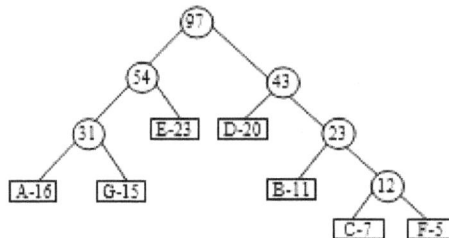

Figure 6.189 Huffman tree

Now, only a single tree is left, and this is the final Huffman tree. The weighted path length for this tree is:

16*3 + 15*3 + 23*2 + 20*2 + 11*3 + 7*4 + 5*4
=260

In the above procedure, we have seen that when two trees are combined, anyone can be made the left or the right subtree of the new tree, and if there is more than one tree with equal weights in the roots, then we can arbitrarily choose any one for combining. So, the Huffman tree produced by the Huffman algorithm is not unique. There can be different Huffman trees for the same set of weights, but the weighted path length for all of them would be the same, irrespective of the shape of the tree. The following figure shows two more Huffman trees for the same set of weights given in the example:

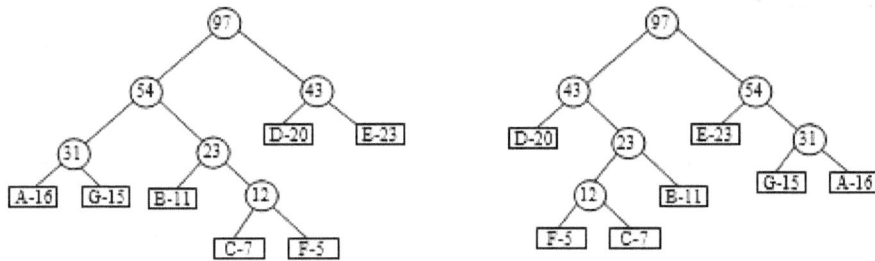

Figure 6.190 Huffman trees for same set of wiights

The weighted path lengths for these two trees are:

16*3 +15*3 + 11*3 + 7*4 + 5*4 + 20*2 +23*2 = 260

20*2 + 5*4 + 7*4 + 11*3 + 23*2 + 15*3 + 16*3 = 260

This algorithm uses the greedy approach because at each step, we choose the two trees that appear to be the best candidates for combining.

6.18.1 Application of Huffman Tree : Huffman Codes

Suppose we have a long message that comprises of different symbols. We want to encode this message with the help of bits (0s and 1s). To do this, we will assign a binary code to each symbol, and then concatenate these individual codes to get the code for the message. If we have n distinct symbols, then we can encode each symbol by using a r-bit code where $2^{r-1} < n \leq 2^r$.

Suppose we have 5 different symbols v, w, x, y, z. We will need a 3-bit code to uniquely represent each symbol.

$2^2 < 5 \leq 2^3$

Suppose the codes assigned to these symbols are:

v	w	x	y	z
000	001	010	011	100

If we use the above codes, then the message "wyxwvyz" can be encoded as:

001011010001000011100

This type of coding is called fixed length coding because the length of the code for each symbol is the same. ASCII and EBCDIC are fixed length codes. If we know the frequency (number of occurrences) of symbols in a message, we can reduce the size of the coded message using variable length codes. Instead of assigning equal bits to all the symbols, we can give shorter codes to symbols that occur more frequently and longer codes to symbols that occur less frequently. These types of codes are called variable length codes because here the length of the code of each symbol is different. This way we can achieve data compression. The following tables show the comparison of fixed length codes and variable length codes.

Fixed length code					Variable length code			
Character	Frequency	Code	Bits		Character	Frequency	Code	Bits
v	5	000	5*3=15		v	5	0100	5*4=20
w	36	001	36*3=108		w	36	00	36*2=72
x	25	010	25*3=75		x	25	011	25*3=75
y	58	011	58*3=174		y	58	1	58*1=58
z	8	100	8*3=24		z	8	0101	8*4=32
Total Bits			396		Total Bits			257

Figure 6.191 Comparison of fixed length codes and variable length codes

In fixed length code, all the symbols are assigned 3-bit codes irrespective of their frequency. The coded message occupies 396 bits in this case. In variable length codes, we have assigned 1 bit code to y since it is most frequent, while v and z are assigned 4-bit codes since they are less frequent. So the same message can be coded using only 257 bits, if variable length codes are used.

Encoding a message using variable length codes is simple, and as in fixed length codes, here also, the individual codes of symbols are just concatenated to get the code for the message. For example, if we use the variable length codes given in the table above, then the message "wyxwvyz" would be encoded as 00101100010010101.

Now, let us see how we can decode the encoded message. When fixed length codes are used, decoding is simple – start reading bits from the left, and just transform each 3 bit sequence to the corresponding symbol. When variable length codes are used, we do not know how many bits to pick. For example, if the encoded message is 0010101011, the code for the first symbol may be 0 or 00 or 001 or 0010. From the table, we can see that 0 is not a code, but 00 is a code for w and no other code starts with 00. So the first two bits can be decoded to get the symbol w. The next bit is 1, which is code of y, and no other code starts with 1. So, the next symbol decoded is y. The next bit is 0, which is not a code; 01 is also not a code, 010 is also not a code, 0101 is the code of z. So, next decoded symbol is z.

This decoding method works because the variable length codes that we have made, are prefix free, i.e., no code is a prefix of other code. For example, 00 is the code for symbol w, and so it is not the prefix of any other code, i.e., no code starts with 00. Similarly, no code starts with 1, since it is a code of y. These types of codes are known as prefix codes. Now the question is, how can we obtain these variable length codes that are prefix free.

The Huffman tree is used to generate these codes, and the resulting codes are called Huffman codes. First, we will create a Huffman tree for the data given in the table. Each external node contains a symbol, and its weight is equal to the frequency of the symbol.

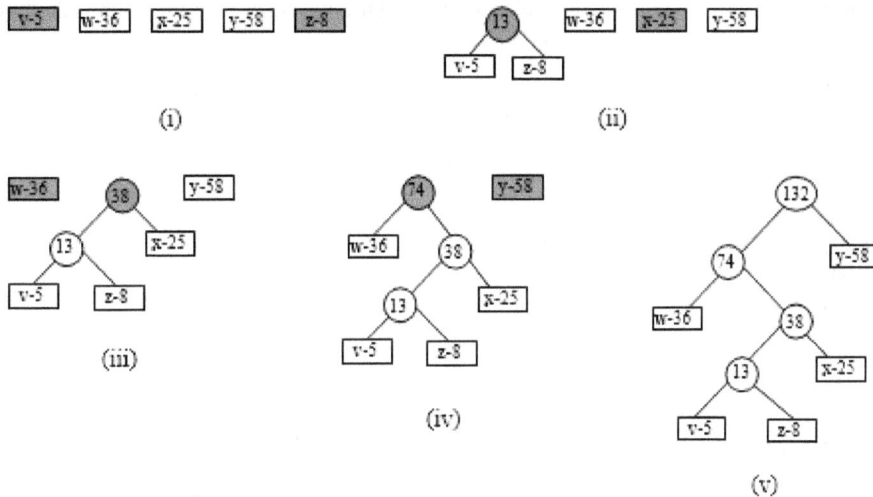

Figure 6.192 Creation of huffman tree

Now, let us see how this Huffman tree can be used to generate Huffman codes. Each branch in the Huffman tree is assigned a bit value. The left branches are assigned 0 and the right branches are assigned 1.

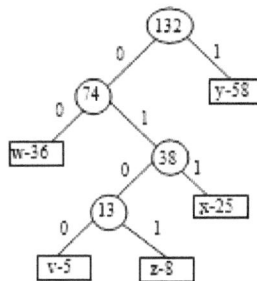

Figure 6.193 Bit values assigned to branches of huffman tree

We can find the code of each symbol by tracing the path that starts from the root, and ends at the leaf node that contains the given symbol. All the bit values in this path are recorded and the bit sequence so obtained is the code for the symbol. For example, to get the code of v, first we move left(0), then right(1), then left(0), and then again left(0). So, the code for v is 0100. Similarly, we can find the codes of other symbols which are:

w	y	x	v	z
00	1	011	0100	0101

Since all the symbols are in the leaf nodes, this method generates codes that are prefix free, and hence, decoding will be unambiguous.

The same Huffman tree is used for decoding data. The encoded data is read bit by bit from the left side. We will start from the root. If there is a 0 in the coded message, we go to the left child, and if there is 1 in the coded message, we go to the right child, and this procedure continues till we reach the leaf node.

On reaching the leaf node, we get the symbol, and then again, we start from the root node. Let us take a coded message and decode it.

```
0001000110101001011
00 01000110101001011                    w
00 0100 0110101001011                   wv
00 0100 011 0101001011                  wvx
00 0100 011 0101 001011                 wvxz
00 0100 011 0101 00 1011                wvxzw
00 0100 011 0101 00 1 011               wvxzwy
00 0100 011 0101 00 1 011               wvxzwyx
```

The drawback with Huffman codes is that we have to scan the data twice: the first time for getting the frequencies and the next time for actual encoding.

6.19 General Tree

We have seen the definition of a general tree in the beginning of this chapter. The following are the three differences in a binary tree and a general tree:

1) A binary tree may be empty, but there should be at least one node in a general tree.

2) In a binary tree, each node can have at most two children, but in a general tree, a node may have more than two children.

3) In a binary tree, every child is the left or the right child, but in a general tree, a child cannot be distinguished as left or right. All the children of a node in a general tree are termed as siblings of each other.

A general tree can be converted to a binary tree by following the procedure given below.

The root of the binary tree will be the same as that of a general tree. The first child of a node in a general tree will be the left child of that node in a binary tree. The next sibling of a node in a general tree will be the right child of that node in a binary tree. Let us take two examples of the general tree and create corresponding binary trees.

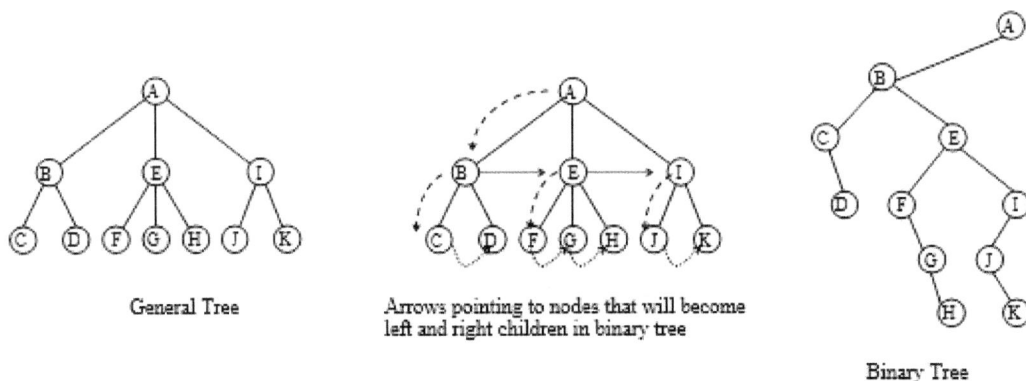

General Tree

Arrows pointing to nodes that will become left and right children in binary tree

Binary Tree

Figure 6.194 Example of general tree to binary tree

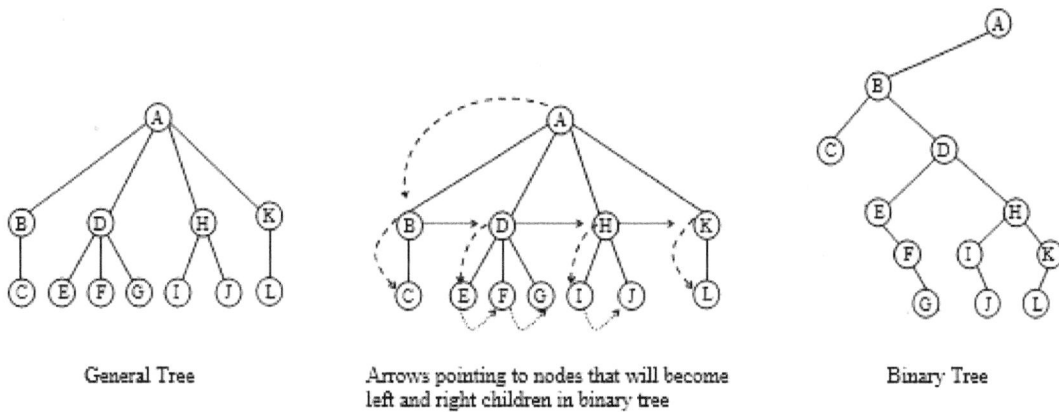

General Tree

Arrows pointing to nodes that will become
left and right children in binary tree

Binary Tree

Figure 6.195 Another example of general tree to binary tree

In both examples, the first figure shows the general tree, the second figure shows the same tree with arrows representing the left and right child of a node in a binary tree, and the third figure shows the corresponding binary tree. Note that in any general tree, the root does not have a sibling, so the root of the corresponding binary tree will not have any right child.

A general tree can easily be represented like a binary tree. The class for a node of a general tree can be taken as:

```
class Node
{
        int info;
        Node *firstChild;
        Node *nextSibling;
};
```

In a binary tree, the left and the right pointers of a node is pointed to the left and right child of the node, respectively. In the general tree, the left pointer will point to the first child or the leftmost child of the node, and the right pointer will point to the next sibling of the node. The linked representation of a general tree is as follows:

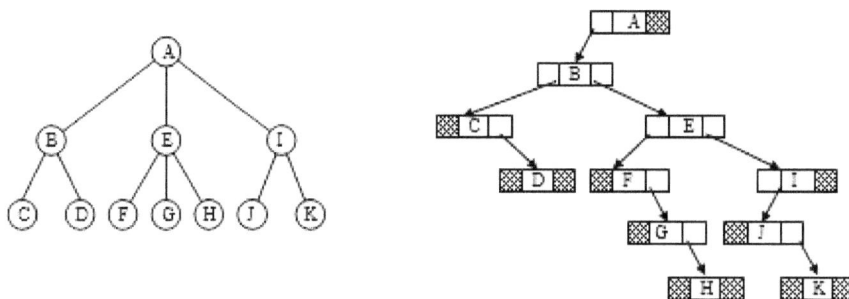

Figure 6.196 Linked representation of a general tree

6.20 Multiway Search Tree

Till now, we have studied about internal searching only, i.e., we have assumed that the data to be searched is present in the primary storage area. Now, we will study external searching, in which data is to be retrieved from the secondary storage such as disk files. We know that the access time in the case of secondary storage is much more than that of primary storage. So, while doing external searching, we should try to reduce the number of accesses. When data is accessed from a disk, a whole block is read instead of a single word. Keeping these points in mind, a data structure was devised, which was specially suited for external searching and is known as multiway search tree. Till now, in all the trees that we have studied, a node can hold only one key value, and can have at most two children. In a multiway search tree, a node can hold more than one value, and can have more than 2 children. Usually, the size of the node is made to coincide with the size of the block of the secondary storage device. Due to the large branching factor of multiway search trees, their height is reduced, and so, the number of nodes traversed to reach a particular record also decreases, which is desirable in external searching.

A multiway search tree of order m is a search tree, in which any node can have at the most m children. The properties of a non-empty m-way search tree of order m are:

(i) Each node can hold a maximum m-1 keys and can have maximum m children.

(ii) A node with n children has n-1 key values, i.e., the number of key values is one less than the number of children. Some of the children can be NULL (empty subtrees).

(iii) The keys in a node are in the ascending order.

(iv) Keys in a non-leaf node will divide the left and right subtrees, where the value of the left subtree keys will be less, and the value of the right subtree keys will be more than that particular key.

To understand these points, let us consider a node of m-way search tree of order 8.

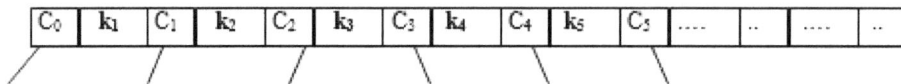

Figure 6.197 Node of m-way search tree of order 8

(i) This node has the capacity to hold 7 keys and 8 children.

(ii) It currently has 5 key values and 6 children. While programming, we can take a variable *numKeys* to keep track of the number of keys that a node currently holds.

(iii) $k_1 < k_2 < k_3 < k_4 < k_5$

(iv) The key k_1 is greater than all the keys in the subtree pointed to by pointer C_0, and less than all the keys in the subtree pointed to by pointer C_1. Similarly, this relation holds true for other keys also.

$$keys(C_0) < k_1 < keys(C_1) < k_2 < keys(C_2) < k_3 < keys(C_3) < k_4 < keys(C_4) < k_5 < keys(C_5)$$

The tree in figure 6.198 is a multiway search tree of order 5:

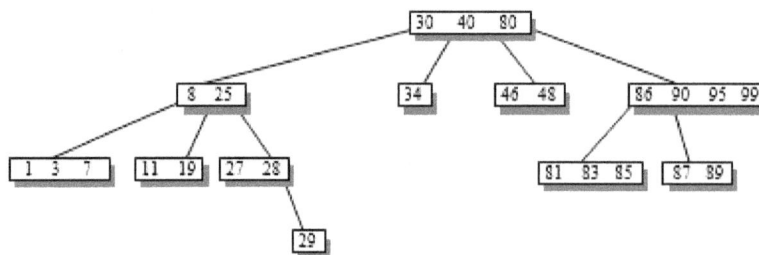

Figure 6.198 Multiway search tree of order 5

From the above explanation, we can say that m-way search trees are a generalized form of Binary search trees, and a Binary search tree can be considered as an m-way search tree of order 2.

6.21 B-tree

In external searching, our aim is to minimize the file accesses, and this can be done by reducing the height of the tree. The height of m-way search tree is less because of its large branching factor, but its height can still be reduced if it is balanced. So, a new tree structure was developed (by Bayer and McCreight in 1972), which was a height **B**alanced m-way search tree and was named B-tree.

A B-tree of order m can be defined as an m-way search tree, which is either empty or satisfies the following properties:

(i) All leaf nodes are at the same level.
(ii) All non leaf nodes (except root node) should have at least $\lceil m/2 \rceil$ children.
(iii) All nodes (except root node) should have at least $\lceil m/2 \rceil$ - 1 keys.
(iv) If the root node is a leaf node (only node in the tree), then it will have no children and will have at least one key. If the root node is a non-leaf node, then it will have at least 2 children and at least one key.
(v) A non leaf node with n-1 key values should have n non NULL children.

From the definition, we can see that any node (except root) in a B-tree is at least half full, and this avoids wastage of storage space. The B-tree is perfectly balanced, so the number of nodes accessed to find a key becomes less.

The following figure shows the minimum and maximum number of children in any non-root and non-leaf node of B-trees of different orders.

Order of the tree	Minimum Children	Maximum Children
3	2	3
4	2	4
5	3	5
6	3	6
7	4	7
....	....	....
M	$\lceil M/2 \rceil$	M

Figure 6.199 Minimum and maximum children for different B-trees orders

Now let us see why the m-way search tree in the previous figure 6.198 is not a B-tree.

(i) The leaf nodes in this tree are [1,3,7], [11,19], [29], [34], [46,48], [81,83,85], [87,89] and it can be clearly seen that they are not at the same level.
(ii) The non leaf node [27, 28] has 2 keys but only one non NULL child, and the non-leaf node [86,90,95,99] has 4 keys but only 2 non NULL children.
(iii) The minimum number of keys for a B-tree of order 5 is $\lceil 5/2 \rceil$-1 = 2, while in the above tree there are 2 nodes [34], [29] which have less than 2 keys.

The tree given in figure 6.200 is a B-tree of order 5.

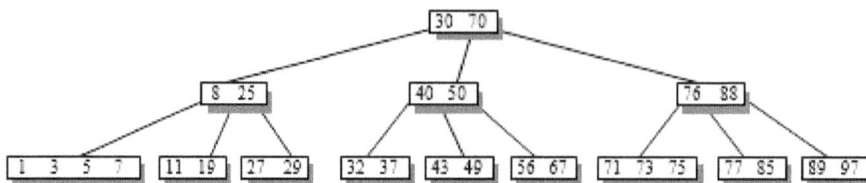

Figure 6.200 B-tree of order 5

While explaining various operations on B-tree, we will take B-trees of order 5. We will denote the maximum number of permissible keys by MAX and a minimum number of permissible keys (except in the root) by MIN. So if the order is 5, MAX = 5-1 = 4, and MIN = $\lceil 5/2 \rceil$-1 = 2.

There are special names given to B-trees of order 3 and 4. A B-tree of order 3 is known as 2-3 tree because any non-root non-leaf node can have 2 or 3 children, and a B-tree of order 4 is known as 2-3-4 tree, because any non-root non-leaf node can have 2, 3 or 4 children.

6.21.1 Searching in B-tree

Searching in B tree is analogous to searching in a binary search tree. In BST, the search starts from the root and at each node, we make a 2-way decision, i.e., we go either to the left child or to the right child. In B tree also, the search starts from the root, but here, we have to make n-way decision at each node, where n is the number of children of the node.

Suppose we want to search for the key 19 in the B-tree of figure 6.200. Searching will start from the root node, so first, we look at the node [30,70]. The key is not there and since 19 < 30, we will move on to the leftmost child of root node, which is [8, 25]. The key is not present in this node also, and the value 19 lies between 8 and 25, and so we move on to node [11,19], where we get the desired key.

If we reach a leaf node and still do not find the value, it implies that the value is not present in the tree. For example, suppose we have to search for the key 35 in the tree of figure 6.200. First, the key is searched in the root node, and since it lies between 30 and 70, we move to the node [40, 50]. Now 35 is less than 40, so we move to the leftmost child of node [40, 50], which is [32, 37]. The key is not present in this node also, and since we have reached a leaf node, the search is unsuccessful.

6.21.2 Insertion in B-tree

Firstly, the key to be inserted is searched in the tree, and if it is already present, we do not proceed further, because duplicate keys are not allowed. If the search is unsuccessful, we will traverse down the tree and reach the leaf node, where the key will be inserted. Now, we can have two cases for inserting the key in the leaf node:
1. Node is not full, i.e., it has less than MAX keys.
2. Node is already full, i.e., it has MAX keys.

In the first case, we can simply insert the key in the node at its proper place, by shifting keys greater than it to the right side.

In the second case, the key is to be inserted into a full node; the full node is split into three parts. The first part consists of all the keys left to the median key, and these keys remain in the same node. The second part consists of the median key, and it is moved to the parent node. The third part consists of all the keys to the right of the median key, and these keys are moved to a new node. The median key is to be moved to the parent node, but what if the parent node is also full. In that case, a split will occur again and this process will continue until we reach a non-full parent node. In extreme cases, we may reach the root node which is full. So here, the root node will be split and a new root will be created which will have the median key, and the height of the tree will increase by one. Let us take some keys and create a B-tree of order 5.

10, 40, 30, 35, 20, 15, 50, 28, 25, 5, 60, 19, 12, 38, 27, 90, 45, 48

(a) Insert 10

Figure 6.201 Insert 10

(b) Insert 40

Figure 6.202 Insert 40

(c) Insert 30

Figure 6.203 Insert 30

30 will be inserted between 10 and 40, since all the keys in a node should be in ascending order.

(d) Insert 35

Figure 6.204 Insert 35

The maximum number of permissible keys for a node of a B-tree of order 5 is 4, and so now, after the insertion of 35, this node has become full.

(e) Insert 20

The node [10, 30, 35, 40] will become overfull [10, 20, **30**, 35, 40], and so, splitting is done at the median key 30. A new node is allocated and keys to the right of the median key, i.e., 35 and 40 are moved to the new node, and the keys to the left of the median key, i.e., 10 and 20, remain in the same node. Generally, after splitting, the median key goes to the parent node, but here the node that is being split, is the root node. So, a new node is allocated, which contains the median key, and now this new node becomes the root of the tree.

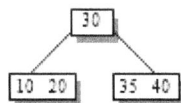

Figure 6.205 Insert 20

Since the root node has been split, the height of the tree has increased by one.

(f) Insert 15, 50, 28

15 and 28 are less than 30, so they are inserted in the left node at the appropriate place, and since 50 is greater than 30, so it is inserted in the right node.

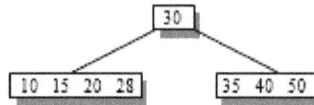

Figure 6.206 Insert 15, 50, 28

(g) Insert 25

The node [10, 15, 20, 28] will become overfull [10, 15, **20**, 25, 28], and so splitting is done and the median key 20 goes to the parent node.

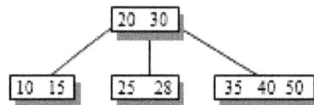

Figure 6.207 Insert 25

(h) Insert 5, 60, 19

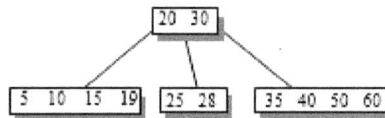

Figure 6.208 Insert 5, 60, 19

(i) Insert 12

The node [5, 10, 15, 19] will become overfull [5, 10, **12**, 15, 19], and so, splitting is done, and the median key 12 goes to the parent node.

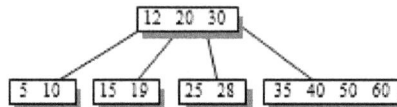

Figure 6.209 Insert 12

(j) Insert 38

The node [35, 40, 50, 60] will become overfull [35, 38, **40**, 50, 60], and so, splitting is done, and the median key 40 goes to the parent node.

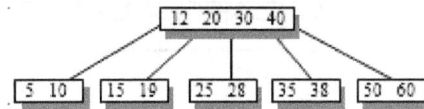

Figure 6.210 Insert 38

(k) Insert 27, 90, 45

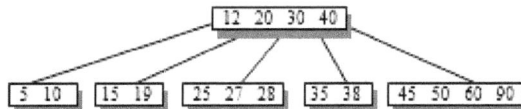

Figure 6.211 Insert 27, 90, 45

(l) Insert 48

The node [45, 50, 60, 90] will become overfull [45, 48, **50**, 60, 90], and so, splitting is done, and the median key 50 goes to the parent node. After insertion of 50, the parent node also becomes overfull [12, 20, **30**, 40, 50], and so, splitting is done again and this time root node is split, so a new root is formed and the tree becomes taller.

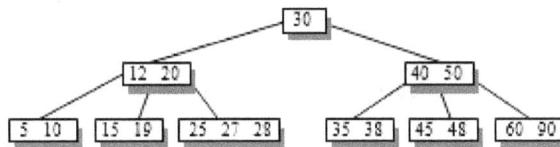

Figure 6.212 Insert 48

6.21.3 Deletion in B-tree

While inserting a key, we had to take care that the number of keys should not exceed MAX. Similarly, while deleting, we have to watch that the number of keys in a node should not become less than MIN. While inserting, when the keys exceeded MAX, we split the node into two nodes, and the median key went to the parent node; while deleting, when the keys will become less than MIN, we will combine two nodes into one.

Now, let us see how all this is done by studying all the cases of deletion. Deletion in a B-tree can be classified into two cases:
(A) Deletion from leaf node
(B) Deletion from non-leaf node

Figure 6.213 shows all the cases of deletion:

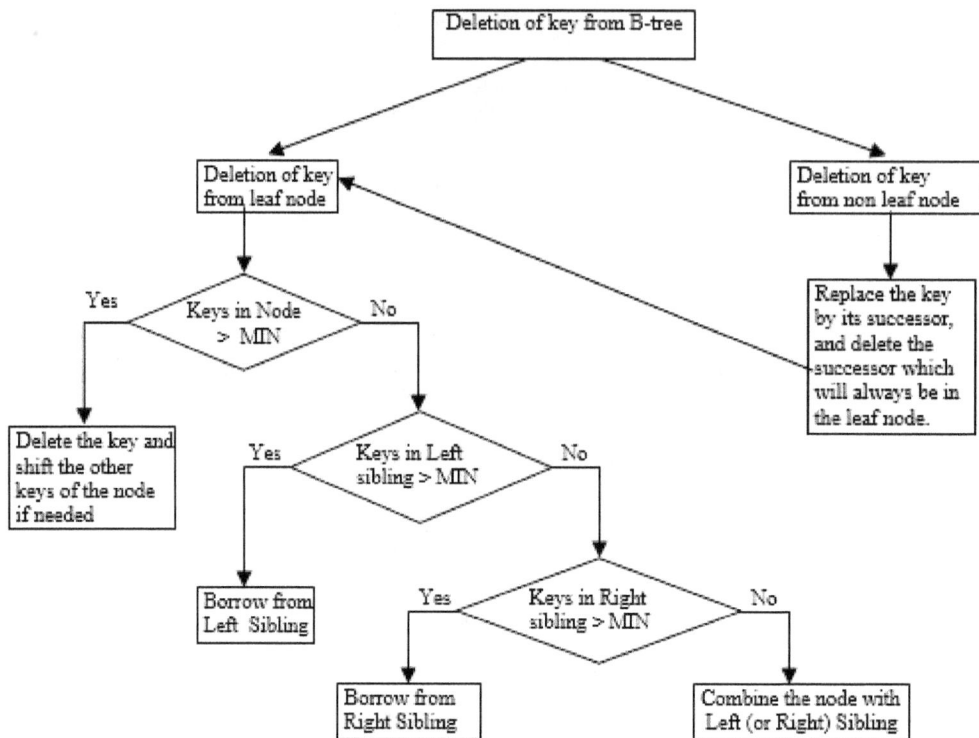

Figure 6.213 Deletion in B-tree

6.21.3.1 Deletion from a Leaf Node

6.21.3.1.1 If Node has More than MIN Keys.

In this case, deletion is very simple and the key can be easily deleted from the node by shifting other keys of the node.

(a) Delete 7, 52 from tree in figure 6.214.

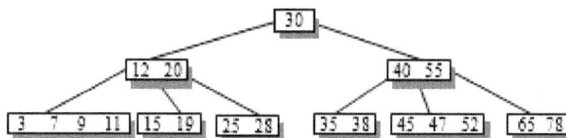

Figure 6.214 Delete 7, 52

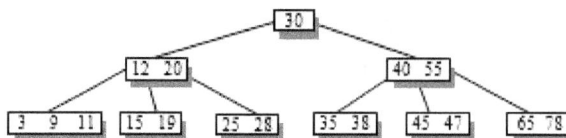

Figure 6.215 B-tree after deletion of 7, 52

9 and 11 can be shifted left to fill the gap created by the deletion of 7. Key 52 is the rightmost key, so other keys in the node need not be shifted.

6.21.3.1.2 If Node has MIN Keys

After deletion of a key, the node will have less than MIN keys, and will become an underflow node. In this case, we can borrow a key from the left or right sibling, if any one of them has more than MIN keys. In our algorithm, we will first try to borrow a key from the left sibling; if the left sibling has only MIN keys, then we will try to borrow from the right sibling. If both siblings have MIN keys, then we will apply another procedure, which we will discuss later.

When a key is borrowed from the left sibling, the separator key in the parent is moved to the underflow node, and the last key from the left sibling is moved to the parent.

When a key is borrowed from the right sibling, the separator key in the parent is moved to the underflow node and the first key from the right sibling is moved to the parent. All the remaining keys in the right sibling are moved one position left.

(b) Delete 15 from the tree in figure 6.216.

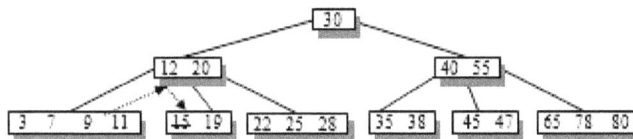

Figure 6.216 Delete 15

Here, key 15 is to be deleted from node [15, 19]. Since this node has only MIN keys, we will try to borrow from its left sibling [3, 7, 9, 11], which has more than MIN keys. The parent of these nodes is node [12, 20] and the separator key is 12. So, the last key of the left sibling(11) is moved to the place of a separator key, and the separator key is moved to the underflow node. The resulting tree after deletion of 15 will be:

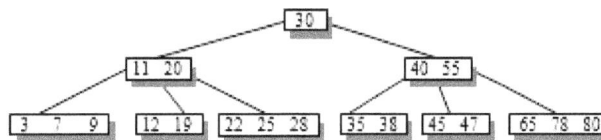

Figure 6.217 B-tree after deletion of 15

The involvement of the separator key is necessary because if we simply borrow 11 and put it in place of 15, then the basic definition of B-tree will be violated.

(c) Delete 19 from the tree in figure 6.218.

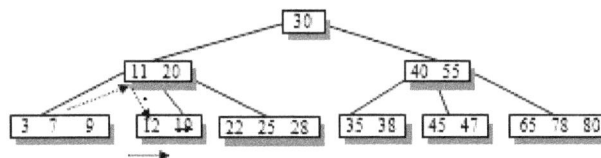

Figure 6.218 Delete 19

We will borrow from the left sibling so key 9 will be moved up to the parent node, and 11 will be moved to the underflow node. In the underflow node, the key 12 will be shifted to the right, to make place for 11. The resulting tree is:

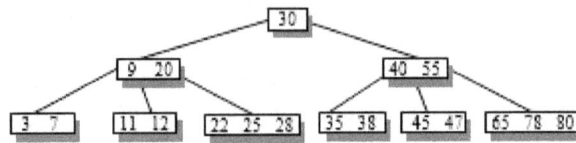

Figure 6.219 B-tree after deletion of 19

(d) Delete 45 from tree in figure 6.220.

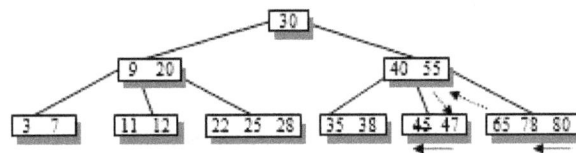

Figure 6.220 Delete 45

The left sibling of [45,47] is [35,38], which has only MIN keys, so we cannot borrow from it. Hence, we will try to borrow from the right sibling [65, 78, 80]. The first key of the right sibling(65) is moved to the parent node and the separator key from the parent node(55) is moved to the underflow node. In the underflow node, 47 is shifted left to make room for 55. In the right sibling, 78 and 80 are moved left to fill the gap created by removal of 65. The resulting tree is:

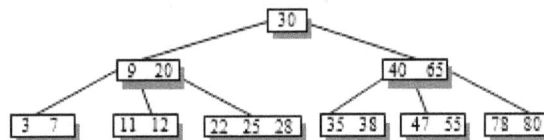

Figure 6.221 B-tree after deletion of 45

If both the left and right siblings of the underflow node have MIN keys, then we can not borrow from any of the siblings. In this case, the underflow node is combined with its left (or right) sibling.

(e) Delete 28 from the tree in figure 6.222.

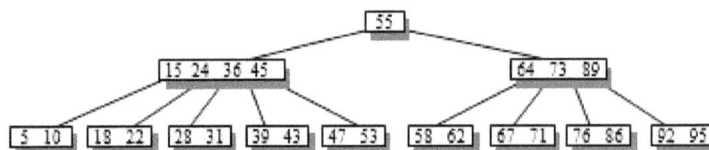

Figure 6.222 Delete 28

We can see that the node [28,31] has only MIN keys, so we will try to borrow from the left sibling [18, 22]. However, it also has MIN keys, so we will look at the right sibling [39,43], which also has only MIN keys. So, after deletion of 28, we will combine the underflow node with its left sibling. For combining these two nodes, the separator key(24) from the parent node will move down in the combined node.

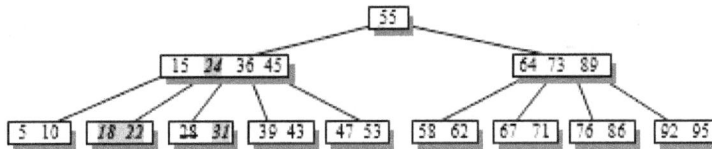

Figure 6.223 Deletion of 28

The resulting tree after deletion of 28 is:

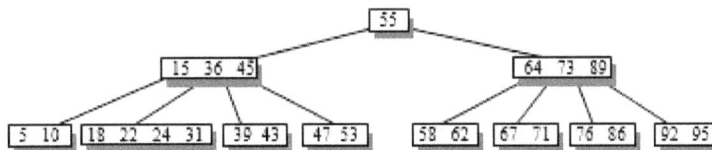

Figure 6.224 B-tree after deletion of 28

(f) Delete 62 from the tree in figure 6.225:

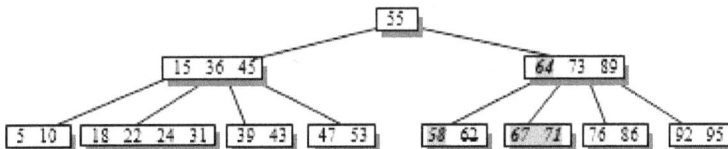

Figure 6.225 Delete 62

Here, the key is to be deleted from [58, 62], which is the leftmost child of its parent, and hence it has no left sibling. So here, we will look at the right sibling for borrowing a key, but the right sibling has only MIN keys. So, we will delete 62 and combine the underflow node with the right sibling. The resulting tree after deletion of 62 is:

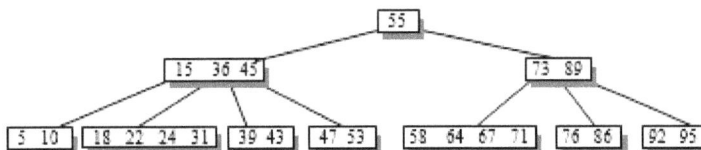

Figure 6.226 B-tree after deletion of 62

(g) Delete 92 from the tree in figure 6.227.

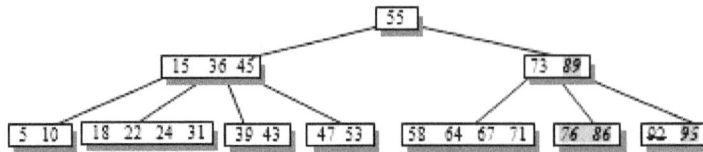

Figure 6.227 Delete 92

After deletion of 92, the underflow node is combined with its left sibling.

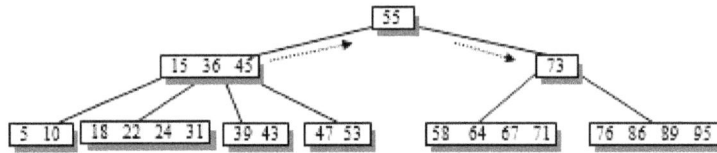

Figure 6.228 Deletion of 92

After combining the two nodes, the parent node becomes underflow[73], so we will borrow a key from its left sibling [15,36,45]. After borrowing, the resulting tree is-

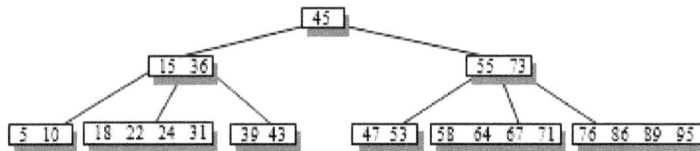

Figure 6.229 B-tree after deletion of 92

Note that before borrowing, the rightmost child of the left sibling was [47,53], and after borrowing, this node becomes the leftmost child of the node [55,73].

(h) Delete 22, 24 from the tree in figure 6.229.

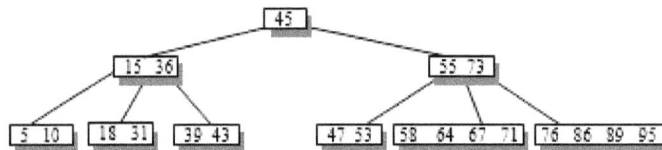

Figure 6.230 B-tree after deletion of 22, 24

(i) Delete 31 from the tree in figure 6.230.

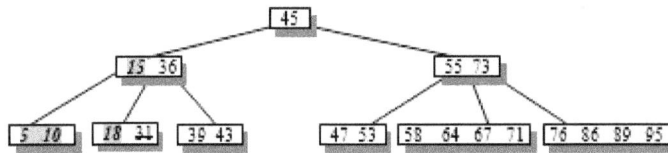

Figure 6.231 Delete 31

The underflow node [18] is combined with its left sibling.

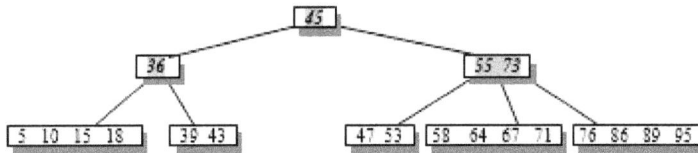

Figure 6.232 Deletion of 31

Now, the parent node [36] has become underflow, and so we will try to borrow a key from its right sibling (since it is leftmost node and has no left sibling). However, the right sibling has MIN keys, and so we will combine the underflow node[36] with its right sibling[55, 73]. The separator key(45) comes down in the combined node, and since it was the only key in the root node, now the root node becomes empty and the combined node becomes the new root of the tree, and the height of the tree decreases by one. The resulting tree is:

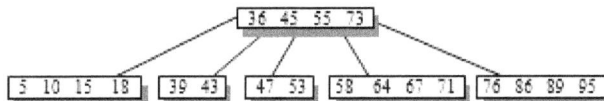

Figure 6.233 B-tree after deletion of 31

These were some examples of deletion from a leaf node. Note that if the key is to be deleted from a node which is the leftmost child of its parent, then no left sibling exists for it, so we will consider only the right sibling for borrowing or combining. For example, consider this tree:

Figure 6.234 B-tree example for deletion of key from leftmost child of its parent

If we have to delete a key from [3,7], then we will have to combine it with its right sibling [12,19], and if we have to delete a key from [35, 38], we have to borrow from its right sibling [65, 78, 80].

6.21.3.2 Deletion from a Non Leaf Node

In this case, the successor key is copied at the place of the key to be deleted, and then the successor is deleted. The successor key is the smallest key in the right subtree and will always be in the leaf node. So, this case reduces to case A of deletion from a leaf node.

(j) Delete 12 from the tree in figure 6.235.

Figure 6.235 Delete 12

The successor key of 12 is 15, and so we will copy 15 at the place of 12. Now our task reduces to deletion of 15 from the leaf node. This deletion is performed by borrowing a key from the right sibling.

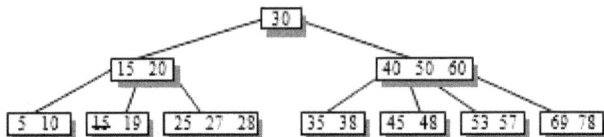

Figure 6.236 Deletion of 12

The tree after deletion of 12 is:

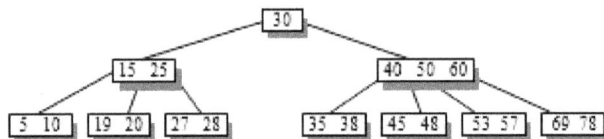

Figure 6.237 B-tree after deletion of 12

(k) Delete 30 from the tree in figure 6.238.

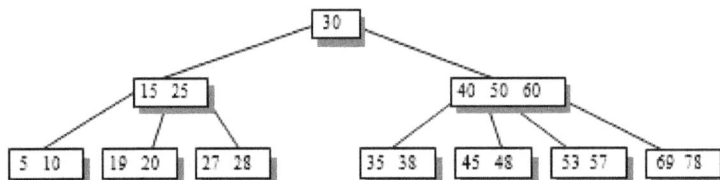

Figure 6.238 Delete 30

Successor of 30 is 35, so it is copied at the place of 30, and now 35 will be deleted from the leaf node.

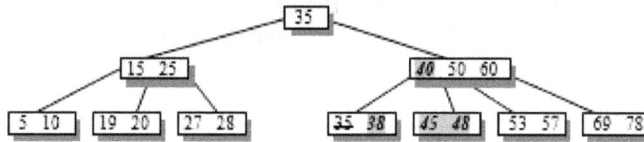

Figure 6.239 Deletion of 30

The resulting tree after deletion of 30 is:

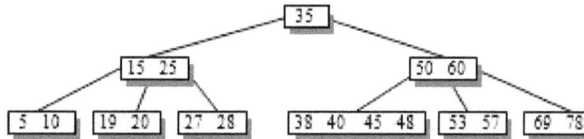

Figure 6.240 B-tree after deletion of 30

These were some examples of deletion from a non-leaf node. We could have taken the predecessor key also instead of the successor, as the predecessor key is the largest key in the left subtree and is always in the leaf node.

Now we will see the implementation of B-tree program.

Here are some constant values used:

```
static const int M = 5; //Order of B-tree
static const int MAX = M-1; //Maximum number of permissible keys in a node
//Minimum number of permissible keys in a node except root
static const int MIN = (M%2==0)?((M/2)-1):(((M+1)/2)-1);
```

This is the class Node of B-tree node:

```
class Node
{
        public:
                int key[MAX+1];
                Node *child[MAX+1];
                int numKeys;
        public:
                Node()
                {
                        numKeys = 0;
                }
};//End of class Node
```

Here, numKeys represents the number of keys currently present in a given node. It is incremented when a key is inserted into the node and decremented when a key is deleted from the node. We have taken two arrays data members, one of type int for the keys, and the other of type Node* for the children. The size of both arrays is MAX+1.

The maximum number of permissible children of a node is MAX+1, so all the elements of the array child will be used. The maximum number of permissible keys in a node is MAX, so we will never use key[0]. Taking the size of array key as MAX+1 simplifies the code. In the program, whenever we will have to shift keys and pointers of a node, we can simply do it by using a for loop. Only the case of child[0] has to be handled separately.

The constant value M represents the order of the B-tree. The maximum number of keys in a node is represented by MAX and is equal to (M-1). The minimum number of keys in a node (except root), is given by MIN which is equal to $\lceil M/2 \rceil$ - 1.

This is the class `BTree` for a B-tree:

```
class BTree
{
        private:
                Node *root;
                void inorder(Node *ptr);
                void display(Node *ptr, int spaces);

                //Functions used in search
                Node* search(int key, Node *p);
                bool searchNode(int key, Node *p, int *n);

                //Functions used in insertion
                bool insert(int key, Node *p, int *iKey, Node **iKeyRchild);
                void insertByShift(Node *p, int n, int iKey, Node *iKeyRchild);
                void split(Node *p, int n, int *iKey, Node **iKeyRchild);

                //Functions used in deletion
                void del(int key, Node *p);
                void delByShift(Node *p, int n);
                void restore(Node *p, int n);
                void borrowLeft(Node *p, int n);
                void borrowRight(Node *p, int n);
                void combine(Node *p, int m);

        public:
                BTree();
                ~BTree(){};
                void display();
                void inorder();
                bool search(int key);
                void insert(int key);
                void del(int key);
}//End of class BTree;
```

This is the constructor of class `BTree`:

```
BTree::BTree()
{
        root = NULL;
}//End of BTree()
```

6.21.4 Searching

The functions used in searching are recursive function `search()` and `searchNode()`. The recursive function `search()` searches a key by moving down the tree using child pointers. It uses a function `searchNode()` to search for the key inside the current node. The recursive function `search()` is called inside public member function `search()`.

```
bool BTree::search(int key)
{
        if(search(key,root) == NULL)
                return false;
        return true;
}//End of search()
Node* BTree::search(int key, Node *p)
{
        if(p == NULL)
                return NULL; //Base case 1 : key is not present in the tree
```

```
        int n=0;
        if(searchNode(key, p, &n) == true) //Base case 2 : key is found in node p
                return p;
        return search(key, p->child[n]); //Recursive case : Search in node p->child[n]
}//End of search()
bool BTree::searchNode(int key, Node *p, int *n)
{
        if(key < p->key[1]) //key is less than leftmost key
        {
                *n = 0;
                return false;
        }

        *n = p->numKeys;
        while(key<p->key[*n] && *n>1)
                (*n)--;
        if(key == p->key[*n])
                return true;
        else
                return false;
}//End of searchNode()
```

Let us first see how the function searchNode() works. This function searches for key in the node p and returns true if the key is present in the node, otherwise it returns false. If the key is found, then *n represents the position of the key in the node; otherwise, the value n is used by the search() function to move to the appropriate child.

If key is less than the leftmost key of the node, then false is returned, indicating that key is not present in this node and value of *n is set to 0, which instructs the function search() to continue its search in the 0th child of node *p. If key is greater than the leftmost key, then we start searching for the key in the node from the right side.

search() is a tail recursive function. It returns NULL if the key is not found in the tree; otherwise, it returns the address of the node in which the key is found. The first argument key, is the key that is to be searched in the tree, and, pointer p represents the root of the tree on which the search proceeds. The variable n is used to give the position of key inside the node.

Recursion can stop in 2 cases: first, when we reach the leaf node, i.e., p==NULL indicating that key is not present in the tree, and second, if searchNode() returns true indicating that key is present in the current node p.

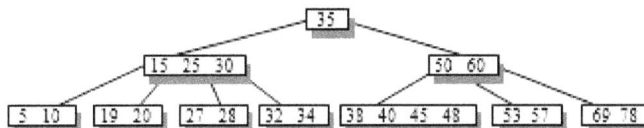

Figure 6.241 B-tree example for searching a key

Search 34 in the tree of figure 6.241:

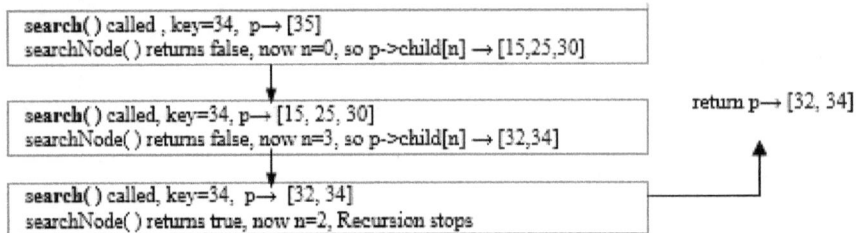

Figure 6.242 Search 34

Here n=2

Search 47 in the tree of figure 6.241:

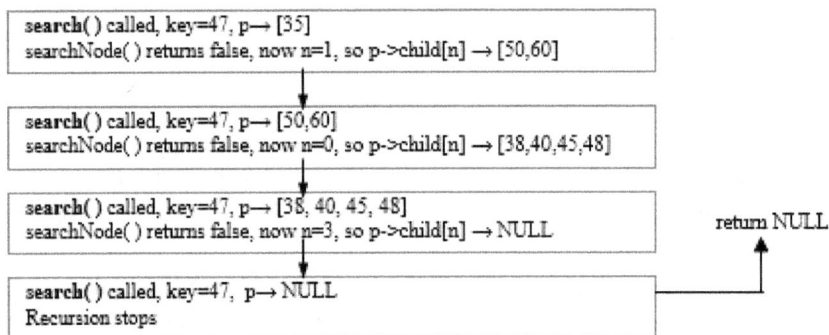

Figure 6.243 Search 47

The key 47 is not present in the tree.

The recursion used in `search()` is tail recursion, and so nothing is done in the unwinding phase.

6.21.5 Insertion

The functions used in insertion are `insert()`, recursive `insert()`, `insertByShift()` and `split()`.

```cpp
void BTree::insert(int key)
{
        int iKey = 0;
        Node *iKeyRchild = NULL;
        bool taller = insert(key, root, &iKey, &iKeyRchild);

        if(taller)      //tree grown in height, new root is created
        {
                Node *temp = new Node();
                temp->child[0] = root;
                temp->key[1] = iKey;
                temp->child[1] = iKeyRchild;
                temp->numKeys = 1;
                root = temp;
        }
}//End of insert()
```

Here, `key` is the key to be inserted in the tree. Inside `insert()`, a recursive function `insert()` is called, which performs the main task of inserting the key into the tree. It takes 4 arguments: the first argument `key` is the key to be inserted, the second argument `root` is the pointer to the root of the tree. The last two arguments are addresses of variables `iKey` and `iKeyRchild`, i.e., this function will set values of variables `iKey` and `iKeyRchild`. The return value of recursive function `insert()` will determine whether the tree has grown in height or not. A B-tree grows in height only when the root node is split (see steps (e) and (l) insertion of 20 and 48). When the root node is split, then a new root has to be created, which needs allocation of a new node. A new node is allocated, which contains the key `iKey`, and the original root node is made its left child, while `iKeyRchild` is made its right child, and finally, this new node is made the new root of the tree.

For example, in step (l) insertion of 48, the root node before insertion was [12, 20, 30, 40], the recursive function `insert()` returns true and sets the value of `iKey` as 30, and makes `iKeyRchild` point to [40,50]. The new root node contains only one key, which is `iKey`, and its right child pointer is `iKeyRchild`. The old root node is its left child pointer. Now, let us discuss the working of this recursive function `insert()`.

In the winding phase, we move down the tree recursively. There can be two base cases, one when we reach a NULL subtree, which means we have to insert the key; and the other is when we find the key in some node, and the key will not be inserted. In the unwinding phase, we insert the key and perform the splitting if required. In unwinding phase, we move up the tree on the path of insertion, and we know that splitting is propagated upwards. So, the insertion of key and splitting is done in this phase.

```
bool BTree::insert(int key, Node *p, int *iKey, Node **iKeyRchild)
{
        if(p == NULL) //First Base case : key not found
        {
                *iKey = key;
                *iKeyRchild = NULL;
                return true;
        }

        int n=0;
        if(searchNode(key, p, &n) == true) //Second Base case : key found
        {
                cout << "Key already present in the tree\n";
                return false; //No need to insert the key
        }

        bool flag = insert(key, p->child[n], iKey, iKeyRchild);
        if(flag == true)
        {
                if(p->numKeys < MAX)
                {
                        insertByShift(p, n, *iKey, *iKeyRchild);
                        return false; //Insertion over
                }
                else
                {
                        split(p, n, iKey, iKeyRchild);
                        return true; //Insertion not over : Median key yet to be inserted
                }
        }

        return false;
}//End of insert()
```

In the unwinding phase, we will insert the key whenever we get a non-full node using `insertByShift()`. Otherwise, we will call `split()`.

The return value of recursive function `insert()` can be true or false. The return value of true indicates that the insertion is not complete and we need to continue work in the unwinding phase. The return value of false means that insertion is finished and there is no need to do any work in the unwinding phase.

Initially, when we reach the base case `(p==NULL)`, `insert()` returns true. When the function `split()` is called, true is returned indicating that the insertion is not over and the median key is still there, waiting to be inserted in the tree. When `insertByShift()` is called, false is returned, indicating that insertion is finished.

When the key is already present in the tree, there is nothing to be done in the unwinding phase, because the key is not inserted in the tree. So in this case also, we return false.

`*iKey` and `*iKeyRchild` represent the key to be inserted, and its right child respectively. Initially, when the recursion stops, `*iKey` is set to `key` and `*iKeyRchild` is set to `NULL`. Whenever `split()` is called, it sets the value of `*iKey` to the median key, and also changes the value of `*iKeyRchild`.

We will take some examples and see how the key is actually inserted. Let us insert key 17 in the tree given in figure 6.244:

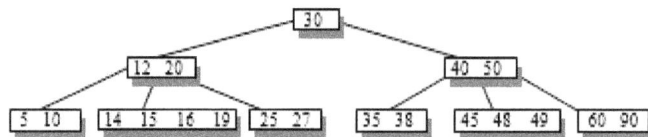

Figure 6.244 B-tree example for inserting 17

For insertion of 17, splitting is required and the resulting tree is:

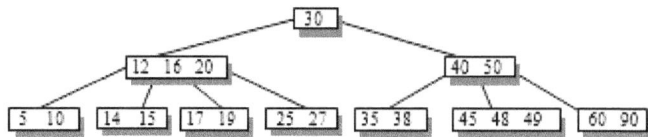

Figure 6.245 B-tree after insertion of 17

Now let us trace and see how this insertion happens in our program.

1) Initially `insert()` calls the recursive function `insert()` with p pointing to root node[30]. Inside recursive function `insert()`, since p is not `NULL`, `searchNode()` is called, which sets n=0, and a recursive call is made to `insert()` with 0th child of p, i.e., [12,20].

2) In the second recursive call of `insert()`, p points to node [12,20] which is not `NULL`, so `searchNode()` is called, which sets n=1. A recursive call is made to `insert()` with the 1st child of p, i.e., [14,15,16,19].

3) In the third recursive call of `insert()`, p points to node [14,15,16,19], `searchNode()` sets n=3. Now, a recursive call is made with the 3rd child of p, which is `NULL`.

4) In the fourth recursive call of `insert()`, p is `NULL`. Hence, we have reached the base case and the recursion stops. `*iKey` is set to 17, and `*iKeyRchild` is set to `NULL`, which means that the key to be inserted is 17, and the child to its right will be `NULL`. This recursive call of `insert()` returns true and the unwinding phase begins.

5) Now, we go back to the 3rd recursive call of `insert()`, where p points to node [14,15,16,19]. The fourth recursive call had returned true, and so, the value of flag is true, which means that insertion is not

yet over. So, we check the number of keys in the node. Since keys are equal to MAX, we need to call the function `split()`. This function splits the node and now sets `*iKey` to 16, `*iKeyRchild` points to [17,19]. This means that now, the key to be inserted is 16, and its right child will be [17,19]. The 3rd recursive call finishes and it returns true.

6) Now, we go back to the 2nd recursive call of `insert()`, where p points to node [12, 20]. The third recursive call had returned true, and so, the value of flag is true, which means that insertion is not yet over. So, we check the number of keys in the node. Since keys are less than MAX, we call the function `insertByShift()`. This function inserts the key at proper place in this node. The 2nd recursive call finishes and it returns false.

7) Now, we go back to the 1st recursive call of `insert()`, where p points to node [30]. The second recursive call had returned false, and so, the value of flag is false, which means that insertion is over. The value false is returned.

8) Now we go back to `insert()`. The outermost call of recursive `insert()` returned false indicating that insertion is over.

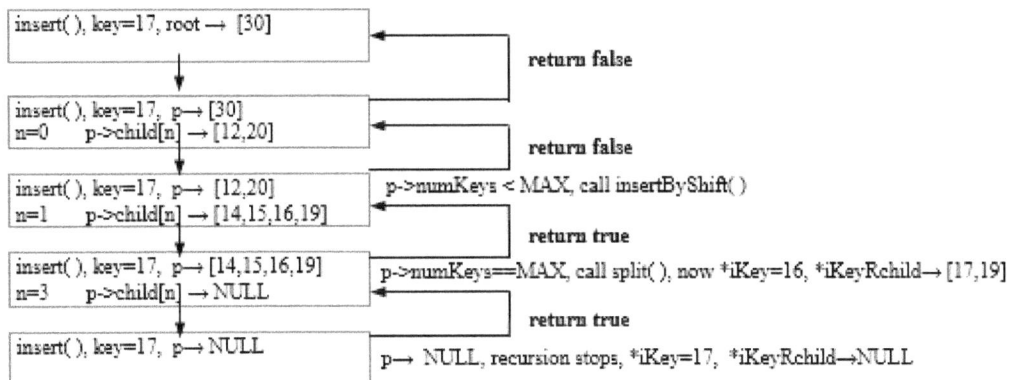

Figure 6.246 Insertion of 17

Now, let us insert key 95 in the tree given in figure 6.247:

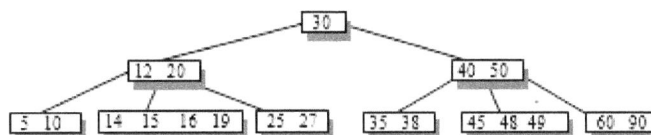

Figure 6.247 B-tree example for inserting 95

95 can be inserted in the leaf node, so no splitting is required. The resulting tree after insertion is:

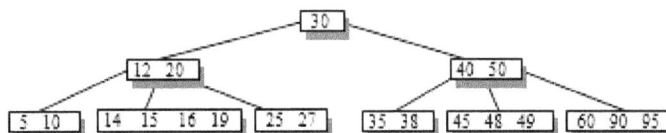

Figure 6.248 B-tree after insertion of 95

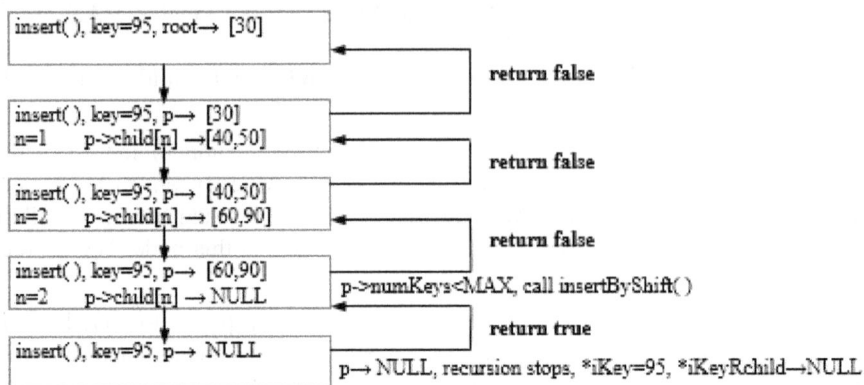

Figure 6.249 Insertion of 95

Now, let us insert key 80 in the tree given in figure 6.250:

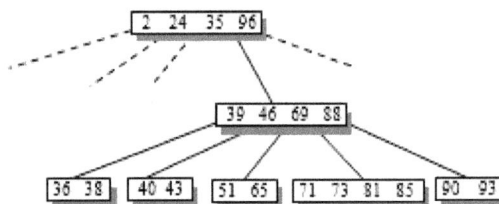

Figure 6.250 B-tree example for inserting 80

In this case, the splitting is propagated up to the root node. The root node is split and a new root is created, and the height of tree increases.

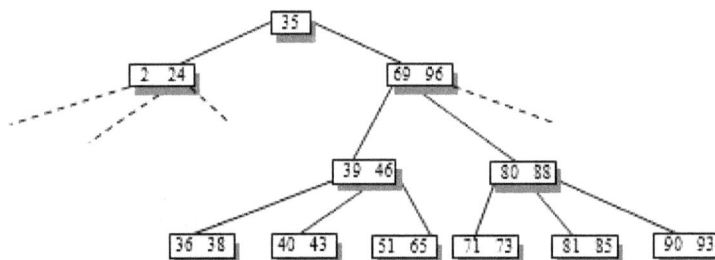

Figure 6.251 B-tree after insertion of 80

Here, the outermost (first) recursive call returns true to `insert()`, indicating that insertion has not completed, and still the key 35 remains to be inserted. Inside `insert()`, the value of taller becomes true and a new root is created and 35 is inserted into it.

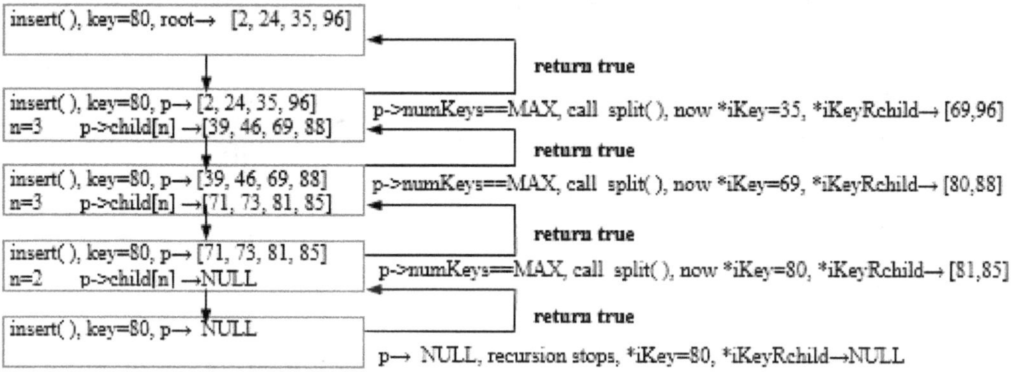

Figure 6.252 Insertion of 80

Now, let us see how the functions `insertByShift()` and `split()` work.

```
void BTree::insertByShift(Node *p, int n, int iKey, Node *iKeyRchild)
{
        for(int i=p->numKeys; i>n; i--)
        {
                p->key[i+1] = p->key[i];
                p->child[i+1] = p->child[i];
        }

        p->key[n+1] = iKey;
        p->child[n+1] = iKeyRchild;
        p->numKeys++;
}//End of insertByShift()
```

This function will be called only if node p contains less than MAX keys, i.e., when there is no chance of overflow if a new key is inserted into it, and the key can simply be inserted, by shifting some keys to the right. This function will insert the key `iKey` and pointer `iKeyRchild` into the node p at the $(n+1)^{th}$ position. For this, initially all keys and pointers which are after the nth position, are shifted right one position to make room for key `iKey` and `iKeyRchild`. After this, these two are inserted at the $(n+1)^{th}$ position in the node and the `numKeys` of node p is incremented.

```
void BTree::split(Node *p, int n, int *iKey, Node **iKeyRchild)
{
        int i, j;
        int lastKey;
        Node *lastChild;

        if(n == MAX)
        {
                lastKey = *iKey;
                lastChild = *iKeyRchild;
        }
        else
        {
                lastKey = p->key[MAX];
                lastChild = p->child[MAX];

                for(i=p->numKeys-1; i>n; i--)
                {
                        p->key[i+1] = p->key[i];
                        p->child[i+1] = p->child[i];
                }
                p->key[i+1] = *iKey;
```

```
                p->child[i+1] = *iKeyRchild;
        }

        int d = (M+1)/2;
        int medianKey = p->key[d];
        Node *newNode = new Node();
        for(i=1,j=d+1; j<=MAX; i++,j++)
        {
                newNode->key[i] = p->key[j];
                newNode->child[i] = p->child[j];
        }
        newNode->key[i] = lastKey;
        newNode->child[i] = lastChild;
        newNode->numKeys = M-d; //Number of keys in the right splitted node
        newNode->child[0] = p->child[d];
        p->numKeys = d-1; //Number of keys in the left splitted node
        *iKey = medianKey;
        *iKeyRchild = newNode;
}//End of split()
```

This function will be called only if node p contains MAX keys.

The node cannot accommodate values more than MAX, and so when a node becomes overflow, we will save the last key value into another variable named lastKey. If the new key is to be inserted at the end, then that new key is stored in the variable lastKey. For example, here 55 is the key to be inserted, and its place among all the keys is last, so it is saved in variable lastKey.

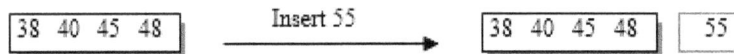

Figure 6.253 Insert 55

If the new key is to be inserted somewhere in between the node, then firstly, the last key of the node is saved in the variable lastKey, and then the new key is inserted by shifting other keys to the right. For example, if 39 is the key to be inserted, then, first 48 is saved in variable lastKey, and then 40, 45 are shifted right, and 39 is inserted in the node.

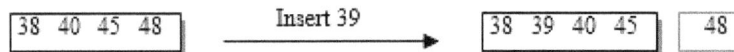

Figure 6.254 Insert 39

The pointer value is also simultaneously saved in variable lastChild.

Now, the space for a new node is allocated. The variable d denotes the median value ceil(M/2). The median key, i.e., the dth key is the key that will be moved up to the parent, so it is stored in *iKey, and *iKeyRchild will have newNode.

When a node is full, it contains MAX keys, and after the arrival of a new key, the total number of keys becomes (MAX+1). This number is equal to M, which is the order of the tree. Now, we have to split these M keys. The first (d-1) keys which are to the left of dth key, remain in the same node, and the remaining M-d keys which are to the right of dth key, will move into a new node.

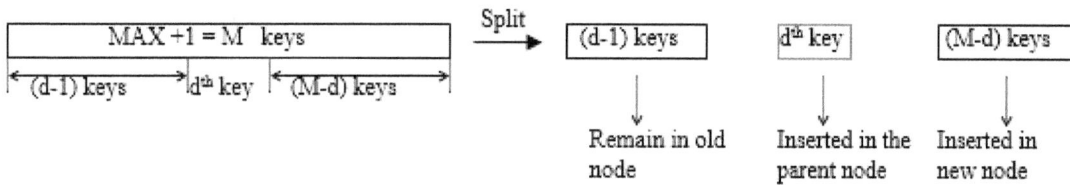

Figure 6.255 Split the keys

6.21.6 Deletion

The functions used in deletion are: `del()`, recursive function `del()`, `delByShift()`, `restore()`, `borrowLeft()`, `borrowRight()`, and `combine()`.

```
void BTree::del(int key)
{
        if(root != NULL)
        {
                del(key, root);

                //If tree becomes shorter, root is changed
                if(root!=NULL && root->numKeys==0)
                {
                        Node *temp = root;
                        root = root->child[0];
                        delete temp;
                }
        }
        else
                cout << "Tree is empty\n";
}//End of del()
```

`del()` function calls another recursive function `del()`, which performs the main deletion process. We know that after the deletion, if the root node becomes empty, then the height of the tree decreases (see step (i), deletion of 31). So, after recursive function `del()` has deleted the key from the tree, `del()` checks whether the root node has become empty or not. If there is no key left in the root node, then the 0th child of the root becomes the new root. The recursive function `del()` is:

```
void BTree::del(int key, Node *p)
{
        int n;
        if(p == NULL) //reached leaf node, key does not exist
        {
                cout << "Key " << key << "not found\n";
        }
        else
        {
                if(searchNode(key, p, &n)) //If found in current node p
                {
                        if(p->child[n] == NULL) //Node p is a leaf node
                        {
                                delByShift(p, n);
                        }
                        else    //Node p is a non leaf node
                        {
                                Node *succ = p->child[n]; //point to the right subtree
```

```
                                while(succ->child[0] != NULL) //move down till leaf node
                                        succ = succ->child[0];

                                p->key[n] = succ->key[1];
                                del(succ->key[1], p->child[n]);
                        }
                }
                else     //Not found in current node p
                {
                        del(key, p->child[n]);
                }
                if(p->child[n] != NULL) //If p is not a leaf node
                {
                        if(p->child[n]->numKeys < MIN) //Check underflow in p->child[n]
                                restore(p, n);
                }
        }
}//End of del()
```

In recursive function `del()`, there are two recursive calls. In both of them, the second argument is same, i.e.,

`p->child[n]` where n is obtained by `searchNode()`. This procedure of traversing down the tree through n^(th) child of p is the same as in recursive function `insert()`. If `del()` is called with p as `NULL`, then it means that the key is not present in the tree.

The function `searchNode()` is called, which searches for the key in the current node. If it is found, then we check whether the current node is a leaf node or a non-leaf node. If it is a leaf node, then the key is simply deleted by shifting the other keys using function `delByShift()`, and if it is a non-leaf node, then the successor key is copied at the place of `key`. This successor key is stored in `succ->key[1]`, and now our task is to delete this successor key. So now, `del()` is called with the first argument as `succ->key[1]`.

When we call `delByShift()`, underflow might occur in the node. We will check for this underflow when we return from the recursive calls, i.e., in the unwinding phase. If there is underflow, we will call `restore()`, which performs all the processes of borrowing keys or combining nodes. This function will need the parent of the underflow node. This is why in the code, we are checking count of `p->child[n]` and not that of p. If `p->child[n]` underflows, we will send its parent to the `restore()` function. If p is a leaf node, then the underflow is not checked, because in this case, `p->child[n]` will be `NULL`.

This process of checking underflow will check underflow in all nodes that come in the unwinding phase, except the root node. The root node is different from other nodes since the minimum number of keys for the root node is 1. If the root node underflows, i.e., it becomes empty, then the `del()` function will handle this case of underflow of the root node.

Consider the tree given in figure 6.256 and delete 19 from it:

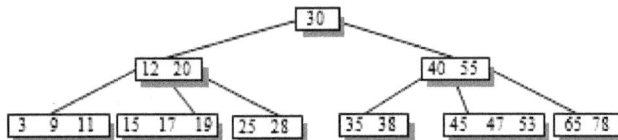

Figure 6.256 B-tree example for deleting 19

Deletion of 19 is simple since the node [15, 17, 19] contains more than MIN keys. The tree after deletion is:

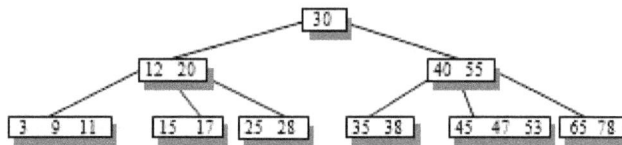

Figure 6.257 B-tree after deletion of 19

When the recursive function del() is called with p→[15, 17, 19], searchNode() returns true as 19 is present in this node. Now, since node p is a leaf node, delByShift() is called, and 19 is deleted from the node. This is the base case of recursion, and so now, recursion terminates and unwinding phase starts. In the unwinding phase, we will check whether underflow has occurred in any node or not.

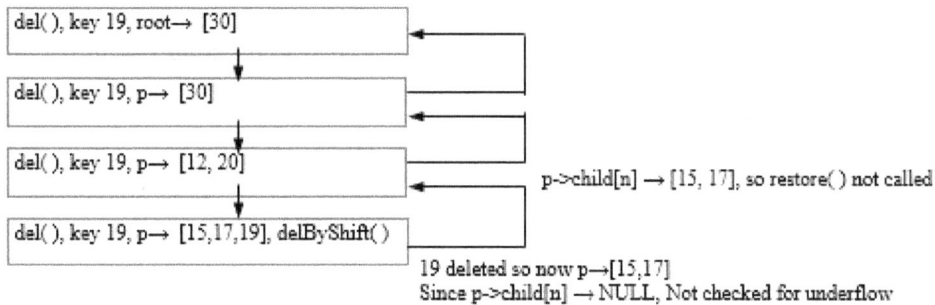

Figure 6.258 Deletion of 19

Consider the tree given in figure 6.259 and delete 69 from it:

Figure 6.259 B-tree example for deleting 69

Here, key 69 is present in a non-leaf node, and so, successor key 71 will be copied at its place, and then 71 will be deleted from the leaf node. The resulting tree after deletion is:

Figure 6.260 B-tree after deletion of 69

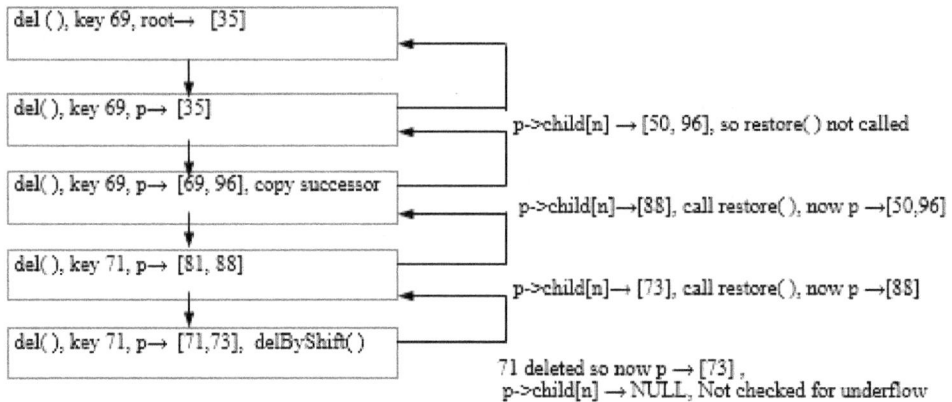

Figure 6.261 Deletion of 69

(iii) Consider the tree given below and delete 45 from it:

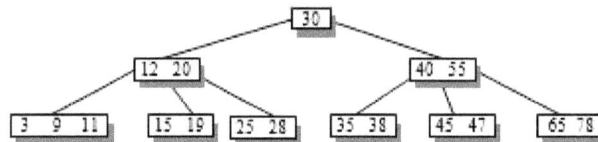

Figure 6.262 B-tree example for deleting 45

After deletion of 45, the height of the tree decreases. The resulting tree after deletion is:

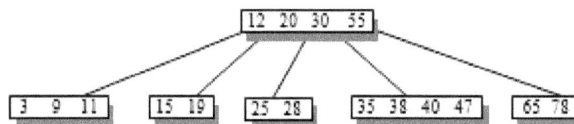

Figure 6.263 B-tree after deletion of 45

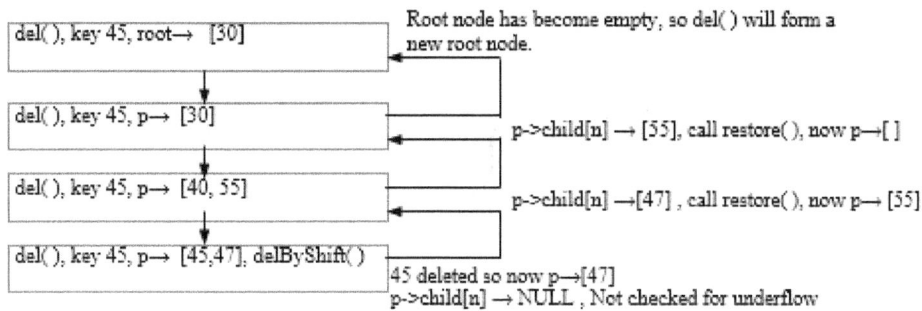

Figure 6.264 Deletion of 45

The code to copy the successor is:

```
Node *succ = p->child[n]; //point to the right subtree
while(succ->child[0] != NULL) //move down till leaf node
        succ = succ->child[0];
p->key[n] = succ->key[1];
```

This code will be required when a deletion is to be performed in a non-leaf node. The task of this code is to replace the nth key of node p, i.e., p->key[n] by its successor key. We know that the successor key is the leftmost key in the right subtree. We will take a pointer succ and use it to move down the right subtree, and since we want to reach the leftmost key, we will move only leftwards using the leftmost child, child[0]. We will stop when we reach the leaf node and the leftmost key of this node is the successor key of p->key[n].

The function delByShift() is:

```
void BTree::delByShift(Node *p, int n)
{
        for(int i=n+1; i<=p->numKeys; i++)
        {
                p->key[i-1] = p->key[i];
                p->child[i-1] = p->child[i];
        }
        p->numKeys--;
}//End of delByShift()
```

This function will be called only if node p contains more than MIN keys, i.e., when there is no chance of underflow if a key is deleted from the node, and the key can be simply deleted by shifting some keys to the left. This function will delete the nth key and its right child pointer from the node p, i.e., key[n] and child[n] are removed from this node. For this, all the keys and pointers which are to the right of the nth position are shifted one position left, and the numKeys of the node p is decremented.

The function restore() is:

```
void BTree::restore(Node *p, int n)
{
        if(n!=0 && p->child[n-1]->numKeys > MIN)
                borrowLeft(p, n);
        else if(n!=p->numKeys && p->child[n+1]->numKeys > MIN)
                borrowRight(p, n);
        else
        {
                if(n==0) //If underflow node is leftmost node
                        combine(p, n+1); //combine nth child of p with its right sibling
                else
```

```
                combine(p, n); //combine nth child of p with its left sibling
        }
}//End of restore()
```

The function `restore()` is called when a node underflows. The underflow node is the nth child of the node p. Let us recall how we proceed in the case of an underflow. First, we try to borrow from the left sibling and then from the right sibling. If borrowing is not possible, then we combine the node with the left sibling, and if the left sibling does not exist, then we combine it with the right sibling.

Since the underflow node is the nth child of the node p, (n-1)[th] child of p is the left sibling and (n+1)[th] child of p is the right sibling of the underflow node. The left sibling will not exist if the underflow node is the leftmost child of its parent (n==0), and the right sibling will not exist if the underflow node is the rightmost child of its parent (n==p->numKeys). So, before borrowing, we have to check for these two conditions also. If the underflow node is not the leftmost child and the left sibling contains more than MIN keys, then we can borrow from left. Otherwise, if the underflow node is not the rightmost child, and the right sibling contains more than MIN keys, then we can borrow from the right. If both these conditions fail, we will combine the node with the left sibling, but if the node is leftmost, we will combine it with the right sibling.

When we combine with the right sibling, the second argument is n+1, and with left sibling, it is n. While combining with the left sibling, the second argument is not n-1. We will come to know the reason for this after studying function `combine()`.

The function `borrowLeft()` is:

```
void BTree::borrowLeft(Node *p, int n)
{
        Node *u = p->child[n];          //underflow node
        Node *ls = p->child[n-1];       //left sibling of node u

        //Shift all the keys and children in underflow node u one position right
        for(int i=u->numKeys; i>0; i--)
        {
                u->key[i+1] = u->key[i];
                u->child[i+1] = u->child[i];
        }
        u->child[1] = u->child[0];
        //Move the separator key from parent node p to underflow node u
        u->key[1] = p->key[n];
        u->numKeys++;
        //Move the rightmost key of node ls to the parent node p
        p->key[n] = ls->key[ls->numKeys];
        //Rightmost child of ls becomes leftmost child of node u
        u->child[0] = ls->child[ls->numKeys];
        ls->numKeys--;
}//End of borrowLeft()
```

The node u represents the underflow node, ls is its left sibling and p is their parent node. Initially, all the keys and pointers in node u are shifted one position right to make room for the new key (in the figure 6.265, key 20 is shifted right). After this, the separator key(18) from the parent is moved to the underflow node. The rightmost key of the left sibling(14) is moved to the parent node. The rightmost child of ls (node [15,16]) becomes the leftmost child of node u.

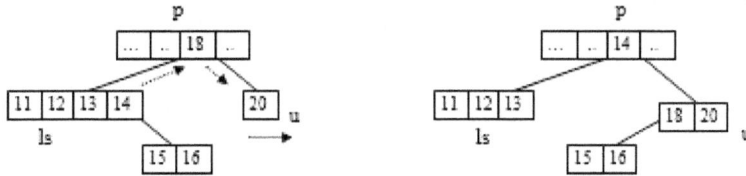

Figure 6.265 Borrow left

All keys and children are not shown in this figure.

The function `borrowRight()` is:

```
void BTree::borrowRight(Node *p, int n)
{
        Node *u = p->child[n];          //underflow node
        Node *rs = p->child[n+1];       //right sibling of node u
        //Move the separator key from the parent node p to the underflow node u
        u->numKeys++;
        u->key[u->numKeys] = p->key[n+1];
        //Leftmost child of node rs becomes the rightmost child of node u
        u->child[u->numKeys] = rs->child[0];
        //Move the leftmost key from node rs to parent node p
        p->key[n+1] = rs->key[1];
        rs->numKeys--;

        //Shift all the keys and children of node rs one position left
        rs->child[0] = rs->child[1];
        for(int i=1; i<=rs->numKeys; i++)
        {
                rs->key[i] = rs->key[i+1];
                rs->child[i] = rs->child[i+1];
        }
}//End of borrowRight()
```

The node u represents the underflow node, rs is its right sibling and p is the parent node. Initially, move the separator key (in the figure 6.266, key 6) from the parent node p to the underflow node u. Note that here, shifting of keys in the underflow node is not needed. The leftmost child of rs (node [7,9]) becomes the rightmost child of u. The leftmost key from node rs (10) is moved to the parent node p. At last, all the remaining keys and pointers in node rs (11,12,13) are shifted one position left to fill the gap created by removal of key 10.

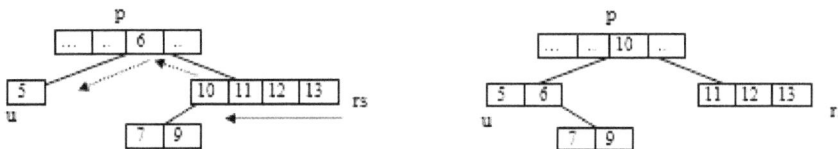

Figure 6.266 Borrow right

All keys and children are not shown in this figure.

The function `combine()` is:

```
void BTree::combine(Node *p, int m)
{
        Node *x = p->child[m];
```

```
        Node *y = p->child[m-1];
        //Move the separator key from parent node p to node y
        y->numKeys++;
        y->key[y->numKeys] = p->key[m];

        //Shift all the keys and children in node p one position left to fill the gap
        for(int i=m; i<p->numKeys; i++)
        {
                p->key[i] = p->key[i+1];
                p->child[i] = p->child[i+1];
        }
        p->numKeys--;
        //Leftmost child of x becomes rightmost child of y
        y->child[y->numKeys] = x->child[0];

        //Insert all the keys and children of node x at the end of node y
        for(int i=1; i<=x->numKeys; i++)
        {
                y->numKeys++;
                y->key[y->numKeys] = x->key[i];
                y->child[y->numKeys] = x->child[i];
        }
        delete x;
}//End of combine()
```

This function combines the two nodes x and y. The node x is the mth child and node y is the $(m-1)^{th}$ child of node p. Initially, the separator key (key e in the figure 6.267) from the parent node is moved to node y, and all the keys that were on the right side of key e in the node p are shifted left to fill the gap created by the removal of e. Now, the leftmost child of x (node [f,g]) becomes the rightmost child of y. At last, all the keys and pointers of node x are inserted at the end of node y, and the memory occupied by node x is released using delete.

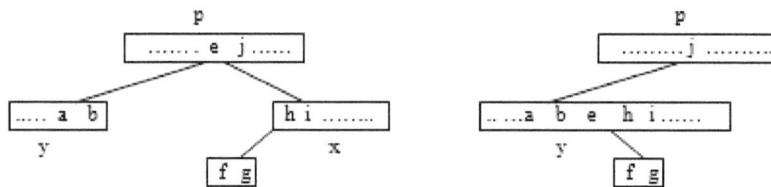

Figure 6.267 Combining two nodes

In the function restore(), we have used combine like this:

```
{
        if(n==0) //If underflow node is leftmost node
                combine(p, n+1); //combine nth child of p with its right sibling
        else
                combine(p, n); //combine nth child of p with its left sibling
}
```

combine(p,n)
m=n, x is n^{th} node, y is $(n-1)^{th}$ node
Here, x is underflow node and y is its left sibling.

combine(p,n+1)
m=n+1, x is $(n+1)^{th}$ node and y is n^{th} node
Here, y is an underflow node and x is its right sibling.

The function `inorder()` is:

```
void BTree::inorder(Node *ptr)
{
        if(ptr != NULL)
        {
                int i;
                for(i=0; i<ptr->numKeys; i++)
                {
                        inorder(ptr->child[i]);
                        cout << ptr->key[i+1] << " ";
                }
                inorder(ptr->child[i]);
        }
}//End of inorder()
void BTree::inorder()
{
        inorder(root);
}//End of inorder()
```

This function prints the inorder traversal of the B-tree. In inorder traversal, the key is processed after its left subtree and before its right subtree. The left subtrees of the keys are processed in the first recursive call. The rightmost subtree of the current node is traversed by the second recursive call outside the for loop.

The function `display()` is:

```
void BTree::display(Node *p, int spaces)
{
        if(p != NULL)
        {
                int i;
                for(i=1; i<=spaces; i++)
                        cout << " ";
                for(i=1; i<=p->numKeys; i++)
                        cout << p->key[i] << " ";
                cout << "\n";
                for(i=0; i<=p->numKeys; i++)
                        display(p->child[i], spaces+10);
        }
}//End of display()
void BTree::display()
{
        display(root, 0);
}//End of display()
```

The function `main()` for B-tree is:

```
//BTree.cpp : Program for B-tree.
#include<iostream>
using namespace std;

int main()
{
        BTree btree;
        cout << "Tree after inserting 10\n";
        btree.insert(10);
        btree.display();
        cout << "\n";
        cout << "Tree after inserting 40\n";
        btree.insert(40);
        btree.display();
        cout << "\n";
```

```
cout << "Tree after inserting 30\n";
btree.insert(30);
btree.display();
cout << "\n";
cout << "Tree after inserting 35\n";
btree.insert(35);
btree.display();
cout << "\n";
cout << "Tree after inserting 20\n";
btree.insert(20);
btree.display();
cout << "\n";
cout << "Tree after inserting 15\n";
btree.insert(15);
btree.display();
cout << "\n";
cout << "Tree after inserting 50\n";
btree.insert(50);
btree.display();
cout << "\n";
cout << "Tree after inserting 28\n";
btree.insert(28);
btree.display();
cout << "\n";
cout << "Tree after inserting 25\n";
btree.insert(25);
btree.display();
cout << "\n";
cout << "Tree after inserting 5\n";
btree.insert(5);
btree.display();
cout << "\n";
cout << "Tree after inserting 60\n";
btree.insert(60);
btree.display();
cout << "\n";
cout << "Tree after inserting 19\n";
btree.insert(19);
btree.display();
cout << "\n";
cout << "Tree after inserting 12\n";
btree.insert(12);
btree.display();
cout << "\n";
cout << "Tree after inserting 38\n";
btree.insert(38);
btree.display();
cout << "\n";
cout << "Tree after inserting 27\n";
btree.insert(27);
btree.display();
cout << "\n";
cout << "Tree after inserting 90\n";
btree.insert(90);
btree.display();
cout << "\n";
cout << "Tree after inserting 45\n";
btree.insert(45);
btree.display();
cout << "\n";
cout << "Tree after inserting 48\n";
```

```
        btree.insert(48);
        btree.display();
        cout << "\n";

        cout << "Tree after deleting 28\n";
        btree.del(28);
        btree.display();
        cout << "\n";
        cout << "Tree after deleting 40\n";
        btree.del(40);
        btree.display();
        cout << "\n";
        cout << "Tree after deleting 15\n";
        btree.del(15);
        btree.display();
        cout << "\n";

        //Search in B-tree
        cout << "search(48) : " << (btree.search(48) ? "True" : "False");
        cout << "\n";
        cout << "search(15) : " << (btree.search(15) ? "True" : "False");
        cout << "\n";
        return 0;
}//End of main()
```

6.22 B+ Tree

A disadvantage of the B-tree is inefficient sequential access. If we want to display the data in ascending order of keys, we can do an inorder traversal, but it is time consuming. Let us see the reason for it. While doing inorder traversal, we have to go up and down the tree several times, i.e., the nodes have to be accessed several times. Whenever an internal node is accessed, only one element from it is displayed, and we have to go to another node. We know that each node of a B-tree represents a disk block, and so, moving from one node to another means moving from one disk block to another, which is time consuming. So, for efficient sequential access, the number of node accesses should be as few as possible.

B+ tree which is a variation of B tree, is well suited for sequential access. The two main differences in B-tree and B+ tree are as follows:

(i) In B-tree, all the nodes contain keys, their corresponding data items (records or pointers to records), and child pointers, but in B+ tree, the structures of leaf nodes and internal nodes are different. The internal nodes store only keys and child pointers, while the leaf nodes store keys and their corresponding data items. So the data items are present only in the leaf nodes. The keys in the leaf nodes may also be present in the internal nodes.

(ii) In B+ tree, each leaf node has a pointer that points to the next leaf node, i.e., all leaf nodes form a linked list.

The figure 6.268 shows a B-tree and the figure 6.269 shows a B+ tree containing the same data.

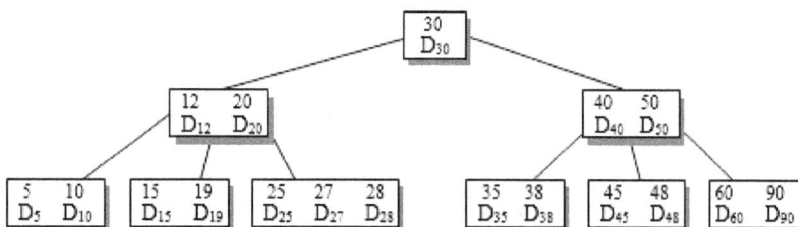

Figure 6.268 B-tree example

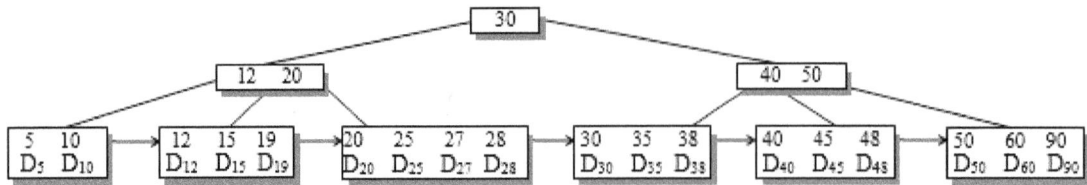

Figure 6.269 B+ tree example

The alphabet 'D' with subscript shown under the key value represents the data item. While discussing B tree, we had not shown this data item in the figures, so that the figures remain small.

In B+ tree, the internal nodes contain only keys and pointers to child nodes, while the leaf nodes contain keys, data items and the pointer to the next leaf node. The internal nodes are used as index for searching data, and so, they are also called index nodes. The leaf nodes contain data items, and they are also called data nodes. The index nodes form an index set, while the data nodes form a sequence set. All the leaf nodes form a linked list, and this feature of B+ tree helps in sequential access, i.e., we can search for a key and then access all the keys following it in a sequential manner. Traversing all the leaves from left to right gives us all the data in ascending order. So, both random and sequential accesses are simultaneously possible in B+ tree.

6.22.1 Searching

In the B tree, our search terminated when we found the key, but this will not be the case in B+ tree. In a B+ tree, it is possible that a key is present in the internal node but is not present in the leaf node. This happens because when any data item is deleted from the leaf node, the corresponding key is not deleted from the internal node. So, the presence of a key in an internal node does not indicate that the corresponding data item will be present in the leaf node. Hence, the searching process will not stop if we find a key in an internal node but it will continue till we find the key in the leaf node. The data items are stored only in the leaf nodes, and so, we have to go to the leaf nodes to access the data.

Suppose we want to search the key 20 in the B+ tree of figure 6.269. Searching will start from the root node, so first, we look at node [30], and since 20 < 30, we will move to left child, which is, [12, 20]. The key value is equal to 20, and so we will move to the right child, which is the leaf node and there we find the key 20 with its data item.

B+ tree supports efficient range queries, i.e., we can access all data in a given range. For this, we need to search the starting key of the range, and then sequentially traverse the leaf nodes till we get the end key of the range.

6.22.2 Insertion

First, a search is performed and if the key is not present in the leaf node then we can have two cases depending on whether the leaf node has maximum keys or not.

If the leaf node has less than maximum keys, then the key and data are simply inserted in the leaf node in ordered manner and the index set is not changed.

If the leaf node has maximum keys, then we will have to split the leaf node. The splitting of a leaf node is slightly different from splitting of a node in a B-tree. A new leaf node is allocated and inserted in the sequence set (linked list of leaf nodes) after the old node. All the keys smaller than the median key remain in the old leaf node, all the keys greater than or equal to the median key are moved to the new node, and the corresponding data items are also moved. The median key becomes the first key of the new node, and this key (without data item) is copied (not moved) to the parent node, which is an internal node. So now, this median key is present both in the leaf node and in the internal node, which is the parent of the leaf node.

Splitting of a leaf node

keys < median   remain in old leaf node
keys >= median   go to new leaf node
Median key is copied to parent node.

If after splitting of leaf node, the parent becomes full, then again a split has to be done. The splitting of an internal node is similar to that of splitting of a node in a B-tree. When an internal node is split the median key is moved to the parent node.

Splitting of an internal node

keys < median   remain in old node
keys > median   go to new node
Median key is moved to parent node.

This splitting continues until we get a non-full parent node. If the root node is split, then a new root node has to be allocated.

Suppose we have to insert data with keys 42 and 24 in B+ tree of figure 6.269.

The key 42 can be simply inserted in the leaf node [40, 45, 48]. After inserting 24 in the tree, we get an overflow leaf node [20, 24, 25, 27, 28] which needs to be splitted. A new leaf node is allocated and keys 25, 27, 28 with data items are moved to this node. The median key 25 is copied to the parent node and is present in the leaf node also.

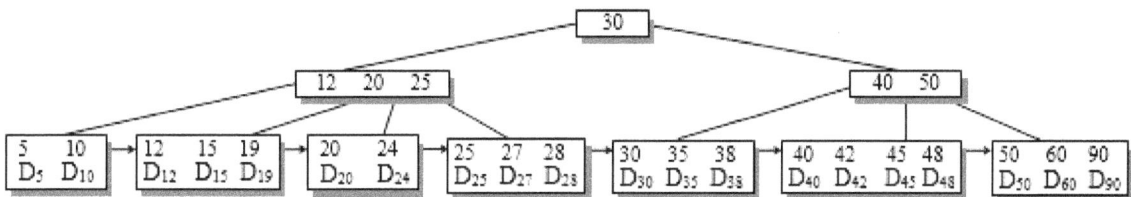

Figure 6.270 B+ tree after insertion of 42, 24

6.22.3 Deletion

First, a search is performed, and if the key is present in the leaf, then we can have two cases depending on whether the leaf node has minimum keys or more than that.

If the leaf node has more than minimum keys, then we can simply delete the key and its data item, and move other keys of the leaf node if required. In this case, the index set is not changed, i.e., if the key is present in any internal node also, then it is not deleted from there. This is because the key still serves as a separator key between its left and right children.

If the key is present in a leaf which has a minimum number of keys, then we have two cases:

(A) If any one of the siblings has more than minimum keys, then a key is borrowed from it and the separator key in the parent node is updated accordingly.

If we borrow from the left sibling, then the rightmost key (with data item) of the left sibling is moved to the underflow node. Now this new leftmost key in the underflow node becomes the new separator key.

If we borrow from right sibling, then the leftmost key (with data item) of right sibling is moved to the underflow node. Now the key which is leftmost in the right sibling, becomes the new separator key.

(B) If both siblings have minimum keys, then we need to merge the underflow leaf node with its sibling.

This is done by moving the keys (with data) of underflow leaf node to the sibling node and deleting the underflow leaf node. The separator key of the underflow node and its sibling is deleted from the parent node, and the corresponding child pointer in the parent node is also removed.

The merging of leaf nodes may result in an underflow parent node, which is an internal node. For internal nodes, borrowing and merging is performed in the same manner as in B-tree.

(i) Delete data with keys 12, 38, 40, 50 from B+ tree of figure 6.269:

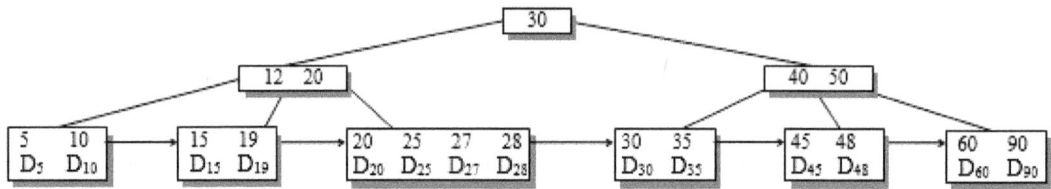

Figure 6.271 B+ tree after deletion of 12, 38, 40, 50

(ii) Delete 15 from B+ tree of figure 6.271 (borrow from right sibling):

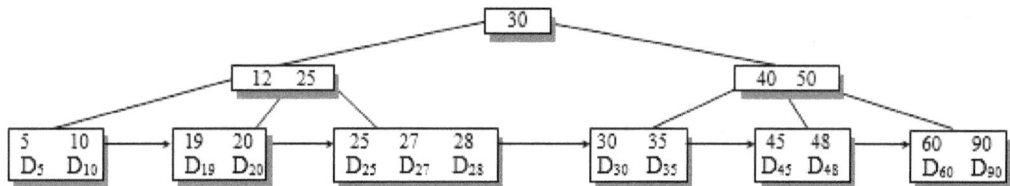

Figure 6.272 B+ tree after deletion of 15

(iii) Delete 48 from B+ tree of figure 6.272:

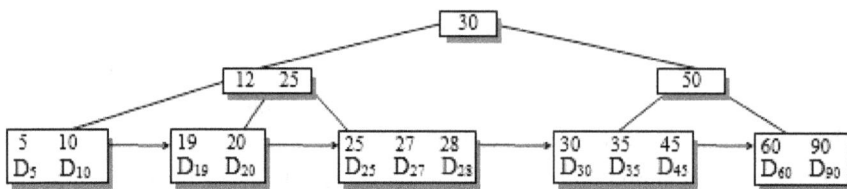

Figure 6.273 Deletion of 48

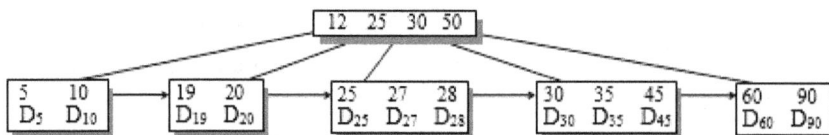

Figure 6.274 B+ tree after deletion of 48

6.23 Digital Search Trees

A digital search tree is a binary tree in which a key and data pair is stored in every node, and the position of keys is determined by their binary representation.

The procedure of insertion and searching is similar to that of the binary search tree, but with a small difference. In the binary search tree, the decision to move to the left or the right subtree was made by comparing the given key with the key in the current node, while here, this decision is made by a bit in the key. The bits in the given key are scanned from the left to right, and when we have 0 bit, we move to the left subtree, and when we have a 1 bit, we move to the right subtree.

Let us insert some keys into an initially empty digital search tree.

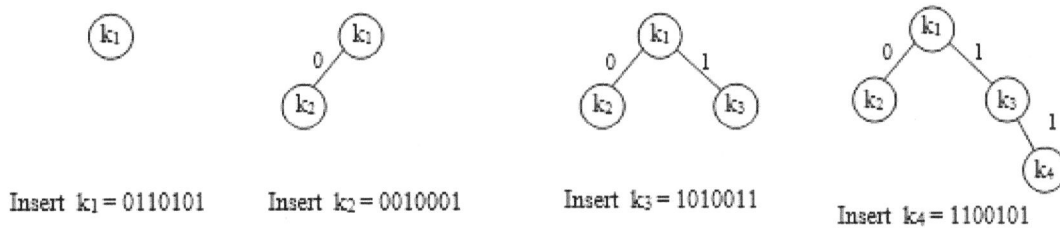

Insert k_1 = 0110101   Insert k_2 = 0010001   Insert k_3 = 1010011   Insert k_4 = 1100101

Figure 6.275 Inserting keys into digital search tree

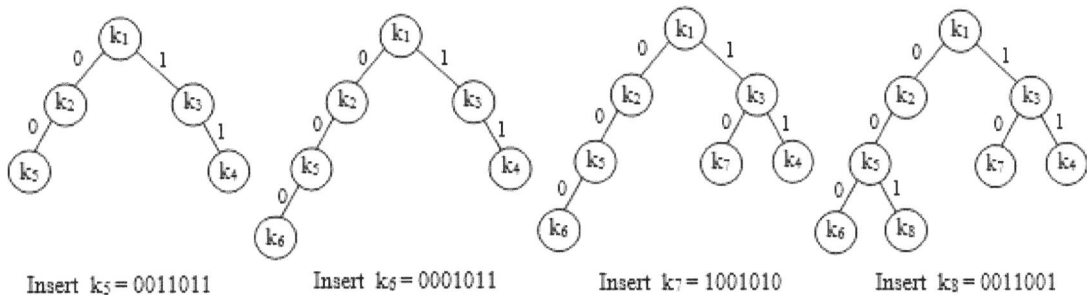

Insert k_5 = 0011011   Insert k_6 = 0001011   Insert k_7 = 1001010   Insert k_8 = 0011001

Figure 6.276 Inserting keys into digital search tree continued

The first key k_1 is to be inserted in an empty tree, and so it becomes the root of the tree. The next key to be inserted is k_2 = 0010001, and since this key is not equal to the key in the root, we move down the tree. The first bit from left is 0, and so we have to move left. Since the left pointer is NULL, we allocate a new node which becomes the left child of root node and insert the key k_2 in that node.

The next key to be inserted is k_3 = 1010011, and since this key is not equal to the key in the root, we move down the tree. The first bit from left is 1, and so we have to move right. Since the right pointer is NULL, we allocate a new node which becomes the right child of the root node, and insert the key k_3 in that node.

The next key to be inserted is k_4 = 1100101, and since this key is not equal to the key in the root, we move down the tree. First bit from left is 1, and so we move to the right child. The key in the right child is not equal to the given key, and so we examine the second bit in the key k_4, which is 1. Now again, we have to move to the right and in this case, the right pointer is NULL. So, we allocate a new node and insert the key there. Similarly, other keys are also inserted.

For searching a key, we proceed down the tree in a similar manner. If at any point, the search key is equal to the key in current node, the search is successful. Reaching a NULL pointer implies that key is not present in the tree.

Deletion in DST is much simpler than in BST. If the key to be deleted is in a leaf node, then we can simply remove the leaf node by replacing it with NULL pointer. If the key to be deleted is in a non-leaf node, then that key can be replaced with a key from any leaf node in any of its subtree, and after that, the particular leaf node may be deleted. For example, suppose we want to delete key k_2 from the last figure. This key can be replaced by any of the keys k_6 or k_8, and then the leaf node may be deleted.

All the above operations are performed in O(h) time, where h is the height of the tree. The maximum height of a digital search tree can be p+1, where p is the numbers of bits in the key and so this tree remains balanced.

6.24 Trie

In earlier data structures, we have seen that complete keys are compared. The key can be considered as a sequence of characters, and these characters can be compared to establish a search path. We can implement the tree node, which will have pointers for these characters. For example, if the key is numeric, it can have 10 pointers. If the key is alphabetic, it can have 26 pointers. These pointers will point to child nodes. We can also have a flag eok, which indicates the end of the key. So in the case of alphabetic key, 0th pointer is for the character 'a', and the 25th pointer is for character 'z'. This is called the Trie data structure (from the word re**trie**val, prononced as try). This can be useful in scenarios where keys have to be searched, based on the prefix of the key.

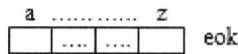

Figure 6.277 Node for trie (alphabetic keys)

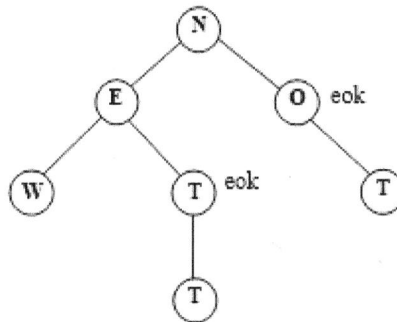

Figure 6.278 Keys in trie

In figure 6.278, the trie has keys: NEW, NET, NETT, NO, NOT. The keys NET and NO are prefix of another key, and they are identified as key with eok is set to true.

This is the class `Node` for trie:

```
class Node
{
        public:
                Node* links[maxSize]; //links to the child node
```

```
              bool eok;  //end of key
              Node()
              {
                      eok = false;
                      for(int i=0; i<maxSize; i++)
                              links[i] = NULL;
              }
};//End of class Node
```

Initially, end of key (eok) is `false` and links to the child node are set to NULL.

The Trie has the following operations:
- Insert
- Serach
- Delete

6.24.1 Insertion of Key in Trie

The key is a sequence of characters, and so each character is checked one by one with the corresponding child pointer of the node. If the pointer is not NULL, then move to the child node. If it is NULL, then create a new node for the child and assign it to that links pointer. We can continue the same process for other characters of the key. Once all the characters of the key are finished, then set the end of key (eok) to `true`.

6.24.2 Searching the Key in Trie

Searching of a key requires checking the child pointer for each character of key. If the child pointer is NULL, that means the key is not there, and so, returns false. If the pointer is not NULL, then move to the child node. We can continue the same process for other characters of the key. Once all the characters of the key are finished, then return the value of eok. eok is true if it is the key and false if it is the prefix of the key.

6.24.3 Deletion of Key in Trie

Deletion of a key requires reaching to the appropriate node in the path for last character of the key. Now we can set the eok false, so now the key is not available. However, there are unnecessary nodes lying in the tree, which need to be deleted. If all the child pointers of the node are NULL, then we have to delete the node. We have to delete the prevoius nodes in the path, if the node child pointers do not point to any child node. This can be done by having all the node pointers of path in stack.

Here is the complete program of trie:

```
//Trie.cpp : Program to implement trie.
#include<iostream>
#include<string>
using namespace std;

static const int maxSize = 26;

class Node
{
      public:
              Node *links[maxSize]; //links to the child node
              bool eok; //end of key

              Node()
              {
                      eok = false;
                      for(int i=0; i<maxSize; i++)
                              links[i] = NULL;
```

```
        }
};//End of class Node
class Trie
{
        private:
                Node *root;
        private:
                void display(Node *ptr, string prefix);
                void destroy(Node *ptr);
        public:
                Trie();
                ~Trie();
                void insert(string key);
                bool search(string key);
                bool startsWith(string prefix);
                void del(string key);
                void display();
};//End of class Trie
Trie::Trie()
{
        root = new Node();
}//End of Trie()
Trie::~Trie()
{
        destroy(root);
        root = NULL;
}//End of ~Trie()
void Trie::destroy(Node *ptr)
{
        for(int i=0; i<maxSize; i++)
        {
                if(ptr->links[i] != NULL)
                {
                        //cout << char(i+'a') << " : " <<  ptr->links[i] << "\n";
                        destroy(ptr->links[i]);
                }
        }
        //cout << "Deleting : " << ptr << "\n";
        delete ptr;
}//End of destroy()
void Trie::insert(string key)
{
        Node *ptr = root;
        for(int i=0; i<key.length(); i++)
        {
                //If letter of key is not there
                if(ptr->links[key[i]-'a'] == NULL)
                {
                        ptr->links[key[i]-'a'] = new Node();
                }
                ptr = ptr->links[key[i]-'a']; //Move to the next child node
        }
        ptr->eok = true; //end of key
}//End of insert()
bool Trie::search(string key)
{
        Node *ptr = root;
        for(int i=0; i<key.length(); i++)
```

```
        {
                if(ptr->links[key[i]-'a'] == NULL)
                {
                        //key is not in the Trie
                        return false;
                }
                ptr = ptr->links[key[i]-'a']; //Move to the next child node
        }
        return ptr->eok;
}//End of search()
bool Trie::startsWith(string prefix)
{
        Node *ptr = root;
        for(int i=0; i<prefix.length(); i++)
        {
                if(ptr->links[prefix[i]-'a'] == NULL)
                {
                        //No prefix
                        return false;
                }
                ptr = ptr->links[prefix[i]-'a']; //Move to the next child node
        }

        //prefix found
        return true;
}//End of startsWith()
void Trie::display(Node *ptr, string prefix)
{
        if(ptr->eok)
                cout << prefix << "\n";

        for(int i=0; i<maxSize; i++)
        {
                if(ptr->links[i] != NULL)
                {
                        display(ptr->links[i], prefix+char('a'+i));
                }
        }
}//End of display()
void Trie::display()
{
        string str;
        display(root,str);
}//End of display()
void Trie::del(string key)
{
        Node *ptr = root;
        for(int i=0; i<key.length(); i++)
        {
                if(ptr->links[key[i]-'a'] == NULL)
                {
                        cout << "key is not in the Trie\n";
                        return;
                }
                ptr = ptr->links[key[i] - 'a']; //Move to the next child node
        }

        if(ptr->eok == false)
                cout << "key is not in the Trie\n";
```

```
                else
                        ptr->eok = false;
}//End of del()
int main()
{
        Trie trie;

        trie.insert("lucknow");
        trie.insert("lucknowcity");
        trie.insert("luxembourg");
        trie.insert("lux");

        //Search in trie
        cout << "search(\"lucknowp\") : " << (trie.search("lucknowp") ? "True" : "False");
        cout << "\n";

        cout << "search(\"luxembourg\") : " << (trie.search("luxembourg") ? "True" :
        "False");
        cout << "\n";

        //Prefix in trie
        cout << "startsWith(\"luxe\") : " << (trie.startsWith("luxe") ? "True" : "False");
        cout << "\n";

        cout << "Trie keys are :\n";
        trie.display();

        //Deletion of key in trie
        trie.del("luxembourg");

        cout << "After deleting luxembourg, trie keys are :\n";
        trie.display();

        return 0;
}//End of main()
```

Exercise

1. Draw all possible non-similar binary trees having (i) 3 nodes (ii) 4 nodes.

2. Draw all possible binary trees of 3 nodes having preorder XYZ.

3. Draw all possible binary search trees of 3 nodes having key values 1, 2, 3.

4. Construct a BST by inserting the following data sequentially.
   45 32 70 67 21 85 92 40

5. If we construct a binary search tree by inserting the following data sequentially, then what is the height of the tree formed?
   71 32 12 82 45 91 38 70 40 61
   If the binary search tree is constructed by inserting this data in sorted order, then what will be the height of that tree?

6. The preorder traversal of a binary search tree T is 23 12 11 9 6 45 32 67 56. What are the inorder and postorder traversals of the tree T?

7. Show a binary tree for which preorder and inorder traversals are same.

8. Show a binary tree for which postorder and inorder traversals are same.

9. Construct binary trees from inorder and preorder traversals.
   (i) Inorder : 12 31 10 45 66   Preorder : 12 31 10 45 66
   (ii) Inorder : 35 26 93 21 68   Preorder : 68 21 93 26 35
   (iii) Inorder : 16 22 31 15 46 77 19   Preorder : 15 22 16 31 77 46 19
   (iv) Inorder : 11 12 23 24 25 32 43 46 54 65 Preorder : 32 23 11 12 24 25 43 54 46 65

10. Construct binary trees from inorder and postorder traversals.
   (i) Inorder : 12 31 10 45 66   Postorder : 12 31 10 45 66
   (ii) Inorder : 35 26 93 21 68   Postorder : 68 21 93 26 35
   (iii) Inorder : 20 19 24 8 11 13 6 Postorder : 20 24 19 11 6 13 8
   (iv) Inorder : 4 5 6 11 19 23 43 50 54 98 Postorder : 4 6 5 19 11 50 98 54 43 23

11. For the following binary search trees, show the possible sequences in which the data was entered in these trees.

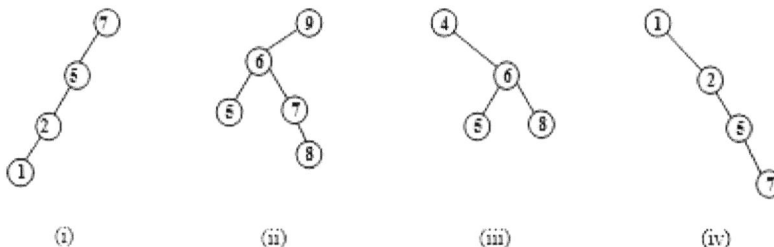

Figure 6.279 Binary search trees

12. Suppose a binary search tree is constructed by inserting the keys 1, 2, 3, 4……n in any order.
    (a) If there are x nodes in the right subtree of the root, which key was inserted in the beginning?
    (b) If there are y nodes in the left subtree of the root, which key was inserted in the beginning?

13. We know that preorder and postorder traversals cannot uniquely define a binary tree. Show an example of binary trees that have the same preorder and postorder traversals.

14. Construct a binary search tree whose preorder traversal is:
    67 34 12 45 38 60 80 78 95 90

15. Construct a binary search tree whose postorder traversal is:
    10 11 40 48 44 32 65 73 88 77 72 56

16. Construct a full binary tree, whose preorder is:
    F B G I C K L

17. Write a function that returns the size of a binary tree, i.e., the total number of nodes in the tree.

18. Write a function that returns the total number of leaf nodes in a binary tree and displays the info part of each leaf node.

19. Write a function to find the length of the shortest path from root to a leaf node. This length is also known as the minimum height of the binary tree. For example, the minimum height of this tree is 3.

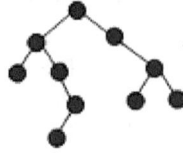

Figure 6.280 Binary tree example to find minimum height

20. Write a function to display all the ancestors of a node in a binary search tree.

21. Write a function that displays all root to leaf paths in a binary tree.

22. Two binary trees are similar if their structure is same. Write a function to check whether two binary trees are similar.

23. Write a function to check whether two binary trees are identical. Two binary trees are identical or copies if their structure as well as data is the same.

24. Write a function to swap right and left children of a binary tree, i.e., all right children become the left children and vice versa. The new tree is the mirror image of the original tree.

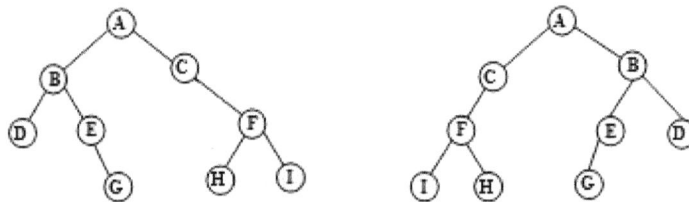

Figure 6.281 Mirror image

25. Write a function to find whether two binary trees are mirror image of each other.

26. Write a function to check whether a binary tree is a binary search tree.

27. Write a recursive function that inputs a level number of a binary tree and returns the number of nodes at that level.

28. Width of a binary tree is the number of nodes on the level that has the maximum nodes. For example, width of the following binary tree is 4. Write a function that returns the width of a binary tree.

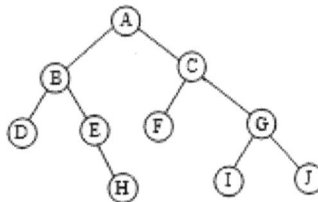

Figure 6.282 Binary tree example to find width

29. Write a function that inputs a level and displays nodes on that level from left to right, right to left in a binary tree.

30. Write a function to traverse a binary tree in a zigzag order. The zigzag traversal of a binary tree in figure 6.282 is:

A C B D E F G J I H

31. Draw an expression tree for the following algebraic expression and write the prefix and postfix forms of the expression by traversing the expression tree in preorder and postorder.

$(a + b / c) - (d + e * f)$

32. The level order traversal of a max heap is 50 40 30 25 16 23 20. What will be the level order traversal after inserting the elements 28, 43, 11?

33. Generate Huffman code for the letters a, b, c, d, e, f having frequencies 16, 8, 4, 2, 1, 1.

34. Construct an AVL tree by inserting the following values sequentially.

23 34 12 11 6 2 45 4 25 24

35. Construct a B-tree of order 5 by inserting the following key values sequentially.

35 63 24 10 12 39 89 72 11 8 4 18 78 14 80 70 21

36. Write a function to check whether a BST is an AVL tree.

Join our book's Discord space

Join the book's Discord Workspace for Latest updates, Offers, Tech happenings around the world, New Release and Sessions with the Authors:

https://discord.bpbonline.com

Graphs

A graph G = (V, E) is a collection of sets V and E, where V is the collection of vertices and E is the collection of edges. An edge is a line or arc connecting two vertices, denoted by a pair (i, j) where i, j belong to the set of vertices V. A graph can be of two types: Undirected graph, or Directed graph.

7.1 Undirected Graph

A graph, which has unordered pair of vertices, is called undirected graph. If there is an edge between vertices u and v then it can be represented as either (u, v) or (v, u).

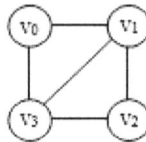

Figure 7.1 Undirected graph

$V(G) = \{ v_0, v_1, v_2, v_3 \}$
$E(G) = \{ (v_0,v_1), (v_0,v_3), (v_1,v_2), (v_1,v_3), (v_2,v_3) \}$
This graph is undirected; it has 4 vertices and 5 edges.

7.2 Directed Graph

A directed graph or digraph is a graph which has ordered pair of vertices (u,v) where u is the tail and v is the head of the edge. In this type of graph, a direction is associated with each edge, i.e., (u,v) and (v,u) represent different edges.

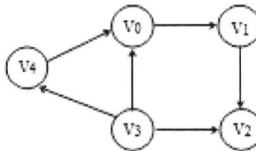

Figure 7.2 Directed graph

$V(G) = \{ v_0, v_1, v_2, v_3, v_4 \}$
$E(G) = \{ (v_0,v_1), (v_1,v_2), (v_3,v_2), (v_3,v_0), (v_3,v_4), (v_4,v_0) \}$
This graph is directed; it has 5 vertices and 6 edges.

7.3 Graph Terminology

The definitions and terms associated with graph data structures are explained with the help of example graphs shown in figure 7.3.

Weighted graph: A graph is weighted if its edges have been assigned some non-negative value as weight. A weighted graph is also known as network. Graph G9 is a weighted graph. The weight on the edge may represent cost, length or distance associated with the edge.

Subgraph: A graph H is said to be a subgraph of another graph G, if the vertex set of H is subset of vertex set of G, and edge set of H is subset of edge set of G.

Adjacency: Adjacency is a relation between two vertices of a graph. A vertex v is adjacent to another vertex u if there is an edge from vertex u to vertex v, i.e., edge $(u,v) \in E$.

In an undirected graph, if we have an edge (u,v), it means that there is an edge from u to v, and also an edge from v to u. So the adjacency relation is symmetric for undirected graphs, i.e., if (u,v) is an edge, then u is adjacent to v, and v is adjacent to u. For example, in G2, vertex v_0 is adjacent to v_3, and v_3 is adjacent to v_0. Vertex v_0 is not adjacent to v_2 since there is no edge between them.

In a digraph if (u,v) is an edge, then v is adjacent *to* u, but u is not adjacent to v since there is no edge from v to u. The vertex u is said to be adjacent *from* v. For example, in G5, v_1 is adjacent to v_0, but v_0 is not adjacent to v_1. The vertex v_0 is adjacent from v_1.

Incidence: Incidence is a relation between a vertex and an edge of a graph. In an undirected graph, the edge (u,v) is incident on vertices u and v. For example, in G2, edge(v_0,v_3) is incident on vertices v_0 and v_3.

In a digraph, the edge (u,v) is incident from vertex u and is incident to vertex v. For example, in G5, the edge(v_0,v_1) is incident from vertex v_0 and incident to vertex v_1.

Path: A path from vertex u_1 to vertex u_n is a sequence of vertices $u_1, u_2, u_3,................,u_{n-1}, u_n$ such that u_2 is adjacent to u_1, u_3 is adjacent to u_2, ... , u_n is adjacent to u_{n-1}. In other words, we can say that (u_1,u_2), (u_2,u_3) ....(u_{n-1},u_n) are all edges or $(u_i, u_{i+1}) \in E$ for i=1,2,3......n-1. For example, in digraph G5, $v_3-v_4-v_0-v_1-v_2$ is a path, while $v_3-v_2-v_1$ is not a path since v_1 is not adjacent to v_2. In undirected graph G12, $v_5-v_2-v_3$ and $v_0-v_1-v_4-v_3-v_1$ are examples of path.

Length of a path: The length of a path is the total number of edges included in the path. For a path with vertices $u_1, u_2, u_3,............,u_{n-1}, u_n$, the length of path is n-1. For example, the length of path $v_3-v_4-v_0-v_1-v_2$ in G5 is 4.

Reachable: If there is a path P from vertex u to vertex v, then vertex v is said to be reachable from vertex u via path P. For example, in digraph G5, vertex v_2 is reachable from vertex v_4 via path $v_4-v_0-v_1-v_2$ while vertex v_3 is not reachable from vertex v_4, as there is no path from v_4 to v_3.

Simple path: A simple path is a path in which all the vertices are distinct. For example, in graph G12, path $v_0-v_1-v_3-v_4-v_6$ is a simple path while path $v_0-v_1-v_3-v_4-v_6-v_3-v_2$ is not a simple path because vertex v_3 is repeated.

Cycle: In a digraph, a path $u_1, u_2, ..., u_{n-1},u_n$ is called a cycle if it has at least two vertices and the first and last vertices are same, i.e., $u_1 = u_n$. In graph G7, path $v_0-v_2-v_1-v_0$ is a cycle and in graph G9, path $v_0-v_1-v_0$ is a cycle.

In an undirected graph, a path $u_1, u_2, ..., u_{n-1}, u_n$ is called a cycle if it has at least three vertices and the first and last vertices are the same, i.e., $u_1 = u_n$. In undirected graph, if (u,v) is an edge, then u–v–u should not be considered a cycle since (u,v) and (v,u) represent the same edge. So, for a path to be a cycle in an undirected graph, there should be at least three vertices. For example, in graph G12, $v_1-v_4-v_6-v_3-v_1$ is a cycle of length 4, path $v_6-v_4-v_3-v_6$ is a cycle of length 3.

Simple Cycle: A cycle $u_1, u_2, u_3,......,u_{n-1}, u_n$ is simple if the vertices $u_2, u_3, ... ,u_{n-1}, u_n$ are distinct. For example, in graph G12, $v_1-v_4-v_3-v_2-v_0-v_1$ is a simple cycle but $v_1-v_4-v_3-v_6-v_2-v_3-v_1$ is not a simple cycle because vertex v_3 is repeated.

Cyclic graph: A graph that has one or more cycles is called a cyclic graph. Graphs G1, G3, G7, G9, G11 and G12 are examples of cyclic graphs.

Acyclic graph: A graph that has no cycle is called an acyclic graph. Graphs G2, G4, G5, G6, G8 and G10 are examples of acyclic graphs.

DAG: A directed acyclic graph is named DAG after its acronym. Graph G5 is an example of a dag.

Degree: In an undirected graph, the degree of a vertex is the number of edges incident on it. In graph G12, the degree of vertex v_0 is 2, the degree of v_1 is 3, the degree of v_2 is 4, the degree of v_3 is 4, the degree of v_4 is 3, the degree of v_5 is 2 and the degree of v_6 is 4. In a digraph, each vertex has an indegree and an outdegree. The degree of a vertex in a digraph is the sum of its indegree and outdegree.

Indegree: The indegree of a vertex v is the number of edges entering the vertex v, or in other words, the number of edges incident to vertex v. In graph G8, the indegree of vertices v_0, v_1, v_3, and v_6 are 0, 2, 6, and 1, respectively.

Outdegree: The outdegree of vertex v is the number of edges leaving the vertex v, or in other words, the number of edges that are incident from v. In graph G8, outdegrees of vertices v_0, v_1, v_3, v_5, and v_6 are 3, 1, 0, 3, and 2 respectively.

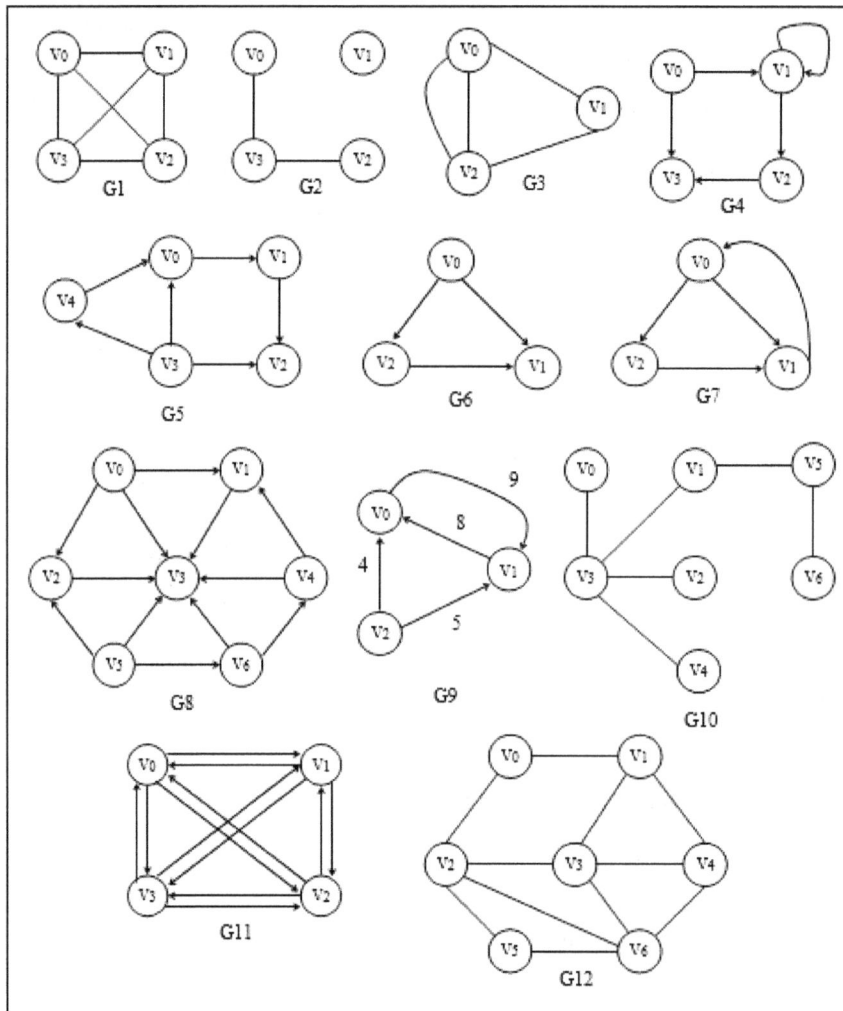

Figure 7.3 Graphs examples

Source: A vertex that has no incoming edges but has outgoing edges is called a source. The indegree of a source is zero. In graph G8, vertices v_0 and v_5 are sources.

Sink: A vertex that has no outgoing edges but has incoming edges is called a sink. The outdegree of a sink is zero. In graph G8, vertex v_3 is a sink.

Pendant vertex: A vertex in a digraph is said to be a pendant if its indegree equals 1 and its outdegree equals 0.

Isolated vertex: If the degree of a vertex is 0, then it is called an isolated vertex. In graph G2, vertex v_1 is an isolated vertex.

Successor and predecessor: In a digraph, if a vertex v is adjacent to vertex u, then v is said to be the successor of u, and u is said to be the predecessor of v. In graph G8, v_0 is the predecessor of v_1, while v_1 is the successor of v_0.

Maximum edges in a graph: If n is the total number of vertices in a graph, then an undirected graph can have maximum n(n-1)/2 edges, and a digraph can have maximum n(n-1) edges. For example, an undirected graph with 3 vertices can have a maximum of 3 edges, and an undirected graph with 4 vertices can have a maximum of 6 edges. A digraph with 3 vertices can have a maximum of 6 edges and a digraph with 4 vertices can have maximum 12 edges.

Complete graph: A graph is complete if any vertex in the graph is adjacent to all the vertices of the graph or we can say that there is an edge between any pair of vertices in the graph. A complete graph contains maximum number of edges, and so, an undirected complete graph with n vertices will have n(n-1)/2 edges, and a directed complete graph with n vertices will have n(n-1) edges. Graph G1 is a complete undirected graph, and graph G11 is a complete directed graph.

Multiple edges: If there is more than one edge between a pair of vertices, then the edges are known as multiple edges or parallel edges. In graph G3, there are multiple edges between vertices v_0 and v_2.

Loop: An edge is called loop or self edge if it starts and ends on the same vertex. Graph G4 has a loop at vertex v_1.

Multigraph: A graph that contains loop or multiple edges is known as multigraph. Graphs G3 and G4 are multigraphs.

Simple graph: A graph that does not have a loop or multiple edges, is known as a simple graph.

Regular graph: A graph is regular if every vertex is adjacent to the same number of vertices. Graph G1 is regular since every vertex is adjacent to 3 vertices.

Planar graph: A graph is called planar if it can be drawn in a plane without two edges intersecting. Graph G1 is not a planar graph, while graphs G2, G3, G4 are planar graphs.

Null graph: A graph that has only isolated vertices is called a null graph.

7.4 Connectivity in Undirected Graph

7.4.1 Connected Graph

An undirected graph is connected if there is a path from any vertex to any other vertex or if any vertex is reachable from any other vertex. A connected graph of n vertices has at least n-1 edges. The following are some examples of connected graphs:

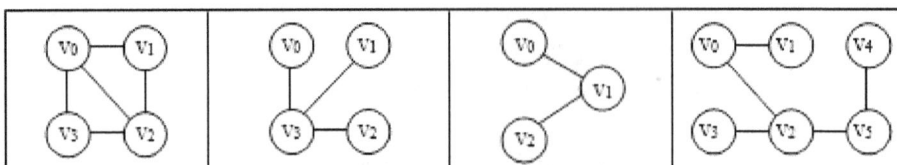

Figure 7.4 Connected graphs

The following three graphs are not connected graphs:

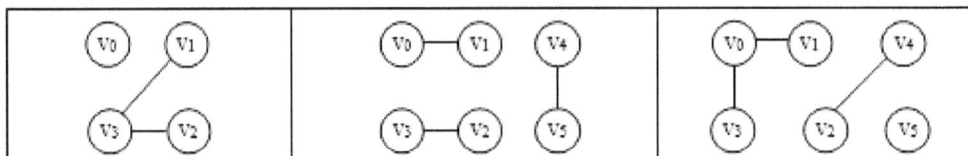

Figure 7.5 Graphs which are not connected

7.4.2 Connected Components

An undirected graph which is not connected, may have different parts of the graph, which are connected. These parts are called connected components.

A connected component of an undirected graph is a subgraph in which all vertices are connected by paths, and it is not possible to add any other vertex to it, while retaining its connectivity property. This way we can define a connected component as a maximal connected subgraph. Figure 7.6 shows three graphs with their connected components.

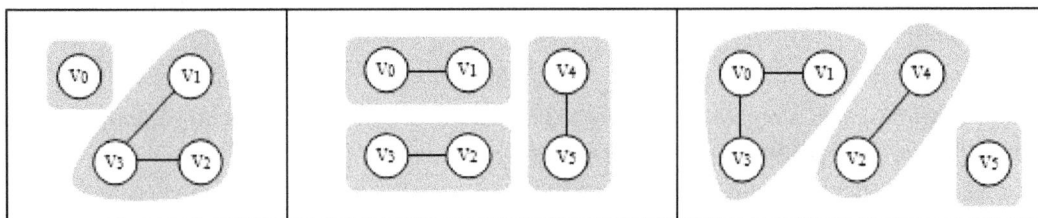

Figure 7.6 Connected components

If a graph is connected, it has only one connected component, which consists of the whole graph.

7.4.3 Bridge

If on removing an edge from a connected graph, the graph becomes disconnected, then that edge is called a bridge. Consider the following graph. We will remove all the edges one by one from it and see if the graph becomes disconnected.

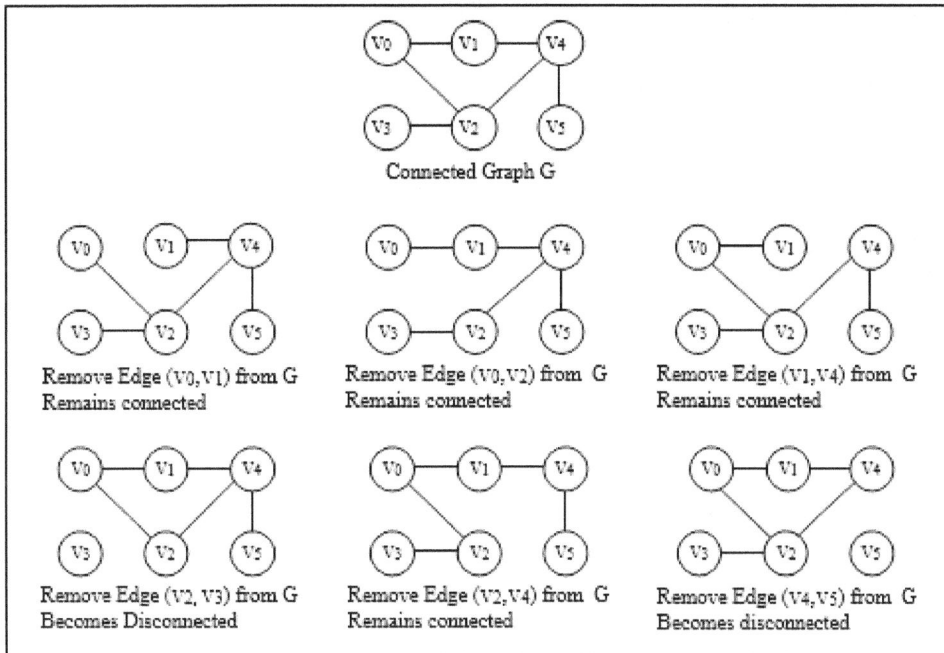

Figure 7.7 Graphs examples to find bridge

From the figure 7.7, we find that removal of edge (v_2, v_3) as well as edge (v_4, v_5), makes the graph disconnected. Thus, these edges are bridges.

7.4.4 Articulation Point

If on removing a vertex from a connected graph, the graph becomes disconnected, then that vertex is called the articulation point or a cut vertex. Consider the graph in figure 7.8. We will remove all the vertices one by one from it and see if the graph becomes disconnected.

From figure 7.8, we find that the removal of vertex v_2 and vertex v_4 makes the graph disconnected. Thus, these are the articulation points of this graph.

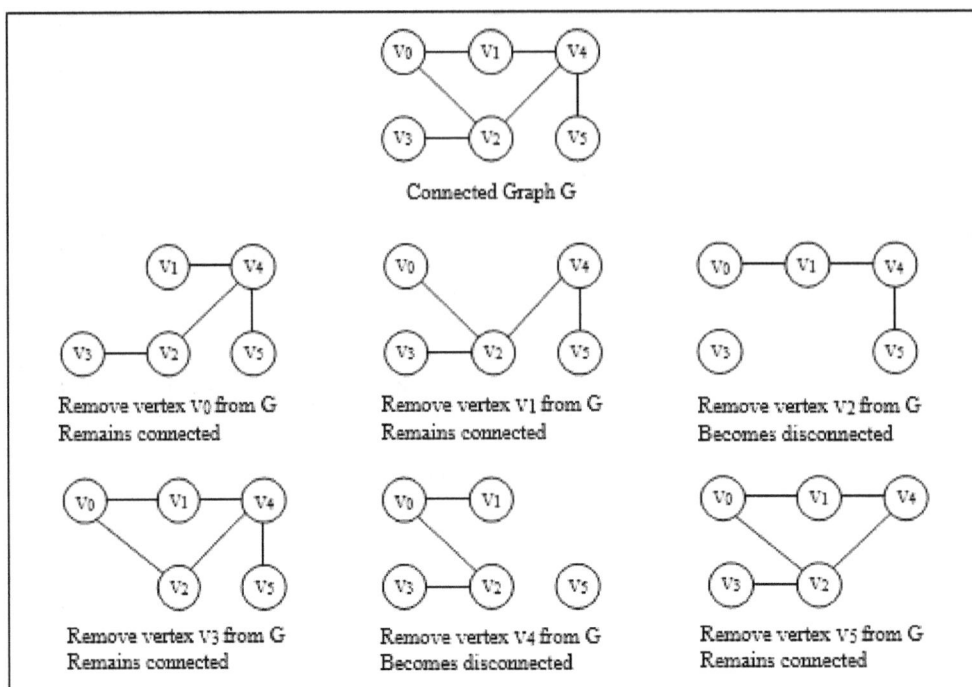

Figure 7.8 Graphs examples to find articulation points

Here are some more examples of graphs with articulation points.

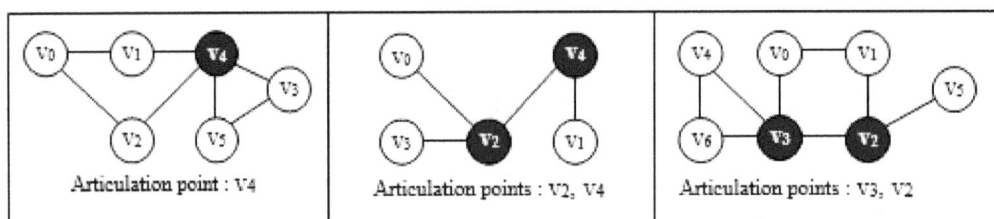

Figure 7.9 More examples of graphs with articulation points

7.4.5 Biconnected Graph

A connected graph with no articulation points is called a biconnected graph. Thus, a biconnected graph is a graph that is connected, and does not have any vertex whose removal can disconnect the graph. Some examples of biconnected graphs are:

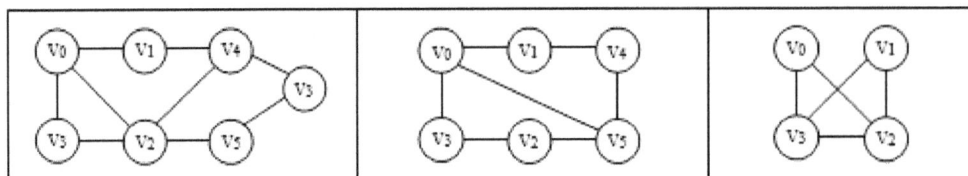

Figure 7.10 Biconnected graphs examples

7.4.6 Biconnected Components

A biconnected component is a maximal biconnected subgraph. It is a maximal set of edges such that any two edges of this set lie on a common simple cycle.

In figure 7.11, the black vertices indicate articulation points, bold edges indicate bridges and edges in the separate shaded regions indicate biconnected components.

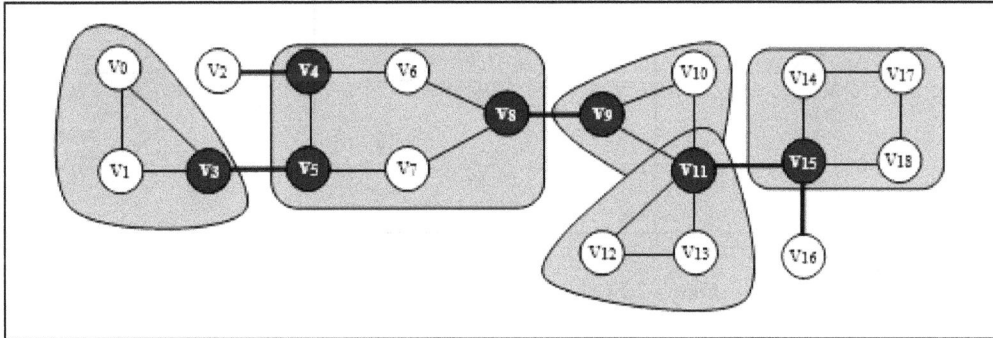

Figure 7.11 Biconnected components

7.5 Connectivity in Directed Graphs

7.5.1 Strongly Connected Graph

A digraph is strongly connected if there is a directed path from any vertex of graph to any other vertex. We can also say that a digraph is strongly connected, if for any pair of vertices u and v, there is a path from u to v and also a path from v to u. The three graphs given next are the examples of strongly connected graphs:

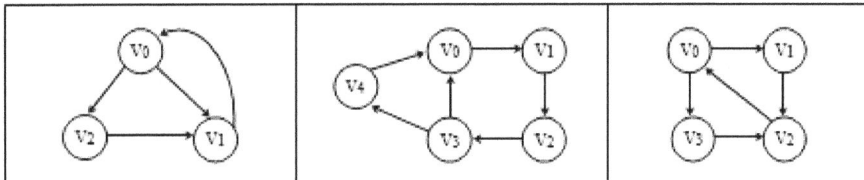

Figure 7.12 Strongly connected graphs

Here are some graphs which are not strongly connected:

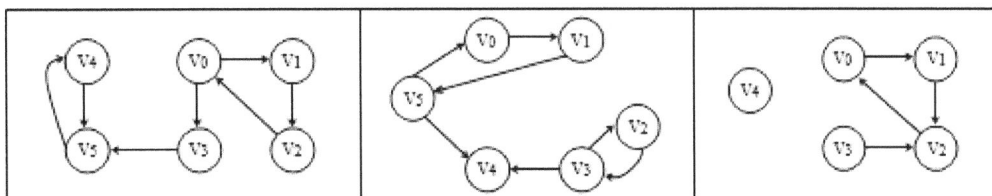

Figure 7.13 Graphs which are not strongly connected

7.5.2 Strongly Connected Components

A digraph that is not strongly connected may have different parts of the graph that are strongly connected. These parts are called strongly connected components. A strongly connected component of a graph is a maximal strongly connected subgraph. The following figure shows some graphs with their strongly connected components:

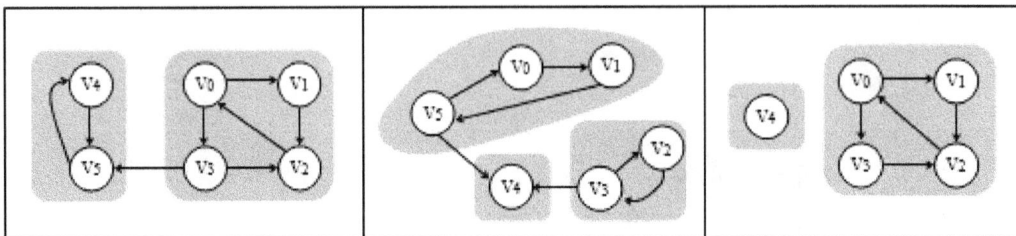

Figure 7.14 Strongly connected components

7.5.3 Weakly Connected

A digraph is called weakly connected or unilaterally connected if, for any pair of vertices u and v, there is a path from u to v or a path from v to u or both. From a digraph, if we remove the directions and the resulting undirected graph is connected, then that digraph is weakly connected. In the following figure, the first graph is weakly connected, while the second one is not.

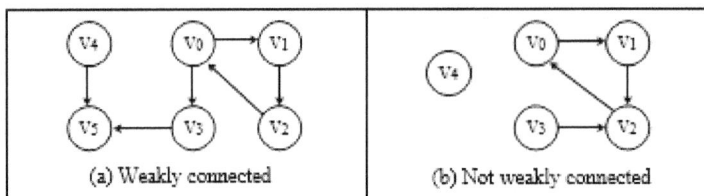

Figure 7.15 Weakly connected and not weakly connected graph

7.6 Tree

An undirected connected graph T is called a tree if there are no cycles in it. There is *exactly* one simple path between any two vertices u and v of T. If there is more than one path between any two vertices, then it would mean that there is a cycle in the graph, and if there is no path between any two vertices, then it would mean that the graph is not connected. So, according to the definition of a tree, there will be exactly one simple path between any pair of vertices of the tree. A tree with n vertices will have exactly n-1 edges. The following are some examples of trees:

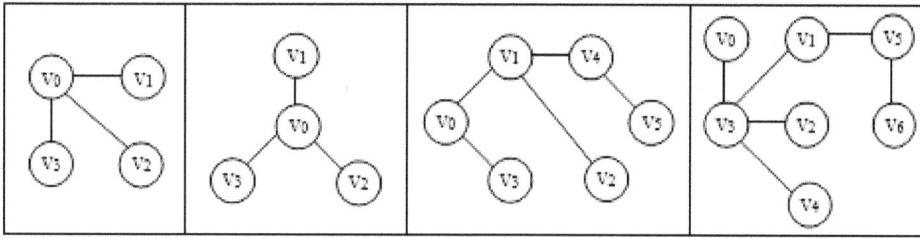

Figure 7.16 Examples of trees

The following examples are graphs which are not trees:

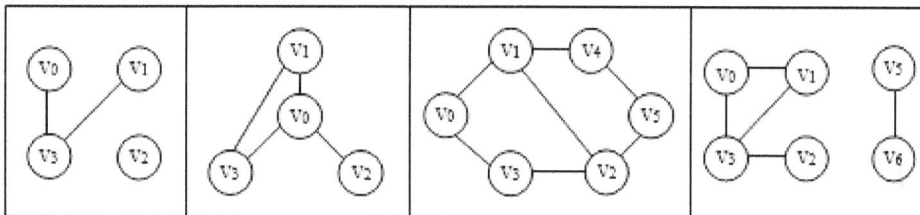

Figure 7.17 Graphs which are not trees

In figure 7.17, the first graph is not a tree as it is not connected; the next two graphs are not trees as they are cyclic, and the last graph is not a tree as it is not connected and is cyclic.

If any edge is removed from a tree, then the graph will not remain connected, i.e., all edges in a tree are bridges. If any edge is added to the tree, then a simple cycle is formed.

7.7 Forest

A forest is a disjoint union of trees. In a forest, there is *at most* one path between any two vertices; this means that there is either no path or a single path between any two vertices.

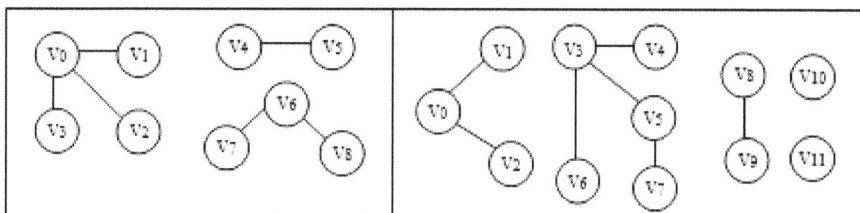

Figure 7.18 Forest

The first forest in figure 7.18 consists of 3 trees, and the second forest consists of 5 trees.

7.8 Spanning Tree

A subgraph T of a connected graph G, which contains all the vertices of G and is a tree, is called a spanning tree of G. It is called a spanning tree because it spans over all vertices of graph G.

So, a spanning tree of a graph G is a subgraph that includes all vertices of G and some (or all) edges of G, such that all the vertices are connected and there are no cycles.

A spanning tree of a graph is not unique; there can be more than one spanning tree of a graph. Figure 7.19 shows a connected graph and its six different spanning trees.

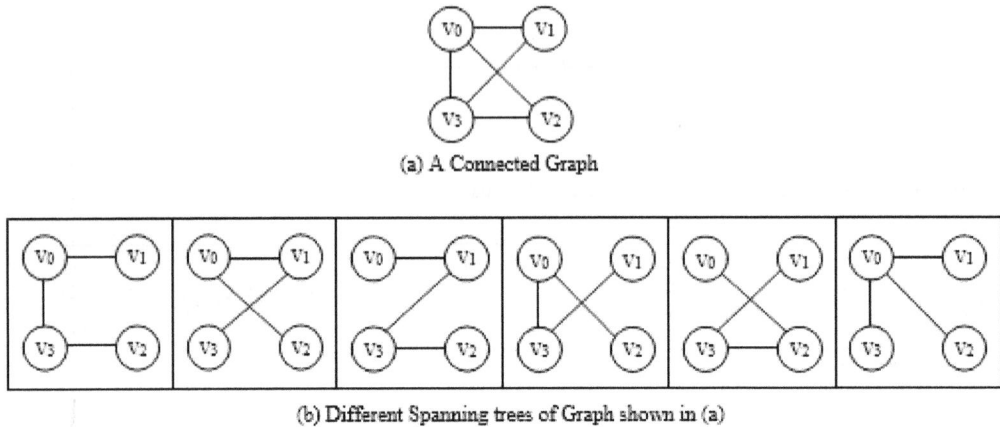

(a) A Connected Graph

(b) Different Spanning trees of Graph shown in (a)

Figure 7.19 Connected graph and its different spanning trees

If a graph is connected, then it will always have a spanning tree. If a graph G is not connected then there will be no spanning tree of G.

7.9 Spanning Forest

A spanning forest is a subgraph that consists of a spanning tree for each connected component of a graph. The following figure shows a graph and its spanning forest. There can be many other spanning forests for this graph:

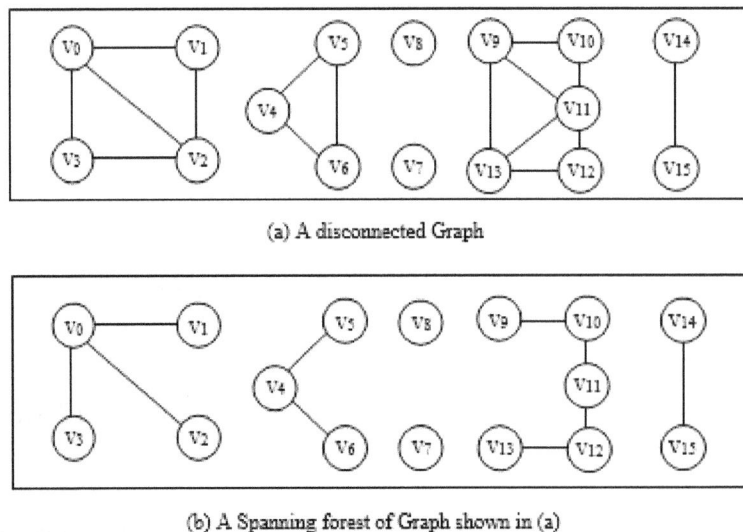

(a) A disconnected Graph

(b) A Spanning forest of Graph shown in (a)

Figure 7.20 Graphs and its spanning forest

7.10 Representation of Graph

A graph mainly has two parts, vertices and edges, and we have to design a data structure keeping these parts in mind. There are two ways of representing a graph: the sequential representation (adjacency matrix) and the linked representation (adjacency list).

7.10.1 Adjacency Matrix

Adjacency matrix is a matrix that maintains the information of adjacent vertices. In other words, we can say that this matrix tells us whether a vertex is adjacent to any other vertex or not. Suppose there are 4 vertices in a graph. Then, the first row represents vertex 1, the second row represents vertex 2, and so on. Similarly, the first column represents vertex 1, the second column represents vertex 2, and so on. The entries of this adjacency matrix are filled using this definition:

$$A(i,j) = \begin{cases} 1 & \text{If there is an edge from vertex } i \text{ to vertex } j \\ 0 & \text{If there is no edge from vertex } i \text{ to vertex } j \end{cases}$$

Figure 7.21 Adjacency matrix definition

Hence, all the entries of this matrix are either 1 or 0. Let us take a directed graph and write the adjacency matrix for it:

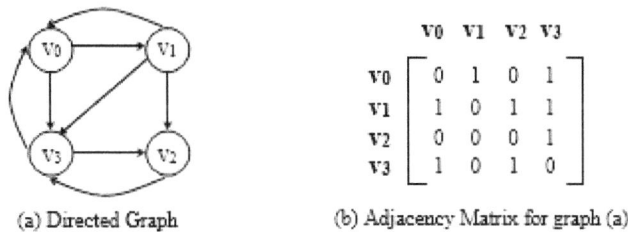

	V0	V1	V2	V3
V0	0	1	0	1
V1	1	0	1	1
V2	0	0	0	1
V3	1	0	1	0

(a) Directed Graph   (b) Adjacency Matrix for graph (a)

Figure 7.22 Adjacency matrix for a directed graph

Here, the matrix entry is $A(0,1) = 1$, which means that there is an edge in the graph from vertex v_0 to vertex v_1. Similarly, $A(2,0) = 0$, which means that there is no edge from vertex v_2 to vertex v_0. In the adjacency matrix of a directed graph, rowsum represents the outdegree and columnsum represents the indegree of that vertex. For example, from the above matrix, we can see that the rowsum of vertex v_1 is 3, which is its outdegree and columnsum is 1 which is its indegree.

Let us take an undirected graph and write the adjacency matrix for it:

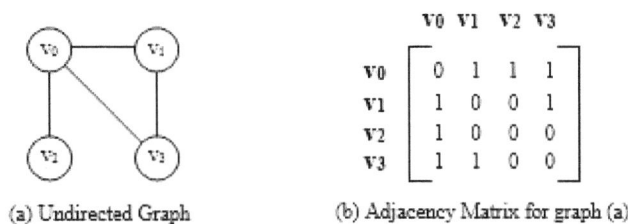

	V0	V1	V2	V3
V0	0	1	1	1
V1	1	0	0	1
V2	1	0	0	0
V3	1	1	0	0

(a) Undirected Graph   (b) Adjacency Matrix for graph (a)

Figure 7.23 Adjacency matrix for an undirected graph

In an undirected graph, if there is an edge form i to j, then there will also be an edge from j to i, i.e., A(i,j) = A(j,i) for every i and j. Hence, the adjacency matrix for an undirected graph will be a symmetric matrix. In an undirected graph, rowsum and columnsum for a vertex are equal and represent the degree of that vertex.

If a graph has some weights on its edges, then the elements of adjacency matrix can be defined as:

$$A(i,j) = \begin{cases} \text{Weight on edge} & \text{If there is an edge from vertex i to vertex j.} \\ 0 & \text{Otherwise} \end{cases}$$

Figure 7.24 Weighted adjacency matrix definition

Let us take a directed weighted graph and write the weighted adjacency matrix for it:

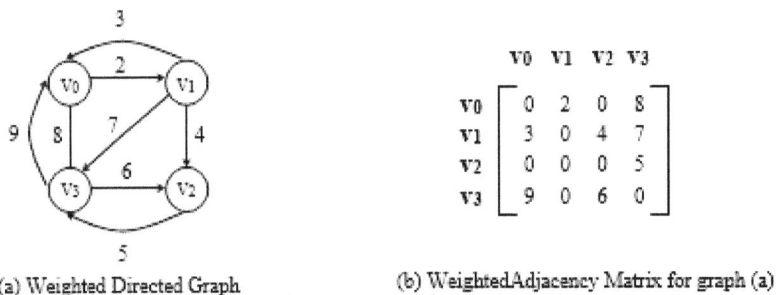

(a) Weighted Directed Graph

	V0	V1	V2	V3
V0	0	2	0	8
V1	3	0	4	7
V2	0	0	0	5
V3	9	0	6	0

(b) WeightedAdjacency Matrix for graph (a)

Figure 7.25 Adjacency matrix for a weighted directed graph

Here, all the non-zero elements of the matrix represent the weight on the corresponding edge.

We know that in C++, we can represent a matrix by a two dimensional array, where the first subscript represents row and the second subscript represents a column of that matrix.

Suppose, we have n vertices in a graph, and these vertices are represented by integers from 0 to n-1. The adjacency matrix of this graph can be maintained with a 2 dimensional integer array `adj[n][n]`.

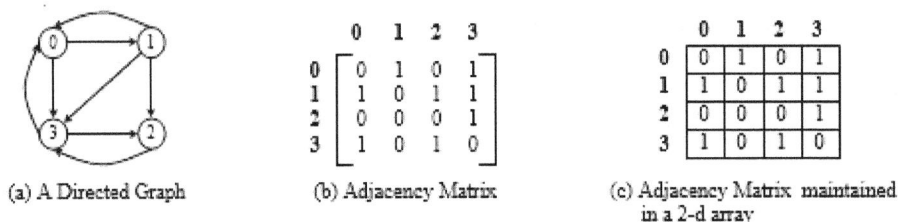

(a) A Directed Graph

	0	1	2	3
0	0	1	0	1
1	1	0	1	1
2	0	0	0	1
3	1	0	1	0

(b) Adjacency Matrix

	0	1	2	3
0	0	1	0	1
1	1	0	1	1
2	0	0	0	1
3	1	0	1	0

(c) Adjacency Matrix maintained in a 2-d array

Figure 7.26 Adjacency matrix of a graph maintained in a 2-d array

This adjacency matrix is maintained in the array `adj[4][4]`.

We will have class `Vertex` for vertex:

```
class Vertex
```

```
{
        public:
                string name;
        public:
                Vertex(string name)
                {
                        this->name = name;
                }
};//End of class Vertex
```

We will have class `DirectedGraph` for directed graph:

```
class DirectedGraph
{
        private:
                int nVertices;
                int nEdges;
                int adj[maxSize][maxSize];
                Vertex *vertexList[maxSize];
        private:
                int getIndex(string vertexName);
                bool isAdjacent(int u, int v);
        public:
                DirectedGraph();
                ~DirectedGraph();
                void insertVertex(string vertexName);
                void insertEdge(string source, string destination);
                void deleteEdge(string source, string destination);
                void display();
                bool edgeExists(string source, string destination);
                int getOutdegree(string vertex);
                int getIndegree(string vertex);
};//End of class DirectedGraph
```

All the vertices will be in `Vertex` array `vertexList`. The member function `getIndex()` will provide the index of the vertex in `vertexList`.

All the edge information will be in two-dimensional array `adj` of nVertices x nVertices. The value of `adj[u][v]` will say if there is an edge from u to v. If `adj[u][v]` is 1, then there is an edge from u to v, and if `adj[u][v]` is 0, then there is no edge from u to v.

The insertion of vertex will add a new vertex in `vertexList`.

`vertexList[nVertices++] = new Vertex(vertexName);`

Insertion of an edge (i, j) requires changing the value of `adj[i][j]` from 0 to 1.

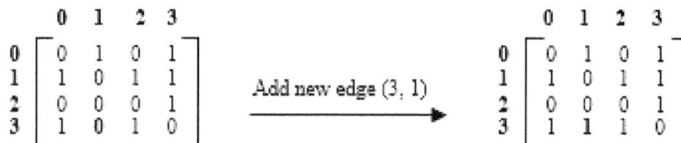

Figure 7.27 Insertion of an edge

Initially, there was no edge from vertex 3 to vertex 1, and so, there was 0 in the 4th row 2nd column. After insertion of edge (3, 1), this 0 changes to 1.

Deletion of an edge (i, j) requires changing the value of `adj[i][j]` from 1 to 0:

$$\begin{array}{c} \\ 0 \\ 1 \\ 2 \\ 3 \end{array} \begin{array}{cccc} 0 & 1 & 2 & 3 \\ \begin{bmatrix} 0 & 1 & 0 & 1 \\ 1 & 0 & 1 & 1 \\ 0 & 0 & 0 & 1 \\ 1 & 0 & 1 & 0 \end{bmatrix} \end{array} \xrightarrow{\text{Delete edge } (1,2)} \begin{array}{c} \\ 0 \\ 1 \\ 2 \\ 3 \end{array} \begin{array}{cccc} 0 & 1 & 2 & 3 \\ \begin{bmatrix} 0 & 1 & 0 & 1 \\ 1 & 0 & 0 & 1 \\ 0 & 0 & 0 & 1 \\ 1 & 0 & 1 & 0 \end{bmatrix} \end{array}$$

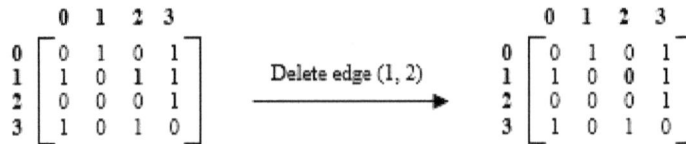

Figure 7.28 Deletion of an edge

Initially, an edge existed from vertex 1 to vertex 2, so there is 1 in the 2nd row, 3rd column. After this edge is deleted, the 1 changes to 0.

getOutDegree() will give information of the number of outgoing edges from a vertex and getInDegree() will give information of number of incoming edges to a vertex.

Let us see the complete program of the directed graph using adjacency matrix:

```cpp
//DirectedGraph.cpp : Program for directed graph using adjacency matrix.
#include<iostream>
#include<string>
using namespace std;

static const int maxSize = 30;

class Vertex
{
    public:
        string name;
    public:
        Vertex(string name)
        {
            this->name = name;
        }
};//End of class Vertex

class DirectedGraph
{
    private:
        int nVertices;
        int nEdges;
        int adj[maxSize][maxSize];
        Vertex *vertexList[maxSize];
    private:
        int getIndex(string vertexName);
        bool isAdjacent(int u, int v);
    public:
        DirectedGraph();
        ~DirectedGraph();
        void insertVertex(string vertexName);
        void insertEdge(string source, string destination);
        void deleteEdge(string source, string destination);
        void display();
        bool edgeExists(string source, string destination);
        int getOutdegree(string vertex);
        int getIndegree(string vertex);
};//End of class DirectedGraph

DirectedGraph::DirectedGraph()
{
    nVertices = 0;
    nEdges = 0;
    for(int i=0; i<maxSize; i++)
    {
```

```
                for(int j=0; j<maxSize; j++)
                {
                        adj[i][j] = 0;
                }
        }
}//End of DirectedGraph()

DirectedGraph::~DirectedGraph()
{
        for(int i=0; i<nVertices; i++)
        {
                delete vertexList[i];
        }
}//End of ~DirectedGraph()

void DirectedGraph::insertVertex(string vertexName)
{
        vertexList[nVertices++] = new Vertex(vertexName);
}//End of insertVertex()

int DirectedGraph::getIndex(string vertexName)
{
        for(int i=0; i<nVertices; i++ )
        {
                if(vertexName == vertexList[i]->name)
                        return i;
        }
        throw exception("Invalid Vertex");
}//End of getIndex()

void DirectedGraph::insertEdge(string source, string destination)
{
        int u = getIndex(source);
        int v = getIndex(destination);
        if(u == v)
                cout << "Not a valid edge\n";
        else if(adj[u][v] != 0)
                cout << "Edge already present\n";
        else
        {
                adj[u][v] = 1;
                nEdges++;
        }
}//End of insertEdge()

void DirectedGraph::deleteEdge(string source, string destination)
{
        int u = getIndex(source);
        int v = getIndex(destination);
        if(adj[u][v] != 0)
        {
                adj[u][v] = 0;
                nEdges--;
        }
        else
                cout << "Edge does not exist\n";
}//End of deleteEdge()

void DirectedGraph::display()
{
        for(int i=0; i<nVertices; i++)
        {
                for(int j=0; j<nVertices; j++)
                        cout << adj[i][j] << " ";
```

```
                cout <<"\n";
        }
}//End of display()
bool DirectedGraph::isAdjacent(int u, int v)
{
        return (adj[u][v] != 0);
}//End of isAdjacent()
bool DirectedGraph::edgeExists(string source, string destination)
{
        return isAdjacent(getIndex(source), getIndex(destination));
}//End of edgeExists()
//Returns number of edges going out from a vertex
int DirectedGraph::getOutdegree(string vertex)
{
        int u = getIndex(vertex);
        int outdegree = 0;
        for(int v = 0; v<nVertices; v++)
        {
                if(adj[u][v] != 0)
                        outdegree++;
        }
        return outdegree;
}//End of getOutdegree()

//Returns number of edges coming to a vertex
int DirectedGraph::getIndegree(string vertex)
{
        int u = getIndex(vertex);
        int indegree = 0;
        for(int v=0; v<nVertices; v++)
        {
                if(adj[v][u] != 0)
                        indegree++;
        }
        return indegree;
}//End of getIndegree()

int main()
{
        DirectedGraph dGraph;
        try
        {
                //Creating the graph, inserting the vertices and edges
                dGraph.insertVertex("0");
                dGraph.insertVertex("1");
                dGraph.insertVertex("2");
                dGraph.insertVertex("3");
                dGraph.insertEdge("0","3");
                dGraph.insertEdge("1","2");
                dGraph.insertEdge("2","3");
                dGraph.insertEdge("3","1");
                dGraph.insertEdge("0","2");
                //Display the graph
                dGraph.display();
                cout << "\n";
                //Deleting an edge
                dGraph.deleteEdge("0","2");
                //Display the graph
                dGraph.display();
                //Check if there is an edge between two vertices
```

```
                    cout << "Edge exists : " << (dGraph.edgeExists("2","3") ? "True" :
                    "False") << "\n";
                    //Display Outdegree and Indegree of a vertex
                    cout << "Outdegree : " << dGraph.getOutdegree("3") << "\n";
                    cout << "Indegree : " << dGraph.getIndegree("3") << "\n";
        }//End of try
        catch(exception e)
        {
                    cout << e.what() << "\n";
        }
        return 0;
}//End of main()
```

For undirected graph, when we insert the edge (i,j), then `adj[i][j]` and `adj[j][i]` will be assigned with value 1.

```
adj[i][j] = 1;
adj[j][i] = 1;
```

When we delete the edge, then `adj[i][j]` and `adj[j][i]` will be assigned with 0 value:

```
adj[i][j] = 0;
adj[j][i] = 0;
```

For directed weighted graph, `insertEdge()` will have one more parameter for weight, and when we insert the edge (i,j), `weight` will be assigned to `adj[i][j]`.

```
adj[i][j] = weight;
```

7.10.2 Adjacency List

If the graph is not dense, i.e., the number of edges is less, then it is efficient to represent the graph through an adjacency list.

In the adjacency list representation of the graph, we maintain two linked lists. The first linked list is the vertex list that keeps track of all the vertices in the graph, and the second linked list is the edge list that maintains a list of adjacent vertices for each vertex. Suppose there are n vertices. Then, we will create one list which will keep information of all n vertices in the graph, and after that, we will create n lists, where each list will keep information of all adjacent vertices of that particular vertex. So, we will have class `VertexNode` for vertex linked list and class `EdgeNode` for edge linked list.

Here is the class `VertexNode` for the vertex linked list:

```
class VertexNode
{
        public:
                    string name;
                    VertexNode *nextVertex; //next vertex in the linked list of vertices
                    EdgeNode *firstEdge; //first Edge of the adjacency list of this vertex
        public:
                    VertexNode(string name)
                    {
                            this->name = name;
                            nextVertex = NULL;
                            firstEdge = NULL;
                    }
};//End of class VertexNode
```

Here is the class `EdgeNode` for the edge linked list:

```
class EdgeNode
{
        public:
                    VertexNode *endVertex; //Destination vertex of the Edge
```

```
            EdgeNode *nextEdge;      //next Edge of the adjacency list
    public:
            EdgeNode(VertexNode *v)
            {
                    this->endVertex = v;
                    nextEdge = NULL;
            }
};//End of class EdgeNode
```

Figure 7.29 shows a directed graph and its adjacency list:

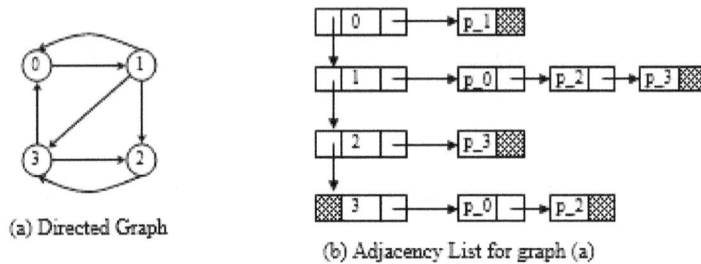

(a) Directed Graph

(b) Adjacency List for graph (a)

Figure 7.29 Adjacency list for a directed graph

In figure 7.29 (b), on the left, we have a linked list (vertically drawn) of the vertices of the graph. In the graph, we have four vertices, so there are four nodes in the linked list of vertices. For each vertex, we have a separate list which stores pointers to adjacent vertices. For example, the vertices 0, 2, 3 are adjacent to vertex 1, i.e., there are edges from vertex 1 to these vertices. So, in the linked list of vertex 1, we have three nodes containing pointers to vertices 0, 2, and 3. There is only one vertex adjacent to vertex 0, so in the list of vertex 0, there is only one node, and it contains a pointer to vertex 1. In the figure, p_0, p_1, p_2, p_3 represent pointers to nodes 0, 1, 2, 3 respectively.

We can also have similar adjacency lists for undirected graphs. In the case of an undirected graph, the space requirement doubles, since each edge appears in two lists. Figure 7.30 shows an undirected graph and its adjacency list structure.

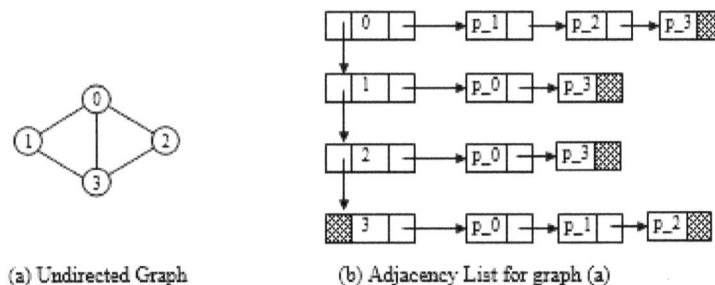

(a) Undirected Graph

(b) Adjacency List for graph (a)

Figure 7.30 Adjacency list for an undirected graph

Here is the class `DirectedGraphList` for the directed graph:

```
class DirectedGraphList
{
    private:
            int nVertices;
            int nEdges;
```

```
public:
        VertexNode *start;
private:
        VertexNode* findVertex(string vertexName);
        void deleteFromEdgeLists(string vertexName);
        void deleteFromVertexList(string vertexName);
public:
        DirectedGraphList();
        ~DirectedGraphList();
        void insertVertex(string vertexName);
        void insertEdge(string source, string destination);
        void deleteVertex(string vertexName);
        void deleteEdge(string source, string destination);
        void display();
        bool edgeExists(string source, string destination);
        int getOutdegree(string vertex);
        int getIndegree(string vertex);
};//End of class DirectedGraphList
```

7.10.2.1 Vertex Insertion

Insertion of a vertex in an adjacency list only requires insertion of that vertex in the linked list of vertices. The new vertex is unconnected, i.e., it has no edges. Edges to this new vertex have to be inserted separately. Let us insert a vertex 4 in the graph of figure 7.29 so that we have the following new graph:

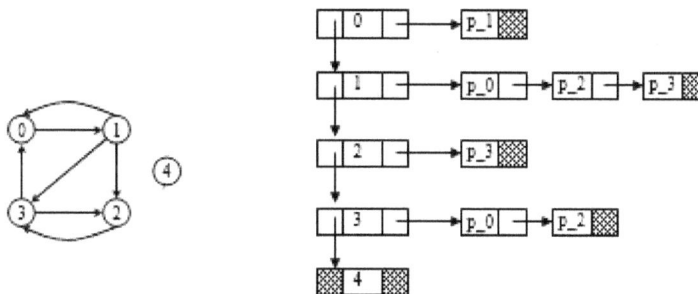

Figure 7.31 Insertion of a vertex

7.10.2.2 Edge Insertion

Insertion of an edge requires an insertion operation in the list of the starting vertex of the edge. Suppose we want to add an edge (2, 0) in the graph of figure 7.29. For this, we have to add a node in the edge list of vertex 2, and this new node will contain a pointer to vertex 0.

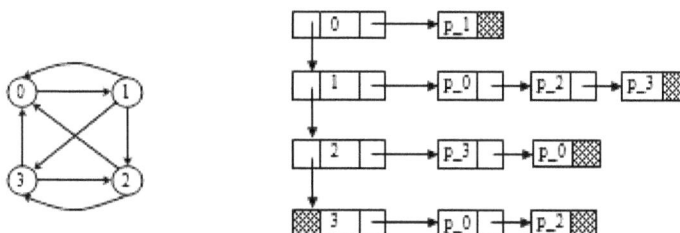

Figure 7.32 Insertion of an edge

This was the procedure for edge insertion in a directed graph. In an undirected graph, the insertion operation has to be done in the lists of both the start and the end vertices of the edge.

7.10.2.3 Edge Deletion

Deletion of an edge requires the deletion operation in the list of the starting vertex of edge. Suppose we want to delete the edge (1,2) from the graph of figure 7.29. For this, deletion will be performed in the list of vertex 1, and the node that will be deleted is the node that contains a pointer to vertex 2.

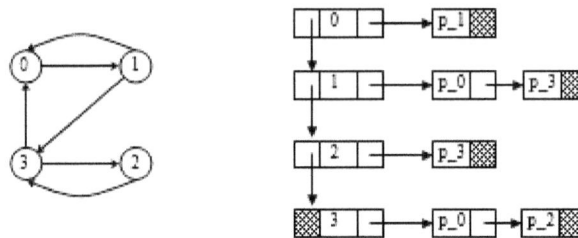

Figure 7.33 Deletion of an edge

In an undirected graph, the deletion operation has to be performed in lists of both start and end vertices of the edge.

7.10.2.4 Vertex Deletion

Deletion of a vertex requires deletion of that particular vertex from the linked list of vertices. Before deleting the vertex, it is necessary to delete all its incoming and outgoing edges.

Suppose we want to delete the vertex 2 from the graph of figure 7.29. Then, first we will delete all edges where vertex 2 is the end node. For this, we have to search the edge lists of all the vertices. The pointer to vertex 2 is found in the adjacency lists of vertices 1 and 3. So, it is deleted from there and hence, the edges (1,2) and (3,2) are deleted from the graph. After this, the adjacency list of vertex 2 is deleted, which removes all edges where vertex 2 is the start node. In the graph of figure 7.29, there is only one node in the adjacency list of vertex 2, and so, it is deleted and after that, vertex 2 is deleted from the linked list of vertices.

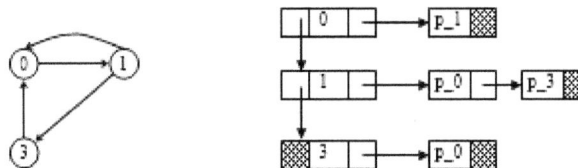

Figure 7.34 Deletion of a vertex

Here is the complete program of the directed graph using adjacency list:

```
//DirectedGraphList.cpp : Program for directed graph using adjacency list.
#include<iostream>
#include<string>
using namespace std;
class VertexNode;
class EdgeNode;
```

```
class VertexNode
{
      public:
              string name;
              VertexNode *nextVertex;
              EdgeNode *firstEdge;
      public:
              VertexNode(string name)
              {
                      this->name = name;
                      nextVertex = NULL;
                      firstEdge = NULL;
              }
};//End of class VertexNode
class EdgeNode
{
      public:
              VertexNode *endVertex;
              EdgeNode *nextEdge;
      public:
              EdgeNode(VertexNode *v)
              {
                      this->endVertex = v;
                      nextEdge = NULL;
              }
};//End of class EdgeNode
class DirectedGraphList
{
      private:
              int nVertices;
              int nEdges;
      public:
              VertexNode *start;
      private:
              VertexNode* findVertex(string vertexName);
              void deleteFromEdgeLists(string vertexName);
              void deleteFromVertexList(string vertexName);
      public:
              DirectedGraphList();
              ~DirectedGraphList();
              void insertVertex(string vertexName);
              void insertEdge(string source, string destination);
              void deleteVertex(string vertexName);
              void deleteEdge(string source, string destination);
              void display();
              bool edgeExists(string source, string destination);
              int getOutdegree(string vertex);
              int getIndegree(string vertex);
};//End of class DirectedGraphList
DirectedGraphList::DirectedGraphList()
{
      nVertices = 0;
      nEdges = 0;
      start = NULL;
}//End of DirectedGraphList()
DirectedGraphList::~DirectedGraphList()
{
      VertexNode *vertexPtr, *tempVertex;
      EdgeNode *edgePtr, *tempEdge;
```

```cpp
            vertexPtr = start;
            while(vertexPtr != NULL)
            {
                    edgePtr = vertexPtr->firstEdge;
                    while(edgePtr != NULL)
                    {
                            tempEdge = edgePtr;
                            edgePtr = edgePtr->nextEdge;
                            delete tempEdge;
                    }
                    tempVertex = vertexPtr;
                    vertexPtr = vertexPtr->nextVertex;
                    delete tempVertex;
            }
}//End of ~DirectedGraphList()
void DirectedGraphList::insertVertex(string vertexName)
{
        VertexNode *ptr, *temp;
        bool vertexFound = false;
        ptr = start;
        if(ptr == NULL)
        {
                temp = new VertexNode(vertexName);
                start = temp;
                nVertices++;
        }
        else
        {
                while(ptr->nextVertex != NULL)
                {
                        if(ptr->name == vertexName)
                        {
                                vertexFound = true;
                                break;
                        }
                        ptr = ptr->nextVertex;
                }//End of while
                if(vertexFound || ptr->name == vertexName)
                {
                        cout << "Vertex already present\n";
                }
                else
                {
                        temp = new VertexNode(vertexName);
                        ptr->nextVertex = temp;
                        nVertices++;
                }
        }//End of else
}//End of insertVertex()
VertexNode* DirectedGraphList::findVertex(string vertexName)
{
        VertexNode *ptr = start;
        while(ptr != NULL)
        {
                if(ptr->name == vertexName)
                        break;
                ptr = ptr->nextVertex;
        }
        return ptr;
}//End of findVertex()
```

```
void DirectedGraphList::insertEdge(string source, string destination)
{
        VertexNode *u, *v;
        EdgeNode *edgePtr, *temp;
        bool edgeFound = false;
        if(source == destination)
        {
                cout << "Invalid Edge : source and destination vertices are same\n";
        }
        else
        {
                u = findVertex(source);
                v = findVertex(destination);
                if(u == NULL)
                {
                        cout << "Source vertex not present, first insert vertex " <<
                        source << "\n";
                }
                else if(v == NULL)
                {
                        cout << "Destination vertex not present, first insert vertex "
                        << destination << "\n";
                }
                else
                {
                        if(u->firstEdge == NULL)
                        {
                                temp = new EdgeNode(v);
                                u->firstEdge = temp;
                                nEdges++;
                        }
                        else
                        {
                                edgePtr = u->firstEdge;
                                while(edgePtr->nextEdge != NULL)
                                {
                                        if(edgePtr->endVertex->name == v->name)
                                        {
                                                edgeFound = true;
                                                break;
                                        }
                                        edgePtr = edgePtr->nextEdge;
                                }//End of while
                                if(edgeFound || edgePtr->endVertex->name == destination)
                                {
                                        cout << "Edge already present\n";
                                }
                                else
                                {
                                        temp = new EdgeNode(v);
                                        edgePtr->nextEdge = temp;
                                        nEdges++;
                                }
                        }//End of else
                }//End of else
        }//End of else
}//End of insertEdge()

void DirectedGraphList::deleteVertex(string vertexName)
{
```

```
                deleteFromEdgeLists(vertexName);
                deleteFromVertexList(vertexName);
}//End of deleteVertex()

//Delete incoming edges
void DirectedGraphList::deleteFromEdgeLists(string vertexName)
{
        VertexNode *vertexPtr;
        EdgeNode *edgePtr, *temp;
        vertexPtr = start;
        while(vertexPtr != NULL)
        {
                if(vertexPtr->firstEdge != NULL)
                {
                        if(vertexPtr->firstEdge->endVertex->name == vertexName)
                        {
                                temp = vertexPtr->firstEdge;
                                vertexPtr->firstEdge = vertexPtr->firstEdge->nextEdge;
                                delete temp;
                                nEdges--;
                                continue;
                        }
                        edgePtr = vertexPtr->firstEdge;
                        while(edgePtr->nextEdge != NULL)
                        {
                                if(edgePtr->nextEdge->endVertex->name == vertexName)
                                {
                                        temp = edgePtr->nextEdge;
                                        edgePtr->nextEdge = edgePtr->nextEdge->nextEdge;
                                        delete temp;
                                        nEdges--;
                                        continue;
                                }
                                edgePtr = edgePtr->nextEdge;
                        }
                }//End of if
                vertexPtr = vertexPtr->nextVertex;
        }//End of while
}//End of deleteFromEdgeLists()

//Delete outgoing edges and vertex
void DirectedGraphList::deleteFromVertexList(string vertexName)
{
        VertexNode *vertexPtr, *tempVertex=NULL;
        EdgeNode *edgePtr, *tempEdge;
        if(start == NULL)
        {
                cout << "No vertices to be deleted\n";
                return;
        }
        if(start->name == vertexName)
        {
                tempVertex = start;
                start = start->nextVertex;
        }
        else    //vertex to be deleted is in between or at last
        {
                vertexPtr = start;
                while(vertexPtr->nextVertex != NULL)
                {
                        if(vertexPtr->nextVertex->name == vertexName)
                                break;
```

```
                              vertexPtr = vertexPtr->nextVertex;
                       }
                       if(vertexPtr->nextVertex != NULL)
                       {
                              tempVertex = vertexPtr->nextVertex;
                              vertexPtr->nextVertex = vertexPtr->nextVertex->nextVertex;
                       }
                       else
                       {
                              cout << "Vertex not found\n";
                       }
               }//End of else
               if(tempVertex)
               {
                       //Before deleting the tempVertex, delete all the edges going from this
                       //vertex
                       edgePtr = tempVertex->firstEdge;
                       while(edgePtr != NULL)
                       {
                              tempEdge = edgePtr;
                              edgePtr = edgePtr->nextEdge;
                              delete tempEdge;
                              nEdges--;
                       }
                       delete tempVertex;
                       nVertices--;
               }
}//End of deleteFromVertexList()
void DirectedGraphList::deleteEdge(string source, string destination)
{
       VertexNode *vertexPtr;
       EdgeNode *edgePtr, *temp;
       vertexPtr = findVertex(source);
       if(vertexPtr == NULL)
       {
               cout << "Edge not found\n";
       }
       else
       {
               edgePtr = vertexPtr->firstEdge;
               if(edgePtr == NULL)
               {
                       cout << "Edge not found\n";
               }
               else
               {
                       if(edgePtr->endVertex->name == destination)
                       {
                              vertexPtr->firstEdge = edgePtr->nextEdge;
                              delete edgePtr;
                              nEdges--;
                       }
                       else
                       {
                              while(edgePtr->nextEdge != NULL)
                              {
                                      if(edgePtr->nextEdge->endVertex->name ==
                                      destination)
                                      {
                                             break;
```

```
                                             }
                                             edgePtr = edgePtr->nextEdge;
                                     }
                                     if(edgePtr->nextEdge == NULL)
                                     {
                                             cout << "Edge not found\n";
                                     }
                                     else
                                     {
                                             temp = edgePtr->nextEdge;
                                             edgePtr->nextEdge = edgePtr->nextEdge->nextEdge;
                                             delete temp;
                                             nEdges--;
                                     }
                             }//End of else
                     }//End of else
             }//End of else
}//End of deleteEdge()
void DirectedGraphList::display()
{
        VertexNode *vertexPtr;
        EdgeNode *edgePtr;
        vertexPtr = start;
        while(vertexPtr != NULL)
        {
                cout << "Vertex : " << vertexPtr->name << "\n";
                edgePtr = vertexPtr->firstEdge;
                while(edgePtr != NULL)
                {
                        cout << "Edge : " << vertexPtr->name << " -> "
                             << edgePtr->endVertex->name << "\n";
                        edgePtr = edgePtr->nextEdge;
                }
                vertexPtr = vertexPtr->nextVertex;
        }
}//End of display()
bool DirectedGraphList::edgeExists(string source, string destination)
{
        VertexNode *vertexPtr;
        EdgeNode *edgePtr;
        bool edgeFound = false;
        vertexPtr = findVertex(source);
        if(vertexPtr)
        {
                edgePtr = vertexPtr->firstEdge;
                while(edgePtr != NULL)
                {
                        if(edgePtr->endVertex->name == destination)
                        {
                                edgeFound = true;
                                break;
                        }
                        edgePtr = edgePtr->nextEdge;
                }
        }
        return edgeFound;
}//End of edgeExists()
int DirectedGraphList::getOutdegree(string vertex)
{
        VertexNode *vertexPtr;
```

```
        EdgeNode *edgePtr;
        int outdegree = 0;
        vertexPtr = findVertex(vertex);
        if(vertexPtr == NULL)
                throw exception("Invalid Vertex");
        edgePtr = vertexPtr->firstEdge;
        while(edgePtr != NULL)
        {
                outdegree++;
                edgePtr = edgePtr->nextEdge;
        }
        return outdegree;
}//End of getOutdegree()
int DirectedGraphList::getIndegree(string vertex)
{
        VertexNode *vertexPtr;
        EdgeNode *edgePtr;
        int indegree = 0;
        if(findVertex(vertex) == NULL)
                throw exception("Invalid Vertex");
        vertexPtr = start;
        while(vertexPtr != NULL)
        {
                edgePtr = vertexPtr->firstEdge;
                while(edgePtr != NULL)
                {
                        if(edgePtr->endVertex->name == vertex)
                        {
                                indegree++;
                        }
                        edgePtr = edgePtr->nextEdge;
                }
                vertexPtr = vertexPtr->nextVertex;
        }
        return indegree;
}//End of getIndegree()
int main()
{
        DirectedGraphList dGraph;
        try
        {
                //Creating the graph, inserting the vertices and edges
                dGraph.insertVertex("0");
                dGraph.insertVertex("1");
                dGraph.insertVertex("2");
                dGraph.insertVertex("3");
                dGraph.insertEdge("0","3");
                dGraph.insertEdge("1","2");
                dGraph.insertEdge("2","3");
                dGraph.insertEdge("3","1");
                dGraph.insertEdge("0","2");
                //Display the graph
                dGraph.display();
                cout << "\n";

                //Deleting an edge
                dGraph.deleteEdge("0","2");
                //Display the graph
                dGraph.display();
                cout << "\n";
```

```
            //Deleting a vertex
            dGraph.deleteVertex("0");
            //Display the graph
            dGraph.display();

            //Check if there is an edge between two vertices
            cout << "Edge exist : " << (dGraph.edgeExists("2","3") ? "True" : "False")
            << "\n";
            //Display Outdegree and Indegree of a vertex
            cout << "Outdegree : " << dGraph.getOutdegree("3") << "\n";
            cout << "Indegree : " << dGraph.getIndegree("3") << "\n";
      }//End of try
      catch(exception e)
      {
            cout << e.what() << "\n";
      }
      return 0;
}//End of main()
```

7.11 Transitive Closure of a Directed Graph and Path Matrix

The transitive closure of a graph G is a graph G′, where G′ contains the same set of vertices as G and whenever there is a path from any vertex i to vertex j in G, there is an edge from i to j in G′.

The path matrix or reachability matrix of a graph G with n vertices is an n x n boolean matrix, whose elements can be defined as:

$$P[i][j] = \begin{cases} 1 & \text{if there is a path from vertex } i \text{ to vertex } j \\ 0 & \text{Otherwise.} \end{cases}$$

Figure 7.35 Path matrix definition

Thus, the path matrix of a graph G is actually the adjacency matrix of its transitive closure G′. The path matrix of a graph is also known as the transitive closure matrix of the graph.

We will now study two methods to compute the path matrix. The first method is by using powers of the adjacency matrix, and the second one is Warshall's algorithm. Here are some inferences that we can draw by looking at the path matrix:

(i) If the element P[i][j] is equal to 1,
    There is a path from vertex i to vertex j
(ii) If any main diagonal element, i.e., any element P[i][i] in the path matrix is 1,
    Graph contains a cycle
(iii) If all the elements in the path matrix are 1,
    Graph is strongly connected

7.11.1 Computing Path Matrix from Powers of Adjacency Matrix

Let us take a graph and compute the path matrix for it from its adjacency matrix:

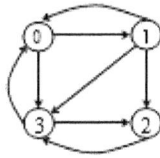

The graph and its adjacency matrix:

$$\text{Adjacency Matrix A} = \begin{array}{c} \\ 0 \\ 1 \\ 2 \\ 3 \end{array} \begin{array}{cccc} 0 & 1 & 2 & 3 \\ \left[\begin{array}{cccc} 0 & 1 & 0 & 1 \\ 1 & 0 & 1 & 1 \\ 0 & 0 & 0 & 1 \\ 1 & 0 & 1 & 0 \end{array}\right] \end{array}$$

Figure 7.36 Adjacency matrix (A) for finding path matrix

Now we compute the matrix AM_2 by multiplying the adjacency matrix A with itself:

$$AM_2 = A^2 = \begin{array}{c} \\ 0 \\ 1 \\ 2 \\ 3 \end{array} \begin{array}{cccc} 0 & 1 & 2 & 3 \\ \left[\begin{array}{cccc} 2 & 0 & 2 & 1 \\ 1 & 1 & 1 & 2 \\ 1 & 0 & 1 & 0 \\ 0 & 1 & 0 & 2 \end{array}\right] \end{array}$$

Figure 7.37 Matrix A^2

In this matrix, the value of $AM_2[i][j]$ will represent the number of paths of path length 2 from vertex i to vertex j. For example, vertex 0 has two paths of path length 2 to vertex 2, and vertex 3 has two paths of path length 2 to itself. Vertex 2 has one path of path length 2 to vertex 0, and there is no path of path length 2 from vertex 2 to vertex 1. These paths may not be simple paths, i.e., all vertices in these paths need not be distinct. Now, we compute the matrix AM_3 by multiplying the adjacency matrix A with AM_2.

$$AM_3 = AM_2*A = A^3 = \begin{array}{c} \\ 0 \\ 1 \\ 2 \\ 3 \end{array} \begin{array}{cccc} 0 & 1 & 2 & 3 \\ \left[\begin{array}{cccc} 1 & 2 & 1 & 4 \\ 3 & 1 & 3 & 3 \\ 0 & 1 & 0 & 2 \\ 3 & 0 & 3 & 1 \end{array}\right] \end{array}$$

Figure 7.38 Matrix A^3

Here, $AM_3[i][j]$ will represent the number of paths of path length 3 from vertex i to vertex j. For example, vertex 0 has 4 paths of path length 3 to vertex 3 (paths 0-3-2-3, 0-3-0-3, 0-1-2-3, 0-1-0-3), and vertex 3 has no path of path length 3 to vertex 1. Similarly, we can find out the matrix AM_4:

$$AM_4 = AM_3*A = A^4 = \begin{array}{c} \\ 0 \\ 1 \\ 2 \\ 3 \end{array} \begin{array}{cccc} 0 & 1 & 2 & 3 \\ \left[\begin{array}{cccc} 6 & 1 & 6 & 4 \\ 4 & 3 & 4 & 7 \\ 3 & 0 & 3 & 1 \\ 1 & 3 & 1 & 6 \end{array}\right] \end{array}$$

Figure 7.39 Matrix A^4

In general, we can say that if AM_k is equal to A^k, then any element $AM_k[i][j]$ represents the number of paths of path length k from vertex i to vertex j.

Let us define a matrix X where:

$$X = AM_1 + AM_2 + \ldots\ldots\ldots\ldots\ldots + AM_n$$

X[i][j] denotes the number of paths, of path length n or less than n, from vertex i to vertex j. Here, n is the total number of vertices in the graph.

For the graph in figure 7.36, the value of X will be:

$$
X = \begin{array}{c} \\ 0 \\ 1 \\ 2 \\ 3 \end{array}
\begin{array}{cccc} 0 & 1 & 2 & 3 \\ \end{array}
\left[\begin{array}{cccc}
9 & 4 & 9 & 10 \\
9 & 5 & 9 & 13 \\
4 & 1 & 4 & 4 \\
5 & 4 & 5 & 9
\end{array} \right]
$$

Figure 7.40 Matrix X

From the definition of path matrix, we know that P[i][j]=1 if there is a path from i to j, and this path can have length n or less than n. Now in the matrix X, if we replace all nonzero entries by 1, then we will get the path matrix or reachability matrix.

$$
\begin{array}{c} \\ 0 \\ 1 \\ 2 \\ 3 \end{array}
\begin{array}{cccc} 0 & 1 & 2 & 3 \\ \end{array}
\left[\begin{array}{cccc}
1 & 1 & 1 & 1 \\
1 & 1 & 1 & 1 \\
1 & 1 & 1 & 1 \\
1 & 1 & 1 & 1
\end{array} \right]
$$

Figure 7.41 Path matrix of graph

This graph is strongly connected since all the entries are equal to 1.

```cpp
//DirectedGraph.cpp : Program to find out the path matrix by powers of adjacency matrix.
#include<iostream>
#include<string>
using namespace std;

static const int maxSize = 30;

class Vertex
{
        public:
                string name;
        public:
                Vertex(string name)
                {
                        this->name = name;
                }
};//End of class Vertex

class DirectedGraph
{
        private:
                int nVertices;
                int nEdges;
                int adj[maxSize][maxSize];
                Vertex *vertexList[maxSize];
        private:
                int getIndex(string vertexName);
        public:
                DirectedGraph();
                ~DirectedGraph();
```

```cpp
        void insertVertex(string vertexName);
        void insertEdge(string source, string destination);
        void display();
        void pathMatrix();
};//End of class DirectedGraph
void DirectedGraph::pathMatrix()
{
        int adjp[maxSize][maxSize], x[maxSize][maxSize], temp[maxSize][maxSize];
        int path[maxSize][maxSize];
        //Initialize x
        for(int i=0; i<nVertices; i++)
        {
                for(int j=0; j<nVertices; j++)
                {
                        x[i][j] = 0;
                }
        }
        //Initially adjp and x is equal to adj
        for(int i=0; i<nVertices; i++)
        {
                for(int j=0; j<nVertices; j++)
                {
                        x[i][j] = adjp[i][j] = adj[i][j];
                }
        }
        //Get the matrix x by adding all the adjp
        for(int p=2; p<=nVertices; p++)
        {
                //adjp(1...n) x adj
                for(int i=0; i<nVertices; i++)
                {
                        for(int j=0; j<nVertices; j++)
                        {
                                temp[i][j]=0;
                                for(int k=0; k<nVertices; k++)
                                {
                                        temp[i][j] = temp[i][j] + adjp[i][k]*adj[k][j];
                                }
                        }
                }
                //Now adjp will be equal to temp
                for(int i=0; i<nVertices; i++)
                {
                        for(int j=0; j<nVertices; j++)
                        {
                                adjp[i][j] = temp[i][j];
                        }
                }
                //x = adjp1 + adjp2 + ...... + adjpn
                for(int i=0; i<nVertices; i++)
                {
                        for(int j=0; j<nVertices; j++)
                        {
                                x[i][j] = x[i][j] + adjp[i][j];
                        }
                }
        }//End of for
        //Display x
        cout << "x matrix is :\n";
        for(int i=0; i<nVertices; i++)
```

```
        {
                for(int j=0; j<nVertices; j++)
                {
                        cout << x[i][j] << " ";
                }
                cout <<"\n";
        }
        //Assign values to path matrix
        for(int i=0; i<nVertices; i++)
        {
                for(int j=0; j<nVertices; j++)
                {
                        if(x[i][j] == 0)
                                path[i][j] = 0;
                        else
                                path[i][j] = 1;
                }
        }
        //Display path matrix
        cout << "Path matrix is :\n";
        for(int i=0; i<nVertices; i++)
        {
                for(int j=0; j<nVertices; j++)
                        cout << path[i][j] << " ";
                cout <<"\n";
        }
}//End of pathMatrix()

int main()
{
        DirectedGraph dGraph;
        try
        {
                //Creating the graph, inserting the vertices and edges
                dGraph.insertVertex("0");
                dGraph.insertVertex("1");
                dGraph.insertVertex("2");
                dGraph.insertVertex("3");
                dGraph.insertEdge("0","1");
                dGraph.insertEdge("0","3");
                dGraph.insertEdge("1","0");
                dGraph.insertEdge("1","2");
                dGraph.insertEdge("1","3");
                dGraph.insertEdge("2","3");
                dGraph.insertEdge("3","0");
                dGraph.insertEdge("3","2");
                //Display the graph
                dGraph.display();
                cout << "\n";

                cout << "Find the path matrix :\n";
                dGraph.pathMatrix();
        }//End of try
        catch(exception e)
        {
                cout << e.what() << "\n";
        }
        return 0;
}//End of main()
```

The constructor, destructor, `insertVertex()`, `getIndex()`, `insertEdge()`, and `display()` functions are the same as in the directed graph program.

7.11.2 Warshall's Algorithm

We have seen that we can find the path matrix P of a given graph G by using powers of the adjacency matrix. Warshall gave an efficient technique for finding the path matrix of a graph known as Warshall's algorithm. Let us take a graph G of n vertices 0, 1, 2,...........n-1. We will define the Boolean matrices P_{-1}, P_0, P_1, ... P_{n-1} where $P_k[i][j]$ is defined as:

$$P_k[i][j] = \begin{cases} 1 & \text{If there is a simple path from vertex i to vertex j which does not use any intermediate vertex greater than k, i.e. all intermediate vertices belong to the set } \{0,1,......k\} \\ 0 & \text{Otherwise} \end{cases}$$

Figure 7.42 $P_k[i][j]$ definition

$P_{-1}[i][j] = 1$ If there is a simple path from vertex i to vertex j, which does not use any intermediate vertex.

$P_0[i][j] = 1$ If there is a simple path from vertex i to vertex j, which does not use any other intermediate vertex except possibly vertex 0.

$P_1[i][j] = 1$ If there is a simple path from vertex i to vertex j, which does not use any other intermediate vertex except possibly 0,1.

$P_2[i][j] = 1$ If there is a simple path from vertex i to vertex j which does not use any other intermediate vertices except possibly vertices 0,1,2.

....
....

$P_k[i][j] = 1$ If there is a simple path from vertex i to vertex j which does not use any other intermediate vertices except possibly 0,1,.......k.

....
....

$P_{n-1}[i][j] = 1$ If there is a simple path from vertex i to vertex j which does not use any other intermediate vertices except possibly 0, 1, ...n-1.

Here P_{-1} represents the adjacency matrix and P_{n-1} represents the path matrix. Let us see why.

$P_{-1}[i][j]=1$, If there is a simple path from vertex i to vertex j, which does not use any vertex. The only way to go from i to j without using any vertex is to go directly from i to j. Hence: $P_{-1}[i][j]=1$ means that there is an edge from i to j. So P_{-1} will be the adjacency matrix.

$P_{n-1}[i][j]=1$, If there is a simple path from i to j which does not use any vertices except 0, 1,...n-1. There are total n vertices, which means that this path can use all n vertices; hence, from the definition of path matrix, we observe that P_{n-1} is the path matrix.

We know that P_{-1} is equal to the adjacency matrix, which we can easily find out from the graph. We have to find matrices P_0, P_1, ... P_{n-1}. If we know how to find matrix P_k from matrix P_{k-1}, then we can find all these matrices. So now let us see how to find the value of $P_k[i][j]$ by looking at the matrix P_{k-1}.

If $P_{k-1}[i][j]$ is 1, $P_k[i][j]$ will also be 1. Let us see why.

$P_{k-1}[i][j]=1$, implies that there is a simple path (say P1) from i to j, which does not use any vertices except possibly 0, 1, ...k-1 or we can say that this path does not use any vertices numbered higher than k-1. So it is obvious that this path does not use any vertices numbered higher than k also, or we can say that this path does not use any other vertices except possibly 0, 1, ... k. So $P_k[i][j]$ will be equal to 1.

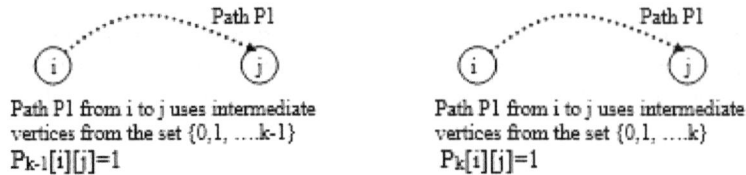

Path P1 from i to j uses intermediate vertices from the set {0,1, ...k-1}
$P_{k-1}[i][j]=1$

Path P1 from i to j uses intermediate vertices from the set {0,1, ...k}
$P_k[i][j]=1$

Figure 7.43 Finding $P_{k-1}[i][j]$ and $P_k[i][j]$ values

Now, we will consider the case when $P_{k-1}[i][j] = 0$. In this case, $P_k[i][j]$ can be 0 or it can be 1. Let us find out the condition in which $P_k[i][j]$ will be 1 when $P_{k-1}[i][j]$ is 0.

$P_{k-1}[i][j]$ is 0, meaning there is no path from i to j using intermediate vertices 0,1, ...,k-1.
$P_k[i][j]$ is 1, means there is a path from i to j using intermediate vertices 0,1,.....k.

This means that when we use only vertices 0,1,.....,k-1, we have no path from i to j, but when we use vertices 0,1,.....,k we get a path (say P2) from i to j. This path P2 will definitely pass through vertex k so that we can break it into two subpaths:
(i) Path P2a from i to k using vertices 0,1,.......k-1.
(ii) Path P2b from k to j using vertices 0,1,.......k-1.

Since we have taken out k and the path P2 is simple (k cannot be repeated), the paths P2a and P2b will have intermediate vertices from the set {0,1,2.....k-1}.
From path P2a, we can write that $P_{k-1}[i][k]=1$
From path P2b, we can write that $P_{k-1}[k][j]=1$

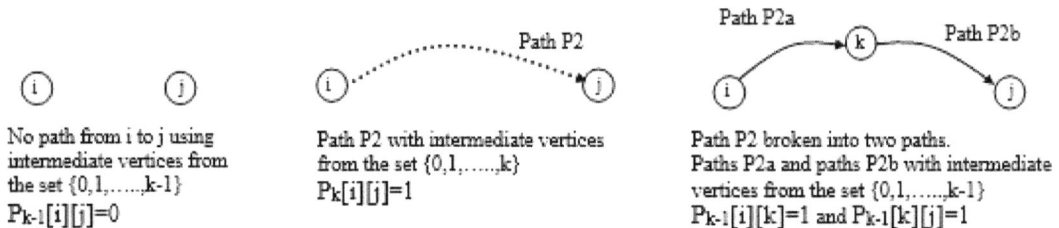

No path from i to j using intermediate vertices from the set {0,1,.....,k-1}
$P_{k-1}[i][j]=0$

Path P2 with intermediate vertices from the set {0,1,.....,k}
$P_k[i][j]=1$

Path P2 broken into two paths.
Paths P2a and paths P2b with intermediate vertices from the set {0,1,.....,k-1}
$P_{k-1}[i][k]=1$ and $P_{k-1}[k][j]=1$

Figure 7.44 Finding path matrix values

For existence of path P2, the paths P2a and P2b should exist, i.e., for $P_k[i][j]$ to be 1 when $P_{k-1}[i][j]$ is zero, the values of $P_{k-1}[i][k]$ and $P_{k-1}[k][j]$ should be 1.

We can conclude that if $P_{k-1}[i][j]=0$, then $P_k[i][j]$ can be equal to 1 only
if $P_{k-1}[i][k]=1$ and $P_{k-1}[k][j]=1$.

So we have two situations when $P_k[i][j]$ can be 1:
1. $P_{k-1}[i][j] = 1$ or
2. $P_{k-1}[i][k] = 1$ and $P_{k-1}[k][j] = 1$

To find any element $P_k[i][j]$ we will proceed as:

First see $P_{k-1}[i][j]$. If it is equal to 1, then $P_k[i][j] = 1$, done
If $P_{k-1}[i][j] = 0$, then see $P_{k-1}[i][k]$ and $P_{k-1}[k][j]$. If both are 1, then $P_k[i][j] = 1$, done
Otherwise $P_k[i][j] = 0$

Let us take the same graph as in figure 7.36 and find out the values of P_{-1}, P_0, P_1, P_2, P_3.

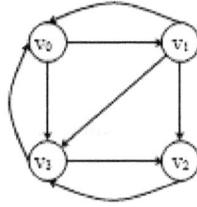

Figure 7.45 Graph example for finding path matrix

The first matrix P_{-1} is the adjacency matrix:

$$
P_{-1} = \begin{array}{c} \\ 0 \\ 1 \\ 2 \\ 3 \end{array}
\begin{array}{cccc}
0 & 1 & 2 & 3 \\
\left[\begin{array}{cccc}
0 & 1 & 0 & 1 \\
1 & 0 & 1 & 1 \\
0 & 0 & 0 & 1 \\
1 & 0 & 1 & 0
\end{array}\right]
\end{array}
$$

Figure 7.46 Matrix P_{-1}

Now we have to find the matrix P_0.

To find any element $P_0[i][j]$, we will proceed as:

First, see $P_{-1}[i][j]$. If it is equal to 1, then $P_0[i][j] = 1$
Otherwise, if $P_{-1}[i][j] = 0$, then see $P_{-1}[i][0]$ and $P_{-1}[0][j]$. If both are 1, then $P_0[i][j] = 1$
Otherwise, $P_0[i][j] = 0$.

Calculation of some elements of matrix P_0:

* Find $P_0[2][3]$
  $P_{-1}[2][3] = 1$ so $P_0[2][3] = 1$

* Find $P_0[3][1]$
  $P_{-1}[3][1] = 0$, so look at $P_{-1}[3][0]$ and $P_{-1}[0][1]$, both are 1; hence, $P_0[3][1] = 1$

* Find $P_0[2][1]$
  $P_{-1}[2][1] = 0$, so look at $P_{-1}[2][0]$ and $P_{-1}[0][1]$, one of them is 0; hence, $P_0[2][1] = 0$

* Find $P_0[2][2]$
  $P_{-1}[2][2] = 0$, so look at $P_{-1}[2][0]$ and $P_{-1}[0][2]$, both are 0; hence, $P_0[2][2] = 0$

It is clear that if an entry is 1 in matrix P_{-1}, then it will also be 1 in P_0. So we can just copy all the 1s and see if the zero entries of P_{-1} can be changed to 1 in P_0. Changing a zero entry to 1 implies we get a path if we use 0 as the intermediate vertex.

$$
P_0 = \begin{array}{c} \\ 0 \\ 1 \\ 2 \\ 3 \end{array}
\begin{array}{cccc}
0 & 1 & 2 & 3 \\
\left[\begin{array}{cccc}
0 & 1 & 0 & 1 \\
1 & 1 & 1 & 1 \\
0 & 0 & 0 & 1 \\
1 & 1 & 1 & 1
\end{array}\right]
\end{array}
$$

Figure 7.47 Matrix P_0

Now we have to find matrix P_1:
* Find $P_1[0][2]$
  $P_0[0][2] = 0$, so look at $P_0[0][1]$ and $P_0[1][2]$, both are 1; hence $P_1[0][2] = 1$
* Find $P_1[2][1]$
  $P_0[2][1] = 0$, so look at $P_0[2][1]$ and $P_0[1][1]$, one of them is zero; hence $P_1[2][1] = 0$

$$P_1 = \begin{array}{c c} & \begin{array}{cccc} 0 & 1 & 2 & 3 \end{array} \\ \begin{array}{c} 0 \\ 1 \\ 2 \\ 3 \end{array} & \left[\begin{array}{cccc} 1 & 1 & 1 & 1 \\ 1 & 1 & 1 & 1 \\ 0 & 0 & 0 & 1 \\ 1 & 1 & 1 & 1 \end{array} \right] \end{array}$$

Figure 7.48 Matrix P_1

* Find $P_2[2][1]$
  $P_1[2][1] = 0$, so look at $P_1[2][2]$ and $P_1[2][1]$, both are zero; hence $P_2[2][1] = 0$

$$P_2 = \begin{array}{c c} & \begin{array}{cccc} 0 & 1 & 2 & 3 \end{array} \\ \begin{array}{c} 0 \\ 1 \\ 2 \\ 3 \end{array} & \left[\begin{array}{cccc} 1 & 1 & 1 & 1 \\ 1 & 1 & 1 & 1 \\ 0 & 0 & 0 & 1 \\ 1 & 1 & 1 & 1 \end{array} \right] \end{array}$$

Figure 7.49 Matrix P_2

$$\text{And} \qquad P_3 = \begin{array}{c c} & \begin{array}{cccc} 0 & 1 & 2 & 3 \end{array} \\ \begin{array}{c} 0 \\ 1 \\ 2 \\ 3 \end{array} & \left[\begin{array}{cccc} 1 & 1 & 1 & 1 \\ 1 & 1 & 1 & 1 \\ 1 & 1 & 1 & 1 \\ 1 & 1 & 1 & 1 \end{array} \right] \end{array}$$

Figure 7.50 Matrix P_3

Here, P_{-1} is the adjacency matrix, and P_3 is the path matrix of the graph. In the program, all the calculation can be done in place using a single two-dimensional array P.

```cpp
//DirectedGraph.cpp : Program to find out the path matrix using warshall's algorithm.
#include<iostream>
#include<string>
using namespace std;

static const int maxSize = 30;

class Vertex
{
      public:
              string name;
      public:
              Vertex(string name)
              {
                      this->name = name;
              }
};//End of class Vertex
```

```
class DirectedGraph
{
        private:
                int nVertices;
                int nEdges;
                int adj[maxSize][maxSize];
                Vertex *vertexList[maxSize];
        private:
                int getIndex(string vertexName);
        public:
                DirectedGraph();
                ~DirectedGraph();
                void insertVertex(string vertexName);
                void insertEdge(string source, string destination);
                void display();
                void warshallsAlgorithm();
};//End of class DirectedGraph
void DirectedGraph::warshallsAlgorithm()
{
        int P[maxSize][maxSize];

        //Initializing P_-1
        for(int i=0; i<nVertices; i++)
        {
                for(int j=0; j<nVertices; j++)
                {
                        P[i][j] = adj[i][j];
                }
        }

        //P_0,P_1......P_n-1
        for(int k=0; k<nVertices; k++)
        {
                for(int i=0; i<nVertices; i++)
                {
                        for(int j=0; j<nVertices; j++)
                        {
                                P[i][j] = (P[i][j] || (P[i][k] && P[k][j]));
                        }
                }
                //Display P
                cout << "P" << k << " :\n";
                for(int i=0; i<nVertices; i++)
                {
                        for(int j=0; j<nVertices; j++)
                                cout << P[i][j] << " ";
                        cout <<"\n";
                }
        }//End of for
}//End of warshallsAlgorithm()
int main()
{
        DirectedGraph dGraph;
        try
        {
                //Creating the graph, inserting the vertices and edges
                dGraph.insertVertex("0");
                dGraph.insertVertex("1");
                dGraph.insertVertex("2");
                dGraph.insertVertex("3");
                dGraph.insertEdge("0","1");
```

```
                dGraph.insertEdge("0","3");
                dGraph.insertEdge("1","0");
                dGraph.insertEdge("1","2");
                dGraph.insertEdge("1","3");
                dGraph.insertEdge("2","3");
                dGraph.insertEdge("3","0");
                dGraph.insertEdge("3","2");
                //Display the graph
                dGraph.display();
                cout << "\n";

                cout << "Find the path matrix :\n";
                dGraph.warshallsAlgorithm();
        }//End of try
        catch(exception e)       .
        {
                cout << e.what() << "\n";
        }
        return 0;
}//End of main()
```

The constructor, destructor, `insertVertex()`, `getIndex()`, `insertEdge()`, `display()` functions are the same as in the directed graph program.

7.12 Traversal

Traversal in graph is different from traversal in tree or list because of the following reasons:

(a) There is no first vertex or root vertex in a graph. Hence, the traversal can start from any vertex. We can choose any arbitrary vertex as the starting vertex. A traversal algorithm will produce different sequences for different starting vertices.

(b) In a tree or list, when we start traversing from the first node, all the elements are visited, but in a graph, only those vertices will be visited that are reachable from the starting vertex. So, if we want to visit all the vertices of the graph, we have to select another starting vertex from the remaining vertices in order to visit all the vertices left.

(c) In tree or list while traversing, we never encounter a node more than once, while in graph we may reach a vertex more than once. This is because in a graph, a vertex may have cycles and there may be more than one path to reach a vertex. So, to ensure that each vertex is visited only once, we have to keep the status of each vertex whether it has been visited or not.

(d) In a tree or list, we have unique traversals. For example, if we are traversing a binary tree in inorder, there can be only one sequence in which vertices are visited. But in the graph, for the same technique of traversal, there can be different sequences in which vertices can be visited. This is because there is no natural order among the successors of a vertex, and thus the successors may be visited in different orders producing different sequences. The order in which successors are visited, may depend on the implementation.

Like binary trees, in graph too, there can be many methods by which a graph can be traversed. However, two of them are standard and known as breadth first search and depth first search.

7.12.1 Breadth First Search

In this technique, we first visit the starting vertex and then visit all the vertices adjacent to the starting vertex. After this, we pick these adjacent vertices one by one and visit their adjacent vertices, and this process goes on. This traversal is equivalent to level order traversal of trees. Let us take a graph and traverse it using breadth first search traversal.

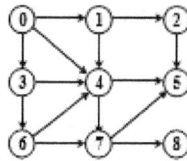

Figure 7.51 Graph for breadth first search traversal

Let us take vertex 0 as the starting vertex. First, we will visit the vertex 0. Then, we will visit all vertices adjacent to vertex 0, i.e., 1, 4, 3. Here, we can visit these three vertices in any order. Suppose we visit the vertices in order 1, 3, 4. Now the traversal is:

<u>0</u> <u>1 3 4</u>

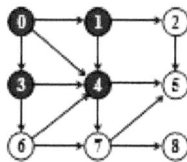

Figure 7.52 Visit start vertex 0, then visit 1, 3, 4

Now, we first visit all the vertices adjacent to 1, then all the vertices adjacent to 3, and then all the vertices adjacent to 4. So first we will visit 2, then 6, and then 5, and 7. Note that vertex 4 is adjacent to vertices 1 and 3, but it has already been visited, and so we have ignored it. Now the traversal is:

<u>0</u> <u>1 3 4</u> <u>2 6 5 7</u>

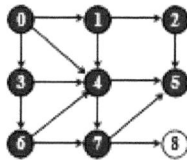

Figure 7.53 Visit 2, 6, 5, 7

Now we will visit all the vertices one by one, that are adjacent to vertices 2, 6, 5, 7. We can see that vertex 5 is adjacent to vertex 2, but it has already been visited, and so we will just ignore it and proceed further. Now, vertices adjacent to vertex 6 are vertices 4 and 7, which have already been visited so we will ignore them also. Vertex 5 has no adjacent vertices. Vertex 7 has vertices 5 and 8 adjacent to it, out of which vertex 8 has not been visited. So visit vertex 8. Now the traversal is:

<u>0</u> <u>1 3 4</u> <u>2 6 5 7</u> <u>8</u>

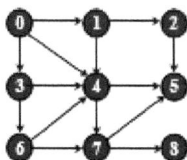

Figure 7.54 Visit 8

Now, we have to visit vertices adjacent to vertex 8, but there is no vertex adjacent to vertex 8. so our procedure stops.

This was the traversal when we take vertex 0 as the starting vertex. Suppose we take vertex 1 as the starting vertex. Then applying the above technique, we will get the following traversal:

1 2 4 5 7 8

Here are different traversals when we take different starting vertices:

Start Vertex	Traversal
0	0 1 3 4 2 6 5 7 8
1	1 2 4 5 7 8
2	2 5
3	3 4 6 5 7 8
4	4 5 7 8
5	5
6	6 4 7 5 8
7	7 5 8
8	8

Note that these traversals are not unique; there can be different traversals depending on the order in which we visit the successors.

We can see that all the vertices are not visited in some cases. The vertices which are visited are those vertices which are reachable from starting vertex. So, to make sure that all the vertices are visited, we need to repeat the same procedure for each unvisited vertex in the graph. The breadth first search is implemented through the queue.

7.12.1.1 Implementation of Breadth First Search Using Queue

During the algorithm, any vertex will be in one of the three states: initial, waiting, visited. At the start of the algorithm, all vertices will be in the initial state. When a vertex will be inserted in the queue, its state will change from initial to waiting. When a vertex will be deleted from queue and visited, its state will change from waiting to visited. The procedure is as follows.

Initially, the queue is empty, and all vertices are in the initial state.
1. Insert the starting vertex into the queue, change its state to waiting.
2. Delete the front element from the queue and visit it; change its state to visited.
3. Look for the adjacent vertices of the deleted element, and from these, insert only those vertices into the queue that are in the initial state. Change the state of all these inserted vertices from initial to waiting.
4. Repeat steps 2, 3 until the queue is empty.

Let us take vertex 0 as the starting vertex for traversal in the graph of figure 7.51. In each step, we will show the traversal and the contents of the queue. In the figure, the different states of the vertices are shown by different colors. The white color indicates the initial state, grey indicates the waiting state, and black indicates the visited state.

(i) Insert the vertex 0 into the queue.
Queue: 0

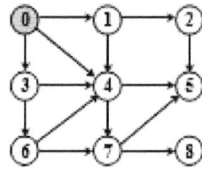

Figure 7.55 Insert 0 into the queue

(ii) Delete vertex 0 from queue, and visit it.
Traversal: 0
Vertices adjacent to vertex 0 are vertices 1, 3, 4 and all of these are in initial state, so insert them into the queue.
Queue: 1, 3, 4

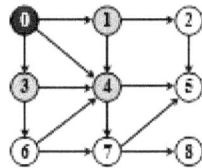

Figure 7.56 Visit 0, insert 1, 3, 4 into the queue

(iii) Delete vertex 1 from queue, and visit it.
Traversal: 0, 1
Vertices adjacent to vertex 1 are vertices 2 and 4. Vertex 4 is in the waiting state because it is in the queue, so it is not inserted into the queue. Vertex 2 is in the initial state, so insert it into the queue.
Queue: 3, 4, 2

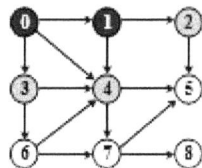

Figure 7.57 Visit 1, insert 2 into the queue

Here, we can see why we have taken the concept of a waiting state. Vertex 4 is in waiting state, i.e., it is already present in the queue, and so, it is not inserted into the queue. The concept of the waiting state helps us avoid insertion of duplicate vertices in the queue.

(iv) Delete vertex 3 from queue, and visit it.
Traversal: 0, 1, 3
Vertices adjacent to vertex 3 are vertices 4 and 6. Vertex 4 is in the waiting state, and vertex 6 is in the initial state, so insert only vertex 6 into the queue.
Queue: 4, 2, 6

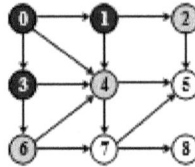

Figure 7.58 Visit 3, insert 6 into the queue

(v) Delete vertex 4 from queue, and visit it.
Traversal: 0, 1, 3, 4
Vertices adjacent to vertex 4 are vertices 5 and 7, and both are in the initial state, so insert them into the queue.
Queue: 2, 6, 5, 7

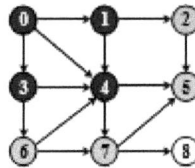

Figure 7.59 Visit 4, insert 5, 7 into the queue

(vi) Delete vertex 2 from queue, and visit it.
Traversal: 0, 1, 3, 4, 2
Vertex adjacent to vertex 2 is vertex 5. Vertex 5 is in a waiting state because it is already in the queue, so it is not inserted into the queue.
Queue: 6, 5, 7

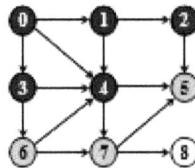

Figure 7.60 Visit 2

(vii) Delete vertex 6 from queue, and visit it.
Traversal: 0, 1, 3, 4, 2, 6
Vertices adjacent to vertex 6 are vertices 4 and 7. Vertex 4 is in a visited state, and vertex 7 is in a waiting state, so nothing is inserted into the queue.
Queue: 5, 7

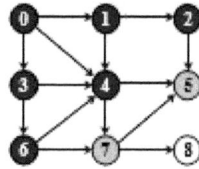

Figure 7.61 Visit 6

Here, we can see why we have taken the concept of visited state. Vertex 4 is in a visited state, i.e., it has been included in the traversal, so there is no need to insert it into the queue. The concept of visited state helps us avoid visiting a vertex more than once.

(viii) Delete vertex 5 from queue, and visit it.
Traversal: 0, 1, 3, 4, 2, 6, 5
Vertex 5 has no adjacent vertices.
Queue: 7

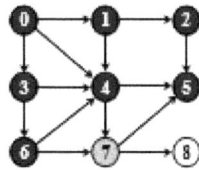

Figure 7.62 Visit 5

(ix) Delete 7 from queue, and visit it.
Traversal: 0, 1, 3, 4, 2, 6, 5, 7
Vertices adjacent to vertex 7 are vertices 5 and 8. Vertex 5 is in the visited state and vertex 8 is in the initial state, so insert only vertex 8 into the queue.
Queue: 8

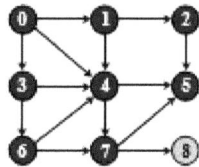

Figure 7.63 Visit 7, insert 8 into the queue

(x) Delete vertex 8 from queue, and visit it.
Traversal: 0, 1, 3, 4, 2, 6, 5, 7, 8
There is no vertex adjacent to vertex 8
Queue: EMPTY

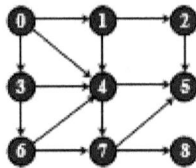

Figure 7.64 Visit 8

Now, the queue is empty, so we will stop our process. This way, we get the breadth first traversal when vertex 0 is taken as the starting vertex.

```cpp
//DirectedGraph.cpp : Program for traversing a directed graph through BFS.
//Visiting only those vertices that are reachable from start vertex.
#include<iostream>
#include<string>
#include<queue>
using namespace std;
static const int maxSize = 30;
class Vertex
{
    public:
            string name;
            int state;
    public:
            Vertex(string name)
            {
                    this->name = name;
            }
};//End of class Vertex
class DirectedGraph
{
    private:
            int nVertices;
            int nEdges;
            int adj[maxSize][maxSize];
            Vertex *vertexList[maxSize];
            int INITIAL;
            int WAITING;
            int VISITED;
    private:
            int getIndex(string vertexName);
            bool isAdjacent(int u, int v);
            void bfs(int vertex);
    public:
            DirectedGraph();
            ~DirectedGraph();
            void insertVertex(string vertexName);
            void insertEdge(string source, string destination);
            void display();
            void bfsTraversal(string vertexName);
            void bfsTraversalAll(string vertexName);
};//End of class DirectedGraph
DirectedGraph::DirectedGraph()
{
    nVertices = 0;
    nEdges = 0;
```

```
                for(int i=0; i<maxSize; i++)
                {
                        for(int j=0; j<maxSize; j++)
                        {
                                adj[i][j] = 0;
                        }
                }
                INITIAL = 0;
                WAITING = 1;
                VISITED = 2;
}//End of DirectedGraph()
void DirectedGraph::bfs(int vertex)
{
        queue<int> bfsQueue;
        //Inserting the start vertex into queue and changing its state to WAITING
        bfsQueue.push(vertex);
        vertexList[vertex]->state = WAITING;

        while(!bfsQueue.empty())
        {
                //Deleting front element from the queue and changing its state to VISITED
                vertex = bfsQueue.front();
                bfsQueue.pop();
                vertexList[vertex]->state = VISITED;
                cout << vertexList[vertex]->name << " ";

                //Looking for the adjacent vertices of the deleted element, and from
                //these insert only those vertices into the queue which are in the
                //INITIAL state. Change the state of all these inserted vertices from
                //INITIAL to WAITING
                for(int i=0; i<nVertices; i++)
                {
                        //Checking for adjacent vertices with INITIAL state
                        if(isAdjacent(vertex,i) && vertexList[i]->state==INITIAL)
                        {
                                bfsQueue.push(i);
                                vertexList[i]->state = WAITING;
                        }
                }
        }//End of while
        cout << "\n";
}//End of bfs()
void DirectedGraph::bfsTraversal(string vertexName)
{
        //Initially all the vertices will have INITIAL state
        for(int i=0; i<nVertices; i++)
        {
                vertexList[i]->state = INITIAL;
        }
        bfs(getIndex(vertexName));
}//End of bfsTraversal()
```

The destructor, `insertVertex()`, `getIndex()`, `insertEdge()`, `display()`, and `isAdjacent()` functions are the same as in the directed graph program.

This process can visit only those vertices which are reachable from the starting vertex. For example, if we start traversing from vertex 4 instead of vertex 0, then all the vertices will not be visited. The traversal would be – 4 5 7 8.

If we want to visit all the vertices, then we can take any unvisited vertex as the starting vertex and again start the breadth first search from there. This process will continue until all the vertices are visited. So, if we want to visit all the vertices when 4 is the start vertex, we have to select another start vertex after visiting 5, 7 and 8. Suppose we take 0 as the next start vertex. Now, the traversal would be – 4 5 7 8 0 1 3 2 6. Thus, all the vertices are visited and so there is no need to choose any other start vertex.

In the program, we have to make a small addition in the bfsTraversal() function. After the call to bfs() with the start vertex, we will check all vertices one by one in a loop. If we get any vertex that is in the initial state,
we will call bfs() with that vertex. We can have a separate function bfsTraversalAll() for visiting all the vertices.

```
//Visiting all vertices
void DirectedGraph::bfsTraversalAll(string vertexName)
{
        //Initially all the vertices will have INITIAL state
        for(int i=0; i<nVertices; i++)
        {
                vertexList[i]->state = INITIAL;
        }
        bfs(getIndex(vertexName));
        for(int v=0; v<nVertices; v++)
        {
                if(vertexList[v]->state == INITIAL)
                        bfs(v);
        }
}//End of bfsTraversalAll()
```

Here is the main() function of the program:

```
int main()
{
        DirectedGraph dGraph;
        try
        {
                //Creating the graph, inserting the vertices and edges
                dGraph.insertVertex("0");
                dGraph.insertVertex("1");
                dGraph.insertVertex("2");
                dGraph.insertVertex("3");
                dGraph.insertVertex("4");
                dGraph.insertVertex("5");
                dGraph.insertVertex("6");
                dGraph.insertVertex("7");
                dGraph.insertVertex("8");
                dGraph.insertEdge("0","1");
                dGraph.insertEdge("0","3");
                dGraph.insertEdge("0","4");
                dGraph.insertEdge("1","2");
                dGraph.insertEdge("1","4");
                dGraph.insertEdge("2","5");
                dGraph.insertEdge("3","4");
                dGraph.insertEdge("3","6");
                dGraph.insertEdge("4","5");
                dGraph.insertEdge("4","7");
                dGraph.insertEdge("6","4");
                dGraph.insertEdge("6","7");
                dGraph.insertEdge("7","5");
                dGraph.insertEdge("7","8");
                //Display the graph
                dGraph.display();
```

```
        cout << "\n";

        //BFS traversal visiting only those vertices that are reachable from
        //start vertex
        dGraph.bfsTraversal("4");
        //BFS traversal visiting all the vertices
        dGraph.bfsTraversalAll("0");
    }//End of try
    catch(exception e)
    {
        cout << e.what() << "\n";
    }
    return 0;
}//End of main()
```

Now suppose that while performing breadth first search, we assign two values to each vertex in the graph – a predecessor and a distance value. Whenever we insert a vertex in the queue, we set its predecessor and distance values.

The predecessor of starting vertex is taken as NIL(-1). The distance value of the starting vertex is taken as 0 and the distance value of any other vertex is one more than the distance value of its predecessor. If we take the case of an example described in section 7.12.1.1, then the predecessor and distance values set in different steps would be:

In step (i) pred[0] = -1
         d[0] = 0
In step (ii) pred[1] = pred[3] = pred[4] = 0
         d[1] = d[3] = d[4] = d[0] + 1 = 0 + 1 = 1
In step (iii) pred[2] = 1
         d[2] = d[1]+1 = 1+1 = 2
In step (iv) pred[6]=3
         d[6] = d[3]+1 = 1+1 = 2
In step (v) pred[5] = pred[7] = 4
         d[5] = d[7] = d[4]+1 = 1+1 =2
In step (ix) pred[8] = 7
         d[8] = d[7] +1 = 2+1 = 3

In steps (vi), (vii), (viii), (x), nothing is inserted in the queue, and so, no value is set in these steps. The following figures show the graph with predecessor and distance values:

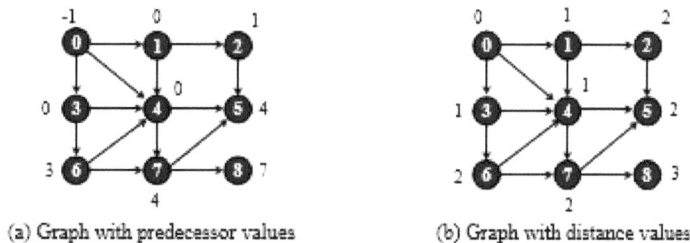

(a) Graph with predecessor values   (b) Graph with distance values

Figure 7.65 Graph with predecessor and distance values

The distance value of a vertex u gives us the shortest distance (number of edges) of u from the starting vertex. For example, the shortest distance from vertex 0 to vertex 8 is 3. This shortest path can be obtained by following the predecessors values, till we get the start vertex as a predecessor. Let us see how we can get this path in the case of 8. Predecessor of 8 is 7, predecessor of 7 is 4, predecessor of 4 is 0, and so, the shortest path is 0 4 7 8.

There may be other paths from vertex 0 to vertex 8, but the length of none of them would be less than 3. Hence, the breadth first search can be used to find the shortest distances to all vertices reachable from the start vertex in unweighted graphs. The length of the shortest path is given by the distance value and this shortest path can be obtained by following the predecessor values.

```cpp
//DirectedGraph.cpp : Program for traversing a directed graph through BFS and finding
//shortest distance and shortest path of any vertex from start vertex.
#include<iostream>
#include<string>
#include<queue>
using namespace std;

static const int maxSize = 30;
class Vertex
{
        public:
                string name;
                int state;
                int predecessor;
                int distance;
        public:
                Vertex(string name)
                {
                        this->name = name;
                }
};//End of class Vertex

class DirectedGraph
{
        private:
                int nVertices;
                int nEdges;
                int adj[maxSize][maxSize];
                Vertex *vertexList[maxSize];
                int INITIAL;
                int WAITING;
                int VISITED;
                int NIL;
                int INFINITY;
        private:
                int getIndex(string vertexName);
                bool isAdjacent(int u, int v);
                void bfs(int vertex);
        public:
                DirectedGraph();
                ~DirectedGraph();
                void insertVertex(string vertexName);
                void insertEdge(string source, string destination);
                void display();
                void bfsTraversal(string vertexName);
                void bfsShortestPath(string source, string destination);
};//End of class DirectedGraph

DirectedGraph::DirectedGraph()
{
        nVertices = 0;
        nEdges = 0;
        for(int i=0; i<maxSize; i++)
        {
                for(int j=0; j<maxSize; j++)
                {
                        adj[i][j] = 0;
```

```
                }
        }
        INITIAL = 0;
        WAITING = 1;
        VISITED = 2;
        NIL = -1;
        INFINITY = 9999;
}//End of DirectedGraph()
void DirectedGraph::bfs(int vertex)
{
        queue<int> bfsQueue;
        //Inserting the start vertex into queue and changing its state to WAITING
        bfsQueue.push(vertex);
        vertexList[vertex]->state = WAITING;
        vertexList[vertex]->predecessor = NIL;
        vertexList[vertex]->distance = 0;

        while(!bfsQueue.empty())
        {
                //Deleting front element from the queue and changing its state to
                //VISITED
                vertex = bfsQueue.front();
                bfsQueue.pop();
                vertexList[vertex]->state = VISITED;

                //Looking for the adjacent vertices of the deleted element, and from
                //these insert only those vertices into the queue which are in the
                //INITIAL state. Change the state of all these inserted vertices from
                //INITIAL to WAITING
                for(int i=0; i<nVertices; i++)
                {
                        //Checking for adjacent vertices with INITIAL state
                        if(isAdjacent(vertex,i) && vertexList[i]->state==INITIAL)
                        {
                                bfsQueue.push(i);
                                vertexList[i]->state = WAITING;
                                vertexList[i]->predecessor = vertex;
                                vertexList[i]->distance = vertexList[vertex]->distance +
                                1;
                        }
                }
        }//End of while
}//End of bfs()
void DirectedGraph::bfsTraversal(string vertexName)
{
        //Initially all the vertices will have INITIAL state
        for(int i=0; i<nVertices; i++)
        {
                vertexList[i]->state = INITIAL;
                vertexList[i]->predecessor = NIL;
                vertexList[i]->distance = INFINITY;
        }
        bfs(getIndex(vertexName));
}//End of bfsTraversal()
void DirectedGraph::bfsShortestPath(string source, string destination)
{
        bfsTraversal(source);
        if(vertexList[getIndex(destination)]->distance == INFINITY)
        {
                cout << "There is no path from " << source << " to " << destination <<
                "\n";
```

```
        }
        else
        {
                cout << "Shortest distance is : " << vertexList[getIndex(destination)]
                ->distance << "\n";
                int v = getIndex(destination);
                int x, y = v;
                int count=0;
                int path[maxSize];
                while(y != NIL)
                {
                        count++;
                        path[count] = y;
                        x = vertexList[y]->predecessor;
                        y = x;
                }
                cout << "Shortest Path is :\n";
                int i;
                for(i=count; i>1; i--)
                {
                        cout << vertexList[path[i]]->name << "->";
                }
                cout << vertexList[path[i]]->name << "\n";
        }//End of else
}//End of bfsShortestPath()

int main()
{
        DirectedGraph dGraph;
        try
        {
                //Creating the graph, inserting the vertices and edges
                dGraph.insertVertex("0");
                dGraph.insertVertex("1");
                dGraph.insertVertex("2");
                dGraph.insertVertex("3");
                dGraph.insertVertex("4");
                dGraph.insertVertex("5");
                dGraph.insertVertex("6");
                dGraph.insertVertex("7");
                dGraph.insertVertex("8");
                dGraph.insertEdge("0","1");
                dGraph.insertEdge("0","3");
                dGraph.insertEdge("0","4");
                dGraph.insertEdge("1","2");
                dGraph.insertEdge("1","4");
                dGraph.insertEdge("2","5");
                dGraph.insertEdge("3","4");
                dGraph.insertEdge("3","6");
                dGraph.insertEdge("4","5");
                dGraph.insertEdge("4","7");
                dGraph.insertEdge("6","4");
                dGraph.insertEdge("6","7");
                dGraph.insertEdge("7","5");
                dGraph.insertEdge("7","8");
                //Display the graph
                dGraph.display();
                cout << "\n";

                //BFS traversal, finding shortest distance and shortest path
                dGraph.bfsShortestPath("0","8");
        }//End of try
```

```
        catch(exception e)
        {
                cout << e.what() << "\n";
        }
        return 0;
}//End of main()
```

The destructor, `insertVertex()`, `getIndex()`, `insertEdge()`, `display()`, and `isAdjacent()` functions are same as in the directed graph program.

In the program, we initialize the distance values of all vertices to INFINITY (a very large number), and the predecessor values are initialized to NIL(-1). Since our vertices start from 0, we can take the value of NIL equal to -1. We use `bfsTraversal()`, as we do not have to find out shortest distances and paths to vertices that are not reachable.

Now, let us look at the graph with predecessor values. If we draw only those edges that join a vertex to its predecessor, then we get the predecessor subgraph, which is a spanning tree of the graph. This spanning tree is called the breadth first search spanning tree.

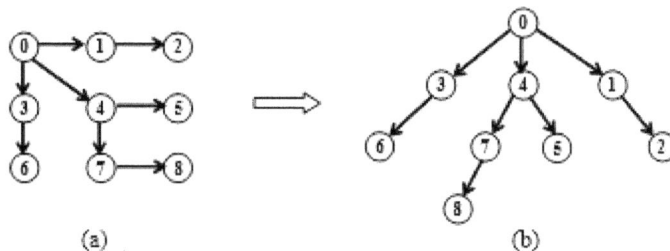

Figure 7.66 Breadth first search spanning tree

Figure 7.66 (a) shows the breadth first search spanning tree. This figure is redrawn on the right, so that it looks like a tree with vertex 0 as the root.

If all vertices are not reachable form start vertex, then we get a BFS spanning forest having more than one spanning tree. For example, if in the above graph we start traversing from vertex 4, then we get two spanning trees. Starting at vertex 4, we can visit only vertices 5,7,8 as these are the only vertices reachable from 4. After this, we select vertex 0 as the next start vertex, and then the rest of the vertices are visited. So we get a BFS spanning forest consisting of two spanning trees.

(a) Graph traversed with start vertices 4 and 0   (b) Spanning Forest

Figure 7.67 Breadth first search spanning forest

In the spanning forest, the arbitrarily chosen vertex is the root of the spanning tree. All the edges that are in the spanning forest are called tree edges. We can output all the tree edges by adding a small line in the `bfs()` function:

```
void DirectedGraph::bfs(int vertex)
{
        queue<int> bfsQueue;
        //Inserting the start vertex into queue and changing its state to WAITING
        bfsQueue.push(vertex);
        vertexList[vertex]->state = WAITING;

        while(!bfsQueue.empty())
        {
                //Deleting front element from the queue and changing its state to VISITED
                vertex = bfsQueue.front();
                bfsQueue.pop();
                vertexList[vertex]->state = VISITED;

                //Looking for the adjacent vertices of the deleted element, and from
                //these insert only those vertices into the queue which are in the
                //INITIAL state. Change the state of all these inserted vertices from
                //INITIAL to WAITING
                for(int i=0; i<nVertices; i++)
                {
                        //Checking for adjacent vertices with INITIAL state
                        if(isAdjacent(vertex,i) && vertexList[i]->state==INITIAL)
                        {
                                bfsQueue.push(i);
                                vertexList[i]->state = WAITING;
                                cout << "Tree Edge - (" << vertexList[vertex]->name << ","
                                    << vertexList[i]->name << ")\n";
                        }
                }
        }//End of while
}//End of bfs()
```

The breadth first search in an undirected graph is performed in the same manner as in a directed graph. Consider the undirected graph given as follows:

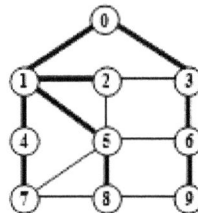

Figure 7.68 Undirected graph, traversed with start vertex 0

If we take 0 as the start vertex, the breadth first traversal would be:

0 1 3 2 4 5 6 7 8 9

As stated before, this traversal is not unique; there may be other traversals depending on the order of visiting of successors.

If the undirected graph is connected, then we can reach all the vertices, taking any vertex as the start vertex. If the graph is not connected, then we can visit only those vertices which are in the same connected component as the start vertex. So we can pick another unvisited vertex, and start traversing from there, and continue this procedure until all vertices are visited. The following figure shows a disconnected undirected graph and its BFS spanning forest. There is a spanning tree corresponding to each connected component of the graph.

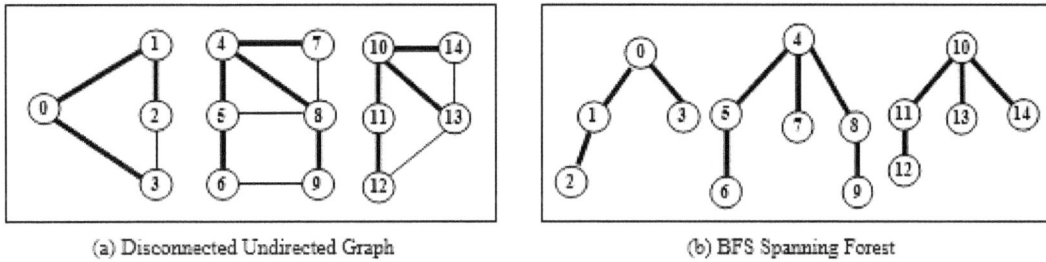

(a) Disconnected Undirected Graph   (b) BFS Spanning Forest

Figure 7.69 BFS spanning forest for disconnected undirected graph

The breadth first search traversal of the graph of figure 7.69 (a) taking 0, 4, and 10 as the start vertices is:

0 1 3 2   4 5 7 8 6 9   10 11 13 14 12

An application of BFS could be to determine whether an undirected graph is connected. An undirected graph is connected if we can visit all the vertices taking any arbitrary start vertex, and there is no need to choose another start vertex.

In the program, after calling function `bfs()` for the start vertex, if even a single vertex is left in the `INITIAL` state, then the graph is not connected.

```
bool UndirectedGraph::isConnected()
{
        bool connected = true;
        //Initially all the vertices will have INITIAL state
        for(int i=0; i<nVertices; i++)
        {
                vertexList[i]->state = INITIAL;
        }
        bfs(0); //Start traversal from vertex 0
        for(int v=0; v<nVertices; v++)
        {
                if(vertexList[v]->state == INITIAL)
                {
                        connected = false;
                        break;
                }
        }
        return connected;
}//End of isConnected()
```

We can find all the connected components using the breadth first search. To find the connected components, all vertices in the graph are given a label such that the vertices in the same component get the same label. For example, in the graph 7.69 (a), we have three connected components. All vertices in the first component have label 1, vertices in the second component have label 2, and, vertices in the third component have label 3.

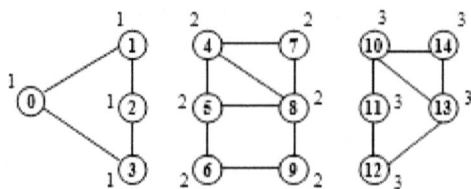

Figure 7.70 Connected components with label

```cpp
//UndirectedGraph.cpp : Program to find connected components in an undirected graph.
#include<iostream>
#include<string>
#include<queue>
using namespace std;

static const int maxSize = 30;

class Vertex
{
    public:
            string name;
            int state;
            int componentNumber;
    public:
            Vertex(string name)
            {
                    this->name = name;
            }
};//End of class Vertex

class UndirectedGraph
{
    private:
            int nVertices;
            int nEdges;
            int adj[maxSize][maxSize];
            Vertex *vertexList[maxSize];
            int INITIAL;
            int WAITING;
            int VISITED;
    private:
            int getIndex(string vertexName);
            bool isAdjacent(int u, int v);
            void bfs(int vertex, int cn);
    public:
            UndirectedGraph();
            ~UndirectedGraph();
            void insertVertex(string vertexName);
            void insertEdge(string source, string destination);
            void display();
            void connectedComponent();
};//End of class UndirectedGraph

UndirectedGraph::UndirectedGraph()
{
    nVertices = 0;
    nEdges = 0;
    for(int i=0; i<maxSize; i++)
    {
            for(int j=0; j<maxSize; j++)
```

```
                {
                        adj[i][j] = 0;
                }
        }
        INITIAL = 0;
        WAITING = 1;
        VISITED = 2;
}//End of UndirectedGraph()

UndirectedGraph::~UndirectedGraph()
{
        for(int i=0; i<nVertices; i++)
        {
                delete vertexList[i];
        }
}//End of ~UndirectedGraph()

void UndirectedGraph::insertVertex(string vertexName)
{
        vertexList[nVertices++] = new Vertex(vertexName);
}//End of insertVertex()

int UndirectedGraph::getIndex(string vertexName)
{
        for(int i=0; i<nVertices; i++)
        {
                if(vertexName == vertexList[i]->name)
                        return i;
        }
        throw exception("Invalid Vertex");
}//End of getIndex()

void UndirectedGraph::insertEdge(string source, string destination)
{
        int u = getIndex(source);
        int v = getIndex(destination);
        if(u == v)
                cout << "Not a valid edge\n";
        else if(adj[u][v] != 0)
                cout << "Edge already present\n";
        else
        {
                adj[u][v] = 1;
                adj[v][u] = 1;
                nEdges++;
        }
}//End of insertEdge()

void UndirectedGraph::display()
{
        for(int i=0; i<nVertices; i++)
        {
                for(int j=0; j<nVertices; j++)
                        cout << adj[i][j] << " ";
                cout <<"\n";
        }
}//End of display()

bool UndirectedGraph::isAdjacent(int u, int v)
{
        return (adj[u][v] != 0);
}//End of isAdjacent()

void UndirectedGraph::bfs(int vertex, int cn)
{
```

```cpp
        queue<int> bfsQueue;
        //Inserting the start vertex into queue and changing its state to WAITING
        bfsQueue.push(vertex);
        vertexList[vertex]->state = WAITING;

        while(!bfsQueue.empty())
        {
                //Deleting front element from the queue and changing its state to VISITED
                vertex = bfsQueue.front();
                bfsQueue.pop();
                vertexList[vertex]->state = VISITED;
                vertexList[vertex]->componentNumber = cn;

                //Looking for the adjacent vertices of the deleted element, and from
                //these insert only those vertices into the queue which are in the
                //INITIAL state. Change the state of all these inserted vertices from
                //INITIAL to WAITING
                for(int i=0; i<nVertices; i++)
                {
                        //Checking for adjacent vertices with INITIAL state
                        if(isAdjacent(vertex,i) && vertexList[i]->state==INITIAL)
                        {
                                bfsQueue.push(i);
                                vertexList[i]->state = WAITING;
                        }
                }
        }//End of while
}//End of bfs()
void UndirectedGraph::connectedComponent()
{
        int componentNumber = 0;
        //Initially all the vertices will have INITIAL state
        for(int i=0; i<nVertices; i++)
        {
                vertexList[i]->state = INITIAL;
        }
        componentNumber++;
        bfs(0, componentNumber);        //Start BFS from vertex 0
        for(int v=0; v<nVertices; v++)
        {
                if(vertexList[v]->state == INITIAL)
                {
                        componentNumber++;
                        bfs(v, componentNumber);
                }
        }
        cout << "Number of connected components = " << componentNumber << "\n";
        if(componentNumber == 1)
        {
                cout << "Graph is connected\n";
        }
        else
        {
                cout << "Graph is not connected\n";
                for(int v=0; v<nVertices; v++)
                {
                        cout << vertexList[v]->name << " -> Component Number : "
                             << vertexList[v]->componentNumber << "\n";
```

```
                        }
              }
}//End of connectedComponent()

int main()
{
        UndirectedGraph uGraph;
        try
        {
                //Creating the graph, inserting the vertices and edges
                uGraph.insertVertex("0");
                uGraph.insertVertex("1");
                uGraph.insertVertex("2");
                uGraph.insertVertex("3");
                uGraph.insertVertex("4");
                uGraph.insertVertex("5");
                uGraph.insertVertex("6");
                uGraph.insertVertex("7");
                uGraph.insertVertex("8");
                uGraph.insertVertex("9");
                uGraph.insertVertex("10");
                uGraph.insertVertex("11");
                uGraph.insertVertex("12");
                uGraph.insertVertex("13");
                uGraph.insertVertex("14");

                uGraph.insertEdge("0","1");
                uGraph.insertEdge("0","3");
                uGraph.insertEdge("1","2");
                uGraph.insertEdge("2","3");
                uGraph.insertEdge("4","5");
                uGraph.insertEdge("4","7");
                uGraph.insertEdge("4","8");
                uGraph.insertEdge("5","6");
                uGraph.insertEdge("5","8");
                uGraph.insertEdge("6","9");
                uGraph.insertEdge("7","8");
                uGraph.insertEdge("8","9");
                uGraph.insertEdge("10","11");
                uGraph.insertEdge("10","13");
                uGraph.insertEdge("10","14");
                uGraph.insertEdge("11","12");
                uGraph.insertEdge("12","13");
                uGraph.insertEdge("13","14");
                //Display the graph
                uGraph.display();
                cout << "\n";

                //Find the connected components of graph
                uGraph.connectedComponent();
        }//End of try
        catch(exception e)
        {
                cout << e.what() << "\n";
        }
        return 0;
}//End of main()
```

7.12.2 Depth First Search

Traversal using depth first search is like traveling a maze. We travel along a path in the graph and when a dead end comes, we backtrack. This technique is named so because search proceeds deeper in the graph, i.e., we traverse along a path as deep as possible.

First, the starting vertex is visited, and then we will pick up any path that starts from the starting vertex and visit all the vertices in this path till we reach a dead end. This means visit the starting vertex (say v1) and then any vertex adjacent to it (say v2). Now, if v2 has any vertex adjacent to it which has not been visited, then visit it, and so on, till we come to a dead end. Dead end means we reach a vertex which does not have any adjacent vertex or all of its adjacent vertices have been visited. After reaching the dead end, we will backtrack along the path that we have visited till now. Suppose the path that we have traversed is v1-v2-v3-v4-v5. After traversing v5, we reached a dead end. Now, we will move backwards until we reach a vertex, that has any unvisited adjacent vertex. We move back and reach v4, but see that it has no unvisited adjacent vertices. So, we will reach vertex v3. Now, if v3 has an unvisited vertex adjacent to it, we will pick up a path that starts from v3, and visit it until we reach a dead end. Then again, we will backtrack. This procedure finishes when we reach the starting vertex and there are no vertices adjacent to it which have to be visited.

Let us take a graph and perform a depth first search, taking vertex 0 as the start vertex. The successors of a vertex can be visited in any order.

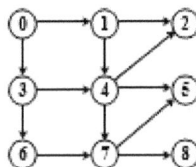

Figure 7.71 Graph for depth first search traversal

First, we will visit vertex 0. Vertices adjacent to vertex 0 are 1 and 3. Suppose we visit vertex 1. Now we look at the adjacent vertices of 1; from the two adjacent vertices 2 and 4, we choose to visit 2. Till now, the traversal is:

0 1 2

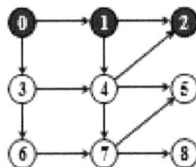

Figure 7.72 Visit vertex 0, 1, 2

There is no vertex adjacent to vertex 2. It means that we have reached the end of the path or a dead end from where we cannot go forward. So, we will move backward. We reach vertex 1 and see if there is any vertex adjacent to it, and not visited yet. Vertex 4 is such a vertex and therefore we visit it. Now, vertices 5 and 7 are adjacent to 4 and unvisited, and from these, we choose to visit vertex 5. Till now the traversal is:

0 1 2 4 5

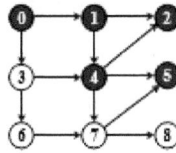

Figure 7.73 Visit vertex 4, 5

There is no vertex adjacent to vertex 5, so we will backtrack. We reach vertex 4, and its unvisited adjacent vertex is 7, so we visit it. Now, vertex 8 is the only unvisited vertex adjacent to 7, and so we visit it too. Till now, the traversal is:

0 1 2 4 5 7 8

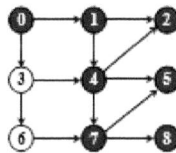

Figure 7.74 Visit vertex 7, 8

Vertex 8 has no unvisited adjacent vertex, and so we backtrack and reach vertex 7. Now, vertex 7 also has no unvisited adjacent vertex, and so we backtrack and reach vertex 4. Vertex 4 also has no unvisited adjacent vertex, and so we backtrack and reach vertex 1. Vertex 1 also has no unvisited adjacent vertex, and so we backtrack and reach vertex 0. Vertex 3 is adjacent to vertex 0, and is unvisited, so we visit vertex 3. Vertex 6 is adjacent to vertex 3 and is unvisited, so we visit vertex 6. Till now the traversal is:

0 1 2 4 5 7 8 3 6

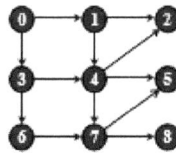

Figure 7.75 Visit vertex 3, 6

Now, vertex 6 has no unvisited adjacent vertex, and so we backtrack and reach vertex 3. Vertex 3 also has no unvisited adjacent vertex, so we backtrack and reach vertex 0. Vertex 0 also has no unvisited adjacent vertex left, and it is the start vertex. So now, we cannot backtrack and hence, our traversal finishes. The traversal is:

0 1 2 4 5 7 8 3 6

The depth first search can be implemented through a stack or recursively.

7.12.2.1 Implementation of Depth First Search Using Stack

During the algorithm, any vertex will be in one of the two states: initial or visited. At the start of the algorithm, all vertices will be in the initial state, and when a vertex is popped from the stack, its state will change to visited. The procedure is as follows:

Initially, the stack is empty, and all vertices are in initial state.

1. Push starting vertex on the stack.
2. Pop a vertex from the stack.
3. If the popped vertex is in the initial state, visit it and change its state to visited. Push all unvisited vertices adjacent to the popped vertex.
4. Repeat steps 2 and 3 until stack is empty.

There is no restriction on the order in which the successors of a vertex are visited, and so we can push the successors of a vertex in any order. Here, we are pushing the successors in the descending order of their numbers. For example, if the successors are 2, 4, and 6, then we will push 6 first and then 4 and then 2. Let us find the depth first traversal of the following graph using stack:

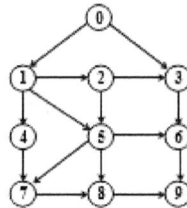

Figure 7.76 Graph for depth first traversal

Start vertex is 0, so initially push vertex 0 on the stack:

Pop 0: Visit 0	Push 3, 1	Stack : 3 1
Pop 1: Visit 1	Push 5, 4, 2	Stack : 3 5 4 2
Pop 2: Visit 2	Push 5, 3	Stack : 3 5 4 5 3
Pop 3: Visit 3	Push 6	Stack : 3 5 4 5 6
Pop 6: Visit 6	Push 9	Stack : 3 5 4 5 9
Pop 9: Visit 9		Stack : 3 5 4 5
Pop 5: Visit 5	Push 8, 7	Stack : 3 5 4 8 7
Pop 7: Visit 7	Push 8	Stack : 3 5 4 8 8
Pop 8: Visit 8		Stack : 3 5 4 8
Pop 8:		Stack : 3 5 4
Pop 4: Visit 4		Stack : 3 5
Pop 5:		Stack : 3
Pop 3:		Stack : Empty

Depth first traversal is : 0 1 2 3 6 9 5 7 8 4

In BFS, if a vertex was already present in the queue, then it was not inserted again in the queue. So, there we changed the state of a vertex from initial to waiting as soon as it was inserted in the queue, and never inserted a vertex in the queue that was in the waiting state. In DFS, we do not have the concept of waiting state, and so there may be multiple copies of a vertex in the stack.

If we do not insert a vertex already present in the stack, then we will not be able to visit the vertices in depth first search order. For example, if we traverse the graph of figure 7.76 in this manner, then we get the traversal as 0 1 2 4 7 8 9 5 6 3, which is clearly not in the depth first order.

```
//DirectedGraph.cpp : Program for traversing a directed graph through DFS.
//Visiting only those vertices that are reachable from start vertex.
#include<iostream>
#include<string>
#include<stack>
using namespace std;
```

```
static const int maxSize = 30;
class Vertex
{
        public:
                string name;
                int state;
        public:
                Vertex(string name)
                {
                        this->name = name;
                }
};//End of class Vertex
class DirectedGraph
{
        private:
                int nVertices;
                int nEdges;
                int adj[maxSize][maxSize];
                Vertex *vertexList[maxSize];
                int INITIAL;
                int VISITED;
        private:
                int getIndex(string vertexName);
                bool isAdjacent(int u, int v);
                void dfs(int vertex);
        public:
                DirectedGraph();
                ~DirectedGraph();
                void insertVertex(string vertexName);
                void insertEdge(string source, string destination);
                void display();
                void dfsTraversal(string vertexName);
                void dfsTraversalAll(string vertexName);
};//End of class DirectedGraph
DirectedGraph::DirectedGraph()
{
        nVertices = 0;
        nEdges = 0;
        for(int i=0; i<maxSize; i++)
        {
                for(int j=0; j<maxSize; j++)
                {
                        adj[i][j] = 0;
                }
        }
        INITIAL = 0;
        VISITED = 1;
}//End of DirectedGraph()
void DirectedGraph::dfs(int vertex)
{
        stack<int> dfsStack;
        //Push the start vertex into stack
        dfsStack.push(vertex);

        while(!dfsStack.empty())
        {
                vertex = dfsStack.top();
                dfsStack.pop();
                if(vertexList[vertex]->state == INITIAL)
                {
```

```
                        vertexList[vertex]->state = VISITED;
                        cout << vertexList[vertex]->name << " ";
                }

                //Looking for the adjacent vertices of the popped element, and from
                //these push only those vertices into the stack which are in the
                //INITIAL state.
                for(int i=nVertices-1; i>=0; i--)
                {
                        //Checking for adjacent vertices with INITIAL state
                        if(isAdjacent(vertex,i) && vertexList[i]->state==INITIAL)
                        {
                                dfsStack.push(i);
                        }
                }
        }//End of while
        cout << "\n";
}//End of dfs()
void DirectedGraph::dfsTraversal(string vertexName)
{
        //Initially all the vertices will have INITIAL state
        for(int i=0; i<nVertices; i++)
        {
                vertexList[i]->state = INITIAL;
        }

        dfs(getIndex(vertexName));
}//End of dfsTraversal()
```

The destructor, `insertVertex()`, `getIndex()`, `insertEdge()`, `display()`, and `isAdjacent()` functions are the same as in the directed graph program.

If all vertices are not reachable from the start vertex, then we need to repeat the procedure, taking some other start vertex. This is similar to the process we had done in the breadth first search. In the function `dfsTraversal()`, we will add a loop which will check the state of all vertices after the first DFS. If we get any vertex that is in the initial state, we will call `dfs()` with that vertex. We can have a separate function `dfsTraversalAll()` for visiting all the vertices.

```
//Visiting all vertices
void DirectedGraph::dfsTraversalAll(string vertexName)
{
        //Initially all the vertices will have INITIAL state
        for(int i=0; i<nVertices; i++)
        {
                vertexList[i]->state = INITIAL;
        }
        dfs(getIndex(vertexName));
        for(int v=0; v<nVertices; v++)
        {
                if(vertexList[v]->state == INITIAL)
                        dfs(v);
        }
}//End of dfsTraversalAll()
```

Here is the `main()` function of the program:

```
int main()
{
        DirectedGraph dGraph;
        try
        {
                //Creating the graph, inserting the vertices and edges
```

```
                dGraph.insertVertex("0");
                dGraph.insertVertex("1");
                dGraph.insertVertex("2");
                dGraph.insertVertex("3");
                dGraph.insertVertex("4");
                dGraph.insertVertex("5");
                dGraph.insertVertex("6");
                dGraph.insertVertex("7");
                dGraph.insertVertex("8");

                dGraph.insertEdge("0","1");
                dGraph.insertEdge("0","3");
                dGraph.insertEdge("1","2");
                dGraph.insertEdge("1","4");
                dGraph.insertEdge("3","4");
                dGraph.insertEdge("3","6");
                dGraph.insertEdge("4","2");
                dGraph.insertEdge("4","5");
                dGraph.insertEdge("4","7");
                dGraph.insertEdge("6","7");
                dGraph.insertEdge("7","5");
                dGraph.insertEdge("7","8");
                //Display the graph
                dGraph.display();
                cout << "\n";

                //DFS traversal visiting only those vertices that are reachable from
                //start vertex
                dGraph.dfsTraversal("4");
                //DFS traversal visiting all the vertices
                dGraph.dfsTraversalAll("0");
        }//End of try
        catch(exception e)
        {
                cout << e.what() << "\n";
        }
        return 0;
}//End of main()
```

As in BFS, here also we can assign a predecessor to each vertex and get the predecessor subgraph, which would be a spanning tree or spanning forest of the given graph depending on the reachability of all vertices from the start vertex.

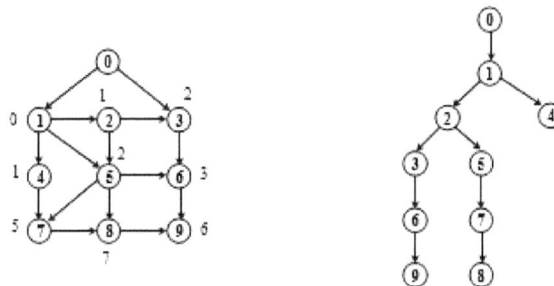

Graph with Predecessor of each vertex   Spanning Tree

Figure 7.77 Graph with predecessor of each vertex and spanning tree

```cpp
void DirectedGraph::dfs(int vertex)
{
        stack<int> dfsStack;
        //Push the start vertex into stack
        dfsStack.push(vertex);

        while(!dfsStack.empty())
        {
                vertex = dfsStack.top();
                dfsStack.pop();
                if(vertexList[vertex]->state == INITIAL)
                {
                        vertexList[vertex]->state = VISITED;
                }

                //Looking for the adjacent vertices of the popped element, and from
                //these push only those vertices into the stack which are in the
                //INITIAL state.
                for(int i=nVertices-1; i>=0; i--)
                {
                        //Checking for adjacent vertices with INITIAL state
                        if(isAdjacent(vertex,i) && vertexList[i]->state==INITIAL)
                        {
                                dfsStack.push(i);
                                vertexList[i]->predecessor = vertex;
                        }
                }
        }//End of while
}//End of dfs()

void DirectedGraph::dfsTraversalAll(string vertexName)
{
        //Initially all the vertices will have INITIAL state
        for(int i=0; i<nVertices; i++)
        {
                vertexList[i]->state = INITIAL;
                vertexList[i]->predecessor = NIL;
        }

        dfs(getIndex(vertexName));
        for(int v=0; v<nVertices; v++)
        {
                if(vertexList[v]->state == INITIAL)
                        dfs(v);
        }
}//End of dfsTraversalAll()

void DirectedGraph::dfsTreeEdges(string vertexName)
{
        dfsTraversalAll(vertexName);
        int p;
        for(int v=0; v<nVertices; v++)
        {
                p = vertexList[v]->predecessor;
                if(vertexList[v]->predecessor != -1)
                        cout << "Vertex : " << vertexList[v]->name << " , Predecessor :
                        " << vertexList[p]->name << "\n";
                else
                        cout << "Vertex : " << vertexList[v]->name << " , Predecessor :
                        " << vertexList[v]->predecessor << "\n";
        }
```

```
        int u;
        for(int v=0; v<nVertices; v++)
        {
                u = vertexList[v]->predecessor;
                if(vertexList[v]->predecessor != -1)
                        cout << "Tree Edge - (" << vertexList[u]->name << ","
                        << vertexList[v]->name << ")\n";
        }
}//End of dfsTreeEdges()
```

For an undirected graph, the depth first search will proceed in the same manner. Like breadth first search, we can use the depth first search also to find whether a graph is connected or not, and for finding all the connected components.

7.12.2.2 Recursive Implementation of Depth First Search

In the recursive implementation, we will take the three states of a vertex as initial, visited and finished. At the start, all vertices are in the initial state, and after a vertex is visited, its state becomes visited. The state of a vertex becomes finished when we backtrack from it, i.e., if it has been visited and it has no adjacent vertices or all its adjacent vertices are in finished state.

```
//DirectedGraph.cpp : Program for traversing a directed graph through DFS using recursion.
//Visiting only those vertices that are reachable from start vertex.
//Visiting all vertices
#include<iostream>
#include<string>
using namespace std;
static const int maxSize = 30;
class Vertex
{
        public:
                string name;
                int state;
        public:
                Vertex(string name)
                {
                        this->name = name;
                }
};//End of class Vertex
class DirectedGraph
{
        private:
                int nVertices;
                int nEdges;
                int adj[maxSize][maxSize];
                Vertex *vertexList[maxSize];
                int INITIAL;
                int VISITED;
                int FINISHED;
        private:
                int getIndex(string vertexName);
                bool isAdjacent(int u, int v);
                void dfs(int vertex);
        public:
                DirectedGraph();
                ~DirectedGraph();
                void insertVertex(string vertexName);
                void insertEdge(string source, string destination);
```

```cpp
                void display();
                void dfsTraversal(string vertexName);
                void dfsTraversalAll(string vertexName);
};//End of class DirectedGraph

DirectedGraph::DirectedGraph()
{
        nVertices = 0;
        nEdges = 0;
        for(int i=0; i<maxSize; i++)
        {
                for(int j=0; j<maxSize; j++)
                {
                        adj[i][j] = 0;
                }
        }
        INITIAL = 0;
        VISITED = 1;
        FINISHED = 2;
}//End of DirectedGraph()

void DirectedGraph::dfs(int vertex)
{
        cout << vertexList[vertex]->name << " ";
        vertexList[vertex]->state = VISITED;
        for(int i=0; i<nVertices; i++)
        {
                //Checking for adjacent vertices with INITIAL state
                if(isAdjacent(vertex,i) && vertexList[i]->state==INITIAL)
                {
                        dfs(i);
                }
        }
        vertexList[vertex]->state = FINISHED;
}//End of dfs()

void DirectedGraph::dfsTraversal(string vertexName)
{
        //Initially all the vertices will have INITIAL state
        for(int i=0; i<nVertices; i++)
        {
                vertexList[i]->state = INITIAL;
        }
        dfs(getIndex(vertexName));
        cout << "\n";
}//End of dfsTraversal()

void DirectedGraph::dfsTraversalAll(string vertexName)
{
        //Initially all the vertices will have INITIAL state
        for(int i=0; i<nVertices; i++)
        {
                vertexList[i]->state = INITIAL;
        }
        dfs(getIndex(vertexName));
        for(int v=0; v<nVertices; v++)
        {
                if(vertexList[v]->state == INITIAL)
                        dfs(v);
        }
        cout << "\n";
}//End of dfsTraversalAll()

int main()
```

```
{
        DirectedGraph dGraph;
        try
        {
                //Creating the graph, inserting the vertices and edges
                dGraph.insertVertex("0");
                dGraph.insertVertex("1");
                dGraph.insertVertex("2");
                dGraph.insertVertex("3");
                dGraph.insertVertex("4");
                dGraph.insertVertex("5");
                dGraph.insertVertex("6");
                dGraph.insertVertex("7");
                dGraph.insertVertex("8");
                dGraph.insertEdge("0","1");
                dGraph.insertEdge("0","3");
                dGraph.insertEdge("1","2");
                dGraph.insertEdge("1","4");
                dGraph.insertEdge("3","4");
                dGraph.insertEdge("3","6");
                dGraph.insertEdge("4","2");
                dGraph.insertEdge("4","5");
                dGraph.insertEdge("4","7");
                dGraph.insertEdge("6","7");
                dGraph.insertEdge("7","5");
                dGraph.insertEdge("7","8");
                //Display the graph
                dGraph.display();
                cout << "\n";

                //DFS traversal visiting only those vertices that are reachable from
                //start vertex
                dGraph.dfsTraversal("4");
                //DFS traversal visiting all the vertices
                dGraph.dfsTraversalAll("0");
        }//End of try
        catch(exception e)
        {
                cout << e.what() << "\n";
        }
        return 0;
}//End of main()
```

The destructor, insertVertex(), getIndex(), insertEdge(), display(), and isAdjacent() functions are the same as in the directed graph program.

Figure 7.78 shows the depth first search for the graph of figure 7.71, vertices which are visited are in grey color, and vertices which are finished are in black. We have also given two numbers to each vertex, discovery time and finishing time. The discovery time of a vertex is assigned when the vertex is first discovered and visited, i.e., when it becomes grey. The finishing time of a vertex is assigned when we backtrack from it, and it becomes black. As earlier, we have chosen to visit the successors in the ascending order of their number, i.e., if a vertex has 1 and 3 as successors, then first we will visit 1 and then 3.

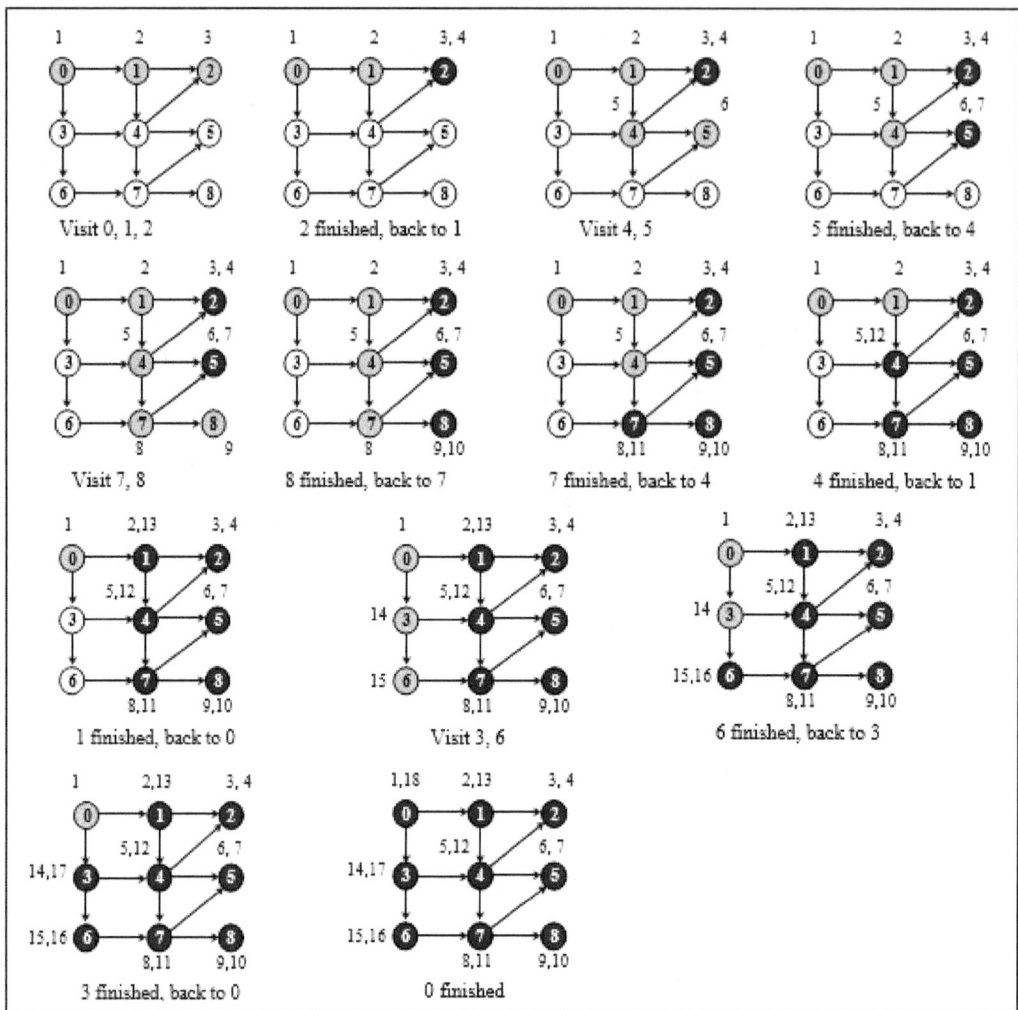

Figure 7.78 Recursive DFS showing discovery time and finishing time

The recursive calls to DFS for the given graph would be:
(Ad means adjacent and In means initial)

▶Call DFS(0) , visit 0
▶1 is Ad to 0 and In : ■ Call DFS(1), visit 1
        ■ 2 is Ad to 1 and In : - Call DFS(2) , visit 2
                               - Vertex 2 finished
        ■ 4 is Ad to 1 and In : ● Call DFS(4) , visit 4
                        ● 5 is Ad to 4 and In : - Call DFS(5) , visit 5
                                               - Vertex 5 finished
                        ● 7 is Ad to 4 and In : * Call DFS(7) , visit 7
                                          * 8 is Ad to 7 and In :- Call DFS(8) , visit 8
                                                               -Vertex 8 finished
                                          * Vertex 7 finished
                        ● Vertex 4 finished
        ■ Vertex 1 finished

►3 is Ad to 0 and In : ♦ Call DFS(3) , visit 3

♦ 6 is Ad to 3 and In : - Call DFS(6) , visit 6

- Vertex 6 finished

♦ Vertex 3 finished

►Vertex 0 finished

If we number all these steps, then we can get the discovery time and finishing time of all the vertices.

<u>1</u>. Call DFS(0) , visit 0

<u>2</u>. 1 is Ad to 0 and In : Call DFS(1) , visit 1

<u>3</u>. 2 is Ad to 1 and In : Call DFS(2) , visit 2

<u>4</u>. Vertex 2 finished

<u>5</u>. 4 is Ad to 1 and In : Call DFS(4) , visit 4

<u>6</u>. 5 is Ad to 4 and In : Call DFS(5) , visit 5

<u>7</u>. Vertex 5 finished

<u>8</u>. 7 is Ad to 4 and In : Call DFS(7) , visit 7

<u>9</u>. 8 is Ad to 7 and In : Call DFS(8) , visit 8

<u>10</u>.Vertex 8 finished

<u>11</u>. Vertex 7 finished

<u>12</u>. Vertex 4 finished

<u>13</u>. Vertex 1 finished

<u>14</u>. 3 is Ad to 0 and In : Call DFS(3) , visit 3

<u>15</u>. 6 is Ad to 3 and In : Call DFS(6) , visit 6

<u>16</u>. Vertex 6 finished

<u>17</u>. Vertex 3 finished

<u>18</u>. Vertex 0 finished

We can make simple additions in our recursive algorithm for recording the discovery time and finishing time of each vertex. We will take a variable `time`, and initialize it to 0, and increment it whenever we visit a vertex or finish a vertex. The class `Vertex` will have data members `discoveryTime` and `finishingTime`.

```
void DirectedGraph::dfs(int vertex)
{
        cout << vertexList[vertex]->name << " ";
        vertexList[vertex]->state = VISITED;
        vertexList[vertex]->discoveryTime = ++time;   //discovery time

        for(int i=0; i<nVertices; i++)
        {
                //Checking for adjacent vertices with INITIAL state
                if(isAdjacent(vertex,i) && vertexList[i]->state==INITIAL)
                {
                        dfs(i);
                }
        }

        vertexList[vertex]->state = FINISHED;
        vertexList[vertex]->finishingTime = ++time;   //finishing time
}//End of dfs()
```

7.12.2.3 Classification of Edges in DFS

DFS can be used to classify the edges of a directed graph into four different groups. The edges can be divided into these groups based on the spanning forest:

(i) Tree edge: An edge included in the DFS spanning forest.
(ii) Back edge: An edge from a vertex to its spanning tree ancestor.
(iii) Forward edge: An edge from a vertex to a spanning tree non son descendant.

(iv) Cross edge: All remaining edges are cross edges. An edge between two vertices u and v is a cross edge, when there is no ancestor or descendent relationship between u and v in the spanning forest. The cross edges can be between the vertices of the same spanning tree or the vertices of different spanning trees.

Let us take a directed graph and apply DFS on it taking 0 as the start vertex.

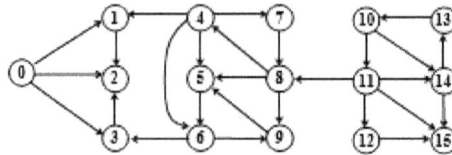

Figure 7.79 Directed graph for DFS

Vertices 1, 2, 3 are reachable from 0, and so, these are visited, and then we select 4, as the next start vertex. The vertices 5, 6,7 8,9 are reachable from 4, and so these are visited, and then we select 10 as the next start vertex. All the remaining vertices are reachable from 10. The traversal would be:

0, 1, 2, 3, 4, 5, 6, 9, 7, 8, 10, 11, 12, 15, 14, 13

The DFS spanning forest for the graph of figure 7.79 and different types of edges are shown in the figure 7.80.

The following function dfs () classifies all the edges in a directed graph:

```cpp
void DirectedGraph::dfs(int vertex)
{
        vertexList[vertex]->state = VISITED;
        vertexList[vertex]->discoveryTime = ++time;

        for(int i=0; i<nVertices; i++)
        {
                if(isAdjacent(vertex,i))
                {
                        if(vertexList[i]->state==INITIAL)
                        {
                                cout << "Tree Edge - (" << vertexList[vertex]->name <<
                                "-" << vertexList[i]->name << ")\n";
                                dfs(i);
                        }
                        else if(vertexList[i]->state==VISITED)
                        {
                                cout << "Back Edge - (" << vertexList[vertex]->name << "-"
                                << vertexList[i]->name << ")\n";
                        }
                        else if(vertexList[vertex]->discoveryTime < vertexList[i]
                        ->discoveryTime)
                        {
                                cout << "Forward Edge - (" << vertexList[vertex]->name
                                << "-" << vertexList[i]->name << ")\n";
                        }
                        else
                        {
                                cout << "Cross Edge - (" << vertexList[vertex]->name <<
                                "-" << vertexList[i]->name << ")\n";
                        }
```

```
        }
    }//End of for

    vertexList[vertex]->state = FINISHED;
    vertexList[vertex]->finishingTime = ++time;
}//End of dfs()
```

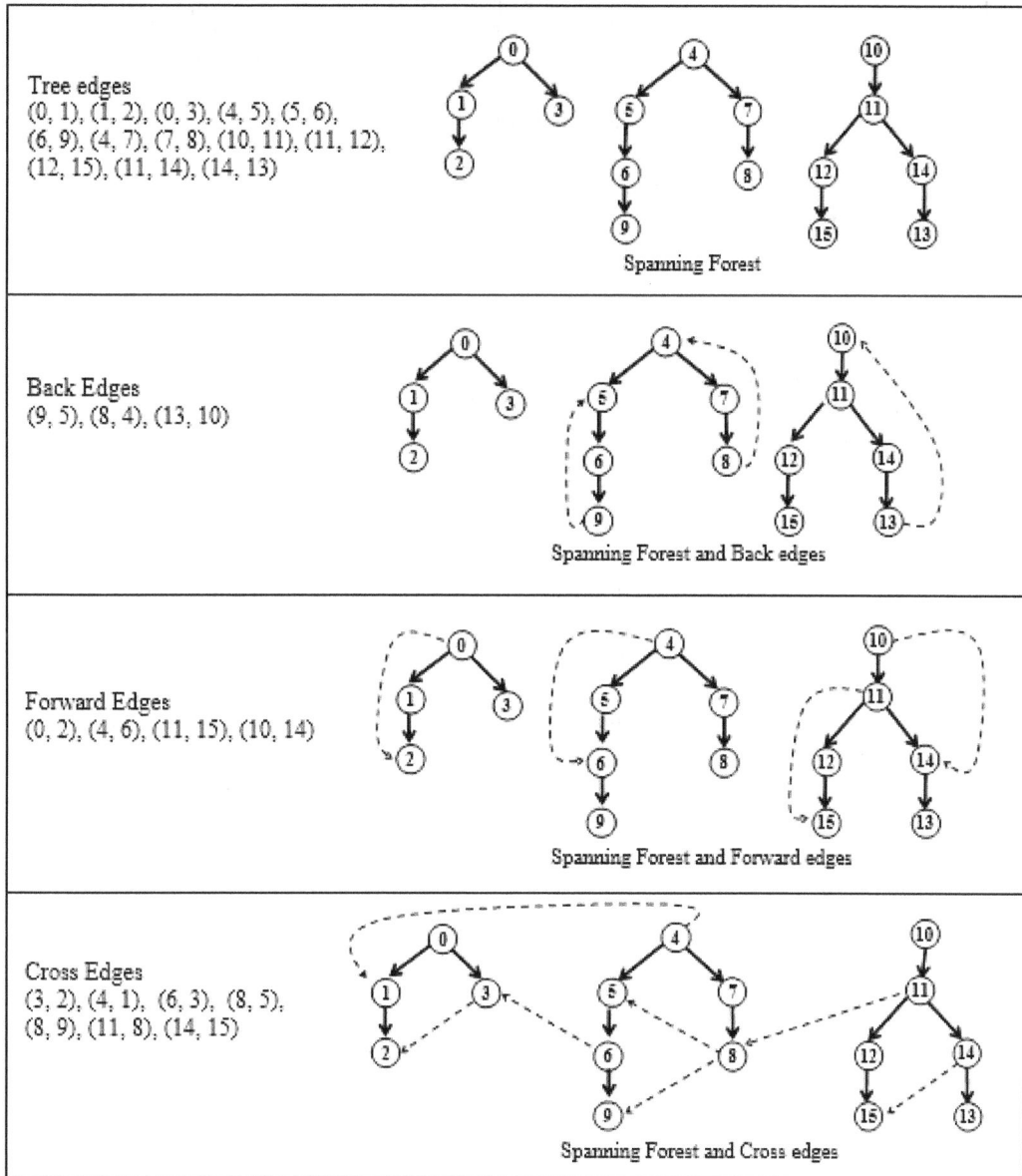

Figure 7.80 DFS spanning forest and diffeternt types of edges

Now let us take an undirected graph and perform a depth first search on it:

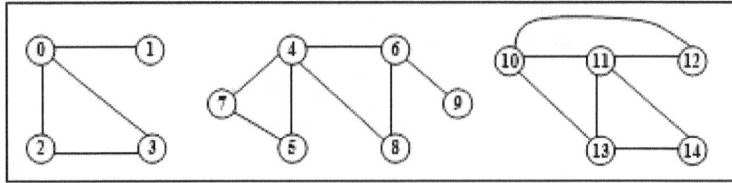

Figure 7.81 Undirected graph for DFS

The depth first traversal of this graph would be:

0 1 2 3   4 5 7 6 8 9   10 11 12 13 14

The spanning forest for this graph would be:

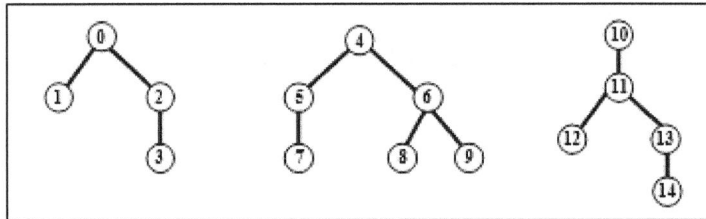

Figure 7.82 Spanning forest for undirected graph

In an undirected graph, there is no difference between back edges and forward edges because all edges are bidirectional. So in an undirected graph, any edge between a vertex and its non son descendant is a back edge. Cross edges are also not possible in the depth first search of an undirected graph. Therefore, in the depth first search of an undirected graph, every edge is classified as either a tree edge or a back edge. The following figure shows the tree edges and back edges for the undirected graph given above:

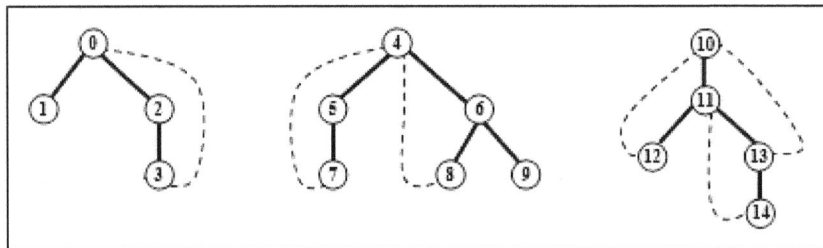

Figure 7.83 Tree edges and back edges for the undirected graph

From this figure, it is clear that in an undirected edge, there can be no distinction between a forward edge and back edge, and so, all edges from a vertex to non-son descendants are back edges. Now, let us see why cross edges are not possible. Suppose there was an edge in the graph from 12 to 14. Then it seems to be a candidate for a cross edge, looking at this spanning forest. But had the edge (12, 14) existed in the graph, the last spanning tree would have been different. In that case, 14 would be visited after 12 and so, 14 would be the son of 12. Hence, we cannot have cross edges in a spanning tree of the forest. Similarly, we cannot have cross edges between different spanning trees. The following function `dfs()` shows how to classify the tree edges and back edges in an undirected graph.

```
void UndirectedGraph::dfs(int vertex)
{
        vertexList[vertex]->state = VISITED;

        for(int i=0; i<nVertices; i++)
        {
                if(isAdjacent(vertex,i) && vertexList[vertex]->predecessor!=i)
                {
                        if(vertexList[i]->state == INITIAL)
                        {
                                vertexList[i]->predecessor = vertex;
                                cout << "Tree Edge - (" << vertexList[vertex]->name <<
                                "," << vertexList[i]->name << ")\n";
                                dfs(i);
                        }
                        else if(vertexList[i]->state == VISITED)
                        {
                                cout << "Back Edge - (" << vertexList[vertex]->name <<
                                "," << vertexList[i]->name << ")\n";
                        }
                }//End of if
        }//End of for
        vertexList[vertex]->state = FINISHED;
}//End of dfs()
```

In an undirected graph, an edge between two vertices v1 and v2 is considered twice during DFS, once from v1 with v2 as its adjacent vertex, and once from v2 with v1 as its adjacent vertex. This can cause confusion in classifying the edges. To avoid this confusion, an edge between v1 and v2 is classified according to whether (v1,v2) or (v2,v1) is encountered first during the traversal; for example, if there is an edge between vertices 5 and 8 of a graph. Now, if vertex 5 is visited first, then we will call edge (5,8) as a tree edge. Vertex 5 will be made the predecessor of vertex 8. Now, when vertex 8 will be visited, we will not consider edge (8,5). This is because we know that this edge has already been considered since 5 is the predecessor of 8.

The depth first search can be used to find out whether a graph is cyclic. In both directed and undirected graphs, if we get a back edge during depth first traversal, then the graph is cyclic.

7.12.2.4 Strongly Connected Graph and Strongly Connected Components

In section 7.5, we read about a strongly connected graph and strongly connected components. Now, we will apply the depth first search to find whether a graph is strongly connected or not and to find the strongly connected components of a graph.

To prove that a graph G is strongly connected, we need to prove that these two statements are true for any vertex v of graph G:

1. All vertices of G are reachable from v, i.e., there is a path from v to every vertex.
2. v is reachable from all other vertices of G, there is a path from every vertex to v.

Now let us see why proving these two statements true is enough to prove that the graph is strongly connected. Let u and w be two vertices in graph G. To prove that G is strongly connected, we need to show that there is a path from u to w and from w to u. If statements 1 and 2 are true, then we can show that these paths will exist.

For going from u to w, we can go from u to v (by st. 2) and then from v to w (by st. 1). Similarly, for going from w to v, we can go from w to v (by st. 2) and then from v to u (by st.1). So, to prove that a graph is strongly connected, we need to prove that the 2 statements given above are true. We can perform DFS(v) and if it visits all the vertices, then we can say that the first statement is true.

For proving the second statement, we need to reverse the graph G, i.e., we have to reverse the direction of all the edges in G. Suppose G^R is the reverse graph; now we will perform DFS(v) on G^R, and if it visits all the vertices, then the second statement is also true. The whole procedure is as follows:

Take any vertex v of the graph G.

1. Perform depth first search on G, starting at vertex v.
2. If it does not visit all the vertices,

   Graph is not strongly connected, Return

   Else

   Reverse the graph G to get graph G^R
3. Perform depth first search on G^R, starting at vertex v.
4. If it does not visit all the vertices

   Graph is not strongly connected.

   Else

   Graph is strongly connected.

Now, let us see how we can find the Strongly Connected Components (SCC) of a graph.

Take any vertex v of the graph G.

1. Perform depth first search on G, starting at vertex v, and mark the finishing time of each vertex.
2. Reverse the graph G to get graph G^R
3. Perform depth first search on G^R, always picking the vertex with highest finishing time for a new DFS.

The depth first trees in the depth first forest thus formed are the strongly connected components of G.

While performing DFS on the reverse graph, we start from the vertex that has the highest finishing time; all vertices reachable from this vertex will be in the same SCC. Now, from the remaining vertices, we pick the vertex that has the highest finishing time, and start DFS from there. All vertices reachable from this vertex will be in the same SCC. This process continues till all the vertices are visited. Let us take a graph and find strongly connected components for it.

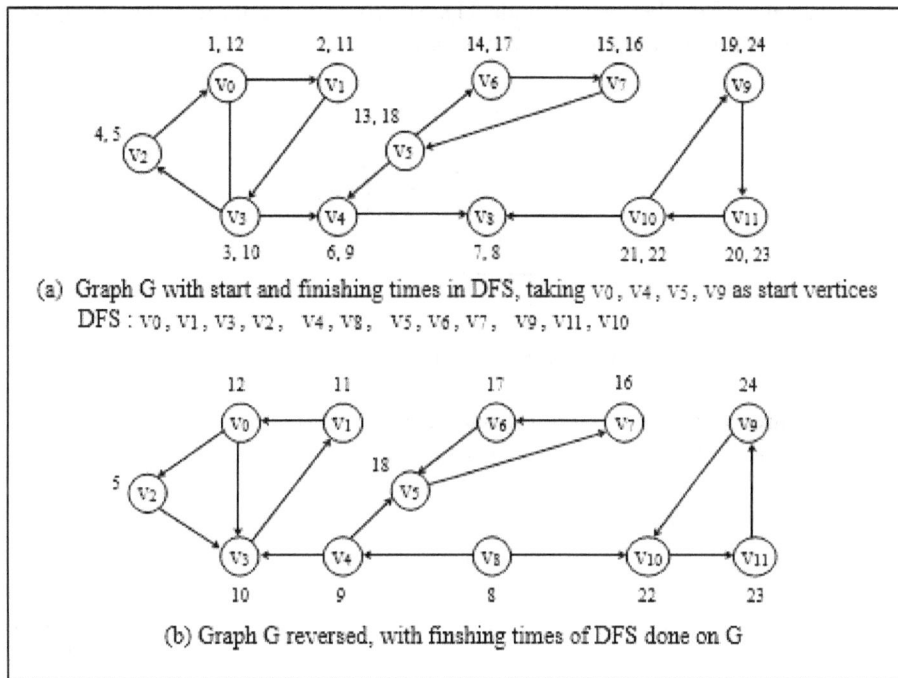

(a) Graph G with start and finishing times in DFS, taking v_0, v_4, v_5, v_9 as start vertices
DFS : v_0, v_1, v_3, v_2, v_4, v_8, v_5, v_6, v_7, v_9, v_{11}, v_{10}

(b) Graph G reversed, with finshing times of DFS done on G

Figure 7.84 Finding strongly connected graph and strongly connected components

In figure 7.84 (a), the graph is shown with the start and finishing time of each vertex when DFS is done with v_0, v_4, v_5, v_9 as start vertices. In figure 7.84 (b), the graph G is reversed and the finishing time from (a) is shown for each vertex.

To find strongly connected components, we will start DFS of the reverse graph from vertex v_9 since it had the highest finishing time in the previous DFS. The vertices v_9, v_{10}, v_{11} are visited, and so they form one SCC. Now, from the remaining vertices, v_5 has the highest finishing time and so we start DFS from there. The vertices v_5, v_7, v_6 are visited, and so they form another SCC. Now, from the remaining vertices, v_0 has the highest finishing time, and so we start DFS from there. The vertices v_0, v_2, v_3, v_1 are visited, and so they form another SCC. Next, v_4 has the highest finishing time. So, DFS starts from there and only v_4 is visited. Thus, it forms one SCC. The remaining vertex v_8 also forms a SCC. The strongly connected components are:

{ v_9, v_{10}, v_{11} }, {v_5, v_7, v_6}, {v_0, v_2, v_3, v_1 }, {v_4}, {v_8}

7.13 Shortest Path Problem

There can be several paths for going from one vertex to another vertex in a weighted graph, but the shortest path is the path in which the sum of weights of the included edges is the minimum. Consider the weighted directed graph in figure 7.85.

Suppose we have to go from vertex 0 to vertex 4. We can take the path 0→2→3→4 and the length of this path would be 16. But this is not the only path from vertex 0 to vertex 4; there are other paths which may be shorter. We are interested in finding the shortest of these paths. The other two paths are

0→2→5→3→4 (length=12)   0→1→4 (length=11). So from all the three paths, the shortest one is 0→1→4. It is not necessary that the shortest path is unique.

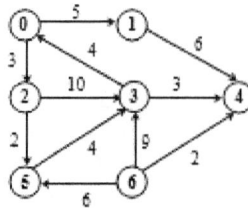

Figure 7.85 Weighted directed graph

We will study these three algorithms for finding out the shortest paths in a weighted graph:
(i) Dijkstra's Algorithm: Single source, non-negative weights.
(ii) Bellman Ford Algorithm: Single source, general weights.
(iii) Floyd's or Modified Warshall's algorithm: All pairs shortest paths.

The first two algorithms are single source shortest paths algorithms (this source is different from the 0 indegree source defined in section 7.3). In these shortest path problems, a vertex is identified as the source vertex, and the shortest path from this vertex to all other vertices is found out. This source vertex can also be called the start vertex. Dijkstra's algorithm works only for non-negative weights, while Bellman Ford algorithm can be used for negative weights also.

There is no algorithm that finds shortest path from source to a single destination, and is faster than the single source shortest paths algorithms. So, finding the shortest paths from a single source to all vertices is as simple as finding the shortest path to a single destination.

Floyd's algorithm is an all pairs shortest path problem. Here, we get the shortest paths between each pair of vertices of the graph. This is also called Modified Warshall's algorithm, because it is based on the Warshall's algorithm that we studied earlier in section 7.11.2.

The shortest paths can be helpful in various situations. For example, suppose our weighted graph represents a transport system, where each vertex is a city and weights on the edges represent the distance of one city from another. We would be interested in taking the shortest route to reach our destination. Similarly, the graph may represent an airlines network or a railway track system, and the weights on the edges may represent the distance, time or cost. In all these cases, the knowledge of shortest paths helps us select the best option. Electric supply systems and water distribution systems also follow this approach. In computers, it is very useful in the network for routing concepts.

7.13.1 Dijkstra's Algorithm

Dijkstra's algorithm is named after E. W. Dijkstra, who developed this technique of finding shortest paths in 1959. In this algorithm, we find the shortest distance from the source vertex to all other vertices in the graph. This algorithm works correctly only if all the weights in the graph are non-negative.

Consider the graph given in figure 7.86. If we assume 0 as the source vertex, then the table next to it shows the shortest paths to all other vertices of the graph.

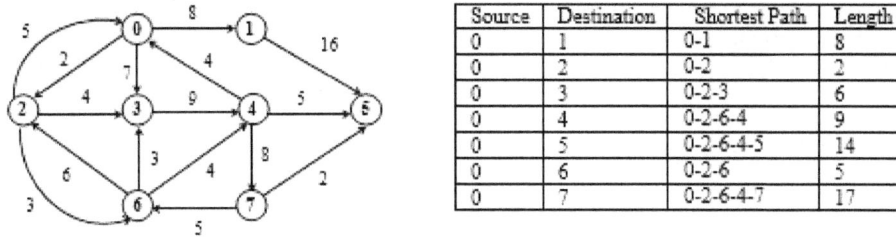

Source	Destination	Shortest Path	Length
0	1	0-1	8
0	2	0-2	2
0	3	0-2-3	6
0	4	0-2-6-4	9
0	5	0-2-6-4-5	14
0	6	0-2-6	5
0	7	0-2-6-4-7	17

Figure 7.86 Shortest path from vertex 0 to others vertices for the graph

Now, we will see how we can obtain these shortest paths using Dijkstra's algorithm. Each vertex is given a status, which can be permanent or temporary. If a vertex is temporary, then it means that the shortest path to it has not been found, and if a vertex is permanent, then it means shortest path to it has been found. Initially all the vertices are temporary, and at each step of the algorithm, a temporary vertex is made permanent.

We label each vertex with pathLength and predecessor. At any point of the algorithm, the pathLength of a vertex v will denote the length of the shortest path – known till now – from the source vertex to v. The predecessor of v will denote the vertex that precedes v in this path.

Initially, the pathLength of all vertices is initialized to a very large number which denotes that at the start of algorithm, we do not know of any path from the source to any vertex. We will call this number as infinity. The predecessor value of all vertices is initialzed to NIL. In the program, we can take NIL to be any number that does not represent a valid vertex. We will take it -1 in our program, since our vertices start from 0.

At the end of the algorithm, pathLength of a vertex will represent the shortest distance of that vertex from the source vertex, and the predecessor will represent the vertex which precedes the given vertex in the shortest path from source.

As the algorithm proceeds, the values of pathLength and predecessor of a vertex may be updated many times provided the vertex is temporary. Once a vertex is made permanent, the values of pathLength and predecessor for it become fixed and are not changed thereafter. It means that the temporary vertices can be relabeled if required, but permanent vertices cannot be relabeled.

When a temporary vertex is made permanent, it means that the shortest distance for it has been finalized. So the pathLength of a permanent vertex represents the length of the shortest path from the source to this vertex, i.e., no other path shorter than this is possible.

At any point of the algorithm, the pathLength of a temporary vertex represents the length of the best known path – from source to this vertex – till now, it is possible that there may be some other better path which is shorter than this one. So, whenever we will find a shorter path, we will update the pathLength and predecessor values of this temporary vertex. We will try to find shorter paths by examining the edges incident from the vertex which is made permanent most recently.

We have stated that at each step, a vertex will be made permanent. Now, the question is, which vertex should be chosen to become permanent. For this, we use the greedy approach. In greedy algorithms, we generally perform an action which appears best at the moment. Greedy algorithms do not always give optimal results in general, but in this case, we get the correct result and we will see the proof at the end. Applying the greedy approach, in each step, the temporary vertex that has the smallest value of pathLength is made permanent.

Now, let us look at the whole algorithm stepwise, and see how the pathLength and predecessor values are updated to get shorter paths, and how we finally get the shortest paths for all the vertices. The procedure is as follows:

(A) Initialize the pathLength of all vertices to infinity and the predecessor of all vertices to NIL. Make the status of all vertices temporary.

(B) Make the pathLength of source vertex equal to 0.

(C) From all the temporary vertices in the graph, find out the vertex that has the minimum value of pathLength. Make it permanent and now, this is our current vertex. (If there are many with the same value of pathlength, then anyone can be selected).

(D) Examine all the temporary vertices adjacent to the current vertex. The value of pathLength is recalculated for all these temporary successors of the current vertex, and relabelling is done if required. Let us see how this is done.

Suppose s is the source vertex, `current` is the current vertex and v is a temporary vertex adjacent to `current`.

(i) If   pathLength(`current`) + weight(`current`, v) < pathLength(v)
It means that the path from s to v via `current` is smaller than the path currently assigned to v. We have found a shorter path, and so the pathLength(v) is updated and assigned the length of this smaller path. Also the predecessor of v is changed to `current`, since now, the `current` is the predecessor of the vertex v in the shortest path. So, in this case, the vertex v is relabelled. Relabelling means discarding the previous path from s to v and updating it to a new path, which consists of a path from s to `current` and a direct edge from `current` to v.

Now   pathLength(v) = pathLength(`current`) + weight(`current`, v)
           predecessor(v) = current

(ii) If   pathLength(`current`) + weight(`current`, v) >= pathLength(v),
It means that using `current` vertex in the path from s to v does not offer any shorter path. So, in this case, vertex v is not relabelled and values of pathLength and predecessor for vertex v remain unchanged.

(E) Repeat steps C and D until no temporary vertex is left in the graph, or all the temporary vertices left have pathLength of infinity.

Now, we will take the graph given in figure 7.86 and find out the shortest paths taking 0 as the source vertex.

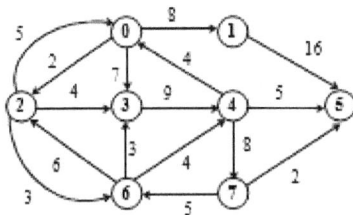

Figure 7.87 Graph for finding shortest paths

Initially, no paths are known, so the pathLength values for all the vertices are set to a very large number (which is larger than length of longest possible path). We will represent this by ∞ in the figure. The predecessor of all vertices is NIL in the beginning. Source vertex 0 is assigned a pathLength of 0. In the figures, all vertices will be joined to their predecessors. A permanent vertex will be joined to its predecessor by a bold arrow.

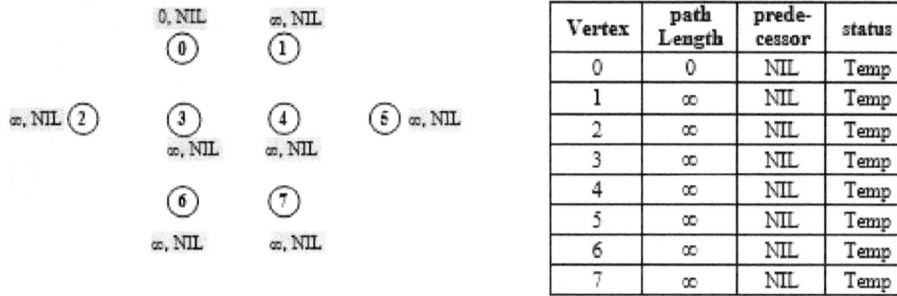

Figure 7.88 Initial graph and table for path length, predecessor, status of vertex

From all the temporary vertices, vertex 0 has the smallest pathLength, so make it permanent. Its predecessor will remain NIL. Now, vertex 0 is the current vertex.

Vertices 1, 2, 3 are temporary vertices adjacent to vertex 0.

pathLength(0) + weight(0,1) < pathLength(1)   0+8 < ∞
Relabel 1, pathLength[1] = 8, predecessor[1] = 0

pathLength(0) + weight(0,2) < pathLength(2)   0+2 < ∞
Relabel 2, pathLength[2] = 2, predecessor[2] = 0

pathLength(0) + weight (0,3) < pathLength(3)   0+7 < ∞
Relabel 3, pathLength[3] = 7, predecessor[3] = 0

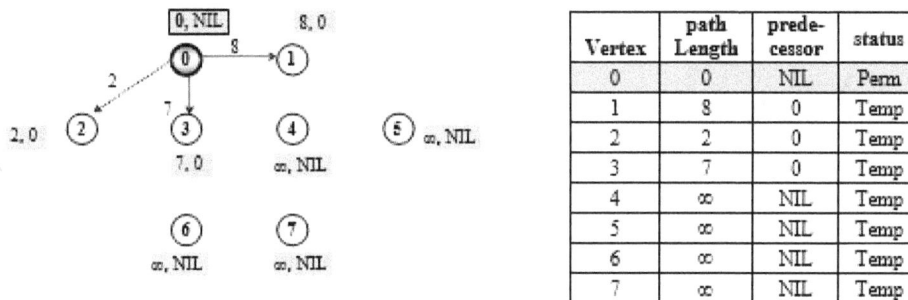

Figure 7.89 Make vertex 0 permanent

From all the temporary vertices, vertex 2 has the smallest pathlength, so make it permanent. Now, vertex 2 is the current vertex.

Vertices 3, 6 are temporary vertices adjacent to vertex 2.

pathLength(2) + weight(2,3) < pathLength(3)   2+4 < 7
Relabel 3, pathLength[3] = 6, predecessor[3] = 2

pathLength(2) + weight(2,6) < pathLength(6)   2+3 < ∞
Relabel 6, pathLength[6] = 5, predecessor[6] = 2

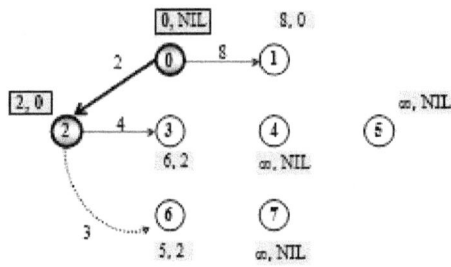

Figure 7.90 Make vertex 2 permanent

From all the temporary vertices, vertex 6 has the smallest pathlength, so make it permanent. Now, vertex 6 is our current vertex.

Vertices 3, and 4 are temporary vertices adjacent to vertex 6.

pathLength(6) + weight(6,3) > pathLength(3)   5+3 > 6
Do not relabel 3

pathLength(6) + weight(6,4) < pathLength(4)   5+4 < ∞
Relabel 4, pathLength[4] = 9, predecessor[4] = 6

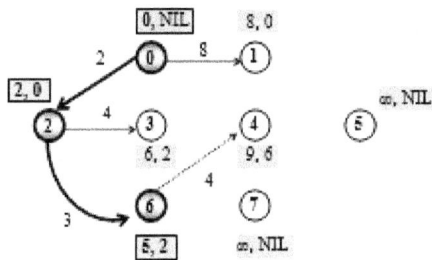

Figure 7.91 Make vertex 6 permanent

From all temporary vertices, vertex 3 has the smallest pathlength, so make it permanent. Now, vertex 3 is the current vertex.

Vertex 4 is the temporary vertex adjacent to 3.

pathLength(3) + weight(3,4) > pathLength(4)   6+9 > 9
Do not relabel 4

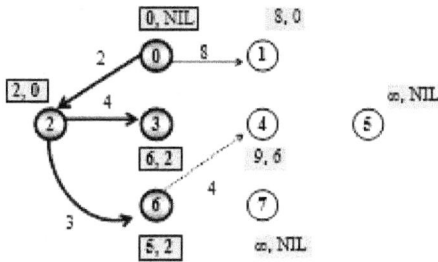

Figure 7.92 Make vertex 3 permanent

From all temporary vertices, vertex 1 has the smallest pathlength, so make it permanent. Now, vertex 1 is the current vertex.

Vertex 5 is the temporary vertex adjacent to 1.

pathLength(1) + weight(1,5) < pathLength(5) $8+16 < \infty$
Relabel 5, pathLength[5] = 24, predecessor[5] = 1

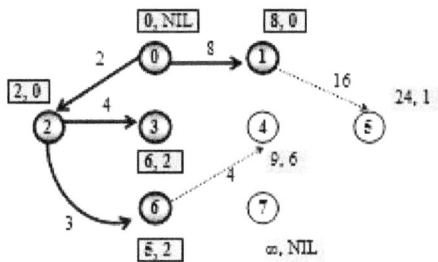

Figure 7.93 Make vertex 1 permanent

Fom all temporary vertices, vertex 4 has the smallest pathLength, so make it permanent. Now, vertex 4 is the current vertex.

Vertices 5 and 7 are temporary vertices adjacent to 4.

pathLength(4) + weight(4,5) < pathLength(5) $9+5 < 24$
Relabel 5, pathLength[5] = 14, predecessor[5] = 4

pathLength(4) + weight(4,7) < pathLength(7) $9+8 < \infty$
Relabel 7, pathLength[7] = 17, predecessor[7] = 4

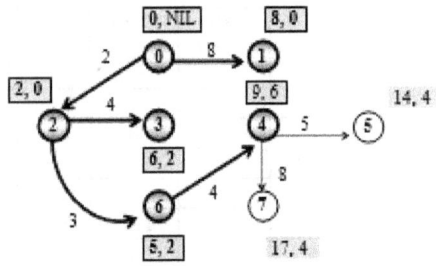

Vertex	path Length	prede -cessor	status
0	0	NIL	Perm
1	8	0	Perm
2	2	0	Perm
3	6	2	Perm
4	9	6	Perm
5	14	4	Temp
6	5	2	Perm
7	17	4	Temp

Figure 7.94 Make vertex 4 permanent

From all temporary vertices, vertex 5 has the smallest pathlength, so make it permanent. Now, vertex 5 is the current vertex.

There is no vertex adjacent to 5.

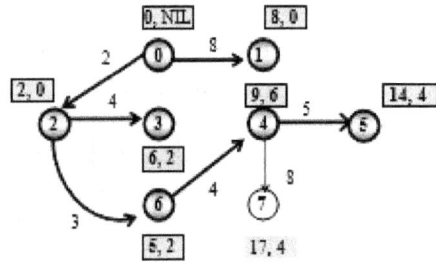

Vertex	path Length	prede -cessor	status
0	0	NIL	Perm
1	8	0	Perm
2	2	0	Perm
3	6	2	Perm
4	9	6	Perm
5	14	4	Perm
6	5	2	Perm
7	17	4	Temp

Figure 7.95 Make vertex 5 permanent

Now, 7 is the only temporary vertex left, and it has a pathLength 17, so make it permanent.

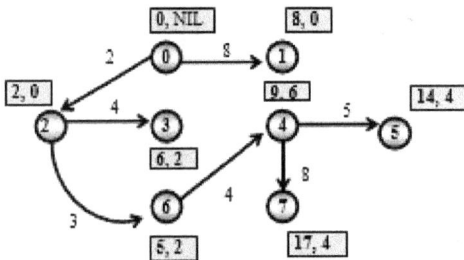

Vertex	path Length	prede- cessor	status
0	0	NIL	Perm
1	8	0	Perm
2	2	0	Perm
3	6	2	Perm
4	9	6	Perm
5	14	4	Perm
6	5	2	Perm
7	17	4	Perm

Figure 7.96 Make vertex 7 permanent

Now, all the vertices have become permanent.

At the end, we get a shortest path tree which includes all the vertices reachable from the source vertex. The source vertex is the root of this tree and the shortest paths from source to all vertices are given by the branches. Each vertex has a predecessor, so we can easily establish the path after completing the whole process. To find the shortest path from the source to any destination vertex, we look at the last table, start from the destination vertex, and keep on following successive predecessors until we reach the source vertex.

If the destination vertex is 3,
predecessor of 3 is 2, predecessor of 2 is 0
Shortest Path is 0 - 2 - 3

If the destination vertex is 5.
predecessor of 5 is 4, predecessor of 4 is 6, predecessor of 6 is 2, predecessor of 2 is 0
Shortest path is 0 - 2 - 6 - 4 - 5

If we want to find the shortest distance between the source and a single destination only, then we can stop our algorithm as soon as the destination vertex is made permanent.

In the example we have taken, all the vertices of the graph were reachable from the source vertex. So, all the vertices were permanent in the last table. If there are one or more vertices in the graph that are not reachable from the source vertex, then the shortest path to all these vertices cannot be found. So, they will never become permanent. For example, in the graph given below, the vertices 1 and 7 are not reachable from source vertex 0.

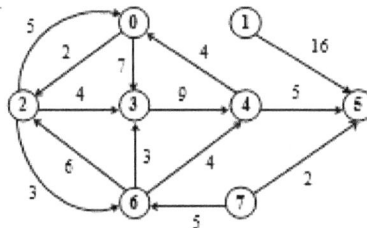

Figure 7.97 Graph with some vertices not reachable

Following the same procedure, vertices 0, 2, 6, 3, 4, 5 will be made permanent and then the pathLength and predecessor values of all vertices will be:

Vertex	path Length	prede- cessor	status
0	0	NIL	Perm
1	∞	NIL	Temp
2	2	0	Perm
3	6	2	Perm
4	9	6	Perm
5	14	4	Perm
6	5	2	Perm
7	∞	NIL	Temp

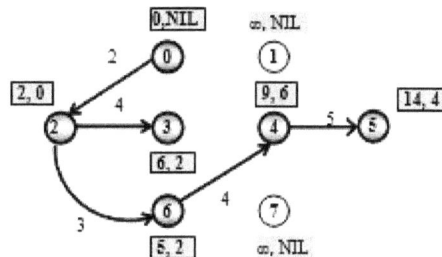

Figure 7.98 1 and 7 left temporary for the graph

Now, all the temporary vertices left have pathLength equal to infinty. While stating the procedure of Dijkstra's algorithm, we had mentioned that the procedure will stop when either no temporary vertices are left or all temporary vertices left have pathLength equal to infinity. So, in this example, we will stop after making vertex 5 permanent, and the vertices 1 and 7 will never be made permanent. These vertices are not reachable from the source vertex.

```cpp
//DirectedWeightedGraph.cpp : Program to find shortest paths using Dijkstra's algorithm.
#include<iostream>
#include<string>
using namespace std;

static const int maxSize = 30;

class Vertex
{
    public:
            string name;
            int status;
            int predecessor;
            int pathLength;
    public:
            Vertex(string name)
            {
                    this->name = name;
            }
};//End of class Vertex

class DirectedWeightedGraph
{
    private:
            int nVertices;
            int nEdges;
            int adj[maxSize][maxSize];
            Vertex *vertexList[maxSize];
            int TEMPORARY;
            int PERMANENT;
            int INFINITY;
            int NIL;
    private:
            int getIndex(string vertexName);
            bool isAdjacent(int u, int v);
            void dijkstrasAlgorithm(int s);
            int getMinimumTemporary();
            void findPath(int s, int v);
    public:
            DirectedWeightedGraph();
            ~DirectedWeightedGraph();
            void insertVertex(string vertexName);
            void insertEdge(string source, string destination, int weight);
            void display();
            void findPaths(string source);
};//End of class DirectedWeightedGraph

DirectedWeightedGraph::DirectedWeightedGraph()
{
    nVertices = 0;
    nEdges = 0;
    for(int i=0; i<maxSize; i++)
    {
            for(int j=0; j<maxSize; j++)
            {
                    adj[i][j] = 0;
            }
    }
    TEMPORARY = 0;
```

```
        PERMANENT = 1;
        INFINITY = 9999;
        NIL = -1;
}//End of DirectedWeightedGraph()

DirectedWeightedGraph::~DirectedWeightedGraph()
{
        for(int i=0; i<nVertices; i++)
        {
                delete vertexList[i];
        }
}//End of ~DirectedWeightedGraph()

void DirectedWeightedGraph::insertVertex(string vertexName)
{
        vertexList[nVertices++] = new Vertex(vertexName);
}//End of insertVertex()

int DirectedWeightedGraph::getIndex(string vertexName)
{
        for(int i=0; i<nVertices; i++)
        {
                if(vertexName == vertexList[i]->name)
                        return i;
        }
        throw exception("Invalid Vertex");
}//End of getIndex()

void DirectedWeightedGraph::insertEdge(string source, string destination, int weight)
{
        int u = getIndex(source);
        int v = getIndex(destination);
        if(u == v)
                cout << "Not a valid edge\n";
        else if(adj[u][v] != 0)
                cout << "Edge already present\n";
        else
        {
                adj[u][v] = weight;
                nEdges++;
        }
}//End of insertEdge()

void DirectedWeightedGraph::display()
{
        for(int i=0; i<nVertices; i++)
        {
                for(int j=0; j<nVertices; j++)
                        cout << adj[i][j] << " ";
                cout <<"\n";
        }
}//End of display()

bool DirectedWeightedGraph::isAdjacent(int u, int v)
{
        return (adj[u][v] != 0);
}//End of isAdjacent()

//Returns the temporary vertex with minimum value of pathLength,
//Returns NIL if no temporary vertex left or all temporary vertices left have pathLength
//INFINITY
int DirectedWeightedGraph::getMinimumTemporary()
{
        int min = INFINITY;
        int k = NIL;
```

```
        for(int i=0; i<nVertices; i++)
        {
                if(vertexList[i]->status==TEMPORARY && vertexList[i]->pathLength<min)
                {
                        min = vertexList[i]->pathLength;
                        k=i;
                }
        }
        return k;
}//End of getMinimumTemporary()
void DirectedWeightedGraph::dijkstrasAlgorithm(int s)
{
        //Make all vertices temporary
        for(int i=0; i<nVertices; i++)
        {
                vertexList[i]->status = TEMPORARY;
                vertexList[i]->predecessor = NIL;
                vertexList[i]->pathLength = INFINITY;
        }
        //Make pathLength of source vertex equal to 0
        vertexList[s]->pathLength = 0;
        while(true)
        {
                //Search for temporary vertex with minimum pathLength and make it current
                //vertex
                int current = getMinimumTemporary();
                if(current == NIL)
                        break;
                //Make current vertex PERMANENT
                vertexList[current]->status = PERMANENT;
                for(int v=0; v<nVertices; v++)
                {
                        //Checks for adjacent temporary vertices
                        if(isAdjacent(current,v) && vertexList[v]->status==TEMPORARY)
                        {
                                if((vertexList[current]->pathLength + adj[current][v])
                                < vertexList[v]->pathLength)
                                {
                                        vertexList[v]->predecessor = current; //Relabel
                                        vertexList[v]->pathLength = vertexList[current]
                                        ->pathLength + adj[current][v];
                                }
                        }
                }//End of for
        }//End of while
}//End of dijkstrasAlgorithm()
void DirectedWeightedGraph::findPath(int s, int v)
{
        int path[maxSize];            //stores the shortest path
        int shortestDistance=0;       //length of shortest path
        int count=0;                  //number of vertices in the shortest path
        int u;
        //Store the full path in the array path
        while(v!=s)
        {
                count++;
                path[count] = v;
                u = vertexList[v]->predecessor;
                shortestDistance += adj[u][v];
```

```
                v = u;
        }
        count++;
        path[count] = s;

        cout << "Shortest Path : ";
        for(int i=count; i>=1; i--)
                cout << vertexList[path[i]]->name << " ";
        cout << "\n";
        cout << "Shortest Distance : " << shortestDistance << "\n";
}//End of findPath()
void DirectedWeightedGraph::findPaths(string source)
{
        int s = getIndex(source);
        dijkstrasAlgorithm(s);
        cout << "Source : " << source << "\n";
        for(int v=0; v<nVertices; v++)
        {
                cout << "Destination : " << vertexList[v]->name << "\n";
                if(vertexList[v]->pathLength == INFINITY)
                        cout << "There is no path from " << source << " to vertex "
                             << vertexList[v]->name << "\n";
                else
                        findPath(s, v);
        }
}//End of findPaths()

int main()
{
        DirectedWeightedGraph dwGraph;
        try
        {
                //Creating the graph, inserting the vertices and edges
                dwGraph.insertVertex("0");
                dwGraph.insertVertex("1");
                dwGraph.insertVertex("2");
                dwGraph.insertVertex("3");
                dwGraph.insertVertex("4");
                dwGraph.insertVertex("5");
                dwGraph.insertVertex("6");
                dwGraph.insertVertex("7");
                dwGraph.insertEdge("0","1",8);
                dwGraph.insertEdge("0","2",2);
                dwGraph.insertEdge("0","3",7);
                dwGraph.insertEdge("1","5",16);
                dwGraph.insertEdge("2","0",5);
                dwGraph.insertEdge("2","3",4);
                dwGraph.insertEdge("2","6",3);
                dwGraph.insertEdge("3","4",9);
                dwGraph.insertEdge("4","0",4);
                dwGraph.insertEdge("4","5",5);
                dwGraph.insertEdge("4","7",8);
                dwGraph.insertEdge("6","2",6);
                dwGraph.insertEdge("6","3",3);
                dwGraph.insertEdge("6","4",4);
                dwGraph.insertEdge("7","5",2);
                dwGraph.insertEdge("7","6",5);
                //Display the graph
                dwGraph.display();
                cout << "\n";
                //Finding path from source vertex to other vertices
```

```
            dwGraph.findPaths("0");
    }//End of try
    catch(exception e)
    {
            cout << e.what() << "\n";
    }
    return 0;
}//End of main()
```

Now, after studying the whole procedure, let us see why this algorithm works and gives the optimal result:

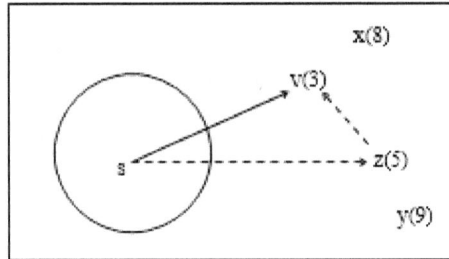

Figure 7.99 Shortest distance from s to v

Suppose we have 4 temporary vertices x, y, z, v. Vertices inside the circle are permanent vertices and vertices outside the circle are temporary vertices. We take the vertex with the smallest pathLength and declare that shortest path to it has been finalized, and make it permanent. In this case, v has the shortest value of pathlength, so it is declared permanent. Let us see why this is the shortest path for v.

If this is not the shortest path for v, then suppose there exists a hypothetical shorter path going through z. This path goes from s to z, and then z to v. Now, the length of this path is equal to the sum of pathLength(z) and weight(z,v). We are claiming that this path is shorter, so the value pathLength(z)+weight(z,v) should be smaller than pathLength(v). If this is so, then the pathLength(z) will also be smaller than pathLength(v). Here comes the contradiction - if pathLength(z) is smaller than pathLength(v), then our greedy approach would have chosen z, to be made permanent instead of v. So we have proved by contradiction that pathLength(v) is the shortest distance from s to v.

7.13.2 Bellman Ford Algorithm

Dijkstra's algorithm works properly only for non-negative weights. For example, consider the graph given as follows:

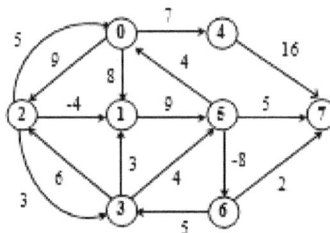

Figure 7.100 Weighted directed graph with negative values

The shortest distances from the source vertex 0 to all other vertices as computed by Dijkstra's algorithm are as follows:

Source	Destination	Shortest Path	Length
0	1	0-1	8
0	2	0-2	9
0	3	0-2-3	12
0	4	0-4	7
0	5	0-2-3-5	16
0	6	0-2-3-5-6	8
0	7	0-2-3-5-6-7	10

Figure 7.101 Shortest path in graph by dijkstra's algorithm

Using Dijkstra's algorithm, the shortest path from 0 to 1 is the path 0→1 of length 8. But if we observe the graph carefully, we see that there exists a shorter path 0→2→1 of length 5. Similarly, for destination vertex 5, there exists a path 0→2→1→5 of length 14 which Dijkstra's algorithm was unable to identify.

So, we can see that Dijkstra's algorithm fails if the graph consists of negative weights. This is so because in Dijkstra's algorithm, once a vertex is made permanent, we do not relabel it, i.e., the shortest path to it is finalized. It is possible that after making the vertex permanent, we find an edge of negative weight that can be used to reach the vertex, and hence, we get a shorter path. But we have already finalized the shortest path of the vertex by making it permanent, so we cannot record this shorter path.

In the graph of figure 7.100, if we apply Dijkstra's algorithm, then the vertices are made permanent in the order- 0 4 1 2 3 5 6 7.

After making vertex 2 permanent, the edge 2→1 of length -4 is considered and we find a shorter path 0→2→1 but it is not recorded, as vertex 1 is already permanent.

In Dijkstra's algorithm, we make a vertex permanent at each step, i.e., the shortest distance to a vertex is finalized at each step, but in Bellman Ford algorithm, the shortest distances are not finalized till the end of the algorithm. Thus in Bellman-Ford algorithm, we drop the concept of making vertices permanent. This is why Dijkstra's algorithm is known as the label setting algorithm and Bellman Ford algorithm is known as label correcting algorithm.

Each vertex is labeled with a pathLength and a predecessor value as in Dijkstra's algorithm. The procedure for Bellman Ford algorithm is as follows:

(A) Initialize the pathLength of all vertices to infinity and predecessor of all vertices to NIL.

(B) Make the pathLength of source vertex equal to 0 and insert it into the queue.

(C) Delete a vertex from the front of the queue and make it the current vertex.

(D) Examine all the vertices adjacent to the current vertex. Check the condition of minimum weight for these vertices and do the relabeling if required, as in Dijkstra's algorithm.

(E) Each vertex that is relabeled is inserted into the queue, provided it is not already present in the queue.

(F) Repeat the steps (C), (D), and (E) till the queue becomes empty.

The whole procedure for the graph of figure 7.100 is shown in the following table:

Current Vertex	Adjacent vertices				Queue
0	1, 2, 4	1	0+8 < ∞	pathLength(1) = 8, pred(1) = 0, Enqueue 1	1 2 4
		2	0+9 < ∞	pathLength(2) = 9, pred(2) = 0, Enqueue 2	
		4	0+7 < ∞	pathLength(4) = 7, pred(4) = 0, Enqueue 4	
1	5	5	8+9 < ∞	pathLength(5) = 17, pred(5) = 1, Enqueue 5	2 4 5
2	0, 1, 3	0	9+5 > 0		4 5 1 3
		1	9 +(- 4) < 8	pathLength(1) = 5, pred(1) = 2, Enqueue 1	
		3	9+3 < ∞	pathLength(3) = 12,pred(3) = 2, Enqueue 3	
4	7	7	7+16 < ∞	pathLength(7) = 23, pred(7) = 4, Enqueue 7	5 1 3 7
5	0, 6, 7	0	17+4 > 0		1 3 7 6
		6	17+(-8) < ∞	pathLength(6) = 9, pred(6) = 5, Enqueue 6	
		7	17+5 < 23	pathLength(7) = 22, pred(7) = 5, 7 already in queue	
1	5	5	5 +9 < 17	pathLength(5) = 14, pred(5) = 1, Enqueue 5	3 7 6 5
3	1, 2, 5	1	12+3 > 5		7 6 5
		2	12 +6 > 9		
		5	12+4 > 14		
7	-	-			6 5
6	3, 7	3	9+5 > 12		5 7
		7	9+2 < 22	pathLength(7) = 11, pred(7) = 6, Enqueue 7	
5	0, 6,7	0	14+4>0		7 6
		6	14+(-8) < 9	pathLength(6) = 6, pred(6) = 5, Enqueue 6	
		7	14+5 > 11		
7	-	-			6
6	3, 7	3	6+5 < 12	pathLength(3) = 11, pred(3) = 6, Enqueue 3	3 7
		7	6 +2 < 11	pathLength(7) = 8, pred(7) = 6, Enqueue 7	
3	1, 2, 5	1	11+3 > 5		7
		2	11+6 > 9		
		5	11+4 > 14		
7	-	-			Empty

Figure 7.102 Bellman ford algorithm procedure for a graph

The shortest paths in this way computed by Bellman Ford algorithm for source vertex 0 are as follows:

Source	Destination	Shortest Path	Length
0	1	0-2-1	5
0	2	0-2	9
0	3	0-2-1-5-6-3	11
0	4	0-4	7
0	5	0-2-1-5	14
0	6	0-2-1-5-6	6
0	7	0-2-1-5-6-7	8

Figure 7.103 Shortest path by bellman ford algorithm

This algorithm will not work properly if the graph contains a negative cycle reachable from source vertex, i.e., a cycle consisting of edges whose weights add up to a negative number. For example, consider the following graph which contains a negative cycle 0→1→3→0 of length -3.

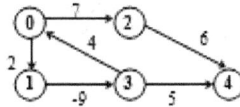

Figure 7.104 Graph with negative cycle

Now, suppose we have to find the shortest path from vertex 0 to vertex 3. One path from vertex 0 to vertex 3 is 0→1→3 of length -7. But there is a shorter path which is 0→1→3→0→1→3 of length -10. Each time we visit the negative cycle, the length of the shortest path will decrease by -3 and hence, the length of shortest path from vertex 0 to vertex 3 is -∞. So, if the graph contains a negative cycle, then the number of edges in the shortest path is not finite, and hence, shortest paths are not defined for such graphs.

In the Bellman Ford algorithm, each vertex can be inserted into the queue maximum n times. If any vertex is inserted more than n times, it indicates that there is negative cycle present in the graph. In this case, we will be stuck in an infinite loop. To come out of it, we can count the number of insertions of any vertex and if it is greater than n, we will come out of the loop stating that the graph has a negative cycle. In the program, we will count the number of insertions of source vertex.

```
//DirectedWeightedGraph.cpp : Program to find shortest paths using Bellman Ford algorithm.
#include<iostream>
#include<string>
#include<queue>
using namespace std;

static const int maxSize = 30;

class Vertex
{
        public:
                string name;
                int predecessor;
                int pathLength;
                bool inQueue;
        public:
                Vertex(string name)
                {
                        this->name = name;
                }
};//End of class Vertex

class DirectedWeightedGraph
{
        private:
                int nVertices;
                int nEdges;
                int adj[maxSize][maxSize];
                Vertex *vertexList[maxSize];
                int INFINITY;
                int NIL;
        private:
                int getIndex(string vertexName);
                bool isAdjacent(int u, int v);
```

```
                void bellmanFordAlgorithm(int s);
                void findPath(int s, int v);
        public:
                DirectedWeightedGraph();
                ~DirectedWeightedGraph();
                void insertVertex(string vertexName);
                void insertEdge(string source, string destination, int weight);
                void display();
                void findPaths(string source);
};//End of class DirectedWeightedGraph
DirectedWeightedGraph::DirectedWeightedGraph()
{
        nVertices = 0;
        nEdges = 0;
        for(int i=0; i<maxSize; i++)
        {
                for(int j=0; j<maxSize; j++)
                {
                        adj[i][j] = 0;
                }
        }
        INFINITY = 9999;
        NIL = -1;
}//End of DirectedWeightedGraph()
void DirectedWeightedGraph::bellmanFordAlgorithm(int s)
{
        queue<int> qu;
        int current;
        int k=0;
        for(int i=0; i<nVertices; i++)
        {
                vertexList[i]->predecessor = NIL;
                vertexList[i]->pathLength = INFINITY;
                vertexList[i]->inQueue = false;
        }
        vertexList[s]->pathLength = 0; //Make pathLength of source vertex equal to 0
        qu.push(s);                   //Insert the source vertex in the queue
        vertexList[s]->inQueue = true;

        while(!qu.empty())
        {
                current = qu.front();
                qu.pop();
                vertexList[current]->inQueue = false;
                if(s == current)
                        k++;
                if(k > nVertices)      //Negative cycle reachable from source vertex
                {
                        throw exception("There is negative cycle in graph.");
                }

                for(int v=0; v<nVertices; v++)
                {
                        if(isAdjacent(current,v))
                        {
                                if((vertexList[current]->pathLength + adj[current][v])
                                < vertexList[v]->pathLength)
                                {
                                        vertexList[v]->predecessor = current; //Relabel
                                        vertexList[v]->pathLength = vertexList[current]
                                        ->pathLength + adj[current][v];
```

```
                                        if(vertexList[v]->inQueue == false)
                                        {
                                                qu.push(v);
                                                vertexList[v]->inQueue = true;
                                        }
                                }
                        }//End of if
                }//End of for
        }//End of while
}//End of bellmanFordAlgorithm()
void DirectedWeightedGraph::findPath(int s, int v)
{
        int path[maxSize];              //stores the shortest path
        int shortestDistance=0;         //length of shortest path
        int count=0;                    //number of vertices in the shortest path
        int u;

        //Store the full path in the array path
        while(v!=s)
        {
                count++;
                path[count] = v;
                u = vertexList[v]->predecessor;
                shortestDistance += adj[u][v];
                v = u;
        }
        count++;
        path[count] = s;

        cout << "Shortest Path : ";
        for(int i=count; i>=1; i--)
                cout << vertexList[path[i]]->name << " ";
        cout << "\n";
        cout << "Shortest Distance : " << shortestDistance << "\n";
}//End of findPath()
void DirectedWeightedGraph::findPaths(string source)
{
        int s = getIndex(source);
        bellmanFordAlgorithm(s);

        cout << "Source : " << source << "\n";
        for(int v=0; v<nVertices; v++)
        {
                cout << "Destination : " << vertexList[v]->name << "\n";
                if(vertexList[v]->pathLength == INFINITY)
                        cout << "There is no path from " << source << " to vertex "
                        << vertexList[v]->name << "\n";
                else
                        findPath(s, v);
        }
}//End of findPaths()

int main()
{
        DirectedWeightedGraph dwGraph;
        try
        {
                //Creating the graph, inserting the vertices and edges
                dwGraph.insertVertex("0");
                dwGraph.insertVertex("1");
                dwGraph.insertVertex("2");
                dwGraph.insertVertex("3");
```

```
              dwGraph.insertVertex("4");
              dwGraph.insertVertex("5");
              dwGraph.insertVertex("6");
              dwGraph.insertVertex("7");

              dwGraph.insertEdge("0","1",8);
              dwGraph.insertEdge("0","2",9);
              dwGraph.insertEdge("0","4",7);
              dwGraph.insertEdge("1","5",9);
              dwGraph.insertEdge("2","0",5);
              dwGraph.insertEdge("2","1",-4);
              dwGraph.insertEdge("2","3",3);
              dwGraph.insertEdge("3","1",3);
              dwGraph.insertEdge("3","2",6);
              dwGraph.insertEdge("3","5",4);
              dwGraph.insertEdge("4","7",16);
              dwGraph.insertEdge("5","0",4);
              dwGraph.insertEdge("5","6",-8);
              dwGraph.insertEdge("5","7",5);
              dwGraph.insertEdge("6","3",5);
              dwGraph.insertEdge("6","7",2);
              //Display the graph
              dwGraph.display();
              cout << "\n";

              dwGraph.findPaths("0");
       }//End of try
       catch(exception e)
       {
              cout << e.what() << "\n";
       }
       return 0;
}//End of main()
```

The destructor, `insertVertex()`, `getIndex()`, `insertEdge()`, `display()`, and `isAdjacent()` functions are same as in the Dijkstra's algorithm program.

7.13.3 Modified Warshall's Algorithm (Floyd's Algorithm)

We have studied two algorithms to find the shortest paths; both of them were single source problems. Now the algorithm that we will study is an all pairs shortest path problem, i.e., it finds the shortest path between all pairs of vertices in the graph.

We may apply Dijkstra's algorithm n times, once for each vertex as the source vertex, and find the shortest path between all pairs of vertices. The time complexity in this case would be $O(n^3)$, and the time complexity of our Floyd's algorithm is also $O(n^3)$. However, Floyd's algorithm is much simpler and faster if the graph is dense. Moreover, negative weights are also allowed in Floyd's algorithm. The only restriction is that the graph should not have any negative cycle.

We have seen Warshall's algorithm (section 7.11.2), which computes the path matrix of a graph and tells us whether there is a path between any two vertices i and j. Now, our problem is to find the shortest path between any two vertices i and j. We will take Warshall's algorithm as the base and modify it to find out the shortest path matrix D, such that D[i][j] represents the length of the shortest path from vertex i to vertex j. This resulting algorithm is known as a modified Warshall's algorithm or Floyd's algorithm or Floyd Warshall algorithm as its basic structure was given by Warshall and it was implemented by Robert. W. Floyd. Any element D[i][j] of the shortest path matrix can be defined as:

$$D[i][j] = \begin{cases} \text{Length of shortest path from vertex i to vertex j} \\ \infty \ (\text{if there is no path from vertex i to j}) \end{cases}$$

Figure 7.105 Shortest path matrix element D[i][j] definition

Here, ∞ is assumed to be a very large number.

We will also find a predecessor matrix that will help us construct the shortest path. Any element Pred[i][j] of this predecessor matrix can be defined as:

$$\text{Pred}[i][j] = \begin{cases} \text{Predecessor of vertex j in shortest path from vertex i to vertex j} \\ \text{NIL} \ (\text{if there is no path from vertex i to j}) \end{cases}$$

Figure 7.106 Predecessor matrix element Pred[i][j] definition

We will take a graph with n vertices, numbered from 0 to n-1, so we can take NIL to be equal to -1.

In Warshall's algorithm, we had worked on the adjacency matrix; here, we will work on a weighted adjacency matrix because to find the shortest paths, we need to know the weight (or length) of each edge. In Warshall's algorithm, we had found the matrices P_{-1}, P_0, P_1, ...P_{n-1}. Here, we will find the matrices D_{-1}, D_0, D_1,......D_{n-1} where an element $D_k[i][j]$ can be defined as:

$$D_k[i][j] = \begin{cases} \text{length of shortest path from vertex j to vertex j,} \\ \text{using only vertices } 0,1,2,........k \text{ as intermediate vertices.} \\ \infty \ (\text{if there is no path from vertex i to vertex j using vertices } 0,1,2,.....k) \end{cases}$$

Figure 7.107 $D_k[i][j]$ definition

We will also find predecessor matrices Pred_{-1}, Pred_0,....... Pred_{n-1}, where any element $\text{Pred}_k[i][j]$ can be defined as:

$$\text{Pred}_k[i][j] = \begin{cases} \text{Predecessor of j on the shortest path from vertex i to vertex j,} \\ \text{using only vertices } 0,1,2,........k \text{ as intermediate vertices.} \\ -1 \ (\text{if there is no path from vertex i to vertex j using vertices } 0,1,2,.....k) \end{cases}$$

Figure 7.108 $\text{Pred}_k[i][j]$ definition

Hence, we can say that:

$D_{-1}[i][j]$ = length of an edge from i to j
$D_0[i][j]$ = length of shortest path from i to j using only vertex 0
$D_1[i][j]$ = length of shortest path from i to j using only vertices 0, 1
$D_2[i][j]$ = length of shortest path from i to j using only vertices 0, 1, 2
....

$D_{n-1}[i][j]$ = length of shortest path from i to j using only vertices 0, 1, 2, ………. n-1
We can find matrix D_{-1} from the weighted adjacency matrix by replacing all zero entries by ∞.

$$D_{-1}[i][j] = \begin{cases} \text{length of edge from vertex i to vertex j} \\ \infty \quad \text{(if there is no edge from vertex i to vertex j)} \end{cases}$$

Figure 7.109 Matrix $D_{-1}[i][j]$ definition

The elements of matrix $Pred_{-1}$ can be defined as:

$$Pred_{-1}[i][j] \begin{cases} i \quad \text{(if there is an edge from vertex i to vertex j)} \\ -1 \quad \text{(if there is no edge from vertex i to vertex j)} \end{cases}$$

Figure 7.110 $Pred_{-1}[i][j]$ definition

If there are n vertices in the graph, then matrix D_{n-1} will represent the shortest path matrix D. Now, our purpose is to find out matrices $D_0, D_1, D_2, \dots\dots, D_{n-1}$. We have already found matrix D_{-1} by the weighted adjacency matrix. Now, if we know how to find out the matrix D_k from matrix D_{k-1}, then we can easily find out matrices $D_0, D_1, D_2 \dots\dots D_{n-1}$ also. So, let us see how we can find out matrix D_k from matrix D_{k-1}.

We have seen in Warshall's algorithm, that $P_k[i][j]=1$ if any of these two conditions is true:

1. $P_{k-1}[i][j]=1$
2. $P_{k-1}[i][k]=1$ and $P_{k-1}[k][j]=1$

This means that there can be a path from vertex i to j using vertices 0,1, 2,………k in two conditions:

1. There is a path from vertex i to vertex j using only vertices 0, 1,……..k-1   (path P1)
2. There is a path from vertex i to vertex k using only vertices 0, 1,……..k-1 and there is a path from vertex k to vertex j using only vertices 0,1,……….k-1. (path P2)

Length of first path P1 will be $D_{k-1}[i][j]$
Length of second path P2 will be $D_{k-1}[i][k] + D_{k-1}[k][j]$

Now we will compare the length of these two paths.

(i) If $(D_{k-1}[i][k] + D_{k-1}[k][j]) < D_{k-1}[i][j]$
This means that the path from i to j will be shorter if we use k as an intermediate vertex.
Thus $D_k[i][j] = D_{k-1}[i][k] + D_{k-1}[k][j]$
$Pred_k[i][j] = Pred_{k-1}[k][j]$

(ii) If $(D_{k-1}[i][k] + D_{k-1}[k][j]) >= D_{k-1}[i][j]$
This means that the path from i to j is not improved if we use k as an intermediate vertex.
Thus $D_k[i][j] = D_{k-1}[i][j]$
$Pred_k[i][j] = Pred_{k-1}[i][j]$

We select the smaller one from the two paths P1 and P2.

Hence, the value of $D_k[i][j] = Minimum(D_{k-1}[i][j] , D_{k-1}[i][k] + D_{k-1}[k][j])$

Now, let us take a graph and find out the shortest path matrix for it.

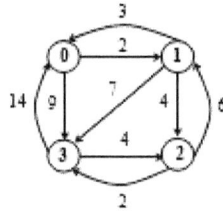

Figure 7.111 Graph for finding shortest path

Weighted adjacency matrix for this graph is:

$$W = \begin{array}{c c} & \begin{array}{c c c c} 0 & 1 & 2 & 3 \end{array} \\ \begin{array}{c} 0 \\ 1 \\ 2 \\ 3 \end{array} & \left[\begin{array}{c c c c} 0 & 2 & 0 & 9 \\ 3 & 0 & 4 & 7 \\ 0 & 6 & 0 & 2 \\ 14 & 0 & 4 & 0 \end{array} \right] \end{array}$$

Figure 7.112 Weighted adjacency matrix for the graph

We can easily write matrices D_{-1} and $Pred_{-1}$ from matrix W, as shown:

$$D_{-1} = \begin{array}{c c} & \begin{array}{c c c c} 0 & 1 & 2 & 3 \end{array} \\ \begin{array}{c} 0 \\ 1 \\ 2 \\ 3 \end{array} & \left[\begin{array}{c c c c} \infty & 2 & \infty & 9 \\ 3 & \infty & 4 & 7 \\ \infty & 6 & \infty & 2 \\ 14 & \infty & 4 & \infty \end{array} \right] \end{array} \qquad Pred_{-1} = \begin{array}{c c} & \begin{array}{c c c c} 0 & 1 & 2 & 3 \end{array} \\ \begin{array}{c} 0 \\ 1 \\ 2 \\ 3 \end{array} & \left[\begin{array}{c c c c} -1 & 0 & -1 & 0 \\ 1 & -1 & 1 & 1 \\ -1 & 2 & -1 & 2 \\ 3 & -1 & 3 & -1 \end{array} \right] \end{array}$$

Figure 7.113 Matrix D_{-1} and $Pred_{-1}$

Now, let us see how we can find matrix D_0 from matrix D_{-1}. If we go through vertex 0 and find a smaller path, then we replace the older path with this smaller one. The calculation of some entries of the matrix is as follows:

- Find $D_0[0][0]$

  $D_{-1}[0][0] + D_{-1}[0][0] > D_{-1}[0][0]$ => No change
  (9999 + 9999 > 9999)

- Find $D_0[1][0]$

  $D_{-1}[1][0] + D_{-1}[0][0] > D_{-1}[1][0]$ => No change
  (3 + 9999 > 3)

- Find $D_0[1][1]$

  $D_{-1}[1][0] + D_{-1}[0][1] < D_{-1}[1][1]$
  (3 + 2 < 9999)
  $D_0[1][1] = D_{-1}[1][0] + D_{-1}[0][1] = 5$
  $Pred_0[1][1] = Pred_{-1}[0][1] = 0$

- Find $D_0[3][1]$

  $D_{-1}[3][0] + D_{-1}[0][1] < D_{-1}[3][1]$
  (14   +   2   < 9999)

  $D_0[3][1] = D_{-1}[3][0] + D_{-1}[0][1] = 16$
  $Pred_0[3][1] = Pred_{-1}[0][1] = 0$

The changed values are shown in bold in the matrix:

$$
D_0 = \begin{array}{c c} & \begin{array}{c c c c} 0 & 1 & 2 & 3 \end{array} \\ \begin{array}{c} 0 \\ 1 \\ 2 \\ 3 \end{array} & \left[\begin{array}{c c c c} \infty & 2 & \infty & 9 \\ 3 & \underline{5} & 4 & 7 \\ \infty & 6 & \infty & 2 \\ 14 & \underline{16} & 4 & \underline{23} \end{array} \right] \end{array}
\qquad
Pred_0 = \begin{array}{c c} & \begin{array}{c c c c} 0 & 1 & 2 & 3 \end{array} \\ \begin{array}{c} 0 \\ 1 \\ 2 \\ 3 \end{array} & \left[\begin{array}{c c c c} -1 & 0 & -1 & 0 \\ 1 & \underline{0} & 1 & 1 \\ -1 & 2 & -1 & 2 \\ 3 & 0 & 3 & 0 \end{array} \right] \end{array}
$$

Figure 7.114 Matrix D_0 and $Pred_0$

Now, we have to find the matrices D_1 and $Pred_1$, and the calculation of some entries is as follows:

- Find $D_1[1][3]$

  $D_0[1][1] + D_0[1][3] > D_0[1][3] \Rightarrow$ No change
  ($5 + 7 > 7$)

- Find $D_1[2][0]$

  $D_0[2][1] + D_0[1][0] < D_0[2][0]$
  ($6 + 3 < 9999$)

  $D_1[2][0] = D_0[2][1] + D_0[1][0] = 9$
  $Pred_1[2][0] = Pred_0[1][0] = 1$

- Find $D_1[2][2]$

  $D_0[2][1] + D_0[1][2] < D_0[2][2]$
  ($6 + 4 < 9999$)

  $D_1[2][2] = D_0[2][1] + D_0[1][2] = 10$
  $Pred_1[2][2] = Pred_0[1][2] = 1$

- Find $D_1[3][0]$

  $D_0[3][1] + D_0[1][0] > D_0[3][0] \Rightarrow$ No change
  ($16 + 3 > 14$)

$$
D_1 = \begin{array}{c c} & \begin{array}{c c c c} 0 & 1 & 2 & 3 \end{array} \\ \begin{array}{c} 0 \\ 1 \\ 2 \\ 3 \end{array} & \left[\begin{array}{c c c c} \underline{5} & 2 & \underline{6} & 9 \\ 3 & 5 & 4 & 7 \\ \underline{9} & 6 & \underline{10} & 2 \\ 14 & 16 & 4 & 23 \end{array} \right] \end{array}
\qquad
Pred_1 = \begin{array}{c c} & \begin{array}{c c c c} 0 & 1 & 2 & 3 \end{array} \\ \begin{array}{c} 0 \\ 1 \\ 2 \\ 3 \end{array} & \left[\begin{array}{c c c c} \underline{1} & 0 & \underline{1} & 0 \\ 1 & 0 & 1 & 1 \\ \underline{1} & 2 & \underline{1} & 2 \\ 3 & 0 & 3 & 0 \end{array} \right] \end{array}
$$

Figure 7.115 Matrix D_1 and $Pred_1$

Similarly, we can find matrices D_2, $Pred_2$, D_3 and $Pred_3$:

$$D_2 = \begin{array}{c} \\ 0 \\ 1 \\ 2 \\ 3 \end{array}\begin{array}{cccc} 0 & 1 & 2 & 3 \\ \left[\begin{array}{cccc} 5 & 2 & 6 & 8 \\ 3 & 5 & 4 & 6 \\ 9 & 6 & 10 & 2 \\ 13 & 10 & 4 & 6 \end{array}\right] \end{array} \qquad Pred_2 = \begin{array}{c} \\ 0 \\ 1 \\ 2 \\ 3 \end{array}\begin{array}{cccc} 0 & 1 & 2 & 3 \\ \left[\begin{array}{cccc} 1 & 0 & 1 & 2 \\ 1 & 0 & 1 & 2 \\ 1 & 2 & 1 & 2 \\ 1 & 2 & 3 & 2 \end{array}\right] \end{array}$$

Figure 7.116 Matrix D_2 and $Pred_2$

$$D = D_3 = \begin{array}{c} \\ 0 \\ 1 \\ 2 \\ 3 \end{array}\begin{array}{cccc} 0 & 1 & 2 & 3 \\ \left[\begin{array}{cccc} 5 & 2 & 6 & 8 \\ 3 & 5 & 4 & 6 \\ 9 & 6 & 6 & 2 \\ 13 & 10 & 4 & 6 \end{array}\right] \end{array} \qquad Pred = Pred_3 = \begin{array}{c} \\ 0 \\ 1 \\ 2 \\ 3 \end{array}\begin{array}{cccc} 0 & 1 & 2 & 3 \\ \left[\begin{array}{cccc} 1 & 0 & 1 & 2 \\ 1 & 0 & 1 & 2 \\ 1 & 2 & 3 & 2 \\ 1 & 2 & 3 & 2 \end{array}\right] \end{array}$$

Figure 7.117 Matrix D_3 and $Pred_3$

The matrix D_3 is the shortest path matrix D and the matrix $Pred_3$ is the predecessor matrix.

Suppose we have to find the shortest path from vertex 3 to vertex 0. The value of D[3][0] is 13, which is the length of this shortest path. We can construct the path from matrix Pred.

Pred[3][0] is 1 => predecessor of vertex 0 on shortest path from 3 to 0 is vertex 1
Pred[3][1] is 2 => predecessor of vertex 1 on shortest path from 3 to 1 is vertex 2
Pred[3][2] is 3 => predecessor of vertex 2 on shortest path from 3 to 2 is vertex 3

So, the shortest path is $3{\rightarrow}2{\rightarrow}1{\rightarrow}0$

If any value D[i][j] is infinity, it means that there is no path from vertex i to vertex j. In the above example, we do not have any infinity in the shortest path matrix.

This algorithm can also be used for cycle detection. If there is no cycle in the graph, then all diagonal elements will be infinity in the last matrix; otherwise, there will be finite values along the diagonal corresponding to vertices, which are in the cycle. For example, if D[i][i] is a finite value, then it denotes that vertex i is a part of the cycle. If this finite value is negative, then it denotes the presence of a negative cycle in the graph, and in this case, shortest paths are not defined.

```cpp
//DirectedWeightedGraph.cpp : Program to find shortest path matrix by Modified Warshall's
//(Floyd) algorithm.
#include<iostream>
#include<string>
using namespace std;

static const int maxSize = 30;

class Vertex
{
      public:
            string name;
      public:
            Vertex(string name)
            {
                  this->name = name;
            }
};//End of class Vertex

class DirectedWeightedGraph
{
      private:
```

```cpp
                int nVertices;
                int nEdges;
                int adj[maxSize][maxSize];
                Vertex *vertexList[maxSize];
                int D[maxSize][maxSize];        //Shortest Path Matrix
                int Pred[maxSize][maxSize];     //Predecessor Matrix
                int INFINITY;
        private:
                int getIndex(string vertexName);
                bool isAdjacent(int u, int v);
                void display(int mat[maxSize][maxSize]);
                void floydWarshallsAlgorithm(int s);
                void findPath(int s, int v);
        public:
                DirectedWeightedGraph();
                ~DirectedWeightedGraph();
                void insertVertex(string vertexName);
                void insertEdge(string source, string destination, int weight);
                void display();
                void findPaths(string source);
};//End of class DirectedWeightedGraph

DirectedWeightedGraph::DirectedWeightedGraph()
{
        nVertices = 0;
        nEdges = 0;
        for(int i=0; i<maxSize; i++)
        {
                for(int j=0; j<maxSize; j++)
                {
                        adj[i][j] = 0;
                }
        }
        INFINITY = 9999;
}//End of DirectedWeightedGraph()

void DirectedWeightedGraph::display(int mat[maxSize][maxSize])
{
        for(int i=0; i<nVertices; i++)
        {
                for(int j=0; j<nVertices; j++)
                        cout << mat[i][j] << " ";
                cout <<"\n";
        }
}//End of display()

void DirectedWeightedGraph::display()
{
        for(int i=0; i<nVertices; i++)
        {
                for(int j=0; j<nVertices; j++)
                        cout << adj[i][j] << " ";
                cout <<"\n";
        }
}//End of display()

void DirectedWeightedGraph::floydWarshallsAlgorithm(int s)
{
        //Getting D_{-1}, Pred_{-1}
        for(int i=0; i<nVertices; i++)
        {
                for(int j=0; j<nVertices; j++)
                {
```

```
                           if(adj[i][j] == 0)
                           {
                                   D[i][j] = INFINITY;
                                   Pred[i][j] = -1;
                           }
                           else
                           {
                                   D[i][j] = adj[i][j];
                                   Pred[i][j] = i;
                           }
                   }
           }//End of for

           //Getting D_k, Pred_k
           for(int k=0; k<nVertices; k++)
           {
                   for(int i=0; i<nVertices; i++)
                   {
                           for(int j=0; j<nVertices; j++)
                           {
                                   if(D[i][k]+D[k][j] < D[i][j])
                                   {
                                           D[i][j] = D[i][k]+D[k][j];
                                           Pred[i][j] = Pred[k][j];
                                   }
                           }
                   }
           }//End of for

           //Finding negative cycle
           for(int i=0; i<nVertices; i++)
           {
                   if(D[i][i] < 0)
                   {
                           throw exception("There is negative cycle in graph.");
                   }
           }
           cout << "Shortest Path Matrix :\n";
           display(D);
           cout << "\nPredecessor Matrix :\n";
           display(Pred);
}//End of floydWarshallsAlgorithm()
void DirectedWeightedGraph::findPath(int s, int v)
{
           int path[maxSize];              //stores the shortest path
           int count=-1;
           if(D[s][v] == INFINITY)
           {
                   cout << "No path\n";
           }
           else
           {
                   do
                   {
                           path[++count] = v;
                           v = Pred[s][v];
                   }while(v!=s);
                   path[++count] = s;
                   cout << "Shortest Path : ";
                   for(int i=count; i>=0; i--)
                           cout << vertexList[path[i]]->name << " ";
```

```
                cout << "\n";
        }
}//End of findPath()
void DirectedWeightedGraph::findPaths(string source)
{
        int s = getIndex(source);
        floydWarshallsAlgorithm(s);
        cout << "Source : " << source << "\n";
        for(int v=0; v<nVertices; v++)
        {
                cout << "Destination : " << vertexList[v]->name << "\n";
                findPath(s, v);
                cout << "Shortest Distance : " << D[s][v] << "\n";
        }
}//End of findPaths()
int main()
{
        DirectedWeightedGraph dwGraph;
        try
        {
                //Creating the graph, inserting the vertices and edges
                dwGraph.insertVertex("0");
                dwGraph.insertVertex("1");
                dwGraph.insertVertex("2");
                dwGraph.insertVertex("3");
                dwGraph.insertEdge("0","1",2);
                dwGraph.insertEdge("0","3",9);
                dwGraph.insertEdge("1","0",3);
                dwGraph.insertEdge("1","2",4);
                dwGraph.insertEdge("1","3",7);
                dwGraph.insertEdge("2","1",6);
                dwGraph.insertEdge("2","3",2);
                dwGraph.insertEdge("3","0",14);
                dwGraph.insertEdge("3","2",4);
                //Display the graph
                dwGraph.display();
                cout << "\n";

                dwGraph.findPaths("0");
        }//End of try
        catch(exception e)
        {
                cout << e.what() << "\n";
        }
        return 0;
}//End of main()
```

The destructor, insertVertex(), getIndex(), insertEdge(), and isAdjacent() functions are the same as in the Dijkstra's algorithm program.

7.14 Minimum Spanning Tree

The sum of weights of edges of different spanning trees of a graph may be different. A spanning tree of graph G whose sum of weights is minimum amongst all spanning trees of G, is called the Minimum Spanning Tree of G.

Let us take a graph and draw its different spanning trees:

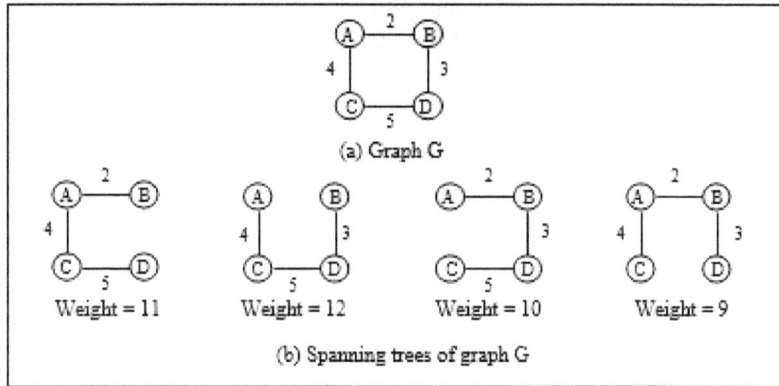

Figure 7.118 Graph and its spanning trees

Here, the tree with weight 9 is the minimum spanning tree. It is not necessary that a graph has unique minimum spanning tree. If there are duplicate weights in the graph, then more than one minimum spanning trees are possible, but if the all weights are unique, then there will be only one minimum spanning tree.

A minimum spanning tree gives us the most economical way of connecting all the vertices in a graph. For example, in a network of computers, we can connect all the computers with the least cost if we construct a minimum spanning tree for the graph where the vertices are computers. Similarly, in a telephone communication network, we can connect all the cities in the network with the least possible cost.

There are many ways to create a minimum spanning tree, but the most famous methods are Prim's and Kruskal's algorithms. Both these methods use the greedy approach.

7.14.1 Prim's Algorithm

In this algorithm, we start with an arbitrary vertex as the root, and at each step, a vertex is added to the tree until all the vertices are in the tree.

The method of making a minimum spanning tree from Prim's algorithm is like Dijkstra's algorithm for the shortest paths. Each vertex is given a status, which can be permanent or temporary. Initially, all the vertices are temporary and at each step of the algorithm, a temporary vertex is made permanent. The process stops when all the vertices are made permanent. Making a vertex permanent means that it has been included in the tree. The temporary vertices are those vertices which have not been added to the tree.

We label each vertex with length and predecessor. The label length represents the weight of the shortest edge connecting the vertex to a permanent vertex, and predecessor represents that permanent vertex. Once a vertex is made permanent, it is not relabeled. Only temporary vertices will be relabeled if required.

Applying the greedy approach, the temporary vertex that has the minimum value of length is made permanent. In other words, we can say that the temporary vertex which is adjacent to a permanent vertex by an edge of least weight is added to the tree.

The steps for making a minimum spanning tree by Prim's algorithm are as follows:

(A) Initialize the length of all vertices to infinity and predecessors of all vertices to NIL. Make the status of all vertices temporary.

(B) Select any arbitrary vertex as the root vertex and make its length label equal to 0.

(C) From all the temporary vertices in the graph, find out the vertex that has smallest value of length, make it permanent, and now, this is our current vertex. (If there are many with the same value of length, then anyone can be selected)

(D) Examine all the temporary vertices adjacent to the current vertex. Suppose `current` is the current vertex and `v` is a temporary vertex adjacent to `current`.

    (i) If weight (`current`,v) < length(v)
        Relabel the vertex v
      Now   length(v) = weight(`current`,v)
               predecessor(v) = `current`
    (ii) If weight (`current`,v) >= length(v)
        Vertex v is not relabelled

(E) Repeat steps (C) and (D) till there are no temporary vertices left, or all the temporary vertices left have length equal to infinity. If the graph is connected, the procedure will stop when all n vertices are made permanent and n-1 edges are added to the spanning tree. If the graph is not connected, then those vertices that are not reachable from the root vertex will remain temporary with length infinity. In this case, no spanning tree is possible.

Let us take an undirected connected graph and construct the minimum spanning tree.

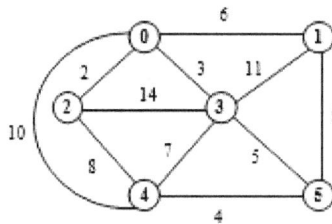

Figure 7.119 Weighted undirected connected graph

Initially, length values for all the vertices are set to a very large number (larger than the weight of any edge). Suppose ∞ is such a number. We have taken the predecessor of all vertices NIL (-1) in the beginning.

Initially, all the vertices are temporary. We select the vertex 0 as the root vertex and make its length label equal to zero.

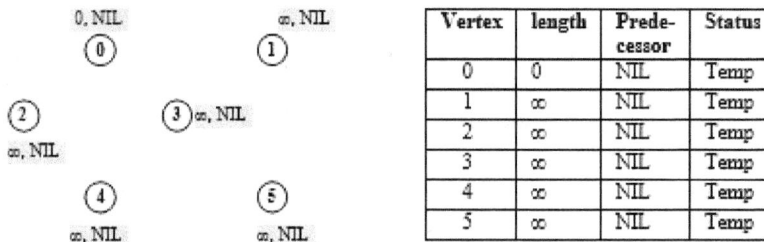

Vertex	length	Prede-cessor	Status
0	0	NIL	Temp
1	∞	NIL	Temp
2	∞	NIL	Temp
3	∞	NIL	Temp
4	∞	NIL	Temp
5	∞	NIL	Temp

Figure 7.120 Initial tree and table for length, predecessor, status of vertex

From all the temporary vertices, vertex 0 has the smallest length, and so it will be made permanent.

This is the first vertex to be included in the tree. Its predecessor will remain NIL. Now, vertex 0 is the current vertex.

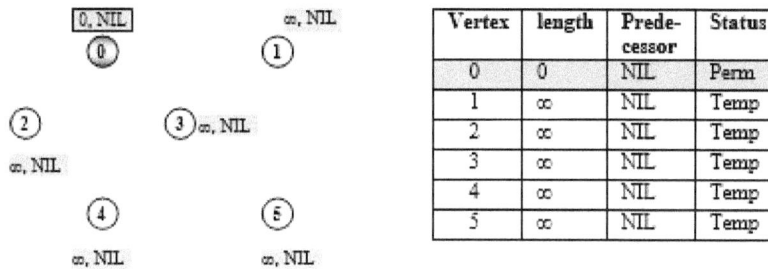

Vertex	length	Prede-cessor	Status
0	0	NIL	Perm
1	∞	NIL	Temp
2	∞	NIL	Temp
3	∞	NIL	Temp
4	∞	NIL	Temp
5	∞	NIL	Temp

Figure 7.121 Make vertex 0 permanent

Vertices 1, 2, 3, 4 are temporary vertices adjacent to 0

weight(0,1) < length(1)   6 < ∞   Relabel 1
predecessor[1]=0 , length[1]=6
weight(0,2) < length(2)   2 < ∞   Relabel 2
predecessor[2]=0 , length[2]=2
weight(0,3) < length(3)   3 < ∞   Relabel 3
predecessor[3]=0 , length[3]=3
weight(0,4) < length(4)   10 < ∞   Relabel 4
predecessor[4]=0, length[4]=10

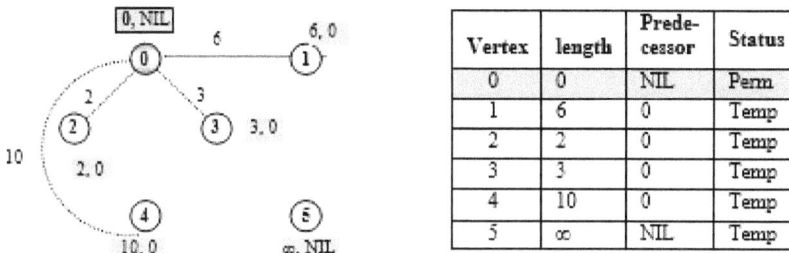

Vertex	length	Prede-cessor	Status
0	0	NIL	Perm
1	6	0	Temp
2	2	0	Temp
3	3	0	Temp
4	10	0	Temp
5	∞	NIL	Temp

Figure 7.122 Relabel 1, 2, 3, 4

From all the temporary vertices, vertex 2 has the smallest length, so make it permanent, i.e., include it in the tree. Its predecessor is 0, so the edge that is added to the tree is (0,2). Now, vertex 2 is the current vertex. Vertices 3, 4 are temporary vertices adjacent to vertex 2.

weight(2,3) > length(3)   14 > 3   Do not Relabel 3
weight(2,4) < length(4)   8 < 10   Relabel 4
predecessor[4]=2 , length[4]=8

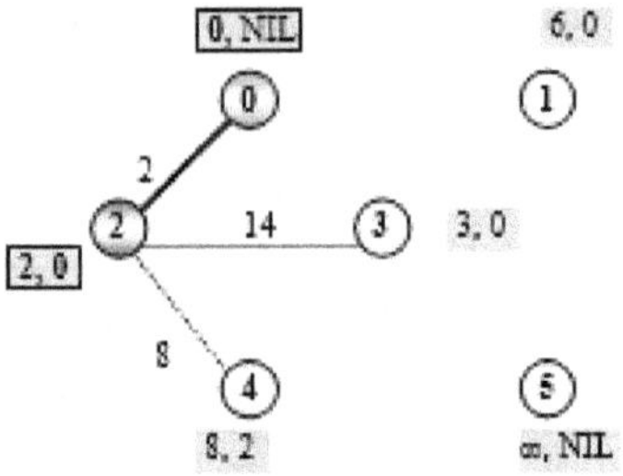

Vertex	length	Prede-cessor	Status
0	0	NIL	Perm
1	6	0	Temp
2	2	0	Perm
3	3	0	Temp
4	8	2	Temp
5	∞	NIL	Temp

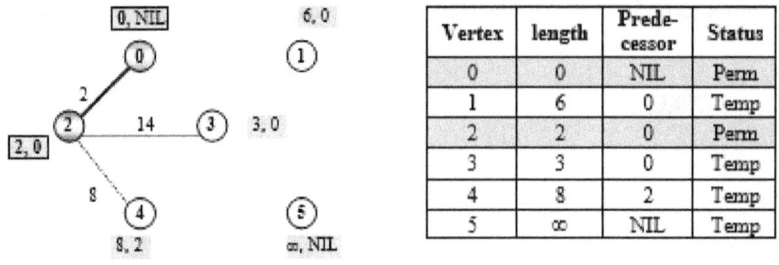

Figure 7.123 Make vertex 2 permanent, relabel 4

From all temporary vertices, vertex 3 has the smallest value of length. So, make it permanent. Its predecessor is 0, so the edge (0,3) is included in the tree. Now, the vertex 3 is the current working vertex. Vertices 1, 4, 5 are temporary vertices adjacent to vertex 3.

weight(3,1) > length(1) 11>6 Do not relabel 1
weight(3,4) < length(4) 7 < 8 Relabel 4
predecessor[4]=3 , length[4]=7
weight(3,5) < length(5) 5 < ∞ Relabel 5
predecessor[5]=3 , length[5]=5

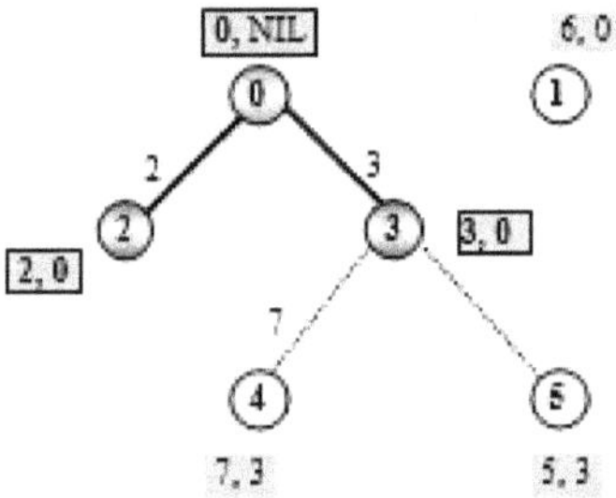

Vertex	length	Prede-cessor	Status
0	0	NIL	Perm
1	6	0	Temp
2	2	0	Perm
3	3	0	Perm
4	7	3	Temp
5	5	3	Temp

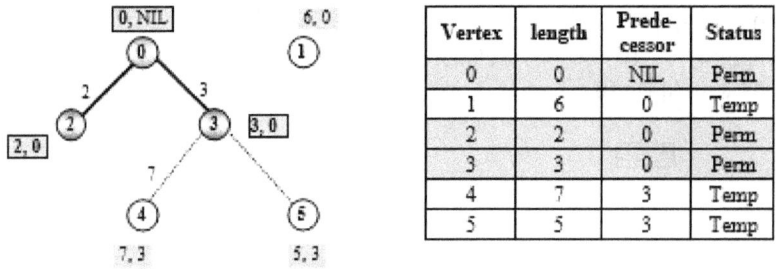

Figure 7.124 Make vertex 3 permanent, relabel 4, 5

From all temporary vertices, vertex 5 has the smallest length, so make it permanent. Its predecessor is 3 so include edge (3,5) in the tree. Now, vertex 5 is the current vertex. Vertices 1, 4 are temporary vertices adjacent to vertex 5.

weight(5,1) > length(1) 9 > 6 Do not relabel 1
weight(5,4) < length(4) 4 < 7 Relabel 4
predecessor[4] = 5, length[4] = 4

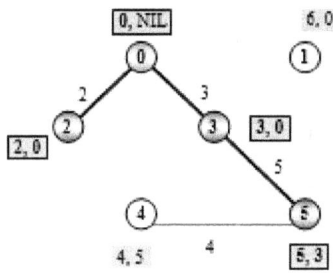

Figure 7.125 Make vertex 5 permanent, relabel 4

From all temporary vertices, vertex 4 has the smallest length, so make it permanent. Its predecessor is 5, so include edge (5,4) in the tree. Now, vertex 4 is the current vertex. There are no temporary vertices adjacent to 4.

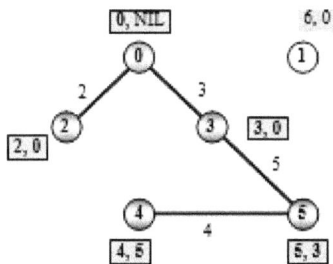

Figure 7.126 Make vertex 4 permanent

Vertex 1 is the only temporary vertex left and its length is 6, so make it permanent. Its predecessor is 0, so edge (0,1) is included in the tree.

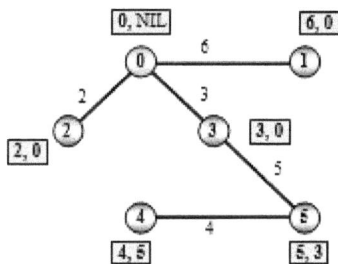

Figure 7.127 Make vertex 1 permanent

Now all the vertices are permanent, so we stop our procedure.

Now, we have a complete minimum spanning tree. The edges that belong to the minimum spanning tree are:

(0,1), (0,2), (0,3), (5,4), (3,5)

Weight of the minimum spanning tree will be:

$6 + 2 + 3 + 4 + 5 = 20$

Now let us take a graph that is not connected.

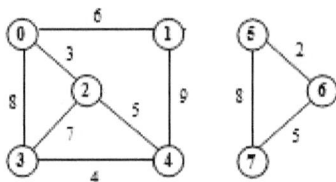

Figure 7.128 Not connected graph

After making vertices 0, 2, 4, 3, 1 permanent, the situation would be:

Vertex	length	Prede-cessor	Status
0	0	NIL	Perm
1	6	0	Perm
2	3	0	Perm
3	4	4	Perm
4	5	2	Perm
5	∞	NIL	Temp
6	∞	NIL	Temp
7	∞	NIL	Temp

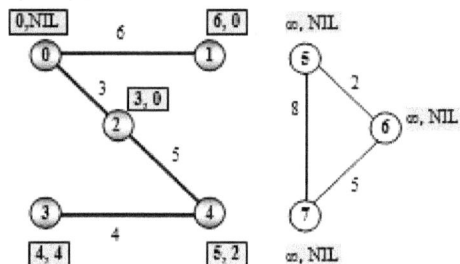

Figure 7.129 Vertex 5, 6, 7 are left temporary

Vertices 5, 6, 7 are temporary with length infinity, so, we stop the procedure and state that the graph is not connected, and hence, no spanning tree is possible.

```cpp
//UndirectedWeightedGraph.cpp : Program to create minimum spanning tree using prim's
//algorithm.
#include<iostream>
#include<string>
using namespace std;

static const int maxSize = 30;

class Vertex
{
      public:
            string name;
            int status;
            int predecessor;
            int length;
      public:
            Vertex(string name)
            {
                  this->name = name;
            }
};//End of class Vertex

class Edge
{
      public:
            int u;
            int v;
```

```
};//End of class Edge
class UndirectedWeightedGraph
{
        private:
                int nVertices;
                int nEdges;
                int adj[maxSize][maxSize];
                Vertex *vertexList[maxSize];
                Edge treeEdges[maxSize];
                int TEMPORARY;
                int PERMANENT;
                int INFINITY;
                int NIL;
        private:
                int getIndex(string vertexName);
                bool isAdjacent(int u, int v);
                void primsAlgorithm(int s);
                int getMinimumTemporary();
        public:
                UndirectedWeightedGraph();
                ~UndirectedWeightedGraph();
                void insertVertex(string vertexName);
                void insertEdge(string source, string destination, int weight);
                void display();
                void minimumSpanningTree(string source);
};//End of class UndirectedWeightedGraph
UndirectedWeightedGraph::UndirectedWeightedGraph()
{
        nVertices = 0;
        nEdges = 0;
        for(int i=0; i<maxSize; i++)
        {
                for(int j=0; j<maxSize; j++)
                {
                        adj[i][j] = 0;
                }
        }
        TEMPORARY = 0;
        PERMANENT = 1;
        INFINITY = 9999;
        NIL = -1;
}//End of UndirectedWeightedGraph()
UndirectedWeightedGraph::~UndirectedWeightedGraph()
{
        for(int i=0; i<nVertices; i++)
        {
                delete vertexList[i];
        }
}//End of ~UndirectedWeightedGraph()
void UndirectedWeightedGraph::insertVertex(string vertexName)
{
        vertexList[nVertices++] = new Vertex(vertexName);
}//End of insertVertex()
int UndirectedWeightedGraph::getIndex(string vertexName)
{
        for(int i=0; i<nVertices; i++)
        {
```

```
                if(vertexName == vertexList[i]->name)
                        return i;
        }
        throw exception("Invalid Vertex");
}//End of getIndex()
```

```cpp
void UndirectedWeightedGraph::insertEdge(string source, string destination, int
weight)
{
        int u = getIndex(source);
        int v = getIndex(destination);
        if(u == v)
                cout << "Not a valid edge\n";
        else if(adj[u][v] != 0)
                cout << "Edge already present\n";
        else
        {
                adj[u][v] = weight;
                adj[v][u] = weight;
                nEdges++;
        }
}//End of insertEdge()
```

```cpp
void UndirectedWeightedGraph::display()
{
        for(int i=0; i<nVertices; i++)
        {
                for(int j=0; j<nVertices; j++)
                        cout << adj[i][j] << " ";
                cout <<"\n";
        }
}//End of display()
```

```cpp
bool UndirectedWeightedGraph::isAdjacent(int u, int v)
{
        return (adj[u][v] != 0);
}//End of isAdjacent()
```

```cpp
//Returns the temporary vertex with minimum value of length,
//Returns NIL if no temporary vertex left or all temporary vertices left have length
//INFINITY
int UndirectedWeightedGraph::getMinimumTemporary()
{
        int min = INFINITY;
        int k = NIL;

        for(int i=0; i<nVertices; i++)
        {
                if(vertexList[i]->status==TEMPORARY && vertexList[i]->length<min)
                {
                        min = vertexList[i]->length;
                        k=i;
                }
        }
        return k;
}//End of getMinimumTemporary()
```

```cpp
void UndirectedWeightedGraph::primsAlgorithm(int r)
{
        int count = 0; //Number of edges in the tree

        //Initialize all vertices
        for(int i=0; i<nVertices; i++)
```

```
                {
                        vertexList[i]->status = TEMPORARY;
                        vertexList[i]->predecessor = NIL;
                        vertexList[i]->length = INFINITY;
                }

        //Make length of source vertex equal to 0
        vertexList[r]->length = 0;

        while(true)
        {
                //Search for temporary vertex with minimum length and make it current
                //vertex
                int current = getMinimumTemporary();

                if(current == NIL)
                {
                        if(count == nVertices-1)
                        {
                                break;  //No temporary vertex left
                        }
                        else            //Temporary vertices left with length INFINITY
                        {
                                throw exception("Graph is not connected, spanning tree
                                is not possible.");
                        }
                }

                //Make current vertex PERMANENT
                vertexList[current]->status = PERMANENT;

                //Insert the edge (vertexList[current]->predecessor,current) into the
                //tree, except when the current vertex is root
                if(current != r)
                {
                        count++;
                        treeEdges[count].u = vertexList[current]->predecessor;
                        treeEdges[count].v = current;
                }

                for(int v=0; v<nVertices; v++)
                {
                        //Checks for adjacent temporary vertices
                        if(isAdjacent(current,v) && vertexList[v]->status==TEMPORARY)
                        {
                                if((adj[current][v]) < vertexList[v]->length)
                                {
                                        vertexList[v]->predecessor = current; //Relabel
                                        vertexList[v]->length = adj[current][v];
                                }
                        }
                }//End of for
        }//End of while
}//End of primsAlgorithm()
void UndirectedWeightedGraph::minimumSpanningTree(string root)
{
        int r = getIndex(root);
        int treeWeight=0;
```

```
        primsAlgorithm(r);
        cout << "Root vertex : " << root << "\n";
        cout << "Minimum Spanning Tree Edges :\n";
        for(int i=1; i<=nVertices-1; i++)
        {
                cout << "Edge - (" << vertexList[treeEdges[i].u]->name << "-"
                << vertexList[treeEdges[i].v]->name << ")\n";
                treeWeight += adj[treeEdges[i].u][treeEdges[i].v];
        }
        cout << "Minimum Spanning Tree Weight : " << treeWeight << "\n";
}//End of minimumSpanningTree()
int main()
{
        UndirectedWeightedGraph uwGraph;
        try
        {
                //Creating the graph, inserting the vertices and edges
                uwGraph.insertVertex("0");
                uwGraph.insertVertex("1");
                uwGraph.insertVertex("2");
                uwGraph.insertVertex("3");
                uwGraph.insertVertex("4");
                uwGraph.insertVertex("5");

                uwGraph.insertEdge("0","1",6);
                uwGraph.insertEdge("0","2",2);
                uwGraph.insertEdge("0","3",3);
                uwGraph.insertEdge("0","4",10);
                uwGraph.insertEdge("1","3",11);
                uwGraph.insertEdge("1","5",9);
                uwGraph.insertEdge("2","3",14);
                uwGraph.insertEdge("2","4",8);
                uwGraph.insertEdge("3","4",7);
                uwGraph.insertEdge("3","5",5);
                uwGraph.insertEdge("4","5",4);
                //Display the graph
                uwGraph.display();
                cout << "\n";

                uwGraph.minimumSpanningTree("0");
        }//End of try
        catch(exception e)
        {
                cout << e.what() << "\n";
        }
        return 0;
}//End of main()
```

7.14.2 Kruskal's Algorithm

This approach of constructing a minimum spanning tree was formulated by J.B.Kruskal and is named after him as Kruskal's algorithm.

In this algorithm, initially, we take a forest of n distinct trees for all n vertices of the graph. So, at the start of the algorithm, each tree is a single vertex tree and no edges are there. In each step of the algorithm, an edge is examined and it is included in the spanning tree if its inclusion does not form a cycle. If this edge forms a cycle, then it is rejected.

Now, the question arises as to which edge should be considered for examining. Here, we apply the greedy approach and use the edge with the minimum weight. For this, we can maintain a list of edges sorted in ascending order of their weights. At each step, we take an edge from this list and include it if it does not form a cycle. If the edge forms a cycle, we reject it. The algorithm completes when n-1 edges have been included. If the graph contains less than n-1 edges, then it means that graph is not connected and no spanning tree is possible.

Initially, we have a forest of n trees, and whenever an edge is included, two distinct trees are joined into a single tree. So, at any stage of this algorithm, we do not have a single tree as in Prim's, but we have a forest of trees. Whenever an edge is inserted, the number of trees in the forest decreases by one, and at the end, when n-1 edges have been included, we are left with only one tree which is our minimum spanning tree. Let us take a graph and create a minimum spanning tree using Kruskal's algorithm.

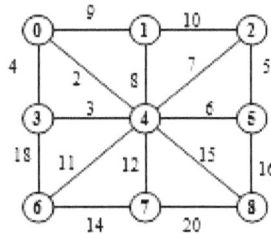

Figure 7.130 Weighted undirected connected graph

Initially, we take a forest of 9 trees, each consisting of a single vertex. All edges are examined in increasing order of their weight:

Edge 0-4, wt = 2	Inserted, see figure 7.131 (b)
Edge 3-4, wt = 3	Inserted, see figure 7.131 (c)
Edge 0-3, wt = 4	Not inserted, forms cycle 0-3-4-0 in figure 7.131 (c)
Edge 2-5, wt = 5	Inserted, see figure 7.131 (d)
Edge 4-5, wt = 6	Inserted, see figure 7.131 (e)
Edge 2-4, wt = 7	Not inserted, forms cycle 2-4-5-2 in figure 7.131 (e)
Edge 1-4, wt = 8	Inserted, see figure 7.131 (f)
Edge 0-1, wt = 9	Not inserted, forms cycle 0-1-4-0 in figure 7.131 (f)
Edge 1-2, wt = 10	Not inserted, forms cycle 1-2-5-4-1 in figure 7.131 (f)
Edge 4-6, wt = 11	Inserted, see figure 7.131 (g)
Edge 4-7, wt = 12	Inserted, see figure 7.131 (h)
Edge 6-7, wt = 14	Not inserted, forms cycle 4-6-7-4 in figure 7.131 (h)
Edge 4-8, wt = 15	Inserted, see figure 7.131 (i)

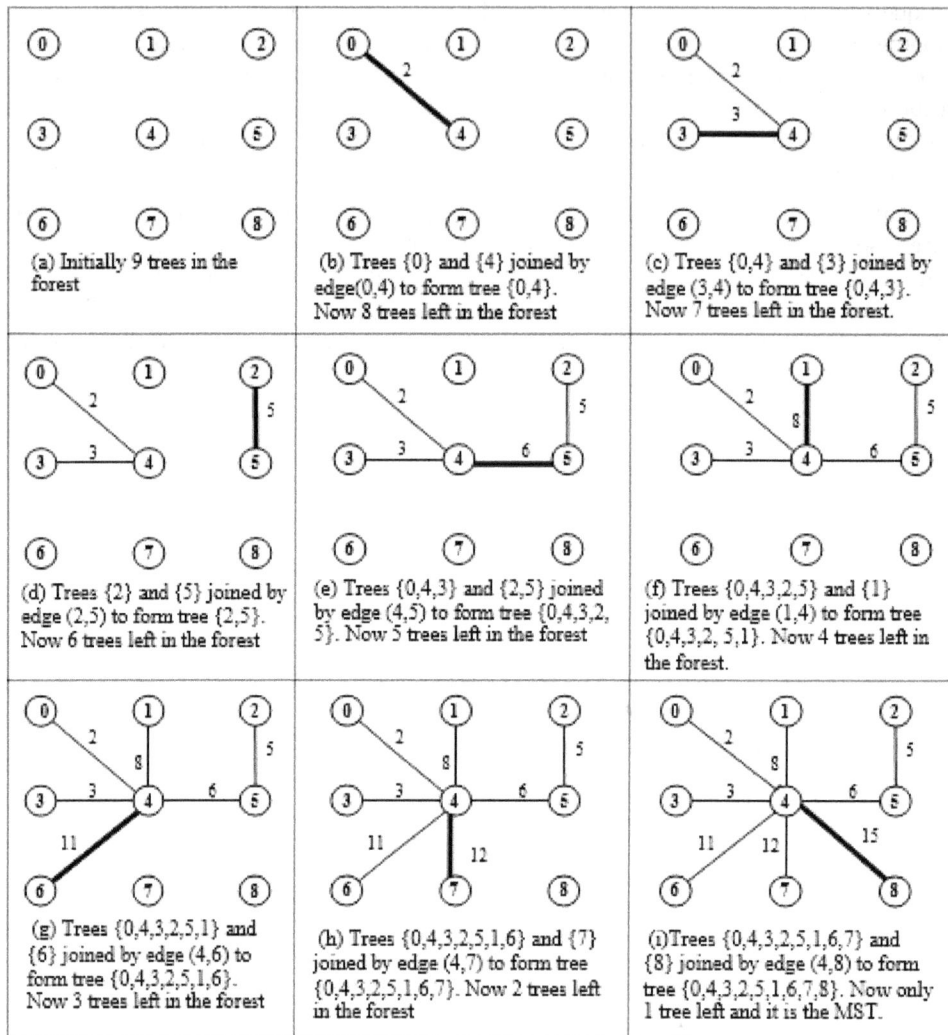

Figure 7.131 Kruskal's algorithm procedure to create a minimum spanning tree

The resulting minimum spanning tree is:

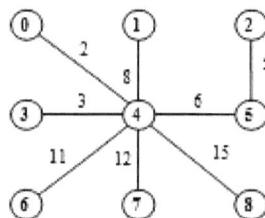

Figure 7.132 Minimum spanning tree for the graph

Let us see how we can implement this algorithm. We examine all the edges one by one, starting from the smallest edge. To decide whether the selected edge should be included in the spanning tree or not, we will examine the two vertices connecting the edge. If the two vertices belong to the same tree, it means that they are already connected, and adding this edge would result in a cycle. So we will insert an edge in the spanning tree, only if its vertices are in different trees.

Now, the question is how to decide whether two vertices are in the same tree or not. We will keep a record of the father of every vertex. Since this is a tree, every vertex will have only one distinct father. We will recognize each tree by a root vertex and a vertex will be a root if its father is NIL(-1). Initially, we have only single vertex trees; each vertex is a root vertex, so we will take the father of all vertices as NIL. To find out to which tree a vertex belongs, we will find out the root of that tree. So we will traverse all the ancestors of the vertex till we reach a vertex whose father is NIL. This will be the root of the tree to which the vertex belongs.

Now we know the root of both vertices of an edge. If the roots are same, this means both vertices are in the same tree and are already connected, so this edge is rejected. If the roots are different, then we will insert this edge into the spanning tree and will join the two trees that have these two vertices. For joining the two trees, we will make the root of one tree as the father of root of another tree.

After joining two trees, all the vertices of both trees will be connected and have the same root. Initially, the father of every vertex is NIL(-1), and hence, every vertex is a root vertex.

```
vertex  0   1   2   3   4   5   6   7   8
father  N   N   N   N   N   N   N   N   N
```

Edge	Wt	v1	v2	root of v1	root of v2	Result		
0-4	2	0	4	0	4	Inserted father[4]=0	vertex 0 1 2 3 4 5 6 7 8	father N N N N 0 N N N N
3-4	3	3	4	3	0	Inserted father[0]=3	vertex 0 1 2 3 4 5 6 7 8	father 3 N N N 0 N N N N
0-3	4	0	3	3	3	Not inserted	vertex 0 1 2 3 4 5 6 7 8	father 3 N N N 0 N N N N
2-5	5	2	5	2	5	Inserted father[5]=2	vertex 0 1 2 3 4 5 6 7 8	father 3 N N N 0 2 N N N
4-5	6	4	5	3	2	Inserted father[2]=3	vertex 0 1 2 3 4 5 6 7 8	father 3 N 3 N 0 2 N N N
2-4	7	2	4	3	3	Not inserted	vertex 0 1 2 3 4 5 6 7 8	father 3 N 3 N 0 2 N N N
1-4	8	1	4	1	3	Inserted father[3]=1	vertex 0 1 2 3 4 5 6 7 8	father 3 N 3 1 0 2 N N N
0-1	9	0	1	1	1	Not inserted	vertex 0 1 2 3 4 5 6 7 8	father 3 N 3 1 0 2 N N N
1-2	10	1	2	1	1	Not inserted	vertex 0 1 2 3 4 5 6 7 8	father 3 N 3 1 0 2 N N N
4-6	11	4	6	1	6	Inserted father[6]=1	vertex 0 1 2 3 4 5 6 7 8	father 3 N 3 1 0 2 1 N N
4-7	12	4	7	1	7	Inserted father[7]=1	vertex 0 1 2 3 4 5 6 7 8	father 3 N 3 1 0 2 1 1 N
6-7	14	6	7	1	1	Not inserted	vertex 0 1 2 3 4 5 6 7 8	father 3 N 3 1 0 2 1 1 N
4-8	15	4	8	1	8	Inserted father[8]=1	vertex 0 1 2 3 4 5 6 7 8	father 3 N 3 1 0 2 1 1 1

Figure 7.133 Kruskal's algorithm implementation approach

The minimum spanning tree should contain n-1 edges, where n is the number of vertices in the graph. This graph contains 9 vertices, so after including 8 edges in the spanning tree, we will not examine other edges of the graph and stop our process.

Edges included in this spanning tree are (0,4), (3,4), (2,5), (4,5), (1,4), (4,6), (4,7), (4,8)

Weight of this spanning tree is $2 + 3 + 5 + 6 + 8 + 11 + 12 + 15 = 62$

We will have a data member `father` in class `Vertex`. The `father` of a vertex will have the value of the index of another vertex in `vertexList`, so this vertex will represent the father of that vertex.

To obtain the edges in ascending order, we can insert them in a priority queue in increasing order of their weights.

In Prim's algorithm, we have a single tree at all the stages of the algorithm, while in Kruskal's algorithm, we have a tree only in the end. Kruskal's algorithm is faster than Prim's because in the latter, we may have to consider an edge several times, but in the former, an edge is considered only once.

```cpp
//UndirectedWeightedGraph.cpp : Program to create minimum spanning tree using Kruskal's
//algorithm.
#include<iostream>
#include<string>
#include<queue>
using namespace std;

static const int maxSize = 30;

class Vertex
{
    public:
        string name;
        int father;
    public:
        Vertex(string name)
        {
            this->name = name;
        }
};//End of class Vertex

class Edge
{
    public:
        int u;
        int v;
        int wt;
    public:
        Edge(){};
        Edge(int u, int v, int wt);
};//End of class Edge

Edge::Edge(int u, int v, int wt)
{
    this->u = u;
    this->v = v;
    this->wt = wt;
};//End of Edge()

class UndirectedWeightedGraph
{
    private:
        int nVertices;
        int nEdges;
        int adj[maxSize][maxSize];
        Vertex *vertexList[maxSize];
```

```
              Edge treeEdges[maxSize];
              int NIL;
      private:
              int getIndex(string vertexName);
              bool isAdjacent(int u, int v);
              void kruskalsAlgorithm();
      public:
              UndirectedWeightedGraph();
              ~UndirectedWeightedGraph();
              void insertVertex(string vertexName);
              void insertEdge(string source, string destination, int weight);
              void display();
              void minimumSpanningTree();
};//End of class UndirectedWeightedGraph
UndirectedWeightedGraph::UndirectedWeightedGraph()
{
      nVertices = 0;
      nEdges = 0;
      for(int i=0; i<maxSize; i++)
      {
              for(int j=0; j<maxSize; j++)
              {
                      adj[i][j] = 0;
              }
      }
      NIL = -1;
}//End of UndirectedWeightedGraph()
class CompareWeight
{
      public:
              bool operator()(Edge a, Edge b)
              {
                      return a.wt > b.wt;
              }
};//End of class CompareWeight
void UndirectedWeightedGraph::kruskalsAlgorithm()
{
      int count = 0; //Number of edges in the tree
      priority_queue<Edge, vector<Edge>, CompareWeight> edgeQueue;

      //Inserting all the edges in priority queue
      for(int u=0; u<nVertices; u++)
      {
              for(int v=u; v<nVertices; v++)
              {
                      if(isAdjacent(u,v))
                      {
                              edgeQueue.push(Edge(u,v,adj[u][v]));
                      }
              }
      }

      //Initialize the father of vertices to NIL
      for(int i=0; i<nVertices; i++)
      {
              vertexList[i]->father = NIL;
      }

      int v1, v2, v1Root=NIL, v2Root=NIL;
      Edge edge;
      while(!edgeQueue.empty() && count < nVertices-1)
```

```
        {
                edge = edgeQueue.top();
                edgeQueue.pop();
                v1 = edge.u;
                v2 = edge.v;
                while(v1!=NIL)
                {
                        v1Root = v1;
                        v1 = vertexList[v1]->father;
                }
                while(v2!=NIL)
                {
                        v2Root = v2;
                        v2 = vertexList[v2]->father;
                }
                if(v1Root != v2Root)    //Include the edge in tree
                {
                        count++;
                        treeEdges[count].u = edge.u;
                        treeEdges[count].v = edge.v;
                        vertexList[v2Root]->father = v1Root;
                }
        }//End of while
        if(count < nVertices-1)
        {
                throw exception("Graph is not connected, spanning tree is not possible.");
        }
}//End of kruskalsAlgorithm()
void UndirectedWeightedGraph::minimumSpanningTree()
{
        int treeWeight=0;

        kruskalsAlgorithm();

        cout << "Minimum Spanning Tree Edges :\n";
        for(int i=1; i<=nVertices-1; i++)
        {
                cout << "Edge - (" << vertexList[treeEdges[i].u]->name << "-"
                << vertexList[treeEdges[i].v]->name << ")\n";
                treeWeight += adj[treeEdges[i].u][treeEdges[i].v];
        }
        cout << "Minimum Spanning Tree Weight : " << treeWeight << "\n";
}//End of minimumSpanningTree()

int main()
{
        UndirectedWeightedGraph uwGraph;
        try
        {
                //Creating the graph, inserting the vertices and edges
                uwGraph.insertVertex("0");
                uwGraph.insertVertex("1");
                uwGraph.insertVertex("2");
                uwGraph.insertVertex("3");
                uwGraph.insertVertex("4");
                uwGraph.insertVertex("5");
                uwGraph.insertVertex("6");
                uwGraph.insertVertex("7");
                uwGraph.insertVertex("8");

                uwGraph.insertEdge("0","1",9);
```

```
        uwGraph.insertEdge("0","3",4);
        uwGraph.insertEdge("0","4",2);
        uwGraph.insertEdge("1","2",10);
        uwGraph.insertEdge("1","4",8);
        uwGraph.insertEdge("2","4",7);
        uwGraph.insertEdge("2","5",5);
        uwGraph.insertEdge("3","4",3);
        uwGraph.insertEdge("3","6",18);
        uwGraph.insertEdge("4","5",6);
        uwGraph.insertEdge("4","6",11);
        uwGraph.insertEdge("4","7",12);
        uwGraph.insertEdge("4","8",15);
        uwGraph.insertEdge("5","8",16);
        uwGraph.insertEdge("6","7",14);
        uwGraph.insertEdge("7","8",20);
        //Display the graph
        uwGraph.display();
        cout << "\n";

        uwGraph.minimumSpanningTree();
    }//End of try
    catch(exception e)
    {
        cout << e.what() << "\n";
    }
    return 0;
}//End of main()
```

The destructor, `insertVertex()`, `getIndex()`, `insertEdge()`, `display()`, and `isAdjacent()` functions are the same as in the Prim's algorithm program.

7.15 Topological Sorting

Topological sorting of a directed acyclic graph is the linear ordering of all the vertices, such that if there is a path from vertex u to vertex v, then u comes before v in the ordering. The sequence of vertices in the linear ordering is known as topological order or topological sequence. An example of a graph and its linear ordering is given in figure 7.134.

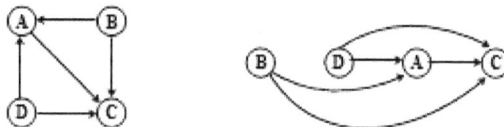

Figure 7.134 Graph and its topological order

We can see that the process of topological sorting linearizes the graph, i.e., we can write all the vertices in a horizontal line such that all the directed edges go from left to right only. This phenomenon is entirely different from the usual sorting techniques.

Topological sorting is possible only in acyclic graphs; i.e., if the graph contains a cycle, then no topological order is possible. This is because for any two vertices u and v in the cycle, u precedes v and v precedes u.

There may be more than one topological sequence for a given directed acyclic graph. For example, another topological ordering for the graph of figure 7.134 is:

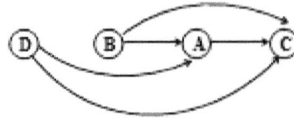

Figure 7.135 Another topological order of the previous graph

Before studying the algorithm for topological sorting, let us first see where it can be used. There are many applications where execution of one task is necessary before starting another task. For example, understanding of 'C++' and programming is necessary before starting 'Data Structures and Algorithms in C++'. Similarly, in this book also, we can go to heap sort or binary tree sort only after understanding tree.

To model these types of problems where tasks depend on one another, we can draw a directed graph in which vertices represent tasks, and if task x has to be completed before task y, then there is a directed edge from x to y.

Suppose a student needs to pass some courses to acquire a degree. The curriculum includes 7 courses named A, B, C, D, E, F, and G. Some courses have to be taken before others; for example, course B can be studied only after studying courses A, C, D. The prerequisite courses for each course are given in the following table:

Course	Prerequisite courses
A	-
B	A, C, D
C	-
D	C
E	B, D, G
F	A, B, E, G
G	-

Figure 7.136 Courses and prerequisite courses for a course

Now, we have to find the sequence in which the student should take the courses, such that before taking any course, all its prerequisite courses are completed. We can represent the information given in the table in the form of a directed graph. If course u is a prerequisite for course v, then there is an edge directed from u to v.

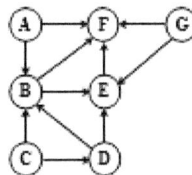

Figure 7.137 Directed graph representing the table

Now, from this directed graph, we can find out the topological order, which is the required sequence in which students should take the courses. We have seen earlier that there may be more than one topological sequence possible; one of such sequences for the above graph is A-C-G-D-B-E-F.

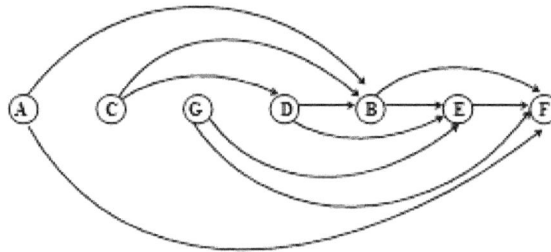

Figure 7.138 Topological order of the graph

Now we will study the algorithm for topological sorting. It finds out the solution using the greedy approach. The procedure is as follows:

1. Select a vertex with no predecessors (vertex with zero indegree).
2. Delete this vertex and all edges going out from it.
3. Repeat this procedure till all the vertices are deleted from the graph.

If, in the middle of this procedure, we arrive at a situation when no vertex can be deleted, i.e., there is no vertex left with zero indegree; all the vertices in the graph have predecessors, then it means that the graph has a cycle. In this case, no solution is possible.

Now, let us see how we can implement this algorithm. To keep track of all the vertices with zero indegree, we can use either a stack or queue. Here, we will use a queue and it will temporarily store the vertices with zero indegree. We will take a one-d array `topoOrder`, which will be used to represent the topological order of the vertices. The vertices will be stored in this array in the sequence of their deletion from the queue.

Initially, the indegree of all the vertices is computed and the vertices that have zero indegree are inserted into the initially empty queue. A vertex from the queue is deleted and listed in the `topoOrder` array. The edges going from this vertex are deleted, and the indegrees of its successors are decremented by 1. A vertex is inserted into the queue as soon as its indegree becomes 0. This process continues till all the vertices in the graph are deleted.

Let us take a graph and apply the topological sorting:

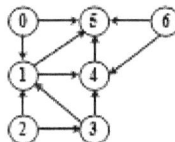

Figure 7.139 Directed graph for topological sorting

Indegree of vertices are:

In(0)=0, In(1)=3, In(2)=0, In(3)=1, In(4)=3, In(5)=4,In(6)=0

The vertices with zero indegree are 0, 2 and 6. They can be inserted in the queue in any order, this is why more than one topological orders are possible.

Queue: 0, 2, 6

Step 1 - Delete the vertex 0 and edges going from vertex 0.
Queue: 2, 6   topoOrder: 0
Updated indegree of vertices: In(1)=2, In(3)=1, In(4)=3, In(5)=3

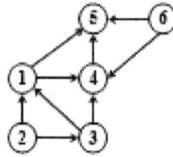

Figure 7.140 Delete the vertex 0 and edges going from vertex 0

Step 2 - Delete the vertex 2 and edges going from vertex 2
Queue: 6   topoOrder : 0, 2
Updated indegree of vertices: In(1)=1, In(3)=0, In(4)=3, In(5)=3
Insert vertex 3 into the queue
Queue: 6, 3

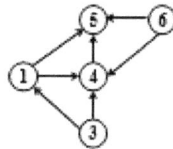

Figure 7.141 Delete the vertex 2 and edges going from vertex 2

Step 3 - Delete the vertex 6 and edges going from vertex 6.
Queue: 3   topoOrder: 0, 2, 6
Updated indegree of vertices: In(1)=1, In(4)=2, In(5)=2

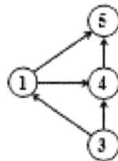

Figure 7.142 Delete the vertex 6 and edges going from vertex 6

Step 4 - Delete the vertex 3 and edges going from vertex 3.
Queue: Empty   topoOrder: 0, 2, 6, 3
Updated indegree of vertices: In(1)=0, In(4)=1, In(5)=2
Insert vertex 1 into the queue
Queue: 1

Figure 7.143 Delete the vertex 3 and edges going from vertex 3

Step 5 - Delete the vertex 1 and edges going from vertex 1.
Queue: Empty   topoOrder: 0, 2, 6, 3, 1
Updated indegree of vertices: In(4) = 0, In(5) = 1
Insert vertex 4 into queue
Queue: 4

Figure 7.144 Delete the vertex 1 and edges going from vertex 1

Step 6 - Delete the vertex 4 and edges going from vertex 4
Queue: Empty   topoOrder: 0, 2, 6, 3, 1, 4
Updated indegree of vertices: In(5) = 0
Insert vertex 5 into the queue
Queue: 5

Figure 7.145 Delete the vertex 4 and edges going from vertex 4

Step 7 - Delete the vertex 5 and edges going from vertex 5
Queue: Empty   topoOrder: 0, 2, 6, 3, 1, 4, 5

Now we have no more vertices in the graph. So, the topological sorting of the graph will be:

0, 2, 6, 3, 1, 4, 5

If there are vertices remaining in the graph and the queue becomes empty at the end of any step, it implies that the graph contains cycle, and so we will stop our procedure. In the program, we will take an array `indeg`, which will store the indegree of vertices.

```cpp
//DirectedGraph.cpp : Program for topological sorting of directed acyclic graph.
#include<iostream>
#include<string>
#include<queue>
using namespace std;

static const int maxSize = 30;

class Vertex
{
        public:
                string name;
        public:
```

```cpp
                    Vertex(string name)
                    {
                            this->name = name;
                    }
};//End of class Vertex
class DirectedGraph
{
        private:
                int nVertices;
                int nEdges;
                int adj[maxSize][maxSize];
                Vertex *vertexList[maxSize];
        private:
                int getIndex(string vertexName);
                int getIndegree(int vertex);
        public:
                DirectedGraph();
                ~DirectedGraph();
                void insertVertex(string vertexName);
                void insertEdge(string source, string destination);
                void display();
                void topologicalOrder();
};//End of class DirectedGraph

//Returns number of edges coming to a vertex
int DirectedGraph::getIndegree(int vertex)
{
        int indegree = 0;
        for(int v=0; v<nVertices; v++)
                if (adj[v][vertex])
                        indegree++;
        return indegree;
}//End of getIndegree()

void DirectedGraph::topologicalOrder()
{
        int topoOrder[maxSize], indegree[maxSize];
        queue<int> q;
        int v, count;

        //Get the indegree of each vertex
        for(v=0; v<nVertices; v++)
        {
                indegree[v] = getIndegree(v);
                if(indegree[v] == 0)
                        q.push(v);
        }
        count=0;
        while(!q.empty() && count<nVertices)
        {
                v = q.front();
                q.pop();
                topoOrder[++count] = v; //Add vertex v to topoOrder array
                //Delete all the edges going from vertex v
                for(int i=0; i<nVertices; i++)
                {
                        if(adj[v][i] != 0)
                        {
                                adj[v][i] = 0;
                                indegree[i] = indegree[i]-1;
```

```
                              if(indegree[i] == 0)
                                   q.push(i);
                    }
              }
        }//End of while
        if(count < nVertices)
        {
              throw exception("Graph contains cycle. Topological order is not
              possible.");
        }
        cout << "Vertices in topological order are :\n";
        for(int i=1; i<=count; i++)
              cout << vertexList[topoOrder[i]]->name << " ";
        cout << "\n";
}//End of topologicalOrder()

int main()
{
        DirectedGraph dGraph;
        try
        {
              //Creating the graph, inserting the vertices and edges
              dGraph.insertVertex("0");
              dGraph.insertVertex("1");
              dGraph.insertVertex("2");
              dGraph.insertVertex("3");
              dGraph.insertVertex("4");
              dGraph.insertVertex("5");
              dGraph.insertVertex("6");

              dGraph.insertEdge("0","1");
              dGraph.insertEdge("0","5");
              dGraph.insertEdge("1","4");
              dGraph.insertEdge("1","5");
              dGraph.insertEdge("2","1");
              dGraph.insertEdge("2","3");
              dGraph.insertEdge("3","1");
              dGraph.insertEdge("3","4");
              dGraph.insertEdge("4","5");
              dGraph.insertEdge("6","4");
              dGraph.insertEdge("6","5");
              //Display the graph
              dGraph.display();

              dGraph.topologicalOrder();
        }//End of try
        catch(exception e)
        {
              cout << e.what() << "\n";
        }
        return 0;
}//End of main()
```

The constructor, destructor, `insertVertex()`, `getIndex()`, `insertEdge()`, `display()`, and `isAdjacent()` functions are the same as in the directed graph program.

Exercise

1. Draw a graph corresponding to the following adjacency matrix.

$$
\begin{array}{c|ccccc}
 & 0 & 1 & 2 & 3 & 4 \\
\hline
0 & 0 & 1 & 0 & 1 & 0 \\
1 & 0 & 0 & 0 & 0 & 0 \\
2 & 0 & 1 & 0 & 1 & 1 \\
3 & 1 & 1 & 0 & 0 & 0 \\
4 & 0 & 0 & 0 & 0 & 0 \\
\end{array}
$$

Figure 7.146 Adjacency matrix

(i) Find indegree and outdegree of each vertex.
(ii) Find the path matrix for this graph.
(iii) Is the graph strongly connected?
(iv) Is the graph acyclic.

2. For the following undirected graphs, find the sum of degrees of all the vertices.

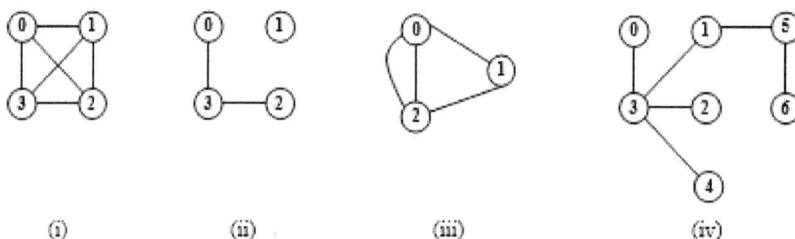

Figure 7.147 Undirected graphs

What is the relation between the number of edges and the sum of degrees of all the vertices?

3. In a graph, the vertices having odd degree are called odd vertices and the vertices having even degree are called even vertices. Prove that the number of odd vertices in a graph is even.

4. For the following directed graphs, find the sum of indegrees and the sum of outdegrees of all the vertices.

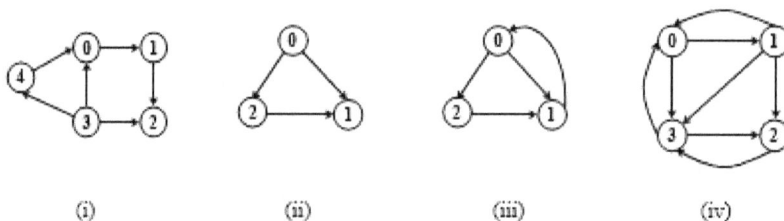

Figure 7.148 Directed graphs

What is the relation between the number of edges, the sum of indegrees, and the sum of outdegrees of all the vertices?

5. How many edges are there in a regular graph of n vertices having degree d?
   (i) A regular graph of degree 2 has 5 vertices. How many edges are there in the graph?
   (ii) A regular graph of degree 3 has 4 vertices. How many edges are there in the graph?
   (iii) A regular graph of degree 3 has 5 vertices. How many edges are there in the graph?

6. Find the articulation points in the following graphs.

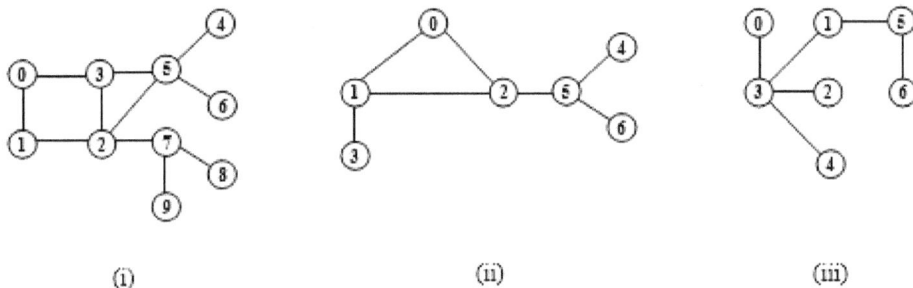

Figure 7.149 Graphs to find articulation point

7. Find whether the following graphs are strongly connected or not.

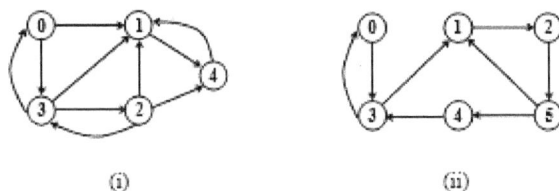

Figure 7.150 Graphs to check if it is strongly connected

8. Find the strongly connected components in the following graph.

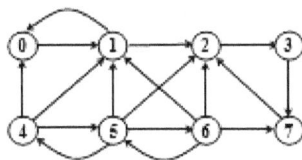

Figure 7.151 Graph to find strongly connected components

9. For the following graph, compute the shortest paths from vertex 0 to all other vertices using Dijkstra's algorithm.

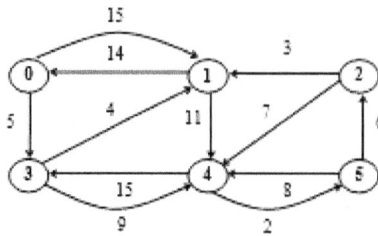

Figure 7.152 Graph to find shortest path using dijkstra's algorithm

10. Consider a complete graph having vertices 0, 1, 2, ... n-1.
    (i) Construct a minimum spanning tree if weight on any edge (u,v) is u+v
    (ii) Construct a minimum spanning tree if weight on any edge (u,v) is | u-v |
    (iii) Construct a minimum spanning tree if weight on any edge (u,v) is 5 | u-v |

Join our book's Discord space

Join the book's Discord Workspace for Latest updates, Offers, Tech happenings around the world, New Release and Sessions with the Authors:

https://discord.bpbonline.com

Sorting

8

Sorting means arranging the data according to their values in some specified order, where order can be either ascending or descending. For example, if we have a list of numbers {6, 2, 8, 1, 4}, then after sorting them in ascending order, we get {1, 2, 4, 6, 8}, and after sorting them in descending order, we get {8, 6, 4, 2, 1}. Here, the data we sorted consists only of numbers, but it may be anything like strings or records. Generally, we have to sort a list of records where each record contains several information fields. Sorting is done with respect to a key, where the key is a part of the record. Sorting these records means rearranging the records so that the key values are in order. The key on which sorting is performed, is also known as the sort key.

Suppose we have several records of employees, where each record contains three fields, viz. name, age, and salary. We can sort the records by taking any one of these fields as the sort key. The following table shows the unsorted list of records and the sorted lists having name, age and salary as the sort keys one by one.

Name	Age	Salary		Name	Age	Salary		Name	Age	Salary		Name	Age	Salary
Sumit	25	4500		Amit	37	7800		Priya	23	9000		Priya	23	9000
Amit	37	7800		Chetna	34	8000		Sumit	25	4500		Chetna	34	8000
Deepak	45	6000		Deepak	45	6000		Neelam	29	3200		Amit	37	7800
Neelam	29	3200		Kiran	39	5500		Chetna	34	8000		Shaman	50	6500
Priya	23	9000		Neelam	29	3200		Amit	37	7800		Deepak	45	6000
Shaman	50	6500		Priya	23	9000		Kiran	39	5500		Kiran	39	5500
Kiran	39	5500		Shaman	50	6500		Deepak	45	6000		Sumit	25	4500
Chetna	34	8000		Sumit	25	4500		Shaman	50	6500		Neelam	29	3200

Unsorted List L	List L sorted by name in ascending order	List L sorted by age in ascending order	List L sorted by salary in descending order

Figure 8.1 Sorting on different keys

We can see that sorting the data according to different keys arranges the data in different orders.

In our algorithms, we will perform sorting on a list of integer values only, so that we can focus on the logic of the algorithm. The extension of these algorithms to sort a list of records is simple.

Now let us see what the requirement of sorting is and why it is important to keep our data in sorted order. In our daily lives, we can see many places where data is kept in sorted order, like dictionaries, telephone directories, indexes of books, bank accounts, merit lists, roll numbers, etc. Imagine the time taken to search for a word in a dictionary, if the words were not arranged alphabetically, or consider the case when you have to search for a name in a telephone directory and the names are not sorted. Suppose you want to know where the topic "Queue" is given in this book; you will go to the index of this book to find the page number; you directly go to the words starting with 'Q', and in an instant, you find your word. This was possible because words in the index were sorted. If the index was not sorted, then you had only one option for searching a particular word, i.e., one by one. So we see that it is easier and faster to search for an item in data that is sorted. Similarly, in computer applications, sorting helps in faster information retrieval, and hence, the data processing operations become more efficient if data is arranged in some specific order. So, practically, there is no data processing application that does not perform sorting.

8.1 Sort Order

We can sort the data either in ascending (increasing) or descending (decreasing) order. If the order is not mentioned, it is assumed to be ascending order. In this chapter, we will use ascending order in our examples and algorithms. By making simple modifications, these algorithms can also work for descending order.

In the case of numbers, the ascending or descending order is clear. Alphabetic and nonalphabetic characters are generally ordered according to their ASCII values. Strings can be ordered using string comparison.

8.2 Types of Sorting

There are two types of sorting: internal sorting and external sorting. If the data to be sorted is small enough to be placed in the main memory at a time, then the sorting process can take place in the main memory, and this sorting is called internal sorting. So in internal sorting, all the data to be sorted is kept in the main memory during the sorting process.

If there is a large amount of data to be sorted that cannot be placed in the main memory at a time, then the data that is currently being sorted is brought into the main memory, and the rest is on secondary memory, i.e., on external files like disks and tapes. This type of sorting is called external sorting.

In internal sort, all the data is in the main memory, and so it is easy to access any element, while it is not so in external sort. In this chapter, we will discuss internal sorting only.

8.3 Sort Stability

Sort stability comes into the picture if the key on which data is being sorted is not unique for each record, i.e., two or more records have identical keys. For example, consider a list of records where each record contains the name and age of a person. We will take name as the sort key and sort all the records according to the names. The unsorted list of these records is given in the first table while the next three tables have sorted list.

Name	Age		Name	Age		Name	Age		Name	Age
Vineet	25		Amit	37		Amit	37		Amit	37
Amit	37		Deepa	56		Deepa	20		Deepa	67
Deepa	67		Deepa	67		Deepa	56		Deepa	20
Shriya	45		Deepa	20		Deepa	67		Deepa	56
Deepa	20		Kiran	18		Kiran	18		Kiran	18
Kiran	18		Shriya	45		Shriya	45		Shriya	45
Deepa	56		Vineet	25		Vineet	25		Vineet	25

Unsorted list   Sorted list (Unstable Sort)   Sorted list (Unstable Sort)   Sorted list (Stable Sort)

Figure 8.2 Stable and unstable sort

Any sorting algorithm would place (Amit,37) in the first position, (Kiran,18) in the fifth position, (Shriya,45) in the sixth position, and (Vineet,25) in the seventh position. There are three records with identical keys (names): (Deepa,67), (Deepa,20), and (Deepa,56). Any sorting algorithm would place them in adjacent locations, i.e., second, third, and fourth locations, but not necessarily in the same relative order.

A sorting algorithm is said to be stable if it maintains the relative order of the duplicate keys in the sorted output i.e., if keys are equal, then their relative order in the sorted output is the same. For example, if records R_i and R_j have equal keys, and if record R_i precedes record R_j in the input data, then R_i should precede R_j in the sorted output data, as well, if the sort is stable. If the sort is not stable, then R_i and R_j may be in any order in the sorted output. So, in an unstable sort, the duplicate keys may occur in any order in the sorted output.

In our example, the first two sorted lists did not maintain the relative order of the duplicate keys, while the third one did. So, we can say that the first two sorted lists were obtained by unstable sorting algorithms while the last one was obtained by a stable sorting algorithm.

Sometimes, we need to sort the records according to different keys at different times, i.e., records that are sorted on one key are again sorted on another key. In these situations, an unstable sort is not desirable. Let us take an example and see why it is so.

Suppose we have a list of all the students of a school, consisting of their names and classes, and the list is alphabetically sorted on name, i.e., all the names are in alphabetical order. Now suppose we want to sort this list with respect to class. Any sorting algorithm will place the names of all classmates in adjacent locations, but only a stable sort will place the names of students in a particular class alphabetically.

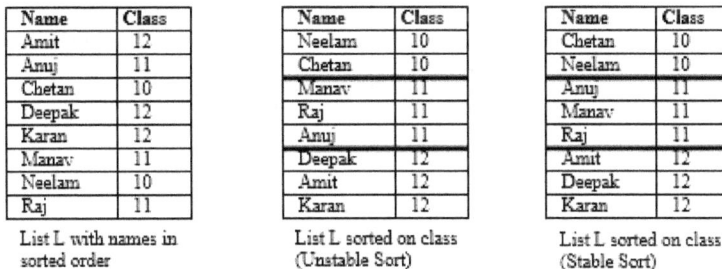

Name	Class
Amit	12
Anuj	11
Chetan	10
Deepak	12
Karan	12
Manav	11
Neelam	10
Raj	11

List L with names in sorted order

Name	Class
Neelam	10
Chetan	10
Manav	11
Raj	11
Anuj	11
Deepak	12
Amit	12
Karan	12

List L sorted on class (Unstable Sort)

Name	Class
Chetan	10
Neelam	10
Anuj	11
Manav	11
Raj	11
Amit	12
Deepak	12
Karan	12

List L sorted on class (Stable Sort)

Figure 8.3 Sorting on different keys

We can see that in stable sort, we got the names of students of each class in alphabetical order, while unstable sort disturbed the initial order of students who were in the same class.

8.4 Sort by Address (Indirect Sort)

Sorting can be done in two ways: by actually moving the records or by maintaining an auxiliary array of pointers and rearranging the pointers in that array. Let us first see how the sorting is done by moving the records.

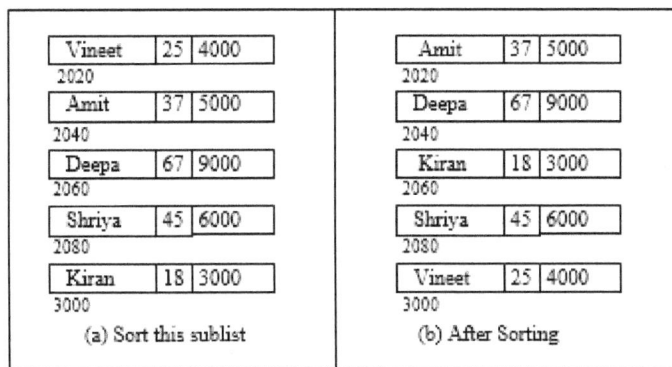

Figure 8.4 Sorting by moving records

Here, we can see that the records are moved from one place to another in the memory. For example, the record (Vineet, 25, 4000) was initially stored at address 2020, but after sorting, it is at address 3000.

If the records to be sorted are very large, then this process of moving records can be an expensive task. In this case, we can take an array of pointers, which contains the addresses of the records in memory. Now instead of rearranging the records, we rearrange the addresses inside the pointer array. In figure 8.5, we have performed sorting on the same records, but this time by adjusting pointers in the pointer array.

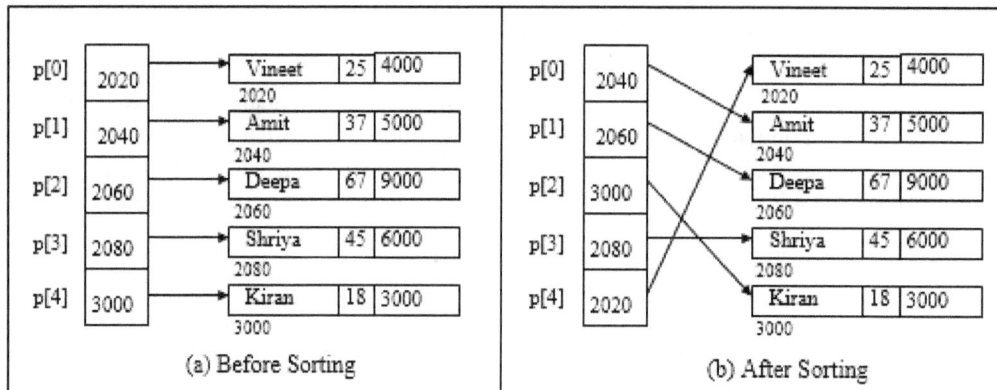

Figure 8.5 Sorting by rearranging pointers

Here, we can see that records are at the same position, but the pointers, which are pointing to records, are in different sequences but still pointing to the same record. For example, the record (Vineet, 25, 4000) was stored at address 2020 before and after the sorting. Before sorting, the first pointer of the array was pointing to the first record, the second pointer to the second record, and so on. After sorting, the first pointer will point to the first record of the sorted list, the second pointer will point to the second record of the sorted list, and so on.

This process of sorting by adjusting pointers is called sorting by address or indirect sort, because we can indirectly refer to the records in sorted order. If the records are elements of an array then we can store the indices of these elements in an auxiliary array instead of storing the addresses and sorting can be done indirectly by rearranging the values of indices contained inside the auxiliary array.

In the programs that we take in this chapter, we will perform the sorting by moving the data and the extension of these programs to perform sorting by address is simple.

Another way to avoid movement of records while sorting, is to store the records in a linked list. In that case, we will have to only change the pointers instead of moving the records. Here, we have overhead of an extra pointer field, but if the records are very large, then this overhead is negligible.

8.5 In-Place Sort

In-place sorting methods generally use the same storage space occupied by input data to store the output data while sorting. These methods do not need any extra storage except possibly a very small amount of working storage that can be neglected. So, the additional space requirements of these types of sorts are O(1).

Other sorting methods may need extra storage to store intermediate results of the sorting. Eventually, the sorted data is copied back to the original storage. In these methods, the amount of extra storage needed is proportional to the size of the data.

For example, suppose we have to sort an array of n elements, and we need another array of size n to perform this sort. Then, we are not doing an in-place sort. If we need only a constant number of extra variables, i.e., the number of variables required is independent of the size of the array, then the sort is in-place sort. The in-place sorts are also known as minimal storage sorting methods. If the size of the array to be sorted is very large, then it is beneficial to use an in-place sort.

Merge sort is not an in-place sort because it requires an extra array of size n to sort an array of size n. Selection sort, bubble sort, and insertion sort methods are in-place sort methods.

8.6 Sort Pass

The process of sorting requires traversing the given list many times. Depending on the algorithm, these traversals may be on the whole list or a part of it. This procedure of sequentially traversing the list or a part of it is called a pass. Each pass can be considered a step in sorting, and after the last pass, we get the sorted list.

8.7 Sort Efficiency

Sorting is an important and frequent operation in many applications and so the aim is not only to get the sorted data, but to get it in the most efficient manner. Therefore, many algorithms have been developed for sorting, and to decide which one to use, we need to compare them using some parameters. The choice is made using these three parameters:

- Coding time
- Space requirement
- Run time or execution time

If data is small and sorting is needed only on a few occasions, then any simple sorting technique would be adequate. In these cases, a simple or less efficient technique would behave at par with the complex techniques developed to minimize run time and space requirements. So, there is no point in spending a lot of time searching for the best sorting algorithm or implementing a complicated technique.

We have already discussed the space requirement of sorting, and we have seen that if the data to be sorted is in a large quantity, then it is better to use an in-place sort.

The most important parameter is the running time of the algorithm. If the amount of data to be sorted is large , then it is crucial to minimize run time by choosing an efficient sorting technique.

The two basic operations in any sorting algorithm are comparisons and record movements. The record moves or any other operations are generally a constant factor of the number of comparisons, and moreover, the record moves can be considerably reduced, so the run time is calculated by measuring the number of comparisons. Calculating the exact number of comparisons may not always be possible, so an approximation is given by big-O notation. Thus, the run time efficiency of different algorithms is expressed in terms of O notation. The efficiency of most of the sorting algorithms is in between $O(n \log n)$ and $O(n^2)$.

In some sorting algorithms, the time taken to sort depends on the order in which elements appear in the original data, i.e., these algorithms behave differently when the data is already sorted or when it is in reverse order. For example, if the data to be sorted is {4, 6, 8, 9, 10}, then an intelligent algorithm will immediately find out that the data is already sorted, and it will not waste time doing anything. Some sorting algorithms always take the same time to sort, irrespective of the order of data.

The run time of a data-sensitive algorithm may be different for different orders of data; hence we need to analyze the sorting algorithms in three different cases which are:

(i) Input data is in sorted order (ascending), e.g. { 1, 2, 3, 4, 5, 6, 7, 8 }

(ii) Input data is in random order, i.e., all the elements are dispersed in the data, and there is no specific order among these elements; for example, { 4, 8, 1, 6, 5, 2, 3, 7 }. In this case, it is assumed that all n! permutations of data are equally likely where n is the size of the data.

(iii) Input data is in reverse sorted order (descending); for example,{ 8, 7, 6, 5, 4, 3, 2, 1}.

There are numerous sorting algorithms, but none of them can be termed best or most efficient; each algorithm has its advantages and disadvantages. The choice of a sorting algorithm depends on the specific situation. For example, if we know in advance that our data is almost sorted, then it would be useful to use an algorithm that can identify this order. The size of data is also considered while deciding which algorithm to choose. The amount of space available also determines our choice of algorithm. If we have no extra space, then we have to go for in-place algorithms. Thus, we can see that the implementation of a particular sorting technique depends not only on the order of that technique, but also on the situation and type of data. Now after this introduction of sorting, we are ready to study various sorting algorithms and their analysis.

8.8 Selection Sort

Suppose that you are given some numbers and asked to arrange them in ascending order. The most intuitive way to do this would be to find the smallest number and put it in the first place, and then find the second smallest number and put it in the second place, and so on. This is the simple technique on which the selection sort is based. It is named so because, in each pass, it selects the smallest element and keeps it in its exact place.

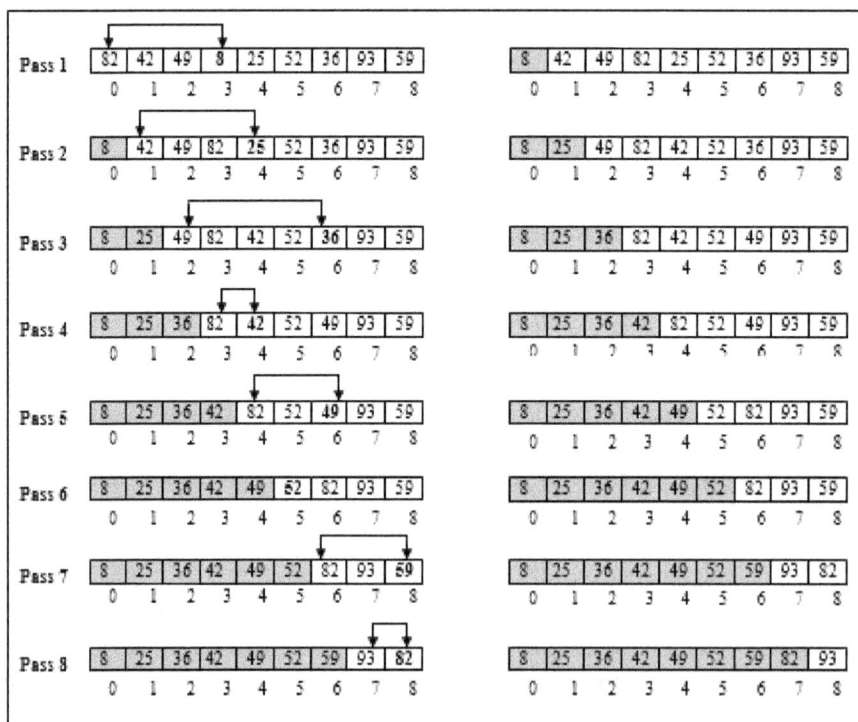

Figure 8.6 Selection sort

Suppose we have n elements stored in an array `arr`. First, we will search the smallest element from `arr[0]`........`arr[n-1]` and exchange it with `arr[0]`. This will place the smallest element of the list at 0th position of the array. Now we will search for the smallest element from the remaining elements `arr[1]`........`arr[n-1]` and exchange it with `arr[1]`. This will place the second smallest element of the list at the 1st position of array. This process continues till the whole array is sorted. The whole process is as follows:

Pass 1 :
1. Search the smallest element from arr[0]........arr[n-1].
2. Exchange this element with arr[0].
Result : arr[0] is sorted.

Pass 2 :
1. Search the smallest element from arr[1].........arr[n-1].
2. Exchange this element with arr[1].
Result : arr[0], arr[1] are sorted.

....
....

Pass n-1 :
1. Search the smallest element from arr[n-2] and arr[n-1].
2. Exchange this element with arr[n-2].
Result : arr[0], arr[1],....................arr[n-2] are sorted.

Now, all the elements except the last one have been put in their proper place. The remaining last element `arr[n-1]` will definitely be the largest of all, and so it is automatically at its proper place. So we need only `n-1` passes to sort the array. Let us take a list of elements in an unsorted order and sort it by applying selection sort (refer to figure 8.6).

In the first pass, 8 is the smallest element among `arr[0]`........`arr[8]`, and so it is exchanged with `arr[0]` i.e., 82. In the second pass, 25 is the smallest among `arr[1]`.......`arr[8]`, and so it is exchanged with `arr[1]` i.e., 42. Similarly, other passes also proceed. The shaded portion shows the elements that have been put in their final place.

Here is the complete program of selection sort. For the rest of the sorting algorithms, only the function will be shown, as `main()` is almost the same.

```cpp
//SelectionSort.cpp : Program of sorting using selection sort.
#include<iostream>
using namespace std;

static const int maxSize = 30;

void selectionSort(int arr[], int n)
{
        int min, temp;

        for(int i=0; i<n-1; i++)
        {
                //Find the index of smallest element
                min = i;
                for(int j=i+1; j<n ; j++)
                {
                        if(arr[min] > arr[j])
                                min = j;
                }
                if(i != min)
                {
                        temp = arr[i];
                        arr[i] = arr[min];
```

```
                        arr[min] = temp ;
                }
        }//End of for
}//End of selectionSort()
int main()
{
        int arr[maxSize] = {82, 42, 49, 8, 25, 52, 36, 93, 59, 15};
        int n = 10;

        cout << "Unsorted list is :\n";
        for(int i=0; i<n; i++)
                cout << arr[i] << " ";
        cout << "\n";

        selectionSort(arr,n);

        cout << "Sorted list is :\n";
        for(int i=0; i<n; i++)
                cout << arr[i] << " ";
        cout << "\n";
}//End of main()
```

Each iteration of the outer `for` loop corresponds to a single pass. In each iteration of the outer `for` loop, we have to exchange `arr[i]` with the smallest element among `arr[i]...arr[n-1]`. The inner `for` loop is used to find the index of the smallest element and it is stored in `min`. Initially, the variable `min` is initialized with `i`. After this, `arr[min]` is compared with each of the elements `arr[i+1]`, `arr[i+2]`........`arr[n-1]`, and whenever we get a smaller element, its index is assigned to `min`.

After finding the smallest element, it is exchanged with `arr[i]`. We have preceded this swap operation with a condition to avoid swapping an element with itself. This situation arises when an element is already in its proper place. In the pass 6 of figure 8.6, `arr[5]` has to be swapped with `arr[5]`, which is obviously redundant.

8.8.1 Analysis of Selection Sort

In selection sort, the number of comparisons does not depend on the order of data i.e., selection sort is not data sensitive. The number of comparisons performed is the same whether input data is sorted, reverse sorted or in random order. In the first pass, `arr[0]` is compared with `arr[1]`........`arr[n-1]`, so there will be `n-1` comparisons; in the second pass, `arr[1]` is compared with `arr[2]`........`arr[n-1]`, so there will be `n-2` comparisons. In the last pass, `arr[n-2]` is compared with `arr[n-1]`, and so there will be only one comparison. The total number of comparisons will be:

$(n-1) + (n-2) + (n-3) +...............+ 3 + 2 +1 = n(n-1)/2 = O(n^2)$

So, the efficiency of the selection sort is $O(n^2)$ in all three cases.

Selection sort is simple to implement and requires only one temporary variable for swapping elements. The main advantage of selection sort is that data movement is very less. If an element is at its proper place, then it will not be moved at all. Thus, if many elements are at the proper place, i.e., the list is almost sorted, then there will be very little data movement. Therefore, we see that the number of swaps depends on the order of data, and it can never be more than `n-1`. The swaps are very less as compared to insertion and bubble sorts. If the records are large, then the cost of moving data is more than the cost of comparisons. Thus, if the records are large, it is better to use selection sort.

Selection sort is not a stable sort. It requires only one temporary variable so it is an in-place sort, and space complexity is $O(1)$.

8.9 Bubble Sort

Bubble sort proceeds by scanning the list and exchanging the adjacent elements if they are out of order with respect to each other. It compares each element with its adjacent element and swaps them if they are not in order i.e., `arr[i]` will be compared with `arr[i+1]`, and if `arr[i]>arr[i+1]`, then they will be swapped.

In selection sort, we searched for the smallest element and then performed the swap, while here, a swap will be performed as soon as we find two adjacent elements out of order. So in selection sort, there was only one swap in a pass, while in bubble sort, there may be many swaps in a single pass. Hence, bubble sort is not an efficient sorting technique, but it is simple and easy to implement.

After the first pass, the largest element will be at its proper position in the array, i.e., $(n-1)^{th}$ position; after the second pass, the second largest element will be placed at its proper position, i.e., $(n-2)^{th}$ position. Similarly, after each pass, the next larger elements will be moved to the end of the list and placed at their proper positions. If there are `n` elements, then only `n-1` passes are required to sort the array, and the procedure is as follows:

Pass 1 :
Compare arr[0] and arr[1] If arr[0] > arr[1], then exchange them,
Compare arr[1] and arr[2], If arr[1] > arr[2], then exchange them,
Compare arr[2] and arr[3], If arr[2] > arr[3], then exchange them,

....
....
Compare arr[n-2] and arr[n-1], If arr[n-2] > arr[n-1], then exchange them.
Result : Largest element is placed at $(n-1)^{th}$ position
arr[n-1] is sorted.

Pass 2 :
Compare arr[0] and arr[1], If arr[0] > arr[1], then exchange them,
Compare arr[1] and arr[2], If arr[1] > arr[2], then exchange them,
Compare arr[2] and arr[3], If arr[2] > arr[3], then exchange them,

....
Compare arr[n-3] and arr[n-2], If arr[n-3] > arr[n-2], then exchange them.
Result : Second largest element is placed at $(n-2)^{th}$ position
arr[n-2], arr[n-1] are sorted.

....
....

Pass n-2 :
Compare arr[0] and arr[1], If arr[0] >arr[1], then exchange them,
Compare arr[1] and arr[2], If arr[1] >arr[2], then exchange them.
Result : arr[2],.........arr[n-2], arr[n-1] are sorted.

Pass n-1 :
Compare arr[0] and arr[1], If arr[0] >arr[1], then exchange them.
Result : arr[1], arr[2],.........arr[n-2], arr[n-1] are sorted.

In the second pass, comparisons will be done only up to $(n-2)^{th}$ position, i.e., the last comparison is done between `arr[n-3]` and `arr[n-2]`, because the largest element has already been placed at its proper position, i.e., position `(n-1)`. In the third pass, the last comparison is done between `arr[n-4]` and `arr[n-3]`, because the second largest element has already been placed at its proper position, i.e., position `(n-2)`. In the last pass, there is only one comparison, which is between `arr[0]` and `arr[1]`. The remaining element `arr[0]` will definitely be the smallest element, and so the whole list is sorted after `n-1` passes.

Let us take an array in unsorted order and sort it by applying bubble sort.

40   20   50   60   30   10

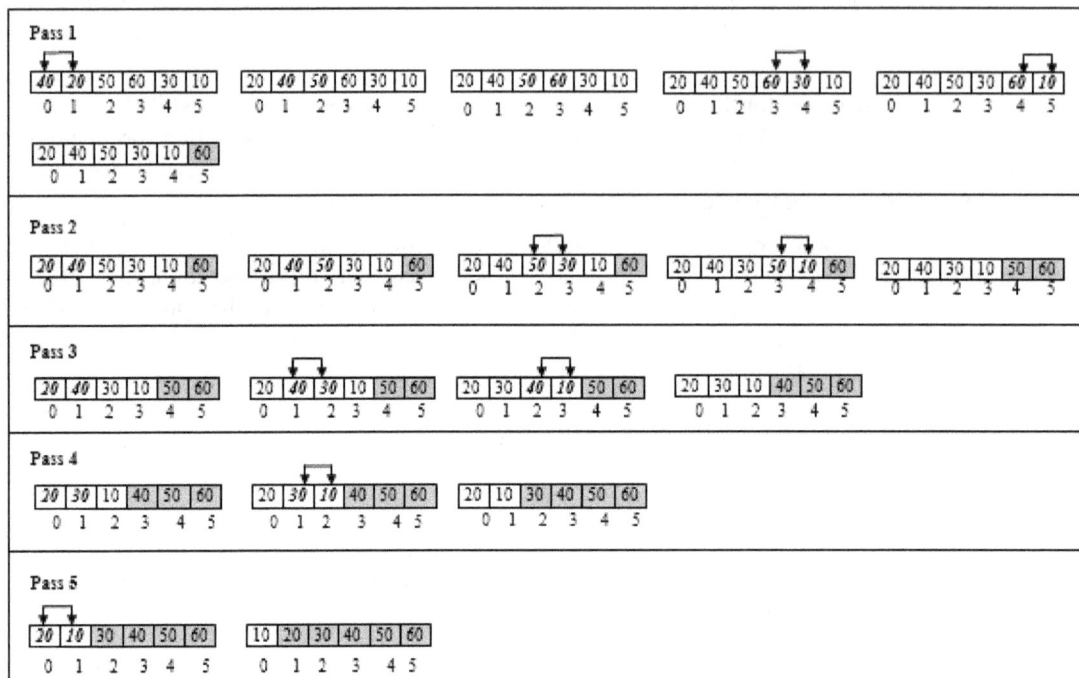

Figure 8.7 Bubble sort

Let us see what happens in the first pass. First, `arr[0]` is compared with `arr[1]`, and since 40>20, they are swapped. Now `arr[1]` is compared with `arr[2]`, and since 40<50, they are not swapped. Now, `arr[2]` is compared with `arr[3]`, and since 50<60, they are not swapped. Now, `arr[3]` is compared with `arr[4]`, and since 60>30, they are swapped. Now `arr[4]` is compared with `arr[5]`, and since 60>10, they are swapped. At the end of this pass, the largest element 60, is placed at the last position. The elements that are being compared, are shown in italics, and the elements which have been placed in the proper place, are shaded.

Sometimes, it is possible that a list of n elements becomes sorted in less than `n-1` passes. For example, consider this list: 40   20   10   30   60   50
After the first pass, the list is: 20   10   30   40   50   60
After the second pass, the list is: 10   20   30   40   50   60

The list of 6 elements becomes sorted in only 2 passes. Hence, other passes are unnecessary and there is no need to proceed further. Now, the question is how we will be able to know that the list has become sorted. If no swaps occur in a pass, it means that the list is sorted. For example, in the above case, there will be no swaps in the third pass. We can take a variable that keeps a record of the number of swaps in a pass, and if no swaps occur, then we can terminate our procedure.

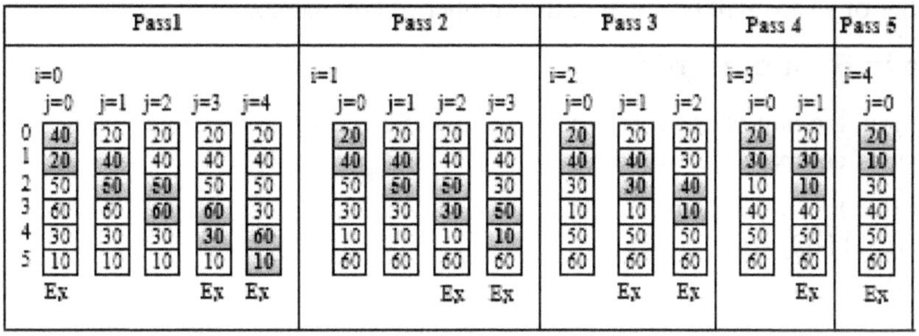

Pass1					Pass 2				Pass 3			Pass 4		Pass 5
i=0					i=1				i=2			i=3		i=4
j=0	j=1	j=2	j=3	j=4	j=0	j=1	j=2	j=3	j=0	j=1	j=2	j=0	j=1	j=0

Figure 8.8 (bubble sort procedure table with element values through passes)

Figure 8.8 Bubble sort procedure example

Figure 8.8 shows the procedure of bubble sort along with the values of i and j. Each iteration of the outer `for` loop corresponds to a single pass. Here is the `bubbleSort()` function:

```
void bubbleSort(int arr[], int n)
{
        int temp, xchanges;
        for(int i=0; i<n-1 ;i++)
        {
                xchanges = 0;
                for(int j=0; j<n-1-i; j++)
                {
                        if(arr[j] > arr[j+1])
                        {
                                temp = arr[j];
                                arr[j] = arr[j+1];
                                arr[j+1] = temp;
                                xchanges++;
                        }
                }
                if(xchanges == 0) //If list is sorted
                        break;
        }//End of for
}//End of bubbleSort()
```

8.9.1 Analysis of Bubble Sort

The number of passes will depend on the order of data. There can be a minimum of 1 pass and a maximum of (n-1) pass.

8.9.1.1 Data in Sorted Order

If all the elements are sorted, then only one pass is required, and so, there will be only one iteration of the outer `for` loop. The number of comparisons will be (n-1), and all elements are in their proper place. So, there will be no swaps. Hence, the time complexity in this case is O(n).

8.9.1.2 Data in Reverse Sorted Order

If the array elements are in reverse order, (n-1) passes are required, and so, there will be (n-1) iterations of the outer `for` loop. In the first iteration, there will be (n-1) comparisons; in the second iteration, there will be (n-2) comparisons; in the third iteration, there will be (n-3) comparisons, and so on. So the total number of comparisons are:

(n-1) + (n-2) + (n-3) + ...+ 3 + 2 + 1
= n(n-1)/2 = O(n²)

The total number of swaps will be equal to the number of comparisons.

8.9.1.3 Data in Random Order

In the ith iteration, the number of comparisons is n-i. So if p passes are required to sort the data, then the total number of comparisons would be:

(n-1) + (n-2) + (n-3) + ...(n-p)
= p/2[2(n-1) + (p-1) (-1)]
= $(2pn - p^2 - p)/2$

It can be shown that the number of passes p in average case is O(n), and so the comparisons will be $O(n^2)$. The main advantage of this algorithm is that it is simple and easy to implement; the additional space requirement is only one temporary variable, and it behaves O(n) for a sorted array of elements. Bubble sort should not be used for large lists; it should generally be used for smaller lists.

Bubble sort is a stable sort. It requires only one temporary variable so it is an in-place sort, space complexity is O(1).

8.10 Insertion Sort

The insertion sort proceeds by inserting each element at the proper place in a sorted list. This is the same technique used by card players for arranging cards. When they receive a card, they place it in the appropriate place among the cards that they have already arranged.

We will consider our list to be divided into two parts: sorted and unsorted. Initially, the sorted part contains only the first element of the list, and the unsorted part contains the rest of the elements. In each pass, the first element from the unsorted part is taken and inserted into the sorted part at the appropriate place. If there are n elements in the list, then after n-1 passes, the unsorted part disappears and our whole list becomes sorted. The process of inserting each element in the proper place is as:

Pass 1 :
Sorted part : arr[0]
Unsorted part : arr[1], arr[2], arr[3], ...,arr[n-1]
arr[1] is inserted before or after arr[0].
Result : arr[0] and arr[1] are sorted.

Pass 2 :
Sorted part : arr[0], arr[1]
Unsorted part : arr[2],arr[3], ...,arr[n-1]
arr[2] is inserted before arr[0], or in between arr[0] and arr[1] or after arr[1].
Result : arr[0], arr[1] and arr[2] are sorted.

Pass 3 :
Sorted part : arr[0], arr[1], arr[2]
Unsorted part : arr[3], arr[4],..........,arr[n-1]
arr[3] is inserted at its proper place among arr[0], arr[1], arr[2]
Result : arr[0], arr[1], arr[2], arr[3] are sorted.
....
....

Pass n-1 :
Sorted part : arr[0], arr[1], ...arr[n-2]
Unsorted part : arr[n-1]
arr[n-1] is inserted at its proper place among arr[0], arr[1], ...arr[n-2]
Result : arr[0], arr[1],arr[2],...............arr[n-1] are sorted.

To insert an element in the sorted part, we need a vacant position, and this space is created by moving all the larger elements one position to the right. Now, let us take a list of elements in unsorted order and sort them by applying insertion sort.

82   42   49   8   25   52   36   93   59

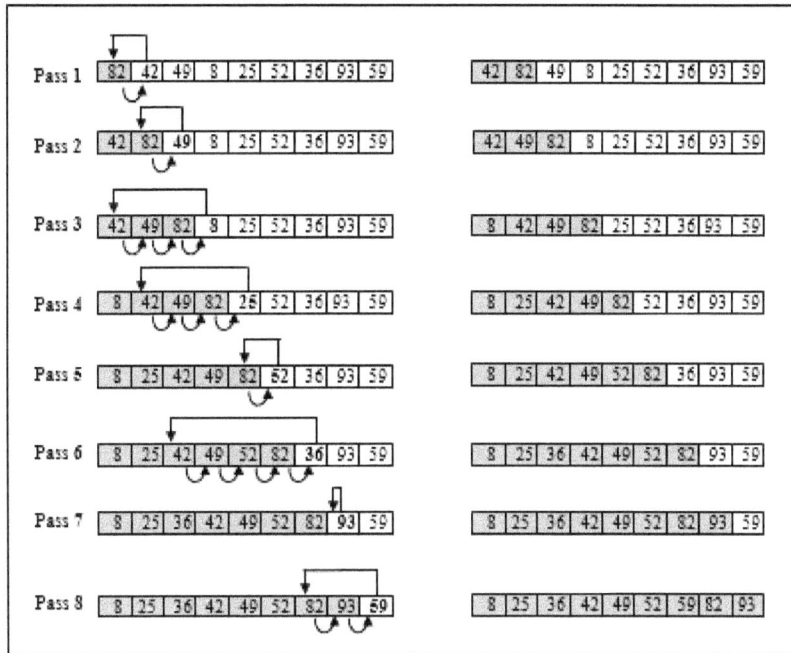

Figure 8.9 Insertion sort

The shaded portion shows the sorted part of the list, and the arrows show the movement of elements. To insert an element, we have to scan the sorted part and search for the appropriate place where this element can be inserted. We will use the sequential search for this purpose. We also need a vacant position for inserting this element, and for this, all the larger elements are moved one position right. For example, in pass 6, the elements 42, 49, 52 and 82 are moved one position right to make space for insertion of 36.

If we start our search from the end of the sorted part, instead of its beginning, then we can simultaneously shift the elements also. Here is the `insertionSort()` function:

```
void insertionSort(int arr[], int n)
{
        int i,j,k;

        for(i=1; i<n; i++)
        {
                k = arr[i];
                for(j=i-1; j>=0 && arr[j]>k; j--)
                        arr[j+1] = arr[j];
                arr[j+1] = k;
        }//End of for
}//End of insertionSort()
```

In each iteration of the `for` loop, the first element of the unsorted part is inserted into the sorted part. The element to be inserted (`arr[i]`) is stored in the variable `k`. In the inner `for` loop, the sorted part is scanned to find the exact location for the insertion of the element `arr[i]`. The search starts from the end of the sorted part, and so, variable `j` is initialized to `i-1`. The search stops when we either reach the beginning of the sorted part, or we get an element less than `k`. Inside the inner `for` loop, the elements are moved right by one position, and obviously, these are elements that are greater than `k`. At the end, `k` is inserted at its proper place.

8.10.1 Analysis of Insertion Sort

The outer `for` loop will always have `n-1` iterations. The iterations of the inner `for` loop will vary according to the data. For each iteration of the outer `for` loop, the inner `for` loop executes 0 to `i` times, i.e., the inner `for` loop can be executed a minimum of 0 times and a maximum of `i` times.

arr[i] has to be put in any of these i+1 positions 0,1,2,3......., i-1, i

- If arr[i] is already at the proper place, i.e., position i is the proper place for arr[i]
  1 comparison, arr[i] compared with arr[i-1]
  No move inside inner for loop and 2 moves for loading and unloading k

- If arr[i] has to be placed at position i-1
  2 comparisons, arr[i] compared with arr[i-1], arr[i-2]
  1 move inside inner for loop and 2 moves for loading and unloading k

- If arr[i] has to be placed at position i-2,
  3 comparisons, arr[i] compared with arr[i-1], arr[i-2],arr[i-3]
  2 moves inside inner for loop and 2 moves for loading and unloading k

- If arr[i] has to be placed at position 2
  i-1 comparisons, arr[i] compared with arr[i-1], arr[i-2],arr[i-3],.......,arr[1]
  i-2 moves inside inner for loop and 2 moves for loading and unloading k

- If arr[i] has to be placed at position 1,
  i comparisons, arr[i] compared with arr[i-1], arr[i-2],arr[i-3],.......,arr[1],arr[0]
  i-1 moves inside inner for loop and 2 moves for loading and unloading k

- If arr[i] has to be placed at position 0
  i comparisons, arr[i] compared with arr[i-1], arr[i-2],arr[i-3],.......,arr[1],arr[0]
  i moves inside inner for loop and 2 moves for loading and unloading k

8.10.1.1 Data in Sorted Order

The best case occurs if the list is in sorted order. In each iteration of the outer `for` loop, `arr[i]` is always in the proper place. We have seen that if `arr[i]` is at the proper place, then there is only one comparison. So there will be only one comparison in each iteration of the outer `for` loop, and the outer `for` loop always iterates `n-1` times. Thus, there will be a total of `n-1` comparisons in all, which is O(n).

The body of the inner `for` loop will never be entered, and so, in each iteration of the outer `for` loop, there will be only 2 moves and hence the total number of moves will be `2(n-1)`. All these moves are unnecessary.

8.10.1.2 Data in Reverse Sorted Order

The worst case occurs when the list is sorted in reverse order. In any i^{th} iteration of the outer `for` loop, the element `arr[i]` will be less than each of these elements `arr[0]`, `arr[1]`, ...`arr[i-1]`. So, arr[i] will always be inserted at the 0th position. We have seen above that if the element `arr[i]` has to be placed at the 0th position, then there will be i comparisons. So in the first iteration of the outer `for` loop, there will be 1 comparison; in the second iteration of the outer `for` loop, there will be 2 comparisons; and in the $(n-1)^{th}$ iteration of the outer `for` loop, there will be `n-1` comparisons. So the total number of comparisons will be:

$$\sum_{i=1}^{n-1} i = 1 + 2 + 3 + \ldots + (n\text{-}1) = n(n\text{-}1)/2 = O(n^2)$$

If `arr[i]` is to be placed at the 0th position, then the number of moves in the ith iteration of `for` loop is i+2, and the total number of moves will be:

$$\sum_{i=1}^{n-1} i+2 = n(n\text{-}1)/2 + 2(n\text{-}1) = O(n^2)$$

There is a variation in the above two cases, so now, let us analyze the efficiency of the insertion sort, when data is in random order.

8.10.1.3 Data in Random Order

Here, we assume an equal probability of occupying all array locations.

The average number of comparisons in the ith iteration of outer `for` loop:

$$\frac{1+2+3+\ldots+ (i\text{-}1)+ i + i}{i+1}$$

$$= [\, i(i+1)] / 2(i+1) + i/(i+1)$$

$$= i/2 + 1 - 1/(i+1)$$

Total number of comparisons:

$$= \sum_{i=1}^{n-1} i/2 + \sum_{i=1}^{n-1} 1 - \sum_{i=1}^{n-1} 1/(i+1)$$

$$= n(n\text{-}1)/4 + (n\text{-}1) - \sum_{i=1}^{n-1} 1/(i+1)$$

$$= n(n\text{-}1)/4 + n - \sum_{j=1}^{n} 1/j$$

$$\approx n(n\text{-}1)/4 + n - \log_e n$$

$$= O(n^2)$$

Average number of moves in the ith iteration of outer `for` loop:

$$\frac{0+1+2+ \ldots + (i\text{-}1)+i}{(i+1)}$$

$$= [i(i+1)] / [2(i+1)]$$

$$= i/2$$

Total number of moves

$$= \sum_{i=1}^{n-1} i/2 = n(n\text{-}1)/4$$

$$= O(n^2)$$

The advantage of insertion sort is its simplicity, and it is very efficient when the number of elements to be sorted is very less because for smaller file size n, the difference between $O(n^2)$ and $O(n \log n)$ is very less, and $O(n \log n)$ generally requires a complex sorting technique. Insertion sort is also efficient for lists that are almost sorted.

We can simplify the inner `for` loop, or reduce a condition in the inner `for` loop, by taking a sentinel value in `arr[0]`. This value is taken to be smaller than the smallest value possible. So, we can avoid the test `j>=0`. This condition is true only when the element to be inserted is the smallest, and has to be inserted in the beginning of the array. The elements to be sorted can be stored in `arr[1]` to `arr[n]` and a sentinel value in `arr[0]`. So now only a single test is sufficient, and this will simplify the inner loop.

We can reduce the number of comparisons by using binary search for finding the proper place of insertion. But still, the elements have to be shifted right to one position, which is $O(n^2)$. So, the use of binary search would not improve the efficiency of the insertion sort.

A disadvantage of this sorting is the number of movements. The elements of the sorted part also have to move to make place for another element. When the data items to be sorted are large, then these movements can prove costly.

Sometimes elements are at their proper place in the list, but still, they are moved. For example, consider this data:

75   19   34   55   12

Here, 19, 34, and 55 are at their proper places, and so, their movement is redundant.

Insertion sort is a stable sort. It requires only one temporary variable, and so, it is an in-place sort, and space complexity is $O(1)$.

8.11 Shell Sort (Diminishing Increment Sort)

Insertion sort is not efficient because many moves are performed, and the reason for so many moves is that elements are moved only one position at a time. The elements are moved only in one position because only adjacent elements are compared. If we can compare elements that are far apart, then we can considerably reduce the number of moves, thereby making insertion sort more efficient. This is what happens in Shell sort which is an improved version of insertion sort and was given by Donald. L. Shell in 1959. It works by first comparing elements that are far apart. Then, it compares closer elements; the distance between the elements to be compared reduces with every pass until the last pass, where adjacent elements are compared.

Now, let us see the procedure of this sorting technique. In each pass, we take a number 'h' called the increment. This number decreases in subsequent passes and finally in the last pass, it is always 1. In each pass, we divide the list into h sublists. Each sublist is created by taking elements that are at a distance of h from each other. For example, if we have an array of 17 elements and we take the increments as 5, 3, 1, then the sublists will be created as:

Pass 1: (increment = 5)
5 sublists are created
Sublist 1 :   a[0], a[5], a[10], a[15]
Sublist 2 :   a[1], a[6], a[11], a[16]
Sublist 3 :   a[2], a[7], a[12]
Sublist 4 :   a[3], a[8], a[13]
Sublist 5 :   a[4], a[9], a[14]

Pass 2 : (increment = 3)
3 sublists are created
Sublist 1 :   a[0], a[3], a[6], a[9], a[12], a[15]
Sublist 2 :   a[1], a[4], a[7], a[10], a[13], a[16]
Sublist 3 :   a[2], a[5], a[8], a[11], a[14]

Pass 3 : (increment =1)
1 sublist is created
Sublist 1 :   a[0], a[1], a[2], a[3], a[4], a[5], a[6],a[7], a[8], a[9], a[10], a[11], a[12], a[13], a[14], a[15], a[16]

These sublists are separately sorted among themselves by insertion sort and at the end of the pass these sorted sublists are combined. The list that we get after each pass is partially sorted. In the last pass, increment is 1, so only one sublist is created, which consists of all the elements. Thus, insertion sort is performed on the whole list and we get our sorted list.

Since the value of increment continually decreases, this sort is also known as diminishing increment sort. Now, we will take an array of 17 elements and see how they can be sorted by shell sort, if the increments are taken to be 5, 3, 1. The sorting procedure is shown in figure 8.10.

Original list	19	63	2	6	7	10	1	18	9	4	45	3	5	17	16	12	56
Pass 1 : Partiton into 5 sublists	19	–	–	–	–	10	–	–	–	–	45	–	–	–	–	12	–
	–	63	–	–	–	–	1	–	–	–	–	3	–	–	–	–	56
	–	–	2	–	–	–	–	18	–	–	–	–	5	–	–	–	–
	–	–	–	6	–	–	–	–	9	–	–	–	–	17	–	–	–
	–	–	–	–	7	–	–	–	–	4	–	–	–	–	16	–	–
Sort above 5 sublists	10	–	–	–	–	12	–	–	–	–	19	–	–	–	–	45	–
	–	1	–	–	–	–	3	–	–	–	–	56	–	–	–	–	63
	–	–	2	–	–	–	–	5	–	–	–	–	18	–	–	–	–
	–	–	–	6	–	–	–	–	9	–	–	–	–	17	–	–	–
	–	–	–	–	4	–	–	–	–	7	–	–	–	–	16	–	–
Combine these 5 sorted sublists	10	1	2	6	4	12	3	5	9	7	19	56	18	17	16	45	63
Pass 2 : Partition into 3 sublists	10	–	6	–	3	–	7	–	18	–	45						
	–	1	–	4	–	5	–	19	–	17	–	63					
	–	2	–	12	–	9	–	56	–	16	–						
Sort above 3 sublists	3	–	6	–	7	–	10	–	18	–	45						
	–	1	–	4	–	5	–	17	–	19	–	63					
	–	2	–	9	–	12	–	16	–	56	–						
Combine these 3 sorted sublists	3	1	2	6	4	9	7	5	12	10	17	16	18	19	56	45	63
Pass 3 : Only one sublist	3	1	2	6	4	9	7	5	12	10	17	16	18	19	56	45	63
	1	2	3	4	5	6	7	9	10	12	16	17	18	19	45	56	63

Figure 8.10 Shell sort

In the first pass, 5 sublists are created and these sublists are sorted among themselves using insertion sort. For example, the first and second sublists are { 19, 10 , 45 ,12 } and { 63, 1, 3, 56 }, and after sorting, they become { 10, 12, 19 , 45 } and { 1, 3, 56, 63}. Similarly, other 3 sublists are also sorted and then all the five sorted sublists are combined. The list that we get after the first pass is partially sorted, i.e., all the elements that are at a distance of 5 from each other, are sorted. This list is also called 5-sorted list and the procedure is called 5-sort. Similarly, in the second pass, 3-sort is performed and we get 3-sorted list. In the last pass, 1-sort is done and we get our sorted list.

Initially, the elements which are far apart are compared and then the elements which are closer and so on. The distance between elements being compared decreases with each pass and finally in the last pass adjacent elements are compared. This way, we have improved over insertion sort because here elements can be moved long distances instead of only one place at a time.

We know that if the list is in almost sorted order, then insertion sort proves to be very efficient. Another feature of insertion sort is that it is very efficient on small lists. These two aspects of insertion sort are the basis of Shell sort.

Initially, when the increment value is large, the size of sublists is small, so insertion sort is fast. After each pass, the elements move closer to their final positions, i.e., the list becomes nearly sorted. The increment value decreases with each pass, thus leading to larger sublists, and insertion sort is not suitable for large lists. But insertion sort works fast on these larger sublists also because they are nearly sorted. When we reach the last pass, the list becomes almost sorted, i.e., the elements are very close to their final positions, so the insertion sort on the whole list goes very rapidly. Thus, we can see that in shell sort, the previous passes help in making the list almost sorted so that the insertion sort in the last pass is very fast.

Now, let us talk about the choice of increments. There is no restriction on sequence of increments except that it should be 1 in the last pass. The increment sequence suggested by Shell originally was to take first increment equal to half the size of list and divide the increment value by 2 in each pass.

If we have a list of 17 elements, then the increment sequence will be 8, 4, 2, 1. The sublists formed in this case are given below (only subscripts are shown):

Increment = 8   { 0, 8, 16 }, {1, 9 }, { 2, 10 }, { 3, 11 }, { 4, 12 }, { 5, 13 }, {6, 14}, { 7, 15 }
Increment = 4   { 0, 4, 8, 12, 16 }, { 1, 5, 9, 13 }, { 2, 6, 10, 14 }, { 3, 7, 11, 15 }
Increment = 2   { 0, 2, 4, 6, 8, 10, 12, 14, 16 }, { 1, 3, 5, 7, 9, 11, 13,15 }
Increment = 1   { 0, 1, 2, 3, 4, 5, 6, 7, 8, 9, 10, 11, 12, 13, 14, 15, 16 }

We can see that elements in the even and odd positions will not be compared till the last pass, and so this increment sequence is not a good choice. We can improve this sequence by adding 1 to the increment if it is even.

In general, it is better not to choose increments which are multiples of each other like 1,3,6,9 or 1,2,4,8, because the elements compared at one pass will be compared again at the next pass. We can achieve greater efficiency if the values of increments are relatively prime. Many increment sequences have been suggested, but till now, none of them has been singled out as perfect. Knuth suggested the following sequence:

$h_1=1$, $h_{i+1}= 3h_i+1$, stop at h_i when $h_i > (n-1)/9$

For example, if n=10000, then increments would be 1, 4, 13, 40, 121, 364, 1093, 3280.

Now, we will see how we can implement Shell sort. One method that naturally comes to mind is that in each pass, we sort all the sublists one by one using insertion sort. We will use another simple method which will make our code look like insertion sort. We can take all elements of the list one by one and insert each element among the elements of its sublist. Here the elements will move h positions instead of one position. Here is the `shellSort()` function:

```
void shellSort(int arr[], int n)
{
        int i,j,k;
        int incr = 5; //maximum increment (odd value)
        while(incr >= 1)
        {
                for(i=incr; i<n; i++)
                {
                        k=arr[i];
                        for(j=i-incr; j>=0 && k<arr[j]; j=j-incr)
                                arr[j+incr]=arr[j];
                        arr[j+incr]=k;
                }//End of for
                incr=incr-2; //Decrease the increment
        }//End of while
```

```
}//End of shellSort()
```

This is similar to the `insertionSort()` function, except for a few changes.

8.11.1 Analysis of Shell Sort

The coding of shell sort technique is simple but its analysis is quite difficult and no one has been able to analyze it mathematically. The only results that are available are based on empirical studies. The running time depends on the number of increments and their value. The empirical studies show that for a particular sequence of increments, it is of $O(n(\log n)^2)$ and for another sequence, it is $O(n^{1.25})$. Shell sort is not a stable sort. It is an in-place sort, and space complexity is $O(1)$.

8.12 Merge Sort

Merge sort was developed by Jon von Neumann in 1945, and it has $O(n \log n)$ performance in both worst and average cases. The main task in merge sort is merging two sorted lists into a single sorted list; so let us first examine the process of merging two sorted lists.

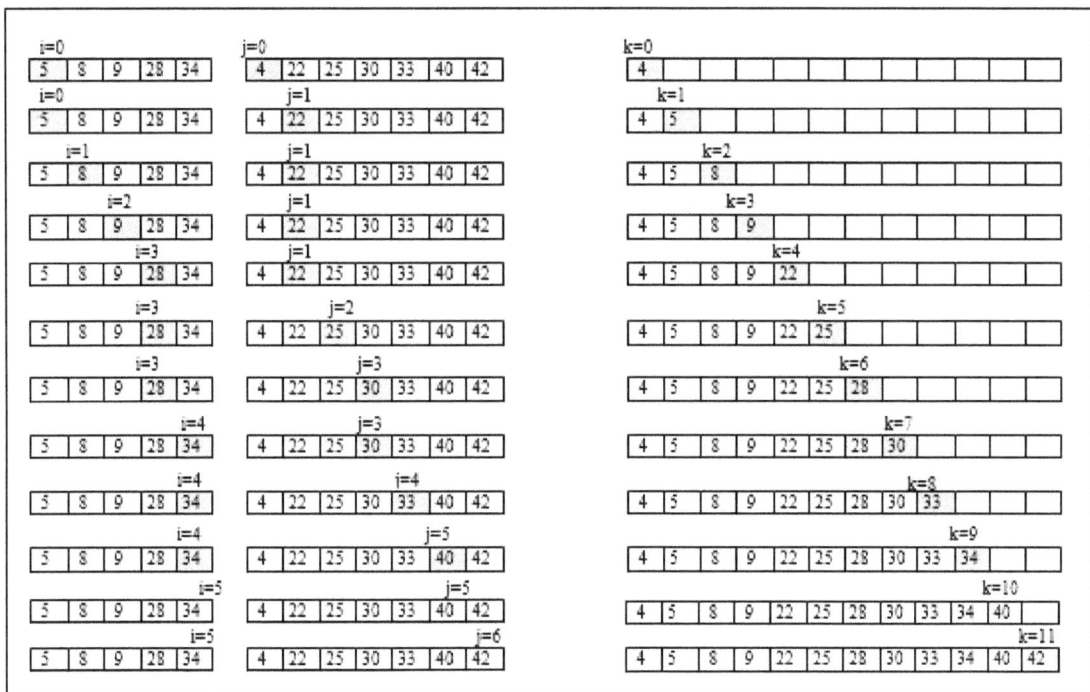

Figure 8.11 Merging

If there are two sorted arrays, then the process of combining these sorted arrays into another sorted array is called merging. A simple approach could be to place the second array after the first and then sort the whole by applying any sorting technique, but by doing this, we are not utilizing the fact that both arrays are sorted. Since both arrays are sorted, we can merge them efficiently by making only one pass through each array. Let us take two arrays `arr1` and `arr2`, in sorted order; we will combine them into a third sorted array `arr3`.

arr1- 5 8 9 28 34   arr2- 4 22 25 30 33 40 42

We will take one element from each array, compare them, and then put the smaller one in the third array. This process will continue until the elements of one array are finished. Then, the remaining elements of the unfinished array are put in the third array. The whole process for merging is shown in figure 8.11. arr3 is the merged array, and i, j, and k are variables used for subscripts of arr1, arr2, and arr3, respectively.

Initially i, j and k point to the beginning of the three arrays, and so i=0, j=0, k=0. The elements arr1[i] and arr2[j] are compared, and the smaller one is copied to the third array arr3 at position k. The variable k is incremented, and one of the variables i or j is incremented.

```cpp
//Merging.cpp : Program of merging two sorted arrays into a third sorted array.
#include<iostream>
using namespace std;

static const int maxSize = 30;

void merge(int arr1[], int arr2[], int temp[], int n1, int n2)
{
        int i = 0;      //Index for first array
        int j = 0;      //Index for second array
        int k = 0;      //Index for merged array

        while(i<=n1-1  && j<=n2-1)
        {
                if(arr1[i] < arr2[j])
                        temp[k++] = arr1[i++];
                else
                        temp[k++] = arr2[j++];
        }

        //Put remaining elements of arr1 into temp
        while(i <= n1-1)
                temp[k++] = arr1[i++];

        //Put remaining elements of arr2 into temp
        while(j <= n2-1)
                temp[k++] = arr2[j++];
}//End of merge()

int main()
{
        int arr1[maxSize] = {5, 8, 9, 28, 34};
        int n1 = 5;
        int arr2[maxSize] = {4, 22, 25, 30, 33, 40, 42};
        int n2 = 7;
        int temp[2*maxSize];

        cout << "Array 1 in sorted order :\n";
        for(int i=0; i<n1; i++)
            cout << arr1[i] << "   ";

        cout << "\nArray 2 in sorted order :\n";
        for(int i=0; i<n2; i++)
            cout << arr2[i] << "   ";

        merge(arr1,arr2,temp,n1,n2);

        cout << "\nMerged list :\n";
        for(int i=0; i<n1+n2; i++)
                cout << temp[i] << "   ";
        cout << "\n";
}//End of main()
```

Merging of two sorted lists of sizes n1 and n2 is O(n1+n2), since only one pass is made through each of the lists.

The two lists to be sorted need not be different arrays; they can be part of the same array. In the example given next, `arr[0:5]` and `arr[6:11]` are merged into another array `temp[0:11]`.

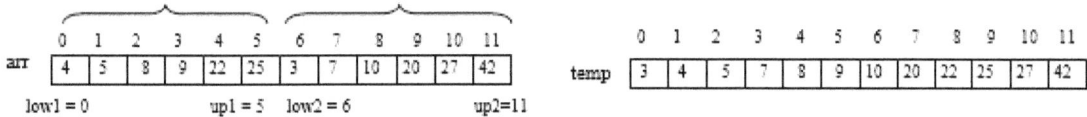

Figure 8.12 Merging of two sorted lists in same array

In the function `merge()` given next, we send the array `arr` and the lower and upper bounds of the lists to be merged. The array `temp` is also sent, which will store the merged array.

```
void merge(int arr[], int temp[], int low1, int up1, int low2, int up2)
{
        int i=low1, j=low2, k=low1;

        while(i<=up1 && j<=up2)
        {
                if(arr[i] < arr[j])
                        temp[k++] = arr[i++];
                else
                        temp[k++] = arr[j++];
        }
        while(i <= up1)
                temp[k++] = arr[i++];

        while(j <= up2)
                temp[k++] = arr[j++];
}//End of merge()
```

If the total number of elements in `arr` is n, then the performance of the above merging algorithm is O(n).

8.12.1 Top Down Merge Sort (Recursive)

This algorithm is based on the divide and conquer technique. The list is recursively divided till we get single element lists which are obviously sorted, and then the lists are merged repeatedly to get a single sorted list. The procedure for top-down merge sort is as follows:

1. Divide the list into two sublists of almost equal size.
2. Sort the left sublist recursively using merge sort.
3. Sort the right sublist recursively using merge sort.
4. Merge the two sorted sublists.

The terminating condition for recursion is when the sublist formed contains only one element. If the list contains an odd number of elements, then we assume that the left half is bigger. Let us take a list of numbers and sort it through merge sort. The list is: 8   5   89   30   42   92   64   4   21   56   3

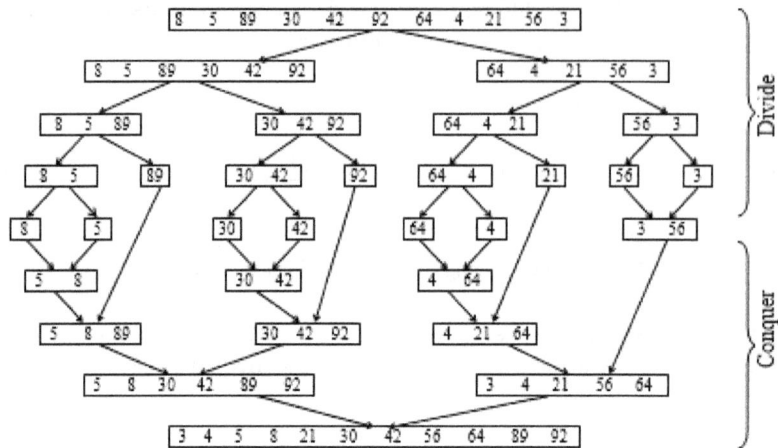

Figure 8.13 Top-down merge sort

■ arr[0:10] is divided into arr[0:5] and arr[6:10]
(8, 5, 89, 30, 42, 92, 64, 4, 21, 56, 3) –> (8, 5, 89, 30, 42, 92) and (64, 4, 21, 56, 3)
  ■ arr[0:5] is divided into arr[0:2] and arr[3:5]
  (8, 5, 89, 30, 42, 92) –> (8, 5, 89) and (30, 42, 92)
    ■ arr[0:2] is divided into arr[0:1] and arr[2]
    (8, 5, 89) –> (8, 5) and (89)
      ■ arr[0:1] is divided into arr[0] and arr[1]
      (8, 5) –> (8) and (5)
      • arr[0] and arr[1] are merged to produce sorted arr[0:1]
      (8) and (5) –> (5, 8)
    • arr[0:1] and arr[2] are merged to produce sorted arr[0:2]
    (5, 8) and (89) –> (5, 8, 89)
    ■ arr[3:5] is divided into arr[3:4] and arr[5]
    (30, 42, 92) –> (30, 42) and (92)
      ■ arr[3:4] is divided into arr[3] and arr[4]
      (30, 42) –> (30) and (42)
      • arr[3] and arr[4] are merged to produce sorted arr[3:4]
      (30) and (42) –> (30, 42)
    • arr[3:4] and arr[5] are merged to give sorted arr[3:5]
    (30, 42) and (92) –> (30, 42, 92)
  • arr[0:2] and arr[3:5] are merged to produce sorted arr[0:5]
  (5, 8, 89) and (30, 42, 92) –> (5, 8, 30, 42, 89, 92)
  ■ arr[6:10] is divided into arr[6:8] and arr[9:10]
  (64, 4, 21, 56, 3) –> (64, 4, 21) and (56, 3)
    ■ arr[6:8] is divided into arr[6:7] and arr[8]
    (64, 4, 21) –> (64, 4) and (21)
      ■ arr[6:7] is divided into arr[6] and arr[7]
      (64, 4) –> (64) and (4)
      • arr[6] and arr[7] are merged to produce sorted arr[6:7]
      (64) and (4) –> (4, 64)
    • arr[6:7] and arr[8] are merged to produce sorted arr[6:8]
    (4, 64) and (21) –> (4, 21, 64)
    ■ arr[9:10] is divided into arr[9] and arr[10]
    (56, 3) –> (56) and (3)
    • arr[9] and arr[10] are merged to produce sorted arr[9:10]
    (56) and (3) –> (3, 56)
  • arr[6:8] and arr[9:10] are merged to produce sorted arr[6:10]
  (4, 21, 64) and (3, 56) –> (3, 4, 21, 56, 64)
• arr[0:5] and arr[6:10] are merged to produce sorted arr[0:10]
(5, 8, 30, 42, 89, 92) and (3, 4, 21, 56, 64) –> (3, 4, 5,8, 21, 30, 42, 56, 64, 89, 92)

Figure 8.14 Top-down merge sort process

```cpp
//MergeSortRecursive.cpp : Program of sorting using merge sort through recursion.
#include<iostream>
using namespace std;

static const int maxSize = 30;

//arr[low1]...arr[up1] and arr[low2]...arr[up2] merged to temp[low1]...temp[up2]
void merge(int arr[], int temp[], int low1, int up1, int low2, int up2)
{
        int i=low1, j=low2, k=low1;

        while(i<=up1 && j<=up2)
        {
                if(arr[i] < arr[j])
                        temp[k++] = arr[i++];
                else
                        temp[k++] = arr[j++];
        }

        while(i <= up1)
                temp[k++] = arr[i++];

        while(j <= up2)
                temp[k++] = arr[j++];
}//End of merge()

void copy(int arr[], int temp[], int low, int up)
{
        for(int i=low; i<=up; i++)
                arr[i] = temp[i];
}//End of copy()

//Recursive merge sort
void mergeSort(int arr[], int low, int up)
{
        int mid, temp[maxSize];

        if(low == up) //if only one element
                return;

        mid = (low+up)/2;
        mergeSort(arr,low,mid);   //Sort arr[low]....arr[mid]
        mergeSort(arr,mid+1,up);  //Sort arr[mid+1]....arr[up]

        //Merge arr[low]...arr[mid] and arr[mid+1]....arr[up] to temp[low]...temp[up]
        merge(arr,temp,low,mid,mid+1,up);

        //Copy temp[low]...temp[up] to arr[low]...arr[up]
        copy(arr,temp,low,up);
}//End of mergeSort()

void mergeSort(int arr[], int n)
{
        mergeSort(arr,0,n-1);
}//End of mergeSort()
```

The `main()` function will be similar to the previous sorting algorithms.

The process is recursive, so the record of the lower and upper bounds of the sublists is implicitly maintained. When recursive `mergeSort()` is called for the first time, the `low` and `up` are set to 0 and `n-1`. The value of `mid` is calculated, which is the index of the middle element. Now, the recursive `mergeSort()` is called for the left sublist, which is `arr[0:mid]`. The `mergeSort()` is recursively called for left sublists till it is called for a one-element sublist. In this call, the value of `low` will not be less than `up`; it will be equal to `up`, so recursion will terminate. Now, recursive `mergeSort()` is called for the right sublist of the previous recursive call. After the return of this call, the two sublists are merged. This continues till the first recursive call returns, after which we get the sorted result. Before returning from recursive `mergeSort()`, the merged list which is in `temp`, is copied back to `arr`. The following figure shows the values of variables `low` and `up` in the recursive calls of the function `mergeSort()`:

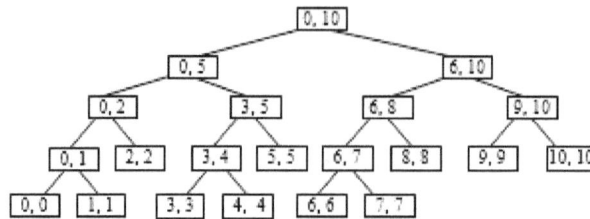

Figure 8.15 Merge sort recursive calls with low and up values

Quick sort also uses a divide-and-conquer approach, but its partition step is difficult while combining is trivial. Here, in the merge sort, the partition is simple, but combining is difficult.

8.12.2 Analysis of Merge Sort

We know that n elements can be repeatedly divided into half approximately $\log_2 n$ times, so after halving the list $\log_2 n$ times we get n sublists of size 1. In each pass, there will be merging of n elements which is O(n), and so, the performance of merge sort is O($n\log_2 n$).

Merge sort is a stable sort. Since the operation of merging is not in-place, merge sort is also not an in-place sort and requires O(n) extra space.

8.12.3 Bottom Up Merge Sort (Iterative)

The stack space needed for recursion can be avoided by implementing a non-recursive version of merge sort. The iterative version works in a bottom-up manner and uses a combine-and-conquer strategy. In this approach, the whole list is initially considered as n sorted sublists of size 1. The adjacent sublists of size 1 are merged pairwise, and we get n/2 sublists of size 2 (and possibly one more sublist of size 1 if n is odd). These sublists of size 2 are then merged, and we get n/4 sublists of size 4 (and possibly one sublist of size 1, 2, or 3). This process continues until only one sublist of size n is left.

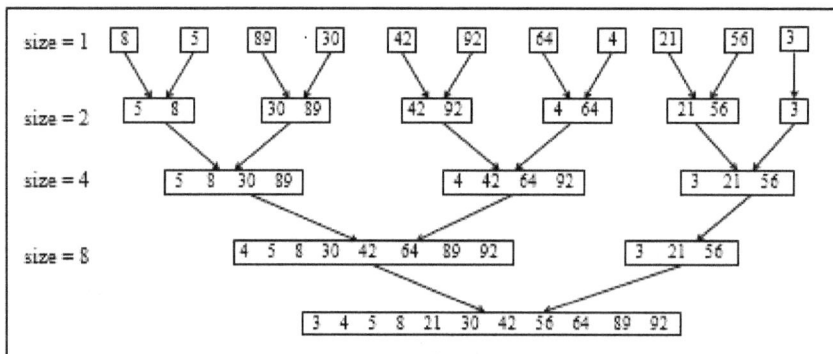

Figure 8.16 Bottom up merge sort

If there is a sublist left in the last that cannot be merged with any sublist, it is just copied to the result. In the example given in figure 8.16, this case occurs in pass 1 where sublist [3] is left alone and in pass 3 where sublist [3, 21, 56] is left alone.

```cpp
//MergeSortIterative.cpp : Program of sorting using merge sort without recursion.
#include<iostream>
using namespace std;

static const int maxSize = 30;
//arr[low1]...arr[up1] and arr[low2]...arr[up2] merged to temp[low1]..temp[up2]
void merge(int arr[], int temp[], int low1, int up1, int low2, int up2)
{
        int i=low1, j=low2, k=low1;

        while(i<=up1 && j<=up2)
        {
                if(arr[i] < arr[j])
                        temp[k++] = arr[i++];
                else
                        temp[k++] = arr[j++];
        }

        while(i <= up1)
                temp[k++] = arr[i++];

        while(j <= up2)
                temp[k++] = arr[j++];
}//End of merge()

//copies temp[low]....temp[up] to arr[low]...arr[up]
void copy(int arr[], int temp[], int n)
{
        for(int i=0; i<n; i++)
                arr[i] = temp[i];
}//End of copy()

void mergePass(int arr[], int temp[], int size, int n)
{
        int i, low1, up1, low2, up2;
        low1 = 0;

        while(low1+size <= n-1)
        {
                up1 = low1 + size - 1;
                low2 = low1 + size;
                up2 = low2 + size - 1;
                if(up2 >= n)    //if length of last sublist is less than size
                        up2 = n-1;
                merge(arr,temp,low1,up1,low2,up2);
                low1 = up2 + 1; //Take next two sublists for merging
        }

        for(i=low1; i<=n-1; i++)
                temp[i] = arr[i]; //If any sublist is left alone

        copy(arr,temp,n);
}//End of mergePass()

void mergeSort(int arr[], int n)
{
        int temp[maxSize], size = 1;

        while(size<n)
        {
                mergePass(arr,temp,size,n);
                size = size*2;
        }
}//End of mergeSort()
```

We can avoid copying from `arr` to `temp` by merging alternately from `arr` to `temp` and from `temp` to `arr`. The function `mergeSort()` would be like this:

```
void mergeSort(int arr[], int n)
{
        int temp[maxSize], size = 1;

        while(size<n)
        {
                mergePass(arr,temp,size,n);
                size = size*2;
                mergePass(temp,arr,size,n);
                size = size*2;
        }
}//End of mergeSort()
```

Now, we can delete the last statement from the function `mergePass()`, which is used for copying `temp` to `arr`. The total number of passes required is $\log_2 n$, and in each pass, n elements are merged, so complexity is $O(n\log_2 n)$.

8.12.4 Merge Sort for Linked List

When merge sort is used for linked lists, there is no need for temporary storage because merge operation in linked lists can be performed without temporary storage. Another advantage of the linked list version is that there is no data movement; only the pointers are rearranged. The function for merging is already explained in a single linked list (Chapter 3, Linked Lists). The merge sort functions can be added with a single linked list program. Here are the functions required for merge sort for linked list:

```
void SingleLinkedList::mergeSort()
{
        start = mergeSortRec(start);
}//End of mergeSort()

//Recursive merge sort
Node* SingleLinkedList::mergeSortRec(Node* listStart)
{
        //If the list is empty or has only one node
        if(listStart==NULL || listStart->link==NULL)
                return listStart;

        //If more than one element
        Node *start1 = listStart;
        Node *start2 = divideList(listStart);
        start1 = mergeSortRec(start1);
        start2 = mergeSortRec(start2);
        Node* startM = merge2(start1, start2);

        return startM;
}//End of mergeSortRec()

Node* SingleLinkedList::divideList(Node *p)
{
        Node *q = p->link->link;

        while(q!=NULL && q->link!=NULL)
        {
                p = p->link;
                q = q->link->link;
        }

        Node *start2 = p->link;
        p->link = NULL;

        return start2;
}//End of divideList()
```

The function `divideList()` takes a pointer to the original list and returns a pointer to the start of the second sublist. We have taken two pointers p and q, where pointer p points to the first node and pointer q points to the third node. In a loop, we move pointer p once and pointer q twice so that when the pointer q is NULL, pointer p points to the middle node. The node next to the middle node will be the start of the second sublist. The middle node will be the last node of first sublist, so its link is assigned NULL.

The function `merge2()` takes pointers to the two sorted lists, merges them into a single sorted list, and returns a pointer to the merged list. There is no requirement of any temporary storage for merging of linked lists.

8.12.5 Natural Merge Sort

Merge sort does not consider any sorted sequences inside a given list and sorts in the usual manner. This type of merge sort is called straight merge sort, and in this sort, all the sublists in a pass are of the same size except possibly the last one. Another type of merge sort is natural merge sort, which takes advantage of the presence of sorted sequences (runs) in the list. For example, consider this list:

12 45 67 3 66 21 89 90 98 65 43 56 68 96 23 87

The runs present in this list are (12, 45, 67) (3, 66) (21, 89, 90, 98) (65) (43, 56, 68, 96) (23, 87). In the first pass, the runs are determined and these runs are merged instead of merging sublists of size 1, remaining passes are same as in the merge sort.

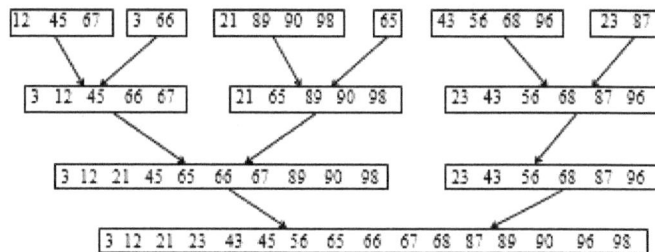

Figure 8.17 Natural merge sort

The disadvantage of this approach is that the size of sublists is different, and we have to keep track of the start and end of each sublist. So, this technique is beneficial only if there are many runs present in the data. Merge sort is not suitable for main memory sorts because it requires extra space of O(n), but this algorithm forms the basis of external sorting techniques. Merge sort is stable because the merge process is stable.

8.13 Quick Sort (Partition Exchange Sort)

Quick Sort was given by C.A.R. Hoare in 1962, and is based on the divide and conquer technique. In this technique, a problem is divided into small problems, which are again divided into smaller problems and so on. Hence solving the bigger problem reduces to solving these smaller ones. As the name suggests, quick sort is a very fast sorting technique and its average case performance is O(n log n). It is an in-place sort, so no additional space is required for sorting. It is also known as partition exchange sort and is efficient because the exchanges occur between elements that are far apart, and so less exchanges are needed to place an element in its final position.

Now let us see how this sorting is performed. We choose an element from the list and place it at its proper position in the list, i.e., at the position where it would be in the final sorted list. We call this element as pivot and it will be at its proper place if:

(i) all the elements to the left of pivot are less than or equal to the pivot

(ii) all the elements to the right of pivot are greater than or equal to the pivot.

Any element of the list can be taken as pivot but for convenience, the first element is taken as the pivot. We will talk more about the choice of pivot later. Suppose our list is [4, 6, 1, 8, 3, 9, 2, 7]. If we take 4 as the pivot, then after placing 4 at its proper place, the list becomes [1, 3, 2, **4**, 6, 8, 9, 7]. Now we can partition this list into two sublists, based on this pivot and these sublists are [1, 3, 2] and [6, 8, 9, 7]. We can apply the same procedure to these two sublists separately i.e., we will select one pivot for each sublist and both the sublists are divided into 2 sublists each, so now we get 4 sublists. This process is repeated for all the sublists that contain two or more elements and in the end we get our sorted list.

Now let us outline the process for sorting the elements through quick sort. Suppose we have an array `arr` with `low` and `up` as the lower and upper bounds.

1. Take the first element of list as pivot.

2. The list is partitioned in such a way that pivot comes at its proper place. After this partition, all elements to the left of pivot are less than or equal to the pivot, and all elements to the right of pivot are greater than equal to the pivot. So one element of the list, i.e., the pivot, is at its proper place. Let the index of pivot be `pivotloc`.

3. Create two sublists left and right side of pivot, left sublist is `arr[low].....arr[pivotloc-1]` and the right sublist is `arr[pivotloc+1]....arr[up]`.

4. The left sublist is sorted using quick sort recursively.

5. The right sublist is sorted using quick sort recursively.

6. The terminating condition for recursion is when the sublist formed contains only one element or no element.

The sublists are kept in the same array, and there is no need of combining the sorted sublists at the end. Let us take a list of elements and sort them through quick sort.

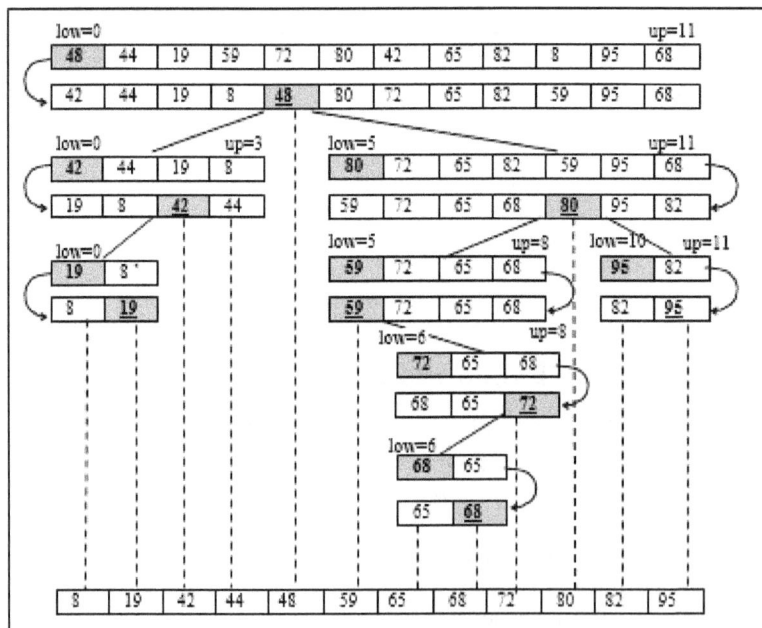

Figure 8.18 Quick sort

Here we are focusing only on the recursion procedure; the logic of placing the pivot at proper place is discussed later. The values of `low` and `up` indicate the lower and upper bounds of the sublists.

Initially the list is [48, 44, 19, 59, 72, 80, 42, 65, 82, 8, 95, 68]. We will take the first element (48) as the pivot and place it in proper place, and so the list becomes [42, 44, 19, 8, **48**, 80, 72, 65, 82, 59, 95, 68]. Now all the elements to the left of 48 are less than it and all elements to the right of 48 are greater than it. We will take two sublists left and right of 48, which are [42, 44, 19, 8] and [80, 72, 65, 82, 59, 95, 68], and sort them separately using the same procedure. Note that the order of the elements in the left sublist or in the right sublist is not the same as it appears in the original list. It depends on the partition process, which is used to place pivot at proper place. For now, you just need to understand that all elements to left of pivot, are less than or equal to pivot and all elements right of pivot are greater than or equal to pivot.

The left sublist is [42, 44, 19, 8] and its pivot is taken as 42. After placing the pivot, the list becomes [19, 8, **42**, 44]. Now 42 is at its proper place; we again divide this list into two sublists, which are [19, 8] and [44]. The list [44] has only one element, so we will stop. The list [19, 8] is taken and here the pivot will be 19 and after placing the pivot at proper place, the list becomes [8, **19**]. The left sublist is [8] and it contains only one element, and so we will not process it. There are no elements to the right of 19, and so, the right sublist is not formed or we can say that right sublist contains zero elements so we will stop.

The right sublist is [80, 72, 65, 82, 59, 95, 68] and 80 is taken as the pivot. After placing the pivot, the list becomes [59, 72, 65, 68, **80**, 95, 82]. Now the two sublists formed are [59, 72, 65, 68] and [95, 82]. In the first sublist, 59 is taken as the pivot and after placing it at the proper place, the sublist becomes [**59**, 72, 65, 68]. There are no elements to the left of 59, so only one sublist is formed, which is [72, 65, 68]. Here, 72 is taken as the pivot and after placing it, the list becomes [68, 65, **72**]. There are no elements to the right of 72, and so, only one sublist is formed which is [68, 65]. In this sublist, 68 is taken as the pivot, and after placing it at the proper place, the sublist becomes [65, **68**]. There are no elements to the right of 68, and the left sublist has only one element so that we will stop.

After this, we will take the sublist [95, 82]. Here, 95 is taken as the pivot and after placing it at proper place, the sublist is [82, **95**]. There are no elements to the right of 95 and the left sublist has only one element, so we will stop.

We can write a recursive function for this procedure. There would be two terminating conditions: when the sublist formed has only 1 element, or when no sublist is formed. If the value of `low` is equal to `up`, then there will be only one element in the sublist, and if the value of `low` exceeds `up`, then no sublist is formed. So, the terminating condition can be written as:

```
if(low >= up)
      return;
```

The recursive function `quickSort()` can be written as:

```
//Recursive quickSort()
void quickSort(int arr[], int low, int up )
{
      if(low >= up)
            return;
      int pivotloc = partition(arr,low,up);
      quickSort(arr,low,pivotloc-1); //process left sublist
      quickSort(arr,pivotloc+1,up);  //process right sublist
}//End of quickSort()
```

The recursive function `quickSort()` will be called here:

```
void quickSort(int arr[], int n)
{
      quickSort(arr, 0, n-1);
}//End of quickSort()
```

The function `partition()` will place the pivot at proper place and then return the location of pivot, so that we can form two sublists left and right of the pivot.

Since the process is recursive, the record of lower and upper bounds of sublists is implicitly maintained. Now, the second main task is to partition a list into two sublists by placing the pivot at the proper place. Let us see how we can do this. Suppose we have an array `arr[low:up]`; the element `arr[low]` will be taken as the pivot. We will take two index variables i and j, where i is initialized to `low+1` and j is initialized to `up`. The following process will put the pivot at its proper place:

(a) Compare the pivot with `arr[i]`, and increment i if `arr[i]` is less than the pivot element. So, the index variable i moves from left to right and stops when we get an element greater than or equal to the pivot.

(b) Now compare the pivot with `arr[j]`, and decrement j if `arr[j]` is greater than the pivot element. So the index variable j moves from right to left and stops when we get an element less than or equal to the pivot.

(c) If i is less than j

Exchange the value of `arr[i]` and `arr[j]`, increment i and decrement j.

else

No exchange, increment i.

(d) Repeat the steps (a), (b), (c) till the value of i is less than or equal to j. We will stop when i exceeds j.

(e) When value of i becomes more than j, we have found proper place for the pivot which is given by j. Hence, now the pivot is to be placed at position j. Pivot was at location `low`, so we can place it at j by exchanging the value of `arr[low]` and `arr[j]`. Now, the pivot is at position j, which is its final position.

Let us now take a list and see how the pivot will be placed at the proper place through this partition process in figure 8.19 and 8.20.

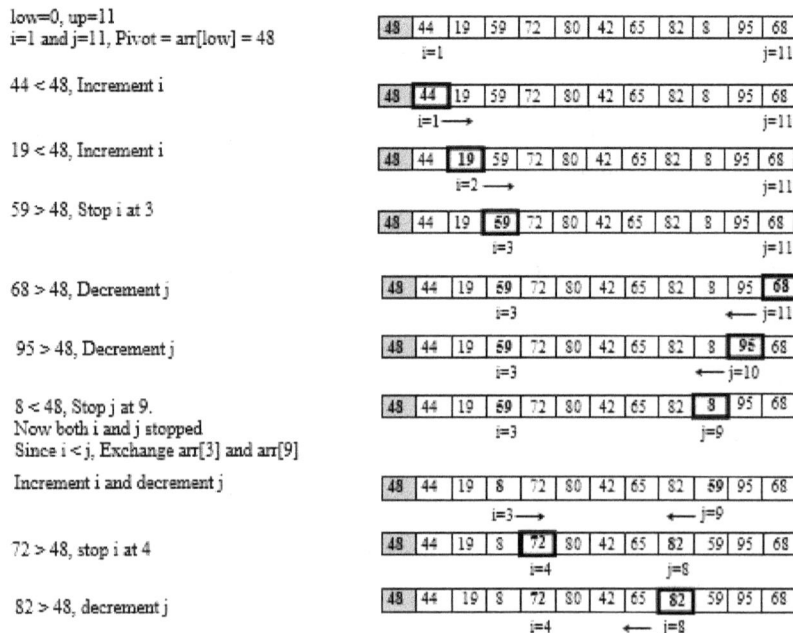

Figure 8.19 Partition process

65 > 48, decrement j

| 48 | 44 | 19 | 8 | 72 | 80 | 42 | **65** | 82 | 59 | 95 | 68 |

i=4 ← j=7

42 < 48, stop j at 6
Both i and j stopped
Since i < j, Exchange arr[4] and arr[6]

| 48 | 44 | 19 | 8 | 72 | 80 | **42** | 65 | 82 | 59 | 95 | 68 |

i=4   j=6

Increment i and decrement j

| 48 | 44 | 19 | 8 | 42 | 80 | 72 | 65 | 82 | 59 | 95 | 68 |

i=4 → ← j=6

80 > 48, stop i at 5

| 48 | 44 | 19 | 8 | 42 | **80** | 72 | 65 | 82 | 59 | 95 | 68 |

i=5,j=5

80 > 48, decrement j

| 48 | 44 | 19 | 8 | 42 | **80** | 72 | 65 | 82 | 59 | 95 | 68 |

i=5
← j=5

42 < 48, stop j at 4
Both i and j stopped.
i is not less than j, so no exchange
i is incremented

| 48 | 44 | 19 | 8 | **42** | 80 | 72 | 65 | 82 | 59 | 95 | 68 |

j=4 i=5 →

Now i > j, so stop movement of i and j.
j is the location for pivot.
Exchange arr[0] and arr[4]

| 48 | 44 | 19 | 8 | 42 | 80 | 72 | 65 | 82 | 59 | 95 | 68 |

j=4   i=6

Pivot placed at proper place

| 42 | 44 | 19 | 8 | **48** | 80 | 72 | 65 | 82 | 59 | 95 | 68 |

← Left sublist → Pivot ← Right sublist →

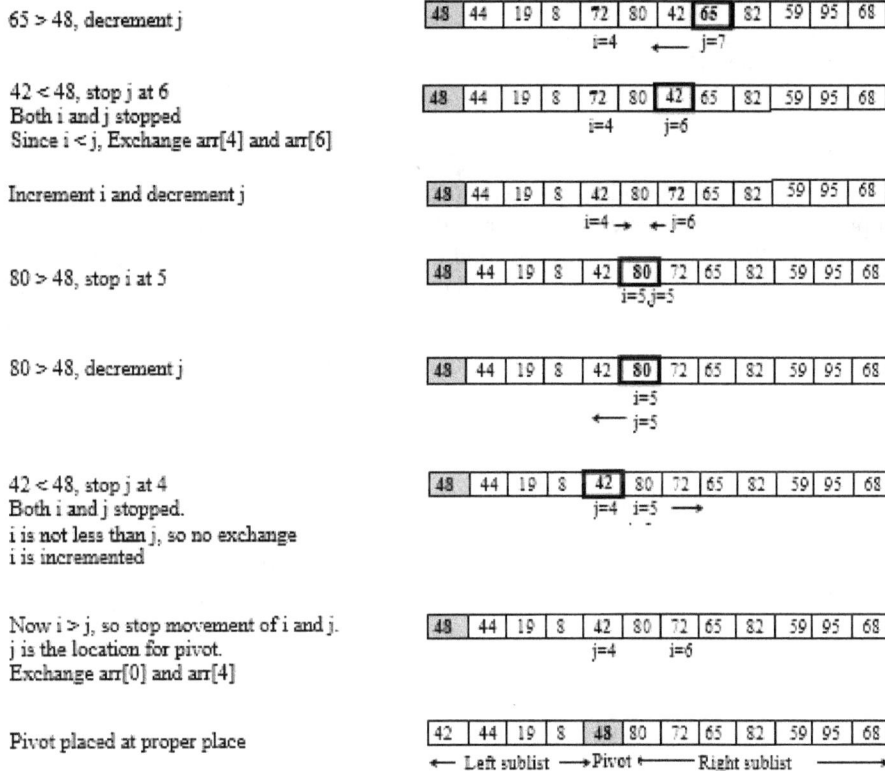

Figure 8.20 Partition process continued

The location for pivot is the value of j, and so the function partition() will return the value of j. Now, for left sublist low=0 and up=3, and for right sublist low=5 and up=11.

```
int partition(int arr[], int low, int up)
{
        int pivot = arr[low];
        int i = low+1; //moves from left to right
        int j = up;    //moves from right to left
        int temp;

        while(i <= j)
        {
                while(arr[i]<pivot && i<up)
                        i++;

                while(arr[j] > pivot)
                        j--;

                if(i < j) //swap arr[i] and arr[j]
                {
                        temp = arr[i];
                        arr[i] = arr[j];
                        arr[j] = temp;
                        i++;
                        j--;
                }
                else    //found proper place for pivot
                        i++;
```

```
}//End of while

//Proper place for pivot is j
arr[low] = arr[j];
arr[j] = pivot;

return j;
}//End of partition()
```

The variable i is moving right, and so we have to prevent it from moving past the array bound. For example, if pivot is the largest element in the array, then there is no element in the array that can stop i, and it just moves on. So we have to check the condition (i<up) before incrementing i. The other way out may be to put a sentinel at the end having the largest possible value. The variable j is moving left, but it will never cross the bound of the array because the pivot is there at the leftmost position.

The function main() will be similar to earlier sorting algorithms. However, the partition process is not stable, so quick sort is not a stable sort.

8.13.1 Analysis of Quick Sort

The time requirement of quick sort depends on the relative size of the two sublists formed. If the partition is balanced and the two sublists are almost equal in size, then the sorting is fast, while if the partition is unbalanced and one sublist is much larger than the other, then the sorting is slow.

The best case for quick sort would be when the pivot is always placed in the middle of the list, i.e., when we get two sublists of equal size. If we have a list of n elements, then we get 2 sublists of size approximately n/2, which are again divided equally, so that we get 4 sublists of size approximately n/4 each. These are again divided, and we get 8 sublists of size approximately n/8 each and so on. We know that n elements can be repeatedly divided into half approximately $\log_2 n$ times, so after halving the list $\log_2 n$ times, we get n sublists of size 1.

Now, let us find out the number of comparisons that will be performed. Initially, we have 1 list of size n for which there will be approximately n comparisons (exactly n-1, but we want Oh notation only so we can take n). We have 2 lists of size approximately n/2 each, and so there will be approximately 2*(n/2) comparisons. Then, we have 4 lists of size approximately n/4 each so that there will be approximately 4*(n/4) comparisons and so on. So the total number of comparisons would be approximately equal to:

n + 2*(n/2) + 4*(n/4) + 8*(n/8) +...................n*(n/n)
n + n + n +... + n   ($\log_2 n$ terms)
= $n\log_2 n$

Thus, in the best case, the performance of quick sort is $O(n\log_2 n)$. Now let us see how quick sort performs in the worst case. If the pivot is the smallest or largest element of the list, then it divides the list into two sublists: one is empty and the other contains n-1 elements. The worst case occurs if this situation arises in every recursive call. If the first element is taken as the pivot, then this worst case occurs when the list is fully sorted (or reverse sorted).

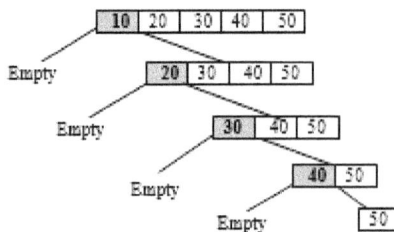

Figure 8.21 Quick sort for already sorted list

If we have a list of n elements, then first we get 2 sublists of sizes 0 and n-1. Now sublist of size n-1 is divided into two sublists of sizes 0 and n-2. The total number of lists that are sorted is n-1 and these are of sizes n, n-1, n-2, …….2. The total number of comparisons will be:

n-1 + n-2 + n-3 + ….. + 1

= n(n-1)/2

= $O(n^2)$

So, in the worst case, the performance of quick sort is $O(n^2)$.

The average case performance is closer to the best case than to the worst case and is found to be $O(n\log_2 n)$. It is not a stable sort. Space complexity for this sort is O(log n).

8.13.2 Choice of Pivot in Quick Sort

The quick sort performs best when the pivot is chosen such that it divides the list into two equal sublists. It performs badly if the pivot value makes an unbalanced partition, i.e., one sublist is very small, and the other one is big. So, the efficiency of quick sort can be improved by choosing a pivot value that makes balanced partitions. The worst case can be avoided by careful selection of the pivot.

The original algorithm given by Hoare selected the first element as the pivot, but the first element is not a good choice because if the list is sorted or almost sorted, then partitions will be unbalanced, and performance will not be good. The last element is also not a good choice for similar reasons. As the chances of a list being sorted or almost sorted are high, it is better to avoid the first and last elements.

Another option is to choose the pivot randomly. For this, we chose a random number k between `low` and `up`, and take `arr[k]` as the pivot. This `arr[k]` is interchanged with the first element before the while loop in the function `partition()` and rest of the code remains same. It seems to be a safe option but random number generators are time consuming.

The ideal choice would be to take the median value of all the elements, but this option is costly. So, we can use the median of three method. In this method, we take the median of the first, middle, and last elements, i.e., median of { `arr[low]`, `arr[(low+up)/2]`, `arr[up]`} and then interchange the median element with the first element.

```
mid = (low+up)/2;
if(arr[low] > arr[mid])
        exchange(arr[low],arr[mid]);
if(arr[low] > arr[up])
        exchange(arr[low],arr[up]);
if(arr[mid] > arr[up])
        exchange(arr[mid],arr[up]);
exchange(arr[low],arr[mid]);
```

In the process of finding the median, we have placed the largest of three at the end, and so, the pivot cannot be greater than the last element, and hence now, there is no need of condition `i<up` before incrementing `i`.

8.13.3 Duplicate Elements in Quick Sort

In our program, we stop variables `i` and `j` when we find an element equal to the pivot. Let us see what other options are and why they are less efficient. There can be 4 options when an element equal to pivot is encountered.

(i) stop i and move j
(ii) stop j and move i
(iii) stop both i and j
(iv) move both i and j

If we stop one pointer and move another, then all elements equal to the pivot would go in one sublist and the partitioning will be unbalanced. For example, if we stop i and move j, then all the equal elements go to the right sublist, and if we stop j and move i, then all the equal elements go to the left sublist. The first two options are not good because they tend to maximize the difference in the sizes of the sublists which reduces the efficiency of quick sort.

To understand which of the last two options is better, let us consider the case when all the elements in the list are equal. If both i and j stop, then there will be many unnecessary exchanges between equal elements, but the good thing is that i and j will meet somewhere in the middle of the list, thus creating two almost equal sublists. If both i and j move, then no unnecessary swaps would be there, but the sublists would be unbalanced. If all the elements are equal, then j will always stop at the leftmost position and so pivot will always be placed at the leftmost position and hence one sublist will always be empty. This is the same situation we studied in the worst case; the running time is $O(n^2)$.

So, it is best to stop i and j when any element equal to the pivot is encountered. It might seem that considering the case of all equal elements is not a good idea as it would rarely occur. A list of all equal elements can be rare but we may get a sublist consisting of all equal elements. For example, suppose we have a list of 500,000 elements, out of which, 10,000 are equal. Since quick sort is recursive so, at some point, there will be a recursive call for these 10,000 identical elements, and if sorting these elements takes quadratic time, then the overall efficiency will be affected.

8.14 Binary Tree Sort

Binary tree sort uses a binary search tree to sort the data. This algorithm has two phases: the construction phase and the traversal phase.

1. Construction Phase: A binary search tree is created from the given data.
2. Traversal Phase: The binary search tree created is traversed in inorder to obtain the sorted data.

The details of creation and traversal of a binary search tree are discussed in the chapter on trees. Let us take an array arr containing unsorted elements and sort them using binary tree sort.

19	35	10	12	46	6	40	3	90	8
0	1	2	3	4	5	6	7	8	9

Figure 8.22 Array elements for binary tree sort

First we will insert all the elements of this array in a binary search tree one by one:

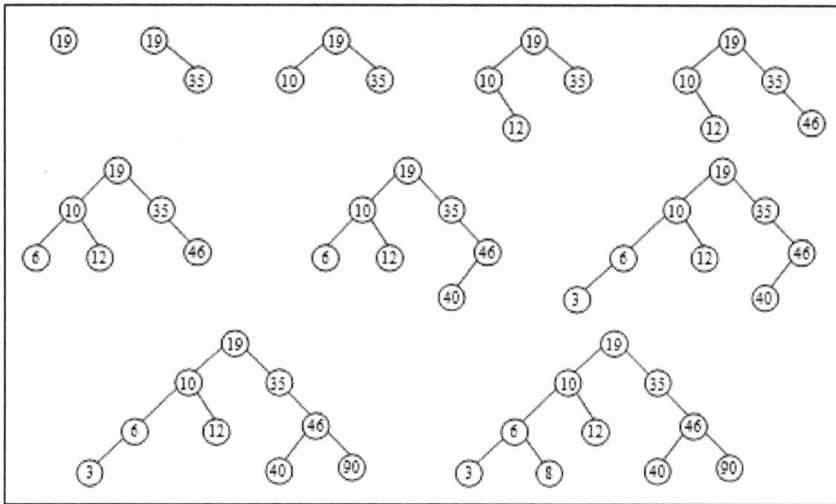

Figure 8.23 Binary tree sort

The inorder traversal of this binary search tree is:

3, 6, 8, 10, 12, 19, 35, 40, 46, 90

These elements are copied back to the array in this order and we get the sorted array:

3	6	8	10	12	19	35	40	46	90
0	1	2	3	4	5	6	7	8	9

Figure 8.24 Array elements in sorted order

```
//BinaryTreeSort.cpp : Program of sorting using binary tree sort.
#include<iostream>
using namespace std;

static const int maxSize = 30;

class BinarySearchTree
{
        private:
                Node *root;
                static int k;
        private:
                void destroy(Node *ptr);
                Node* insert(Node *ptr, int data);
                void inorder(Node *ptr, int arr[]);
        public:
                BinarySearchTree();
                ~BinarySearchTree();
                bool isEmpty();
                void insert(int data);
                void inorder(int arr[]);
};//End of class BinarySearchTree

int BinarySearchTree::k;

//Recursive inorder traversal
void BinarySearchTree::inorder(Node *ptr, int arr[])
{
```

```
        if(ptr == NULL)
                return;

        inorder(ptr->lchild,arr);
        arr[k++] = ptr->info;
        inorder(ptr->rchild,arr);
}//End of inorder()
void BinarySearchTree::inorder(int arr[])
{
        k = 0;
        inorder(root,arr);
}//End of inorder()
void binaryTreeSort(int arr[], int n)
{
        BinarySearchTree bst;

        for(int i=0; i<n; i++)
                bst.insert(arr[i]);
        bst.inorder(arr);
}//End of binaryTreeSort()
```

The class `Node`, other functions of class `BinarySearchTree` here will be same as explained in binary search tree program of Chapter 6, Trees.

8.14.1 Analysis of Binary Tree Sort

We have seen that if a binary tree contains n nodes, then its maximum height possible is n and minimum height possible is $\lceil \log_2(n+1) \rceil$.

The maximum height n occurs when the tree reduces to a chain or linear structure, and in case of a binary search tree, this happens if the elements are inserted in ascending or descending order. The minimum height occurs when the tree is balanced.

The main operation in binary tree sort is the insertion of elements in binary search tree. We have studied if h is the height of a binary search tree, then all the basic operations run in order O(h). The insertion of an element is also O(h) and so, insertion of n elements will be O(nh). If the data that is to be sorted is in ascending or descending order, then the tree that we get by inserting this data will have height n and so the insertion of n elements will be $O(n^2)$. If the data gives us an almost balanced tree, then the insertion of n elements will be O(n log n).

Let us find out this order by counting the number of comparisons. We will take 6 numbers 1, 2, 3, 4, 5, 6 in sorted order, reverse sorted order and random order. The binary search trees obtained by inserting these numbers in different orders are:

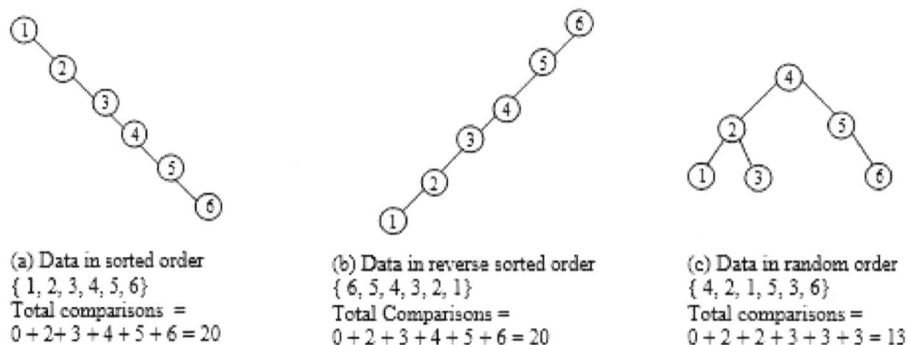

(a) Data in sorted order
{ 1, 2, 3, 4, 5, 6}
Total comparisons =
$0 + 2 + 3 + 4 + 5 + 6 = 20$

(b) Data in reverse sorted order
{ 6, 5, 4, 3, 2, 1}
Total Comparisons =
$0 + 2 + 3 + 4 + 5 + 6 = 20$

(c) Data in random order
{ 4, 2, 1, 5, 3, 6}
Total comparisons =
$0 + 2 + 2 + 3 + 3 + 3 = 13$

Figure 8.25 Binary search trees by inserting numbers in different order

In case (a), no comparison is needed to insert node 1; only 2 comparisons are needed to insert node 2; and 3 comparisons are required in order to insert node 3, and so on. Hence, the total number of comparisons required to insert all the nodes is 20. Similarly, in case (b), no comparison is needed to insert node 6; only 2 comparisons are needed to insert node 5; 3 comparisons are needed to insert node 4, and so on. Here also, the total number of comparisons required to insert all the nodes is 20. In case (c), no comparison is needed to insert node 4, and 2 comparisons each are required to insert nodes 2 and 5, and 3 comparisons each are required for inserting nodes 1, 3, 6, and so, the total number of comparisons in this case is only 13.

If the data is in sorted order or reverse sorted order, then the total number of comparisons is given by:

$0 + 2 + 3 + 4 + 5 + \ldots\ldots\ldots\ldots + n = n(n+1)/2 \Rightarrow O(n^2)$

The main drawback of the binary tree sort is that if data is already in sorted order or in reverse order, then the performance of binary tree sort is not good.

If data is in random order and suppose we get a balanced tree whose height is approximately log n, then the number of comparisons can be given by:

$0 + 2 * 2^1 + 3 * 2^2 + 4 * 2^3 + \ldots\ldots\ldots (h) * 2^{h-1}$

This is because there can be a maximum of 2^L nodes at any level L, and L+1 comparisons are required to insert any node at level L as we have seen in case (c). The root node is at level 0, and the last level is h-1. The efficiency in this case is O(n log n).

So if the tree that we obtain is of height log n, then the performance of binary tree sort is O(n log n). Generally, with random data, the chances of getting a balanced tree are good, and so, we can say that average run time of binary tree sort is O(n log n).

After insertion of elements, some time is needed for traversal also. Binary tree sort is not an in-place sort since it requires additional O(n) space for the construction of tree. It is a stable sort.

8.15 Heap Sort

The heap tree that was introduced in the chapter on trees has an important application in sorting.

Heap sort is performed in two phases:

Phase 1: Build a max heap from the given elements.
Phase 2: Keep on deleting the root till there is only one element in the tree.

The root of a heap always has the largest element, and so, by successively deleting the root, we get the elements in descending order, i.e., first the largest element of list will be deleted, then the second largest, and so on. We can store the deleted elements in a separate array or move them to the end of the same array that represents the heap.

If we have n elements that are to be sorted, first, we build a heap of size n. The elements `arr[1]`, `arr[2]`,......`arr[n]` form the heap. Then, the root is deleted and we get a heap of size n-1. So now the elements `arr[1]`,`arr[2]`,......`arr[n-1]` form the heap, but `arr[n]` is not a part of the heap. The element deleted from the root is the largest element; we can store it in `arr[n]` because `arr[n]` is not a part of the heap now. Now, the root from the heap of size n-1 is deleted and we get a heap of size n-2. The element deleted from root can be stored in `arr[n-1]`. This process goes on till we delete the root from heap of size 2 and get a heap of size 1 and this time, the element deleted from root is stored in `arr[2]`. This way, the array that represented the heap becomes sorted.

Let us take an array and sort it by applying heap tree sort.

arr

25	35	18	9	46	70	48	23	78	12	95
1	2	3	4	5	6	7	8	9	10	11

Figure 8.26 Array elements for heap sort

First, this array is converted to a heap. The procedure of building a heap is described in the chapter on trees. The heap obtained from this array is shown as follows:

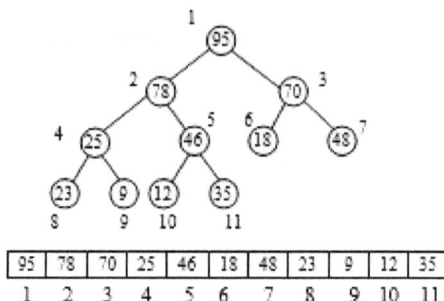

95	78	70	25	46	18	48	23	9	12	35
1	2	3	4	5	6	7	8	9	10	11

Figure 8.27 Heap tree

Now, the root is repeatedly deleted from the heap. The procedure of deletion of root from the heap is described in the chapter on trees.

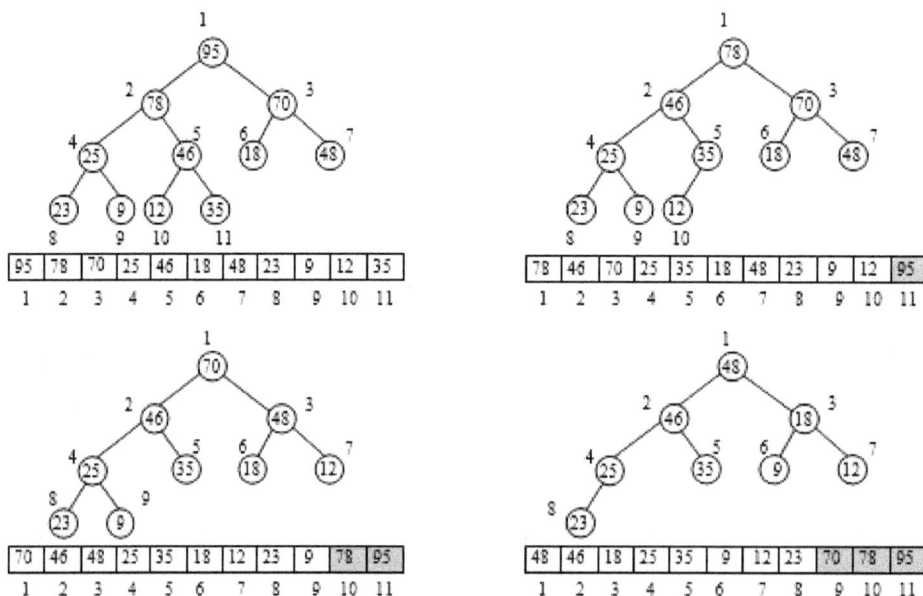

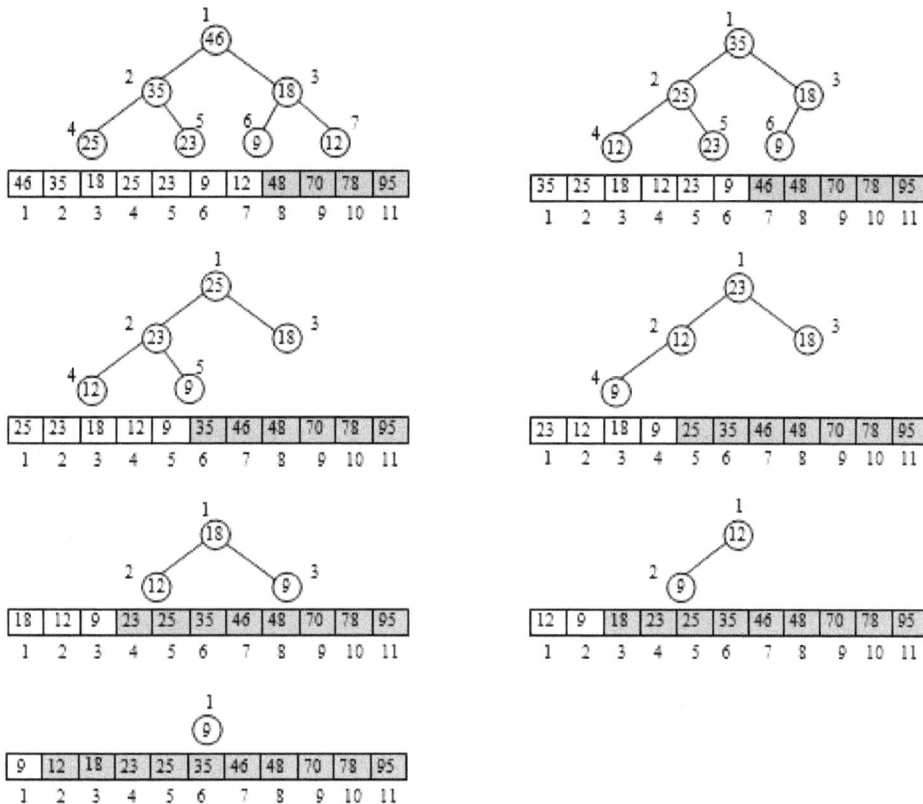

Figure 8.28 Heap sort

This way finally, we see that the array `arr` becomes sorted. If we do not want to change the array that represents the heap, we can take a separate array `sortedArr[]` for the sorted output. The elements deleted from the root can be stored in `sortedArr[n]`, `sortedArr[n-1]` and so on, till `sortedArr[1]`. This time, we have to copy the element in position 1 as well.

```cpp
//HeapSort.cpp : Program of sorting using heap sort.
#include<iostream>
using namespace std;

static const int maxSize = 30;
void buildHeapBottomUp(int arr[], int n)
{
        for(int i=n/2; i>=1; i--)
              restoreDown(i,arr,n);
}//End of buildHeapBottomUp()
void heapSort(int arr[], int n)
{
        buildHeapBottomUp(arr,n);

        cout << "Heap is :\n";
        for(int i=1; i<=n; i++)
              cout << arr[i] << " ";
        cout << "\n";

        //deleting the root and moving it(maxValue) to arr[n]
```

```
        int maxValue;
        while(n > 1)
        {
                maxValue = arr[1];
                arr[1] = arr[n];
                arr[n] = maxValue;
                n--;
                restoreDown(1,arr,n);

                cout << "Heap is :\n";
                for(int i=1; i<=n; i++)
                        cout << arr[i] << " ";
                cout << "\n";
        }
}//End of heapSort()
int main()
{
        int arr[maxSize] = {9999,25,35,18,9,46,70,48,23,78,12,95}; //data is from arr[1]
        int n = 11; //data is from arr[1]...arr[11]

        cout << "Unsorted list is :\n";
        for(int i=1; i<=n; i++)
                cout << arr[i] << " ";
        cout << "\n";

        heapSort(arr,n);

        cout << "Sorted list is :\n";
        for(int i=1; i<=n; i++ )
                cout << arr[i] << " ";
        cout << "\n";
}//End of main()
```

The function `restoreDown()` is the same as in heap tree (Trees) while building a heap.

8.15.1 Analysis of Heap Sort

The algorithm of heap sort proceeds in two phases. In the first phase, we build a heap and its running time is O(n) if we use the bottom up approach. The delete operation in a heap takes O(log n) time, and it is called n-1 times. Hence, the complexity of second phase is O(n log n). So, the worst case complexity of heap sort is O(n log n). The average case and best case complexity is also O(n log n).

Heap sort is good for larger lists but it is not preferable for small list of data. It is not a stable sort. It has no need of extra space other than one temporary variable, and so, it is an in-place sort and space complexity is O(1).

8.16 Radix Sort

Radix sort is a very old sorting technique and was used to sort punch cards before the invention of computers. If we are given a list of some names and asked to sort them alphabetically, we would intuitively proceed by first dividing the names into 26 piles, with each pile containing names that start with the same alphabet. In the first pile, we will put all the names which start with alphabet 'A'; in the second pile, we will put all the names that start with alphabet 'B', and so on. After this, each pile is further divided into subpiles according to the second alphabet of the names. This process of creating subpiles will continue and the list will become totally sorted when the number of times subpiles created, is equal to the number of alphabets in the largest name.

In the above case, where we had to sort names, the radix was 26 (all alphabets). If we have a list of decimal numbers, then the radix will be 10 (digits 0 to 9). We have sorted the names starting from the most significant position (from left to right). While sorting numbers also, we can do the same thing. If all the numbers do not have the same number of digits, then we can add leading zeros. First, all numbers are divided into 10 groups based on the most significant digit, and then these groups are again divided into subgroups based on the next significant digit. The problem with implementing this method is that we have to keep track of many groups and subgroups. The implementation would be much simpler if the sorting starts from the least significant digit (from right to left). These two methods are called Most Significant Digit (MSD) radix sort and Least Significant Digit (LSD) radix sort.

In LSD radix sort, sorting is performed digit by digit, starting from the least significant digit and ending at the most significant digit. In first pass, elements are sorted according to their units (least significant) digits; in second pass, elements are sorted according to their tens digit; in third pass elements are sorted according to hundreds digit and so on, till the last pass where elements are sorted according to their most significant digits.

For implementing this method, we will take ten separate queues for each digit from 0 to 9. In the first pass, numbers are inserted into appropriate queues depending on their least significant digits (units digit). For example, 283 will be inserted in queue 3, and 540 will be inserted in queue 0. After this, all the queues are combined, starting from the digit 0 queue to the digit 9 queue, and a single list is formed. Now in the second pass, the numbers from this new list are inserted in queues based on tens digit. For example, 283 will be inserted in queue 8 and 540 will be inserted in queue 4. These queues are combined to form a single list, which is used in the third pass. This process continues till numbers are inserted into queues based on the most significant digit. The single list that we will get after combining these queues will be the sorted list. We can see that the total number of passes will be equal to the number of digits in the largest number. In figure 8.29, we have taken some numbers in unsorted order and sorted them by applying radix sort.

It is important that in each pass, the sorting on digits should be stable, i.e., the numbers which have the same i^{th} digit (from right) should remain sorted on the $(i-1)^{th}$ digit (from right). After any pass, when we get a single list, we should enter the numbers in the queue in the same order as they are in the list. This will ensure that the digit sorts are stable.

We take the initial input in linked list to simplify the process. If the input is in an array, then we can convert it to the linked list. In the program, we just traverse the linked list and add the number to the appropriate queue. After this, we can combine the queues into one single list by joining the end of a queue, in order to start another queue.

We do not know in advance how many numbers will be inserted in a particular queue in any pass. It may be possible that in a particular pass, the digit is the same for all the numbers, and all numbers may have to be inserted in the same queue. If we use arrays for implementing queues, then each array should be of size n, and we will need space equal to 10*n. So, it is better to take a linked allocation of queues instead of sequential allocation.

Original List : 62, 234, 456, 750, 789, 3, 21, 345, 983, 99, 153, 65, 23, 5, 98, 10, 6, 372

Pass 1 :   Numbers classified according to units digit(least significant digit)

Queue for digit 0	750, 10
Queue for digit 1	21
Queue for digit 2	62, 372
Queue for digit 3	3, 983, 153, 23
Queue for digit 4	234
Queue for digit 5	345, 65, 5
Queue for digit 6	456, 6
Queue for digit 7	
Queue for digit 8	98
Queue for digit 9	789, 99

List after first pass : 750, 10, 21, 62, 372, 3, 983, 153, 23, 234, 345, 65, 5, 456, 6, 98, 789, 99

Pass 2 :   Numbers classified according to tens digit

Queue for digit 0	3, 5, 6
Queue for digit 1	10
Queue for digit 2	21, 23
Queue for digit 3	234
Queue for digit 4	345
Queue for digit 5	750, 153, 456
Queue for digit 6	62, 65
Queue for digit 7	372
Queue for digit 8	983, 789
Queue for digit 9	98, 99

List after second pass : 3, 5, 6, 10, 21, 23, 234, 345, 750, 153, 456, 62, 65, 372, 983, 789, 98, 99

Pass 3 :   Numbers classified according to hundreds digit(most significant digit)

Queue for digit 0	3, 5, 6, 10, 21, 23, 62, 65, 98, 99
Queue for digit 1	153
Queue for digit 2	234
Queue for digit 3	345, 372
Queue for digit 4	456
Queue for digit 5	
Queue for digit 6	
Queue for digit 7	750, 789
Queue for digit 8	
Queue for digit 9	983

List after third pass : 3, 5, 6, 10, 21, 23, 62, 65, 98, 99, 153, 234, 345, 372, 456, 750, 789, 983

Sorted List : 3, 5, 6, 10, 21, 23, 62, 65, 98, 99, 153, 234, 345, 372, 456, 750, 789, 983

Figure 8.29 Radix sort

```cpp
//RadixSort.cpp : Program of sorting using radix sort.
#include<iostream>
using namespace std;

static const int maxSize = 30;

class Node
{
    public:
        int info;
        Node *link;
        Node(int data)
        {
            info = data;
            link = NULL;
        }
};//End of class Node
```

```
//Returns kth digit from right in n
int getDigit(int n, int k)
{
        int digit=0;
        for(int i=1; i<=k; i++)
        {
                digit = n%10 ;
                n /= 10;
        }

        return digit;
}//End of digit()
```

```
//Returns number of digits in the largest element of the list
int digitsInLargest(Node *start)
{
        //Find largest element
        Node *ptr = start;
        int large = 0;

        while(ptr != NULL)
        {
                if(ptr->info > large)
                        large = ptr->info;
                ptr = ptr->link;
        }

        //Find number of digits in largest element
        int ndigits = 0;
        while(large != 0)
        {
                ndigits++;
                large /= 10;
        }

        return ndigits;
}//End of digitsInLargest()
```

```
void radixSort(int arr[], int n)
{
        Node *temp;
        Node *start = NULL;

        //Creating linked list by insertion at beginning from arr[n-1]...arr[0]
        for(int i=n-1; i>=0; i--)
        {
                temp = new Node(arr[i]);
                temp->link = start;
                start = temp;
        }

        Node *rear[10], *front[10];
        int leastSigPos = 1;
        int mostSigPos = digitsInLargest(start);
        int i, digit;
        Node *ptr;

        for(int k=leastSigPos; k<=mostSigPos; k++)
        {
                //Make all the queues empty at the beginning of each pass
                for(i=0; i<=9 ; i++)
                {
                        rear[i] = NULL;
                        front[i] = NULL;
                }
```

```cpp
        for(ptr=start; ptr!=NULL; ptr=ptr->link)
        {
                //Find kth digit from right in the number
                digit = getDigit(ptr->info, k);

                //Insert the node in Queue(dig)
                if(front[digit] == NULL)
                        front[digit] = ptr ;
                else
                        rear[digit]->link = ptr;
                rear[digit] = ptr;
        }

        //Join all the queues to form the new linked list
        i=0;
        while(front[i] == NULL) //Finding first non empty queue
                i++;

        start = front[i];
        while(i <= 8)
        {
                if(rear[i+1] != NULL) //if (i+1)th queue is not empty
                        rear[i]->link = front[i+1]; //join end of ith queue to
                                                    //start of (i+1)th queue
                else
                        rear[i+1] = rear[i]; //continue with rear[i]
                i++;
        }
        rear[9]->link = NULL;
    }//End of for

    //Copying linked list to arr and deleting the linked list
    i=0;
    ptr=start;
    while(ptr != NULL)
    {
            arr[i++] = ptr->info;
            ptr = ptr->link;
            delete start;
            start = ptr;
    }
}//End of radixSort()

int main()
{
        int arr[maxSize] = {62,234,456,750,789,3,21,345,983,99,153,65,23,5,98,10,6,372};
        int n = 18;

        cout << "Unsorted list is :\n";
        for(int i=0; i<n; i++)
                cout << arr[i] << " ";
        cout << "\n";

        radixSort(arr, n);

        cout << "Sorted list is :\n";
        for(int i=0; i<n; i++)
                cout << arr[i] << " ";
        cout << "\n";
}//End of main()
```

8.16.1 Analysis of Radix Sort

The number of passes p is equal to the number of digits in the largest element, and in each pass, we have n operations where n is the total number of elements. In the program, we can see that the outer loop iterates p times and the inner loop iterates n times. So, the run time complexity of the radix sort is given by $O(p*n)$.

If the number of digits in the largest element is equal to n, then the run time becomes $O(n^2)$, and this is the worst performance of the radix sort. It performs best if the number of digits in the largest element is log n. In this case, the run time becomes $O(n \log n)$. So, the radix sort is most efficient when the number of digits in the elements is small. The disadvantage of radix sort is an extra space requirement for maintaining queues and so it is not an in-place sort. It is a stable sort.

8.17 Address Calculation Sort

This technique makes use of the hashing function (explained in Chapter 9, Searching and Hashing) for sorting the elements. Any hashing function $f(x)$ that can be used for sorting should have this property:

If $x < y$, then $f(x) \leq f(y)$

These types of functions are called non-decreasing functions or order-preserving hashing functions. This function is applied to each element, and according to the value of the hashing function, each element is placed in a particular set. When two elements are to be placed in the same set, they are placed in sorted order. Now, we will take some numbers and sort them using address calculation sort.

194, 289, 566, 432, 654, 98, 232, 415, 345, 276, 532, 254, 165, 965, 476

Let us take a function $f(x)$ whose value is equal to the first digit of x. This will obviously be a non decreasing function because if first digit of any number A is less than the first digit of any number B, then A will definitely be less than B.

x	194	289	566	432	654	098	232	415	345	276	532	254	165	965	476
f(x)	1	2	5	4	6	0	2	4	3	2	5	2	1	9	4

Figure 8.30 f(x) values for numbers

Now all the elements will be placed in different sets according to the corresponding values of $f(x)$. The value of function $f(x)$ can be 0, 1, 2.....,9 and so, there will be 10 sets into which these elements are inserted.

0	098
1	165, 194
2	232, 254, 276, 289
3	345
4	415, 432, 476
5	532, 566
6	654
7	
8	
9	965

Figure 8.31 Sets of numbers from f(x) values

We can see that the value of $f(x)$ for the elements 289, 232, 276, 254 is same, and so they are inserted in the same set, but in sorted order, i.e., 232, 254, 276, 289. Similarly, other elements are also inserted in their particular sets in sorted order. All the elements in a set are less than the elements of the next set and elements in a set are in sorted order. So if we concatenate all the sets then we will get the sorted list.

98, 165, 194, 232, 254, 276, 289, 345, 415, 432, 476, 532, 566, 654, 965

Let us sort the same list by taking another non decreasing hash function:

h(x) = (x/k) * 5   (where k is the largest of all numbers)

x	194	289	566	432	654	98	232	415	345	276	532	254	165	965	476
h(x)	1	1	2	2	3	0	1	2	1	1	2	1	0	5	2

Figure 8.32 h(x) values for numbers

Here, the value of function h(x) can be 0, 1, 2, 3, 4, 5, and so, there will be only 6 sets into which these elements are inserted.

0	98, 165
1	194, 232, 254, 276, 289, 345
2	415, 432, 476, 532, 566
3	654
4	
5	965

Figure 8.33 Sets of numbers from h(x) values

The sorted list that is obtained by concatenating these 6 sets is:

98, 165, 194, 232, 254, 276, 289, 345, 415, 432, 476, 532, 566, 654, 965

For implementing this sorting technique, we can represent each set by a linked list. We know that in each set, the elements have to be inserted in sorted order, so we will take sorted linked lists. The starting address of each linked list can be maintained in an array of pointers.

In the case of function f(x), which gives us the first digit of an element, there will be 10 linked lists each corresponding to one set. We can take an array of pointers head[10], and each of its element will be a pointer pointing to the first element of these lists. For example, head[0] will be a pointer that will point to the first element of that linked list, in which all elements starting with digit 0 are inserted. Similarly, head[1], head[2], ...head[9] will be pointers pointing to first elements of other lists.

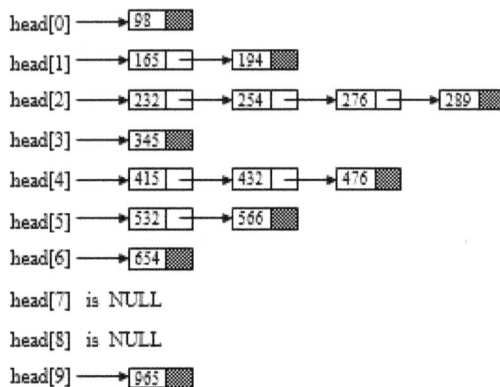

Figure 8.34 Linked lists for f(x) values

These linked lists can be easily concatenated to get the final sorted list. In the case of function h(x) discussed before, there will be only 6 linked lists.

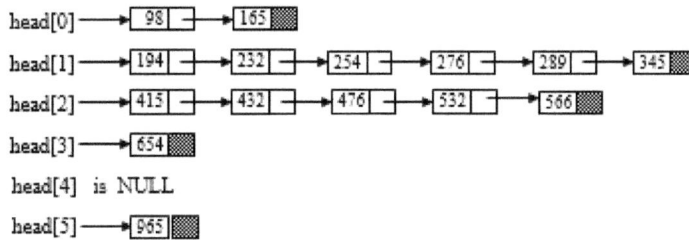

Figure 8.35 Linked lists for h(x) values

```
//AddressCalculationSort.cpp : Program of sorting using address calculation sort.
#include<iostream>
using namespace std;

static const int maxSize = 30;
class Node
{
      public:
              int info;
              Node *link;
              Node(int data)
              {
                      info = data;
                      link = NULL;
              }
};//End of class Node

class SortedLinkedList
{
      private:
              Node *start;
              bool isEmpty() const;
      public:
              SortedLinkedList();
              ~SortedLinkedList();
              void insert(int data);
              Node* getStart();
};//End of class SortedLinkedList

SortedLinkedList::SortedLinkedList()
{
      start = NULL;
}//End of SortedLinkedList()

SortedLinkedList::~SortedLinkedList()
{
      Node *ptr;
      while(start != NULL)
      {
              ptr = start->link;
              delete start;
              start = ptr;
      }
}//End of ~SortedLinkedList()

Node* SortedLinkedList::getStart()
```

```
{
        return start;
}//End of getStart()
inline bool SortedLinkedList::isEmpty() const
{
        return start == NULL;
}//End of isEmpty()
void SortedLinkedList::insert(int data)
{
        Node *temp = new Node(data);

        //List empty or new node to be inserted before first node
        if(isEmpty() || data < start->info)
        {
                temp->link = start;
                start = temp;
        }
        else
        {
                Node *ptr = start;
                while(ptr->link != NULL && ptr->link->info < data)
                        ptr = ptr->link;
                temp->link = ptr->link;
                ptr->link = temp;
        }
}//End of insert()

int hashFn(int x, int large)
{
        float temp;
        temp = (float)x/large;
        return (int)(temp*5);
}//End of hashFn()
void addressCalculationSort(int arr[], int n)
{
        SortedLinkedList list[6];
        int i;

        int large = 0;
        for(i=0; i<n; i++)
        {
                if(arr[i] > large)
                        large = arr[i];
        }

        int x;
        for(i=0; i<n; i++)
        {
                x = hashFn(arr[i],large);
                list[x].insert(arr[i]);
        }

        //Elements of linked lists are copied to array
        Node *ptr;
        i = 0;
        for(int j=0; j<=5; j++)
        {
                ptr = list[j].getStart();
                while(ptr != NULL)
                {
                        arr[i++] = ptr->info;
                        ptr = ptr->link;
```

```
            }
        }//End of for
}//End of addressCalculationSort()
int main()
{
        int arr[maxSize] = {194,289,566,432,654,98,232,415,345,276,532,254,165,965,476};
        int n = 15;

        cout << "Unsorted list is :\n";
        for(int i=0; i<n; i++)
                cout << arr[i] << " ";
        cout << "\n";

        addressCalculationSort(arr,n);

        cout << "Sorted list is :\n";
        for(int i=0; i<n; i++)
                cout << arr[i] << " ";
        cout << "\n";
}//End of main()
```

8.17.1 Analysis of Address Calculation Sort

In address calculation sort, we maintain sorted linked lists and so the time requirement is mainly dependent on the insertion time of elements in the lists. If any list becomes too long i.e., most of the elements have to be inserted in the same list, then the run time becomes close to $O(n^2)$. If all the elements are uniformly distributed among the lists, i.e., almost each element is inserted in a separate list. Then, only a little work has to be done to insert the elements in their respective lists and hence the run time becomes linear i.e., $O(n)$. So, the run time does not depend on the original order of the data, but it depends on how the hashing function distributes the elements among the lists. If the hashing function is such that many elements are mapped into the same list, then the sort is not efficient. This is not an in-place sort, since space is needed for nodes of linked lists and header nodes. It is a stable sort.

Exercise

1. Show with an example that the selection sort is not data sensitive.
2. Write a recursive program for sorting an array through selection sort.
3. Write a program to sort an array in descending order using selection sort.
4. Modify the selection sort program given in the chapter so that in each pass, the larger element moves towards the end.
5. Show the elements of the following array after four passes of the bubble sort.
    34 23 12 9 45 67 21 89 32 10
6. Modify the bubble sort program so that the smallest element is bubbled up in each pass.
7. Modify the bubble sort given in the chapter, so that in each pass, the sorting is done in both directions. i.e., in each pass, the largest element is bubbled up and smallest element is bubbled down. This sorting technique is called bidirectional bubble sort or the shaker sort.
8. Show with the help of an example that the selection sort is not a stable sort.
9. Show with the help of an example that bubble sort is a stable sort i.e., it preserves the initial order of the elements.
10. The elements of an array after three passes of insertion sort are:

2 5 20 34 13 19 5 21 89 3

Show the array after four more passes of the insertion sort are finished.

11. Write a function to sort a linked list using insertion sort.

12. Consider the following array of size 10.

45 3 12 89 54 15 43 78 28 10

Selection sort, bubble sort and insertion sort were applied to this array and the contents of the array after three passes in each sort are given:

(i) 3 12 15 43 45 28 10 54 78 89

(ii) 3 10 12 89 54 15 43 78 28 45

(iii) 3 12 45 89 54 15 43 78 28 10

Identify the sorting technique used in each case.

13. The insertion sort algorithm in the chapter uses linear search to find the position for insertion. Modify this algorithm and use binary search instead of linear search.

14. Suppose we are sorting an array of size 10 using quicksort. The elements of the array after finishing the first partitioning are:

3 2 1 5 8 12 16 11 20 9

Which element (or elements) could be the pivot?

15. Show the contents of the following array after placing the pivot 47 at the proper place.

47 21 23 56 12 87 19 35 11 36 72 12

16. Show how this input is sorted using heap sort.

12 45 21 76 83 97 82 54

17. Write a program to sort a list of strings using the bubble sort.

18. Show the elements of the following array after the first pass of the shell sort with increment 5.

34 21 65 89 11 54 88 23 76 98 17 51 72 91 24 12

19. Write a program to partition an array such that all the even numbers are on the left side of the array and odd numbers are on the right side.

20. Write a program to sort the elements of a matrix (i) Row-wise (ii) Column-wise

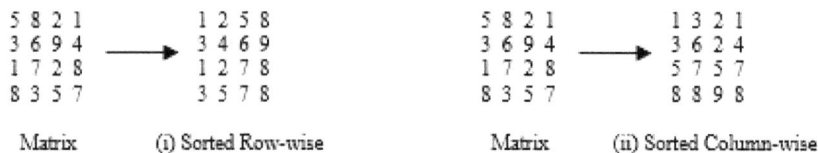

```
5 8 2 1          1 2 5 8          5 8 2 1          1 3 2 1
3 6 9 4    →     3 4 6 9          3 6 9 4    →     3 6 2 4
1 7 2 8          1 2 7 8          1 7 2 8          5 7 5 7
8 3 5 7          3 5 7 8          8 3 5 7          8 8 9 8

 Matrix      (i) Sorted Row-wise     Matrix     (ii) Sorted Column-wise
```

Figure 8.36 Matrices to sort row-wise and column-wise

Searching and Hashing

9

9.1 Sequential Search (Linear Search)

Sequential search is performed in a linear way i.e., it starts from the beginning of the list and continues till we find the item or reach the end of the list. The item to be searched is compared with each element of the list one by one, starting from the first element. For example, consider the array in figure 9.1. Suppose we want to search for value 12 in this array. This value is compared with `arr[0]`, `arr[1]`, `arr[2]`,......`arr[10]`, `arr[11]`. Since the value is found at index 11, the search is successful.

0	1	2	3	4	5	6	7	8	9	10	11	12	13	14	15	16	17	18	19
96	19	85	9	16	29	2	36	41	67	53	12	66	6	75	82	89	23	93	45

Figure 9.1 Sequential search

Now, suppose we have to find value 56 in the above array. This value is compared with `arr[0]`, `arr[1]`, `arr[2]`,........`arr[19]`. The value was not found even after examining all the elements of the array, and so the search is unsuccessful. The program for sequential search is:

```
//LinearSearch.cpp : Program of sequential search (linear search) in an array
#include<iostream>
using namespace std;

static const int maxSize = 30;

int linearSearch(int arr[], int n, int item)
{
        int i=0;
        while(i<n && arr[i]!=item)
                i++;

        if(i<n)
                return i;
        else
                return -1;
}//End of linearSearch()

int main()
{
        int arr[maxSize] = {96, 19, 85, 9, 16, 29, 2, 36, 41, 67};
        int n = 10;
        int item = 29;

        int index = linearSearch(arr, n, item);

        if(index==-1)
                cout << item << " not found in array\n";
        else
                cout << item << " found at position " << index << "\n";

        return 0;
}//End of main()
```

The function `linearSearch()` returns the location of the item if found, and if not, -1.

The number of comparisons required to search for an item depends on the position of the element inside the array. The best case is when the item is present at the first position, and in this case, only one comparison is done. The worst case occurs when the item is not present in the array, and in this case, n comparisons are required where n is the total number of elements. Searching for an item that is present at the ith position requires i comparisons. Now let us find out the average number of comparisons required in a successful search, assuming that the probability of searching of all elements is same.

$$(1 + 2 + 3 + 4 + \ldots\ldots\ldots + n)/n = (n+1)/2$$

So, in both average as well as worst case, the run time complexity of linear search is O(n).

This search is good for data structures such as linked lists, because no random access to elements is required. Sequential search in linked lists is given in Chapter 3, Linked Lists.

In the while loop of the `linearSearch()`, we are making two comparisons in each iteration. The comparison i<n can be avoided by using a sentinel value. In the last location of the array, i.e., `arr[n]`, we can temporarily place the value of the item being searched. This value terminates the search when the search item is not present in the array.

	0	1	2	3	4	5	6	7	8	9	10	11	12	13	14	15	16	17	18	19	20
Search 12	96	19	85	9	16	29	2	36	41	67	53	12	66	6	75	82	89	23	93	45	12

	0	1	2	3	4	5	6	7	8	9	10	11	12	13	14	15	16	17	18	19	20
Search 56	96	19	85	9	16	29	2	36	41	67	53	12	66	6	75	82	89	23	93	45	56

Figure 9.2 Sequential search using sentinel value

The function for sequential search using sentinel is:

```cpp
int linearSearch(int arr[], int n, int item)
{
        arr[n] = item;

        int i=0;
        while(arr[i] != item)
                i++;

        if(i < n)
                return i;
        else
                return -1;
}//End of linearSearch()
```

The number of comparisons in an unsuccessful search can be reduced if the array is sorted. In this case, we need not search for the item until the end of the list; we can terminate our search as soon as we find an element greater or equal to the search item (in ascending array). If the element is equal to the search item, the search is successful; otherwise, it is unsuccessful. The function for sequential search in an ascending order array is:

```cpp
int linearSearch(int arr[], int n, int item)
{
        int i=0;
        while(i<n && arr[i]<item)
                i++;

        if(arr[i] == item)
                return i;
        else
                return -1;
}//End of linearSearch()
```

9.2 Binary Search

The prerequisite for binary search is that the array should be sorted. Firstly, we compare the item to be searched with the middle element of the array. If the item is found there, our search finishes successfully; otherwise, the array is divided into two halves. The first half contains all elements to the left of the middle element, and the other one consists of all the elements to the right of the middle element. Since the array is sorted, all the elements in the left half will be smaller than the middle element, and the elements in the right half will be greater than the middle element. If the item to be searched is less than the middle element, it is searched in the left half. Otherwise, it is searched in the right half.

Now, the search proceeds in the smaller portion of the array (subarray), and the item is compared with its middle element. If the item is the same as the middle element, the search finishes. Otherwise, the subarray is divided again into two halves and the search is performed in one of these halves. This process of comparing the item with the middle element and dividing the array continues, till we find the required item or get a portion which does not have any element.

To implement this procedure, we will take 3 variables, viz. `low`, `up` and `mid`, that will keep track of the status of the lower limit, upper limit, and middle value of that portion of the array, in which we will search the element. If the array contains an even number of elements, there will be two middle elements. We will take the first one as the middle element. The value of the `mid` can be calculated as:

`mid = (low+up)/2 ;`

The middle element of the array would be `arr[mid]`, the left half of the array would be `arr[low]`......
`arr[mid-1]`, and the right half of the array would be `arr[mid+1]`.... `arr[up]`.

The item is compared with the mid element; if it is not found, then the value of `low` or `up` is updated to select the left or right half. When `low` becomes greater than `up`, the search is unsuccessful as there is no portion left in which to search.

If item > arr[mid]
        Search will resume in right half which is arr[mid+1] ....arr[up]
        So low = mid+1, up remains same
If item < arr[mid]
        Search will resume in left half which is arr[low] ....arr[mid-1]
        up = mid-1, low remains same
If item == arr[mid], search is successful
        Item found at mid position
If low > up , search is unsuccessful
        Item not present in array

Let us take a sorted array of 20 elements and search for elements 41, 62, and 63 in this array, one by one. The portion of the array in which the element is searched, is shown with a bold boundary in the following figure.

Search 41

low = 0, up = 19,
mid = (0+19)/2 = 9

|0|1|2|3|4|5|6|7|8|9|10|11|12|13|14|15|16|17|18|19|
|6|9|15|19|23|29|32|36|41|**47**|53|62|66|72|75|82|89|90|93|96|

41 < 47
Search in left half
up = mid-1 = 8

low = 0, up = 8,
mid = (0+8)/2 = 4

|0|1|2|3|4|5|6|7|8|9|10|11|12|13|14|15|16|17|18|19|
|6|9|15|19|**23**|29|32|36|41|47|53|62|66|72|75|82|89|90|93|96|

41 > 23
Search in right half
low = mid+1 = 5

low = 5, up = 8,
mid = (5+8)/2 = 6

|0|1|2|3|4|5|6|7|8|9|10|11|12|13|14|15|16|17|18|19|
|6|9|15|19|23|29|**32**|36|41|47|53|62|66|72|75|82|89|90|93|96|

41 > 32
Search in right half
low = mid+1 = 7

low = 7, up = 8,
mid = (7+8)/2 = 7

|0|1|2|3|4|5|6|7|8|9|10|11|12|13|14|15|16|17|18|19|
|6|9|15|19|23|29|32|**36**|41|47|53|62|66|72|75|82|89|90|93|96|

41 > 36
Search in right half
low = mid+1 = 8

low = 8, up = 8,
mid = (8+8)/2 = 8

|0|1|2|3|4|5|6|7|8|9|10|11|12|13|14|15|16|17|18|19|
|6|9|15|19|23|29|32|36|**41**|47|53|62|66|72|75|82|89|90|93|96|

41 found

Figure 9.3 Search 41

Search 62

low = 0, up = 19,
mid = (0+19)/2 = 9

|0|1|2|3|4|5|6|7|8|9|10|11|12|13|14|15|16|17|18|19|
|6|9|15|19|23|29|32|36|41|**47**|53|62|66|72|75|82|89|90|93|96|

62 > 47
Search in right half
low = mid+1 = 10

low = 10, up = 19,
mid=(10+19)/2 =14

|0|1|2|3|4|5|6|7|8|9|10|11|12|13|14|15|16|17|18|19|
|6|9|15|19|23|29|32|36|41|47|53|62|66|72|**75**|82|89|90|93|96|

62 < 75
Search in left half
up = mid-1 = 13

low =10, up = 13,
mid=(10+13)/2= 11

|0|1|2|3|4|5|6|7|8|9|10|11|12|13|14|15|16|17|18|19|
|6|9|15|19|23|29|32|36|41|47|53|**62**|66|72|75|82|89|90|93|96|

62 found

Figure 9.4 Search 62

Search 63

low = 0, up = 19,
mid = (0+19)/2 = 9

|0|1|2|3|4|5|6|7|8|9|10|11|12|13|14|15|16|17|18|19|
|6|9|15|19|23|29|32|36|41|**47**|53|62|66|72|75|82|89|90|93|96|

63 > 47
Search in right half
low = mid+1 = 10

low = 10, up = 19,
mid=(10+19)/2 =14

|0|1|2|3|4|5|6|7|8|9|10|11|12|13|14|15|16|17|18|19|
|6|9|15|19|23|29|32|36|41|47|53|62|66|72|**75**|82|89|90|93|96|

63 < 75
Search in left half
up = mid-1 = 13

low =10, up = 13,
mid=(10+13)/2= 11

|0|1|2|3|4|5|6|7|8|9|10|11|12|13|14|15|16|17|18|19|
|6|9|15|19|23|29|32|36|41|47|53|**62**|66|72|75|82|89|90|93|96|

63 > 62
Search in right half
low = mid +1 = 12

low =12, up = 13,
mid=(12+13)/2= 12

|0|1|2|3|4|5|6|7|8|9|10|11|12|13|14|15|16|17|18|19|
|6|9|15|19|23|29|32|36|41|47|53|62|**66**|72|75|82|89|90|93|96|

63 < 66
Search in left half
up = mid - 1 = 11

Figure 9.5 Search 63

Now, `low=12` and `up=11`. The value of `low` has exceeded the value of `up`, so the search is unsuccessful.

The program for binary search is:

```cpp
//BinarySearch.cpp : Program of binary search in an array
#include<iostream>
using namespace std;
static const int maxSize = 30;
int binarySearch(int arr[], int n, int item)
{
        int low=0, up=n-1, mid;

        while(low <= up)
        {
                mid = (low+up)/2;
                if(item > arr[mid])
                        low = mid+1;    //Search in right half
                else if(item < arr[mid])
                        up = mid-1;     //Search in left half
                else
                        return mid;
        }

        return -1;
}//End of binarySearch()
int main()
{
        int arr[maxSize] = {2, 9, 16, 19, 29, 36, 41, 67, 85, 96};
        int n = 10;
        int item = 29;

        int index = binarySearch(arr, n, item);

        if(index==-1)
                cout << item << " not found in array\n";
        else
                cout << item << " found at position " << index << "\n";

        return 0;
}//End of main()
```

The function `binarySearch()` returns the location of the `item` if found; otherwise, -1.

The best case of binary search is when the item to be searched is present in the middle of the array, and in this case, the loop is executed only once. The worst case is when the item is not present in the array. In each iteration, the array is divided into half. So if the size of array is n, there will be maximum of log n such divisions. Thus, there will be log n comparisons in the worst case. The run time complexity of the binary search is $O(\log n)$, and so it is more efficient than the linear search. For an array of about 1000000 elements, the maximum number of comparisons required to find any element would be only 20.

Binary search is preferred only where the data is static, i.e., very few insertions and deletions are done. This is because whenever an insertion or deletion is to be done, many elements have to be moved to keep the data in sorted order. Binary search is not suitable for linked list because it requires direct access to the middle element.

The recursive function `rbinarySearch()` for binary search is:

```cpp
int rbinarySearch(int arr[], int low, int up, int item)
{
        int mid;

        if(low > up)
                return -1;
```

```
        mid = (low+up)/2;

        if(item > arr[mid]) //Search in right half
                rbinarySearch(arr, mid+1, up, item);
        else if(item < arr[mid]) //Search in left half
                rbinarySearch(arr, low, mid-1, item);
        else
                return mid;
}//End of rbinarySearch()
```

The recursive function `rbinarySearch()` will be called in non recursive function `rbinarySearch()` as:

```
int rbinarySearch(int arr[], int n, int item)
{
        return rbinarySearch(arr, 0, n-1, item);
}//End of rbinarySearch()
```

9.3 Hashing

We have seen different searching techniques where search time is dependent on the number of elements. Sequential search, binary search and all the search trees are totally dependent on number of elements, and many key comparisons are involved. Now, we will see another approach where less key comparisons are involved, and searching can be performed in constant time i.e., search time is independent of the number of elements.

Suppose we have keys that are in the range 0 to n-1, and all of them are unique. We can take an array of size n and store the records in that array based on the condition that the key and array index are same. For example, suppose we have to store the records of 15 students, and each record consists of the roll number and name of the student. The roll numbers are in the range 0 to 14, and they are taken as keys. We can take an array of size 15 and store these records in it as:

[0]	0	Devanshi
[1]	1	Saachi
[2]	2	Raghav
[3]	3	Supreet
[4]	4	Anushka
[5]	5	Prajwal
[6]	6	Shivani
[7]	7	Parul
[8]	8	Shriya
[9]	9	Samarth
[10]	10	Arnav
[11]	11	Dyuti
[12]	12	Anjali
[13]	13	Sanjana
[14]	14	Niharika

Figure 9.6 Records with roll number as keys

The record with key (roll number) 0 is stored at array index 0, the record with key 1 is stored at array index 1, and so on. Now, whenever we have to search any record with key k, we can directly go to index k of the array because random access is possible in the array. Thus, we can access any record in constant time, and no key comparisons are involved. This method is known as direct addressing or key-indexed search, but it is useful only when the set of possible key values is small.

Consider the case when we have to store records of 500 employees of a company, and their 6 digit employee ID is taken as the key. The employee ID can be anything from 000000 to 999999, so here, the set of possible key values is much more than the number of keys. If we adopt the direct addressing method, then we will need an array of size 10^6; and only 500 locations of this array would be used. In practice, the number of possible key values will be more than the number of keys actually stored, so this direct addressing is rarely used.

Now let us see how we can modify the direct addressing approach, so that there is no wastage of space, and we can still use the value of key to find out its address. For this, we will need some procedure through which we can convert the key into an integer within a range, and this converted value can be used as an index of the array. Instead of taking a key equal to the array index, we can compute the array index from the key. This process of converting a key to an address (index of the array) is called hashing or key to address transformation, and it is done through a hash function. A hash function is used to generate an address from a key, or we can say that each key is mapped on a particular array index through the hash function. The hash function takes a key as input and returns the hash value of that key, which is used as the address for storing the key in the array. Keys may be of any type, like integers, strings, etc, but the hash value will always be an integer.

Key ⟶ Hash Function ⟶ Address

Figure 9.7 Hash function

We can write this as:

```
h(k) = a
```

Here h is the hash function, k is the key, and a is the hash value of the key k. Now, the key k can be stored at array index a, which is also known as its home address. This process of generating addresses from keys is called hashing the key, and the array in which insertion and searching are done through hashing is called a hash table. Each entry of the hash table consists of a key and the associated record.

For inserting a record, we generate an address (index) by applying a hash function to the key and insert the record at that address. For accessing any record, we apply the same hash function to the key and then access the record at the address given by the hash function.

Let us take the example of storing records of books where the ISBN numbers of the books are keys. Suppose we take a hash function that maps a key to an address by adding the digits of the key. For example, if the ISBN is 8183330487, then the record of this book will be stored at index 45. Figure 9.8 shows the records of 4 books stored in a hash table.

[44]		
[45]	8183330487	"C in Depth"
[46]		
[47]		
[48]	8175586440	"Ultimate Python"
[49]	8178082195	"Effective C++"
[50]		
[51]		
[52]		
[53]	8176567418	"DS thru C in depth"
[54]		
[55]		

Figure 9.8 Records of books using ISBN number as keys

Now, suppose we have to store a book with ISBN 8173380843. The sum of the digits is 45, i.e., the address given by our hash function is 45. However, this address is already occupied. This situation is called a **collision**. Collision occurs when the hash function generates the same address for different keys. The keys which are mapped to the same address are called **synonyms**. For resolving collision, we have different collision resolution techniques which we will study in detail later in this chapter. Ideally, a hash function should give unique addresses for all keys, but this is practically not possible. So, we should try to select a hash function that minimizes collision. While making algorithms that use hashing, we have to mainly focus on these two things:

1. Selecting a hash function that converts keys to addresses.
2. Resolving the collision.

9.3.1 Hash Functions

Now we know that the hash function generates a table address from a given key. It works like mapping interface between the key and hash table. If the size of the hash table is m, then we need a hash function that can generate addresses in the range 0 to m-1. Basically, we have two criteria for choosing a good hash function:

1. It should be easy to compute.
2. It should generate addresses with minimum collision, i.e., it should distribute the keys as uniformly as possible in the hash table.

If we know beforehand about the types of keys that will arrive, then we can select a good hash function that gives minimum collision for these keys. However, the nature of keys is generally not known in advance; hence, the general approach is to take a function that can work on the key such that addresses generated are distributed randomly.

Now, we will see some techniques for making hash functions. In all hashing functions that we will discuss, we will assume the key to be an integer. If the key is not an integer, it can easily be converted into one. For example, an alphanumeric key can be converted to an integer by using the ASCII values of the characters.

9.3.1.1 Truncation (or Extraction)

This is the easiest method for computing an address from a key. Here, we take only a part of the key as an address; for example, we may take some rightmost or leftmost digits. Let us take some 8 digit keys and find addresses for them:

82394561, 87139465, 83567271, 85943228

Suppose the table size is 100, and we decide to take the 2 rightmost digits to get the hash table address. Thus, the addresses of the above keys will be 61, 65, 71, and 28, respectively.

This method is easy to compute, but the chances of collision are higher because the last two digits can be the same in many keys.

9.3.1.2 Midsquare Method

In the midsquare method, the key is squared, and some digits or bits from the middle of this square are taken as address. Generally, the selection of digits depends on the size of the table. It is important that the same digits should be selected from the squares of all the keys. Suppose our keys are 4 digit integers, and the size of the table is 1000; we will need 3 digit addresses. We can square the keys and take the 3rd, 4th, and 5th digits from each squared number as the hash address for the corresponding key.

Key:	1337	1273	1391	1026
Squares of key:	17**875**69	16**205**29	19**348**81	10**526**76
Address:	875	205	348	526

If the key is too large to square, then we can take a part of the key and perform the midsquare method on that part rather than on the whole key. For example, if we have a 7 digit key, we can take a part of the key which contains the first 4 digits of the key and square that part.

9.3.1.3 Folding Method

In this method, the key is broken into different parts, and the length of each part is the same as that of the required address, except possibly the last part. After this, these parts are shifted such that the least significant digits of all parts are in the same line and then these parts are added. The address of the key can then be obtained by ignoring the final carry in the sum. Suppose we have a table of size 1000, and we have to find the address for a 12 digit key. Since the address should be of 3 digits, we will break the key into parts containing 3 digits.

738239456527 => 738   239   456   527

After this, these parts are shifted and added.

```
 738
 239
 456
 527
1960
```

Now, ignoring the final carry 1, the hash address for the key is 960. This technique is called shift folding; it can be modified to get another folding technique called boundary folding. In this method, the key is assumed to be written on a paper that is folded at the boundaries of the parts of the key, so all even parts are reversed before addition.

738
932 (Reversed)
456
725 (Reversed)
2851

Now, ignoring the final carry 2, the hash address for the key is 851.

9.3.1.4 Division Method (Modulo-Divison)

In this method, the key is divided by the table size, and the remainder is taken as the address for the hash table. In C++ language, this operation is provided by the % operator. This method ensures that we will get the address in the limited range of the table. If the size of the table is m, then we will get the addresses in the range {0, 1,......, m-1}.

$H(k) = k \bmod m$

Collisions can be minimized if the table size is taken to be a prime number. Let us take a table of size 97 and see how the following keys will be inserted in it.

82394561, 87139465, 83567271

82394561 % 97 = 45
87139465 % 97 = 0
83567271 % 97 = 25

So here, the hash address of the above keys will be 45, 0, and 25.

We can combine other hashing methods with the division method, which will ensure that addresses are within the range of the hash table.

9.3.2 Collision Resolution

An ideal hash function should perform one-to-one mapping between a set of all possible keys and all hash table addresses, but this is almost impossible, and no hash function can completely prevent collisions. A collision occurs whenever a key is mapped to an address that is already occupied, and the different collision resolution techniques suggest an alternate place where this key can be placed. The two collision resolution techniques that we will study are:

1. Open Addressing (Closed Hashing)
2. Separate Chaining (Open Hashing)

Any of these collision resolution techniques can be used with any hash function.

In the process of searching, the given key is compared with many keys and each key comparison is known as a probe. The efficiency of a collision resolution technique is defined in terms of the number of probes required to find a record with a given key.

9.3.2.1 Open Addressing (Closed Hashing)

In open addressing, the key which caused the collision is placed inside the hash table itself but at a location other than its hash address. Initially a key value is mapped to a particular address in the hash table. If that address is already occupied, then we will try to insert the key at some other empty location inside the table. The array is assumed to be closed, and hence this method is named as closed hashing. We will study three methods to search for an empty location inside the table.

(i) Linear Probing
(ii) Quadratic Probing
(iii) Double Hashing

9.3.2.1.1 Linear Probing

If the address given by the hash function is already occupied, then the key will be inserted in the next empty position in the hash table. If the address given by the hash function is `a`, and it is not empty, then we will try to insert the key at the next location, i.e., at address `a+1`. If the address `a+1` is also occupied, then we will try to insert at the next address, i.e., `a+2`, and we will keep on trying successive locations till we find an empty location where the key can be inserted. While probing the array for empty positions, we assume that the array is closed or circular, i.e., if the array size is N, then after (N-1)th position, the search will resume from 0th position of the array.

If a function `h` returns address 5 for a key and the table size is 11, then we will search for empty locations in this sequence - 5, 6, 7, 8, 9, 10, 0, 1, 2, 3, 4. If location 5 is empty, there will be no collision, and we can insert the key there. Otherwise, we will linearly search these locations and insert the key when we find an empty one. Note that we have taken our array to be closed, and so, after the last location(10th), we probe the first location of array(0th).

Let us take a table of size 11, and insert some keys in it, taking a hash function:

h(key) = key % 11

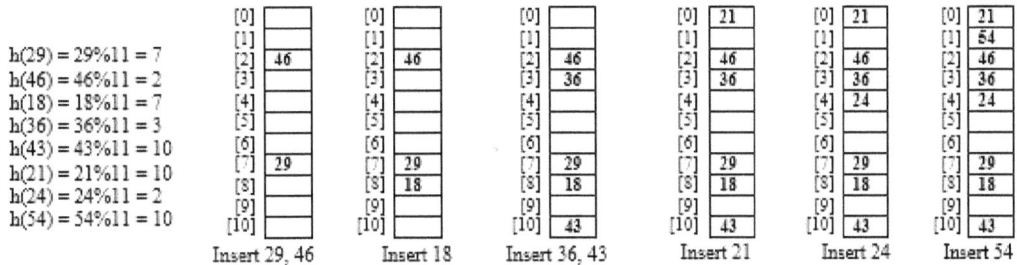

Figure 9.9 Linear probing

First, 29 and 46 are inserted at the 7th and 2nd positions of the array, respectively. Next, 18 is to be inserted, but its hash address 7 is already occupied. So, it will be inserted in the next empty location, which is the 8th position. After this, 36 and 43 are inserted without any collision. Now, 21 is to be inserted, but its hash address 10 is not empty. So, it is inserted in the next empty location, which is the 0th position. Now, 24 is to be inserted, whose hash address is 2 which is not empty. So, the next location 3 is probed, which is also not empty. Finally, it is inserted in the next empty position, which is the 4th position. In a similar manner, 54 is inserted in the 1st position.

The formula for linear probing can be written as:

H(k, i) = (h(k) + i) mod Tsize

Here, the value of `i` varies from 0 to `Tsize-1`. We have done mod `Tsize` so that the resulting address does not cross the valid range of array indices. So, we will search for empty locations in the sequence:

h(key), h(key)+1, h(key)+2, h(key)+3 .... all modulo Tsize

Let us take the example of inserting 54 in the above table:

H(54, 0) = (10 + 0) % 11 = 10 (not empty)
H(54, 1) = (10 + 1)% 11 = 0 (not empty)
H(54, 2) = (10 + 2)% 11 = 1 (Empty, Insert the key)

This is how insertion is done in linear probing. To search for a key, we first check the hash address position in the table. If the key is not available at that position, we sequentially search for the keys after that hash address position. The search terminates if we get the key, reach an empty location, or reach the position where we started. In the last two cases, the search is unsuccessful.

The main disadvantage of the linear probing technique is primary clustering. When about half of the table is full, there is the tendency for cluster formation, i.e., groups of records stored next to each other are created. In the above example, a cluster of indices 10, 0, 1, 2, 3, 4 is formed. If a key is mapped to any of these indices, then it will be stored at index 5, and the cluster will become bigger. Suppose a key is mapped to index 10. Then, it will be stored at 5, far away from its home address. The number of probes for inserting or searching this key will be 7. Clustering increases the number of probes to search or insert a key, and hence, the search and insertion times of the records also increase.

9.3.2.1.2 Quadratic Probing

In linear probing, the colliding keys are stored near the initial collision point, resulting in the formation of clusters. In quadratic probing, this problem is solved by storing the colliding keys away from the initial collision point. The formula for quadratic probing can be written as:

$H(k, i) = (h(k) + i^2) \bmod Tsize$

The value of i varies from 0 to `Tsize-1`, and h is the hash function. Here also, the array is assumed to be closed. The search for empty locations will be in the sequence:

$h(k), \quad h(k)+1, \quad h(k)+4, \quad h(k)+9, \quad h(k)+16, \quad \ldots\ldots\ldots\ldots \text{ all mod Tsize}$

Let us take a table of size 11 and hash function $h(key) = key\%11$, and apply this technique for inserting the following keys.

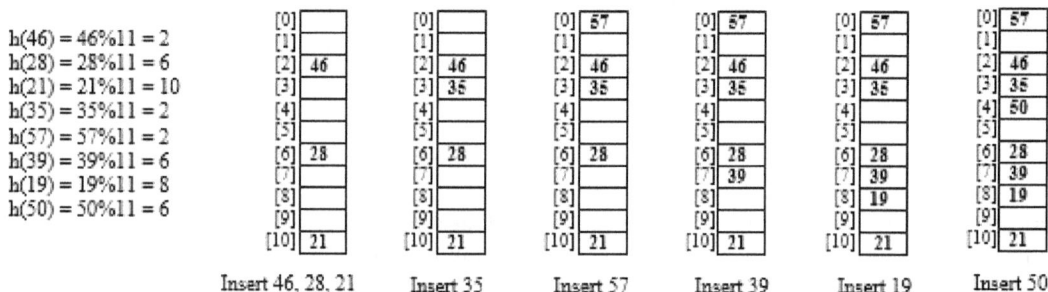

Figure 9.10 Quadratic probing

Keys 46, 28, and 21 are inserted without any collision. Now, 35 is to be inserted whose hash address is 2, which is not empty, and so the next location $(2+1)\%11 = 3$ is tried. It is empty, so 35 is inserted in location 3. To insert 57, first location 2 is tried. It is not empty, so the next location $(2+1)\%11 = 3$ is tried, which is also not empty. Therefore, the next location $(2+4)\%11 = 6$ is tried, which is also not empty. However, the next location $(2+9)\%11 = 0$ is tried, and it is empty. So, 57 is inserted there. Similarly, key 39 is inserted at position 7. The key 19 is inserted without any collision. The key 50 is inserted at location 4.

$H(50, 0) = (6 + 0) \% 11 = 6 \text{ (not empty)}$
$H(50, 1) = (6 + 1^2) \% 11 = 7 \text{ (not empty)}$
$H(50, 2) = (6 + 2^2) \% 11 = 10 \text{ (not empty)}$
$H(50, 3) = (6 + 3^2) \% 11 = 4 \text{ (Empty, Insert the key)}$

Quadratic probing does not have the problem of primary clustering as in linear probing, but it gives another type of clustering problem, known as secondary clustering. Keys that have the same hash address will probe the same sequence of locations, leading to secondary clustering. For example, in the above table, keys 46, 35, and 57 are all mapped to location 2 by the hash function h, so the locations that will be probed in each case are the same.

46 - 2, 3, 6, 0, 7, 5,.....
35 - 2, 3, 6, 0, 7, 5,.....
57 - 2, 3, 6, 0, 7, 5,.....

In secondary clustering, clusters are not formed by records that are next to each other but by records that follow the same collision path.

Another limitation of quadratic probing is that it cannot access all the positions of the table. An insert operation may fail in spite of empty locations inside the hash table. This problem can be alleviated by taking the size of the hash table a prime number, and in that case at least half of the locations of the hash table will be accessed. In linear probing, an insert operation will fail only when the table is fully occupied.

9.3.2.1.3 Double Hashing

In double hashing, the increment factor is not constant as in linear or quadratic probing, but it depends on the key. The increment factor is another hash function, hence, the name double hashing. The formula for double hashing can be written as:

$$H(k, i) = (h(k) + i \, h'(k)) \bmod Tsize$$

The value of i varies from 0 to Tsize-1, and h is the hash function. h′ is the secondary hash function. The search for empty locations will be in the sequence:

h(k), h(k)+ h'(k), h(k)+2 h'(k), h(k)+3 h'(k), ... all mod Tsize

Let us see how some keys can be inserted in the table, taking these two functions:

h(k) = key%11
h'(k) = 7 - (key % 7)

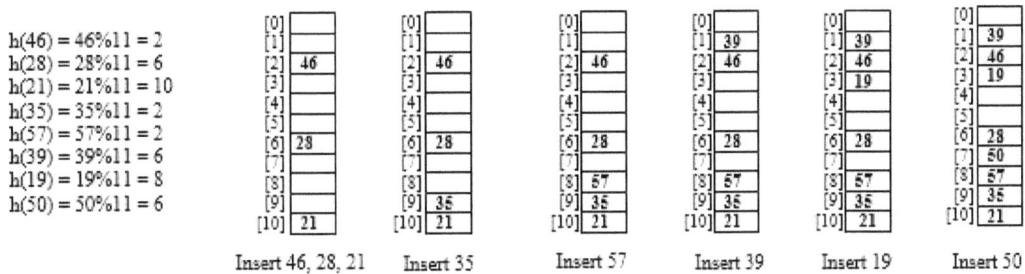

$$h(46) = 46\%11 = 2$$
$$h(28) = 28\%11 = 6$$
$$h(21) = 21\%11 = 10$$
$$h(35) = 35\%11 = 2$$
$$h(57) = 57\%11 = 2$$
$$h(39) = 39\%11 = 6$$
$$h(19) = 19\%11 = 8$$
$$h(50) = 50\%11 = 6$$

Insert 46, 28, 21   Insert 35   Insert 57   Insert 39   Insert 19   Insert 50

Figure 9.11 Double hashing

(i) Insertion of 46, 28, 21: No collision, all are inserted at their home addresses
(ii) Insertion of 35: Collision at 2.
     Next probe is done at: (2 + 1(7-35%7)) %11 = 9,   Location 9 is empty, so 35 is inserted there.
(iii) Insertion of 57: Collision at 2
     Next probe is done at: (2 + 1(7 - 57%7)) % 11 = 8,   Location 8 is empty, so 57 is inserted there
(iv) Insertion of 39: Collision at 6
     Next probe is done at: (6 + 1(7-39%7))%11 = 9,   Location 9 is not empty.
     Next probe is done at: (6 + 2(7-39%7))%11 = 1,   Location 1 is empty, so 39 is inserted there.
 (v) Insertion of 19: Collision at 8
     Next probe is done at: (8 + 1(7-19%7))%11 = 10,   Location 10 is not empty.

Next probe is done at: (8 + 2(7-19%7))%11 = 1,　　Location 1 is not empty

Next probe is done at: (8 + 3(7-19%7))%11 = 3,　　Location 3 is empty, so 19 is inserted there.

(vi) Insertion of 50: Collision at 6

Next probe is done at: (6 + 1(7- 50%7))%11 = 1,　　Location 1 is not empty.

Next probe is done at: (6 + 2(7- 50%7))%11 = 7,　　Location 7 is empty, so 50 is inserted there.

The problem of secondary clustering is removed in double hashing because keys that have the same hash address probe different sequence of locations. For example 46, 35, and 57 all hash to the same address 2, but their probe sequences are different.

46 - 2, 5, 8, 0, 3, 6,.......

35 - 2, 9, 5, 1, 8, 4........

57 - 2, 8, 3, 9, 4, 10.......

While selecting the secondary hash function, we should consider these two points: first, that it should never give a value of 0; second, that the value given by secondary hash function should be relatively prime to the table size.

Double hashing is more complex and slower than linear and quadratic probing because it requires two times calculation of hash function.

The load factor of a hash table is generally denoted by λ and is calculated as:

$\lambda = n/m$

Here, n is the number of records, and m is the number of positions in the hash table.

In open addressing, the load factor is always less than 1, as the number of records cannot exceed the size of the table. To improve efficiency, there should always be some empty locations inside the table, i.e., the size of the table should be more than the number of actual records to be stored. If a table becomes dense, i.e., the load factor is close to 1, then there will be more chances of collision, hence deteriorating the search efficiency. Leaving some locations empty is a waste of space but improves search time, so it is a space vs. time tradeoff.

A disadvantage of open addressing is that key values are far from their home addresses, which increases the number of probes. Another problem is that hash table overflow may occur.

9.3.2.1.4 Deletion in Open Addressed Tables

We have seen how to insert and search records in open addressed hash tables; now, let us see how records can be deleted. Consider the table in figure 9.9, and suppose we want to delete the record with key 21. Suppose we do this by marking location 0 as empty (in whichever way the application denotes empty locations) so that it can be used for inserting any other record. Now consider the case when we have to search for key 54. This key maps to address 10, so it is first searched there, and since it is not present there, it will be searched in the next location, which is the 0th location. The search will terminate at the 0th location because it is empty. So, our search for key 54 failed even though it was in the table. This happened because our search terminated prematurely due to a location that had become empty due to deletion. The same problem can occur in quadratic and double hashing. To avoid this problem, we need to differentiate between positions that are empty and positions that previously contained a record but now are empty (vacated) due to deletion. The search should not terminate when we reach an empty location because a record was deleted from there. In the implementation, we have done this by taking a variable `status` in each record.

9.3.2.1.5 Implementation of Open Addressed Tables

In our program, we will store information of employees in a hash table, and the employee ID of an employee is taken as the key.

Here is the class `Employee` and details of its functions:

```
class Employee
{
        private:
                int employeeId;
                string employeeName;
        public:
                Employee(){};
                Employee(int id, string name);
                int getEmployeeId();
                void setEmployeeId(int id);
                friend ostream& operator<<(ostream& out, const Employee& emp);
};//End of class Employee
Employee::Employee(int id, string name)
{
        employeeId = id;
        employeeName = name;
}//End of Employee()
int Employee::getEmployeeId()
{
        return employeeId;
}//End of getEmployeeId()
void Employee::setEmployeeId(int id)
{
        employeeId = id;
}//End of setEmployeeId()
ostream& operator<<(ostream& out, const Employee& emp)
{
        out << " " << emp.employeeId << " " << emp.employeeName << "  " ;
        return out;
}//End of operator<<
```

Here is the class `HashTable`, which will do all the operations: insert, search, delete, hash and display the employee record with hash table:

```
class HashTable
{
        private:
                Employee *arr;
                int m;  //size of array
                int n;  //number of employee records
                int *status;
                static const int EMPTY = 0;
                static const int DELETED = 1;
                static const int OCCUPIED = 2;
        private:
                int hash(int key);
        public:
                HashTable();
                ~HashTable();
                void insert(Employee emp);
                bool search(int key);
                void del(int key);
                void display();
};//End of class HashTable
```

Here, `arr` is of type `Employee` to keep the employee records, and this is our hash table.

Here, `status` will keep the status of each hash table location. It can have one of these values: `EMPTY`, `DELETED`, `OCCUPIED`. Initially, the status of all hash table locations is set to `EMPTY`.

If `arr[i]` contains a record, then the value of `status[i]` will be OCCUPIED. If `arr[i]` is empty because of deletion of a record, i.e., it is empty now but was previously occupied, then the value of `status[i]` will be DELETED. Otherwise, if `arr[i]` is empty (was never occupied), then the value of `status[i]` will be EMPTY.

The function `search()` returns -1 if the key is not found. Otherwise, it returns the index of the array `arr` where the key was found. Whenever we search for a key, our search will terminate only when we reach a location `arr[i]`, whose status is EMPTY. While inserting, we can stop and insert a new record whenever we reach a location `arr[i]` whose status is EMPTY or DELETED. Deletion of a record stored at location `arr[i]` is done by setting `status[i]` to DELETED.

The search will terminate when an EMPTY location is encountered or the key is found. Thus, it is important that at least one location in the table is left EMPTY so that the search can terminate if the key is not present.

If frequent deletions are performed, then there will be many locations which will be marked as DELETED, and this will increase the search time. In this case, we will have to reorganize the table by reinserting all the records in an empty hash table. So, if many deletions are to be performed, then the open addressing is not a good choice. We have used linear probing in the program; and it can be easily modified for quadratic or double hashing.

Here is the `main()` and other functions of the class `HashTable`:

```cpp
//OpenAddressing.cpp : Program of Open Addressing - Linear Probing
#include<iostream>
#include<string>
using namespace std;
static const int maxSize = 11;
HashTable::HashTable()
{
        m = maxSize;
        n = 0;
        arr = new Employee[m];
        status = new int[m];

        for(int i=0; i<m; i++)
                status[i] = EMPTY;
}//End of HashTable()
HashTable::~HashTable()
{
        delete[] arr;
        delete[] status;
}//End of ~HashTable()
int HashTable::hash(int key)
{
        return key%m;
}//End of hash()
void HashTable::insert(Employee emp)
{
        int key = emp.getEmployeeId();
        int h = hash(key);
        int location = h;

        for(int i=1; i<m; i++)
        {
                if(status[location]==EMPTY || status[location]==DELETED)
                {
                        arr[location] = emp;
                        status[location] = OCCUPIED;
                        n++;
```

```
                        return;
                }
                if(arr[location].getEmployeeId() == key)
                {
                        cout << "Duplicate key\n";
                        return;
                }
                location = (h+i)%m;
        }
        cout << "Table is full\n";
}//End of insert()
bool HashTable::search(int key)
{
        int h = hash(key);
        int location = h;

        for(int i=1; i<m; i++)
        {
                if(status[location]==EMPTY || status[location]==DELETED)
                        return false;
                if(arr[location].getEmployeeId() == key)
                {
                        cout << arr[location] << "\n";
                        return true;
                }

                location = (h+i)%m;
        }

        return false;
}//End of search()
void HashTable::del(int key)
{
        int h = hash(key);
        int location = h;

        for(int i=1; i<m; i++)
        {
                if(status[location]==EMPTY || status[location]==DELETED)
                {
                        cout << "Key not found\n";
                        return;
                }
                if(arr[location].getEmployeeId() == key)
                {
                        status[location] = DELETED;
                        n--;
                        cout <<"Record " << arr[location] << " deleted\n";
                        return;
                }

                location = (h+i)%m;
        }
}//End of del()
void HashTable::display()
{
        for(int i=0; i<m; i++)
        {
                cout << "[" << i << "] --> ";

                if(status[i] == OCCUPIED)
```

```
                        cout << arr[i] << "\n";
            else
                        cout << "___" << "\n";
      }
}//End of display()

int main()
{
      HashTable table;

      table.insert(Employee(15,"Suresh"));
      table.insert(Employee(28,"Manish"));
      table.insert(Employee(20,"Abhishek"));
      table.insert(Employee(45,"Srikant"));
      table.insert(Employee(82,"Rajesh"));
      table.insert(Employee(98,"Amit"));
      table.insert(Employee(77,"Vijay"));
      table.insert(Employee(9,"Alok"));
      table.insert(Employee(34,"Vimal"));
      table.insert(Employee(49,"Deepak"));

      table.display();

      cout << (table.search(15) ? "Key found" : "Key not found") << "\n";

      table.del(15);
      cout << (table.search(15) ? "Key found" : "Key not found") << "\n";

      table.display();

      return 0;
}//End of main()
```

9.3.2.2 Separate Chaining

In this method, linked lists are maintained for elements that have the same hash address. Here, the hash table does not contain actual keys and records, but it is just an array of pointers, where each pointer points to a linked list. All elements having the same hash address i will be stored in a separate linked list, and the starting address of that linked list will be stored in the index i of the hash table. So, array index i of the hash table contains a pointer to the list of all elements that share the hash address i. Each element of the linked list will contain the whole record with key. These linked lists are referred to as chains, and hence, the method is named as separate chaining.

Let us take an example and see how collisions can be resolved using separate chaining. Suppose we take a hash table of size 7 and hash function H(key) = key%7:

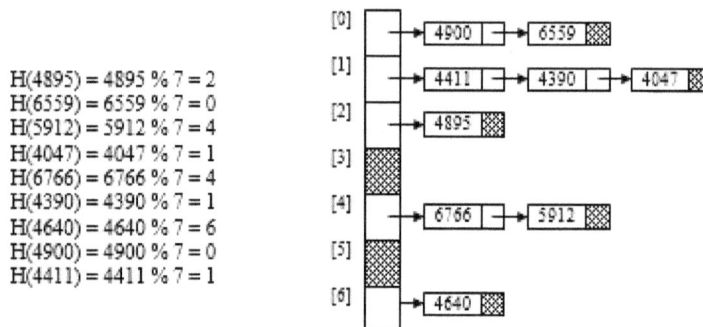

$$H(4895) = 4895 \% 7 = 2$$
$$H(6559) = 6559 \% 7 = 0$$
$$H(5912) = 5912 \% 7 = 4$$
$$H(4047) = 4047 \% 7 = 1$$
$$H(6766) = 6766 \% 7 = 4$$
$$H(4390) = 4390 \% 7 = 1$$
$$H(4640) = 4640 \% 7 = 6$$
$$H(4900) = 4900 \% 7 = 0$$
$$H(4411) = 4411 \% 7 = 1$$

Figure 9.12 Separate chaining

Here, keys 4411, 4390, 4047 all hash to the same address, i.e., array index 1, and so, they are all stored in a separate linked list, whose starting address is stored in location 1 of the array. Similarly, other keys are also stored in respective lists depending on their hash addresses.

If linked lists are short, performance is good. However, if lists become long, then it takes time to search a given key in any list. To improve the retrieval performance, we can maintain the lists in a sorted order.

For inserting a key, first, we will get the hash value through hash function. Then that key will be inserted in the beginning of the corresponding linked list. Searching a key is also the same: first, we will get the hash value through hash function, and then we will search the key in corresponding linked list. For deleting a key, that key will first be searched and then the node holding that key will be deleted from its linked list.

In open addressing, accessing any record involved comparisons with keys which had different hash values which increased the number of probes. In chaining, comparisons are done only with keys that have same hash values.

In open addressing, all records are stored inside the hash table itself, and so there can be a problem of hash table overflow, and to avoid this, enough space has to be allocated at the compilation time. There will be no problem of hash table overflow in separate chaining because linked lists are dynamically allocated. So, there is no limitation on the number of records that can be inserted. It is not necessary that the size of the table will be more than the number of records. Separate chaining is best suited for applications where the number of records is not known in advance.

In open addressing, it is best if some locations are always empty. If records are large, then this results in wastage of space. In chaining, there is no wastage of space because the space for records is allocated when they arrive.

The implementation of insertion and deletion is simple in separate chaining. The main disadvantage of separate chaining is that it needs extra space for pointers. If there are n records and the table size is m, then we need extra space for $n+m$ pointers. If the records are very small, then this extra space can prove to be expensive.

In separate chaining, the load factor denotes the average number of elements in each list and it can be greater than 1.

```cpp
//SeparateChaining.cpp : Program of Separate Chaining
#include<iostream>
#include<string>
using namespace std;

static const int maxSize = 11;

class Node
{
        public:
                Employee info;
                Node *link;
        public:
                Node(Employee data)
                {
                        info = data;
                        link = NULL;
                }
};//End of class Node
class SingleLinkedList
{
        private:
                Node *start;
        public:
```

```
                SingleLinkedList();
                ~SingleLinkedList();
                bool isEmpty();
                void display();
                Node* search(int key);
                void insertAtBeginning(Employee data);
                void deleteNode(int key);
};//End of class SingleLinkedList
SingleLinkedList::SingleLinkedList()
{
        start = NULL;
}//End of SingleLinkedList()
SingleLinkedList::~SingleLinkedList()
{
        Node *ptr;
        while(start != NULL)
        {
                ptr = start->link;
                delete start;
                start = ptr;
        }
}//End of ~SingleLinkedList()
bool SingleLinkedList::isEmpty()
{
        return (start == NULL);
}//End of isEmpty()
void SingleLinkedList::display()
{
        Node *ptr;
        if(!isEmpty())
        {
                ptr = start;
                while(ptr != NULL)
                {
                        cout << ptr->info;
                        ptr = ptr->link;
                }
                cout << "\n";
        }
        else
                cout << "List is empty\n";
}//End of display()
Node* SingleLinkedList::search(int key)
{
        Node *ptr = start;
        while(ptr != NULL)
        {
                if(ptr->info.getEmployeeId() == key)
                        break;
                ptr = ptr->link;
        }
        return ptr;
}//End of search()
void SingleLinkedList::insertAtBeginning(Employee data)
{
        Node *temp;

        temp = new Node(data);
        if(!isEmpty())
```

```cpp
                    temp->link = start;
          start = temp;
}//End of insertAtBeginning()
void SingleLinkedList::deleteNode(int key)
{
          Node *ptr, *temp;

          ptr = start;
          if(isEmpty())
                    cout << "Key " << key << " not present\n";
          else if(ptr->info.getEmployeeId() == key) //Deletion of first node
          {
                    temp = ptr;
                    start = ptr->link;
                    delete temp;
          }
          else //Deletion in between or at the end
          {
                    while(ptr->link != NULL)
                    {
                              if(ptr->link->info.getEmployeeId() == key)
                                        break;
                              ptr = ptr->link;
                    }
                    if(ptr->link == NULL)
                              cout << "Key " << key << " not present\n";
                    else
                    {
                              temp = ptr->link;
                              ptr->link = ptr->link->link;
                              delete temp;
                    }
          }//End of else
}//End of deleteNode()
class HashTable
{
          private:
                    SingleLinkedList *arr;
                    int m;  //size of the array
                    int n;  //number of records
                    int hash(int key);
          public:
                    HashTable();
                    ~HashTable();
                    void insert(Employee emp);
                    bool search(int key);
                    void del(int key);
                    void display();
};//End of class HashTable
HashTable::HashTable()
{
          m = maxSize;
          n = 0;
          arr = new SingleLinkedList[m];
}//End of HashTable()
HashTable::~HashTable()
{
          delete[] arr;
}//End of ~HashTable()
```

```cpp
int HashTable::hash(int key)
{
        return key%m;
}//End of hash()
bool HashTable::search(int key)
{
        int h = hash(key);
        Node *ptr = arr[h].search(key);

        if(ptr != NULL)
        {
                cout << ptr->info;
                return true;
        }

        return false;
}//End of search()
void HashTable::insert(Employee emp)
{
        int key = emp.getEmployeeId();
        int h = hash(key);

        if(search(key))
        {
                cout << " Duplicate key\n";
                return;
        }
        arr[h].insertAtBeginning(emp);
        n++;
}//End of insert()
void HashTable::del(int key)
{
        int h = hash(key);
        arr[h].deleteNode(key);
        n--;
}//End of del()
void HashTable::display()
{
        for(int i=0; i<m; i++)
        {
                cout << "[" << i << "]   -->";

                if(!arr[i].isEmpty())
                        arr[i].display() ;
                else
                        cout << " ___" << "\n";
        }
}//End of display()
int main()
{
        HashTable table;

        table.insert(Employee(15,"Suresh"));
        table.insert(Employee(28,"Manish"));
        table.insert(Employee(20,"Abhishek"));
        table.insert(Employee(45,"Srikant"));
        table.insert(Employee(82,"Rajesh"));
        table.insert(Employee(98,"Amit"));
        table.insert(Employee(77,"Vijay"));
        table.insert(Employee(9,"Alok"));
        table.insert(Employee(34,"Vimal"));
```

```
        table.insert(Employee(49,"Deepak"));
        table.display();

        cout << (table.search(15) ? "Key found" : "Key not found") << "\n";

        table.del(15);
        cout << (table.search(15) ? "Key found" : "Key not found") << "\n";

        table.display();

        return 0;
}//End of main()
```

The class `Employee` and its functions will be same as given previously in open addressing.

9.3.3 Bucket Hashing

This technique postpones collisions but does not resolve them completely. Here, the hash table is made up of buckets, where each bucket can hold multiple records. There is one bucket at each hash address, and this means that we can store multiple records at a given hash address. Collisions will occur only after a bucket is full. In the example given in figure 9.13, we have taken a hash table in which each bucket can hold three records. So, we can store three records at the same hash address without collision. A collision occurs only when a fourth record with the same hash address arrives.

A disadvantage of this technique is the wastage of space since many buckets will not be occupied or will be partially occupied. Another problem is that this method does not prevent collisions but only defers them, and when collisions occur, they have to be resolved using a collision resolution technique like open addressing.

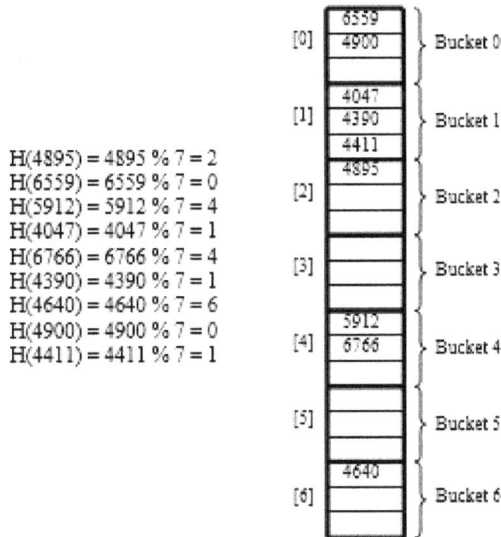

$$H(4895) = 4895 \% 7 = 2$$
$$H(6559) = 6559 \% 7 = 0$$
$$H(5912) = 5912 \% 7 = 4$$
$$H(4047) = 4047 \% 7 = 1$$
$$H(6766) = 6766 \% 7 = 4$$
$$H(4390) = 4390 \% 7 = 1$$
$$H(4640) = 4640 \% 7 = 6$$
$$H(4900) = 4900 \% 7 = 0$$
$$H(4411) = 4411 \% 7 = 1$$

Figure 9.13 Bucket hashing

Exercise

1. An array contains the following 18 elements.
   12 19 23 27 30 34 45 56 59 61 76 79 83 85 88 90 94 97
   Perform binary search to find the elements 27, 32, 61, 97 in the array. Show the values of low, mid and up in each step.

2. Find the hash addresses of the following keys using the midsquare method if the size of the table is 1000.
   342, 213, 432, 542, 132, 763, 298

3. Find the hash addresses of the following keys using the folding method if the size of the table is 1000.
   321982432, 213432183, 343541652, 542313753

4. Find the hash addresses of the keys in exercise 3 using the boundary folding method if the size of the table is 1000.

5. How many collisions occur for the following keys if the hash addresses are generated using the modulo division method, where the table size is 64?
   9893, 2341, 4312, 7893, 4531, 8731, 3184, 5421, 4955, 1496
   How many collisions occur if the table size is changed to 67?

6. Insert the following keys in an array of size 17 using the modulo division method. Use linear probing to resolve collisions.
   94, 37, 29, 40, 84, 88, 102, 63, 67, 120, 122

7. Insert the following keys in an array of size 17 using the modulo division method. Use quadratic probing to resolve collisions.
   94, 37, 29, 40, 84, 88, 102, 63, 67, 120, 122

8. Insert the following keys in an array of size 17 using the modulo division method. Use double hashing to resolve collisions. Take $h'(k) = (key\%7) + 1$ as the second hash function.
   94, 37, 29, 40, 84, 88, 102, 63, 67, 120, 122

9. What is the length of the longest chain if the following keys are inserted in a table of size 11 using modulo division and separate chaining?
   1457 2134 8255 4720 6779 2709 1061 3213

Join our book's Discord space

Join the book's Discord Workspace for Latest updates, Offers, Tech happenings around the world, New Release and Sessions with the Authors:

https://discord.bpbonline.com

Storage Management

We have seen data structures which are used to implement different concepts in a programming language. In each one of them, we specify the need for storage space to implement these data structures. For example, in the case of a linked list, we allocate the space for the node at the time of insertion and free the storage space at the time of deletion. This allocation and freeing of space can be done at run time because C++ language supports dynamic memory allocation. Generally, it is the work of the operating system to provide the specified memory to the user and manage the allocation and release process. Now, we will see different techniques and data structures for storage management.

Dynamic memory allocation requires allocating and releasing different sizes of memory at different times. Many applications might be running on a system, and they can request different sizes of memory. The operating system's memory management system is responsible for managing the memory and fulfilling the users' memory requirements.

Suppose we have 512K of available memory and the programs P1, P2, P3, P4 request for memory blocks of sizes 110K, 90K, 120K, 110K respectively. The memory is allocated sequentially to all these programs.

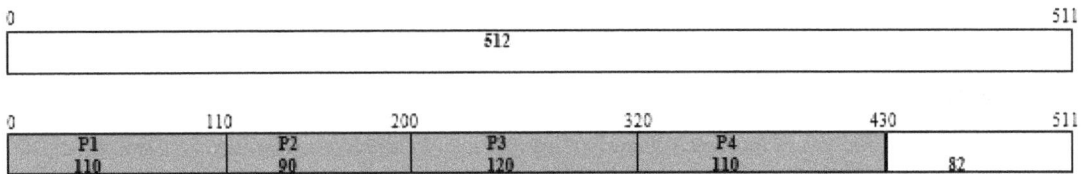

Figure 10.1 Sequential memory allocation

After some time, programs P1 and P3 release their memory.

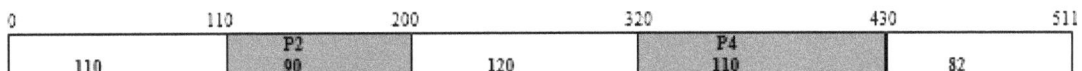

Figure 10.2 P1, P3 released from memory

Now, there are two blocks of memory that are being used, and three blocks that are free; the free blocks can be used to satisfy memory requests. The operating system needs to keep a record of all the free memory blocks, so that they can be allocated whenever required. This is done by maintaining a linked list of all the free blocks, known as **free list**. Each free block contains a link field that contains the address of next free block. The blocks can be of varying sizes, and so a size field is also present in each free block. These fields can be present in some fixed location of the block, so that they can be accessed if the starting address of the block is known. Generally these fields are stored at the start of the block. A pointer named `freeblock` or `avail` is used to point to the first free block of this linked list. Figure 10.3 shows how the free blocks are linked together to form a free list.

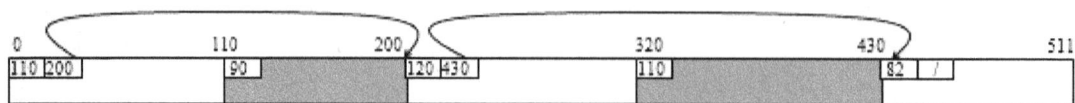

Figure 10.3 Free list by linking of free blocks

Whenever a request for a block of memory comes, memory is allocated from any of the blocks in the free list depending upon the size of the memory requested and the sequential fit method used. If the size of the block is equal to the memory requested, then the whole block is allocated; otherwise, a portion of the block is allocated, and the remaining portion becomes a free block, and it remains in the free list. When a block of memory becomes free, it is joined to this free list.

10.1 Sequential Fit Methods

There are many methods for selecting a free block from the free list during the allocation of memory requested by the user. The three methods we will see are first fit, best fit and worst fit methods. Consider the situation in figure 10.4. Suppose that program P8 requests for 25K memory. Now, let us see how this memory will be allocated using different sequential fit methods.

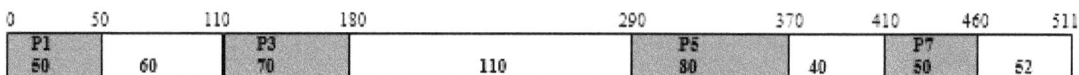

Figure 10.4 Memory allocation for programs

10.1.1 First Fit Method

In this method, the free list is traversed linearly, and memory is allocated from the first free block that is large enough to fulfill the request, i.e., the first free block whose size is greater or equal to the size of memory requested. If the size of the block is equal to the memory requested, the whole block is allocated. Otherwise, it is split into two blocks, one of which is allocated and the other is put on the free list. In figure 10.4, the first free block that has a size greater than the size of memory requested is the block of size 60. So this block is split and a portion of this block is allocated for P8, while the remaining block of 35K remains on the free list.

Figure 10.5 First fit method

Since the link part in each block is stored at the starting of each block, it is better to allocate the second portion of the block for the memory requested. By doing this, there would be no need to change the link part of previous free block. The link part of the split free block would become the link part of the new free block and so there is no need to change it.

10.1.2 Best Fit Method

In this method, the whole list is traversed and the memory is allocated from the free block whose size is closest to the size of the memory requested i.e., from the smallest free block whose size is greater than or equal to the memory requested. In figure 10.4, the free block of size 40 is the one that is closest to size 25, and so a portion from this block is allocated.

Figure 10.6 Best fit method

The advantage of the best fit method is that the bigger blocks are not broken. A disadvantage is that there are many small sized blocks left (here 15K) which are practically unusable.

10.1.3 Worst Fit Method

In this method, the whole list is traversed and memory is always allocated from the free block that is largest in size. In figure 10.4, the largest free block is block of size 110, and so a portion from this block is allocated.

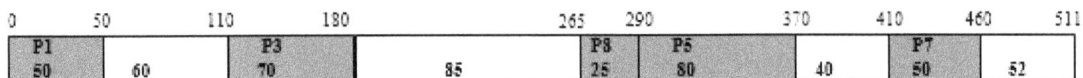

Figure 10.7 Worst fit method

The advantage of this method is that after the allocation of memory, the blocks that are left are of reasonable size and can be used later. For example, here the block left after allocation is of size 85.

The order in which blocks are stored on the free list can improve the search time. For example, the search time in best fit can be reduced if the blocks are arranged in order of increasing size. If the blocks are arranged in order of decreasing size, then the largest block will always be the first one, and so there will be no need for searching in the case of worst fit. For the first fit, the blocks can be arranged in order of increasing memory address. Generally, the first fit method proves to be the most efficient one and is preferred over others.

10.2 Fragmentation

After several allocations and deallocations, we can end up with memory broken into many small parts, which are practically unusable, thus wasting memory. This wastage of memory is known as fragmentation. There are two types of fragmentation problems:

(i) External Fragmentation: This occurs when there are many non contiguous free memory blocks. This results in wastage of memory outside allocated blocks.

Figure 10.8 External fragmentation

In figure 10.8, we have four free memory blocks and the total free memory is 262. Suppose a program requests for memory of size 150. Although the free memory is much more than the memory requested, this requirement cannot be fulfilled because the free memory is divided into non-contiguous blocks, and we do not have 150K of contiguous free memory. External fragmentation can be removed by compaction.

(ii) Internal Fragmentation: This occurs when memory allocated is more than the memory requested, thus wasting some memory inside the allocated blocks. For example, suppose the memory is to be allocated only in sizes of powers of two, i.e., the blocks that can be allocated can be of sizes 1, 2, 4, 8, 16, 32, 64, 128…….. Suppose a request for memory of size 100 comes. Then the memory block of size 128 would be allocated, thereby wasting 28 memory locations inside the allocated block.

10.3 Freeing Memory

Now, let us see what needs to be done when a memory block is freed. Whenever a memory block is freed, it has to be added to the free list. If the free list is not ordered, then it is added at the front of the list. Otherwise, it is put at the appropriate place in the list. This way, after some time, there will be many small free blocks on the free list and it would not be possible to fulfill a request for a large memory block. At the time of allocation, the bigger blocks are split into smaller blocks. Thus, while freeing memory, there should be some combination procedure that combines small free blocks into large blocks.

If any neighbor (left or right or both) of the freed block is free, then we can remove it from the free list and combine these contiguous free blocks to form a larger free block and put this larger free block on the free list. To find out whether a free neighbor exists, we have to traverse the whole free list. Consider the situation given in figure 10.9:

Figure 10.9 Program and free block in memory

Suppose now P5 is freed. We can remove the block at address 180 from the free list and combine these two blocks to form one block and put this larger block of size 190 on the free list.

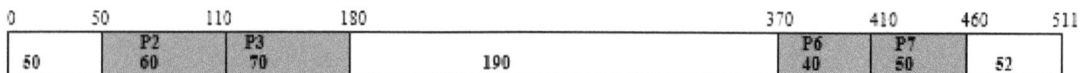

Figure 10.10 Free P5

If the free list is arranged in order of increasing memory address, then we need not search the whole list. For example, suppose we free a block B. We search the list for a block B1 where the address of B1 is greater than address of B.

If the free block B1 is contiguous to B, then B1 is removed from the list and is combined with B. The new combined block is placed in the list at the place of B1. If block B1 is not contiguous to block B, then block B is inserted in the list just before B1.

Suppose block B2 is the free block immediately preceding B1. If B2 is contiguous to block B, then B2 is removed from the list and is combined with B and the new combined block is placed in the list at the place of B2.

10.4 Boundary Tag Method

In the boundary tag method, there is no need to traverse the free list for finding the address and free status of adjacent free blocks. To achieve this, we need to store some extra information in all the blocks.

When a block is freed, we need to locate its left and right neighbors and find whether they are free or not. Let us see how we can calculate the addresses of the left and right neighbors of block B.

Start address of right neighbor of B = Start address of B + size of B
Start address of left neighbor of B = Start address of B - size of left neighbor

For example, in figure 10.11, address of right neighbor of P3 is (110+70) and address of its left neighbor is (110 - 60).

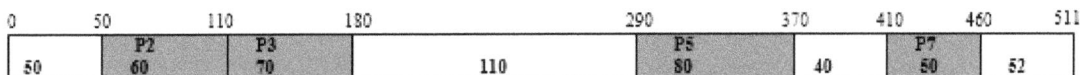

Figure 10.11 Program and free block in memory

Let us assume that a `size` field is stored at a positive offset from the start address, so that we can find size by expression `size(p)`, where p is the start address. Now, suppose a block B at address `k` is freed. Its size would be `size(k)` and the starting address of right neighbor would be `k+size(k)`. To find the start address of the left neighbor, we need the size of left neighbor. However, to access its size, we need to know its start address. We only know the end address of the left neighbor, which is `(k-1)`, so there is no way in which we can find the size of the left neighbor. The solution to this problem is to store a duplicate size field in each block at a negative offset from the end of the block; let us call it `bsize`. If the end address is `q`, then the size of block can be accessed by expression `bsize(q)`. So now, the start address of the left neighbor of B would be `k-bsize(k-1)`.

When a block is freed, we need to know whether its left and right neighbors are free or not. A status field is stored in each block; if the block is free, then this field is 0, and otherwise, it is 1. This status field is stored both at the start and end of the block. If the start address of a block is `p`, then we can access its free status field by `status(p)`, and if `q` is the end address, then we can get its free status field by `bstatus(q)`. So if a block B at start address `k` is being freed, we can access the status field of the right neighbor by `status(k+size(k))` and that of the left neighbor by `bstatus(k-1)`.

Each block needs the size and status fields at both the ends i.e., at both the boundaries and hence the name of this method is boundary tag method.

In boundary tag method, the free list will be stored as a double linked list. This is because we do not reach a block by traversal and hence we do not know its predecessor, which is required for the removal of a block from the list. So each free block will have next and prev pointers, pointing to the next and previous free blocks, and these will be stored at a positive offset from the start of the block.

The structure of a block in boundary tag method is:

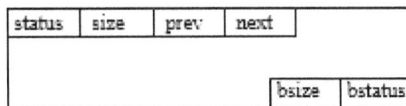

Figure 10.12 Block structure in boundary tag method

Whenever a block is freed, first its free status is set to 0, and then statuses of its left and right neighbors are checked. We can combine the freed block with the next, or previous block or both, if they are free. The free list would be maintained as a circular double linked list with a header. Now, let us take some examples. Suppose we have 86K memory, and some of it is allocated to programs P1, P2, P3 and P4. The free list is shown in figure 10.13:

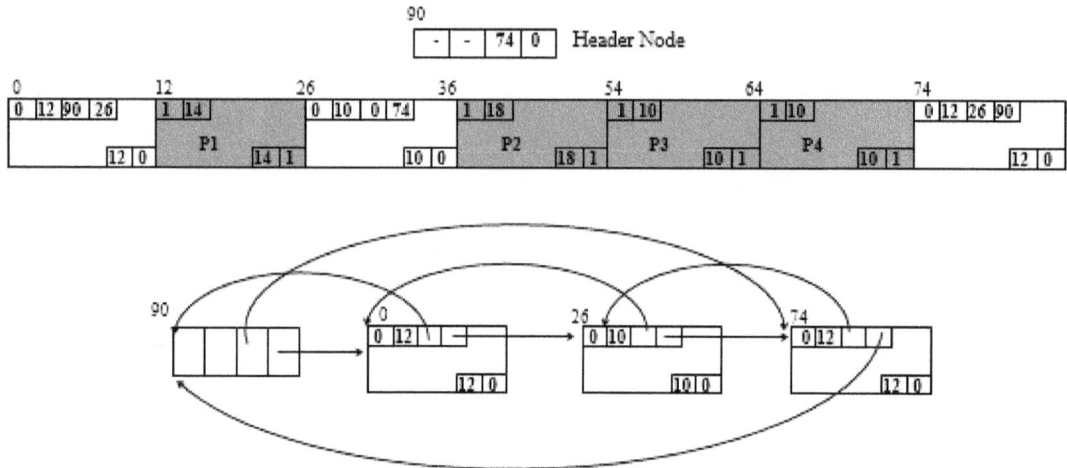

Figure 10.13 Program allocation in memory and free list

Now we will free the memory blocks one by one, and see how the free blocks are combined in the free list.

(i) Free P3 in figure 10.13.

P3 has no free neighbor, so it is just added to the beginning of the free list.

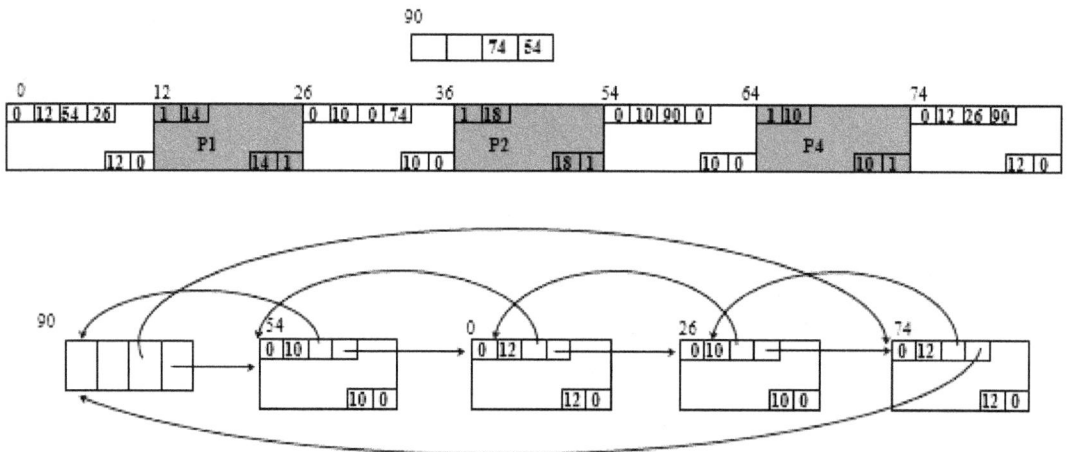

Figure 10.14 Free P3

(ii) Free P4 in figure 10.13.

The left neighbor at 54 is not free, but the right neighbor at 74 is free. So, the block at 74 is removed from the free list and is combined with the freed block and the new block of size 22 is added to the free list.

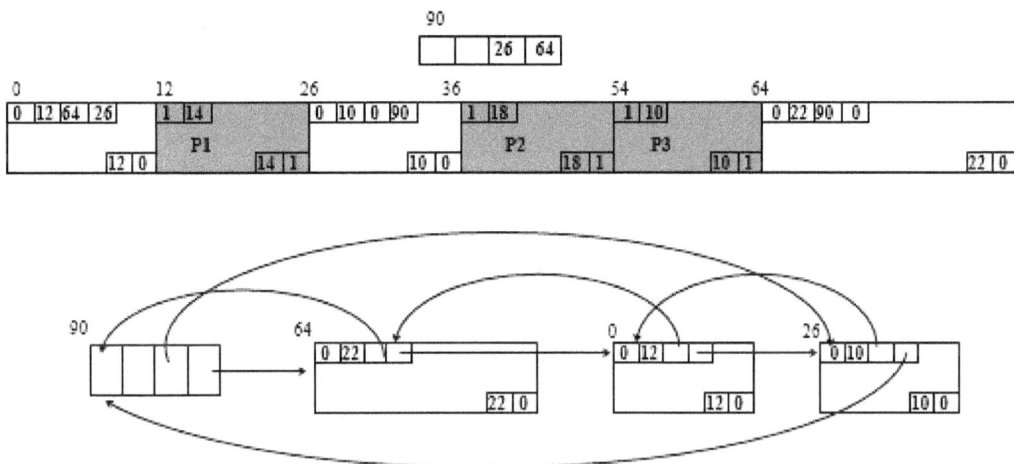

Figure 10.15 Free P4

(iii) Free P2 in figure 10.13

The right neighbor at 54 is not free, but the left neighbor at 26 is free. So, the block at 26 is removed from the free list and is combined with the freed block, and the new block of size 28 is added to the free list.

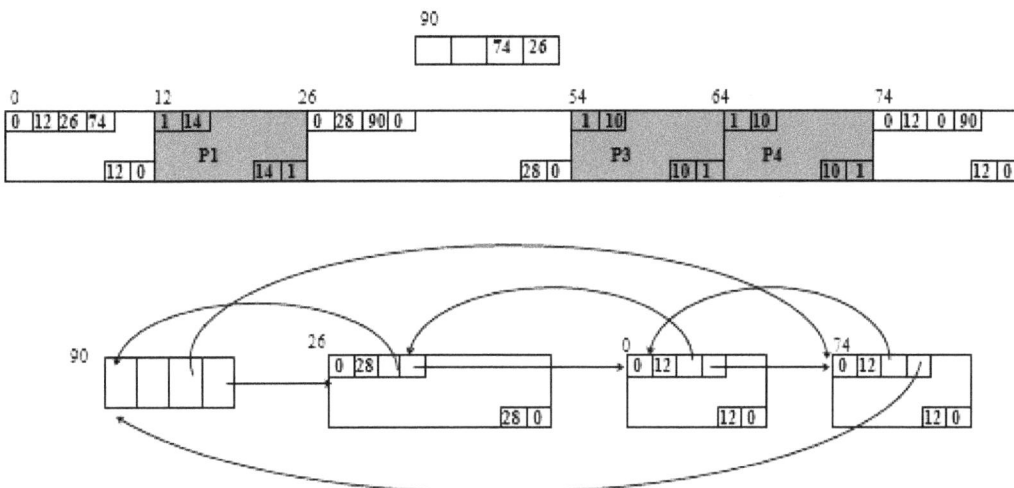

Figure 10.16 Free P2

(iv) Free P1 in figure 10.13

The left neighbor is at 0 and right neighbor is at 26, and both are free. So both these blocks are removed from the free list, and the new combined block of size 36 is added to the free list.

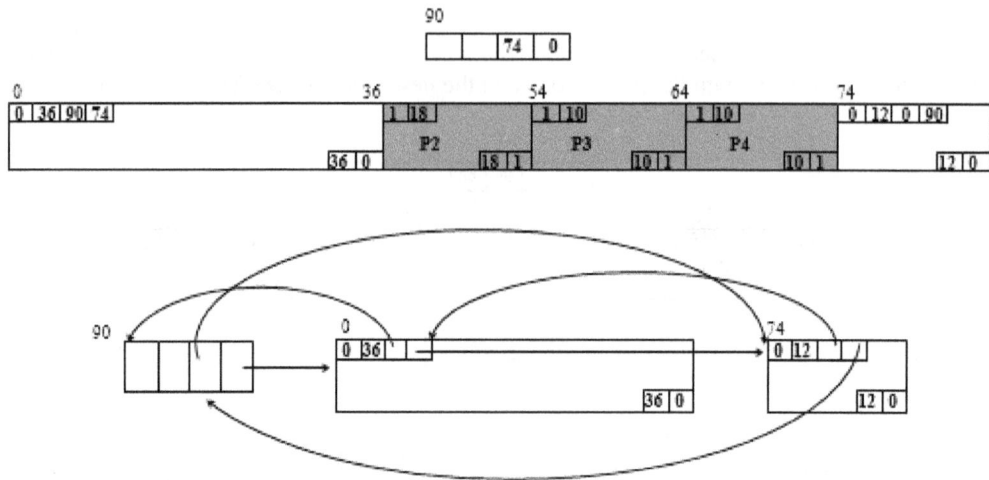

Figure 10.17 Free P1

10.5 Buddy Systems

In buddy systems, the size of memory blocks that can be allocated is restricted to some fixed set i.e., we can have blocks of only some specific sizes. There is a separate free list for each permitted block size. So, in a buddy system, many free lists are maintained, where each free list is a double linked list that contains free blocks of the same size. Any block can be split to form two smaller blocks of permitted sizes, and these blocks are called buddies. Any two buddies i.e., blocks which were split from the same parent block can be combined to rebuild the parent block.

When a memory of size n is requested, a block of size p is allocated where p is the smallest permitted block size that is greater or equal to n. If a block of size p is not free, then the next larger block is split into two blocks called buddies. One of these blocks is added to the appropriate free list and the other block is either allocated (if it is of size p) or again splitted. The process of splitting continues till we get a block of size p.

When a block is freed, first, its buddy is checked, and if the buddy is also free, these two buddies are combined to form a larger block. Two free blocks can be combined only when they belong to the same parent block i.e., only buddies can be combined. If the buddy of the combined block is also free, then it is also combined with its buddy to form a larger block. This combining process continues till there are no buddies left to combine, or we get the largest block after combining. The two common buddy systems are binary buddy system and the Fibonacci buddy system.

10.5.1 Binary Buddy System

In this system, all block sizes are in powers of 2. So the permitted block sizes in this system are 1, 2, 4, 8, 16, 32, 64, 128, 256, 512, 1024 and so on. At the time of split, a block of size 2^i is split into two equal blocks of size 2^{i-1} and at the time of combining, two buddies of size 2^{i-1} are combined to form a block of size 2^i.

For all free blocks, double linked lists will be maintained based on power of 2. An i-block is a block of size 2^i, and the free list that contains all free i-blocks is called an i-list. For example, a 6-block is a block of size 64 (2^6) and a 6-list is a free list of all free 6-blocks.

Suppose initially the total memory available is 2^m. The permitted size of blocks will be 1, 2, 4, 16,........2^m. The free lists that will be maintained are: 0-list, 1-list, 2-list........m-list. Initially the whole memory will be considered as one free block of size 2^m, and this block will be present in the m-list, all other free lists will be empty.

If we want to allocate a memory of size n, then we will find an integer p where $2^{p-1} < n \le 2^p$. Now, we know that we need to allocate a p-block. We will look in the p-list, and if it is not empty, then we will remove a block from it and allocate it. If the p-list is empty, then we will look at the (p+1)-list. If (p+1)-list is not empty, then we will remove a block from it and break it into two buddy blocks where each buddy is a p-block, i.e., each buddy is of size 2^p. Now, one of these buddies will be allocated and the other will be put on the p-list. If both p-list and (p+1)-list are empty, then we will look at the (p+2)-list and take a block from it and split it into two (p+1) blocks. One of these blocks is put into (p+1)-list, and the other is again split into two p-blocks. One of these p-blocks is put into p-list, and the other is allocated. This procedure of splitting will continue till we get a block of size p.

When a block of size 2^i is deallocated, we compute the address of its buddy block. If the buddy block is not free, then the deallocated block is added to the i-list. If the buddy block is free, then we combine the two buddies to form a block of size 2^{i+1}. After combining, we find the address of the buddy of the combined block of size 2^{i+1}. If the buddy of this block is not free, then this block is added to the (i+1)-list. Otherwise, it is combined with its buddy to form a block of size 2^{i+2}. This process continues till we get a block whose buddy is not free or till we get a block of size 2^m.

Suppose we have $2^9 = 512$ K of memory, and the smallest size of block that can be allocated is taken as $2^3 = 8$K. So we will have to maintain 7 free lists viz. 3-list, 4-list, 5-list, 6-list, 7-list, 8-list and 9-list.

(i) Initially all the free lists are empty except the 9-list which contains a block that starts at address 0.

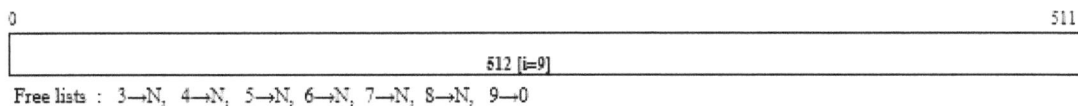

Free lists : 3→N, 4→N, 5→N, 6→N, 7→N, 8→N, 9→0

Figure 10.18 Free list with 9-list

(ii) Allocate 30K for P1.

$2^4 < 30 \le 2^5$ so p=5. We look at the 5-list; it is empty; therefore, we will look at the 6-list so that we can split a 6-block into two 5-block buddies, but the 6-list is also empty. The 7-list and 8-list are also empty. There is a block in the 9-list, so it will be split into two 8-block buddies at addresses 0 and 256. The 8-block at 256 is put into the 8-list, and the other buddy is again split into two 7-block buddies. The 7-block at address 128 is put into the 7-list, and its buddy at address 0 is again split to give two 6-block buddies. The 6-block at address 64 is put into the 6-list, and its buddy is split into two 5-block buddies. The 5-block at address 32 is put into 5-list, and its buddy at address 0 is allocated for P1.

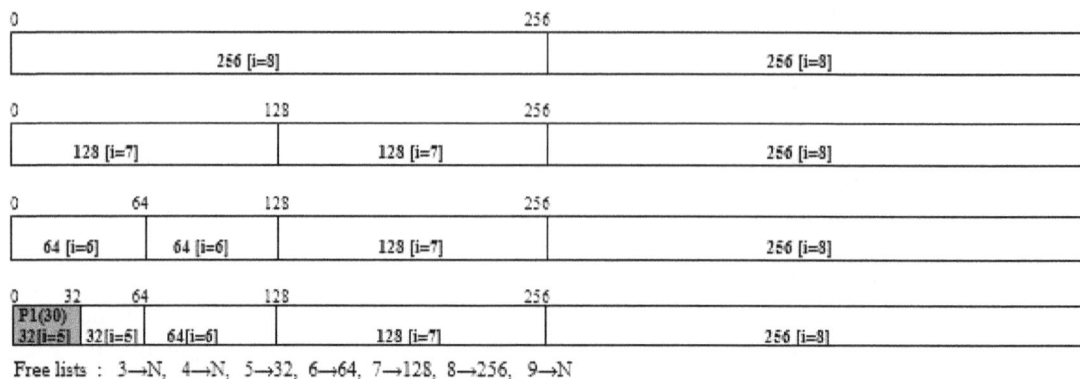

Free lists : 3→N, 4→N, 5→32, 6→64, 7→128, 8→256, 9→N

Figure 10.19 Allocate 30K for P1

(iii) Allocate 105K for P2

$2^6 < 105 <= 2^7$, so p=7. There is a block in 7-list so we will allocate this block for P2.

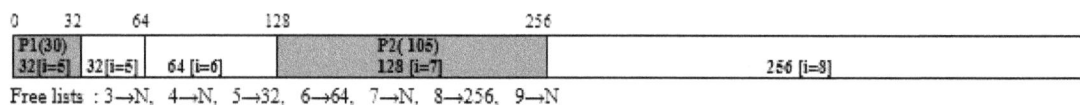

Free lists : 3→N, 4→N, 5→32, 6→64, 7→N, 8→256, 9→N

Figure 10.20 Allocate 105K for P2

(iv) Allocate 100K for P3

$2^6 < 100 <= 2^7$, so p=7. The 7-list is empty so we look at the 8-list which has one block. This block is split into two 7-block buddies at addresses 256 and 384. The 7-block at address 384 is put into the 7-list and its buddy at 256 is allocated for P3.

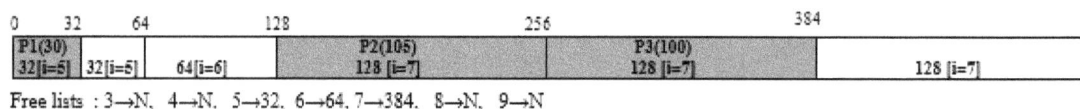

Free lists : 3→N, 4→N, 5→32, 6→64, 7→384, 8→N, 9→N

Figure 10.21 Allocate 100K for P3

(v) Allocate 140K

$2^7 < 140 <= 2^8$, so p=8. The 8-list is empty, so we look at the 9-list which is also empty. Therefore this request cannot be fulfilled.

(vi) Allocate 55K for P4

$2^5 < 55 <= 2^6$, so p=6. There is a block in 6-list, so it is allocated for P4.

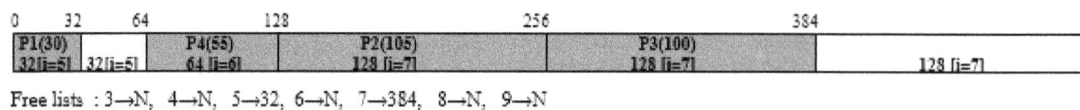

Free lists : 3→N, 4→N, 5→32, 6→N, 7→384, 8→N, 9→N

Figure 10.22 Allocate 55K for P4

(vii) Allocate 80K for P5

$2^6 < 80 <= 2^7$, so p=7. There is a block in 7-list, so it is allocated for P5.

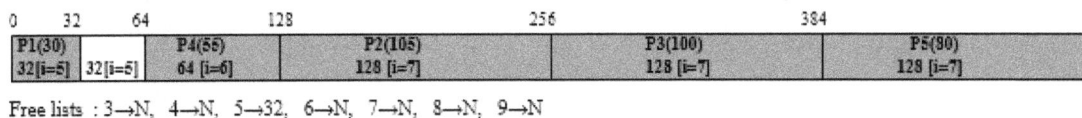

0	32	64	128	256	384	
P1(30)		P4(55)	P2(105)	P3(100)	P5(80)
32[i=5]	32[i=5]	64 [i=6]	128 [i=7]	128 [i=7]	128 [i=7]

Free lists : 3→N, 4→N, 5→32, 6→N, 7→N, 8→N, 9→N

Figure 10.23 Allocate 80K for P5

(viii) Allocate 28K for P6

$2^4 < 28 <= 2^5$, so p=5. There is a block in 5-list, so it is allocated for P6.

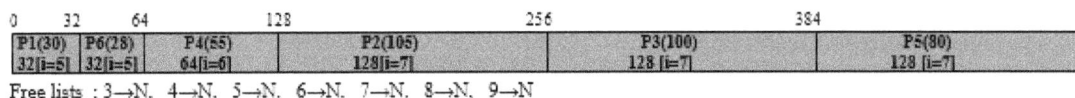

0	32	64	128	256	384	
P1(30)	P6(28)	P4(55)	P2(105)	P3(100)	P5(80)
32[i=5]	32[i=5]	64[i=6]	128[i=7]	128 [i=7]	128 [i=7]

Free lists : 3→N, 4→N, 5→N, 6→N, 7→N, 8→N, 9→N

Figure 10.24 Allocate 28K for P6

When a free block is returned, we need to compute the address of its buddy. A block can have either a left buddy or a right buddy. If the size of block is 2^i and it is situated at address $k * 2^i$, then the block has a right buddy if k is even, while it has a left buddy if k is odd. If the block has a left buddy, then the address of the left buddy would be $(k-1) * 2^i$, and if the block has right buddy, then the address of right buddy would be $(k+1) * 2^i$. For example, a block of size 2^7 situated at address 256($2* 2^7$) will have a right buddy situated at 384($3*2^7$). A block of size 2^5 situated at address 32($1*2^5$) will have a left buddy situated at address 0($0*2^5$).

The address of the left or right buddy of a block of size 2^i can also be determined by complementing the ith bit in the address of the block (if we count the least significant bit as the 0th bit). If the ith bit in the address of a block of size 2^i is 1, then the block has a left buddy, and otherwise, it has a right buddy.

For example, suppose we have block of size 2^5 at address 384,
110 000 000
5th bit is 0, so it will have a right buddy whose address can be obtained by complementing the 5th bit 110 100 000(416).

If we have a block of size 2^7 at address 384,
110 000 000
7th bit is 1, so it will have a left buddy whose address can be obtained by complementing the 7th bit 100 000 000(256).

The address of buddy of a block can be obtained by:

Address of buddy of block B = (Address of block B) xor (Size of block B)

Now let us continue from the figure of step (viii) and start freeing the blocks.

(ix) Free P3

The 7-block at 256 is now free, its buddy at 384 is not free. So the 7-block at 256 is put into the 7-list.

0	32	64	128	256		384	
P1(30) 32[i=5]	P6(28) 32[i=5]	P4(55) 64 [i=6]	P2(105) 128 [i=7]	128 [i=7]		P5(80) 128 [i=7]	

Free lists : 3→N, 4→N, 5→N, 6→N, 7→256, 8→N, 9→N

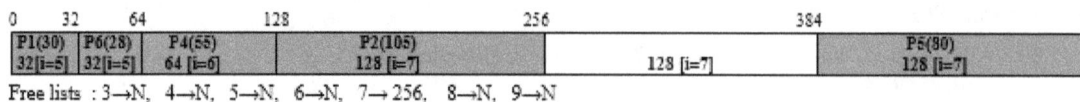

Figure 10.25 Free P3

(x) Free P1

The 5-block at 0 is now free, its buddy at 32 is not free. So the 5-block at 0 is put into the 5-list.

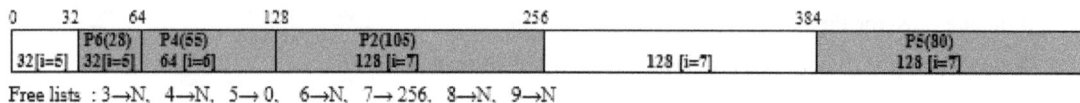

0	32	64	128	256		384	
32[i=5]	P6(28) 32[i=5]	P4(55) 64 [i=6]	P2(105) 128 [i=7]	128 [i=7]		P5(80) 128 [i=7]	

Free lists : 3→N, 4→N, 5→0, 6→N, 7→256, 8→N, 9→N

Figure 10.26 Free P1

(xi) Free P2

The 7-block at 128 is now free. It has an adjacent free 7-block at 256, but it can not be combined with it since both of them are not buddies. The free 7-block at 128 was formed by splitting an 8-block at 0, while the free 7-block at 256 was formed by splitting an 8-block at address 256. So the free 7-block at 128 is put into the 7-list.

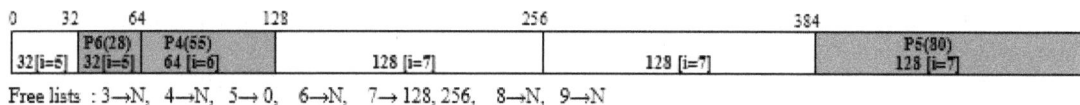

0	32	64	128	256		384	
32[i=5]	P6(28) 32[i=5]	P4(55) 64 [i=6]	128 [i=7]	128 [i=7]		P5(80) 128 [i=7]	

Free lists : 3→N, 4→N, 5→0, 6→N, 7→128, 256, 8→N, 9→N

Figure 10.27 Free P2

Here, note that although we have an adjacent free space of 256K, the largest memory request that can be fulfilled is 128K.

(xii) Free P6

The 5-block at 32 is now free; its buddy is at 0, which is also free, so we combine these buddies to form a 6-block at 0. Now, the buddy of this 6-block at 0 is the 6-block at 64, which is not free. So, the free 6-block at 0 is put into the 6-list.

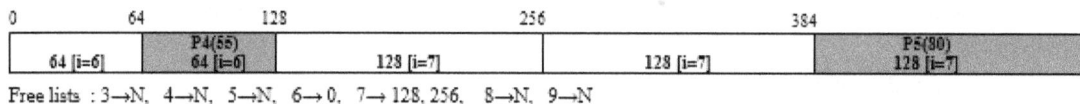

0	64	128	256		384	
64 [i=6]	P4(55) 64 [i=6]	128 [i=7]	128 [i=7]		P5(80) 128 [i=7]	

Free lists : 3→N, 4→N, 5→N, 6→0, 7→128, 256, 8→N, 9→N

Figure 10.28 Free P6

(xiii) Free P5

The 7-block at 384 is now free and its buddy at 256 is also free, so both of them are combined to form an 8-block at 256. The buddy of this 8-block at 256 is 8-block at 0, but it is currently not available as it has been split into smaller blocks. So the free 8-block at 256 is put into the 8-list.

0	64	128	256

64 [i=6]	P4(55) 64 [i=6]	128 [i=7]	256 [i=8]

Free lists : 3→N, 4→N, 5→N, 6→ 0, 7→ 128, 8→256, 9→N

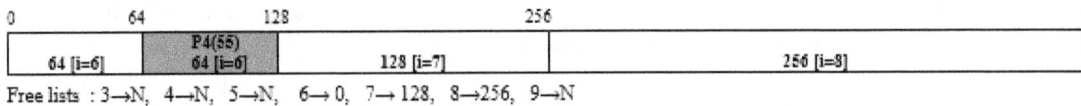

Figure 10.29 Free P5

(xiv) Free P4

The 6-block at 64 is now free, its buddy is at 0 and it is also free, so both of them are combined to form a free 7-block at 0. The buddy of this 7-block at 0 is a 7-block at 128 which is also free so both of these are combined to form a free 8-block at 0. Now the buddy of 8-block at 0 is an 8-block at 256 which is free, so both are combined to form a 9-block at 0. This 9-block is put into the 9-list.

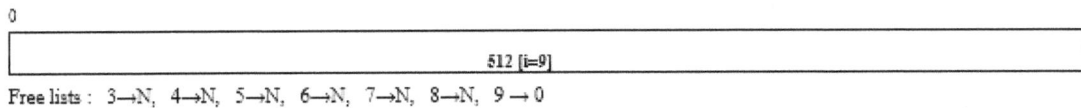

0

512 [i=9]

Free lists : 3→N, 4→N, 5→N, 6→N, 7→N, 8→N, 9 → 0

Figure 10.30 Free P4

Now let us see what information needs to be stored in each block for the implementation of a buddy system. The four fields which are included in all blocks are:

(i) status flag, which denotes whether the block is free or not.
(ii) size, which denotes the size of the block. Instead of storing the exact size, we can store the power of 2. For example, for a block of size 128, we can store 7.
(iii) a left link that points to the previous block on the free list.
(iv) a right link that points to the next block on the free list.

The last two fields are used only when the block is free.

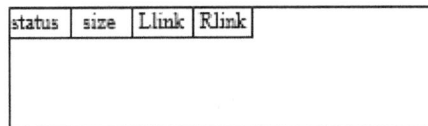

status	size	Llink	Rlink

Figure 10.31 Structure of block for buddy system

To find whether the buddy of a block B is free or not, first we will calculate the address of the buddy. After that, we will see the size of the block located at that address. If the size is not equal to the size of the block B, it means that the buddy of B has been split into smaller blocks. If the size of the block at the calculated address is the same as that of B, then we can check the status flag of the buddy to find whether it is free or not.

For example, in step (xi), a 7-block located at address 128 is freed. It can be calculated that this block has a left buddy situated at address 0. Now the size field of block at address 0 is checked. It is a 5-block, so this means that the buddy of the block that we have freed just now is not available and it has been splitted into smaller blocks.

In step (ix) a 7-block at address 256 is freed. It can be calculated that this block has a right buddy situated at address 384. Now the size field of the block at address 384 is checked and it is found to be a 7-block.

This means the buddy of the block is not split. Now the status flag of the buddy is checked, which shows that the buddy is not free and so the two buddies cannot be combined.

In step (xiii) a 7-block at 384 is freed. It can be calculated that this block has a left buddy situated at address 256. Now the size field of the block at address 256 is checked and it is found to be a 7-block, this means the buddy of the block is not splitted. Now the status flag of the buddy is checked, which shows that the buddy is free and so the two buddies are combined.

For deletion of the buddy from the free list, we need address of its predecessor. We are not reaching the buddy by traversing the free list, but we get its address by calculation i.e., we are directly reaching to any position in a list. So we need to maintain the free lists as double linked list, so that we can get the address of the predecessor of a block while removing it from the list.

In binary buddy system, lot of space is wasted inside the allocated blocks. Only memory requests which are in power of 2 result in no waste, while any other size of memory requested will result in wastage of space. Lot of memory is wasted if the size of memory requested is just a bit larger than the smaller block and is very less than the larger block. For example, if we need memory of size 130, we will have to allocate a block of size 256 thus wasting 126 memory locations. Hence, internal fragmentation is a main disadvantage of the binary buddy system. External fragmentation is also present in buddy systems, as there can be many adjacent free blocks that cannot be combined because they are not buddies.

10.5.2 Fibonacci Buddy System

The Fibonacci sequence can be defined recursively as:

$f_0 = f_1 = 1$
$f_i = f_{i-1} + f_{i-2}$ for $i \geq 2$

The numbers in fibonacci sequence are 1, 2, 3, 5, 8, 13, 21, 34, 55, 89,… Each element is the sum of previous two elements. The Fibonacci buddy system uses these Fibonacci numbers as permitted block sizes. Here an i-block is a block whose size is equal to the ith Fibonacci number. For example a 7-block is a block of size 21. For the implementation of Fibonacci buddy system, an array of Fibonacci numbers needs to be stored so that the ith Fibonacci number can be found easily.

In binary buddy system, when an i-block splits, we get two same size (i-1)-blocks. In the Fibonacci system, we will get buddies of different sizes. When an i-block splits, we get one (i-1)-block and one (i-2)-block. For example, if we split a 10-block (size 89), we get a 9-block (size 55) and a 8-block (size 34). In the binary buddy system, we could easily compute the address of the buddy of a block B, from the address and size of block B. Here, this computation is not simple as the buddies are of different sizes. We need to store some additional information in each block for obtaining the address of its buddy. In each block, a Left Buddy Count (LBC) field is introduced. Initially, the left buddy count of the whole block is 0. This count is changed when a block is split or two buddies are combined.

Splitting:
LBC of left buddy = LBC of parent block + 1
LBC of right buddy = 0

Combining:
LBC of combined block = LBC of left buddy - 1

If the LBC of a block is 0, this means that it is a right buddy. For example, if a block of size 34 has LBC 0, this means that it is a right buddy formed by splitting a block of size 89, and the left buddy is of size 55. If the LBC is 1 or more than 1, this means that it is a left buddy.

Suppose we have 144K of memory, and the smallest size of block that can be allocated is taken as fib(5) = 8K. So we will have to maintain 7 free lists viz. 5-list, 6-list, 7-list, 8-list, 9-list, 10-list, 11-list.

(i) Initially all the free lists are empty except the 11-list which contains a block that starts at address 0. The LBC of this block is 0.

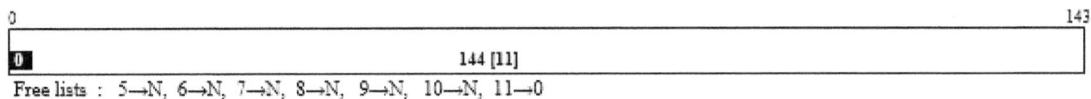

Free lists : 5→N, 6→N, 7→N, 8→N, 9→N, 10→N, 11→0

Figure 10.32 Free list with 11-list

(ii) Allocate 16K for P1

fib(6) < 16 <= fib(7), so we need to allocate a 7-block. The 7-list, 8-list, 9-list, and 10-list are all empty, so the 11-block in the 11-list is split into a 10-block and a 9-block. The 10-block is put on the free list while the 9-block is split into an 8-block and a 7-block. The 8-block is put on the free list and the 7-block is allocated. The left buddy counts have also been updated, as shown in the figure:

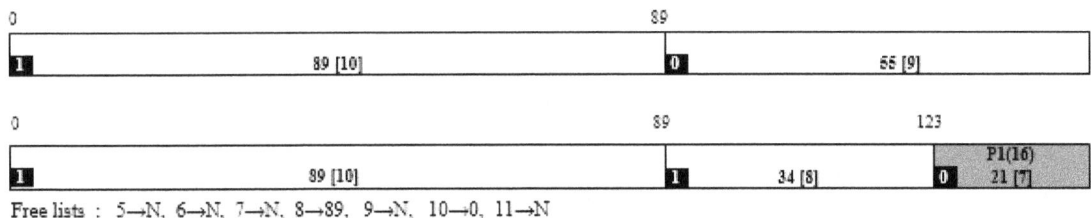

Free lists : 5→N, 6→N, 7→N, 8→89, 9→N, 10→0, 11→N

Figure 10.33 Allocate 16K for P1

(iii) Allocate 20K for P2

fib(6) < 20 <= fib(7), so we need to allocate a 7-block. The 8-block at address 89 is splitted.

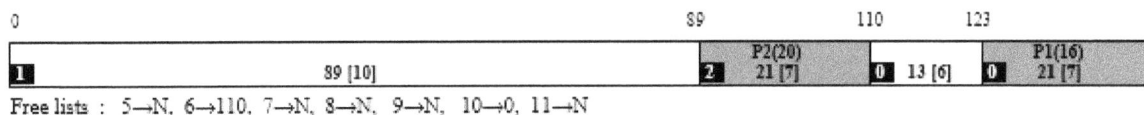

Free lists : 5→N, 6→110, 7→N, 8→N, 9→N, 10→0, 11→N

Figure 10.34 Allocate 20K for P2

(iv) Allocate 30K for P3

fib(7) < 30 <= fib(8), so we need to allocate an 8-block. The 10-block at address 0 is splitted.

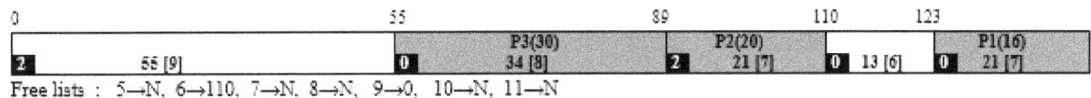

Free lists : 5→N, 6→110, 7→N, 8→N, 9→0, 10→N, 11→N

Figure 10.35 Allocate 30K for P3

(v) Allocate 15K for P4

fib(6) < 15 <= fib(7), so we need to allocate a 7-block. The 9-block at address 0 is splitted.

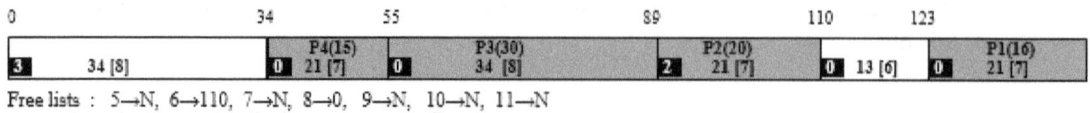

Figure 10.36 Allocate 15K for P4

(vi) Allocate 20K for P5

fib(6) < 20 <= fib(7), so we need to allocate a 7-block. The 8-block at address 0 is splitted.

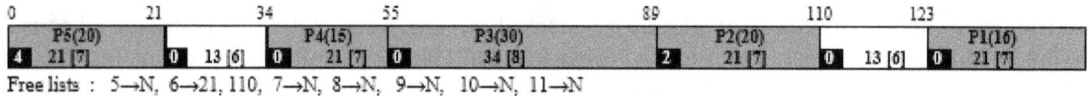

Figure 10.37 Allocate 20K for P5

(vii) Allocate 10K for P6, 8K for P7

fib(5) < 10 <= fib(6), fib(5) < 8 <= fib(6) so we need to allocate two 6-blocks.

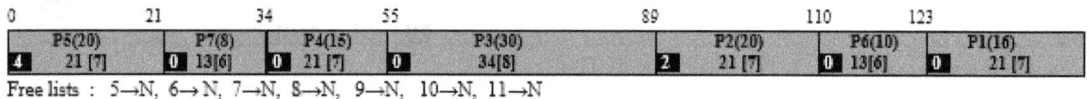

Figure 10.38 Allocate 10K for P6, 8K for P7

(viii) Free P7

The LBC of block P7 is 0, which means that it is a right buddy. Its left buddy would be a 7-block situated at address 0(21 – 21). There is a 7-block at address 0, but it is not free, so no combination takes place.

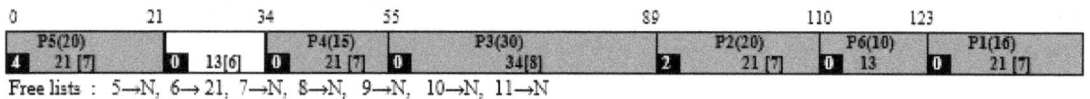

Figure 10.39 Free P7

(ix) Free P4

The LBC of block P4 is 0, which means that it is a right buddy. Its left buddy would be an 8-block situated at address 0(34–34). The block at address 0 is not an 8-block which means that the left buddy has been splitted.

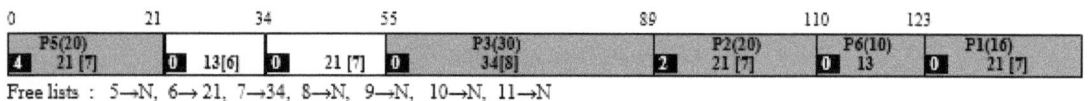

Figure 10.40 Free P4

(x) Free P5

The LBC of P5 is not zero, which means that it is a left buddy. Its right buddy would be a 6-block situated at address 21(0+21). The block at address 21 is a 6-block and is free, and so, a combination takes place.

```
0              34      55              89        110     123          144
┌─┬──────────┬─┬──────┬─┬───────────┬─┬────────┬─┬──────┬─┬─────────┐
│3│  34[8]   │0│ 21[7]│0│  P3(30)   │2│ P2(20) │0│P6(10)│0│ P1(16)  │
│ │          │ │      │ │  34[8]    │ │ 21 [7] │ │13[6] │ │ 21 [7]  │
└─┴──────────┴─┴──────┴─┴───────────┴─┴────────┴─┴──────┴─┴─────────┘
```

Figure 10.41 Free P5

Now, the newly combined node is an 8-block at address 0. Its LBC is 3, indicating that it is a left buddy. Its right buddy would be a 7-block at address 34(0+34). The right buddy is free, so again, a combination takes place.

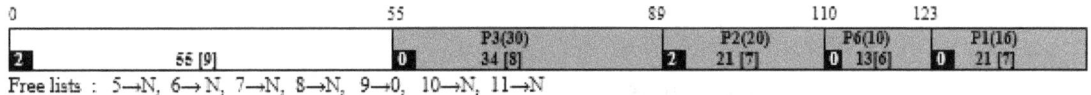

```
0                          55              89        110     123
┌─┬───────────────────────┬─┬───────────┬─┬────────┬─┬──────┬─┬────────┐
│2│        55 [9]         │0│  P3(30)   │2│ P2(20) │0│P6(10)│0│ P1(16) │
│ │                       │ │  34 [8]   │ │ 21 [7] │ │13[6] │ │ 21 [7] │
└─┴───────────────────────┴─┴───────────┴─┴────────┴─┴──────┴─┴────────┘
Free lists :  5→N, 6→N, 7→N, 8→N, 9→0, 10→N, 11→N
```

Figure 10.42 Combination of buddy blocks

(xi) Free P2

The LBC of block P2 is not 0, which means that it is a left buddy. Its right buddy would be a 6-block at address 110(89+21). The right buddy exists but is not free.

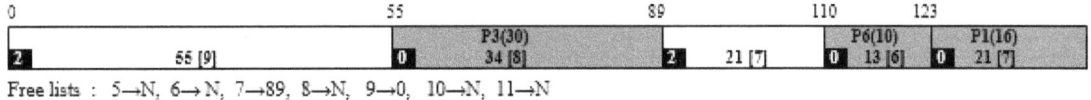

```
0                          55              89        110     123
┌─┬───────────────────────┬─┬───────────┬─┬────────┬─┬──────┬─┬────────┐
│2│        55 [9]         │0│  P3(30)   │2│ 21 [7] │0│P6(10)│0│ P1(16) │
│ │                       │ │  34 [8]   │ │        │ │13 [6]│ │ 21 [7] │
└─┴───────────────────────┴─┴───────────┴─┴────────┴─┴──────┴─┴────────┘
Free lists :  5→N, 6→N, 7→89, 8→N, 9→0, 10→N, 11→N
```

Figure 10.43 Free P2

(xii) Free P1

The LBC is 0, indicating that it is a right buddy. Its left buddy would be an 8-block at address 89(123-34). The left buddy is not currently available.

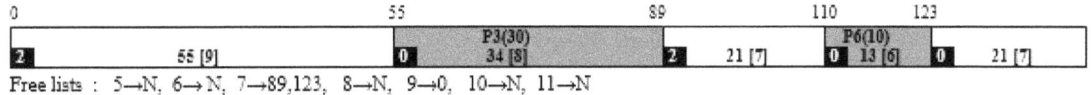

```
0                          55              89        110     123
┌─┬───────────────────────┬─┬───────────┬─┬────────┬─┬──────┬─────────┐
│2│        55 [9]         │0│  P3(30)   │2│ 21 [7] │0│P6(10)│ 21 [7]  │
│ │                       │ │  34 [8]   │ │        │ │13 [6]│         │
└─┴───────────────────────┴─┴───────────┴─┴────────┴─┴──────┴─────────┘
Free lists :  5→N, 6→N, 7→89,123, 8→N, 9→0, 10→N, 11→N
```

Figure 10.44 Free P1

(xiii) Free P6

The LBC is zero indicating that it is a right buddy. Its left buddy would be a 7-block at address 89(110-21). The left buddy is free so they are combined.

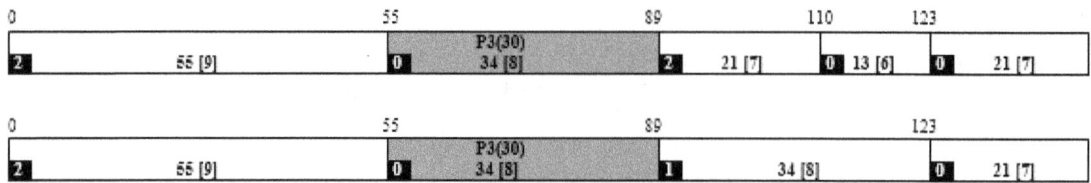

Figure 10.45 Free P6

The LBC of combined block is 1, and hence, it is a left buddy. Its right buddy is a 7-block at address 123(89+34), and it is free. So, they are combined.

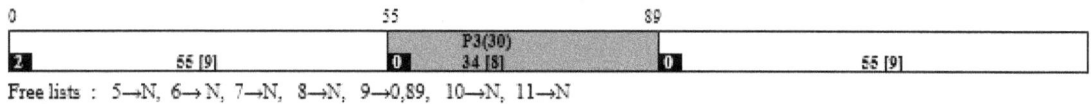

Free lists : 5→N, 6→N, 7→N, 8→N, 9→0,89, 10→N, 11→N

Figure 10.46 Free buddy blocks combined

(xiv) Free P3

The LBC is zero, so it is a right buddy. Its left buddy is a 9-block at address 0(55-55), and it is free, so they are combined.

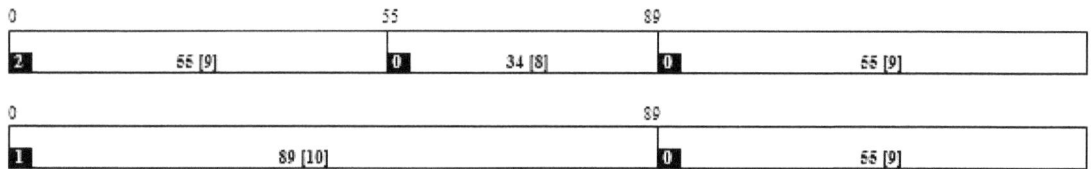

Figure 10.47 Free P3

The LBC of combined block is 1, and hence, it is a left buddy. Its right buddy is a 9-block at address 89(0+89), and it is free so they are combined.

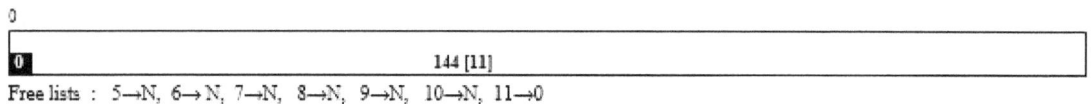

Free lists : 5→N, 6→N, 7→N, 8→N, 9→N, 10→N, 11→0

Figure 10.48 Combined free blocks

In the Fibonacci buddy system, internal fragmentation is reduced since there is a larger variety in the sizes of free blocks.

10.6 Compaction

After repeated allocation and dealloctaion of blocks, the memory becomes fragmented. Compaction is a technique that joins the non-contiguous free memory blocks to form one large block, so that the total free memory becomes contiguous. All the memory blocks that are in use, are moved towards the beginning of the memory i.e., these blocks are copied into sequential locations in the lower portion of the memory. For example, in the following figure, blocks allocated for programs P1, P3, P5, P7 are copied in locations starting from 0 and a single large block of free memory is created.

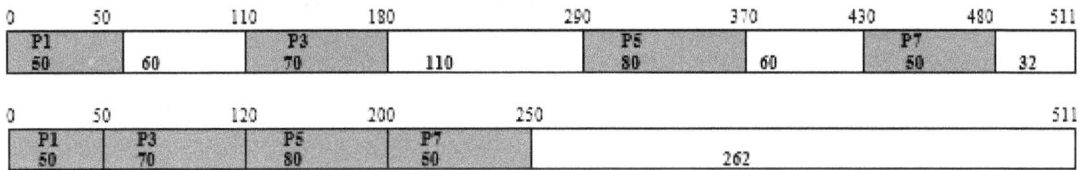

Figure 10.49 Compaction

When compaction is performed, all the user programs come to a halt. A problem can arise if any of the used blocks that are copied contain a pointer value. For example, suppose inside block P5, the location 350 contains address 310. After compaction the block P5 is moved from location 290 to location 120, and so now, the pointer value 310 stored inside P5 should change to 140. So after compaction, the pointer values inside blocks should be identified and changed accordingly.

10.7 Garbage Collection

Garbage refers to those memory blocks that are allocated but not in use; these objects are dead. The garbage collection technique is used to recognize garbage blocks and automatically free them. Garbage collection is also known as automatic memory management, as the dynamically allocated memory is automatically reclaimed by the garbage collector, and there is no need for the programmer to deallocate it explicitly. The main work of a garbage collector is to differentiate between garbage and non garbage blocks and return the garbage blocks to the free list. The two common approaches of garbage collection are:
(i) Reference counting
(ii) Mark and sweep

10.7.1 Reference Counting

Each allocated block contains a reference count, which indicates the number of pointers pointing to this block. This count is incremented each time we create or copy a pointer to the block and decremented each time when a pointer to the block is destroyed. When the reference count of an object becomes zero, it become unreachable and is considered garbage. This garbage block is immediately made reusable by placing it on the free list.

An advantage of reference counting is that a block of memory is freed as soon as it becomes garbage. A major disadvantage of reference counting is that it cannot handle cyclic references correctly. A cyclic reference occurs when an object references itself indirectly. For example, when some block A references block B and block B references block A. The reference count of blocks A and B will never become zero. So, the reference counting mechanism fails to recognize cyclic data structures as garbage and is not able to free them. Another disadvantage is that reference counts have to be frequently updated, thereby increasing processing costs.

10.7.2 Mark and Sweep

The mark and sweep garbage collector is run when the system is very low on memory, and it is not possible to allocate any space for the user. All the application programs come to a halt temporarily when this garbage collector runs, and resume when all the garbage blocks are reclaimed. This garbage collection takes place in two phases: the first phase is the mark phase in which all the non garbage blocks are marked, and the second phase is the sweep phase in which the collector sweeps over the memory and returns all the unmarked (garbage) blocks to the free list.

A root is a program variable that directly points to a block on the heap, and the set of all the roots is called the root set. These roots may be local variables on stack frames, register variables, global variables or static variables. A block is live or reachable if it is directly or indirectly accessible by the root set. The directly accessible blocks are those that are pointed to by any root, and the indirectly accessible blocks are those that are pointed to by any pointer from within a live block. Hence, all the reachable blocks can be found by following pointers from the root set.

So the first task that needs to be done is to find the root set. For this, all the program variables are scanned, and pointers to dynamic memory (heap) are identified as roots. All the blocks that are directly and indirectly referenced by these roots are visited and marked. This is like DFS traversal of a graph and can be implemented recursively. The traversal starts from the set of roots, and all the reachable blocks are visited. Whenever a block is visited, its marked field is set to true. So after the first phase, all live blocks are marked and garbage blocks are not.

In the sweep phase, the garbage collector sequentially scans all the blocks on the heap and reclaims all the unmarked ones by placing them on the free list. The marked blocks are unmarked for the next run of the garbage collector. There is no movement of blocks.

In each memory block, a boolean field is taken to differentiate between the marked and unmarked nodes. This mark field will be true if the block is marked and false if it is unmarked.

A mark and sweep garbage collector can recognize blocks that have already been marked and so there is no problem in the case of cyclic references. Another advantage is that there is no overhead of maintaining reference variables as in the reference count method.

The disadvantage of this method is that it uses a stop-the-world approach i.e., all programs need to stop when garbage collection takes place. This may be undesirable in interactive and real-time applications. Another problem, named thrashing, occurs when most of the memory is being used. In this case the collector can reclaim very less memory which is exhausted in a short duration. This causes the garbage collector to be called again, and this time also, it reclaims only little space. So the garbage collector is called again and again in this case.

Exercise

1. Consider the situation in the given figure and allocate 50K for a program using:
    (i) First Fit method
    (ii) Best Fit Method
    (iii) Worst Fit method

Figure 10.50 Programs and free blocks in memory

2. Deallocate the memory block P2 using Boundary tag method.

90

| - | - | 72 | 0 | Header Node |

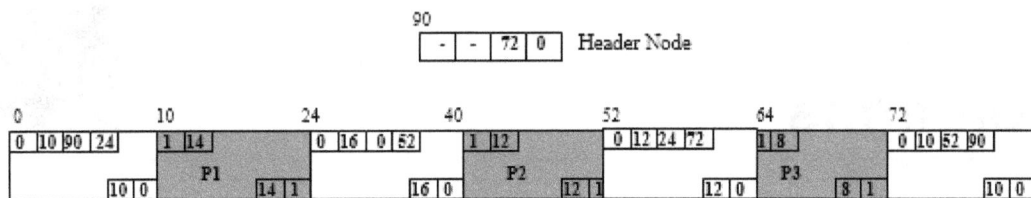

Figure 10.51 Programs and free blocks in memory using boundary tag method

3. Suppose we have 512K of free memory and the smallest block of memory that can be allocated is of size 8K. Use binary buddy system to allocate 100K for P1, 25K for P2, 50K for P3, 60K for P4, 125K for P5.

4. The following memory blocks were allocated using binary buddy system. Deallocate the block P4.

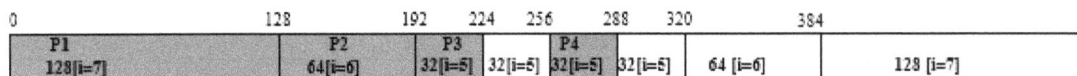

Figure 10.52 Programs and free blocks in memory using binary buddy system

5. Suppose we have 144K of free memory and the smallest block of memory that can be allocated is of size 8K. Use the Fibonacci buddy system to allocate 20K for P1, 30K for P2, 15K for P3, and 35K for P4.

6. The following memory blocks were allocated using the Fibonacci buddy system. Deallocate the block P3.

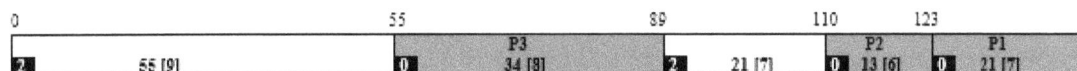

Figure 10.53 Programs and free blocks in memory using fibonacci buddy system

Join our book's Discord space

Join the book's Discord Workspace for Latest updates, Offers, Tech happenings around the world, New Release and Sessions with the Authors:

https://discord.bpbonline.com

Solutions

Chapter 1 Introduction

1. (b)   2. (a)   3. (a)   4. (a)   5. (a)   6. (c)   7. (a)   8. (c)   9. (b)   10. (a)
11. (b)   12. (b)   13. (a)   14. (c)   15. (b)   16. (a)   17. (a)   18. (a)   19. (b)

Chapter 2 Arrays

18. First, transpose the matrix, then reverse the columns of matrix.
19. Selection sort is done up to k pass.
21. Solution 1: Rotate an array by 1 element k times.
Solution 2: Rotate left by k using reverse.
reverse(arr, 0, k-1);
reverse(arr, k, n-1);
reverse(arr, 0, n-1);
22. If array1 element is in array2, then display it.
23. Display all the elements of array1. Then, display all the elements of array2 that are not present in array1.

Check all the programs to see how they are solved. Some problems are solved using nested loop, which can be done using BST or hashing.

Chapter 3 Linked Lists

5. Traverse list L and insert the nodes one by one at the beginning of the new list.
6. We did this in a single pass of bubble sort; here, we will do the swap unconditionally. After swapping two nodes, we will leave them and move to the next node.
7. Unlike a single linked list, here we will not need a pointer to the previous node.
8. While swapping through info, we will need a pointer to the last node. While swapping through links, we will need a pointer to the second last node.
9. Compare adjacent elements and if the first one is greater than second, swap them. This is the technique that we used in a single pass of bubble sort.
10. Compare the first element with all other elements starting from the second one, and if any element is smaller than the first element, swap them. This is the technique that we used in a single pass of selection sort.
13. Here, we need a pointer to the last node of the list.

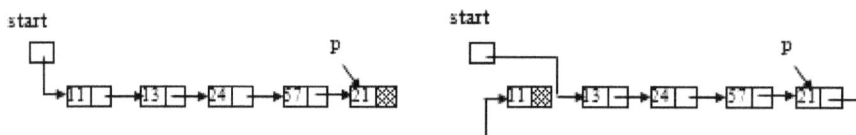

Figure 11.1 Removing first node and inserting at end

14. Here, we need a pointer to the second last node of the list, because we have to put NULL in its link.

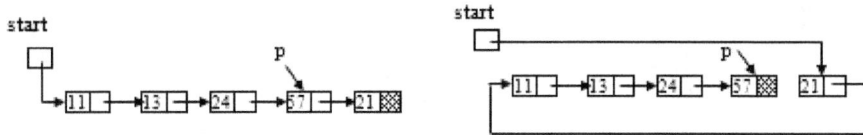

Figure 11.2 Removing last node and inserting at beginning

16. For deleting a node, we need a pointer to the previous node, so that we can change link part of the previous node and make it point to the node which is after the node to be deleted. Here, we are given only a pointer to the node to be deleted, and since the list is a single linked list, we cannot get the pointer to the previous node. We do not have the start pointer so we cannot traverse the list and get the pointer to previous node.

    We copy the data from the next node into the node to be deleted, and then delete the next node.

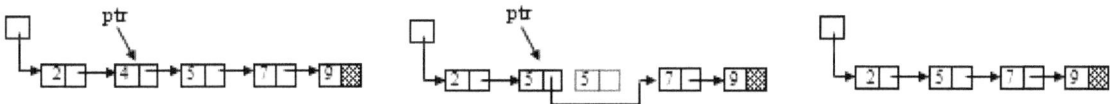

Figure 11.3 Deleting the current node without traversal

    The last node cannot be deleted if only a pointer to it is given because, in that case, we need the previous node so that its link can be set to NULL.

17. Inserting a node after a node pointed by p is simple. For inserting a node before a node pointed by p, we need the pointer to the previous node also. However, we have no other information except the pointer p. So, we can use the trick of copying info as we did in exercise 16.

18. Since the list is sorted, the duplicate elements will be adjacent. We can start traversing from the beginning and compare the data of adjacent nodes. If the data is the same, we can delete the next node and continue. Before deleting any node, we need to store the address of its next node.

19. In an unsorted list, the duplicate elements need not be adjacent. So, here, we can either sort the list and then delete duplicates as in Ex18, or we can use two nested loops to compare the elements of both lists.

24.

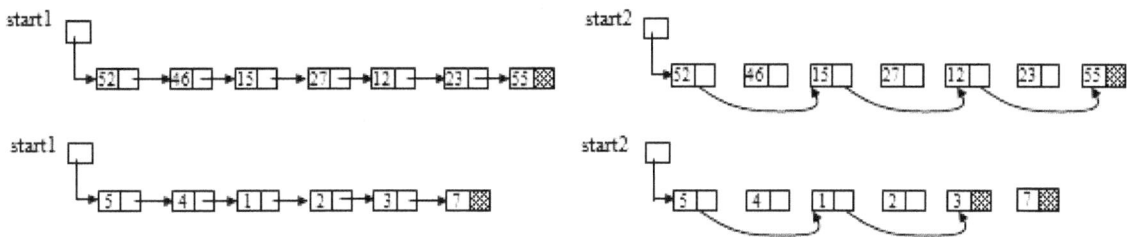

Figure 11.4 Deleting alternate nodes

25. Take two pointers and initially point them to the first node. Move the first pointer n times. Now, move both the pointers simultaneously, and when the first pointer becomes NULL, the second pointer will be pointing to the nth-last node. For example, to find 3rd last node in the list below, move the pointer p1 three times, then move both p1 and p2 until p1 becomes NULL. The pointer p2 will then point to the 3rd last node.

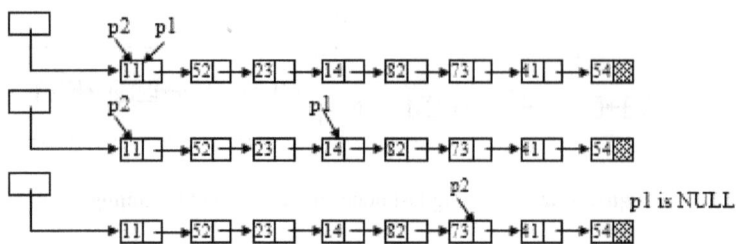

Figure 11.5 Getting n[th] node from end of a single linked list

26. We can use the tortoise and hare algorithm. When the fast pointer becomes NULL, the slow pointer will be at the middle of the list.
27. Reach the middle of the list as in Ex26, and then split the list there.
29.

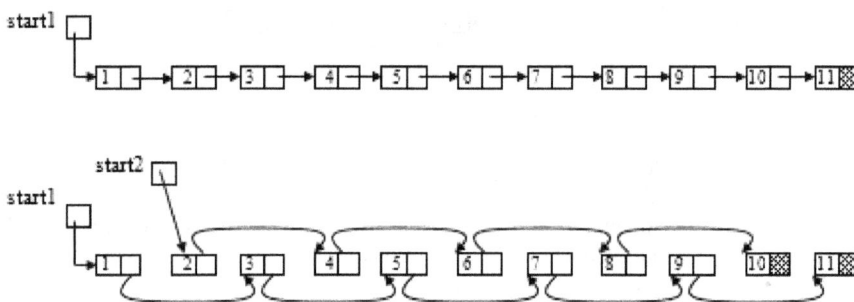

Figure 11.6 Even numbered nodes in new list

30.

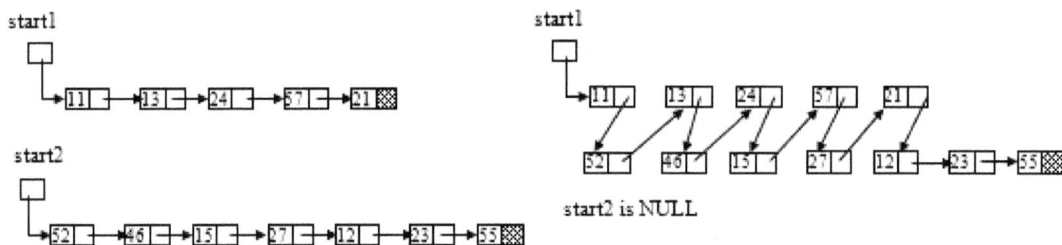

Figure 11.7 Combining alternate nodes of two lists

31.

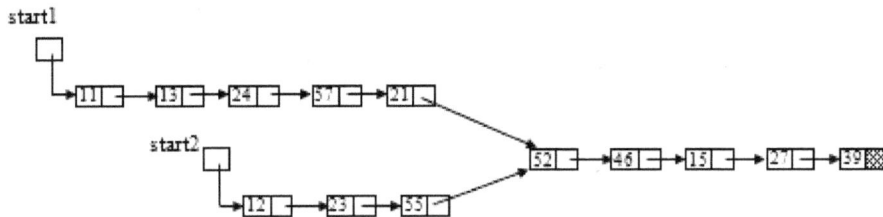

Figure 11.8 Merge point of two lists (Y shaped lists)

Find the length of both lists. Suppose d is the difference of lengths of both lists. Take two pointers pointing to the beginning of the lists. Move the pointer which points to the longer list d times. Now move both pointers simultaneously and compare them. If at any point both the pointers are equal, then we get a merge node. If we reach the end of any lists without getting the merge node, we can conclude that the lists do not intersect at any point. In the example, the merge point is the node containing data 52.

34. First, find the middle of the list as in Ex26. Split the list into two halves, reverse the second half of the list, and compare the two halves. After comparing, reverse the second half and join the two halves to get the original list. There will be different cases for odd and even elements.

Chapter 4 Stacks and Queues

4. The first stack will start from 0th position and the second stack will start from the last position of array. The overflow will occur when the top of the two stacks cross.

(i) Push 4, 8 on stack A, Push 3,6,9 on stack B

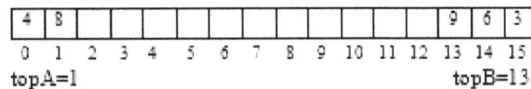

Figure 11.9 Push 4, 8 on stack A, Push 3,6,9 on stack B

(ii) Push 1,2,5,9 on stack A, Push 4,6,1,2,3,8,5 on stack B

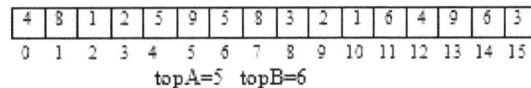

Figure 11.10 Push 1,2,5,9 on stack A, Push 4,6,1,2,3,8,5 on stack B

(iii) Pop from stack A

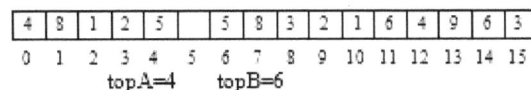

Figure 11.11 Pop from stack A

(iv) Pop from stack B

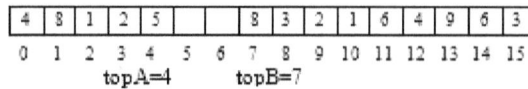

4	8	1	2	5			8	3	2	1	6	4	9	6	3

0　1　2　3　4　5　6　7　8　9　10　11　12　13　14　15

topA=4　　　topB=7

Figure 11.12 Pop from stack B

5. The first queue will start from the 0th position and the second queue will start from the last position of the array.

6.

Enqueue: Push item on instack

Dequeue: If outstack is empty, then move all the items from instack to outstack.
　　　Pop item from outstack.

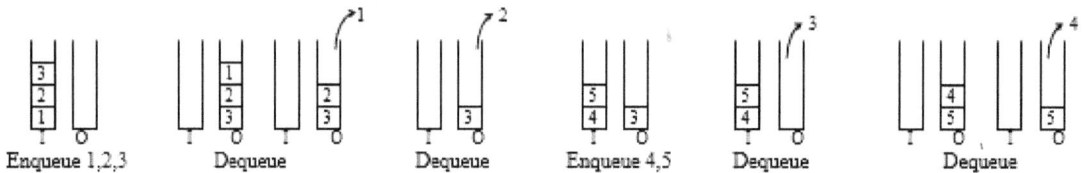

Figure 11.13 Queue using two stacks

This way, we can get the FIFO behavior using two stacks.

7.

Push: Enqueue all the items of Q1 into Q2. Enqueue the new item. Enqueue all the items of Q2 into Q1.
Pop: Delete the front item from Q1.

8.

Push: Enqueue the item. Equeue the front item, delete the front items one by one for size-1 of the queue.
Pop: Delete the front item.

(i) Queue : 1,2,3,4

　Push 5

　Queue - 1,2,3,4,5

　Queue - 2,3,4,5,1

　Queue - 3,4,5,1,2

　Queue - 4,5,1,2,3

　Queue - 5,1,2,3,4

　5 is a front item, which is pushed.

(ii) Queue - 5,1,2,3,4

　Pop

　Queue - 1,2,3,4

　5 is deleted, which is the item popped.

9.

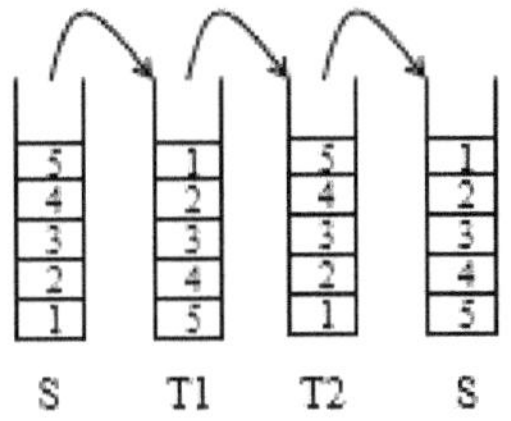

Figure 11.14 Reversing a stack using two stacks

10.

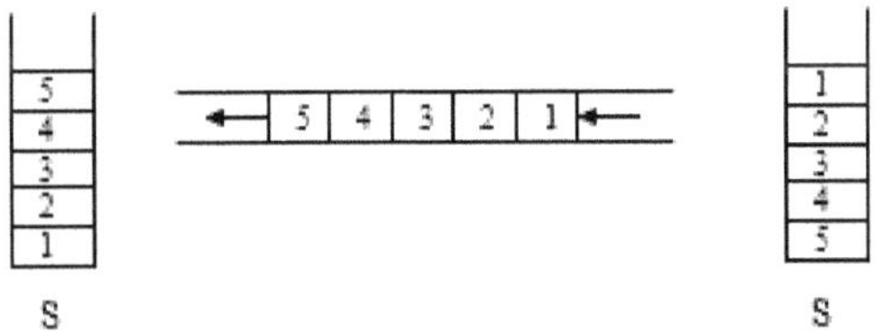

Figure 11.15 Reversing a stack using a queue

11.

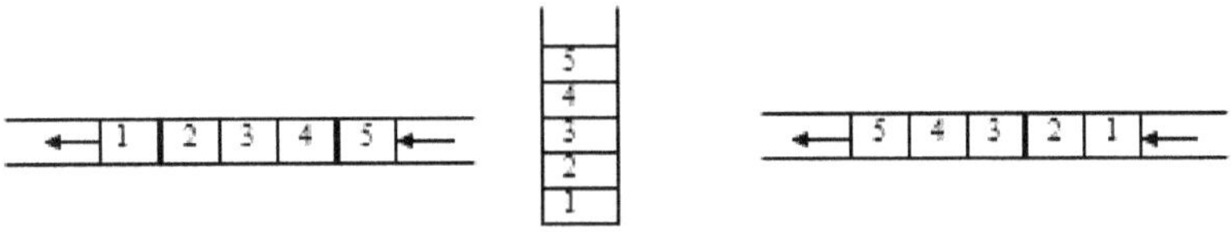

Figure 11.16 Reversing a queue using one stack

12.

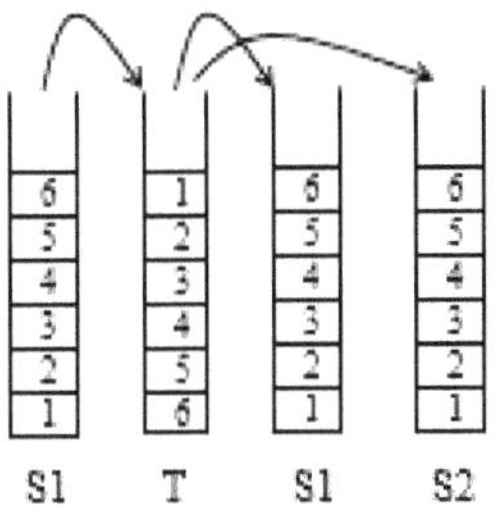

Figure 11.17 Copying content of a stack to another stack

13. Delete the elements from Q1 one by one and insert them both in Q1 and Q2.

Q1- 1 2,3,4,5	Q1- 2,3,4,5,1	Q1- 3,4,5,1,2	Q1- 4,5,1,2,3	Q1- 5,1,2,3,4	Q1- 1,2,3,4,5
Q2-	Q2- 1	Q2- 1,2	Q2- 1,2,3	Q2- 1,2,3,4	Q2- 1,2,3,4,5

14. Take two stacks, one to store all the elements and the other to store the minimum.

    Push: Push the item on the main stack. Push on the minimum stack only if the item to be pushed is less than or equal to the value at the top of the minimum stack.

    Pop: Pop from the main stack. Pop from the minimum stack only if the value popped from the main stack is equal to that on the top of the minimum stack.

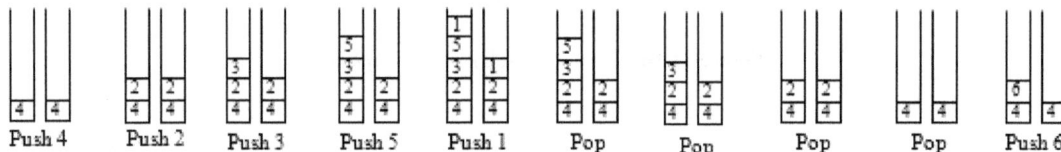

Figure 11.18 Getting minimum element from stack

Another way: We can have a data member min in stack node. When the min of top of stack is more than the pushed data, then the node min is set with pushed data. Otherwise, the min of node is min of top only. The top will have min information.

15. Keep on dividing the number by 2 and pushing the remainder on a stack till the number is reduced to 0. Now pop all the numbers from the stack and display them.

    101

101/2 q=50, r=1	stack=1
50/2, q=25,r=0	stack=1,0
25/2, q=12, r=1	stack=1,0,1
12/2,q=6,r=0	stack=1,0,1,0
6/2,q=3,r=0	stack=1,0,1,0,0
3/2,q=1,r=1	stack=1,0,1,0,0,1
1/2, q=0,r=1	stack=1,0,1,0,0,1,1

    Binary = 1100101

16. Find the prime factors iteratively and push them in a stack. Pop elements from the stack and display them.

17. Scan the infix from right to left. Whenever an operator comes, pop the operators which have priority greater than (not equal to) the priority of the symbol operator. The rest of the procedure is the same as in postfix.

18.

    Postfix (i) AB+CD+* (ii) ACD-%BE*+ (iii) ABC+D*E/- (iv) HJK+^I*S%

    Prefix   (i) *+AB+CD   (ii) +%A-CD*BE (iii) -A/*+BCDE (iv) %*^H+JKIS

19. (i) -/+5342   Value : 0 (ii) ++/63*3^221   Value : 15 (iii) +-*/+8223/213 Value : 16

20. Scan from left to right, when you get an operator; place it before the 2 operands that precede it. For example:

    (i)

    ABC*-DE-F*G/H/+

    A[*BC]-DE-F*G/H/+

    [-A*BC]DE-F*G/H/+

    [-A*BC][-DE]F*G/H/+

    [-A*BC][*-DEF]G/H/+

    [-A*BC][/*-DEFG]H/+

    [-A*BC][//*-DEFGH]+

    +-A*BC//*-DEFGH

    (ii) Prefix: -*/+ABCD^EF   (iii) Prefix : +-A^BC/*DE+FG

21. Scan from right to left; when you get 2 consecutive operands after an operator, take the operator and place it after the two operands. For example:
    (i)
    +-+A/BC*DEF
    +-+A[BC/]*DEF
    +-[ABC/+]*DEF
    +-[ABC/+][DE*]F
    +[ABC/+DE*-]F
    ABC/+DE*-F+
    (ii) Postfix : ABCDE^*/+FGH^*-   (iii) Postfix : ABCD^/+EF*GH+/-
22. (i) 14   (ii) 9   (iii) 17

Chapter 5 Recursion

1. 33 33. Both functions return the sum of all numbers from a to b.
2. 1033, Function returns the sum of all numbers from a to b, added to 1000.
3. 40, func( ) returns the sum of all numbers from 6 to 10. In func1( ), we have infinite recursion, as the terminating condition is never true.
4. func(4,8) returns 30, but in func(3,8), we have the infinite recursion, as the terminating condition is never true.
5. 18 17 16 15 14 13 12 11 10
   10 11 12 13 14 15 16 17 18
6. 10 11 12 13 14 15 16 17 18
   18 17 16 15 14 13 12 11 10
7. 24 0 0, func( ) returns the product of a and b.
8. 5, count( ) returns the number of digits in n.
9. 23, func( ) returns the sum of digits in n.
10. 3, count( ) returns the number of times digit d occurs in number n.
11. 4, func( ) returns the total number of even elements in array arr.
12. 28, func( ) returns the sum of all elements of array arr.
13. func( ) returns the number of times character a occurs in string str.
14. func1( ) prints -   func2( ) prints-
    ```
       ****                      *
       ***                       **
       **                        ***
       *                         ****
    ```
15. 1, func( ) returns the smallest element of the array.
16. 2, func( ) returns the smallest element of the array. The array arr[low], ...arr[high] is divided into two parts arr[low], ...arr[mid] and arr[mid+1], ...arr[high] and, the smallest elements of both parts is computed recursively. The smaller of these two elements is returned as the smallest element of the array. If the size of the array is even, then the size of both parts is same, and if the size of the array is odd, then the size of the first part is one more than the size of the second part. The terminating condition for recursion is when the size of part becomes equal to one i.e., low==high.
23. Proceed as in Ex16.
30.

$$a^n = \begin{cases} 1 & \text{if } n=0 \\ (a*a)^{n/2} & \text{if n is even} \\ a*(a*a)^{(n-1)/2} & \text{if n is odd} \end{cases}$$

Figure 11.19 Computation of a^n

Chapter 6 Trees

1.

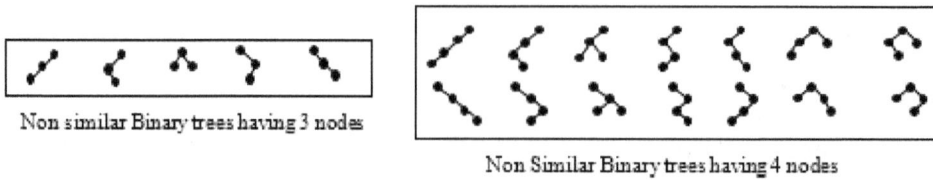

Non similar Binary trees having 3 nodes

Non Similar Binary trees having 4 nodes

Figure 11.20 Non similar binary trees having 3 and 4 nodes

If there are n nodes then the number of possible non-similar binary trees is $^{2n}C_n * 1/(n+1)$
For 3 nodes [6! / (3! * 3!)] * [1/4] = 5
For 4 nodes [8! / (4! * 4!)] * [1/5] = 14
If we want to find out the total number of different binary trees with n different keys, then we can multiply the above value by n!
For example, suppose we have to find the number of possible binary trees of 3 nodes having key values 1,2,3. We have 5 different structures of possible binary trees, as shown in the figure, and in each structure, the values 1,2,3 can be arranged in 3! ways. So, the total number of different binary trees will be 30.

2.

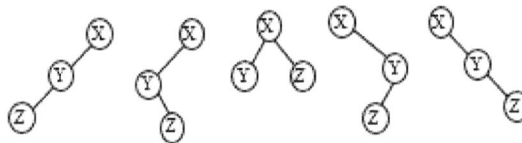

Figure 11.21 Binary trees of 3 nodes having preorder XYZ

3.

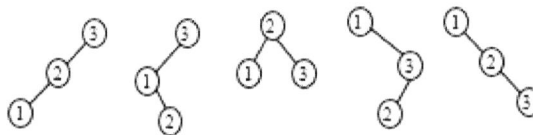

Figure 11.22 Binary search trees of 3 nodes having key values 1,2,3

4.

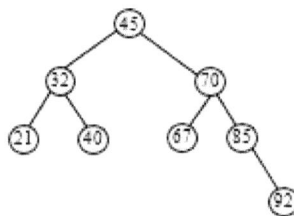

Figure 11.23 Binary search tree

5. Height = 5

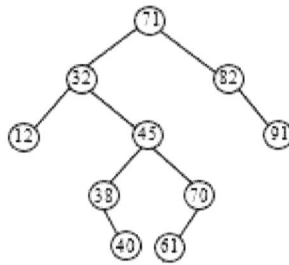

Figure 11.24 Binary search tree

If data is inserted in sorted order, then the height of the binary search tree will be 10.

6. Inorder traversal of binary search tree is always in ascending order, so arranging the data in ascending order gives us inorder traversal.

Inorder - 6 9 11 12 23 32 45 56 67

From inorder and preorder traversals, we can construct the tree and find the postorder traversal.

Postorder - 6 9 11 12 32 56 67 45 23

7.

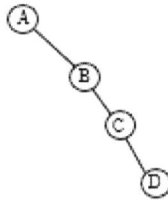

Figure 11.25 Binary tree with same preorder and inorder traversals

Inorder and preorder are A B C D

8.

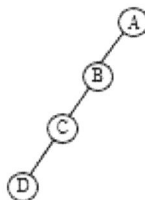

Figure 11.26 Binary tree with same inorder and postorder traversals

Inorder and postorder are D C B A

9.

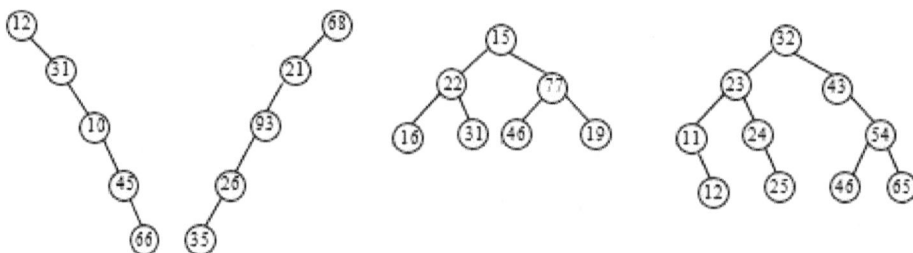

Figure 11.27 Binary trees from inorder and preorder traversals

10.

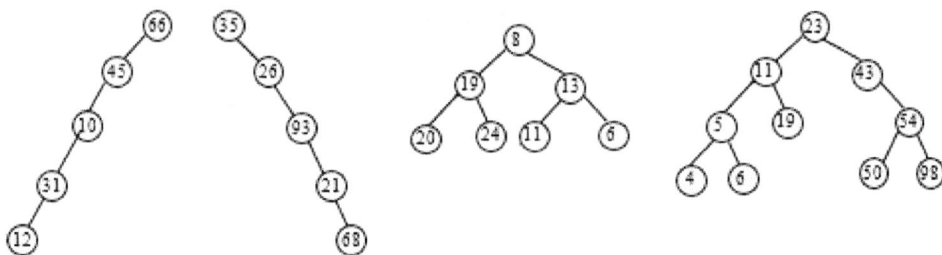

Figure 11.28 Binary trees from inorder and postorder traversals

11. (i) (7, 5, 2, 1)   (ii)   (9, 6, 5, 7, 8) (9, 6, 7, 8, 5) (9, 6, 7, 5, 8)
        (iii) (4, 6, 5, 8) (4, 6, 8, 5)   (iv) (1, 2, 5, 7)
12. (a) (n-x)   (b) y+1
13. For all these trees Preorder = ABC, Postorder = CBA

Figure 11.29 Binary trees with same preorder and postorder traversals

14. 67 is root node, and all values less than 67 will be in the left Subtree and those more than 67 will be in right subtree. By applying this logic for the subtrees, we can also create our BST.

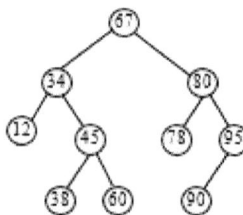

Figure 11.30 Binary search tree from preorder traversal

Alternatively, we can construct the tree as in section 6.9.3. The inorder traversal of a BST can be found by putting the data in sorted order.

15.

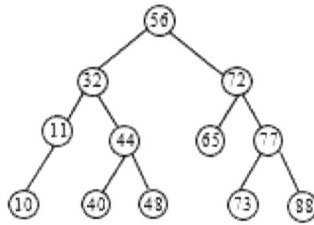

Figure 11.31 Binary search tree from postorder traversal

16. In a full binary tree, the left and right subtrees of a node have the same number of nodes. F is the root node, and from the remaining 6 nodes, three will be in the left subtree, and three in the right subtree.

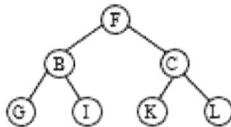

Figure 11.32 Full binary tree from preorder traversal

31.

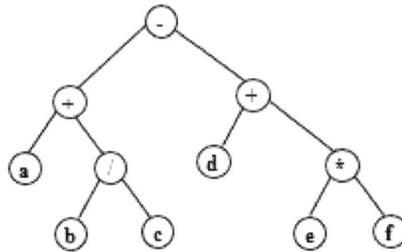

Figure 11.33 Expression tree from algebraic expression

Prefix: -+a/bc+d*ef
Postfix: abc/+def*+-

32. After inserting 28 - 50 40 30 28 16 23 20 25
    After inserting 43 - 50 43 30 40 16 23 20 25 28
    After inserting 11 - 50 43 30 40 16 23 20 25 28 11

33.

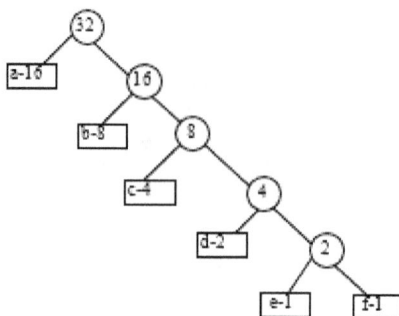

Figure 11.34 Huffman tree

Huffman codes: a-0, b-10, c-110, d-1110, e-11110, f-11111

34.

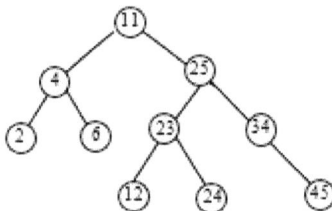

Figure 11.35 AVL tree

35.

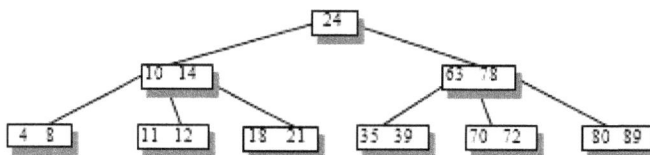

Figure 11.36 B-tree

Chapter 7 Graphs

1.

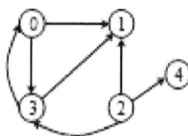

Figure 11.37 Graph from adjacency tree

(i) In(0)=1, In(1)=3, In(2)=0, In(3)=2, In(4)=1, Out(0)=2, Out(1)=0, Out(2)=3, Out(3)=2, Out(4)=0
(ii) The path matrix is:

$$
\begin{array}{c c c c c c}
 & 0 & 1 & 2 & 3 & 4 \\
0 & \begin{bmatrix} 1 & 1 & 0 & 1 & 0 \\ 1 & 0 & 0 & 0 & 0 & 0 \\ 2 & 1 & 1 & 0 & 1 & 1 \\ 3 & 1 & 1 & 0 & 1 & 0 \\ 4 & 0 & 0 & 0 & 0 & 0 \end{bmatrix}
\end{array}
$$

Figure 11.38 Path matrix for the graph

(iii) Since all elements of the path matrix are not 1, the graph is not strongly connected.
(iv) Since all the diagonal elements of the path matrix are not 0, the graph is not acyclic.

2.   (i) Sum of degrees = 3 + 3 + 3 + 3 = 12 (ii) Sum of degrees = 1 + 0 + 1 + 2 = 4
(iii) Sum of degrees = 3 + 2 + 3 = 8   (iv) Sum of degrees = 1 + 2 + 1 + 4 + 1 + 2 + 1 = 12
The sum of degrees of all the vertices is twice the number of edges. This is because each edge contributes 2 to the sum of degrees. This result is called handshaking Lemma. If in a meeting, people are represented by vertices, and a handshake between two people by an edge, then the total number of hands shaken is twice the total number of handshakes.

3.   Sum of degrees = Sum of degrees of even vertices + Sum of degrees of odd vertices.
The sum of degrees of all vertices is even by handshaking lemma, and the sum of degrees of even vertices will be even. The difference of two even numbers is even, so the sum of degrees of odd vertices will be even. The sum of degrees of odd vertices is a sum of only odd terms, and so the sum can be even only if the number of these odd terms is even. So, the number of odd vertices in a graph is even.

4.   (i) Sum of indegrees = 2 + 1 + 2 + 0 + 1 = 6, Sum of outdegrees = 1 + 1 + 0 + 3 + 1 = 6
(ii) Sum of indegrees = 0 + 2 + 1 = 3, Sum of outdegrees = 2 + 0 + 1 = 3
(iii) Sum of indegrees = 1 + 2 + 1 = 4, Sum of outdegrees = 2 + 1 + 1 = 4
(iv) Sum of indegrees = 2 + 1 + 2 + 3 = 8, Sum of outdegrees = 2 + 3 + 1 + 2 = 8
Sum of indegrees of all vertices = Sum of outdegrees of all vertices = Number of edges.
This is handshaking lemma for the directed graphs. Each edge contributes 1 to the sum of indegrees and 1 to the sum of outdegrees.

5.   The sum of degrees of all vertices of a graph is twice the number of edges. In a regular graph of n vertices having degree d, the sum of degrees of all vertices is n*d.
2e = n*d => e = (n*d)/2
(i) 5 (ii) 6
(iii) (3*5)/2 is not a whole number, so this is not possible. In Ex3, we have proved that the number of odd vertices should be even but here it is not so.

6.   (i) 5, 7, 2   (ii) 1, 2, 5   (iii) 3, 1, 5

7.   (i) All vertices are visited by performing a DFS from 0. Now reverse the graph.

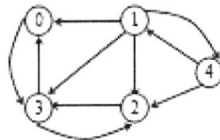

Figure 11.39 Reverse graph

In the reverse graph, all vertices are not visited by performing a DFS from 0. So, the graph is not strongly connected.
(ii) All vertices are visited by performing a DFS from 0. Now reverse the graph.

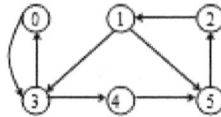

Figure 11.40 Reverse graph

In the reverse graph, all vertices are visited by performing a DFS from 0. So, the graph is strongly connected.

8. DFS taking 0 as the start vertex: 0 1 2 3 7 4 5 6

Discovery time and finishing times of vertices are:

Vertex 0 - (1, 10), Vertex 1 - (2, 9), Vertex 2 - (3, 8), Vertex 3 - (4, 7),

Vertex 4 - (11,16), Vertex 5 - (12, 15), Vertex 6 - (13,14), Vertex 7 - (5, 6)

Now reverse the graph.

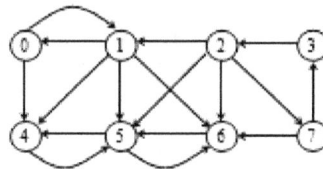

Figure 11.41 Reverse graph

Start DFS from 4 as it has the highest finishing time.

Strongly connected components are: (4, 5, 6) (0,1) (2,3,7)

9. (0, 3, 1) = 9, (0, 3, 4, 5, 2) = 22, (0, 3) = 5, (0, 3, 4) = 14, (0, 3, 4, 5) = 16

10. (i) Edges in MST : (0,1), (0,2), (0,3),.....(0,n-1)

Weight of MST = 1 + 2 + 3 +.........(n-1) = n(n-1)/2

(ii) Edges in MST : (0,1), (1,2),(2,3)......(n-2,n-1)

Weight of MST = 1 + 1 + 1 + ...+ 1 = n-1

(iii) Edges in MST : (0,1), (1,2),(2,3)......(n-2,n-1)

Weight of MST = 5 + 5 + 5 +............+ 5 = 5(n-1)

Chapter 8 Sorting

1. (1 2 3 4 5)   (5 4 3 2 1)   (2 3 1 5 4)

For all these sets of data, the number of comparisons will be 10.

5. 9   12   21   23   32   10   34   45   67   89

8.

12	23_A	42	23_B	6	9	23_C
6	23_A	42	23_B	12	9	23_C
6	9	42	23_B	12	23_A	23_C
6	9	12	23_B	42	23_A	23_C
6	9	12	23_B	42	23_A	23_C
6	9	12	23_B	23_A	42	23_C
6	9	12	23_B	23_A	23_C	42

9. On sorting the data given in Ex8, by bubble sort, we get 6   9   12 23_A 23_B 23_C 42

10. 2   5   5   13   19   20   21   34   89   3

12. (i) Bubble   (ii) Selection   (iii) Insertion

14. 5 or 8 could be the pivot.

15. 11 21 23 12 12 36 19 35 47 87 72 56
16. The contents of array after each pass of heap sort are:

83 76 82 54 45 21 12 _____ 97
82 76 21 54 45 12 _____ 83 97
76 54 21 12 45 _____ 82 83 97
54 45 21 12 _____ 76 82 83 97
45 12 21 _____ 54 76 82 83 97
21 12 _____ 45 54 76 82 83 97
12 _____ 21 45 54 76 82 83 97

18. Sublist 1 : 34 54 17 12   →   12 17 34 54
Sublist 2 : 21 88 51   →   21 51 88
Sublist 3 : 65 23 72   →   23 65 72
Sublist 4 : 89 76 91   →   76 89 91
Sublist 5 : 11 98 24   →   11 24 98
12 21 23 76 11 17 51 65 89 24 34 88 72 91 98 54

Chapter 9 Searching and Hashing

1. Search 27   (0, 8, 17) (0, 3, 7) - 27 found at position 3
Search 32   (0, 8, 17) (0, 3, 7) (4, 5, 7) (4, 4, 4) (5, 4, 4) - 32 not found in array
Search 61   (0, 8, 17) (9, 13, 17) (9, 10, 12) (9, 9, 9) - 61 found at position 9
Search 97   (0, 8, 17) (9, 13, 17) (14, 15, 17) (16, 16, 17) (17, 17, 17) - 97 found at position 17

2. Squaring the keys and taking 2nd, 4th and 6th digits
116964   045369   186624   293764   017424   582169   088804
  194   439   864   974   144   819   884

3. 321 + 982 + 432 = 1735   213 + 432 + 183 = **828**
343 + 541 + 652 = **1536**   542 + 313 + 753 = **1608**
Addresses are 735, 828, 536, 608

4. 321 + 289 + 432 = **1042**   213 + 234 + 183 = **630**
343 + 145 + 652 = **1140**   542 + 313 + 753 = 1608
Addresses are 42, 630, 140, 608

5. H(9893)=37, H(2341)=**37**, H(4312)=24, H(7893)=21, H(4531)=51, H(8731)=27, H(3184)=48
H(5421)=45, H(4955)=**27**, H(1496)=**24**
H(9893)=44, H(2341)=63, H(4312)=24, H(7893)=54, H(4531)=42, H(8731)=21, H(3184)=35
H(5421)=61, H(4955)=64, H(1496)=22

6. Linear Probe

[0]	102
[1]	67
[2]	120
[3]	37
[4]	88
[5]	122
[6]	40
[7]	
[8]	
[9]	94
[10]	
[11]	
[12]	29
[13]	63
[14]	
[15]	
[16]	94

Figure 11.42 Linear probing to resolve collisions

7. Quadratic Probe

[0]	102
[1]	120
[2]	
[3]	37
[4]	88
[5]	
[6]	40
[7]	122
[8]	67
[9]	94
[10]	
[11]	
[12]	29
[13]	63
[14]	
[15]	
[16]	84

Figure 11.43 Quadratic probing to resolve collisions

8. Double hashing

[0]	102
[1]	120
[2]	
[3]	37
[4]	67
[5]	
[6]	40
[7]	122
[8]	88
[9]	94
[10]	
[11]	
[12]	29
[13]	63
[14]	
[15]	
[16]	84

Figure 11.44 Double hashing to resolve collisions

9. Length of the longest chain is 3, and the keys in it are 1457, 8255, 1061

Chapter 10 Storage Management

1. In first fit and worst fit, memory is allocated from 120K free block and in best fit, memory is allocated from 72K free block.

2.

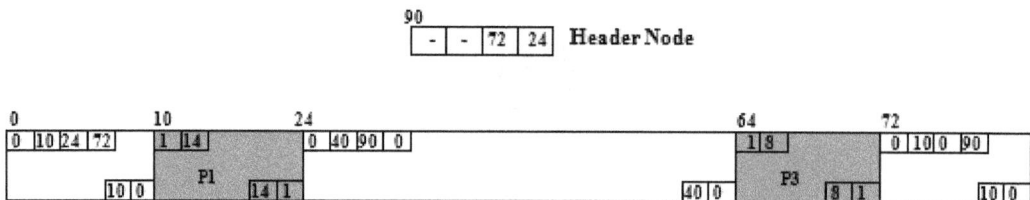

Figure 11.45 Deallocated the memory block P2 using Boundary tag method

3. P1 is allocated in a 7-block starting at 0, P2 is allocated in a 5-block starting at 128
   P3 is allocated in a 6-block starting at 192, P4 is allocated in a 6-block starting at 256
   P5 is allocated in a 7-block starting at 384

4. The address 256 in binary is 100000000 and the 5th bit is 0. So, the 5-block at 256 has a right buddy and the address of the right buddy is 288(100100000).
   The free 5-block at 256 is combined with its right buddy from a free 6-block at 256, which is combined with its right buddy to form a free 7-block at 256. The free 7-block at 256 is combined with its right buddy to form a free 8-block at 256.

5. P1 is allocated in a 7-block starting at 123,   P2 is allocated in a 8-block starting at 89,
   P3 is allocated in a 7-block starting at 55,   P4 is allocated in a 8-block starting at 0

6. The LBC of block P3 is 0, i.e., it is a right buddy. Its left buddy would be a 9-block at address 0 (55 - 55). The left buddy is free, so both are combined to form a free 10-block. The LBC of combined free block will be 1, which implies that it is a left buddy. Its right buddy would be a 9 block at address (0+89). But the block at address 89 is not a 9-block, which means that right buddy is not available.

Join our book's Discord space

Join the book's Discord Workspace for Latest updates, Offers, Tech happenings around the world, New Release and Sessions with the Authors:

https://discord.bpbonline.com

Index

www.ingramcontent.com/pod-product-compliance
Lightning Source LLC
Chambersburg PA
CBHW061737210326
41599CB00034B/6701